MW00978258

CONTRACTORS GUIDE TO BUSINESS, LAW AND PROJECT MANAGEMENT

North Carolina General Contractors
8th Edition

Supplemental forms and links are available at NASCLAforms.org
using access code NC129354.

National Association of State Contractors Licensing Agencies (NASCLA)
23309 N. 17th Drive
Building 1, Unit 110
Phoenix, Arizona 85027
(623) 587-9354
(623) 587-9625 fax
Visit our web site:
www.nascla.org

Contractors Guide to Business, Law and Project Management

North Carolina General Contractors 8th Edition

Revised December 2019

Previously published as *Business and Project Management for Contractors, North Carolina General Contractors Edition* and *Contractors Guide to Business, Law and Project Management, North Carolina General Contractors, 7th Edition*

Copyright © 2001, 2003, 2004, 2006, 2007, 2009, 2012 and 2019 by

National Association of State Contractors Licensing Agencies (NASCLA)
23309 North 17th Drive, Building 1, Unit 110
Phoenix, Arizona 85027

ISBN-10 1-948558-10-6

ISBN-13 978-1-948558-10-5

INTRODUCTION

The construction industry is one of the strongest industries in America. To keep the construction industry thriving and to be a successful construction contractor, you must be knowledgeable in both your trade and managing a business.

Thorough business planning and good management skills are key to success in today's market. A solid business plan lays the foundation for your financial, marketing, and management strategies and helps you maximize your potential. Competition can be fierce in the construction industry. In developing a business plan, you analyze your market and competition and identify where you can gain an edge.

Good management skills entail applying knowledge from all aspects of the business to create a successful operation. Effective managers know how to win customers, satisfy employees, meet all legal obligations, and increase the bottom line. If this is where you want to take your business, this book can help you get there.

About This Book

This book is organized into three sections:

Part 1 focuses on planning and starting your business. This section will help you formulate a business plan, choose a business structure, understand licensing and insurance requirements and gain basic management and marketing skills.

Part 2 covers fundamentals you will need to know in order to operate a successful construction business. This section covers estimating, contract management, scheduling, project management, safety and environmental responsibilities, and building good relationships with employees, subcontractors, and customers.

Part 3 provides valuable information to assist you in running the administrative functions of your business. Financial management, tax basics, and lien laws are covered. Effective management of these areas of business is vital and can cause serious problems if you do not give them proper attention.

Part 1: Getting Your Business Off the Ground

- ✓ Chapter 1 covers tips for writing a business plan and discusses key characteristics of entrepreneurship. A sample business plan is provided in Appendix A and at **NASCLAforms.org** using access code **NC129354**.
- ✓ Chapter 2 describes each type of business entity and summarizes their advantages and disadvantages.
- ✓ Chapter 3 reviews the licensing process and the requirements for getting a license.
- ✓ Chapter 4 discusses insurance and bonding options to protect your business against unmitigated risk.
- ✓ Chapter 5 is your business toolbox with tips on time management, delegation, business ethics, and technology. It also provides information on resources available to assist small businesses.
- ✓ Chapter 6 helps you execute your marketing plan through promotional materials, public relations and effective selling skills.

Part 2: Fundamentals for the Field

✓ Chapter 7 shows you how to formulate estimates and evaluate bid opportunities.

✓ Chapter 8 takes you through the key elements of contracts and what is needed to make them enforceable.

✓ Chapter 9 covers scheduling techniques and the fundamental skills needed to effectively manage construction projects.

✓ Chapter 10 explains the importance of understanding customer expectations and handling change orders effectively. The basics of successful negotiation are also addressed.

✓ Chapter 11 is your resource for employment law, hiring and retaining of good employees, and discipline and termination of employees if unfortunate employment circumstances arise.

✓ Chapter 12 gives you the fundamentals for understanding OSHA laws and setting up a safety program for your company. Environmental considerations and possible permitting situations are covered in the event you are creating or working with environmental hazards.

✓ Chapter 13 covers the basics of finding and hiring good subcontractors and establishing good working relationships with them.

Part 3: Office Administration

✓ Chapter 14 takes you through the accounting cycle, the preparation and analysis of financial statements and payroll procedures.

✓ Chapter 15 gives you federal and state tax basics and helps you understand the forms you need to file.

✓ Chapter 16 covers lien law regulations and the process for filing a lien.

Supplemental forms and links are available at **NASCLAforms.org** using access code **NC129354**.

Whether you are studying for the contractors' licensing exam or need an ongoing reference manual for managing your business, the NASCLA Contractors Guide to Business, Law and Project Management will serve as a valuable resource. We hope you find this reference useful in your daily operations and that the concepts discussed give you the tools for running a successful business.

TABLE OF CONTENTS

PART I
Getting Your Business Off the Ground

PART II
Fundamentals for the Field

PART III
Office Administration

PART 1
Getting Your Business Off the Ground

Chapter 1
THE PLAN

Just as you need trade tools to successfully complete contracting jobs, you need organization tools to successfully manage your business. As a business owner you go from being an expert in your trade to requiring expertise in project management, marketing, employee management, financial management, contract management and much more.

Success Factors: It takes an organized, consistent approach to achieve success in today's market. Businesses fail every day. The top reasons businesses fail are:

✓ poor sales,

✓ competitive weakness,

✓ high operating expenses,

✓ difficulty collecting on invoices,

✓ inventory problems,

✓ too many fixed assets,

✓ poor location, and

✓ fraud.

From this point forward, we will build your business management expertise so you can identify and understand these obstacles, thereby, increasing your chances of building and operating a successful business.

> ### To Sum It Up...
> Poor planning and inadequate management are overriding factors in business failure.

Being an Entrepreneur

Understanding Entrepreneurship: As a business owner, you may be referred to as an entrepreneur. There are many definitions of "entrepreneur." For our purposes, an entrepreneur is a person engaged in strategic activities that involve the initiation and development of a new business, created to build long-term value and steady cash flow streams.

Risk Taking: Entrepreneurs are often regarded as risk takers. There is risk associated with any venture, but entrepreneurs understand the importance of taking calculated risks. A calculated risk is a risk that is well-thought through where all outcomes are considered. This chapter will introduce the business planning process and help you understand the risks and opportunities associated with business ownership and how to manage them.

> ### Something to Consider...
> Entrepreneurship has its rewards as well as its drawbacks. Before embarking on any business venture, an entrepreneur must weigh all of these factors carefully.

Rewards and Challenges: Rewards of owning your own business include:

✓ being your own boss;

✓ having flexibility of time;

✓ having more freedom and independence;

✓ making your own decisions; and

✓ receiving personal satisfaction from completing a job.

Entrepreneurship also has many frustrations and challenges, including:

✓ long working hours;

✓ managing cash flow and payroll;

✓ high potential for overwhelming responsibility;

✓ finding and keeping qualified employees;

✓ paying taxes; and

✓ knowing and following government regulations.

Entrepreneurs need to decide if the rewards of entrepreneurship outweigh the challenges.

The Benefits of a Business Plan

Preparing a business plan that outlines strategies and goals for your business is useful for a newly-formed or early-stage business. It can also be a helpful tool for a company that is making major strategic changes (i.e., providing additional product or service offerings). A business plan should be a living document that changes as your business and the market change.

Think of the business plan as a blueprint for your business. Just as you would not perform your trade without a blueprint or plan from the customer, you should not operate your company without a business plan.

Key Functions: A business plan serves three key functions:

✓ **Planning Tool:** Your business plan is a road map for the growth of the business. Putting together the plan helps you think through all possible scenarios for growth in the market.

✓ **Loan or Investor Document:** If you are planning to seek loan financing or approach an investor, you will need a business plan. Investors or loan officers will review this document to evaluate the qualifications of your management team, your projected growth, and your competitive advantage.

✓ **Benchmarking Tool:** Your business plan should also serve as a base against which to measure and monitor the company's performance. If your company exceeds or falls short of your projections, you can investigate the reasons for the difference.

A business plan will allow you to think through all aspects of your business, thus providing you with a competitive edge.

Elements of a Business Plan

The following are the typical elements found in a business plan:

✓ **Cover Page:** Contact information and a confidentiality statement are stated on the cover page.

✓ **Executive Summary:** Placed after the cover page at the beginning of the business plan, the executive summary includes highlights of the plan and gains the interest of the reader. It is usually written last.

✓ **Company Summary:** The company vision and mission, legal structure, management personnel, business location, and facilities are outlined in the company summary section.

✓ **Products and Services:** Your specific products and services, primary subcontractors and suppliers, the effect of technology on your business, and expansion opportunities are all covered in the products and services section.

✓ **Market Analysis:** Your target market, market trends, and major competitors are defined under market analysis.

✓ **Marketing Strategy:** The uniqueness of your product or service as well as your pricing, advertising, and promotional strategies are outlined in the marketing strategy.

✓ **Financial Plan:** If you already have financial statements, you should include a balance sheet, an income statement, and a cash flow statement as part of your business plan. New and existing businesses can put together financial projections as additional documentation.

A business plan template that can be customized for your company is located in Appendix B. The template provides specific guidance for completing each section.

Samples: The websites listed below offer sample business plans:

✓ www.allbusiness.com

✓ www.bplans.com

✓ www.inc.com

✓ www.sba.gov

✓ www.americanexpress.com/en-us/business/trends-and-insights

✓ www.bizmove.com/small-business/business-plan.htm

Business planning software packages that provide a step-by-step guide to creating a business plan are also available for purchase.

* *

Your business plan is the blueprint for your business.

* *

Business Plan Pitfalls

 As you start creating your business plan, there are guidelines you should follow to make sure you are giving investors an accurate and honest picture of your business.

✓ Make sure your assumptions are realistic.

✓ Keep the language simple. Don't use technical terminology or jargon.

✓ Cover the risks as well as the opportunities.

✓ Analyze your competition thoroughly.

By applying these simple guidelines, your business plan will have a solid foundation.

Final Inspection...

Being an Entrepreneur: Entrepreneurs should take calculated risks and weigh all factors when making business decisions.

The Benefits of a Business Plan: A business plan is sometimes required by bank loan officers or by investors. It can also be used as a planning and benchmarking tool.

Elements of a Business Plan: A business plan typically contains a cover page, an executive summary, a company summary, a listing of products and/or services, a market analysis, an explanation of the marketing strategy, and a financial plan.

Business Plan Pitfalls: It is important to portray an accurate picture of your business when formulating your business plan.

Supplemental Forms

Supplemental forms and links are available at **NASCLAforms.org** using access code **NC129354**.

Business Plan Template	This template gives an outline for the business plan, including questions that help create detailed assumptions for each section of the plan.
Profit and Loss Pro Forma	This spreadsheet automatically calculates totals when you enter profit and loss numbers. You can adjust the numbers to determine your revenue and expense break-even point.

Chapter 2
CHOOSING YOUR BUSINESS STRUCTURE

When starting a business, one of the first things you need to decide is the legal structure your business will take. Each form of business has its advantages and disadvantages. The right choice depends on the nature of your business, plus various tax and liability issues. To ensure you are making the appropriate choice, it is best to consult with an attorney and an accountant.

Sole Proprietorships

Getting Started: Many businesses begin as sole proprietorships, because it is the simplest ownership form to set up. In a sole proprietorship, you are the sole owner of the company. If the sole proprietorship does business under a name different than your own, typically, a fictitious name certificate needs to be filed at a local or state government office.

If you are doing any type of significant business, a sole proprietorship may be a risky legal business structure, because it exposes you to unlimited liability for the business debt.

Key Characteristics of Sole Proprietorships:

✓ **Existence:** You own the assets of the company. If you decide to sell your sole proprietorship business, in actuality you are selling the assets of the business. You would have to close out your business license and the new buyer would have to obtain all appropriate licenses and accounts in his or her name. A sole proprietorship is terminated upon the owner's death.

✓ **Financial Management:** Business and personal expenses must be separated and careful records must be kept, because the IRS may question the handling of these funds and you may be asked to provide documentation.

✓ **Liability:** You bear personal liability for all actions undertaken in the name of the business.

✓ **Taxes:** Your net income from the business is reported as ordinary income. Sole proprietors do not pay corporate income taxes.

Advantages of a Sole Proprietorship:

✓ Minimal legal restrictions

✓ Simple ownership form

✓ Low startup costs

✓ Sole ownership of profits

✓ Freedom in decision-making process

Disadvantages of a Sole Proprietorship:

✓ Unlimited personal liability

✓ Less available capital

✓ Possible difficulty in obtaining long-term financing

✓ Dissolution of the business in the event of the owner's death

Sole proprietorships are easy to form but are risky because the owner has unlimited personal liability.

Partnerships

Partnering Up: A partnership is a relationship between two or more persons who join to carry on a trade or business. Each person contributes money, property, labor, or skill, and each partner expects to share in the profits and losses of the business. A partnership may be considered when neither partner can operate the business alone. Each partner should bring specific advantages to the business. There are two types of partnerships–general and limited. The differences are outlined in the following key characteristics.

Key Characteristics of Partnerships:

✓ ***Existence:*** A general partnership can be formed through an oral agreement, but it is recommended that a written partnership agreement be made. General partners own the assets of the company, just as an individual owns assets in a sole proprietorship. A limited partnership consists of one or more general partners and one or more limited partners. Limited partners have limited liability in the company. A partnership exists as long as the partners agree it will and as long as all of the general partners remain in the partnerships. If a general partner leaves the partnership or dies, the partnership dissolves and the assets of the partnership must be sold or distributed to first pay the creditors and then the partners.

✓ ***Financial Management:*** The partnership should keep separate bank accounts and financial records for the business so that partners know whether there are profits and losses and the distribution of these amounts. The use of an outside accountant for record-keeping is recommended to prevent suspicion or doubt among partners.

✓ ***Liability:*** All owners in a general partnership have personal and unlimited liability for all actions undertaken in the name of the business, including all debts. Each partner is responsible for the acts of other partners when they act in the name of the business. Limited partners have no personal liability for the business of the partnership. Limited partners are liable only for the previously agreed-upon contribution or investment to the business.

✓ ***Taxes:*** Business, income, and sales taxes are the responsibility of every partner. For federal income taxes, partners must file returns on IRS Form 1065.

Advantages of a General Partnership:

✓ Ease of formation

✓ Direct profit rewards

✓ Larger management base than that of a sole proprietorship

Disadvantages of a General Partnership:

✓ Unlimited personal liability of general partners

✓ Multiple decision makers

✓ Limited life of the business

✓ Changes of partners or partnership agreement may be difficult

✓ Partnership dissolves in the event of a general partner's death

Use Caution: Partnerships should be entered into carefully. Potential partners should discuss their expectations of the business before deciding to go into business together.

Questions to ask include these:

✓ Do the partners want to grow and operate a company long-term?

✓ Do the partners want to grow a short-term company to sell?

✓ How will profits be distributed: 100 percent to partners, or a part to the business, the rest to partners? What are the profit distribution percentages?

✓ Do the partners agree on the nature of the business, including the types of jobs the business will accept?

Also, be sure to define each partner's individual responsibilities as well as the group responsibilities.

✓ Who can sign debt instruments, such as notes, bonds, and leases for the partnership?

✓ Who determines the amount and frequency of compensation, salaries, draws, or profit-sharing for the partners?

✓ Who will handle record-keeping?

✓ If required, who oversees recruitment of additional partners or dissolution of the partnership?

✓ Who can make amendments to the partnership agreement?

Partnership Registration in North Carolina: Limited partnerships and limited liability partnerships must register through the North Carolina Secretary of State, Business Registration Division. The application for registration and other partnership forms are available online at www.sosnc.gov/divisions/business_registration.

North Carolina Partnerships: North Carolina-based partnerships must submit domestic forms for registration.

Foreign Partnerships: Out-of-state partnerships and partnerships from other countries (both are called foreign partnerships) must submit foreign forms for registration.

Carefully examine business expectations and responsibilities before entering into a partnership.

C Corporations

Your Corporate Identity: If you decide to do business under a corporate identity, you will have to comply with the formal requirements of state law to create the corporation. A business assumes a corporate identity in North Carolina when it files as a corporation with the North Carolina Secretary of State.

Key Characteristics of Corporations:

✓ **Existence:** Incorporation gives your business a legal existence. That is, the business can own assets and conduct business in its own name. A corporation lasts as long as the stockholders determine it should.
A corporation continues to exist even if one or more of the shareholders die.

✓ **Financial Management:** The corporation needs separate bank accounts and separate business records. The corporation, not the shareholders, owns the money that the shareholders pay to buy the corporation's stock, all the assets, and the money earned by the corporation.

✓ **Liability:** The owners of the corporation, known as stockholders, are not personally liable for the losses of the business. Generally speaking, the corporate entity is responsible for business debts.

✓ **Taxes:** The corporation must file income tax returns and pay taxes on the profits. Dividends paid to shareholders by the corporation are also taxed to each shareholder individually. That is why there is said to be a "double tax" on corporations.

Other requirements for a corporation include:

✓ a board of directors and corporate officers;

✓ stockholders as owners of the company;

✓ periodic board meetings, maintenance of board minutes, and approval of corporate resolutions; and

✓ a board empowered to authorize certain actions such as borrowing money, entering into contracts, and allocating corporate resources beyond routine business transactions.

Advantages of a C Corporation:

✓ Separate legal entity

✓ Limited liability for stockholders

✓ Unlimited life of the business

✓ Availability of capital resources

✓ Transfer of ownership through sale of stock

Disadvantages of a C Corporation:

✓ Complex and expensive organization

✓ Limitations on corporate activities and decisions by the corporate charter

✓ Extensive regulation and record-keeping requirements

✓ Double taxation (one on corporate profits and again on dividends)

Filing for Incorporation in North Carolina: To begin the filing process, contact the Secretary of State, Business Registration Division to obtain the proper forms to complete.

North Carolina Secretary of State

Business Registration Division

2 South Salisbury Street

Raleigh, North Carolina 27601-2903

Telephone: (919) 814-5400

Fax: (919) 807-2063

Website: www.sosnc.gov

Forms are also available on the Secretary of State website.

Your corporation's name must include the following words or abbreviations: Company, Corporation, Incorporated, Limited, Co., Corp., Inc., or Ltd.

Complete the forms with appropriate signatures and turn them in with the appropriate fees.

North Carolina Corporations: North Carolina-based corporations must submit the domestic Articles of Incorporation form.

Foreign Corporations: Out-of-state corporations and corporations from other countries (both are called foreign corporations) must use foreign forms. Foreign corporations file an Application for Certificate of Authority with the Secretary of State, Business Registration Division to conduct business in North Carolina.

Fee Schedule: Filing fees are as follows:

✓ North Carolina (domestic) Profit Corporation: $125

✓ Foreign Profit Corporation: $250

Any significant changes to the Articles of Incorporation or Certificate of Authority in the form of amendments, mergers, consolidations, dissolutions, or withdrawals are also filed with the division. All filings are public record and available for inspection.

Annual Filing: Corporations are required to file an annual report. Annual reports delivered to the Secretary of Revenue are due by the due date for filing the corporation's income and franchise tax returns. Electronically filed annual reports with the Secretary of State are due by the fifteenth day of the fourth month following the close of the corporation's fiscal year.

Corporations are more complex to form and operate but reduce personal liability of the owners.

S Corporations

If your business is an eligible domestic corporation, you can avoid double federal taxation (corporate and shareholder taxes on the same earnings as in a C corporation) by electing to be treated as an S corporation under the rules of Subchapter S of the Internal Revenue Code. In this way, the S corporation passes its items of income, loss, deduction, and credits

through to its shareholders to be included on their separate returns.

Requirements for an S Corporation:

✓ Domestic corporation with one class of stock

✓ No more than 100 shareholders who are citizens or legal residents of the U.S.

✓ All shareholders must consent to S corporation status

✓ Use of a permitted tax year

✓ Filing of IRS Form 2553

S corporations have special tax considerations. Consult with the appropriate financial and legal professionals to find out if this option is right for you.

Limited Liability Company (LLC)

A Hybrid Structure: This legal arrangement shares characteristics of both sole proprietorship and corporate identities. LLCs must consist of at least one member. The ownership in your LLC is invested in memberships rather than shares of stock.

Limited liability companies offer some protection from liability for actions taken by your company or by other members of your company. It does not  protect from liability for personal actions. In this way, it resembles a sole proprietorship rather than a corporation.

Like an S corporation, federal income taxes are paid only on income distributed to members as ordinary income. A limited liability company can be expensive to organize and requires more administrative work. This form of organization is useful to professionals and general partnerships.

Advantages of a Limited Liability Company:

✓ Limited disclosure of owners

✓ Limited documentation

✓ No advance IRS filings

✓ No public disclosure of finances

✓ Limited liability for managers and members

✓ Ability to delegate management to a non-member

Tax Implications: LLCs are not taxed at an entity level. Depending on the number of business owners, the LLC is taxed differently.

- ✓ An LLC with one owner is taxed as a sole proprietorship.
- ✓ An LLC with more than one owner may elect to be taxed as a partnership or as a corporate entity.

Filing Articles of Organization in North Carolina: Limited liability companies (LLCs) are created by filing Articles of Organization with the Secretary of State, Business Registration Division. LLCs offer protection from personal liability for the manager or members for the debts and obligations of the company. LLCs enjoy the benefit of financial and management flexibility with less paperwork than required for corporations.

North Carolina Limited Liability Companies: North Carolina-based limited liability companies must use the domestic Articles of Organization forms.

Foreign Limited Liability Companies: Foreign (formed outside of North Carolina) limited liability companies must file an Application for Certificate of Authority with the Secretary of State, Business Registration Division to conduct business in North Carolina.

Fee Schedule: Filing fees are as follows:

- ✓ North Carolina (domestic) Limited Liability Company: $125
- ✓ Foreign Limited Liability Company: $250

Any significant changes to the Articles of Organization or Certificate of Authority for limited liability companies in the form of amendments, mergers, consolidations, dissolutions, or withdrawals are also filed with the division. All filings are public record and available for inspection.

Annual Filing: Limited liability companies are required to file an annual report. The first annual report is due on April 15th of the year following the creation year and every year thereafter on or before April 15th. Annual reports can be filed electronically or as a pre-populated annual report available for download on the North Carolina Secretary of State website.

Summary of Business Legal Structures

	Ownership	Liability	Formation Documents	Taxation	Management
Sole Proprietorship	One Owner	Unlimited personal liability	Doing Business As (DBA) Filing	Entity not taxed; profits and losses claimed on personal taxes	Owner
General Partnership	Unlimited number of general partners	Unlimited personal liability	General Partnership Agreement	Entity not taxed; profits and losses claimed on personal taxes of general partners	General partners
Limited Partnership	Unlimited number of general and limited partners	Unlimited personal liability of the general partners; limited partners generally have no personal liability	Limited Partnership Certificate Limited Partnership Agreement	Entity not taxed; profits and losses claimed on personal taxes of general and limited partners	General partners
Limited Liability Company (LLC)	Unlimited number of members	Generally no personal liability of the members for obligations of the business	Articles of Organization Operating Agreement	Entity not taxed (unless chosen to be taxed); profits and losses are passed through to the members	Manager or members designated in Operating Agreement
C Corporation	Unlimited number of shareholders	Generally no personal liability of the shareholders	Articles of Incorporation Bylaws Organizational Board Resolutions Stock Certificates Stock Ledger IRS and State S Corporation Election	Corporation taxed on its earnings at the corporate level and the shareholders may have a further tax on any dividends distributed ("double taxation")	Board of Directors
S Corporation	Up to 100 shareholders allowed	Generally no personal liability of the shareholders	Articles of Incorporation Bylaws Organizational Board Resolutions Stock Certificates Stock Ledger IRS and State S Corporation Election	Entity generally not taxed, as profits and losses are passed through to the shareholders ("pass-through" taxation)	Board of Directors

Joint Ventures

Complement Your Strengths: A joint venture is a special business arrangement that exists when two or more companies join to undertake a specific project. The management of a joint venture is often assigned to one individual or company. This arrangement brings together companies with complementary resources and strengths. When forming this type of venture, it is important to consult an attorney to ensure that all aspects of risk are covered.

Naming Your Business

Choose Wisely: Selecting a name is an important part of forming your business. The name you choose affects your customers' impression of your company. The individuality of the name affects future trademarks and service marks. It is important to select a name that is distinctive.

Do your homework before you decide on a name for your company. A search can be conducted using the following sources:

✓ U.S. Patent and Trademark Office (800) 786-9199 or at www.uspto.gov

✓ Secretary of State Office in the state where you intend to do business

✓ Internet search engines such as www.yahoo.com or www.google.com

A business may choose to file for a trademark or service mark. A trademark can be a word, name, symbol, sound, or color used to represent and distinguish a company's products. A service mark can be a word, name, symbol, sound, or color used to represent and distinguish a company's services. A trademark or service mark is not the same as a trade name. Trademarks can be filed on the state and federal level. State information is available through the North Carolina Secretary of State. Federal information is available through the U.S. Patent and Trademark Office.

Registering Your Name in North Carolina

The North Carolina Secretary of State, Business Registration Division is the agency to contact in order to file Articles of Incorporation and Organization, to determine name availability for corporate and limited liability companies (LLCs), to file applications by foreign corporations seeking authority to transact business in North Carolina, and to file annual reports. The Business Registration Division is responsible for the examination, custody, and maintenance of the legal documents filed by more than 400,000 corporations, limited partnerships, and limited liability companies. The duty of the Secretary of State is to ensure uniform compliance with the statutes governing the creation of these entities, record the information required to be kept as a public record, and provide that information to the public. The Business Registration Division acts in an administrative capacity only and cannot give legal advice.

> *North Carolina Secretary of State*
> *Business Registration Division*
> *2 South Salisbury Street*
> *Raleigh, North Carolina 27601-2903*
>
> *Telephone: (919) 814-5400*
> *Fax: (919) 807-2063*
>
> *Website: www.sosnc.gov*

Reserving a Corporate Name: A corporate name may be reserved 120 days prior to incorporation by completing the name reservation application and paying a $30.00 fee.

The name you choose for your corporation must be clearly distinguishable from the names of all other corporations, limited liability companies, and limited partnerships already on file with the Business Registration. You can check the corporate name you have chosen by calling (919) 814-5400. Any clearance you receive from the Business Registration Division by phone for a corporate name is preliminary. There is no guarantee that the name you choose during your preliminary check will still be available when you file your registration paperwork unless you file a formal application to reserve a name.

Formally reserve the name or wait for confirmation of your filing prior to obtaining stationery, business cards, phone listings, bank accounts, etc.

Assumed Name Filing: Most companies, including sole proprietorships, select a business name other than the owner's name and often design a logo to be used on advertising, stationery, and other materials. An assumed name certificate (commonly referred to as a "doing business as" or "DBA" filing) is filed at the Registrar of Deeds in any county where you want to do business. There is no statewide name registration for sole proprietorships or general partnerships.

Final Inspection...

Sole Proprietorships: This business structure offers easy formation and operation. However, unlimited personal liability is a concern because the business and owner are considered the same legal entity.

Partnerships: Partnerships can bring together two or more people with strengths and resources in different areas but also allow for unlimited personal liability of general partners. To reduce conflicts among partners, responsibilities and business goals must be clearly outlined at the beginning of the business arrangement.

C Corporations: C corporations offer liability protection to the owners and easy ownership transfer through stock sales. This business structure is more complex to operate and shareholders may be "double-taxed" on their earnings.

S Corporations: S corporations are similar to C corporations but offer special tax considerations. S corporation status can be filed with the IRS, if companies meet the specified criteria.

Limited Liability Company (LLC): LLCs have characteristics of both sole proprietorships and corporations.

Summary of Business Legal Structures: Each type of business entity has unique ownership, liability, taxation, and management characteristics. Required formation documents differ for each business structure.

Joint Ventures: Joint ventures are generally formed on a project basis in order to integrate positive attributes and resources of two or more companies.

Naming Your Business: An appropriate business name is important and defines how your customers perceive you.

Reserving Your Name in North Carolina: A corporate name may be reserved 120 days prior to incorporation. The name must be distinguishable from other names on file with the Secretary of State.

Supplemental Forms

Supplemental forms and links are available at **NASCLAforms.org** using access code **NC129354**.

Summary of Business Legal Structures	Table showing the primary features of each type of business entity (featured earlier in the chapter).
IRS Form 2553	IRS form to elect S corporation status

Chapter 3
BECOMING A LICENSED CONTRACTOR

Chapter Survey...

⇨ *Purpose of Licensing*

⇨ *North Carolina Licensing Board for General Contractors*

⇨ *When is a Contractor's License Needed for General Contracting?*

⇨ *Licensing Process*

⇨ *License Limitations*

⇨ *License Renewals*

⇨ *Reciprocity*

⇨ *Disciplinary Action*

⇨ *Homeowners Recovery Fund*

Purpose of Licensing

A major purpose of contractor licensing is to protect the health, safety, and welfare of the public. Licensing also defines the work that a contractor is allowed to do under a particular license.

Licensing establishes entrance requirements, standards of practice, and disciplinary authority to protect the public from unqualified, incompetent, and unethical contractors.

✓ **Entrance Requirements:** Licensing ensures that those practicing a trade or occupation have met a minimum set of qualifications, such as experience, training, and required examination.

✓ **Standards of Practice:** Contractors are required to adhere to standards of practice established by law. These workmanship standards ensure an appropriate level of quality is given to the public. Continuing education may be required for certain trades.

✓ **Disciplinary Authority:** Statutes define illegal and prohibited activities. Licensing authorities have a mechanism to conduct investigations and administer discipline to problem contractors. Violations of the general contracting laws and regulations may result in penalties including suspension and revocation of license. The Board may recover reasonable administrative costs associated with the investigation or prosecution of a violation.

North Carolina Licensing Board for General Contractors

The North Carolina Licensing Board for General Contractors was established for the purpose of safeguarding life, health, and property and to promote public welfare. The licensing statutes that govern the Board prescribe certain standards for persons, firms, and corporations who enter into contracts for construction work in the state.

North Carolina Licensing Board for General Contractors
5400 Creedmoor Road
Raleigh, North Carolina 27612

Phone: (919) 571-4183
Fax: (919) 571-4703

Website: www.nclbgc.org

The Board issues general contractor licenses in the following classifications:

✓ building,

✓ residential,

✓ highway,

✓ public utilities,

✓ specialty, and

✓ unclassified (includes all of the above classifications).

Laws and regulations governing general contractors are found in Appendix E and F, at the end of this book.

When is a Contractor's License Needed for General Contracting?

Current laws in North Carolina define general contractors as persons, firms, or corporations who enter into construction contracts in the amount of $30,000 or more. General contractors must obtain a license before bidding, entering into a contract, or undertaking an agreement to superintend or manage these construction projects.

In general, subcontractors working under the supervision of a prime or general contractor do not need to be licensed. You also do not need a license if the land is in your name and you are building a house that is to be solely occupied by you and your family for 12 months after completion.

Licensing Process

You must complete the licensing process to obtain a contractor's license. The following is a summary of this process.

1. Complete the contractor's license application. The application is available for free online on the Board website at www.nclbgc.org.

    Physical application packages are available through the mail by sending a personal check, money order, or cashier's check for $15.00, payable to the North Carolina Licensing Board for General Contractors, to 5400 Creedmoor Rd., Raleigh, NC 27612. Cash is not accepted.

    Applications are available at the Board office for $13.00. The office is located at 5400 Creedmoor Road, Raleigh, North Carolina 27612.

    Application packages include
    ✓ application form and instructions,
    ✓ information for all 21 exams,
    ✓ state requirements, and
    ✓ copy of the laws and regulations applicable to general contracting in the State of North Carolina.

    Applications are reviewed twice per month.

2. The Board, in determining the qualifications of any applicant for examination eligibility, shall, among other things, consider the following:
    ✓ character,
    ✓ competency,
    ✓ ability,
    ✓ integrity,
    ✓ financial ability, and
    ✓ ability to comply with the provisions of the licensing law or any other law of the state.

    The Board sends an examination eligibility letter to notify candidates who are approved.

3. Register for examination through PSI and a pay fee of $79. If an applicant/qualifier is utilizing an exam waiver from an authorized state or the NASCLA exam a North Carolina Law & Regulation Exam will be required before the license can be issued.

    PSI Licensure–Certification
    3210 E. Tropicana
    Las Vegas, Nevada 89121

    Phone: (800) 733-9267
    Fax: (702) 932-2666

    www.psiexams.com

4. Take examination as scheduled through PSI. Official scores are mailed by the Board. If you fail the examination, you may retake the examination 30 days after the previous examination. Reexamination forms are mailed with failing test scores.

5. The Board reviews official examination scores and applicants pay a nonrefundable license fee. Fees are as follows:

Unlimited	$125
Intermediate	$100
Limited	$75

6. The Board issues a license for the appropriate classification.

Display of License: At all times, the license certificate granted by the Board with the chairman's and secretary-treasurer's signatures must be displayed at the licensee's place of business.

Change of Address: License applicants and license holders must notify the Board in writing of a change in address within 30 days from the date of the change.

Complete Application &
Submit to Board Ofice

Board Review of
Application & Distribution
of Eligibility Letter

Register for Examination
& Pay Fee

Take Examination &
Scores Mailed to Board

Review of Official
Examination
Scores

Issuance of License
by Board

License Limitations

License limitations are determined by the amount of
the applicant's working capital. Limitation categories
are as follows:

	Project Limitation	Amount of Working Capital
Limited	Up to $500,000	$17,000
Intermediate	Up to $1,000,000	$75,000
Unlimited	No Restrictions	$150,000

Applicants who submit an application for an
intermediate or an unlimited license must have the
required working capital shown in the chart reflected

in an Agreed Upon Procedures report on the form
provided in the license application or an audited
financial statement prepared by a certified public
accountant or an independent accountant who is
engaged in the public practice of accountancy.

Bonding: Applicants may present a surety bond in
lieu of demonstrating the required amount of working
capital. Required bond amounts are as follows:

	Bond Amount
Limited	$175,000
Intermediate	$500,000
Unlimited	$1,000,000

If the bond is canceled, the surety and applicant must
notify the Board immediately. The applicant's license
is suspended if written proof of financial responsibility
is not provided within 30 days of bond cancellation.

Limitation Increase: To request an increase in
limitation, you must complete an increase application
form. To be considered for an increase, your license
must be active and renewed. An audited financial
statement with an unqualified opinion, a classified
balance sheet, and accompanying notes to the
financial statement must be submitted with the
increase application form and appropriate fee.
The audit must be prepared by a certified public
accountant or an independent accountant who is
engaged in the public practice of accountancy.

License Renewals

North Carolina enacted a law that requires 8 hours of
continuing education annually as a condition to license
renewal effective January 1, 2020 for the license
classifications of Building, Residential and Unclassified.
(See NCGS 93-10.2 in Appendices E & F)

Licenses expire annually on January 1. Renewal fees are
as follows:

Limited	$75
Intermediate	$100
Unlimited	$125

If the license is not renewed within 60 days following
expiration, it becomes invalid.

Contractors with an invalid license are considered
unlicensed. If more than four years pass after the
license expires, the contractor must go through the full
application process.

Renewal applications are delivered electronically to licensed contractors by November 30. Completed renewal applications must have the required financial information or certification and are required to be submitted electronically as prescribed by the Board.

The renewal certificate granted by the Board with the chairman's and secretary-treasurer's signatures must be displayed at all times by the licensee's place of business.

Reciprocity

North Carolina has a reciprocal agreement with Georgia, Louisiana, Mississippi, South Carolina, and Tennessee's contractor licensing boards to waive certain examinations. However, contractors must still complete the application process in order to become licensed in the state of North Carolina. In addition to the state exams listed, North Carolina also accepts the *NASCLA Accredited Examination for Commercial General Building Contractors*. If an applicant is using an authorized exam waiver from another state or the NASCLA exam, the applicant/qualifier will be required to pass the North Carolina Law & Regulation exam before a license will be issued.

Disciplinary Action

Complaints against general contractors are filed with the Board office. All complaints are reviewed by the Board and assigned to a investigator.

Contractor Notification: Once a complaint is received, written notice of the complaint and the charges are sent to the licensee or general contractor for a response.

Investigation: Following a preliminary review of the complaint, an investigator may gather additional evidence by inspecting the construction project or the work in question. Investigators may also interview the contractor, witnesses, or other individuals familiar with the case. When an investigation is completed, the case is forwarded to the Board's review committee, which then determines whether probable cause exists to recommend that the case be presented to the full Board for a disciplinary hearing.

Penalties: The Board may impose discipline by revoking or suspending the license of the general contractor based on a finding of gross negligence, incompetence, misconduct, or willful violations of the licensing laws.

If the general contractor is not licensed to practice general contracting, the Board may only seek entry of a permanent injunction against the contractor in Superior Court. The Board's disciplinary statutes, which describe these procedures, are found at North Carolina General Statutes 87-11(a), 87-13, and 87-13.1.

Homeowners Recovery Fund

The Homeowners Recovery Fund was created to provide some amount of monetary assistance to homeowners who have suffered a reimbursable loss resulting from the dishonest or incompetent conduct of a licensed general contractor. This fund is administered by the Licensing Board for General Contractors.

Eligibility for Assistance: To be eligible for assistance from the fund, a claimant must be the owner or former owner of the single-family residential dwelling in question. The claimant must be able to show the Board that he or she has suffered a reimbursable loss that resulted from the dishonest or incompetent conduct of a licensed general contractor or of an unlicensed contractor who fraudulently represented him- or herself as licensed. No part of the loss may have been paid in any amount by or on behalf of the general contractor or be covered by a bond, surety agreement, or an insurance contract. Claimants must exhaust all other remedies for recovery before being eligible for assistance from the fund.

Other Remedies for Recovery: The claimant must have sued the general contractor in civil court and obtained a judgment that has not been paid by the contractor and remains unsatisfied. If the contractor filed bankruptcy during construction or during the civil action, the claimant must exhaust all remedies in the bankruptcy proceeding. This includes filing a proof of claim and/or following any procedures necessary to obtain consideration in the bankruptcy proceeding. The review committee will not consider a claim involving the bankruptcy of the general contractor until the bankruptcy proceeding is terminated.

Claims Against the Recovery Fund: Once a claim has been received by the Homeowners Recovery Fund, the Board staff opens a case file. The claim form and all attachments are copied and served on the general contractor alleged to be the cause of the reimbursable loss. The contractor has 30 days to respond to the allegations contained in the claim. The staff conducts an investigation to determine if the claimant meets the requirements for reimbursement set forth in the Homeowners Recovery Fund statutes and rules (at N.C.G.S. 87-15.5 and 21 NCAC 12.0900).

Board Review: Once the investigation is complete, the Board staff presents the facts to the Homeowners Recovery Fund Review Committee, which will make an initial decision as to whether the claimant has successfully met the requirements for assistance from the fund. If the review committee determines that the claimant meets the requirements, a formal hearing is scheduled before the Board.

Hearing: At the hearing, the claimant appears before a panel of Board members and presents information regarding the claim. The purpose and focus of this hearing is to determine the actual loss the claimant has incurred as a result of the actions of the general contractor. Board members may ask questions about the claim and the information provided.

Following the presentation of this information, the Board will make a determination as to the amount of assistance, if any, they will award. Only the actual loss is considered. Attorneys' fees, court costs, special damages, consequential damages, punitive damages, etc. are not considered. The Board's decision is final. All awards are a matter of privilege and not of right.

Final Inspection...

Purpose of Licensing: A major purpose of licensing is to protect the health, safety, and welfare of the public.

North Carolina Licensing Board for General Contractors: The North Carolina Licensing Board for General Contractors regulates general contracting activities through examination, licensure, and disciplinary action.

When is a Contractor's License Needed for General Contracting? A contractor's license is required for construction projects valued at $30,000 or more.

Licensing Process: You must complete the licensing process to obtain a contractor license. The license certificate must be displayed at the licensee's place of business.

License Limitations: License limitations are determined by the amount of working capital of the applicant. A bond may be posted in lieu of providing written proof of financial responsibility.

License Renewals: Licenses expire annually on January 1.

Reciprocity: North Carolina has a reciprocal agreement with Georgia, Louisiana, Mississippi, South Carolina, and Tennessee's contractor licensing boards to waive certain examinations.

Disciplinary Action: Penalties for violations include being charged with a misdemeanor, fines, reprimand and suspension or revocation of license.

Homeowners Recovery Fund: This fund was created to provide some amount of monetary assistance to homeowners who have suffered a reimbursable loss resulting from the dishonest or incompetent conduct of a licensed general contractor.

Chapter 4
MANAGING RISK

Managing risk can be one of the biggest challenges you'll face in the construction industry. The weather, site conditions, customer changes, and employees can be just a few of the unpredictable factors in a job. Some of the risks that you face are preventable and others can be minimized.

Risk assessment is one of the most important steps in the risk management process. You must determine the probability of loss occurring and the consequences if the loss occurs. Your approach to a risk with the potential for a large loss and a low probability of occurring is handled differently from a risk with a potential for minimum loss but a high likelihood of occurring.

Potential risk must be examined on both a project and overall business basis. Future chapters will focus on the skills you need to assess, manage, and ultimately protect yourself against risks for certain situations, such as environmental and safety risks.

Risk Management Benefits

Unmanaged risk can harm your business, resulting in financial loss, lower profit margins, and unnecessary liabilities. Risk management involves assessing all areas of your business from operations to administrative functions. Good risk management provides several benefits that can affect your reputation and bottom line:

✓ Lower business and liability insurance premiums

✓ Reduce chances of being sued

✓ Improve chances of prevailing in a lawsuit

Risk is managed in several ways. There may be provisions added to a contract to reduce your risk (discussed in Chapter 8), or safety programs or operating procedures can be put in place. Other risks can be minimized through insurance coverage and bonding, which will be discussed in this chapter.

Insurance

While some risks can be minimized, others are uncontrollable. Insurance is a way to supplement your risk management program to protect your business against unforeseen events, such as accidents and theft. Without it, you could lose your business in a lawsuit as a result of one bad accident. The less coverage your business has, the more risk you assume. As you increase coverage, you reduce your risk.

Insurance Defined: Insurance is a protective measure in which coverage is obtained for a specific risk (or set of risks) through a contract. In this contract or policy, one party indemnifies another against specified loss in return for premiums paid. Indemnity is a way to transfer risk and exemption from loss incurred by any course of action. Sometimes an insurance payout is called an indemnity.

An insurance policy outlines the specifics of the contract between your business and the insurance company. At a minimum, the policy lists the policy term, coverage, premiums, and deductibles.

Finding the Right Insurance Company and Agent: Large companies often employ full-time risk managers. Most small business owners do not have this benefit, and this makes finding the right insurance company and agent important to the risk management process. There are two types of agents: those who work with only one insurance company and independent agents who can shop around for policies with competing companies. Regardless of which type of agent you choose, it is important to find a professional you can trust. Your agent will provide you with a wealth of knowledge on insurance and risk management topics and help you assess your insurance needs.

Required Coverage: The law may require you to carry a certain level of coverage, such as workers' compensation, unemployment, and vehicle insurance.

Many construction contracts require a contractor to maintain certain types of insurance and coverage levels. The following chart gives an example of how insurance coverage requirements might be outlined in a contract.

Type of Insurance	Minimum Insurance Coverage (Combined Single Limit Per Occurrence / Aggregate)
Commercial General Liability including Premises - Operations Products / Completed Operations Contractual Insurance Property Damage Independent Contractors Bodily Injury	$3,000,000 / $3,000,000
Automobile Liability Owned, Non-owned, or Rented	$3,000,000 / $3,000,000
Workers' Compensation and Occupational Diseases	As Required by Applicable Laws
Employer's Liability	$3,000,000

It is important to conduct a site survey to assess any special conditions that may cause added risk to a project. You should also consider the nature of each project to be sure you have adequate coverage for the work you are performing. You may want to talk this over with your insurance agent and add supplemental coverage when necessary.

In this chapter, we will focus on policies that apply to the construction industry, but you should consult with your insurance carrier for a plan that is right for you and provides your business with the best protection.

Property Insurance

Property insurance typically covers your business and personal property when damage, theft, or loss occurs. You can buy property insurance to cover specific risks such as fire or theft or you can purchase a broad-based policy to cover a variety of risks (including fire, theft, vandalism, and "acts of God" such as lightning strikes). In considering property insurance, evaluate your physical location and the region in which you do business to determine which risks are likely to occur, such as hurricanes or floods.

Types of Property You May Want to Cover:

✓ Buildings and other structures (owned or leased)
✓ Furniture, equipment, and supplies
✓ Inventory
✓ Machinery
✓ Computers
✓ Intellectual property, (i.e., books and documents)
✓ Automobiles, trucks, and construction equipment
✓ Intangible property (i.e., good will, trademarks, etc.)
✓ Leased equipment

All-Risk Builders' Risk Insurance

All-risk builders' risk insurance is a form of property insurance that covers property owners and builders for buildings under construction. This type of insurance typically covers machinery, equipment, materials, supplies, and fixtures that are part of the structure or will become part of the structure. Additional coverage can be added for items, such as temporary structures and scaffolding, used during construction. In general, major construction defects such as poor workmanship and faulty design are not covered. Your tools also may not be covered under this type of policy. You should talk to your insurance agent about getting separate coverage for these items.

All-risk coverage provides for direct loss by those perils that are not specifically excluded by the policy. It generally provides coverage for almost all risks, including theft, vandalism, accidental losses, and damage or destruction. Construction must be in progress for coverage to exist.

The American Institute of Architects (AIA) and the Associated General Contractors of America (AGC) publish contract documents useful for owners and contractors (for AIA documents, check the AIA website at www.aiacontracts.org; for AGC documents, see the organization's website at www.agc.org). These standard documents require the purchase of all-risk coverage. An owner has the option of giving the responsibility of purchasing all-risk coverage to the general contractor. If this is the case, the owner is required to notify the general contractor in writing. General contractors may prefer to purchase the insurance because they may have a deeper understanding of the project and the potential risk. The cost of the insurance is then passed on to the owner.

The standard AIA and AGC documents require replacement cost coverage for losses that occur. Replacement cost coverage replaces damaged property without any allowances or deductions, such as depreciation.

If you use documents other than the AIA and AGC standard forms, carefully examine the insurance obligations for both you and the owner and discuss any concerns with your insurance agent.

A subrogation clause is generally included in the builders' risk insurance policy. Subrogation typically occurs when the insurance company pays the insured for damage or loss and then sues the negligent third party to pay for the loss. This can lead to a situation where the contractor is sued by the owner's insurance company for a loss that occurred.

To avoid this situation between the owner, contractor, and subcontractors, the contract may contain a clause waiving the parties' right to sue one another.

Named Peril Builders' Risk Insurance

Named peril builders' risk insurance policies have narrower coverage than all-risk insurance and specify what perils are covered. Typical named peril policies are written for fire and lightning but can also include events such as wind damage, explosion, water damage, terrorism, or earthquake.

Inland Marine/Equipment Theft Insurance

Inland marine insurance is a type of property insurance that you can purchase for your tools and equipment. It provides coverage for goods in transit and projects under construction. The cost of the insurance may be more than the cost of putting preventive measures in place to deter theft. It is important to secure your equipment by using the proper locks, creating limited access through fencing and locked storage areas, and removing keys from the ignition of all vehicles. Equipment theft increases the cost of insurance premiums, and if it happens often, you might find it difficult to obtain coverage.

Equipment Floater Policy

An equipment floater policy is a type of inland marine insurance. Coverage for equipment is available on an all-risk or specified-peril basis. The coverage provided is for direct physical loss to the equipment and is designed to cover mobile equipment while it is stored on premises, in transit, or at temporary locations or jobsites. An endorsement can be added for rented or leased equipment. Normal wear and tear is generally not covered by the equipment floater policy.

Transportation Floater and Motor Truck Cargo Insurance

Both transportation floater and motor truck cargo insurance are types of inland marine insurance. A transportation floater policy protects the transporter against damage that occurs to freight during transport. Motor truck cargo insurance protects the transporter in the event of damaged or lost freight. This protection also applies to contractors who transport equipment or materials to and from the jobsite.

Liability Insurance

Liability insurance is designed to protect against third-party claims that arise from alleged negligence resulting in bodily injury or property damage. Payment is not typically made to the insured but rather to someone suffering loss who is not a party to the insurance contract.

Commercial General Liability (CGL)

Commercial general liability (CGL) insurance offers basic liability coverage. CGL covers four types of injuries, including:

✓ bodily injury that results in actual physical damage or loss for individuals who are not employees;

✓ damage or loss to property not belonging to the business;

✓ personal injury, including slander or damage to reputation; and

✓ advertising injury, including charges of negligence that result from promotion of goods or services.

Most businesses in the construction industry will need to supplement their CGL policy with other types of insurance, such as a vehicle insurance policy.

Umbrella Liability Insurance

An umbrella liability insurance policy can supplement your CGL policy. The umbrella policy provides additional coverage in the areas that are not covered in the CGL policy. This type of insurance takes effect once a certain deductible or self-insured retention level is met. Umbrella insurance coverage can be customized to meet the needs of your business.

Director's and Officer's (D and O)Liability Insurance

Director's and officer's (D and O) liability insurance protects directors and officers from liability due to actions connected with their corporate positions. These actions include such things as misstatement of financial reports, misuse of company funds, and failure to honor an employment contract. This insurance does not cover intentional or illegal acts.

Other Types of Liability Insurance

Other types of liability insurance may be purchased in order to cover exclusions that exist in your CGL policy. Examples of additional liability coverage include:

✓ **Contractual liability insurance** provides contractors with protection for damages that result from their negligence while under written contract.

✓ **Completed operations liability insurance** provides coverage for loss arising out of completed projects.

✓ **Contractor's protective public and property damage liability insurance** protects contractors who supervise and subsequently are held liable for actions of subcontractors from claims for personal injury and property damage.

✓ **Professional liability insurance** (sometimes called errors and omissions insurance) protects contractors from negligence resulting from errors or omissions of designers and architects.

✓ **Construction wrap-up liability insurance** bundles liability and workers' compensation insurance for general contractors and subcontractors on large construction projects. This type of insurance helps eliminate gaps in coverage. To qualify for this type of insurance, certain contract cost requirements must be met. These requirements vary by state.

Business Owner's Policies (BOPs)

Business owner's policies (BOPs) bundle property and liability coverage together. This type of coverage can eliminate gaps or overlaps between separate property and liability policies. Small and mid-sized companies usually qualify for this type of policy. A business selects the amount of liability coverage it needs based on its assets. Additional coverage can be purchased depending on the particular risks of the company.

Automobile Insurance

If you have a company vehicle or a fleet of vehicles, auto insurance provides coverage for liability and physical damage associated with vehicles owned by your company. All states require vehicle owners to carry some level of liability insurance covering bodily injury and property damage incurred in a vehicle accident. Physical damage coverage pays for the damage to the insured vehicle. Different types of automobile insurance are available. Various options include coverage for only vehicles owned; vehicles owned, leased or hired; and for all automobiles, including those not owned, leased, or hired.

Burglary and Theft Insurance

Burglary and theft insurance covers loss or damage by burglary, theft, larceny, robbery, forgery, fraud, and vandalism. However, this type of insurance generally does not cover employee acts.

Fidelity bond or employee theft insurance is used to cover criminal acts of burglary and theft by employees.

Key Man Life Insurance

This type of coverage is beneficial if your company depends on specific individuals for continuing success of your business. For example, if your legal structure is a partnership, the success or ongoing existence of the company would not continue if one of the partners died or became incapacitated. Key man insurance is available as life insurance, disability insurance, or both.

Coverage Gaps and Overlaps

It is important to understand the coverage that each of your policies provides. You must be aware of gaps and overlaps that may exist between policies. Differences in coverage can cause difficulties in claim settlement, particularly when a claim falls in the gray area between coverages. For example, if a claim involves both an automobile and property, there may be a conflict between which policy covers the damage. To minimize these conflicts, you may want one insurer for all policies. If you have overlapping coverage, make sure that each policy has fairly equal reimbursement levels. This will ensure that you receive equal coverage if more than one policy covers a claim.

Carefully evaluate your risk management program and supplement it with the appropriate insurance coverage.

Employment-Related Insurance

Workers' Compensation Insurance

Workers' compensation insurance provides coverage for employees who are injured on the job. The insurance is purchased by the employer; no part of

it should be paid for by employees or deducted from their pay.

North Carolina Coverage Requirements: If you are a sole proprietorship, partnership, or LLC, you are required by law to carry workers' compensation coverage if you have three or more employees. Employees can be full-time, part-time, regular, seasonal, or family members. Sole proprietors, partners, and managers and members of the LLC are not included in the headcount.

All forms of corporations with a total of three or more people are required by law to carry workers' compensation coverage. Everyone is included in the headcount, including corporate officers.

If one or more employees are employed in activities which involve the use or presence of radiation, workers' compensation is required.

Subcontractor Coverage: Any contractor who sublets any part of a contract must first obtain documentation that the subcontractor is in compliance with the North Carolina Workers' Compensation Act. Subcontractors must provide compliance documentation regardless of whether the subcontractor employs fewer than three employees. If proper documentation is not obtained, the party subletting the contract is liable for payment of compensation and other benefits if any of the subcontractor's employees are injured or die from an accident associated with the work covered by the subcontract.

As part of your operating policies, you may require subcontractors to carry workers' compensation coverage even if the subcontractor has less than three employees.

Information on North Carolina's program is available through the Industrial Commission.

North Carolina Industrial Commission
1240 Mail Service Center
Raleigh, North Carolina 27699-1240

Physical Address:
430 N. Salisbury Street
Raleigh, North Carolina 27603

Telephone (919) 807-2501 or 800-688-8349
Fax: (919) 715-0282

Website: www.ic.nc.gov

Chapter 11, Employee Management, covers workers' compensation insurance in more detail.

Follow the Law...

Workers' compensation insurance coverage may be required by law for your business. It is 100 percent employer-paid and premiums cannot be deducted from the employee's pay.

Employer's liability insurance can be purchased to supplement your workers' compensation insurance in the event you are sued for negligence as a result of an employee injury or death.

Unemployment Insurance

Unemployment insurance (UI) programs provide unemployment benefits to eligible workers who become unemployed through no fault of their own and meet certain other eligibility requirements. This program is jointly financed through federal and state employer payroll taxes (federal/state UI tax).

Generally, employers must pay both state and federal unemployment taxes if:

✓ they pay wages to employees totaling $1,500 or more in any quarter of a calendar year; or

✓ they had at least one employee during any day of a week during 20 weeks in a calendar year, regardless of whether or not the weeks were consecutive.

North Carolina Program: The North Carolina Employment Security Law establishes guidelines for state unemployment tax. Business entities are subject to an unemployment payroll tax if they have one or more employees for 20 weeks during a calendar year or pay $1,500 in wages in any calendar quarter during a calendar year in North Carolina.

The tax is payable quarterly. Tax wage base and tax rate may vary from year to year. For the most current information, refer to the North Carolina Division of Employment Security (DES). Current tax rates are available online at www.ncesc.com. New business entities in North Carolina are subject are assigned a new business tax rate for the first two years. The rate may be changed after the entity comes under an experience rating.

Additional information regarding the North Carolina state unemployment tax is available at:

State of North Carolina
Division of Employment Security (DES)
P.O. Box 25903
Raleigh, North Carolina 27611-5903

Tax Telephone: 919-707-1150
Claims Telephone: 888-737-0259

Website: des.nc.gov/des

Chapter 11, Employee Management, covers unemployment insurance in more detail.

Social Security Insurance

The Social Security Administration (SSA) is a federal agency responsible for paying retirement, disability, and survivors' benefits to workers and their families. The SSA is also responsible for administering the Supplemental Security Income program. The SSA issues Social Security numbers, which are required for employees to legally work in the United States. Chapter 15, Tax Basics, explains how to submit Social Security tax for employees.

Insurance Coverage for Subcontractors

When hiring subcontractors, you should verify their insurance coverage to ensure it is adequate enough to cover any liability arising from their work.

There are a few simple questions you can ask to assess proper coverage:

✓ **Does the subcontractor carry the appropriate insurance?** Determine what type of insurance is needed. For example, you may require the subcontractor to carry commercial general liability (CGL) insurance.

✓ **Is the coverage adequate for the type of work being performed?** You can be held responsible for damages not covered by the subcontractor's insurance. Make sure their coverage limits are large enough to cover your project.

✓ **Is the insurance coverage current?** You can check with the insurance company listed on the insurance certificate to verify that the subcontractor's insurance coverage is current and that it will cover your project.

If insurance coverage is required, it is prudent to write the requirements into the contract. Chapter 8, Contract Management, talks about indemnification clauses as a contract provision to limit risk. This provision can also be included in your contract with the subcontractor. Indemnification absolves your company of any losses or damages incurred by the subcontractor.

What is a Bond?

A surety bond is a risk transfer mechanism between a surety, the contractor, and the project owner. The agreement binds the contractor to comply with the terms and conditions of a contract. If the contractor cannot perform the contract, the surety assumes the contractor's responsibilities and ensures that the project is completed.

Statutory and Common-Law Bonds: The federal government uses surety bonds on construction projects as a way to pre-qualify prospective construction firms. A surety bond is often required by law for public projects. It is referred to as a statutory bond. The owner of a private construction project may also opt to require a bond as an added guarantee that a project will be completed on-time, on budget, and within specified requirements. These private construction bonds are sometimes referred to as common-law bonds.

Surety Bonding Companies: When selecting a surety bonding company, check with the U.S. Department of the Treasury or a similar state agency (i.e., Department of Insurance) to ensure that the company is licensed for bonding. The surety company is the primary risk-taker in a bonding agreement, so it is important that it complies with all applicable laws and regulations.

Bond Language

Bonds generally contain four basic requirements.

✓ **Total dollar amount required for the bond**
The bond amount is generally set as a percentage of the estimated cost. This number can vary and can be up to 100 percent of the estimated cost of construction. Maintenance bonds often use a figure of 10 percent of construction cost as the required amount.

✓ **Length of the bond**
Bond lengths are typically required for a fixed rate of time following a project milestone, after which the bond is released. For construction performance bonds, this is usually after completion and final approval of the project.

✓ **Requirements for notice of defect or lack of maintenance**
A period for completion of corrections is generally outlined after a notice of defect. The bond also establishes a time period for response from the bonding company, if the contractor fails to meet the obligations of the contract.

✓ **Bond enforcement**
If the contractor does not successfully complete all required work or violates any requirement of the bond, enforcement measures are outlined to ensure project completion and proper maintenance.

Types of Bonds

A *bid bond* guarantees that the contractor, if awarded the job, will do work at the submitted bid price, enter into a contract with the owner, and furnish the required performance and payment bonds. Bid bonds serve as a deterrent against frivolous or unqualified bidders. If the contractor defaults on the bid agreement, the bid bond can be used to make up the pricing difference with the next lowest bidder.

A **performance bond** guarantees that the contractor will complete a contract within its time frame and conditions.

A **payment bond** guarantees subcontractors and suppliers that they will be paid for work if they perform properly under the contract.

A **maintenance bond** guarantees that for a stated period, typically for one year, no defective workmanship or material will appear in the completed project.

A **completion bond** provides assurance to the financial backers of a construction project that it will be completed on time.

A **fidelity bond** covers business owners for losses due to dishonest acts by their employees.

A **lien bond** guarantees that liens cannot be placed against the owner's property by contractors for payment of services. This type of bond allows someone to "bond around" a labor or materialmen's lien.

Just as the owner may require the general contractor to obtain a performance bond, a payment bond, or both, the general contractor may require the same of the subcontractor. The **subcontractor's bond** protects the general contractor in the event that the subcontractor does not fully perform the contract and/or pay for labor and materials.

A **bank letter of credit** is not a bond but is a cash guarantee to the owner. It is not a guarantee of performance but can be converted to a payment to the owner by a bank or lending institution. The letter of credit typically does not cover 100 percent of the contract but customarily 5 percent to 10 percent of the contract.

Various types of bonds are issued as a protective measure in the event that contractual obligations are not met.

Qualifying for a Bond

Before issuing a bond, a surety company will examine your business thoroughly to make sure it is established, profitable, and well-managed. Some of the items the surety company will evaluate to make this determination include:

✓ good references;

✓ ability to meet current and future obligations;

✓ experience matching contract requirements;

✓ necessary equipment to complete the work;

✓ financial stability;

✓ good credit; and

✓ established bank relationship and line of credit.

A surety's underwriting process consists of an extensive prequalification process in order to guarantee to the project owner that the contractor will fulfill the terms of the contract.

Bonds are priced on the basis of a percentage of the contract amount. Market conditions and prevailing industry practices set the percentage. Bond premiums vary among surety companies, but typically range from a half percent to two percent of the contract amount.

Bond Claims

Filing Process: Construction law and contractual relationships govern the bond claims process. The filing process is outlined in the bond language for common-law bonds. Government statutes outline the filing process for statutory bonds.

Project Changes: Unless specifically outlined in the bond agreement, the surety company will not cover changes to the original contract. In most cases, a request for additional coverage must be made and the bonding company must be notified of the contract changes.

Payment in the Event of Default: In the event of contractor default, the surety has several options. The surety may:

✓ provide additional financing for the contractor to finish the project;

✓ arrange for a new contractor or hire subcontractors to complete the work; or

✓ pay out the amount of the bond.

Laws Governing Bonding of Federal Construction Projects

Miller Act: As a result of the high failure rate for completion of public construction projects, the Heard Act was enacted in 1894, allowing the use of surety bonds for federally funded projects. In 1935, the Miller Act replaced the Heard Act. The Miller Act is the current law requiring performance and payment bonds on all federal construction projects valued at greater than $100,000.

The surety amounts are defined as follows:

✓ A performance bond is required in an amount that the contracting officer regards as adequate. The bond is normally 100 percent of the contracted price.

✓ A separate payment bond is required for the protection of the suppliers of labor and materials. The sum of the payment bond varies, based on the size of the contract. These amounts include:

• Fifty percent of the contract amount for projects less than $1 million

- Forty percent of the contract amount for projects between $1 million and $5 million
- $2.5 million payment bond for contracts in excess of $5 million

Little Miller Acts: Most states and local governments also have similar surety laws on public works projects that are referred to as "Little Miller Acts."

Construction Industry Payment Protection Act of 1999: The Construction Industry Payment Protection Act of 1999 makes several amendments to the Miller Act of 1935. Its purpose is to improve payment bond protections for persons who furnish labor or material for use on federal construction projects. This law was passed because the bonding amounts specified in the Miller Act may not provide subcontractors with adequate protection.

The Construction Industry Payment Protection Act of 1999 outlines three specific requirements:

✓ The general contractor of a project generally must obtain a payment bond in an amount that is equal to the total value of the federal contract, unless a lesser amount is specified by the contracting officer. The payment bond cannot be less than the performance bond.

✓ Subcontractors are permitted to notify contractors of intent to sue by any means which provides written, third-party verification of delivery.

✓ Waivers of Miller Act payment bond protections are void before the work begins. Any waiver of a subcontractor's right to sue on a payment bond must be in writing, signed, and executed after the subcontractor has first furnished labor or materials for use in the project.

Laws Governing Bonding of North Carolina State Public Construction Projects

State public projects meeting the following criteria require the contractor to obtain a performance and payment bond.

✓ The total amount of contracts awarded exceeds $300,000.

✓ The contractor or construction manager's contract exceeds $50,000 on the project.

✓ State departments, state agencies, and the University of North Carolina and its constituent institutions require a performance and payment bond if the total amount of construction contracts awarded for any one project exceeds five hundred thousand dollars ($500,000).

The performance and payment bond must each be in the amount of 100 percent of the construction contract. The bond must be executed by one or more surety companies approved to do business in the State of North Carolina.

Full text of the statutes governing bonding of North Carolina state public projects is found in Appendix G.

Final Inspection...

Risk Management Benefits: Managing risk is challenging but is important to your reputation and bottom line.

Insurance: Insurance should supplement your risk management program. It provides protection against unforeseen events and is sometimes required by law. Several different types of insurance coverage are available to fit the needs of your business.

Property Insurance: Property insurance typically covers your business and personal property when damage, theft, or loss occurs. All-risk builders' risk, named peril builders' risk, inland marine/equipment theft, equipment floater, transportation floater, and motor truck cargo policies are types of property insurance that may benefit your business.

Liability Insurance: Liability insurance is designed to protect against third-party claims that arise from alleged negligence resulting in bodily injury or property damage. Several types of liability insurance policies are available, such as commercial general, umbrella, and director's and officer's liability insurance.

Business Owner's Policies (BOPs): Property and liability coverage are bundled under business owner's policies.

Automobile Insurance: Liability and physical damage associated with vehicles owned or leased by your company are covered under automobile insurance. Several types of coverage are available.

Burglary and Theft Insurance: Loss or damage by burglary, theft, larceny, robbery, forgery, fraud, and vandalism is covered under burglary and theft insurance.

Key Man Life Insurance: This type of insurance is available as life insurance or disability insurance, or both, to protect the continuing success of the business.

Coverage Gaps and Overlaps: It is important to evaluate all of your insurance coverage. Using one insurer may minimize gaps and overlaps in coverage.

Employment-Related Insurance: Workers' compensation, unemployment, and social security are employment-related insurance regulated by state and/or federal government.

Insurance Coverage for Subcontractors: When hiring subcontractors, ensure that they carry proper insurance coverage. These requirements should be outlined in the construction contract.

What is a Bond? Bonds provide protection in the event that contractual obligations are not met.

Bond Language: At a minimum, bonds should contain the total dollar amount, length of the bond, requirements for notice of defect or lack of maintenance, and bond enforcement.

Types of Bonds: Several types of bonds are available depending on the desired coverage.

Qualifying for a Bond: Before issuing a bond, the surety company will review your business to ensure it is established, profitable, and well-managed.

Bond Claims: The bond claim filing process is outlined in the bond language for common-law bonds and in the government statutes for statutory bonds.

Laws Governing the Bonding of Federal Construction Projects: The Miller Act and Construction Industry Payment Protection Act of 1999 outline bonding requirements for federal construction projects.

Laws Governing Bonding of North Carolina State Public Construction Projects: A payment and performance bond is required for the following types of projects: when the total amount of construction contracts for a project is $300,000 or more; the contractor or construction manager's contract exceeds $50,000; or state department, state agency, or the University of North Carolina and its constituent institutions contracts awarded for any one project exceeds five hundred thousand dollars ($500,000). The bonds must be in the amount of 100 percent of the contract price.

Chapter 5
YOUR BUSINESS TOOLBOX

Chapter Survey...

⇨ *Time Management*

⇨ *Delegation*

⇨ *Business Ethics*

⇨ *Technology*

⇨ *Small Business Assistance and Loans*

⇨ *Small Business Certifications*

Just as you need a toolbox filled with the right tools to accomplish your job as an electrician, you need the right skills and resources to operate a successful business. This chapter will introduce a few of these tools and will lay a foundation for tools covered in subsequent chapters.

Time Management

Time Is Money: This familiar phrase holds special meaning for business owners. Your ability to manage time effectively can make the difference between completing a job successfully and failing to meet customer expectations. Time is one of your most important tools. Use it wisely.

Setting Goals: Effective goal setting is a key cornerstone to time management success. Once goals are set, they should be documented. This gives you a visual reminder and ensures proper communication to the whole work team. A methodical approach should be used to move forward towards achieving your goals. Your management team and employees should understand your goals and can help put together the plan tactics.

Four Time Management Tips: These habits will help you organize and manage your time.

1. Prioritize tasks daily
2. Delegate effectively when possible
3. Use checklists and calendars (find a time management system that works for you)
4. Do not procrastinate

Advantage of Technology: Learning about new technology and using it in your operations can save you time. Research ways to automate your operations without taking away from the quality of your products and services. Putting a new technology or process in place can give you more time to focus on strategic activities.

Competitive Edge: Although multitasking is an important skill, effective time management requires that you focus on the necessary task at hand to move forward towards achievement of the set goals. It gives you a competitive edge and helps you anticipate problems before they occur. Planning your time puts you in control, gives you the ability to be proactive and helps reduce anxieties caused by "putting out fires". Your professionalism will be appreciated by your customers, subcontractors, and suppliers.

*Time is money.
Use it wisely.*

Delegation

You Can't Do It All: When you become a business owner, you go from a tradesperson to a manager of many jobs and a business administrator. Delegation is a key tool that will ensure that you get all tasks accomplished. You simply cannot do it all and be efficient.

Preparing to Delegate: Learning to delegate is often difficult because you are giving up control of certain tasks. You may feel that a task won't be done correctly or that it takes longer to explain a task than just doing it yourself.

Delegation is a way of developing your employees and building a solid team. Giving your employees increased responsibility builds their self-confidence, provides motivation, and makes them more productive and loyal. Delegation gives you the chance to concentrate strategically on running your business.

How to Delegate: Here are simple steps on how to delegate:

1. Identify a person for the task.

2. Explain the task clearly and make sure you are understood. You may want to ask the person to repeat their understanding of the task back to you.

3. Follow up with the person throughout the process.

4. Give positive feedback and provide guidance on how the task can be improved, if necessary.

> *Effective delegation increases your efficiency.*

Business Ethics

Your Reputation: Good business ethics are a must if you want to safeguard your reputation in the industry. Practicing good business ethics, when dealing with customers, employees, subcontractors, and suppliers, is not only the right thing to do, it is the best way to avoid litigation.

Defining Ethics: You may ask, "What are ethics?" In general, the term as it applies to business means behaving in a trustworthy, fair, honest, and respectful manner toward everyone with whom you interact. Your core values serve as your moral compass and guide this standard.

> **Studies Say...**
>
> Top management has the strongest influence on employees' ethical behavior. If top managers demonstrate unethical behavior, employees are likely to do the same.

Establishing a code of conduct is the first step to ensuring that good ethics are practiced throughout your company. A code of conduct is a documented way that an organization should operate.

This document can include:

✓ guidelines for employees, management, subcontractors, and suppliers;

✓ standards for doing business; and

✓ a statement of commitment to the community.

You may want to provide your customers with your code of conduct. It will reinforce your commitment to good ethics and demonstrate professionalism.

> *Make the right ethical choices to protect your reputation and avoid litigation.*

Technology

Technology as an Essential Tool: Technology is an essential tool for communicating and keeping your business competitive. Purchasing technology is becoming increasingly cost-effective. There are many technological tools specifically designed for the construction industry. These tools increase efficiency and aid in various tasks, such as:

✓ estimating and bidding,

✓ accounting,

✓ job costing,

✓ scheduling, and

✓ construction management.

If you have not jumped into the technology age, here are a few basics to start with:

Computer/Laptop/Tablet: For a business owner, a computer has many uses which will help in streamlining administrative functions. This is the basic tool you will need to operate programs for applications such as writing, accounting, scheduling, estimating, and email. Some builders opt to have laptop computers or tablets to perform these functions on the jobsite.

Phone: Cell phone, or smart phone, technology has advanced in the area of communications, use of email, photography, text messaging, and calendar management. Regardless of the features you choose for your business cell phone, it is important that you are always accessible to your customers and employees.

Fax Machine: Although email has become a prevalent means for communications, it is still important for businesses to have a fax machine so that copies of important documents can be transmitted quickly and efficiently.

Printer: A printer allows you to produce hard copies of the files you have on your computer. A printer will come in handy when creating customer correspondence and contracts. Portable printers small enough to bring to the jobsite are also available.

Scanner: Documents and small objects can be copied or scanned in a form that can be stored on a computer and then these files can be manipulated and printed for use.

Multifunction Hardware: You can purchase a single machine that works as a photocopier, fax, printer, and scanner. This type of hardware can be convenient and cost-effective if your business uses such functions frequently. However, bear in mind that if the unit breaks, you may lose several or all of the functions until it is repaired or replaced.

Digital Camera or Smart Phone: A digital camera or a smart phone with a camera are great ways to store photos on a computer or cloud server. It is important for you to document your work every step of the way, and digital pictures are a cost effective way to organize that information. Your pictures can be stored on a drive or cloud server with project files and emailed or shared as necessary.

Internet: The Internet is a powerful tool. It can be used for research, communication, or marketing your company. It is also the foundation for a growing number of social media platforms (i.e., Facebook, LinkedIn, Instagram, etc.). Social media allows you to connect with customers in new and unique ways. Most businesses these days have a social media presence on multiple platforms.

Word Processing Software: Word processing can save you a lot of time because the information you need is stored in the computer. Handwritten documents need to be rewritten each time, while documents entered in the computer can be modified and reused. Many word processing programs have templates of commonly used documents for business, and these can be used, modified, and reused at any time. Word processing programs are available as both software and web-based.

Spreadsheet Program: This type of software gives you the flexibility to create financial worksheets on the computer. You can set up the worksheet to automatically calculate figures, reducing mathematical errors. Spreadsheet programs are available as both software and web-based.

A Warning about Software: Although software is designed to streamline your processes, you must still understand the basics. For example, if you purchase accounting software but do not understand the fundamentals of accounting, the software is useless to you. In future chapters, we will cover basic skills that will help you utilize software packages.

Once you become comfortable with technology, you may want to purchase other advanced tools and software.

Using technology can increase your efficiency and keep you competitive.

Small Business Assistance and Loans

Various federal, state and local resources can help you with small business services or education you might need. Many of these services may be free or available at a minimal cost to business owners. Below are some of the resources available to you:

North Carolina Department of Commerce

The North Carolina Department of Commerce has resources for starting and operating your business. The website has several links to topic areas such as financing, licensing, business start up, and technology assistance.

> *North Carolina Department of Commerce*
> *301 North Wilmington Street*
> *Raleigh, North Carolina 27601-1058*
>
> *Mailing Address:*
> *4301 Mail Service Center*
> *Raleigh, North Carolina 27699-4301*
>
> *Telephone: (919) 814-4600*
> *Toll-free: (800) 228-8443*
>
> *Website: www.nccommerce.com*

Local Community Colleges & Universities

Business education opportunities are available through local community colleges and universities. Seminars, workshops, and courses are offered on business skills and small business management.

The Small Business Center Network offered through the North Carolina Community College System conducts training and seminars for business owners, offers business counseling, and has many resources available on their website. To find a local Small Business Center, visit the website at www.ncsbc.net.

America's Small Business Development Center Network utilizes universities, colleges, and state economic development agencies to provide service centers are available to provide no-cost business consulting and low-cost training throughout the United States. To find a location near you, visit the website at www.americassbdc.org.

Small Business Administration (SBA)

The Small Business Administration's mission is to counsel, assist, and protect the interests of small business. The SBA provides training and online help for small businesses.

The SBA website at www.sba.gov has several online resources to Federal, state, and local information for business owners. Resources include:

✓ Starting a Business

✓ Registrations, Licenses, and Permits

✓ Finance and Taxes

✓ Expanding Your Business

✓ Legal Compliance

✓ Industry Specifics

✓ State and Local Resources

A partnership program through the SBA links business owners from across the nation to create a social network and provide access to experts.

The SBA Headquarters is located in Washington, D.C., but you can check the website at www.sba.gov or call 1-800-U-ASK-SBA to find an office near you.

Small Business Administration
North Carolina District Office
6302 Fairview Road, Suite 300
Charlotte, North Carolina 28210

Telephone: (704) 344-6563
Fax: (704) 344-6769

Website: www.sba.gov/offices/district/nc/charlotte

Service Corps of Retired Executives (SCORE)

SCORE is a national volunteer organization of retired executives who can provide counseling and training to

you if you are an entrepreneur and/or business owner. There are several SCORE offices located throughout the state. You can find the SCORE office nearest to you on the website.

SCORE Association
1175 Herndon Parkway
Suite 900
Herndon, VA 20170
Telephone: (800) 634-0245

Website: www.score.org

Appendix C contains additional references and website links on topics covered in this book.

Small Business Certifications

Federal and state governments often have opportunities for businesses to bid on contracts. These contracts are highly sought after for a number of reasons. To level the playing field, the government has established certifications for small, minority-owned, and women-owned businesses. If your company fits the criteria, you can obtain one or more certifications, which can provide additional opportunities for you to bid on government contracts.

The U.S. Small Business Administration has several different certification and assistance programs for small businesses. These programs include the following:

✓ Historically Underutilized Business Zone (HUBZone) Certification

✓ 8(a) Business Development Program

✓ Small Business Certification

✓ Women-Owned Small Business Federal Contract Program

✓ Veteran and Service-Disabled Veteran Owned Business Assistance Program

✓ Native American Owned Business Certification

✓ Alaskan Owned Business Assistance Program

✓ Native Hawaiian Owned Business Assistance Program

Information on these certifications is found on the SBA website at www.sba.gov/federal-contracting/contracting-assistance-programs or by calling 1-800-U ASK SBA (1-800-827-5722). In addition to certification information, the SBA website contains helpful links about government contracting and business development.

Certifications are also available at the state and local level. The Institute (formerly known as the North Carolina Institute of Minority Economic Development) provides technical and financial assistance to existing and emerging minority businesses across the state.

The Institute
114 W. Parrish Street
Durham, North Carolina 27701

Mailing Address
P.O. Box 1331
Durham, NC 27701

Telephone: (919) 956-8889
Fax: (919) 688-7668

Website: theinstitutenc.org

Final Inspection...

Time Management: Effective time management gives you a competitive edge and helps you anticipate problems before they occur.

Delegation: Effective delegation increases your efficiency and helps develop your employees.

Business Ethics: The right ethical choices help protect your reputation and avoid litigation.

Technology: Technology is an essential tool for communicating and keeping your business competitive.

Small Business Assistance and Loans: Several organizations are available to help small businesses with a variety of functions.

Small Business Certifications: Certifications for small, minority, and women-owned businesses are available through the government. If your company qualifies, certifications can provide additional opportunities for you to bid on government contracts.

Chapter 6
MARKETING AND SALES

Chapter Survey...

⇨ *Executing Your Marketing Plan*

⇨ *Logos, Stationery, and Business Cards*

⇨ *Promotional Materials*

⇨ *Public Relations*

⇨ *Effective Selling Skills*

⇨ *Organizing the Sales Process*

⇨ *Your Sales Presentation*

Start Off on the Right Foot: First impressions can tell your potential customers a lot about your business. Customers may judge your professionalism or reputation on this initial contact. Marketing, in some cases, may be the first impression of your business, and you want to make sure customers feel comfortable with you and your company from this point on.

The purpose of marketing is to bring in new customers and retain current customers. A good marketing program helps ensure a steady flow of leads and customers and, more important, a steady flow of incoming cash.

*First impressions are lasting ones.
Make your company's first impression a
positive one.*

Executing Your Marketing Plan

Maximize Your Marketing Potential: When developing your market analysis and marketing strategy (featured in the business plan template in Appendix B), you should answer questions such as these:

✓ What is the vision for my business?

✓ Who are my customers?

✓ What is the best way to reach these customers?

✓ What is my competitive advantage?

✓ What is the best way to promote my products and services (e.g. advertising, public relations, online marketing, direct sales, etc.)?

✓ What will my marketing efforts cost?

✓ How much revenue do I expect to gain as a result of marketing efforts?

✓ Who will manage the marketing program? Will I need to hire outside help to execute the program?

✓ What growth opportunities exist in my industry?

✓ What challenges for growth exist in my industry?

Now it is time to put these thoughts into action. Developing a promotion plan will help you bring these ideas to life.

Logos, Stationery, and Business Cards

Create Your Identity: A simple start to developing your promotion plan is to create a logo. Not only will your name distinguish you in the market but a logo will set you apart from your competitors. Logos become part of your company identity and convey a professional look, which is important for that first impression.

A good logo design should be:

✓ simple and easy to remember;

✓ attractive in color and black and white;

✓ limited to one or two colors;

✓ representative of your company identity; and

✓ scalable up or down and attractive in any size.

Once your logo is created, you should include it on your business cards and stationery.

Promotional Materials

You may also apply your logo to several different promotional items. These items include:

✓ brochures,

✓ direct mailings,

✓ jobsite signs,

✓ truck signs,

✓ yellow pages,

✓ social media sites, and

✓ websites.

Using promotional materials will give you name recognition. When potential customers have an upcoming job, they may be more likely to approach your company to put in a bid because your name is out in the market.

Business promotion through social media has become a prevalent means of marketing. You can create a business account on social media websites, such as Facebook, Twitter, and LinkedIn, to advertise your services, post updates on your business, and gain name recognition. Participation in social media can be an inexpensive way to market and increase traffic to your business website. In addition to creating a business page on social media sites for promotion, these sites have areas where you can buy advertising space.

A good marketing program is an investment that can help you gain customers and strengthen your reputation.

Public Relations

Benefits of Networking: Public relations are an inexpensive but effective marketing tool. It is important to build name recognition; good public relations constantly keeps your business in the eye of the public–your potential customers. The downside to public relations is its labor-intensive nature, but the time invested will give you great rewards. You may use this approach to not only get potential customers

but as a way to get referrals to good sub suppliers, or employees.

In the Public Eye: Here are some ideas to get you started:

✓ **Join local trade associations**
This is a good opportunity to meet new people in your industry. You can also volunteer to speak at meetings and conferences to showcase your knowledge and expertise.

✓ **Participate in a local non-profit initiative (for example, be a volunteer Habitat for Humanity worker)**
High-profile projects will put you in a positive light in the public eye and may get some press coverage.
Volunteer for local leadership opportunities
Leadership positions in organizations such as schools or the local Chamber of Commerce may give you time with other influential people in the community who can make good referrals about you and your business.

✓ **Sponsor community events**
When you sponsor community events, your business name is often featured in event brochures, signage, and media promotions such as newspapers and radio advertisements.

✓ **Send press releases to the local media**
This public relations technique offers exposure to a broad audience and gives you credibility because it is communicated through a third-party. Press releases can report your involvement in the local community, new construction trends, or any ideas that might be interesting to the public and will promote your company.

✓ **Hold an open house**
You can hold an open house at your office or at a job where you can showcase your work. An open house gives you a chance to reinforce current business relationships and make new ones.

Effective Selling Skills

Don't Underestimate Your Selling Skills: Selling is often perceived as a salesperson pitching a product or service and the customer saying yes or no. Many people don't feel comfortable with the process of selling, because it makes them feel pushy and overbearing. Selling should be the simple process of matching your company's skills and expertise with what the customer needs.

Listen Up: Active listening is the golden rule to effective selling. Without listening, you cannot clearly understand what your customer needs. You may ask yourself, "What exactly is active listening?" Here are a few simple rules:

- ✓ Maintain good eye contact.
- ✓ Be attentive.
- ✓ Keep an open mind.
- ✓ Don't interrupt.
- ✓ Ask clarifying questions.
- ✓ Put yourself in the "shoes" of the other person.
- ✓ Pay attention to body language (i.e., facial expressions).

Using these simple guidelines, you will gain a more thorough understanding of your potential customers and be able to target your response to their needs.

A Word of Caution...

Be careful not to make unrealistic or inaccurate statements just to make a sale. You will hurt your business in the long run and potentially leave yourself open to a lawsuit. All advertising and marketing claims must be truthful and not deceptive. Individual state contractor licensing boards may have specific guidelines regarding licensed contractor advertising such as including a licensing number and specific verbiage required by law.

Organizing the Sales Process

Track and Prioritize: Selling is a process. Generally speaking, higher-value sales have a longer selling process than a lower-value sale. To manage this selling process and provide the best service possible, you must be organized. Tracking potential customers is made simple by developing a sales tracking sheet for each contact you make. Your tracking sheet should contain the contact information for the potential customer, the type of work the customer wants, a summary of communication, the source of referral for that customer, and any other information you feel is necessary.

The next step is to prioritize your sales leads. Prioritizing leads is a way to manage your time in the sales process and can give you key insights into the effectiveness of your marketing program. You want to concentrate most of your time on the strong leads.

Tracking and prioritizing leads makes the sales process most effective.

Your Sales Presentation

Present Your Best Side: Once you have determined your strongest sales leads, you should schedule time to make a sales presentation. This is your opportunity to show customers how your company can meet their needs; in the sales presentation you try to gain a commitment to perform the work.

Presentation materials are important visuals and give the customer something concrete to take away and read after the meeting. These materials can include:

- ✓ a company information sheet,
- ✓ brochures,
- ✓ business cards,
- ✓ past customer testimonials,
- ✓ warranty information, and
- ✓ photographs of past projects.

To avoid awkward stumbling in the presentation, have materials prepared ahead of time. This demonstrates your professionalism and ensures that you have thought through the presentation.

Overcoming "No:" Handling objections is one of the more difficult parts of the sales process. This is the time to use your active listening skills and overcome the objection.

- ✓ Repeat the objection to ensure that you completely understand the potential customer's reservation.
- ✓ No question is a stupid question. The person with the objection may just not understand the process.
- ✓ Give an example of a customer with the same question and how you effectively fulfilled his/her needs.

Communication Is Key: Closing the sale is a very important part of the process. Try to gain a commitment from the potential customer, whether it is hiring your company to do the work or just scheduling a follow-up appointment.

Follow up on all sales presentations. This may be as simple as making a phone call or sending a card or small gift. Consistent follow-up ensures that you are at the top of your potential customer's mind and gives you an advantage over competitors.

Clearly understanding your potential customer's needs is imperative.

Final Inspection...

Executing Your Marketing Plan: Once you develop your marketing plan, the next step is implementing it.

Logos, Stationery, and Business Cards: These simple marketing tools can help establish your company's identity.

Promotional Materials: You can extend your marketing program by using various promotional materials.

Public Relations: This is an inexpensive but effective way to market your company.

Effective Selling Skills: Effective selling involves carefully listening to your potential customer's needs.

Organizing the Sales Process: Tracking potential sales leads can help you organize the process of selling.

Your Sales Presentation: Preparation and follow-up are important when presenting to potential customers.

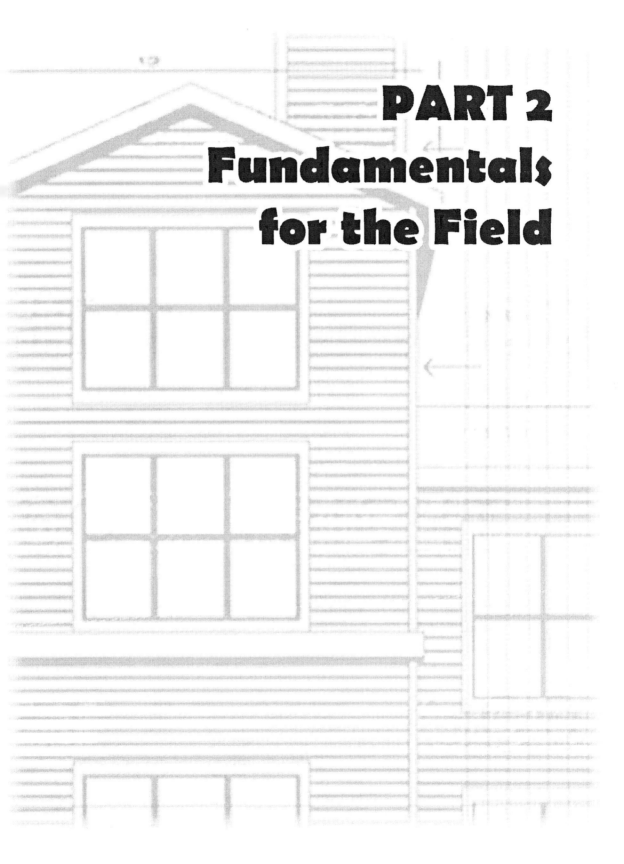

PART 2
Fundamentals for the Field

Chapter 7
BIDDING AND ESTIMATING

Chapter Survey...

- ⇨ *Bid Documents*
- ⇨ *Ethics in Bidding*
- ⇨ *Estimate Planning*
- ⇨ *Estimating Framework*
- ⇨ *Determining Estimated Costs*
- ⇨ *Other Methods of Estimating*
- ⇨ *Estimating Pitfalls*
- ⇨ *Using an Estimator*
- ⇨ *Submitting Your Bid*
- ⇨ *Job Cost Recording System*
- ⇨ *Technology Tools for Estimating*

Accurate estimating is important to the profitability of a construction company. If a job is estimated correctly, the contractor has a good chance at getting the job and making money. If the job is poorly estimated, the contractor may lose the bid or win the bid and lose money on the project.

The estimator must ask these questions when assessing whether to bid on a project:

- ✓ **Company Resources and Type of Work:** Does our company have the resources to perform this work? Is this project consistent with the type of work we do?

- ✓ **Site Considerations:** Are there any special site considerations that we need to consider? Do the site conditions create any additional costs for our company?

- ✓ **Location and Cost Effectiveness:** How can we do the work efficiently and in the most cost effective manner? Does the location present special considerations and added cost through travel time and limited accessibility?

- ✓ **Risk Assessment:** What are the risks and how will we manage them?

- ✓ **Profitability of Project:** What is our profit margin on this work?

If you know you cannot complete the job on time or there is a chance you could lose money on the project, we recommend that you not bid the job. The jobs you choose should contribute to your long-term goals and the reputation you want your company to have in the market.

Bid Documents

In a competitive bid situation, a bid package is often put together that includes:

- ✓ **an invitation to bid** that gives a brief overview of the project, deadlines, and general requirements;

- ✓ **bid instructions** that contain specifics of how the bid should be completed and submitted;

- ✓ **bid forms**, including but not limited to items such as a bid sheet, bid schedule, bidder's questionnaire on experience, financial responsibility and capability, and a copy of the contract; and

- ✓ **supplements**, including items important to the overall bid process such as a property survey and soil analysis.

It is important to follow all the instructions in the bid package carefully and submit all documents according to the required specifications. The bidder can be found unresponsive if information is incorrectly submitted or omitted altogether.

Pre-bid meetings may also be scheduled, especially for larger projects. In a pre-bid meeting, the project specifications and any changes to the bid package are discussed.

If changes are made to a bid package before it is due, an **addendum** is issued. The addendum becomes part of the bid documents and, ultimately, part of the contract when awarded. It is important to carefully review all addenda to evaluate the impact on your bid. Changes in plans and specifications may affect your bid pricing or even your decision to bid at all.

Carefully evaluate whether bidding on a project is the right decision for your company.

Ethics in Bidding

Good ethical conduct is necessary to maintain the integrity of the bidding process. The situations listed below are not only a poor way to do business, but some state statutes forbid these practices on public projects.

✓ **Bid Shopping**
Bid shopping occurs when the general contractor approaches subcontractors other than those who have submitted bids to seek a lower offer than what was quoted in original bids. In this situation, the general contractor reveals the original bids submitted and tries to reduce the price.

✓ **Bid Peddling**
Bid peddling occurs when the subcontractor approaches the general contractor after the project was awarded with the intent of lowering the original price submitted on bid day.

✓ **Bid Rigging**
Bid rigging is a form of collusion where contractors coordinate their bids to fix the award outcome of a project.

Estimate Planning

Once you have determined that you want to submit a bid, you must prepare your estimate. An estimate is the sum of the costs to complete the project, plus your added overhead and profit margin. Before you start putting numbers down on paper, you should understand all the factors that impact the cost of the job. A good estimate will fall within 1 percent to 2 percent of actual construction costs.

Project Documents

A complete set of project documents is required to prepare an accurate cost estimate. These documents include the following:

✓ **Construction or architectural drawings** show a schematic diagram of the job. The drawings may illustrate many different views or elevations of the job.

✓ **Specifications** are details that determine the type of materials or methods to be used in construction. If there is a conflict between the specifications and applicable codes, you must follow the stricter of the two. The codes are the minimum requirements by law. You must always meet or exceed the applicable codes.

✓ **The contract** is the agreement between you and your customer to complete the specified work. The conditions outlining the obligations of each party, such as the owner and contractor, are included in the contract. If your bid is accepted, the construction drawings and specifications become part of the contract package. Contracts are covered in more detail in Chapter 8.

✓ **Bonds** may be required as part of the bid submittal (discussed in Chapter 4). Bonds commonly required are bid and performance bonds.

You should carefully review these documents to understand the project and the expectations of the customer.

Site Visit

There may be specifics about the site that influence the cost estimate. These details cannot always be determined from the construction documents. It is important that you go to the actual site and look at any factors that may impact the project. Soil type, grading, vehicle access, and availability of electricity and water are some of the variables that could affect the cost of the project. You want to anticipate as many of these problems as you can before beginning work.

During this time, you should consider the environmental aspects of the project. If you need to obtain environmental permits, this process will affect your estimated costs. Your project may also require special equipment and processes that should be factored into your estimate. Chapter 12, Jobsite Safety and Environmental Factors, discusses environmental impacts in more depth.

Estimating Framework

Estimating should be a systematic process. Approaching the estimate in an organized way will help you avoid errors or omissions. Taking the extra time to construct a framework for the estimate will increase your accuracy.

Your estimating framework essentially lists the process for completing the job. This can be accomplished by:

✓ defining the phases of the project; and

✓ listing each task and materials needed for each phase.

Once your framework is established, you can enter the time and cost for each task. If you are awarded the job, you can easily convert your estimating framework into your job schedule.

Define the Phases

The first thing you need to consider when you build your estimate is the phases of the project that you are working on. For example, you might list the phases as preconstruction, construction, and post-construction. The order of tasks will drive your scheduling process.

List Each Task and Materials Needed

Once you list the phases of the project, you need to develop a list of tasks and materials for each phase. Be very specific in this step. If you omit an item or add an unnecessary item, your estimate will be inaccurate. The task and material list should also include labor time needed and material amounts. By identifying these items early in the process, you may determine the need for items such as overtime to meet certain project deadlines and temporary storage. All of these items play a part in the cost estimate.

Estimating Checklist

The Construction Specifications Institute publishes a classification system called MasterFormat. This system includes numbers and job tasks grouped by major construction activities. This is a helpful tool when setting up your estimating framework to ensure that you have accounted for all aspects of materials and labor. After you become familiar with

the estimating process, you may develop your own estimating checklist customized for your needs.

Determining Estimated Costs

Quantity Take-off Method

One accurate method of estimating is the quantity take-off method. Using this method, you individually estimate units of materials and labor for each task you listed in your estimating framework.

After estimating materials and labor, the following items are added:

✓ subcontractor fees,

✓ labor burden,

✓ project overhead costs,

✓ project equipment,

✓ contingencies,

✓ allowances,

✓ company overhead, and

✓ profit.

By going through the items individually, you can adjust your estimate to accommodate the unique aspects of the project you may have uncovered when reviewing the construction documents or during your site survey.

 Determine Labor Cost for Each Task

Using your estimating framework, you can begin to enter your labor cost. Information from previous jobs can help you determine accurate job costs. There are also published costs available through books such as the RSMeans cost data series, but this is no substitute for your knowledge of the industry. Your experience with your local labor market and wages should be factored into your estimated costs.

For each labor item on your estimating framework list, use the following formula to determine the labor cost.

Required Labor Hours per Task x Labor Rate = Labor Cost per Task

The required labor hours can vary based on several different factors, such as employee skill level, size of crew, and weather conditions. These factors must be taken into account when determining the required labor hours. Hours spent planning and scheduling must also be figured into the labor cost equation.

Another helpful tool when determining labor cost is your historical cost data. Determining your final labor cost from past projects will help you put together more accurate estimates for future jobs. Developing a cost-tracking system is discussed later in this chapter.

 ## Add Labor Burden

As an employer, you incur costs such as employ-ment taxes and insurance. These obligations add approximately 30 percent to your labor cost. This additional amount is referred to as labor burden.

Labor burden includes items such as:

✓ Medicare and social security (discussed in Chapter 15),

✓ federal unemployment insurance (discussed in Chapter 15),

✓ workers' compensation,

✓ liability insurance,

✓ state unemployment insurance, and

✓ company benefits (such as health insurance, vacations, etc.).

Labor burden must be factored into your total labor cost.

 ## Determine Materials Cost

Just as you plugged labor cost into your estimating framework, you can do the same with materials cost. For each material item listed on your estimating framework, you need to obtain a cost.

Your suppliers can provide you with the materials price per unit or a lump sum. The cost of materials can fluctuate according to the availability of raw materials and demand, so it is important to keep current cost data. In addition to tracking wage, earnings, employment, and benefit statistics, the Bureau of Labor Statistics (www.bls.gov) tracks the prices of major groups of construction materials as part of its Producer Price Index (PPI) program. Periodically reviewing this resource can help you understand potential increases and decreases in materials cost.

You may receive the materials cost as a unit cost. If necessary, use the following formula to determine the total material cost per unit for each of the materials categories on your take-off sheet.

Price per Unit x Number of Units Needed = Total Material Unit Cost

To make sure you are receiving the best price, obtain at least three bids from suppliers. You should also add a small contingency for waste. Depending on the type of material and the job specifications, your waste contingency will vary.

 ## Determine Project Equipment Cost

Equipment needed to complete the job is figured as a direct cost of the project and added to your estimate.

For example, if you need a crane to set an air handling unit on top of a building as part of a HVAC project, it is considered a direct cost.

Small tools and pickup trucks are considered an indirect cost and not part of project equipment. These indirect costs are figured into project overhead.

Figuring the direct cost of equipment differs depending if you rent or own the equipment.

Owned Equipment: To estimate owned equipment, you must arrive at a unit cost for the equipment. To calculate unit cost, consider the following factors:

✓ actual value of equipment factoring in its age and amount of depreciation from the original purchase price;

✓ maintenance and operating costs;

✓ taxes and fees;

✓ labor to operate equipment, including any training or licensing costs; and

✓ insurance.

Unit cost is calculated by estimating the number of hours you will use the equipment per year and dividing this number by the total yearly cost of the equipment calculated by considering the operational factors.

For example, if you figure the total cost of the equipment for the year is $30,000 and you plan to use the equipment for a total of 1,000 hours, your unit cost to operate the equipment is $30 an hour.

If you estimate using the equipment for 40 hours on a project, your estimated project equipment cost for that project is $1,200.

Rental Equipment: The following items are considered when figuring the cost of rental equipment:

✓ equipment rental rate;

✓ labor cost to pick up and return equipment or delivery fees;

✓ labor cost to operate equipment; and

✓ other costs associated with operating the equipment (e.g., cost of fuel).

Subcontracting: You may decide that neither option is cost effective or feasible and subcontract the work. In this case, this line item would appear under subcontractor fees.

Rent, Lease, or Buy? Construction equipment is vital to the completion of construction projects. Equipment can range from cranes to computers. The decision to rent, lease, or purchase this equipment is a challenging one, and there are many considerations to each option.

Leasing is a long-term rental agreement that provides the benefits of using the equipment without purchasing. Lease payments are made to the owner of the equipment in exchange for the use of the equipment. At the end of the lease term, the owner takes possession of the equipment.

Leasing equipment has many advantages. One of the biggest is the ability to use the equipment with a limited capital expenditure. Other advantages compared to purchasing include:

✓ no down payment;

✓ duration of payments over a longer period making them lower;

✓ lease payments (as defined by the IRS) deductible as operating expenses; and

✓ obsolete equipment is returned to the owner at end of the lease.

Equipment ownership allows you to take advantage of certain tax benefits and usually costs less than leasing in the long run. Leases are long-term contractual agreements that generally cannot be cancelled. If you no longer need the equipment, you must still make payments for the full term of the lease.

Purchasing equipment is advantageous when the equipment has a long and useful life and will

not become obsolete in the short-term. You gain ownership of the equipment after the purchase is made but you should consider how the equipment will hold value over a long-term period. For this reason, salvage value is a benefit to purchasing equipment.

Renting equipment may be an alternative to purchasing or leasing. Although renting equipment is usually the costliest, it is the best option in certain circumstances. These include:

✓ short-term, specialized projects;

✓ replacement for equipment being repaired;

✓ equipment with high maintenance costs; and

✓ jobs that require transportation and storage to distant locations.

The decision to rent, purchase, or lease is one that should be analyzed carefully to provide the most cost-effective solution for your company.

Add Subcontractor Fees

Subcontractors will be a consideration if you need to outsource work that your company does not have the resources to complete. Chapter 13 covers hiring and working with subcontractors. You should get at least three bids from subcontractors, so you have a good measure of comparison. Carefully evaluate your subcontractors to determine that they have the proper qualifications, licensure, and insurance coverage. The subcontractor fees must be added to the estimate that you give your customer.

Add Allowances

There may be items that are not specified in the project plans, such as finish materials (carpeting, fixtures, lighting, etc.). For these items, you can specify an allowance in your estimate. This is the owner's budget for these items. If the owner's choices exceed or fall short of the allowance amount, the contract should clearly address who is responsible for the difference. Typically, a change order is created stating the amount under or over what is stated in the contract. Change orders are discussed in Chapter 8.

Add Contingencies

A contingency percentage is sometimes added to an estimate to protect the contractor if an unanticipated problem or condition arises during the course of the project. Contingency markups are generally based on the risk level of the project.

For example, a low risk level project might have a 2 percent contingency markup, but a project that has more unknown factors would have a higher markup.

STEP 8 — Add Project Overhead

Project overhead costs are items that are necessary to complete the project but are not directly associated with labor and materials. These costs typically account for 5 percent to 10 percent of the total bid, but these costs should be itemized as much as possible to achieve the most accurate result.

Examples of project overhead costs include:

✓ bonds,

✓ temporary storage,

✓ temporary office,

✓ security guard,

✓ utilities,

✓ dumpsters, and

✓ portable toilets.

Project overhead differs from company overhead. Company overhead cannot be directly linked with a project.

STEP 9 — Add Company Overhead

Company overhead is the cost of doing business. These expenses are necessary to keeping the operation running. Examples of these expenses are:

✓ office rent,

✓ accounting fees,

✓ taxes,

✓ telephone,

✓ legal fees, and

✓ administrative labor.

Calculating an Overhead Percentage

Using historical information from the past year is the best way to predict overhead for the following year. Overhead percentages generally average between 5 percent and 20 percent, so it is best to calculate the overhead rates specific to your company.

Company Overhead: To arrive at a company overhead percentage, you can make the following calculations.

✓ Add up all of your overhead costs from the previous year. These numbers may also be found on your income statement as part of your administrative expenses.

✓ Divide your overhead costs by your revenues (also found on your income statement) to arrive at your overhead percentage.

Project Overhead: Project overhead is a similar calculation.

✓ Add up all of your project overhead costs from the previous year.

✓ Divide your project overhead costs by your revenues (found on your income statement) to arrive at your overhead percentage.

Adding Overhead to the Bid: You must add these overhead percentages to your estimate to cover your overhead costs.

For example, let's say you calculated the direct costs for your bid at $100,000, your project overhead at 9 percent, and company overhead percentage at 11 percent. Your direct costs are then 80 percent of your total bid price. Since overhead is a percentage of revenue, you should divide the direct costs of your bid by 80 percent (.80).

Here is what the calculation should look like:

$$\$100,000 \div .80 = \$125,000$$

After adding in overhead, the bid price with direct costs and overhead is $125,000.

STEP 10 — Add Markup and Determine Profit Margin

Considerations for properly pricing a job include:

✓ cost estimate,

✓ customer needs and expectations,

✓ local market and competition, and

✓ expected profit margin.

Determining the right pricing based on these factors is important to maximizing your profit and satisfying your customers.

Cost-based pricing is one of the most common ways to price a bid. Essentially, the cost of the project is determined through the cost estimate and an overhead percentage, plus a markup percentage. The markup percentage is divided into the direct costs of the project, just like the overhead costs in the previous example. If you estimated correctly, you will achieve your internal profit margin goals.

The standard industry markup is 15 percent, but you should consider the market and competition. You must be careful to keep your estimate in line with your competition and understand how much your customers are willing to pay for your work.

In your estimate, markup is applied to the direct costs of the project, such as labor, material, project equipment, project overhead, and subcontractors.

If your markup is too low, you may not cover your costs to complete the project, causing you to break even, or lose money on the job. To get the work, you may decide to bid low by lowering your profit markup and make it up on future projects, but this should not be a common practice. You will eventually go out of business if an insufficient amount of profit is achieved over time.

On the flip side, if your markup is too high, you may bid yourself out of jobs. Typically, the higher the markup, the fewer jobs you receive. The lower the markup, the more jobs you receive. You must estimate and choose your markup carefully to ensure a steady flow of jobs and profits for your company.

* *
Attention to detail is important to preparing an accurate estimate.
* *

Other Methods of Estimating

Quantity take-off is generally the most accurate way to estimate, but there are other estimating methods you can use.

✓ A **conceptual estimate** is generally prepared by the architect using cost models from previous projects. The contractor may arrive at a much different cost because of the project's unique characteristics.

✓ Using the **square-foot method** of estimating, the project cost is a calculation of the square footage of the project multiplied by a unit cost. This is a quick way to arrive at an estimated cost, but this method does not account for project specifics that

affect cost. Another variation of this method is putting together an estimate using cubic feet of the project multiplied by a unit cost.

✓ The **unit price method** of estimating bundles all of the cost factors such as labor, materials, equipment, and subcontractors to come up with a unit price for the entire task. For example, let's say you are placing and finishing a 2,000-square-foot concrete slab and you determined that your unit price is $2.00 per square foot for this task. The total unit price is $4,000.

Estimating Pitfalls

Accurate estimating is a vital function for construction businesses and can make the difference between getting the right jobs and making a profit on a job. There are pitfalls that are detrimental to the estimating function that you want to avoid.

Preliminary Estimates

Your customers may be eager to determine what their project will cost and will ask for an estimate on the spot. Quoting a price before you have a chance to make accurate calculations is a risky practice. If you quote a price too high, it is possible that you could lose the bid. If you quote a price too low, the potential customer may be disappointed and feel you were dishonest in your initial contact.

Inaccurate Estimates

Inaccuracies occur when you make errors and omissions in your estimate. To avoid inaccuracies, you should always check your estimates. Errors to look for:

✓ *Mathematical errors:* Always check your work and if possible, have someone else check the mathematical accuracy of the estimate.

✓ *Omissions in labor or materials:* Be as thorough as possible when setting up the framework for your estimate. The use of a standard format, such as MasterFormat, will help you avoid this mistake.

✓ *Non-standard abbreviations:* Non-standard abbreviations may be interpreted as a different measurement or material. Spell out the actual word rather than inventing an abbreviation that is unclear or vague.

✓ **Units of measure:** Define linear, square, and cubic measure accurately. The difference between these measures can make a drastic difference in cost.

The more accurately you prepare your estimates, the better chance you have to make your expected profit.

Accurate estimates help you get the right jobs and make a profit.

Using an Estimator

Estimators develop the cost information business owners or managers need to bid for a contract. Small business owners or managers may perform this function without the use of a professional estimator. Large companies or a large project may need to use an estimator.

Estimators follow the same estimating process: performing the quantity take-off, analyzing subcontractor bids, determining equipment needs and sequence of operations, analyzing physical constraints at the site and contingencies, and determining allowances and overhead costs. The estimator may also have a say in setting the profit for the project and the terms and conditions of the contract. The estimator's job is solely to perform the estimating function and, if used, the estimator is an important member of the project team.

Submitting Your Bid

Once your estimate is complete and you are ready to submit your bid, you must make sure to follow all of the instructions in the bid package. These instructions include submitting all of the required documents and the exact information requested by the bid submission deadline. Even though you may have a template put together for the estimating process, you may need to customize your bid so as to respond to the specifications of the bid. Once your bid is submitted, it is reviewed by the owner. Bid review is generally a 30- to 90-day process. You are notified of the acceptance or rejection of your bid after this review process is complete.

Job Cost Recording System

A job cost recording system provides many benefits to the estimating and project management process.

✓ Current projects are monitored more closely with a cost tracking system. Cost overruns are identified and corrective action is taken sooner.

✓ Information from a job cost recording system helps with future estimates by creating more accurate unit costs.

✓ Many analytical reports can be generated from cost data to review performance by project, activity, year, etc. Using this data can help you make more strategic decisions.

There are many ways to set up a job cost recording system, but to ensure accuracy, it must remain consistent for all projects.

The first step is to develop a cost code system. A cost code system includes the following components.

✓ **Project Number:** A project numbering system could be as simple as starting with the number one (1) and consecutively numbering subsequent projects. A more complex project numbering system might also include a code for the type of project and the year it was started. For example, let's say you are working on a remodel project (R) that started in 2016 (16) and was the first (01) project of the year. Your project number could be R-16-01.

✓ **Activity Classification Code:** You may want to develop your own system or use a classification system such as the CSI MasterFormat. For example, for a finish carpentry job you could use MasterFormat number 06200. If you use the same classifications on your estimate, it will be easier to compare estimated to actual costs.

✓ **Distribution Code:** These are items such as material, labor, equipment, and project overhead. For example, coding might be as simple as one-letter abbreviations:

> Material = M
> Labor = L
> Equipment = E
> Project Overhead = P

This code can be placed behind the activity classification code. For example, the labor for finish carpentry could be classified as 06200L and materials as 06200M.

Once your system is set up, you can begin entering the cost data. Materials, equipment, and project overhead costs can be gathered from purchase orders, receipts, and invoices. Labor costs can be taken from timecards. It is important that employees fill out timecards completely and with enough detail so you can accurately record labor costs. A sample time card is located in Chapter 14.

Technology Tools for Estimating

Many computer tools are available to help streamline the estimating process. This technology provides many benefits:

✓ shorter time to prepare the estimate;

✓ improved accuracy; and

✓ professional presentation to the customer.

Estimating software ranges from a basic spreadsheet format to complex databases. However, the programs share some common features:

✓ databases for unit cost items, such as material and labor;

✓ multiple estimate report formats to present to the customer (hard copy and electronic);

✓ tracking method for historical information;

✓ ability to recall and modify past projects; and

✓ job costing capabilities.

As with any software, you must understand the fundamentals. If you do not know how to estimate, the software available will provide limited benefits to the process.

Final Inspection...

Bid Documents: All bid documents should be completed according to the specific requirements of the bid.

Ethics in Bidding: Good ethical practices are important to maintaining the integrity of the bid process.

Estimate Planning: Careful review of construction documents and a site visit are important first steps to creating an accurate estimate.

Estimating Framework: An estimating framework includes the project phases and the labor and materials needed for each phase.

Determining Estimated Costs: The quantity take-off method is one of the more accurate estimating methods. All direct and indirect costs must be added to ensure the estimate is complete.

Other Methods of Estimating: Estimates can be prepared using different methods with varying degrees of accuracy.

Estimating Pitfalls: It is important to be accurate and detailed when estimating a job. You may not make your expected profit if you make mistakes in your estimate.

Using an Estimator: An estimator is used to perform the estimating function on a project. The estimator may also make recommendations on the project profit margin and terms of the contract.

Submitting Your Bid: All instructions in a bid package must be followed or the bid may be rejected. There is typically a 30- to 90-day bid review process.

Job Cost Recording System: Monitoring current projects, creating more accurate future estimates, and providing reports for analysis are benefits of implementing a job cost recording system.

Technology Tools for Estimating: There are several computer tools to help you create your estimate, but it is still important to fully understand the process.

Chapter 8
CONTRACT MANAGEMENT

Chapter Survey...

Legally Speaking: Contracts are legally binding agreements between two or more parties. The main purpose of contracts is to prevent disputes between parties entering into an agreement. Many times, agreements are made verbally, but it is best to get a contract in writing.

Contracts serve many purposes including:

✓ **defining the obligations of the agreement;**

✓ **outlining payment terms; and**

✓ **limiting the liability of the parties involved.**

Contracts need to be worded carefully to protect your company. It is recommended you consult with an attorney experienced in construction law to ensure you have a legally enforceable contract.

Required Contract Elements

Make it Binding: You may have reached an agreement to do work for a customer, but that does not mean that you have a contract. There are four key elements that must be in effect to make a contract binding.

✓ **Offer and Acceptance**

✓ **Consideration**

✓ **Competent Parties**

✓ **Legal Purpose**

Offer and Acceptance

The Offer is on the Table: An offer specifically outlines the obligations of the contract, including the work to be done and compensation for this work. When you submit an estimate or bid for work, this is considered an offer. All parties must be clear on the essential details and obligations of the contract to have a valid offer. Once an offer is made, you are bound to what you have agreed to do.

An offer generally has a specific amount of time in which an acceptance needs to be made. This time frame is typically 30 days, but it should be stated in the offer. If a deadline for acceptance is not outlined in the offer, it expires in a "reasonable time." Reasonable time is up to court interpretation and is considered on an individual case basis.

Negotiation: Negotiation is the process where the owner and contractor come to an agreement on the price and terms of the contract. Chapter 10 discusses techniques that help guide you through the negotiation process. An offer is usually the outcome of a negotiation, but parties are not bound to the contract terms until an offer is made and acceptance is achieved. It is important to be clear when a communication is for negotiation purposes so it is not misconstrued as an offer.

Acceptance: The next step of the process is acceptance. Acceptance is agreeing to the offer made and generally is done by signing the offer. In some cases, a counteroffer is made. A counteroffer is not considered acceptance. It is only when both parties agree to the contract terms that you obtain acceptance.

Offer Checklist: Your offer should contain certain components because, if accepted, you are contractually bound to it:

✓ Date of offer

✓ Names and contact information of contracting parties

✓ Name and location of project

✓ Description of the work to be performed

✓ Contract time or start and completion date

✓ Payment terms, including progress payment schedule and final payment

✓ Conditions for schedule delays

✓ List of contract documents, including general conditions, drawings, and specifications

✓ Contract sum, including contract type such as lump sum, unit price, or cost plus (discussed later in this chapter)

✓ Expiration date of offer

Once accepted, this agreement becomes part of the contract's Standard Form of Agreement.

Consideration

An Exchange: Both parties must give up something of value to have consideration. Most likely this will be money, but it could be anything of value. Payment terms should be clearly outlined in the contract. Typically, the contractor provides services and in exchange, the owner provides monetary compensation.

Competent Parties

Legal Capacity: The parties in agreement should have the legal capacity to enter into a contract. Simply put, the parties must both be of sound mind in order for the contract to be valid. A situation where parties may not have legal capacity might be if you contracted with someone who is heavily under the influence of drugs or alcohol. The courts may rule someone incompetent if they are mentally disabled. Minors are prohibited from entering into contracts without parental consent.

Legal Purpose

Contracts must be possible to perform, not intended to harm anyone, and cannot require any illegal activity. For example, a contract that requires the contractor to build a house that does not comply with building codes does not have a legal purpose and is invalid.

Consult with an attorney to ensure your contracts are legally enforceable.

Contract Provisions

Make it Clear: Contracts should be clear and concise. It is important that both parties understand the terms of the contract. There are provisions you need to include in your contracts to ensure that all details are clearly outlined. Provisions are simply clauses that outline the stipulations of the contract.

Key Contract Provisions: Contracts are full of provisions, but a few key ones you will want to include:

✓ **Contract Price and Payment Terms**

✓ **Obligation of the Parties**

✓ **Supplemental Conditions**

✓ **Breach of Contract**

Contract Price and Payment Terms

Getting Paid: The contract should specify how the contract price is calculated. Whether you choose to use a lump-sum, unit-price or cost-plus method, include all fees the customer is expected to pay.

Payment terms should be very specific and include:

✓ who is issuing payment,

✓ amount of the payment,

✓ form of payment, and

✓ when the payment will be issued.

Progress Payments: Progress payments are partial payments made after specified phases of construction are complete. Payments are generally calculated by taking the difference between the completed work and materials delivered and a predetermined schedule of unit costs.

Requirements for the schedule of progress payments should be clearly outlined in the construction contract including:

- ✓ number of payments,
- ✓ amount of each payment,
- ✓ stage of progress between payments, and
- ✓ date or stage when each one is due.

It is important to monitor the progress payment schedule to ensure timeliness. You may be required to submit a partial payment estimate to the project architect or engineer prior to the payment due date. The partial payment estimate outlines the work performed and proof of materials and equipment delivery required for the next stage of construction. The architect or engineer certifies each progress payment by confirming the information in the partial payment estimate.

Progress payments have two functions: one, to protect the owner by holding the contractor responsible for following the planned schedule and two, to allow the contractor to pay for labor and material expenditures as they occur. This method of payment also protects both parties in the event of a contract breach on either side.

Retainage: Retainage is used by the owner to ensure completion of the construction project and provide protection against liens, claims, and defaults. It is calculated as a percentage (generally 10 percent) withheld from each progress payment. The retainage amount may be reduced further after substantial completion of the project (for example, retainage amounts may drop to 5 percent after 75 percent completion of the project). Retainage amounts must be clearly stated in the construction contract. Prime contractors generally hold the same percentage of retainage for their subcontractors.

The architect or engineer certifies when the project is complete and the work meets the conditions of the contract documents.

The retained amounts are generally due to the contractor upon completion and acceptance of the work.

Final Payment: Once the structure can be used for its intended purpose, the architect issues a certificate of substantial completion. A certificate of occupancy, issued by a building inspector, deems the structure meets all applicable codes and is safe for occupancy.

Final payment is generally due when all punch list items are complete as agreed between the owner and contractor, proper approvals are obtained, and all paperwork is complete.

To receive a final payment, the following documentation should be prepared and delivered to the owner upon completion of the project:

- ✓ Completion certificates issued by the architect
- ✓ Inspection certificates
- ✓ Guaranties and warranties
- ✓ Affidavits that all subcontractors and project bills have been paid
- ✓ Equipment operation manuals
- ✓ Final lien waivers for those who submitted preliminary notices
- ✓ Final project drawings
- ✓ Any other documents as required by contract

It is important to organize paperwork throughout the construction process. A delay in putting the final paperwork together can consequently delay the final payment.

Obligations of the Parties

Contract Conditions: The obligations of the parties should be specifically outlined in the contract and include both the contractor's obligations and the owner's obligations. The obligations of the parties are the contract conditions.

Contractor's obligations include but are not limited to:

- ✓ having proper licensure;
- ✓ securing building permits;
- ✓ ordering all materials and supplies and arranging for site delivery;
- ✓ furnishing all labor, including obtaining required subcontractors to complete the job;
- ✓ completing all work in compliance with all applicable codes and scheduling inspections on a timely basis;
- ✓ completing all work according to plans and specifications; and
- ✓ keeping the construction site clean and removing all debris during and upon completion of construction.

Owner's obligations include but are not limited to:

✓ ensuring prompt approval of all plans and specifications;

✓ ensuring project meets zoning specifications;

✓ issuing payments according to the specified progress payment schedule;

✓ paying for all required permits, assessments, and charges required by public agencies and utilities;

✓ furnishing all surveys and recording plats and a legal description of the property; and

✓ providing access to the construction site in a timely manner.

Each list of obligations must be customized according to the agreement reached and the individual job being performed. Most contracts require agreement by both parties if obligations are assigned to another party.

Supplemental Conditions

The supplemental conditions modify the general conditions of the contract and are often prepared in a separate document. Supplemental conditions are tailored specifically to each project. They may outline items such as specific insurance requirements, project procedures, and local law requirements.

Be very specific when outlining the obligations of both parties.

Breach of Contract

A breach of contract occurs when one of the parties involved fails to perform in accordance with any of the terms and conditions of the contract.

A breach may occur when a party:

✓ refuses to perform the contract;

✓ performs an act prohibited by the contract; or

✓ prevents the other party from performing its obligations.

There are two types of breaches: **material and immaterial**.

A **material breach** is a serious violation of the contract. For example, if a contractor refuses to perform or complete a job or if an owner refuses to pay for completed or partial jobs, this is considered a breach of contract. This type of

breach may void the contract and will most likely end up in litigation.

The injured party can seek monetary damages for the loss suffered as a result of the breach. Sometimes the damages are written into the contract. These are called **liquidated or stated damages**.

Breach of contract can occur if contracts are not completed within the time frame specified in the contract. If a time is not specified in the contract, the project must be completed in a "reasonable time." If the project has an unexcused delay, the owner may be entitled to liquidated damages for the "loss of use." Some contracts specify a per-day rate for liquidated damages. For example, if a contract specifies a $400 per day assessment and the contractor finishes 30 days late, $12,000 in liquidated damages is assessed to the contractor. An owner who sues for liquidated damages cannot sue for actual damages.

If you sue for breach of contract, you must do so within the statute of limitations. Statutes of limitations are laws that set a maximum period of time within which a lawsuit or claim may be filed. The deadlines vary depending on the circumstances of the case and the type of claim. If a claim is not filed before the statutory deadline, you may lose the right to file a claim.

An **immaterial or partial breach** is a less serious violation and usually does not result in termination of the contract. The injured party may only sue for the value of the damages.

Boilerplate Provisions

Standard Language: The term "boilerplate" refers to standard language or clauses used in a legal contract. Sometimes they are referred to as "miscellaneous" clauses. They generally appear at the end of the contract and their purpose is to protect the business in the event of a lawsuit. Attorney's fees, arbitration, and consent to jurisdiction (meaning where the disputes will be settled) are a few examples of boilerplate provisions. When dealing with contracts, make sure to draft and read the boilerplate provisions carefully. These provisions affect your legal rights just as much as the other parts of the contract.

Provisions to Limit Risk

Allocating Risk: As mentioned at the beginning of the chapter, one of the purposes of a contract is to limit the liabilities of the parties involved. Your contract should address the allocation of risk among parties. Examples of risk allocation provisions are listed below:

✓ **Force majeure** addresses "acts of God" and other external events such as war or labor strikes. This provision is written to either absolve the owner or contractor of costs associated with these occurrences.

✓ **Indemnification** absolves the indemnified party from any payment for losses and damages incurred by a third party. Simply put, it is a way to shift payment or liability for any loss or damage that has occurred. Indemnification clauses must be examined carefully to ensure the proper liability is distributed between the contractor and owner.

✓ **Differing site conditions** provision allocates the responsibility for extra costs due to unexpected site conditions. As discussed in Chapter 7, the site conditions must be investigated and taken into consideration when putting together the bid. The owner is responsible for disclosing all site information during the bid process. If errors or omissions occur, the owner may be responsible for incurring the extra construction cost.

✓ **Warranties or guarantees** define the contractor's responsibility for the repair of defects to the construction project after the completion of work. Warranties are often set forth for a defined time period.

✓ **Delays and extensions of time** provide a contingency in case the completion deadline is not met. Delays at no fault of the contractor, such as changes by the owner or architect and environmental or severe weather delays, are generally not considered breach of contract. These types of delays are considered excusable and are granted time extensions. This contingency needs to be clearly outlined in the contract.

✓ **Schedule acceleration** provides assignment of costs incurred to complete a project ahead of schedule. In general, if the owner requires the contractor to accelerate the schedule, the owner is responsible for all associated costs. If the owner requests the schedule be accelerated due to project delays caused by the contractor, the contractor is generally liable for additional costs incurred.

✓ **Artistic changes clause** addresses changes made by the architect or design professional during the course of the project for artistic or creative purposes. The drawings and specifications outline the technical aspects of the project, but may not show the artistic objectives of the project. Including an artistic changes clause will put a limit on the number of changes that can occur as a result of artistic decisions.

Standard legal language must be used when specifying risk assignments to make the contract enforceable. Since legal language is often difficult to understand, it is recommended that you consult with legal counsel when drafting and/or interpreting these provisions.

What Are Recitals?

Background Information: Recitals are language at the beginning of the contract that provide background to the contract, such as the parties entering into the contract, the contract contents, and reasons for the parties' entering into the contract. Recitals cannot always be enforced by law, so it is important to provide specific terms throughout the contract.

Types of Construction Contracts

The differences in the types of contracts are primarily:

✓ who takes the risk that the work will be performed for the estimated cost;

✓ who pays for cost overruns; and

✓ who keeps the cost savings if the project performed is less than the estimate.

Contracts between the owner and primary contractor may differ from contracts between the primary contractor and subcontractors.

Lump-Sum Contract

In a lump-sum contract, the contractor agrees to complete the project for a predetermined, specified price. The contractor essentially assumes all of the risk under this contract agreement because the contractor is responsible for additional costs associated with unforeseen circumstances. For example, if extra cost is incurred due to inclement weather, the contractor must absorb these costs. Conversely, the contractor gets to keep any cost savings achieved.

If you use this type of contract, you may be required to formally submit a specific schedule and your quality assurance program so your customer knows you are completing the project to the highest standards. You should avoid this type of contract unless plans and specifications are detailed enough that a final cost can be determined in advance.

Unit-Price Contract

A unit-price contract may be used for jobs where the extent of work cannot be fully determined, or the actual quantities of required items cannot be accurately calculated in advance. A price per unit is calculated for each item and the contractor is paid according to the actual quantities used.

Cost-Plus Contract

Using the cost-plus contract method, the contractor is reimbursed for the actual cost of labor and materials and is paid a markup fee for overhead and profit. The cost-plus contract can be calculated different ways. The owner may pay the actual costs, plus a percentage markup or a fixed fee markup.

Contracting Methods

Single Prime

The single prime method is the traditional form of contracting. The project owner typically hires an architectural firm to design the project. The contractor then performs the work according to the specifications of the project and is responsible for the costs of all materials and labor to obtain project completion.

Design/Build

Using the design/build method of construction, the owner contracts with one company to complete the process from start to finish. The company awarded the design/build contract puts together a team of construction professionals, which may include designers, architects, engineers, and contractors that take a project from design through completed construction. The team works closely to satisfy the owner's needs within a predetermined budget.

Construction Management

Under the construction management method, the project owner contracts with a professional construction manager to coordinate and manage the project. The construction manager generally receives a fee to manage, coordinate, and supervise the construction process from the conceptual

development stage through final construction. Work must be performed in a timely manner and on an economical basis.

Turnkey

Turnkey construction is similar to the design/build construction model. In addition to managing the construction and design team, the contractor also obtains financing and land. Under the turnkey model, the construction firm is obligated to complete a project according to pre-specified criteria but with expanded responsibilities and liability. A price is generally fixed at the time the contract is signed.

Fast-Track Construction

Under fast-track construction management, the construction process begins before completion of the contract documents. Fast-track construction involves a phased approach to the project. A contract may be drawn up for each phase. Generally, the cost is not fixed until after construction documents are complete and some construction commitments have already been made.

Multiple Prime Contracts

Large construction projects may involve multiple prime contracts. The owner may contract with two or more prime contractors to complete the same project. This contracting method may integrate elements of the construction management and fast-track construction models. The owner takes on a more active role in managing the different prime contractors. Contractor and owner obligations must be clearly defined in the contract.

Partnering

Partnering starts with setting common objectives and goals for a construction project. All parties involved, such as the owner, design professionals, engineers, and contractors, work together to achieve these objectives and goals. Several meetings are held throughout the bid and construction process to evaluate the decisions made by all parties and adjustments occur when necessary. Partnering increases communication and trust, consequently reducing potential litigation and claims.

Sources of Contracts

Standard forms for contracts are readily available through many sources. There are numerous books available that provide sample contracts and forms. Associations such as the American Institute of Architects (AIA) or the Associated General Contractors (AGC) also have standard forms for contracts.

In situations where the form of the contract is not written by you, it is important to:

✓ read the contract very carefully;

✓ highlight anything that is vaguely worded for further clarification;

✓ make necessary additions;

✓ review changes with the other party;

✓ make sure any requested changes have been added prior to signing; and

✓ review the contract again, prior to signing.

Always make sure you keep a signed copy of every contract you sign, in case you need to refer to it in the future.

Making Changes to the Contract

A **change order** is a written agreement between the owner and contractor to change the contract. Change orders add to, delete from, or otherwise alter the work set forth in the construction documents. Change orders are standard in the construction industry as a legal means for making changes to the contract.

Common reasons for generating a change order include:

✓ change in scope (for example, owner requests a design change or owner exceeds allowance amount);

✓ unforeseen conditions when site conditions differ from the expected; and

✓ errors or omissions in construction plans or specifications.

The AIA and AGC have standardized forms that you can use to execute change orders. Change orders are legally binding and it is important that all of the provisions are clear to both parties. Change orders should include:

✓ date of change order;

✓ description of the change in work;

✓ reason for change;

✓ change in contract price;

✓ change, if any, in contracted time; and

✓ signatures from both parties.

Chapter 10 also discusses how to handle change orders from a customer relations perspective.

Changes prior to the contract award are called **addenda**. Changes made after the contract is signed and executed are called **modifications**.

Resolving Claims

The claims resolution process provides a way for the owner and contractor to resolve disputes about additional amounts owed as a result of contract changes. As discussed in the previous section, the purpose of written change orders is to avoid disputes. If a change is made to the contract without a change order, claims may arise.

Claims Procedure: The contract may stipulate specific procedures for handling claims. Many times, the contract defers to the architect to initially resolve claims. If claims cannot be resolved by the architect, the contractor and owner may proceed to mediation. If mediation fails, the next step is arbitration. The contract should specify the time allowed to request arbitration. A typical deadline for an arbitration request is 30 days from the time the architect makes a decision on the claim.

Project Schedule: During the claims resolution process, the project cannot be delayed. All schedules and deadlines must be followed. The only exception is disputes involving safety. Work must cease on disputed activities until all safety issues are resolved.

Alternative Dispute Resolution

Alternative dispute resolution (ADR) involves settling legal disputes by avoiding the often costly and time intensive process of a government judicial trial. The most common forms of ADR are: negotiation, mediation, collaborative law, and arbitration.

Negotiation: Negotiation is a dialogue entered into for the purpose of resolving disputes or producing an agreed upon course or courses of action. Negotiation is inexpensive and generally the first step in ADR. Negotiation allows for an unstructured discussion between both parties and generally does not involve anyone other than the affected parties. If an agreement is not reached, more formal methods of dispute resolution are required.

Mediation: In mediation, the parties themselves set forth the conditions of any agreement with dialogue facilitated by an independent, third party mediator. The mediator is not a judge or arbitrator who sets forth the terms of an agreement, rather a mediator is a trained professional in negotiations and the process of mediation. The goal of mediation is to find areas of agreement between the parties involved by using strategies and techniques designed to allow the parties to work towards a mutual and fair agreement. If a settlement is not reached, the dispute may go through mediation again or sent to arbitration. The option to take legal disputes to mediation is desirable from a cost perspective because it is generally less expensive and allows for a quicker resolution than going to trial.

Collaborative Law: Collaborative law is a facilitative process wherein all parties agree at the onset to work to identify a solution that is beneficial to all parties involved. In collaborative law, the parties use their advocates, most often their lawyers, to facilitate a mutually beneficial result through the process of negotiation. There is no neutral mediator or arbitrator involved and the parties are expected to reach a settlement without using further methods of ADR or litigation.

Arbitration: Arbitration uses a third-party arbitrator or arbitrators to act as a judge or judges to render a decision by which all parties are legally bound. Arbitration is held in a format less formal than a trial. The arbitrator(s), unlike a mediator, is not involved in the negotiation discussion towards a settlement. Arbitrators may be attorneys or retired judges who serve individually or as a panel. They are either chosen by the parties involved in the dispute or appointed by the court according to the terms of the contract. Arbitrators with industry-specific experience (such as construction litigation experience) may be appointed to certain types of disputes. The decision or arbitral award made by the arbitrator(s) is legally binding unlike in mediation. Many times, contracts call for disputes to be resolved through arbitration over taking matters to a costly trial. Arbitration may be required by law for certain types of disputes. Nearly all states have adopted the federal Uniform Arbitration Act making arbitral awards binding by both state and federal law.

Making Substitutions

When bidding on a project, many contractors bid from their normal manufacturers and suppliers and not the manufacturer that appears on the plans. When bidding, you need to make sure you can pay for the cost of all items and products as specified. Failure to do so could cost you a lot of money.

Substitution Approval Process: The best way to ensure a specific substitution is by the "prior approval" process. A "prior approval" occurs during the bid stage only. If a particular product or item is desired other than the specified item, you must submit a request while the project is being bid. If approved, all bidders will be allowed to use that item or product in their bids. That is why the "prior approval" is done in the bidding stage. It keeps the playing field level for all competitors.

Substitutions After the Bid Process: A substitution may be made after the bid has been accepted. Nevertheless, any substitution must meet certain criteria to even be considered. The specifications should describe the conditions for such substitutions. Usually there are only four reasons that a substitution would be entertained:

- ✓ the specific item or product is no longer available;
- ✓ a cost savings;
- ✓ a time savings; or
- ✓ combination of cost and time savings.

Discontinued Products: A product no longer available is generally the only event that will not require a change order reducing cost and/or time, unless it was approved under the "prior approval" process. Do not forget to note those reductions in the substitution request. The reason a reduction of cost and/or time is required is due to the fact that it is understood that the bid was based on the specific item or product. To make a change, the result must benefit the owner; otherwise, there is no reason to make the substitution.

Substitution Specifications: If there is a basis for the substitution, the next requirement is that the item or product must be equal to that which was specified. Just as the reference of a 2 x 4 to contractors is not measured as 2" x 4", its nomenclature is referred to as "nominal." Many other products are referred to as "nominal" sizing. HVAC systems are especially that way. Just because one manufacturer references a unit as five-tons, it does not mean that it produces the same capacity as a five-ton unit from another manufacturer under the same conditions.

The specifications must be analyzed carefully before submitting the substitution request. Be sure to cover the cost of the specified item, as a substitution may not be granted, not even in the "prior approval" process.

Contract Documents and Project Manual

The project manual is a central location for bid documents, contract provisions, technical specifications, and addenda. This bound manual is a useful tool easily referenced on the jobsite. It can be reproduced and distributed to contractors, subcontractors, and suppliers. The following is a detailed summary of the documents contained in a typical project manual.

Bid Documents:

- ✓ Invitation to bid
- ✓ Bid instructions
- ✓ Bid forms
- ✓ Supplements
- ✓ Addenda

Contract Provisions:

- ✓ Form of agreement
- ✓ General conditions or obligation of parties
- ✓ Supplemental conditions
- ✓ Change orders
- ✓ Index of drawings

Supplemental Forms:

- ✓ Required bonds
- ✓ Certificate of insurance

Technical Specifications are generally organized by a classification system, such as the CSI MasterFormat.

The **construction drawings** are also part of the contract documents. For larger projects, the drawings are divided by design discipline and trades. Drawings may include but are not limited to:

- ✓ architectural,
- ✓ structural,
- ✓ plumbing,
- ✓ electrical,
- ✓ mechanical,
- ✓ landscape, and
- ✓ civil.

The drawings are kept separate but can be indexed in the project manual.

Are Oral Agreements Legally Binding?

Under most circumstances, oral agreements are just as binding as written agreements with a few exceptions. Exceptions include contracts which have a high risk of fraud such as the sale or purchase of land. Oral agreements present a challenge because it is difficult to prove what terms were agreed upon if a dispute arises. Needless to say, it is a risky way to do business and it is best to get everything in writing.

Sometimes parties enter into agreements that are partially oral and partially written. For example, you may have carefully put together a written contract to do work. The customer then verbally gives you a change order. Now you are in a situation where you have an oral agreement for the change. To protect yourself, it is best to follow up with a written change order. In a legal judgment, written agreements always take precedence over oral agreements.

Oral agreements are not a good way to do business. Get it in writing!

Legal Interpretation

Clarity of language and meaning is one of the most important aspects of interpreting contracts and avoiding disputes. It is strongly recommended that you use an attorney when drafting contracts to ensure that the contract will stand up in a dispute. There are also necessary provisions that should be included in a contract. A contract lawyer can advise you on this matter.

The use of plain language is important when establishing intent in a contract. If a dispute arises, the contract will be interpreted using the plain meaning of the words in the contract. If your contract goes to litigation, the judge may not have a background in the construction industry. This is why it is important to clearly state the terms in the contract using plain language.

Technical terminology in contracts between parties who understand their technical meaning may be used. However, many customers may not understand technical jargon so you may want to use caution putting these terms in a contract. Rather, you should express your intentions in layman terms. Disputes may arise when parties do not understand undefined technical language and contract interpretation may not end up in your favor.

If the provision being disputed is vague, the actions of the parties will be examined first. If the parties conducted themselves consistently with what they thought the provision meant at that time, the provision would likely take that meaning. If the contract cannot be clarified based on this method, the interpretation will go against the party who wrote it.

Subcontracting

Subcontractors contract with the general contractor or other subcontractors to complete a portion of a larger project. The same principles that apply to owner/contractor contracts also apply to subcontracts.

Subcontracts should include similar content as owner/contractor contracts, such as:

✓ Date

✓ Names and contact information of contracting parties

✓ Name and location of project

✓ Description of the work to be performed

✓ Subcontract time or start and completion date

✓ Payment terms, including progress payment schedule and final payment

✓ Conditions for schedule delays

✓ Drawings and specifications

✓ Contract sum

✓ Any general and supplemental conditions that apply

✓ Signatures from both parties

Depending on the stipulations in the owner/contractor agreement, the owner may need to approve subcontractors.

It is also important to get subcontracts in writing to avoid disputes. In providing a written contract, both parties have a clear understanding of the agreement. Oral contracts can lead to ambiguity and one party may interpret the agreement differently than the other.

Clarity is very important to an enforceable contract.

Final Inspection...

Required Contract Elements: Required contract elements include offer and acceptance, consideration, competent parties, and legal purpose.

Contract Provisions: Your contract should contain provisions that clearly outline the terms of the contract. A few key provisions you want to include are contract price and payment terms, obligation of the parties, and breach of contract.

Breach of Contract: A breach of contract occurs when one of the parties involved fails to perform in accordance with any of the terms and conditions of the contract.

Boilerplate Provisions: These provisions contain standard language designed to protect you in the event of a lawsuit.

Provisions to Limit Risk: These provisions limit the liability of the contracting parties by addressing allocation of risk.

What Are Recitals? This language appears at the beginning of the contract and is intended to give background information.

Types of Construction Contracts: Different types of contracts address who is responsible for cost savings and overruns for estimated work.

Contracting Methods: Depending on the level of involvement in a construction project, different types of contracting methods are used.

Sources of Contracts: Contracts are available through several different sources, including associations such as the American Institute of Architects (AIA) or the Associated General Contractors (AGC).

Making Changes to the Contract: To change the contract, a change order is written and agreed to by the owner and contractor.

Resolving Claims: The claims resolution process provides a way for the owner and contractor to resolve disputes about additional amounts owed as a result of contract changes.

Alternative Dispute Resolution (ADR): Involves settling legal disputes by avoiding the often costly and time intensive process of a government judicial trial. The most common forms of ADR are: negotiation, mediation, collaborative law, and arbitration.

Making Substitutions: Specifications must be analyzed carefully before submitting the substitution request. Substitutions may be granted if products are discontinued or to provide a cost or time savings.

Contract Documents and Project Manual: The project manual is a central location for bid documents, contract provisions, technical specifications, and addenda.

Are Oral Agreements Legally Binding? Oral agreements can be binding, but it makes good business sense to get a contract in writing.

Legal Interpretation: Clarity of language and meaning in contracts is important to avoid disputes and ensure proper legal interpretation in the event of a lawsuit.

Subcontracting: The same principles that apply to owner/contractor contracts also apply to subcontracts. Similar language is used to ensure that each party is clear on terms and conditions of the contract.

Chapter 9
SCHEDULING AND PROJECT MANAGEMENT

Many construction jobs are performed every day without using a formal scheduling method. Knowing how to schedule and organize tasks helps you complete projects on time, which increases customer satisfaction and ultimately your competitive edge.

Using the quantity take-off method, as explained in Chapter 7, you developed the basis for your project schedule. Each task was assigned the number of labor hours for completion to determine labor cost. Scheduling takes the list of tasks and labor hours and assigns an order of completion.

Scheduling Process

Planning is a key element to formulating an accurate schedule and effectively managing the project. Planning allows you to visualize the project and anticipate potential conflicts and challenges. The project start and completion dates are outlined in the contract. It is the job of the scheduler to fit in all necessary tasks within this time frame in the most efficient manner.

Sequence of Tasks: Understanding the correct sequence of tasks is critical to completing your project on time. As you created your estimate (discussed in Chapter 7), you probably listed your tasks in the order of completion. This determination is particularly important when scheduling subcontractors. Be sure to review the tasks outlined in the estimate and make any necessary corrections to the sequence of tasks.

Some tasks may be completed at the same time while other tasks must come before starting the next task. For example, interior and exterior paint may be applied at the same time but drywall must be completed before paint is applied.

Activity Duration: When creating your estimate, you determined the number of labor hours it takes to complete each task on the project. Using this estimate, you need to determine the duration of the task. The duration of each task depends on a few factors:

✓ size of the project;

✓ labor hours estimated; and

✓ length of time dedicated to the task each day. For example, if a task is estimated at four hours but your crew only has two hours per day to work on the task, the activity duration is two working days.

When determining activity duration, it is important to get input from your subcontractors and the experienced members of your crew.

Once the duration is determined for each activity, you can compare the total time against the project completion time outlined in the contract. If the total time exceeds the project completion time, adjustments must be made. Consideration must be given to increasing labor resources, requiring overtime, or extending the project completion date. These options must be weighed carefully due to added costs and possible timeline conflicts with the owner.

Contingency Time: Contingency time is used as a buffer between tasks to protect against unforeseen task delays. To determine contingency time, the task is analyzed to determine the likelihood of a delay occurring. A few general rules apply to determining contingency time:

✓ Tasks subject to weather delays require more contingency time.

✓ Standard work requires less contingency time than custom work.

✓ Tasks performed in areas with limited access require more contingency time.

With contingency time in place, the likelihood of a delayed task impacting the entire schedule is reduced.

Task Time Ranges: After completing the sequence of tasks, activity duration, and contingency time, the earliest and latest start date and earliest and latest end date are calculated. If the task completion falls outside these dates during the construction process, the project manager has an accurate calculation of the amount of time the project is ahead or behind.

Float Time: Float time is the remaining time after a task is complete and before the next task begins.

✓ The amount of time an activity can be delayed without impacting the early start of the next activity is called free float time.

✓ Total float time refers to the amount of leeway allowed in starting or completing an activity without delaying the project completion date.

✓ Activities with "zero float" are considered critical activities.

Scheduling Methods

A schedule is your blueprint to finishing the project on time. There are three main types of scheduling methods used in the construction industry:

✓ **Calendar Scheduling**

✓ **Bar Chart Scheduling**

✓ **Critical Path Method**

The type of schedule you use depends on factors such as project size, complexity, and location.

Calendar Scheduling

Calendar scheduling is a simple method and can be done on a regular desk calendar. The primary advantage to this method is that you can link project tasks to specific dates, such as:

✓ dates of other projects,

✓ delivery dates of materials,

✓ payment schedules, and

✓ employee vacations and holidays.

To create a calendar schedule, you need to know the sequence of tasks and activity duration. After these factors are determined, you can plug the activities into the calendar.

The following is a sample calendar schedule. Calendar scheduling works for smaller, less complex projects but is not recommended for large ones.

SAMPLE CALENDAR SCHEDULE

Project Name: _____ Start Date: _____ End Date: _____

Sunday	Monday	Tuesday	Wednesday	Thursday	Friday	Saturday
1 Off	**2** Excavation——	**3**	**4** Layout Slab Foundation Forms	**5** Under- ground Plumbing	**6** Pour Concrete	**7** Concrete Cure Time
8 Concrete Cure Time	**9**	**10**	**11** Frame Exterior Walls	**12**	**13** Off	**14** Off
15 Off	**16** Frame Roof—— Install Doors & Windows	**17**	**18**	**19** Lay Roofing Materials	**20**	**21**
22 Off	**23** Electrical Rough-In Plumbing Rough-In	**24**	**25** HVAC	**26** Siding——	**27**	**28** Off
29 Off	**30** Siding Insulation ——	**31**	**1** Install Drywall Paint Exterior	**2**	**3**	**4** Off
5 Off	**6** Install Wood/Tile Flooring	**7**	**8** Install Trim	**9**	**10**	**11** Off
12 Off	**13** Paint Interior	**14**	**15** Finish Electrical Finish Plumbing	**16**	**17** Install Carpeting	**18** Site Clean-up

Bar Chart Scheduling

Similar to the calendar scheduling method, the bar chart schedule shows the activity duration and sequence of tasks to be completed. It is an easy-to-read visual showing a graphical depiction of the schedule in its entirety.

One of the main weaknesses of the bar chart and calendar scheduling methods is that they do not show the interdependencies of activities.

For example, if there is a delay in a task, the bar chart does not show the impact it has on other tasks. The following is a sample bar chart schedule.

SCHEDULE BAR CHART FOR RETAIL STORE CONSTRUCTION

Description of Tasks	March				April				May				June			
	W1	W2	W3	W4	W1	W2	W3	W4	W1	W2	W3	W4	W1	W2	W3	W4
Contract Award	■															
Field Survey		■														
Documents Reviewed		■														
Building Permit			■	■												
Pre-Meeting				■												
Demolition					■											
Door & Windows					■											
Electrical Rough In					■	■										
Plumbing Rough In						■										
Lighting						■										
HVAC						■										
Fire Protection						■										
Ceiling					■	■										
Drywall						■										
Plumbing Fixtures						■										
Caulking & Sealants							■									
Flooring								■								
Cash Wrap									■	■						
Product Racks									■	■						
Electrical Fixtures											■					
Painting											■					
Signage											■					
Construction Cleaning													■			
Project Closeout															■	

Critical Path Method

The critical path method (CPM) of scheduling illustrates the interdependent relationship of tasks. To develop a CPM schedule, you start by determining the sequence of tasks and activity duration as you would with bar chart or calendar scheduling. In addition, you need to outline the following:

✓ Relationship between tasks

✓ Simultaneous events

✓ Critical path

Relationship between Tasks: Most construction tasks are interrelated. For example, you can't start framing until you pour the foundation. A CPM schedule graphically shows which tasks are related and which ones are not. When you create your CPM schedule, you need to determine how each task impacts another.

Simultaneous Events: If you know which tasks can be performed simultaneously, you can shorten project completion time. When creating the CPM schedule, you must show when simultaneous tasks are possible.

Critical Path: The critical path is the sequence of tasks that determines the duration of the project. If a task on the critical path is delayed by one week, the project is delayed by one week. You must know which subsequent tasks cannot begin until a critical path item is completed.

The following diagram illustrates a simple critical path example.

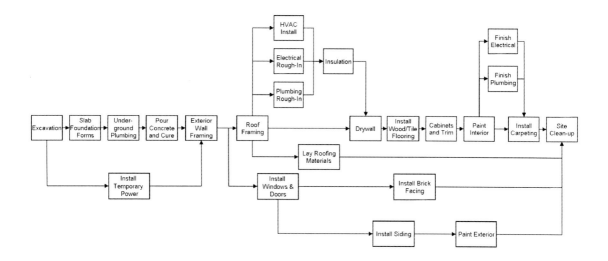

Adding Activity Duration to the CPM Schedule: The CPM schedule can be placed against a timeline. An example of this is illustrated in the bar chart schedule earlier in the chapter. Another alternative is to place the activity duration with each task. You can also put a code with the activity to correlate it to your estimate. If you use your estimating format, you could use the CSI MasterFormat to code the tasks in your schedule. For example, let's say the task of painting the interior has a three-day duration and you use MasterFormat code 09900. Your task might look like this on the CPM chart.

Paint Interior	
09900	3

Many different types of software are available to help you create schedules. You want to choose a program that is right for your needs whether it is simple or more complex. Some programs allow you to adjust the timelines if, for example, you experience a delay in the project. Scheduling software also facilitates the tracking function of a project schedule, which is a key project management tool.

Scheduling and Cash Management

It is important to track incoming cash and expenditures during the construction project to ensure you have enough working capital to complete the job. "Working capital" refers to the amount of cash available after the liabilities or debts are paid. Balancing incoming progress payments and outgoing expenditures is important to manage the project effectively and should be a consideration when preparing your schedule.

If you have more expenditures than incoming cash in any stage of construction, you may not

have enough money to proceed to the next stage of construction or pay your debts.

A preliminary cash flow budget, outlining stages of construction with anticipated revenues and expenditures, should be completed during the scheduling phase to anticipate any cash shortages. Cash flow should be tracked through the duration of the project.

What is Project Management?

Effective project management is a challenging task on a construction project. It requires a carefully balanced combination of management skills with an understanding of the design and construction process. Project managers may manage several projects at the same time with projects at different stages of the process. A project manager not only has to manage time through the scheduling process but must also consider many other factors:

✓ Budget constraints

✓ Quality standards

✓ Project plans and specifications

✓ Resource management such as labor, materials, etc.

Project management has applications that are unique in nearly every industry, including construction.

The ability to effectively manage significantly contributes to the success or failure of the project.

Who is the Project Manager?

Construction project managers plan and coordinate construction projects to meet the overall goals of the project and serve as the main contact with the owner. Responsibilities generally include but are not limited to:

✓ preparing budgets;

✓ reviewing shop drawings to determine appropriate construction methods;

✓ determining labor requirements and preparing schedules;

✓ monitoring overall progress of the project and preparing job records;

✓ monitoring compliance with building and safety codes;

✓ ensuring proper handling of change orders; and

✓ regularly meeting with owners, trade contractors, architects, and other design professionals on project progress.

Construction project managers work closely with the project superintendent who manages daily site operations.

Construction managers may be owners or salaried employees of a construction management or contracting firm, or they may work under contract or as a salaried employee of the owner, developer, contractor, or management firm overseeing the construction project. They may plan and direct a whole project or just a part of a larger project.

> ***What Qualities Does a Good Manager Need?***
> ✓ A good manager must possess several qualities to effectively lead a team.
> ✓ Good communication skills
> ✓ Honesty and integrity
> ✓ Positive attitude
> ✓ Effective delegation skills
> ✓ Team and morale building skills

Project Supervisory Team

While the project manager has a high level understanding of the project, supervisors coordinate and monitor the daily aspects of the project. Depending on the size of the project, the number of supervisory team members may vary.

Superintendent: The superintendent is the onsite supervisor responsible for daily operations. Depending on the size of the project and amount of responsibility the project manager wants to delegate, the superintendent's duties may include:

✓ coordinating project activities and serving as a liaison with subcontractors, architects, utilities, and others;

✓ participating in project construction development and planning;

✓ processing utility requests for construction projects;

✓ representing the company regarding onsite construction quality control reviews;

✓ making recommendations and processing change order requests;

✓ reviewing punch lists;

✓ assuring construction specifications are met;

✓ tracking deviations from project schedules and costs; and

✓ maintaining project records and reports.

Communication between the project manager and superintendent is important to keeping the project on-time and within budget and providing a quality product.

Foreman: The foreman assists the superintendent with daily project operations. The superintendent generally oversees all of the daily operations, but the foreman usually supervises specific areas by trade. For example, a carpentry foreman may supervise rough and finish carpentry while the masonry foreman supervises formwork and concrete installation.

The foreman assists the supervisor by:

✓ reviewing project plans and blueprints;

✓ providing input on estimated time, material, equipment and supplies needed;

✓ developing schedules and crew assignments;

✓ inspecting work areas;

✓ evaluating employee and subcontractor performance;

✓ completing time sheets, accident reports, and work orders; and

✓ training employees.

Materials Expediter: Timely delivery of materials is important to keeping a project schedule on track.

A materials expediter supervises the materials procurement process to ensure accurate and timely delivery of materials.

Later in the chapter, we will discuss the importance of effective materials management.

Architect and Owner's Representative: The owner will sometimes defer to an appointed representative to oversee a project. In this case, the owner's representative and/or architect will deal with the project manager. The owner's representative and architect usually do not have supervisory authority over the employees and subcontractors but they may communicate with the project manager in order to express any concerns with the project work.

In general, the owner's representative and architect have access to the jobsite and work records and can contribute to quality control on the project. The architect (or sometimes the engineer) must certify each progress payment, so it is in the best interest of the project manager to work closely with the architect and owner's representative.

Project Life Cycle

Each project has a start point, project life cycle, and end point. Through each phase of the project life cycle, you must manage each aspect of the project such as customer relations, materials, budget, and subcontractors. Using the customer relations category as an example, the following illustrates various management aspects in the project life cycle.

Contract Award

After you are successfully offered the job, you should get a contract signed as soon as possible. A few weeks before the job starts, schedule a pre-construction meeting with your customer and any other relevant parties (i.e., architect, subcontractors, etc.).

Pre-Construction Phase

During the pre-construction meeting, you should go over customer expectations. Chapter 10 discusses creating realistic expectations for your customer to avoid disappointment. At this time, you should have a preliminary schedule prepared, so potential scheduling conflicts can be discussed. Be sure to follow up with meeting notes and distribute to those in attendance as well as those who could not attend.

Construction Phase

As the project progresses, you should carefully monitor the budget, schedule, and project quality. Regularly meet with your customer to discuss the progress of the project and any issues or questions that arise. If you are billing in progress payments, make sure you are invoicing regularly and collecting payments within the defined terms.

Job Completion and Closeout

After the job is complete, you must do a walkthrough and develop a punch list of follow-up items. Discuss any warranties contained in your contract and how the customer can request warranty repairs. Send a customer satisfaction survey to gather feedback for future improvements.

Key Elements for a Successful Project Outcome

Many elements go into a successful project outcome:

- ✓ Project manager who understands the total project as a big picture
- ✓ Early preparation and planning
- ✓ Good management and front-line supervision
- ✓ Effective responses to problems and changes
- ✓ Active customer involvement
- ✓ Good communication skills

Tracking the Progress of the Project

Daily Reports

Many contractors find that keeping a daily log is a useful project tool. You can use a log to track the progress of a project and as legal back up in case any disputes arise.

The daily log can list:

- ✓ Project name and location
- ✓ Date
- ✓ Weather conditions
- ✓ Personnel on the job
- ✓ Description of work
- ✓ Hours worked on each task
- ✓ Change orders
- ✓ Progress of the job
- ✓ Other relevant information

Personal comments should not be made in the daily report. It should contain only factual information.

There are specific guidelines you should follow to increase the credibility of the daily report, if a legal dispute arises.

- ✓ The report should be completed daily. If there was no work completed, note that fact and the reason for it.
- ✓ Writing should be in ink and not altered.
- ✓ Pages should be in consecutive order and in a bound book.

Photos are a good way to document the progress of a project and can serve as a supplement to the daily log. Photos should be taken of the site prior to starting work and at critical points during the project to document any problem areas. Digital cameras make photo-taking easy with instant results. You also have the flexibility to store photos on your computer and send them through email.

Status Reports

Status reports summarize project highlights, addressing items completed, in progress, and outstanding. This report is a helpful tool to communicate with the customer, managers, subcontractors, and suppliers periodically throughout the project.

To support your status reports, you should have work records easily accessible for review. These work records include:

- ✓ daily reports,
- ✓ project photographs,
- ✓ previous status reports,
- ✓ safety and accident reports,
- ✓ change orders,
- ✓ shop drawings,
- ✓ purchase orders,
- ✓ receiving documentation, and
- ✓ relevant written correspondence.

You should solicit feedback on any anticipated problems or concerns and encourage two-way communication throughout the project. Status reports are a good way to initiate this communication.

Tracking the Schedule

A good project manager makes sure that deadlines are met on time. As discussed earlier, the first step is to develop the schedule. Next, you want to make sure you communicate the schedule to anyone who is impacted by it, such as your crew, subcontractors, and suppliers. You need to make sure they understand the deadlines and their assignments. You may want to present the schedule in a graphical format so team members can get a visual snapshot of the timeline.

Budget and Cost Controls

Project management involves working with budget constraints. A good project manager will control costs and make sure that the project comes in on budget.

If the budget is not monitored carefully, a job that was estimated correctly can turn into a loss for the company.

Materials

Just-In-Time (JIT): Just-in-time deliveries will keep your inventory cost low. This process allows you to time deliveries to arrive as you need the materials in the construction process. Using your schedule, you can closely predict when you need materials according to the work being completed and then coordinate timing with your suppliers. Less inventory onsite will also cut down the risk of theft or vandalism.

Purchase Orders: Using a purchase order system can help you organize and document your materials purchases. If you prepare your purchase orders in advance, you can review these with your customers. This process can potentially reduce change orders by allowing customers to make decisions and sign off on them in advance. Your purchase orders can also serve as delivery date documentation so you can organize just-in-time deliveries.

Receiving: You can control material costs through proper receiving. When materials are delivered, someone should check the materials against the purchase order to confirm the correct quantity and items ordered were received. If there are discrepancies, follow up with the supplier as soon as possible to ensure you receive the proper credits or replacements.

To the best of your ability, you want to estimate and order the correct amount of materials. If you have excess materials, check with your supplier for a return policy. Excess materials should be stored correctly to preserve their condition. Some suppliers charge a restocking fee, but it is generally nominal and worth your time to receive a materials credit.

Budget Tracking

The easiest way to track your budget is to use the cost estimate and a job cost system to determine if you have any cost overruns.

Cost overruns occur when you exceed budgeted amounts in your estimate. These overruns can happen in many areas of the project such as exceeding the amount of labor through improper scheduling and excessive materials waste. Chapter 8, Contract Management, summarizes types of contracts that address who is responsible for cost overruns.

It is important to track costs as the project progresses because cost overruns can indicate a possible problem. The sooner these problems are identified, the easier it will be to take corrective action.

Cost overruns may occur because you have a bad estimate. Tracking your budget will help you or your estimator prepare more accurate estimates in the future.

Cost overruns reduce the amount of profit you make on the job. If you are not making a profit or you are losing money on your projects, you will eventually go out of business.

Quality Assurance

Ensuring the customer receives a quality built product is one of the most important aspects of project management. You may find ways to cut corners, but neglecting quality can cost you in the long run. You may also run into ethical considerations when neglecting quality. Concealing defective work and design flaws can leave you open to a lawsuit and ruin your reputation.

Accurate and Detailed Specifications and Plans

Accurate and detailed specifications and plans are important to setting the quality standards of the project. These items will help you put together a more accurate estimate and should be part of the contract documents. If details are vague, your decisions on material quality and construction methods may differ from the owner's. This misunderstanding can cause conflict and disappoint your customer. It is best to set expectations and obtain agreement from the customer early in the project.

Detailed Shop Drawings

In addition to specifications and plans, shop drawings are often required to detail specific aspects of a project. Shop drawings outline specific details, materials, dimensions, and installation for specific items. Product data and samples may accompany shop drawings to provide additional information. Shop drawings are produced by the material supplier, contractor, subcontractor, or manufacturer. As part of the quality control process, the architect and contractor must review and approve shop drawings.

Quality Assurance Program

Setting up a quality assurance program is a good way to let your employees and customers know the importance of producing a high quality product. Internal inspections should take place at different stages of the construction process to review the completed work and confirm that it meets your quality standards.

Your company philosophy should stress quality. You want your employees to take pride in their work. As an employer, you can create a positive work atmosphere and provide the tools employees need to be successful. Providing ongoing training for employees so they can expand their knowledge base helps improve the quality of their work. Employees should know the standards they are expected to follow. Documenting work standards and conducting regular performance reviews are good ways to create a mutual understanding of the level of quality you expect.

Customer Satisfaction Surveys

Customer satisfaction surveys are also a good tool to receive feedback about the quality of your work. Customer surveys are good for asking about the professionalism of your employees, quality of work, and overall service. Potential customers may be interested that you have a continuous improvement program. Positive feedback from your current or former customers can serve as a good marketing tool to gain new business.

Value Engineering

Value engineering is a project management approach. The objective is to understand the owner's cost, quality, and time priorities to deliver a product of the highest value. Many owners will provide incentives to contractors to meet these objectives. For example, an owner may provide a bonus for a contractor who can cut costs without sacrificing quality while meeting all deadlines. If value engineering bonuses exist, it is important that they are included in the construction contract.

The Society of American Value Engineering International (SAVE) publishes a methodology for the construction industry. The purpose of this methodology is to reduce costs, improve productivity, and develop innovative ways to solve problems.

Final Inspection...

Scheduling Process: During the project scheduling process, the sequence of tasks, activity duration, contingency time, task time ranges, and float time are determined.

Scheduling Methods: The three main types of scheduling are calendar scheduling, bar chart scheduling, and critical path method (CPM).

Scheduling and Cash Management: Effective cash management helps ensure you have enough working capital to complete your project.

What is Project Management? Project management involves managing several different factors including budgets, quality controls, project plans and specifications, and resource management.

Who is the Project Manager? Construction project managers plan and coordinate construction projects to meet the overall goals of the project and serve as the main contact with the owner. The ability to manage effectively contributes significantly to the success or failure of a project.

Project Supervisory Team: Depending on the size of the project, the supervisory team may consist of a superintendent, foreman, materials expediter, architect, and owner's representative.

Project Life Cycle: Through each phase of the project life cycle, you must manage each aspect of the project such as customer relations, materials, budget, and subcontractors.

Tracking the Progress of the Project: A good project manager makes sure that deadlines are met on time. Daily reports and status reports are tools you can use to track your progress.

Budget and Cost Controls: A good project manager will control costs and make sure the project comes in on budget.

Quality Assurance: Ensuring that the customer receives a quality built product is one of the most important aspects of project management.

Value Engineering: Balancing the owner's cost, quality, and time priorities while delivering the highest value product are objectives of the value engineering approach.

Chapter 10
CUSTOMER RELATIONS

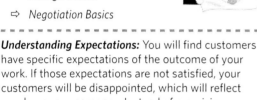

Understanding Expectations: You will find customers have specific expectations of the outcome of your work. If those expectations are not satisfied, your customers will be disappointed, which will reflect poorly on your company. Instead of promising your customers an unrealistic outcome, it is easier to be honest and bring expectations to a realistic level. If customers have a realistic picture of the project, you can avoid disappointing them. The best way to accomplish this is through consistent and effective communication with your customers.

Communication with Customers

It is important for customers to understand the status of their project and have all the information needed to make informed decisions. This communication will not only keep the customer's expectations realistic but also build a trusting relationship with you and your company.

Communication Opportunities: You have several opportunities to communicate with your customers nad keep their expectations at a realistic level, including:

✓ contract negotiations,

✓ contract acceptance,

✓ weekly meetings,

✓ punch list and final walkthrough, and

✓ post-job follow-up.

Establishing communication at these times will ensure that your customer is aware of your progress and of issues that arise during any step of the process.

Communication Basics: Now that we have established when to communicate with customers, let's go over a few basics on how to communicate.

✓ Understand that your customer may not have the same level of technical knowledge as you. Avoid using technical terminology and clarify when necessary.

✓ Give your customer a chance to ask questions and express any concerns. Use active listening skills, and remember that all questions are important to the customer.

✓ When dealing with difficult customers, always remain professional.

✓ Use email or written communication as a follow-up to verbal conversations to document key items discussed and any changes agreed to.

✓ Don't forget the personal touch. Email and fax are great tools, but schedule time to talk to the customer in person.

✓ Return phone calls promptly.

Good communication can build customer trust and help you understand customer expectations.

Handling Customer Change Orders

Proper handling of customer change orders is very important. This is a critical point in the customer-contractor relationship that can result in a positive or negative outcome. If you do not follow through with the change order as the customer expects, it will result in disappointment and mistrust. If you follow through to the customer's specifications, you will reinforce that you are responsive and understand the importance of customer service.

You should always apply a few general rules when change orders arise:

✓ Always obtain a signed change order for significant amounts of change work.

✓ Small changes done with verbal approval should be followed up with a written and signed change order.

✓ Invoice for change order work promptly.

✓ Include any complimentary work done without charge on the invoice.

✓ Show labor and quantity details when pricing change orders as you would when creating your initial estimate.

Negotiation Basics

Good negotiation skills can benefit you personally and in all areas of your business. When a successful negotiation occurs, both parties are satisfied with the outcome.

Preparing to Negotiate: Negotiation is a process and it is important to prepare ahead of time to get the most out of the negotiation. Considering these questions will help:

✓ What are you negotiating (i.e., money, time, conditions, etc.)?

✓ What is the ideal outcome?

✓ How much are you willing to compromise?

✓ What is the other person trying to achieve?

A negotiation may not always involve price. Consider what is valuable to your business. For example, if time is a critical factor to completing your current projects, you may want to negotiate on project timelines. It is important not to compromise your reputation in a negotiation. You don't want to lose your best customer or future referrals.

Confident Negotiations: Now that you are prepared, you can come to the negotiation confident in knowing what you want. Aim high in your negotiation and you will get more. If you ask for more than you want, people will tend to meet you in the middle. It is important to be flexible during the negotiation. Even though you have prepared ahead of time, the other party may change the direction of the negotiation to different terms. For example, you may have prepared

to negotiate on price, but your counterpart may want to deal on the timeline of the work.

When possible, it is important to get the final outcome of your negotiation in writing. Once it is in writing, both parties can sign off on what they agreed to, which will help avoid any disappointment or confusion.

Final Inspection...

Communication with Customers: Good communication helps you build trust and understand customer expectations.

Handling Customer Change Orders: Change orders should be handled carefully and accurately documented.

Negotiation Basics: Come to a negotiation prepared, and, when possible, make sure you get any agreement in writing.

Chapter 11
EMPLOYEE MANAGEMENT

Chapter Survey...

Finding good, hardworking employees can sometimes mean the difference between success and failure in business. It is easier to delegate to good employees and produce high-quality work from employees who care about their job. Poor employees can cost a company wasted time and ultimately money. The first step to finding good employees is taking the extra time to hire the right people for the job.

Employees should start off with a few fundamental qualities. They should be:

✓ qualified for the position;

✓ motivated to do the job and show initiative;

✓ responsible for their work and actions;

✓ dependable to show up on time and keep work commitments; and

✓ open to learning new skills.

These basic qualities will result in an employee who is capable of performing their present job responsibilities and taking on more tasks in the future.

Interviewing and Hiring Employees

Asking Questions: Asking the right interview questions is key to finding the right employee. The wrong interview questions can get you into trouble. You must convey that you are a fair and non-discriminatory employer. If you ask questions implying otherwise, you will open yourself to a lawsuit. Some questions could lead to legal action and are strictly off-limits, especially the following:

✓ How old are you?

✓ Do you have any disabilities?

✓ Are you pregnant?

✓ Are you married?

✓ Do you have children?

✓ What is your religious affiliation?

✓ What is your sexual orientation?

✓ What ethnic background are you?

Now that you know what questions not to ask, here are some areas to cover during the job interview that will be helpful in determining if an employee is the right fit for your company.

Questions should be asked to elicit information about the candidate's:

✓ ability to work with other members of a construction team;

✓ ability to handle conflict;

✓ expectations of the job (e.g. salary, benefits, working hours, etc.);

✓ past work history and reasons for leaving previous jobs;

✓ level of skill or expertise;

✓ training and education;

✓ safety record;

✓ ability to solve problems;

✓ knowledge of your company; and

✓ questions about the job.

Appendix C contains links to websites that provide sample job interview questions for the construction industry that you can customize for your business.

Hiring the right people for the job is the first step to finding good employees.

New Hire Reporting

Reporting Requirements: You are required to report all new employees to the North Carolina New Hire Reporting Program no later than 20 days from the date of hire, rehire or recall. Employers who submit reports magnetically or electronically must submit the reports in two monthly transmissions not more than sixteen days apart.

You can use one of several reporting methods:

✓ **Internet:** SUse the online data entry form or secure file upload at www.scnewhire.com

✓ **Electronic New Hire Reports:** Format new hire information to specifications outlined by the North Carolina New Hire Reporting Program. You can submit this form electronically through the new hire website or via file transfer protocol (FTP).

✓ **New Hire Data Entry Software:** Download the new hire software from the website. Using the software, you can complete the employee information and send it electronically.

✓ **Mail**: Mail W-4 forms, state reporting forms, or other approved paper report to the above address.

✓ **Fax**: Fax W-4 forms, state reporting forms, or other approved paper report to (866) 257-7005.

✓ **Payroll Service:** If you use a payroll service, inquire if it can report new hires for you.

Failure to comply with the New Hire Law could result in a $25 fine per incident for failure to report or, if conspiracy to avoid reporting is determined, a fine of up to $500.

Required Information: The following data must be included for each new hire:

✓ Employer name (use corporate name)

✓ Employer mailing address

✓ Employer federal identification number (If you have more than one FEIN, use the same FEIN you use to report your quarterly wage information when reporting new hires)

✓ Employer state identification number (This is the state employer number used on the NCUI101 Employer Quarterly Tax and Wage Report.)

✓ Employee name

✓ Employee address

✓ Employee social security number

✓ Employee date of birth (if available)

✓ Employee date of hire (if available)

Purpose of New Hire Reporting: New hire information submitted by employers is used to establish and enforce child support orders and detect fraud in unemployment benefits, workers' compensation, and in other government programs, such as welfare and food stamps.

Hiring Minors for Construction Work

The State of North Carolina and the U.S. Department of Labor have strict rules for the hiring of minors. State law requires employers to obtain an employment certificate for minors under the age of 18. The purpose of the employment certificate is to provide conclusive evidence of the minor's age and educational standing. In addition, it confirms that the minor is not employed in a prohibited profession or during prohibited hours

Working Hours:

✓ When school is in session, a minor 14 or 15 years of age cannot begin work before 7 a.m., work later than 7 p.m., or work more than three hours a day or more than 18 hours a week.

✓ When school is not in session, a minor 14 or 15 years of age cannot begin work before 7 a.m., work past 9 p.m., or work more than 8 hours a day or more than 40 hours a week.

✓ When school is in session the next day, a 16- or 17-year old cannot begin work before 5 a.m. and past 11 p.m. The only exception occurs when written permission is obtained from the minor's parents and school principal.

✓ Minors under the age of 16 must be given at least a 30-minute break after five consecutive hours of work.

Prohibited Tasks: Minors are prohibited from working in hazardous or detrimental jobs. Except for office or sales work, most construction jobs fall into the category of hazardous. Specific tasks categorized as hazardous or detrimental that apply to the construction industry (with the exception of apprentices as defined by law) include:

✓ operating power-driven woodworking machines;

✓ roofing operations;

✓ excavation operations;

✓ operating circular and band saws with the exception of machines equipped with full automatic feed and ejection;

✓ operating hoisting machines;

✓ driving any motor vehicle on a public road or in an excavation (prohibited for minors 16 and under; minors 17 and older may drive under certain restrictions);

✓ helper on any motor vehicle unless the minor rides in the cab;

✓ operating power-driven metal forming, punching and shearing machines;

✓ any work involving exposure to lead or its compounds;

✓ welding, brazing, or torch cutting;

✓ any work involving the risk of falling a distance of 10 or more feet;

✓ any work in confined spaces as defined by law; and

✓ any work as an electrician or electrician's helper.

Penalties: Violators of child labor provisions may be subject to a federal civil penalty of up to $11,000 and a criminal fine of up to $10,000. Additional penalties are assessed for minor employee violations that result in serious injury or death. State penalties for each minor employed in violation are $500 for the first violation and $1,000 for each subsequent violation.

Employee Documentation

Once you hire an employee, you should make sure you set up an employee file.

These items should be included in your employee files:

✓ **Form I-9**: The United States Customs and Immigration Service requires this form. It shows that the worker has legal immigration status in the United States. (For more information on I-9s, see the following section on the Immigration and Nationality Act.)

✓ **IRS Form W-4**: This form is required to determine the appropriate level of federal tax withholding. Employees can change the amount of federal tax withholding at anytime by completing a new W-4 form.

✓ **State Tax Form**: This form is required to determine the appropriate level of state tax withholding, if applicable. Employees must complete the NC-4 Employee's Withholding Allowance Certificate to designate the amount of state tax withholding.

✓ **Employment Application:** All employees should complete an application before being hired. It should contain basic information such as the employee's name, address, and phone number. The application should also be signed, giving your company authorization to check references on the employment history section.

✓ **Policy Signoffs**: If you have written policies or an employee handbook, have your employees sign a receipt that the employee has received and reviewed it.

✓ **Emergency Notification Form:** It is important that you know who to contact in the event of an emergency. Make sure to update this information periodically.

The employee file should be maintained throughout employment and other relevant documentation can be added, such as disciplinary action forms or insurance enrollment forms.

Key Employment Laws

There are several key laws governing equal employment opportunities and prohibiting discrimination in employment. It is important to understand and abide by these laws, not only to protect your company from a lawsuit but also to safeguard your reputation as a good employer.

Fair Labor Standards Act (FLSA)

The Fair Labor Standards Act, which prescribes standards for the basic minimum wage and overtime pay, affects most private and public employment. It applies to employers who have one or more employees.

Individual states may also have additional minimum wage requirements.

✓ Effective July 24, 2009, federal minimum wage increased to $7.25 per hour. If the state minimum wage rate differs from the federal rate, the employer must pay the higher of the two rates. Minors under 20 years of age may be paid a minimum wage of not less than $4.25 per hour during the first 90 consecutive calendar days of employment. Employers may not displace any employee to hire someone at the youth minimum wage.

✓ Employers must pay overtime compensation of one-and-one-half-times the regular rate after 40 hours of work in a workweek.

✓ Wages must be paid on the regular payday for the pay period covered.

✓ The act restricts the hours that children under age 16 can work and forbids the employment of children under age 18 in certain jobs deemed too dangerous.

FLSA is administered by the Employment Standards Administration's Wage and Hour Division within the U.S. Department of Labor.

Determining Exemption Status: Some employees are exempt from the overtime pay provisions or both

the minimum wage and overtime pay provisions as defined under the Fair Labor Standards Act (FLSA). This rule would apply to the following examples of employees who might be employed in the construction industry:

✓ Executives

✓ Administrative personnel

✓ Professional employees

✓ Outside sales employees

✓ Employees in certain computer-related occupations as defined in the Department of Labor regulations

Workweek Defined under FLSA: A workweek is a period of 168 hours during seven consecutive 24-hour periods. It may begin on any day of the week and at any hour of the day established by the employer. Generally, for purposes of minimum wage and overtime payment, each workweek stands alone; you may not average two or more workweeks. Employee coverage, compliance with wage payment requirements, and the application of most exemptions are determined on a workweek basis.

Work Hours Defined Under FLSA: Work hours ordinarily include all time during which an employee is required to be on the employer's premises, on duty, or at a prescribed work place.

Bona fide meal periods (typically 30 minutes or more) generally need not be compensated as work time. The employee must be completely relieved from duty for the purpose of eating regular meals. The employee is not relieved if he or she is required to perform any duties, whether active or inactive, while eating.

Employment Practices Not Covered: While FLSA does set basic minimum wage and overtime pay standards and regulates the employment of minors, there are a number of employment practices that FLSA does not regulate.

FLSA does not require:

✓ vacation, holiday, severance, or sick pay;

✓ meal or rest periods, holidays off, or vacations;

✓ premium pay for weekend or holiday work;

✓ pay raises or fringe benefits; or

✓ reason for discharge, immediate payment of final wages to a terminated employee, or discharge notices.

Also, FLSA does not limit the number of hours in a day or days in a week an employee may be required or scheduled to work, including overtime hours, if the employee is at least 16 years old.

Matters not covered by FLSA are left for agreement between the employer and the employees or their authorized representatives. Individual state labor departments may have specific regulations separate from FLSA regarding these requirements.

For more information, contact:

State of North Carolina
Department of Labor
1101 Mail Service Center
Raleigh, North Carolina 27699-1101

Phone: (800) NC LABOR or (800) 625-2267

Website: www.labor.nc.gov

Recordkeeping under FLSA

The FLSA requires employers to keep records on wages, hours, and other items as specified in Department of Labor recordkeeping regulations. Most of this information is maintained by employers in ordinary business practice and in compliance with other laws and regulations. The records do not have to be kept in any particular form, and time clocks need not be used.

Required Information: For employees subject to the minimum wage provisions or both the minimum wage and overtime pay provisions, the following records must be kept:

✓ personal information, including employee's name, home address, occupation, sex, and birth date (if under 19 years of age);

✓ basis on which employee wages are paid ,

✓ hour and day when workweek begins;

✓ total hours worked each workday and each workweek;

✓ total daily or weekly straight-time earnings, regular hourly pay;

✓ regular hourly pay rate;

✓ weekly overtime earnings;

✓ deductions from or additions to wages;

✓ total wages paid each pay period; and

✓ date of payment and pay period covered.

Special information is required for home workers, for employees working under uncommon pay arrangements, for employees to whom lodging or other facilities are furnished, and for employees receiving remedial education.

Chapter 14, Financial Management, covers the basics of payroll accounting and how to process the listed information.

Penalties

Enforcement of FLSA is carried out by investigators stationed across the U.S. They conduct investigations and gather data on wages, hours, and other employment conditions or practices in order to determine compliance with the law. Where violations are found, they may recommend changes in employment practices to bring an employer into compliance.

Retaliation against an employee for filing a complaint or for participating in a legal proceeding under FLSA is against the law.

Willful violations of employment under FLSA may be prosecuted criminally, and the violator fined up to $10,000. A second conviction may result in imprisonment.

Employers who willfully or repeatedly violate the minimum wage or overtime pay requirements are subject to a civil money penalty of up to $1,100 for each violation.

Immigration and Nationality Act

The employment eligibility provisions of the Immigration and Nationality Act require employers to verify the employment eligibility of all individuals hired. Immigration and Naturalization Service forms (I-9) must be kept on file for at least three years after the date of hire or for one year after the date employment ends, whichever is later.

I-9 forms must be completed with required documentation within three days of hire. A sample I-9 form is located at the end of this chapter.

The law does not require businesses to obtain I-9 documentation for independent contractors and their employees.

Unlawful Discrimination: Discrimination based on national origin or citizenship status is prohibited. If an Office of Special Counsel for Unfair Employment-Related Discrimination (OSC) or Equal Employment Opportunity Commission (EEOC) investigation reveals employment discrimination covered by the Immigration and Nationality Act, the employer will be ordered to cease the prohibited practice and may be ordered to take one or more of the following steps:

✓ hire or reinstate, with or without back pay, individuals directly injured by the discrimination;

✓ lift any restrictions on an employee's assignments, work shifts, or movements;

✓ post notices to employees about their rights and about employers' obligations;

✓ educate all personnel involved in hiring and in complying with the employer sanctions and anti-discrimination laws; and

✓ remove a false performance review or false warning from an employee's personnel file.

Employers may also be ordered to pay civil monetary penalties of $375 to $3,200 per individual discriminated against for the first offense, $3,200 to $6,500 per individual discriminated against for the second offense, and $4,300 to $16,000 per individual discriminated against for subsequent offenses.

Completing the I-9 Form for New Hires

Form I-9 is available for download on the U.S. Citizenship and Immigration Services website at www.uscis.gov or by calling (800) 870-3676. The National Customer Service Center at (800) 375-5283 can answer questions on USCIS forms and information on immigration laws, regulations and procedures.

The following gives step-by-step instructions on how to complete the form properly.

Section One
The employee completes section one of the I-9 form at the start of employment. The employee's name, address, date of birth, and social security number (optional unless the employer participates in the USCIS E-Verify Program), certification of legal status, and expiration date for temporary work authorization are required. Permanent aliens and authorized aliens must fill in either their alien number or authorization number. The employee must sign and date the form. If a preparer or translator is used, the appropriate signature block must be completed. If a preparer or translator is used, the appropriate signature block must be completed.

Section Two
An authorized employee representative completes section two by examining one document from list A or by examining one document from list B and one document from list C (a summary of approved documents is listed in the following section and a complete list is on the back of the I-9 form). The representative must view original documentation and keep copies of the front and back of this documentation on file.

Acceptable Documentation: The purpose of providing documentation is to establish identity and employment eligibility. Listed below are common forms of identification used when completing the I-9 form. A complete list is included on the back of the I-9 form located at the end of this chapter. I-9 forms must be updated when identity and employment eligibility documents are changed or renewed.

Employees can provide one of the following documents that establishes both identity and employment eligibility:

✓ U.S. passport

✓ Certificate of U.S. citizenship

✓ Certificate of naturalization

✓ Unexpired foreign passport with I-551 stamp or attached I-94 form indicating current employment authorization

✓ Permanent resident card or alien registration receipt with photograph

Employees also have the option of providing two documents–one to establish identity and the other to establish employment eligibility.

Documents that establish identity include

✓ state-issued driver's license with photo;

✓ ID card with photo issued by federal, state or local government agencies;

✓ voter's registration card; and

✓ U.S. military card.

Documents that establish employment eligibility include:

✓ U.S. Social Security card issued by the Social Security Administration;

✓ original or certified birth certificate;

✓ U.S. citizen ID card (form I-197);

✓ resident ID card; and

✓ Native American tribal document.

Certification: The date to be used in the certification section must correspond with the current employment date. The authorized employee representative must sign and date this section.

Additional Information: U.S. Citizen and Immigration Services publishes a Handbook for Employers, which is a helpful resource for completing the I-9 form. This publication is available online at www.uscis.gov/i-9-central/handbook-employers-m-274

Americans with Disabilities Act (ADA)

This law prohibits discrimination against persons with disabilities and applies to employers with 15 or more employees. In general, the employment provisions of the ADA require:

✓ equal opportunity in selecting, testing, and hiring qualified applicants with disabilities;

✓ job accommodation for applicants and workers with disabilities when such accommodations would not impose "undue hardship;" and

✓ equal opportunity in promotion and benefits.

Employment Discrimination: ADA prohibits discrimination in all employment practices, including job application procedures, hiring, firing, advancement, compensation, training, and other terms, conditions, and privileges of employment. It applies to recruitment, advertising, tenure, layoff, leave, fringe benefits, and all other employment-related activities.

Qualified Individuals with Disabilities: Employment discrimination is prohibited against "qualified individuals with disabilities" including applicants for employment and employees. An individual is considered to have a "disability" if that individual has a physical or mental impairment that substantially limits one or more major life activities or has a record of such an impairment, or is regarded as having such an impairment.

Conditions Covered: The ADA applies to persons who have impairments that substantially limit major life activities such as seeing, hearing, speaking, walking, breathing, performing manual tasks, learning, caring for oneself, and working.

Examples include an individual with:

✓ epilepsy,

✓ paralysis,

✓ HIV infection,

✓ AIDS,

✓ substantial hearing or visual impairment,

✓ mental retardation, or

✓ specific learning disability.

An individual with a minor, non-chronic condition of short duration, such as a sprain, broken limb, or the flu, generally would not be covered by the ADA.

Reasonable Accommodations: An employer is required to accommodate a "known" disability of a qualified applicant or employee unless it imposes an "undue hardship" on the operation of the employer's business. A reasonable accommodation is any modification or adjustment to a job or the work environment that will enable a qualified applicant or employee with a disability to participate in the application process or to perform essential job functions. Reasonable accommodations also include adjustments to assure that a qualified individual with a disability has rights and privileges in employment equal to those of employees without disabilities.

Additional Resources: The Equal Employment Opportunity Commission has developed several resources to help employers and people with disabilities understand and comply with the employment provisions of the ADA. Resources include:

✓ a technical assistance manual that provides "how-to" guidance on the employment provisions of the ADA as well as a resource directory to help individuals find specific information; and

✓ a variety of brochures, booklets, and fact sheets.

For more information about the ADA, contact:

U.S. Equal Employment Opportunity Commission
131 M Street, NE
Fourth Floor, Suite 4NWO2F
Washington, D.C. 20507

Phone: (202) 663-4000
TTY: (202) 663-4494
Website: www.eeoc.gov

Other Labor Laws

Many other labor laws protect the rights of employees.

✓ The **Davis-Bacon Act** requires payment of prevailing wage rates and fringe benefits on federally-financed or assisted construction.

✓ The **Walsh-Healey Public Contracts Act** requires payment of minimum wage rates and overtime pay on contracts that provide goods to the federal government.

✓ The **Service Contract Act** requires payment of prevailing wage rates and fringe benefits on contracts to provide services to the federal government.

✓ The **Contract Work Hours and Safety Standards Act** sets overtime standards for service and construction contracts on federal projects.

✓ The **Wage Garnishment Law** limits the amount of an individual's income that may be legally garnished and prohibits firing an employee whose pay is garnished for payment of a single debt.

✓ The **Employee Polygraph Protection Act** prohibits most private employers from using any type of lie detector test, either for pre-employment screening of job applicants or for testing current employees during the course of employment.

✓ The **Family and Medical Leave Act** entitles eligible employees of covered employers to take up to 12 weeks of unpaid job-protected leave each year, with the maintenance of group health insurance, for the birth and care of a child, for the placement of a child for adoption or foster care, for the care of a child, spouse, or parent with a serious health condition, or for the employee's serious health condition.

✓ **Title VII of the Civil Rights Act of 1964** prohibits discrimination on the basis of race, color, religion, national origin, and sex. Sexual harassment is considered a form of sex discrimination and is a violation of Title VII. An amendment to Title VII provides protection against sex discrimination on the basis of pregnancy, childbirth, and related medical conditions.

✓ The **Equal Pay Act of 1963** prohibits employers from paying different wages to men and women who perform essentially the same work under similar working conditions.

✓ The **Age Discrimination in Employment Act (ADEA)** prohibits discrimination against individuals who are age 40 or older. It applies to employers with 20 or more employees.

✓ The **Worker Adjustment and Retraining Notification Act (WARN)** offers protection to workers, their families, and communities by requiring employers to provide notice 60 days in advance of covered plant closings and covered mass layoffs.

✓ **Title III of the Consumer Credit Protection Act (CCPA)** protects employees from being discharged by their employers because their wages have been garnished for any one debt and limits the amount of employees' earnings that may be garnished in any one week.

✓ The **Uniformed Services Employment and Reemployment Rights Act (USERRA)** protects service members' reemployment rights when returning from a period of service in the uniformed services, including those called up from the reserves or National Guard, and prohibits employer discrimination based on military service or obligation.

✓ **Numerous labor organizing, collective bargaining and dispute resolution acts** give employees the right to organize, join labor unions, bargain collectively, and strike.

✓ **Right-to-work laws** secure the right of employees to decide for themselves whether or not to join or financially support a union. North Carolina is a right-to-work state.

North Carolina Wage and Hour Laws

The North Carolina Department of Labor is the regulating agency for the state wage and hour laws.

Listed below is a summary of the rules that may apply to your business.

✓ **Wage Payment:** Wages are due on the regular payday. If requested, final paychecks must be mailed.

✓ **Payment on Termination:** The employer must pay an employee who is voluntarily or involuntarily terminated within 48 hours or the next regular payday, not to exceed 30 days after termination.

✓ **Withholding of Wages:** No employer may withhold or divert any portion of an employee's wages unless required or empowered by state or federal law, or unless the employer has written authorization from the employee.

✓ **Employer to Furnish Certain Information:** Employees must be notified of paydays, pay rates, policies on vacation and sick leave, commissions, bonuses, and other pay matters. Employers must notify employees in writing or through a posted notice maintained in a place accessible to employees, of any reduction in the amount of promised wages at least 24 hours before the change.

✓ **Wage Disputes:** When the amount of wages is in dispute, the employer's payment of the undisputed portion cannot restrict the right of the employee to continue his or her claim for the rest of the wages. The Department of Labor will, upon complaint, investigate wage complaints to determine if any violations have occurred.

✓ **Overtime:** Time and a half must be paid after 40 hours of work in any one workweek. The state overtime provision does not apply to some employers or to employees who are exempt.

. . . .

Be aware of the labor laws that apply to your business.

. . . .

Required Postings

Some of the statutes and regulations enforced by agencies within the U.S. Department of Labor require that posters or notices be posted in the workplace. A complete list of postings can be found at www.dol.gov. Postings that may apply to you are listed below:

Poster	Description of Employers Required to Post Notice
Safety and Health Protection on the Job	Employers located in states with OSHA-approved state plans should obtain and post the state's equivalent poster.
Equal Opportunity is the Law	Businesses holding federal contracts or subcontracts or federally assisted construction contracts of $10,000 or more.
Employee Rights for Workers with Disabilities/Special Minimum Wage Poster	All employers having workers employed under special minimum wage certificates must post this notice.
National Labor Relations Act (NLRA) Poster (effective January 31, 2012)	All private-sector employers (excluding agricultural, railroad and airline employers) must post this notice.
Your Rights Under the Family and Medical Leave Act	Public agencies (including state, local, and federal employers), public and private elementary and secondary schools, as well as private sector employers who employ 50 or more employees in 20 or more work weeks and who are engaged in commerce or in any industry or activity affecting commerce, including joint employers and successors of covered employers
Fair Labor Standards Act (FLSA): Minimum Wage Poster	All private, federal, state and local government employers subject to the FLSA
Uniformed Services Employment and Reemployment Rights Act	The full text of the notice must be provided by each employer to persons entitled to rights and benefits under USERRA.

Poster	Description of Employers Required to Post Notice
Notice to All Employees Working on Federal or Federally Financed Construction Projects	Any contractor/ subcontractor engaged in contracts in excess of $2,000 for the actual construction, alteration/ repair of a public building or public work or building or work financed in whole or in part from federal funds, federal guarantee, or federal pledge
Notice to Employees Working on Government Contracts	Every contractor or subcontractor engaged in a contract with the United States or the District of Columbia in excess of $2,500 the principal purpose of which is to furnish services in the U.S. through the use of service employees.
Notice: Employee Polygraph Protection Act	Any employer engaged in or affecting commerce or in the production of goods for commerce. Does not apply to federal, state and local governments, or to circumstances covered by the national defense and security exemption.
Notification of Employee Rights Under Federal Labor Laws	Federal contractors and subcontractors are required to post the prescribed employee notice conspicuously in plants and offices where employees covered by the National Labor Relations Act (NLRA) perform contract-related activity, including all places where notices to employees are customarily posted both physically and electronically.

Additional postings may be required for federal contractors.

North Carolina state law requires posting the following notices:

✓ Safety and Health (OSHA)–N.C. Department of Labor Responsibilities, Employer Rights and Responsibilities, Employee Rights and Responsibilities, and Other OSHA Information

✓ Wage and Hour Act–Minimum Wage, Overtime, Youth Employment, Wage Payment, Complaints, and Right to Work Laws

✓ Unemployment Insurance–Certificate of Coverage and Notice to Workers as to Benefit Rights (Form NCESC 524)

✓ Workers' Compensation Notice Posters (NCIC Form No. 17)

Required state postings are available for download on the Department of Labor website at www.nclabor.com. Other state agencies may also require display of specific documents in the workplace. Contact the appropriate agencies directly to verify any poster display requirements.

Posters are periodically updated. Ensure you post the most current version, if required.

Employee Handbook and Policies

Having clear and well-documented policies helps employees understand the rules of the workplace and protects you if a disgruntled employee files a lawsuit or complaint against you.

Enforcing Policies and Procedures: An employee handbook is a document you put together that lists company policies and employee benefits and rights. It is important for employees to sign a receipt that they have read and understood the contents of the handbook. This documentation is helpful in enforcing the policies and procedures of your company.

Changing Your Handbook: An employee handbook is not a static document. You can add items to the handbook but make sure you distribute these amendments to employees and have them sign off on the changes.

Writing Your Employee Handbook

It may be difficult to determine where to start when writing your employee handbook and policies. Consider the following sections when putting your handbook together:

- ✓ Company history
- ✓ Compensation guidelines (i.e., introductory period, full-time status requirements, etc.)
- ✓ Payroll distribution dates and times
- ✓ Benefits
- ✓ Normal working hours
- ✓ Overtime pay
- ✓ Vacation time
- ✓ Sick days
- ✓ Policy on sexual harassment
- ✓ Policy on the use of illegal drugs or alcohol
- ✓ Non-discrimination policy
- ✓ Rules of conduct (i.e., disciplinary action for insubordination, fighting, etc.)
- ✓ Safety policies
- ✓ Equipment and tool policies
- ✓ Disciplinary action procedures

You may want to have an attorney review your employee handbook. In many states, the employee handbook is considered an employment contract. There may be certain wording and disclaimers in your employee handbook to protect you against legal action.

Employee Satisfaction

Benefits of Employee Satisfaction: Keeping your employees happy and motivated can have a tremendous effect on the performance of your work teams. Your company can benefit from satisfied employees in several ways:

- ✓ Stronger company loyalty and corporate culture
- ✓ Higher quality work and customer satisfaction
- ✓ Lower employee turnover
- ✓ Increased productivity

Maintaining employee satisfaction is not as easy as it sounds. Even though employers may have good intentions, when faced with tight deadlines and day-to-day operations, employee satisfaction sometimes drops to the bottom of the priority list.

Motivating Employees: The following checklist includes simple ways you can motivate your employees and give them a feeling of achievement:

- ✓ Provide informal and formal training opportunities for employees to learn new skills.
- ✓ Empower employees to make decisions and give positive and constructive feedback.
- ✓ Provide clear expectations for your employees.
- ✓ Conduct performance reviews on a regular basis.
- ✓ Mentor your employees and tell them about advancement opportunities in your company and the industry.
- ✓ Recognize and reward employees for good work.

The Value of Job Descriptions

Job descriptions give employees a guideline for the responsibilities of their job. Job descriptions benefit the employee because employees understand your expectation for their performance. It also makes it easier for you to monitor their performance, give reviews, and conduct disciplinary action if necessary.

Job descriptions should contain a few basic elements:

- ✓ Job title
- ✓ Job description, including who the position reports to and summary of job purpose
- ✓ Key responsibilities
- ✓ Required licenses and/or certifications
- ✓ Skills and knowledge needed

Sample Job Description: Listed below is a sample job description for a construction superintendent position using the above categories. All job descriptions must be carefully reviewed and modified to fit the individual company's requirements.

Job Title: Construction Superintendent

Description: Under general direction of the company owner, the construction superintendent serves as a member of the construction management team with broad authority over assigned projects, participating in all phases of construction from project planning to completion. Emphasis is on quality control, evaluation of change order requests, and timely completion of construction schedules.

Key Responsibilities: The duties listed below are intended only as illustrations of the various types of work that may be performed by the construction superintendent:

✓ Coordinates activities associated with the company's construction projects.

✓ Serves as liaison with subcontractors, architects, utilities, and others.

✓ Participates in project construction development and planning.

✓ Processes utility requests for construction projects.

✓ Represents the company regarding onsite construction quality control reviews.

✓ Makes recommendations and processes change order requests.

✓ Reviews punch lists.

✓ Assures construction specifications are met.

✓ Notes deviations from project schedules and costs.

✓ Maintains records and prepares reports.

The omission of specific statements of duties does not exclude them from the position if the work is similar, related, or a logical assignment to this class.

Required Licenses or Certifications: Requires a valid driver's license.

Skills and Knowledge Needed:

✓ Principles and practices of construction management, building operation and maintenance, quality assurance programs and systems, budget administration, construction specifications, and bidding processes.

✓ Ability to plan, organize, and manage time to track progress and elements of assigned construction projects effectively.

✓ Establish and maintain effective working relationships with coworkers, employees of subcontractors, and outside entities.

✓ Prepare or participate in the development of construction and other budgets and monitor performance against the approved budget.

✓ Communicate effectively, both orally and in writing.

✓ Ability to lift up to 50 pounds.

Providing Benefits

Offering benefit plans can be an effective means of attracting and retaining good employees, keeping up

with the competition, and boosting employee morale. Traditional employee plans include:

✓ health insurance,

✓ dental insurance,

✓ vision insurance,

✓ long-term disability,

✓ life insurance, and

✓ 401(k) or other retirement plan.

Some employers also opt to offer more creative benefit options, such as tuition reimbursement, gym subsidies, and child care referral services.

However you decide to package your benefits plan, a few key laws are important.

Workers' Compensation Laws provide monetary compensation to employees who are injured or disabled on the job. These laws also provide benefits for dependents of those workers who are killed because of work-related accidents or illnesses. Some laws protect employers by limiting the amount an injured employee can recover from an employer and by eliminating the liability of coworkers in most accidents. Workers' compensation laws and programs are established at the state level for most employment.

Workers' compensation fraud is committed when an individual willfully intends to provide false or inaccurate information to receive workers' compensation benefits. Examples of fraud include:

✓ reporting an injury as work-related when it was not;

✓ continuing to work and receive benefits at the same time; and

✓ misrepresenting an injury.

Employers are in the best position to identify workers' compensation fraud. Workers' compensation fraud is illegal. Your workers' compensation administrator should be notified if you suspect fraud.

Workers' compensation insurance is purchased by the employer; no part of it should be paid for by employees or deducted from their pay.

North Carolina Program: If you are a sole proprietorship, partnership, or LLC, you are required by law to carry workers' compensation coverage if you have three or more employees. Employees can be full time, part-time, regular, seasonal, or family members.

Sole proprietors, partners, and managers and members of the LLC are not included in the headcount.

All forms of corporations with a total of three or more people are required by law to carry workers' compensation coverage. Everyone is included in the headcount, including corporate officers.

If one or more employees are employed in activities which involve the use or presence of radiation, workers' compensation is required.

Coverage is provided through the following ways:

✓ **Self-Insurance:** You may qualify to become self-insured. To receive information on this process, contact the Department of Insurance at (855) 408-1212.

✓ **Self-Insured Fund:** Your business may be placed in a self-insured fund. To receive a list of the self-insured funds in North Carolina, contact the Department of Insurance at (855) 408-1212.

✓ **Coverage through Private Carrier:** You may find coverage in the conventional and open market. To do so, contact an independent insurance agent and request assistance in providing your business with coverage.

✓ **Assigned Risk Pool:** You may be placed in the assigned risk pool, which is administered by the North Carolina Rate Bureau. You may contact them directly for information at (919) 783-9790, or you may ask your insurance agent for information.

Any contractor who sublets any part of a contract must first obtain documentation that the subcontractor is in compliance with the North Carolina Workers' Compensation Act. Subcontractors must provide compliance documentation regardless of whether the subcontractor employs fewer than three employees. If proper documentation is not obtained, the party subletting the contract is liable for payment of compensation and other benefits if any of the subcontractor's employees are injured or die from an accident associated with the work covered by the subcontract. As part of your operating policies, you may require subcontractors to carry workers' compensation coverage even if the subcontractor has less than three employees.

N.C. Gen. Stat. §97-94(b) outlines penalties for non-compliance of workers' compensation laws. Employers are subject to penalties of $50.00 to $100.00 for each day of noncompliance until proper coverage is obtained.

Contractors cannot obtain a building permit until proof of proper workers' compensation coverage is provided to the building official issuing the permit.

Information on North Carolina's program is available through the Industrial Commission.

> *North Carolina Industrial Commission*
> *1240 Mail Service Center,*
> *Raleigh, NC 27699-1240*
>
> *Physical Address:*
> *430 N. Salisbury Street*
> *Raleigh, North Carolina 27603*
>
> *Telephone (919) 807-2501 or (800) 688-8349*
> *Fax: (919) 715-0282*
>
> *Website: www.ic.nc.gov*

Unemployment Compensation programs provide unemployment benefits to eligible workers who become unemployed through no fault of their own and meet certain other eligibility requirements. This program is jointly financed through federal and state employer payroll taxes through the federal/state unemployment insurance tax.

Generally, employers must pay both state and federal unemployment taxes if:

✓ they pay wages to employees totaling $1,500 or more in any quarter of a calendar year; or

✓ they had at least one employee during any day of a week during 20 weeks in a calendar year, regardless of whether or not the weeks were consecutive.

North Carolina Program: The North Carolina Employment Security Law establishes guidelines for state unemployment tax. Business entities are subject to an unemployment payroll tax if they have one or more employees for 20 weeks during a calendar year or pay $1,500 in wages in any calendar quarter during a calendar year in North Carolina.

The tax is payable quarterly. Tax wage base and tax rate may vary from year to year. For the most current information, refer to the North Carolina Division of Employment Security. Current tax rates are available online at des.nc.gov. New business entities in North Carolina are assigned a new business tax rate for the first two years. The rate may be changed after the entity comes under an experience rating.

Employers liable to one or more states for unemployment insurance tax receive a federal unemployment tax (FUTA) credit for timely tax payments made to the state(s). The FUTA tax base and tax rate is calculated at the current prevailing rate. The current federal tax information is available online at www.irs.gov.

The state taxable wage base differs from the federal taxable wage base and is recomputed each year. Employers are notified of the taxable wage base applicable for the coming calendar year on their tax rate notification. The taxable wage base is also printed on the Employer's Quarterly Tax and Wage Report. Employers must pay 100 percent of federal and state unemployment tax due. Deductions cannot be made from employee payroll for the purpose of paying this tax.

All employers doing business in North Carolina are required to complete and file form NCUI 604, Status Report to determine their liability for unemployment insurance.

To report unemployment taxes, you must file form NCUI 101, Employer's Quarterly Tax and Wage Report. Payment of state unemployment tax is made quarterly by the end of the month following the end of each calendar quarter. State unemployment tax reports are due by January 31 (for the fourth quarter of the previous calendar year), April 30, July 31, and October 31.

All employers must maintain records for each person they employ (including corporate officers). These records must show:

✓ the employee's name and social security number;

✓ the beginning and ending dates worked;

✓ the amount of wages paid; and

✓ all other payments made to the employee including vacation pay, tips, reasonable value of board and lodging, and other compensation for services.

Records must be maintained for at least five years and be available for inspection by authorized personnel of the Division of Employment Security.

SUTA Dumping: SUTA dumping is a transfer of employees between businesses for the purpose of obtaining a lower unemployment compensation tax rate. SUTA dumping is prohibited and subject to criminal and/or civil penalties according to state law.

The Division of Employment Security investigates suspicious activity in the transfer or acquisition of a business or shifting of employees to identify SUTA dumping.

Contact Information: Additional information regarding the North Carolina state unemployment tax is available at:

> State of North Carolina
> Division of Employment Security (DES)
> P.O. Box 25903
> Raleigh, North Carolina 27611-5903
>
> Tax Telephone: (919) 707-1150
> Claims Telephone: (888) 737-0259
>
> Website: des.nc.gov

The **Consolidated Omnibus Budget Act of 1985 (COBRA)** includes provisions for continuing health care coverage. These provisions apply to group health plans of employers with 20 or more employees on 50 percent of the typical working days in the previous calendar year. COBRA gives "qualified beneficiaries" (a covered employee's spouse and dependent children) the right to maintain, at their own expense, coverage under their health plan that would be lost due to a "qualifying event," such as termination of employment, at a cost comparable to what it would be if they were still members of the employer's group.

Health Insurance Portability and Accountability Act of 1996 (HIPAA) provides for improved portability and continuity of health insurance coverage connected with employment. These provisions include rules relating to exclusions of preexisting conditions, special enrollment rights, and prohibition of discrimination against individuals based on health status-related factors. HIPAA also addresses an employee's right to privacy concerning their health information. As an employer, you need to be aware of this act and keep records concerning any employee's medical conditions in a confidential file.

Disciplining Employees

Corrective action may be necessary from time to time for employees who are not following employment policies and procedures properly. Employers need to administer discipline fairly to promote a respectful work environment and to avoid trouble later.

Progressive Discipline: Progressive discipline is a method of corrective action where the consequences of the improper behavior become more significant if it continues. Progressive discipline gives the employee a chance to take corrective action to prevent future disciplinary action. There are certain offenses that may be cause for immediate termination (i.e., theft, endangering the safety of others, etc.) and are not subject to progressive discipline.

The employee manual is a good place to have written disciplinary policies and a comprehensive list of offenses that lead to immediate dismissal.

Terminating Employees

At one time or another, most employers run into circumstances where they need to terminate employees. It is not a fun or rewarding task but sometimes a necessary one. When terminating an employee, you want to make sure you have followed the proper procedures to minimize your risk of a wrongful termination lawsuit.

Employment relationships are either contractual or at-will; the definition of the relationship influences the procedures for termination.

Contractual Employees

Union employees and some executives have employment contracts. When terminating a contractual employee, it is important to comply with the terms of the contract. If the contract is breached, you may be subject to a lawsuit.

At-Will Employees

"At-will employment" means that either the employer or the employee may terminate employment at any time without notice or cause. It is not exactly that easy, and there are restrictions that you should be aware of as an employer. These restrictions include:

✓ An employer may not terminate an employee for discriminatory reasons (i.e., race, gender, etc.).

✓ An employer cannot terminate an employee for taking time off to serve on a jury.

✓ Reporting health and safety violations and abuses of power cannot lead to termination. There are "whistle-blower laws" that protect employees if this circumstance does occur.

✓ All employers should use good faith and fair dealing throughout employment. This is why documenting poor performance is strongly recommended. Without documentation, the termination may be perceived as a breach of good faith.

These are general guidelines, and it is recommended you consult with an expert in Human Resources or an attorney regarding specific situations.

Proper documentation is important when disciplining and terminating employees.

Final Inspection...

Interviewing and Hiring Employees: Your interviews should focus on skills, experience, and qualities. There are certain questions you should avoid because they are not legal to ask.

New Hire Reporting: North Carolina has mandatory requirements for reporting new hires.

Hiring Minors for Construction Work: The State of North Carolina and the U.S. Department of Labor have strict rules about the hiring of minors, including restricted working hours and prohibited tasks.

Employee Documentation: Employee files should be maintained throughout employment with relevant documents, such as tax forms and disciplinary forms.

Key Employment Laws: There are several employment laws that you must comply with, such as the Fair Labor Standards Act (FLSA), Immigration and Nationality Act, and the Americans with Disabilities Act (ADA).

Fair Labor Standards Act (FLSA): Standards for basic minimum wage and overtime pay are outlined in the Fair Labor Standards Act. The Act applies to most private and public employers who have one or more employees.

Immigration and Nationality Act: Employers are required to verify the employment eligibility of all individuals hired through I-9 forms. These forms must be kept on file for at least three years after the date of hire or for one year after the date employment ends, whichever is later.

Americans with Disabilities Act (ADA): This law prohibits discrimination against persons with disabilities. It applies to employers with 15 or more employees.

Other Labor Laws: Several other labor laws protect the rights of employees. Specific laws exist that set guidelines for federal contractors, wage garnishment, and an employee's right to join a union. Other laws provide protection against the discriminatory actions of employers.

North Carolina Wage and Hour Laws: The North Carolina Department of Labor regulates specific laws pertaining to employment, such as payment of wages, overtime, payment on termination, withholding of wages, wage disputes, and an employer's obligation to furnish certain information.

Required Postings: Employers must post certain notices for employees under federal and state law.

Employee Handbook and Policies: An employee handbook is a useful document for communicating your policies and procedures.

Employee Satisfaction: Your company can benefit in several ways from putting employee satisfaction programs in place.

Providing Benefits: There are some mandatory benefits you must provide employees. Other benefits, such as health insurance, may also be offered to attract and retain employees.

Disciplining Employees: Discipline should be administered in a fair manner and documented appropriately.

Terminating Employees: Using proper termination procedures will help minimize your risk of a wrongful termination lawsuit.

Americans with Disabilities Act (ADA)	ADA guide for small businesses published by the U.S. Department of Justice
Job Description Template	Form featured earlier in the chapter that shows a sample job description
Employer's Tax Guide (Circular E)	Publication used to determine federal income tax withholding for employees

Supplemental Forms

Supplemental forms and links are available at **NASCLAforms.org** using access code **NC129354**.

IRS Form W-4	IRS form to determine federal income tax withholding
Form I-9	Required form to confirm legal immigration status
Fair Labor Standards Act (FLSA)	Copy of the FLSA law from the U.S. Department of Labor

Chapter 12
JOBSITE SAFETY AND ENVIRONMENTAL FACTORS

Chapter Survey...

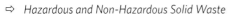

Safety First: Creating a safe working environment is not only a good way to run your business, it is the

law. Effective management and implementation of workplace safety and health programs add significant value to individuals and companies by reducing the extent, severity, and consequences of work-related injury and illness. Businesses spend approximately $171 billion a year on costs associated with occupational injuries and illnesses. As a whole, businesses spend between $145 billion to $290 billion a year in indirect and direct costs associated with occupational injuries and illnesses.

✓ Workplace injuries and illnesses are reduced by approximately 20 to 40 percent when employers establish safety and health programs.

✓ Workers' compensation premiums, employee retraining costs, and absenteeism are decreased by reducing workplace injuries and illnesses.

✓ Increased workplace safety results in increased productivity and morale and ultimately, profits.

Safety Standards

Understanding OSHA: The Occupational Safety and Health Administration (OSHA) was established by the Occupational Safety and Health Act of 1970 (OSH Act). All employers are subject to federal OSHA requirements and some states have adopted a state plan. State standards are at least as strict as the federal plan. The first step to complying with OSHA is to learn the published standards.

The OSHA standards that apply to the construction industry are:

✓ 29 CFR 1926, Safety and Health Regulations for the Construction Industry;

✓ 29 CFR 1910, Occupational Safety and Health Standards; and

✓ 29 CFR 1904, Recording and Reporting Occupational Injuries and Illnesses.

It is the employer's responsibility to understand the OSHA standards and quickly correct any violations. Putting together a safety program with these standards in mind can help maximize employee safety and prevent violations before they occur.

OSHA Poster: All employers must post the OSHA poster (or state plan equivalent) in a prominent location in the workplace. In construction, employees are generally dispersed to different sites and the OSHA poster must be posted at the location to which employees report each day.

The OSHA poster is downloadable from the OSHA website (www.osha.gov). This website also has useful links to many safety and environmental topics including compliance assistance and laws and regulations. For more information about OSHA, contact:

> *Occupational Safety and Health Administration (OSHA)*
> *Office of Small Business Assistance*
> *Directorate of Cooperative and State Programs*
> *200 Constitution Avenue, NW*
> *Washington, DC 20210*
>
> *Telephone: (800) 321-6742 (OSHA)*
>
> *Website: www.osha.gov*

OSHA Construction Safety Act: TThe Contract Work Hours and Safety Standards Act, commonly known as the Construction Safety Act, sets safety standards for construction contracts on federal projects.

North Carolina Safety Program: North Carolina does not have a state-adopted OSHA plan and falls under federal OSHA laws. The Department of Labor, Occupational Safety & Health Division is responsible for assisting employers in complying with federal OSHA requirements and reducing work-related injuries and illnesses.

> *North Carolina Department of Labor*
> *Occupational Safety & Health Division*
> *1101 Mail Service Center*
> *Raleigh, North Carolina 27699-1101*
>
> *Telephone: (919) 707-7876*
>
> *Website: www.labor.nc.gov/safety-and-health/ occupational-safety-and-health*

The Division has several services available to employers:

✓ Complaint, accident and fatality investigations

✓ Random inspections

✓ Free safety consultation services

✓ Training classes on safety and health issues

✓ Safety awards

Safe Hiring and Training

Hire Safe: The first step to improving safety in the workplace is to hire employees who have a good safety track record. The majority of accidents are caused by unsafe actions, not unsafe conditions. It is important to do thorough applicant screening and check all employment references. If you find that an applicant had safety accidents with a previous employer, chances for additional accidents while working for you are greater.

Regular Training: Training on safety practices and policies should be conducted regularly. New employees should receive a copy of your safety policies and sign off on them. Brief 10-minute training sessions can be conducted at the jobsite with your crew daily. During these training sessions, you can review policies and receive feedback from your employees on potential hazards that exist on the jobsite.

> *Conduct regular safety training for your employees.*

Substance Abuse Policies

Your Bottom Line: Substance abuse in the workplace can have a profound effect on your business and significantly impact your bottom line. This problem costs American businesses more than $100 billion every year. This loss occurs in:

✓ workers' compensation claims,

✓ medical costs,

✓ absenteeism,

✓ lost productivity, and

✓ employee turnover.

For this reason, you should develop a substance free workplace program and make sure that all employees know that substance abuse is not permitted.

Employee Program: Develop your program together with your employees. Talk about the benefits of having a substance free workplace and your concern for them to have a safe and healthy work environment. Eliminating substance abuse increases productivity, reduces accidents, and lowers insurance claim costs. Solicit input from your employees on how to implement the program in the workplace and any other suggestions they have.

> ### Consider this...
>
> Ninety percent of large businesses have drug-free workplace programs in place today, while 5 percent to 10 percent of small- and medium-sized businesses have implemented similar programs. The irony here is that 75 percent of employed Americans work for small- and medium-sized businesses.

Communicate Your Policy: Once you have developed a program, distribute the policy to all employees and have them sign off on it. Your policies should expressly prohibit the illegal use of drugs and/or abuse of alcohol by any employee and spell out the consequences of policy violations. All new employees should receive your policy as part of their orientation. You should also check with your workers' compensation carrier to see if you can receive a credit for having this policy in place.

Encourage employee participation in developing company safety programs.

Safety Equipment

Prevent Injuries: Using the proper safety equipment can lower the occurrence of injuries on the job. This equipment might include:

✓ hard hats,

✓ safety shoes/boots,

✓ protective eyewear,

✓ gloves,

✓ fall protection,

✓ hearing protection,

✓ respirators,

✓ protective coveralls, and

✓ face shields.

Make sure you consult OSHA safety standards to determine what safety equipment is required by law and assess your jobsite to determine additional equipment you want your employees to have.

Emergency Action Plan

Your Plan of Action: OSHA regulations require you have an emergency action plan. If you have more than 10 employees, your plan must be in writing. If you have fewer than 10 employees, you may communicate the plan orally to employees. The emergency action plan must include procedures for:

✓ reporting a fire or other emergency;

✓ emergency evacuation;

✓ employees who remain for critical operations before evacuating;

✓ accounting for all employees after evacuation; and

✓ employees performing rescue or medical duties.

The plan should also include the name or job title of the plan administrator. You must review the plan with your employees, designate and train employees to assist in a safe evacuation, and have a distinctive signal that serves as an employee alarm system.

Other OSHA recommendations, although not required, for inclusion in the emergency action plan are:

✓ a description of the employee alarm system defining each of the alarm signals and corresponding employee action;

✓ an alternative site for communication in the event of a fire or explosion; and

✓ a secure location, either onsite or offsite, where important information, such as accounting documents, legal files, and employee emergency contact numbers, can be stored.

OSHA Recordkeeping

For the Record: Every employer covered by OSHA who has more than 10 employees, except for employers in certain low-hazard industries in the retail, finance, insurance, real estate, and service sectors, must maintain three types of OSHA-specified records of job-related injuries and illnesses.

These forms are located at the end of the chapter:

✓ **OSHA Form 300**

✓ **OSHA Form 300A**

✓ **OSHA Form 301**

The **OSHA Form 300** is an injury/illness log, with a separate line entry for each recordable injury or illness. Such events include work-related deaths, injuries, and illnesses other than minor injuries that require only first aid treatment and that do not involve medical treatment, loss of consciousness, restriction of work, days away from work, or transfer to another job. Construction site operations that last for more than one year must keep a separate OSHA 300 log.

Each year, the employer must conspicuously post in the workplace a **Form 300A**, which includes a summary of the previous year's work-related injuries and illnesses. The data from Form 300 is used to complete this form. Form 300A must be posted by February 1 and kept in place until at least April 30 following the year covered by the form.

OSHA Form 301 is an individual incident report that provides added detail about each specific recordable injury or illness. An alternative form, such as an insurance or workers' compensation form that provides the same details may be substituted for OSHA Form 301.

Who Needs to Complete the Forms? Employers with 10 or fewer employees are exempt from maintaining these records. However, such employers must keep these records if they receive an annual illness and injury survey form either from the Bureau of Labor Statistics (BLS) or from OSHA. Employers selected for these surveys will be notified before the end of the prior year to begin keeping records during the year covered by the survey.

Timeframe to Retain Records: OSHA records must be kept by the employer for five years following the year to which they pertain.

Exposure Records and Medical Records: Exposure records (including employee exposure to toxic substances and harmful physical agents) must be maintained for 30 years and medical records for the duration of employment plus 30 years. Analysis using exposure or medical records must be kept for 30 years.

Toxic substances and harmful agents include:

✓ any material listed in the National Institute for Occupational Safety and Health (NIOSH) Registry of Toxic Effects of Chemical Hazards (RTECHS);

✓ substances which have evidenced an acute or chronic health hazard in testing conducted by or known to the employer; and

✓ substances in a material safety data sheet kept by or known to the employer, indicating that the material may pose a health hazard.

Reporting Fatalities and Hospitalizations: When a work-related fatality or incident that requires hospitalization of three or more employees occurs:

✓ employers must orally report the fatality or incident to the nearest OSHA Area Office within eight hours; and

✓ if a death occurs within 30 days of the incident, employers must report it within eight hours.

Employers do not need to report a death occurring more than 30 days after a work-related incident.

Recordable Illnesses and Injuries: Cases that meet the general recording criteria involve a significant injury or illness diagnosed by a physician or other licensed health care professional, even if it does not result in death, days away from work, restricted work or job transfer, medical treatment beyond first aid, or loss of consciousness.

Medical Treatment Defined: Medical treatment means the management and care of a patient to combat a disease or disorder. It does not include:

✓ visits to a physician or other licensed health care professional solely for observation or counseling;

✓ conduct of diagnostic procedures, such as x-rays and blood tests, including the administration of prescription medications used solely for diagnostic purposes (i.e., eye drops to dilate pupils); or

✓ first aid.

First Aid Defined: The following treatments are considered first aid according to 29 CFR 1904:

✓ Using a non-prescription medication at the non-prescription strength

✓ Administering tetanus immunizations (other immunizations, such as the Hepatitis B vaccine or rabies vaccine, are considered medical treatment)

✓ Cleaning, flushing or soaking wounds on the surface of the skin

✓ Using wound coverings such as bandages, Band-Aids™, gauze pads, etc.; or using butterfly bandages or Steri-Strips™; other wound closing devices such as sutures, staples, etc., are considered medical treatment

✓ Using hot or cold therapy

✓ Using any non-rigid means of support, such as elastic bandages, wraps, non-rigid back belts, etc.; devices with rigid stays or other systems designed to immobilize parts of the body are considered medical treatment for recordkeeping purposes

✓ Using temporary immobilization devices while transporting an accident victim (i.e., splints, slings, neck collars, back boards, etc.)

✓ Drilling of a fingernail or toenail to relieve pressure or draining fluid from a blister

✓ Using eye patches

✓ Removing foreign bodies from the eye using only irrigation or a cotton swab

✓ Removing splinters or foreign material from areas other than the eye by irrigation, tweezers, cotton swabs or other simple means

✓ Using finger guards

✓ Using massages; physical therapy or chiropractic treatment are considered medical treatment for recordkeeping purposes

✓ Drinking fluids for relief of heat stress

OSHA Injury Decision Tree

The OSHA injury decision tree shows the steps involved in making the determination for recording work-related injuries or illnesses.

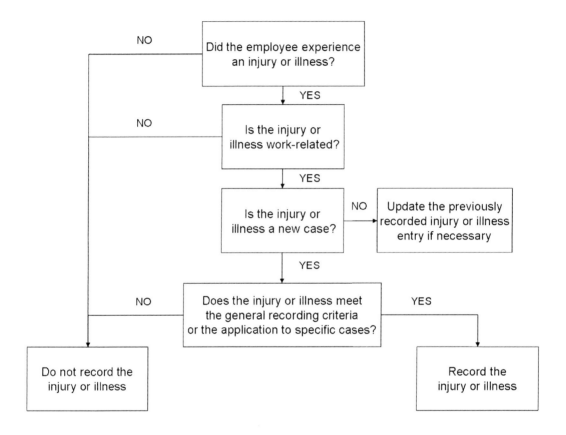

Material Safety Data Sheets (MSDS)

Chemical Safety: Material safety data sheets (MSDS) are a requirement of OSHA's Hazard Communication Standard (HCS). The purpose of the HCS is to ensure chemical safety in the workplace. Requirements of the MSDS program include:

✓ Manufacturers and importers of hazardous materials are required to conduct hazard evaluations of the products they manufacture or import.

✓ If a product is found to be hazardous under the terms of the standard, the manufacturer or importer must so indicate on containers of the material, and the first shipment of the material to a new customer must include a material safety data sheet (MSDS).

✓ Employers must use these MSDSs to train their employees to recognize and avoid the hazards presented by the materials.

Emergency Treatment: Employers must keep MSDSs on hand for all chemicals used in the workplace. The MSDS provides emergency information in case of contact with the chemical either internally or externally. The MSDS also explains the proper precautions to take when using a chemical. In the event of an OSHA inspection, the compliance officer will confirm that all MSDSs are at the worksite.

Inspection Guidelines: OSHA publishes inspection guidelines for enforcement of the Hazard Communication Standard. A summary of items that are reviewed during an inspection is included below:

✓ Is there a written hazard communication plan?

✓ Who is responsible for obtaining and maintaining MSDSs?

✓ Is there an MSDS for every chemical used?

✓ How are the MSDSs maintained (i.e., in notebooks in the work area(s), in a pickup truck at the jobsite, etc.) and do employees have proper access to them?

✓ Who is responsible for conducting training on chemicals and what are the elements of the training program?

The detailed procedure can be downloaded off the OSHA website (www.osha.gov).

Underground Utility Safety

Excavating without identifying underground utilities is a safety issue and can cost you unnecessary fines, repair costs, and utility outages. Although laws on marking underground utilities vary from state to state, contractors should identify underground utilities before digging on:

✓ public and private property;

✓ public streets;

✓ alleys;

✓ utility easements; and

✓ all other rights-of-way.

In order to request a locater to come out to your site and locate underground utilities, the Common Ground Alliance (CGA) can be reached by calling 811. Your call is then routed to a local One Call Center. If you prefer to contact your local One Call Center directly, contact information for each state is located on the CGA website at www.call811.com/state-specific.aspx.

Overhead Power Line Safety

OSHA has several programs focused on safety for those who work around overhead power lines. Listed below are a few key points from OSHA to consider when formulating a health and safety program and worksite planning.

Considerations include the following:

✓ perform a thorough site survey prior to beginning construction work;

✓ stay at least 10 feet away from overhead power lines;

✓ assume that all power lines are energized unless confirmed by proper authorities;

✓ call the utility company if overhead lines are present to determine voltage and if the lines can be shut off or insulated during construction work;

✓ use non-conductive ladders when working around overhead power lines;

✓ keep conductive objects at least 10 feet away from overhead power lines unless otherwise trained and qualified to use insulated tools specifically designed for high voltage lines; and

✓ perform thorough research on the location and voltage of overhead power lines when using cranes and heavy equipment to determine a minimum safe distance for operation.

Additional information on overhead power line safety is available on the OSHA website at www.osha.gov.

Benefits of Providing a Safe and Healthy Workplace

Ignoring safety and health regulations in the workplace is detrimental in many ways. Employees are put at risk, company reputation is at stake, and costs are high when accidents happen which effects overall company profits.

Ensuring workers are healthy and safe provides many direct benefits to employers:

✓ lower workers' compensation insurance costs;

✓ reduced medical expenditures;

✓ smaller expenditures for return-to-work programs;

✓ fewer faulty products;

✓ lower costs for job accommodations for injured workers;

✓ less money spent for overtime benefits.

Following safety and health regulations and proper procedures has indirect benefits as well:

✓ increased productivity;

✓ higher quality products;

✓ increased morale;

✓ better labor/management relations;

✓ reduced turnover;

✓ better use of human resources.

The impact of a safety and health program extends beyond the workplace providing employees and their families the security that their incomes are protected, family life is not hindered by injury, and overall reduced stress.

Employee Rights

The OSH Act grants employees several important rights. Among them are the rights to:

✓ complain to OSHA about safety and health conditions in their workplace and, to the extent permitted by law, have their identities kept confidential from their employer;

✓ contest the amount of time OSHA allows for correcting violations of standards; and

✓ participate in OSHA workplace inspections.

Retaliation is Prohibited: Private sector employees who exercise their rights under OSHA can be protected against employer reprisal. Employees must notify OSHA within 30 days of the time they learned of the alleged discriminatory action. OSHA will then investigate. If it agrees that discrimination has occurred, OSHA will ask the employer to restore any lost benefits to the affected employee. If necessary, OSHA can initiate legal action against the employer. In such cases, the worker pays no legal fees. The OSHA-approved state plans have similar employee rights provisions, including protections against employer reprisal.

Penalties

OSHA Enforcement: Every establishment covered by the OSH Act is subject to inspection by OSHA compliance safety and health officers (CSHOs). These individuals are chosen for their knowledge and experience in occupational safety and health. They are thoroughly trained in OSHA standards and in the recognition of occupational safety and health hazards. In states with their own OSHA-approved state plan, state officials conduct inspections, issue citations for violations, and propose penalties in a manner that is at least as strict as the federal program.

The following table illustrates penalty types, descriptions, and amounts assessed to the employer.

Penalty Type and Description	Penalty Amount
Other Than Serious Violation - A violation that has a direct relationship to workplace safety and health, but probably would not cause death or serious physical harm.	Discretionary penalty up to $7,000 for each violation
Serious Violation - A violation where there is substantial probability that death or serious physical harm could result and that the employer knew, or should have known, of the hazard.	Mandatory penalty up to $7,000 for each violation

Willful Violation - A violation that the employer knowingly commits or commits with plain indifference to the law. The employer either knows that what he or she is doing constitutes a violation, or is aware that a hazardous condition existed and made no reasonable effort to eliminate it.	Penalties of up to $70,000 with a minimum penalty of $5,000 for each violation. If an employer is convicted of a willful violation of a standard that has resulted in the death of an employee, the offense is punishable by a court-imposed fine or by imprisonment for up to six months, or both. A fine of up to $250,000 for an individual, or $500,000 for a corporation, may be imposed for a criminal conviction.
Repeated Violation - A violation of any standard, regulation, rule, or order where, upon reinspection, a substantially similar violation is found.	Penalties of up to $70,000
Penalty Type and Description	**Penalty Amount**
Failure to Abate Prior Violation – A violation given when a previous violation has not been corrected.	Civil penalty of up to $7,000 for each day the violation continues beyond the prescribed abatement date
De Minimis Violation – A violation of standards which have no direct or immediate relationship to safety or health.	Violation documented but not cited

Violations may be adjusted depending on the employer's good faith (demonstrated by efforts to comply with the act), history of previous violations, and size of business.

Additional violations for which citations and proposed penalties may be issued upon conviction include the following:

✓ Falsifying records, reports, or applications can bring a fine of $10,000 or up to six months in jail, or both.

✓ Violations of posting requirements can bring a civil penalty of up to $7,000.

✓ Assaulting a compliance officer, or otherwise resisting, opposing, intimidating, or interfering with a compliance officer while they are engaged in the performance of their duties is a criminal offense, subject to a fine of not more than $5,000 and imprisonment for not more than three years.

Citation and penalty procedures may differ somewhat in states with their own occupational safety and health programs.

Inspections: OSHA conducts two general types of inspections: **programmed** and **unprogrammed**.

✓ **Programmed inspections** are performed on establishments with high injury rates.

✓ **Unprogrammed inspections** are used in response to fatalities, catastrophes, and complaints.

Various OSHA publications and documents detail OSHA's policies and procedures for inspections and the penalties for violations.

Environmental Considerations

You need to be aware of the environmental considerations surrounding construction during all phases of the project.

✓ During the **pre-bid phase**, you must learn the regulations that pertain to the project and factor in the cost of compliance into the estimate.

✓ Obtaining the necessary permits occurs during the **pre-construction phase** and environmental responsibilities should be assigned to the construction crew.

✓ Self-audits help ensure compliance during the **construction phase**.

✓ For **post-construction**, you need to ensure that all the close-down procedures were done properly.

Going Green: Integrating eco-friendly practices in your business may help you control costs, tap into a new customer base, and enhance your socially responsible reputation. The demand for energy-efficient building design and construction is increasing. The Energy Star website at www.energystar.gov provides numerous resources on home improvement and commercial and residential construction. The EPA website at archive.epa.gov/greenbuilding has information on components of green building, national, state and local funding opportunities, and publications on various environmental topics

U.S. Environmental Protection Agency

Environmental Regulation: The U.S. Environmental Protection Agency (EPA) leads the nation's environmental science, research, education, and assessment efforts. The EPA works to develop and enforce regulations that implement environmental laws enacted by Congress. The EPA is responsible for researching and setting national standards for a variety of environmental programs and delegates to states the responsibility for issuing permits and for monitoring and enforcing compliance. If national standards are not met, the EPA can issue sanctions and take other steps to assist the states in reaching the desired levels of environmental quality.

Compliance Assistance: The EPA publishes a guide called Managing Your Responsibilities: A Planning Guide for Construction and Development. This publication is available for download at: archive.epa.gov/compliance/resources/publications/assistance/sectors/web/html

This guide provides comprehensive information for all types of environmental hazards and compliance requirements. Summarized briefly below are some of the environmental hazards impacting construction projects.

North Carolina Department of Environmental Quality (NCDEQ)

The North Carolina Department of Environmental Quality (NCDEQ) preserves and protects North Carolina's natural resources through proactive programs and enforcement of environmental regulations. Regulatory programs are designed to protect air quality, water quality, and the public's health. NCDEQ also offers technical assistance to businesses and local governments. Through its natural resource divisions, NCDEQ works to protect fish, wildlife, and wilderness areas.

North Carolina Department of Environmental Quality
1601 Mail Service Center
Raleigh, North Carolina 27699-1601

Telephone: 1-877-623-6748
Environmental Emergency: 1-800-858-0368
Fax: (919) 715-3060

Website: deq.nc.gov

Before beginning a project, you should assess the jobsite and determine if you need an environmental permit. The NCDENR website has several resources available to help with the permitting process. The online Customer Service Center offers Express Permitting, One Stop Permit Coordination, and an interactive database to help businesses find the required permits.

Environmental Law

There are several environmental laws that may impact your construction activities.

✓ The **Clean Water Act** establishes the basic structure for regulating discharges of pollutants into the waters of the United States. This act gives the EPA authority to implement pollution control programs, such as setting wastewater standards for the industry and water quality standards for all contaminants in surface waters. This act is discussed in more depth later in this chapter.

✓ Through the **Clean Air Act**, the EPA sets limits on how much of a pollutant is allowed in the air anywhere in the United States.

✓ The **Endangered Species Act (ESA)** protects threatened or endangered species from further harm. You should consider the impact of your construction activities on these species before you start your project.

✓ The **National Environmental Policy Act (NEPA)** applies to your construction project only if it is considered a "federal action." This act ensures that federal agencies consider environmental impacts in federal planning and decision making and covers construction and post-construction activities.

✓ The **National Historic Preservation Act (NHPA)** applies to your construction project if your project might have a potential impact on a property that is eligible for or included on the National Register of Historic Places (NRHP).

A thorough environmental assessment of your construction site is recommended for all projects. This assessment allows you to understand the environmental impacts of your project early, causing fewer delays and problems.

Air Quality

Outdoor Air Quality: Air regulations for construction activities are designed to limit the generation of particulate and ozone depleting substances.

Air quality issues that may impact your business are:

✓ uncontrolled open burning of debris,

✓ dust generation,

✓ vehicle emissions,

✓ combustion gases from oil-fired equipment, and

✓ releases of chlorofluorocarbons (CFCs).

Indoor Air: Indoor air quality can be just as important as outdoor air quality. For the safety of those on the construction site, you should give special consideration to materials that contain harmful chemicals including

✓ paint/primers,

✓ adhesives,

✓ floor coatings,

✓ carpet, and

✓ plywood/particle board.

Properly installed HVAC units and drain pans are important to avoid biological contaminants that breed in stagnant water. Most air permitting requirements for construction activities are at the state and local level.

Division of Air Quality: The Division of Air Quality within the North Carolina Department of Environmental Quality is responsible for issuing air quality permits. North Carolina General Statute 143-215.108A specifies that the following activities require a permit:

✓ establishing or operating any air containment source;

✓ building, erecting, using, or operating any equipment that may result in the emission of an air contaminant or that is likely to cause air pollution; or

✓ altering or changing the construction or method of operation of any equipment or process from which air contaminants are or may be emitted.

The law also allows for certain activities to take place before securing a permit. These activities include:

✓ clearing and grading;

✓ construction of access roads, driveways, and parking lots;

✓ building and installing underground pipe work including water, sewer, electric, and telecommunications utilities; and

✓ building ancillary structures, including fences and office buildings that are not a necessary component of an air contaminant source, equipment, or associated air cleaning device as defined by law.

Air Quality Contacts:

Main Number: (919) 707-8100

Emergency Management: (800) 858-0368 or (919) 707-8425

Air Quality Regional Offices:

Asheville: (828) 296-4500
Fayetteville: (910) 433-3300
Mooresville: (704) 663-1699
Raleigh: (919) 791-4200
Washington: (252) 946-6481
Wilmington: (910) 796-7215
Winston-Salem: (336) 771-5000

Be aware of both indoor and outdoor pollution.

Asbestos

Before beginning any demolition or renovation activities on existing buildings, you should evaluate the potential for releasing asbestos. Exposure to asbestos can cause serious health problems and the EPA and OSHA have published rules regulating its production, use, and disposal.

Evaluation Guidelines: When evaluating whether or not asbestos may be present, you want to note possible asbestos-containing material, such as:

✓ Insulation, including blown, rolled and wrapped

✓ Resilient floor coverings (tiles)

✓ Asbestos siding shingles

✓ Asbestos-cement products

✓ Asphalt roofing products

✓ Vermiculite insulation

The EPA has a comprehensive list of suspected asbestos-containing materials at: www.epa.gov/asbestos

Inspections: If you are working with asbestos, you should have your site inspected by a certified asbestos inspector prior to construction. You must submit a written notice of intent 10 working days prior to starting construction activities. Written notices should be submitted to your delegated state/local pollution control agency and your EPA Regional Office.

Permit and Notification: Removal and demolition projects containing asbestos require a permit and notification. Applications are available on the Health Hazards Control Unit website at epi.dph.ncdhhs.gov.

> *Health Hazards Control Unit*
> *NCDHHS-Division of Public Health*
> *12001 Mail Service Center*
> *Raleigh, NC 27699-2000*
>
> *Telephone: (919) 707-5950*
> *Fax: (919) 870-4808*

Buncombe, Forsyth and Mecklenburg counties have additional asbestos-related ordinances:

> *Buncombe County*
> *WNC Regional Air Pollution Control Agency*
> *(828) 255-5655*
>
> *Forsyth County*
> *Environmental Affairs Department*
> *(336) 727-8064*
>
> *Mecklenburg County*
> *Land Use and Environmental Services Agency, Air Quality*
> *(704) 336-5430*

Open burning is regulated through the Division of Air Quality:

> *Open Burning Line*
> *(877) OPEN BURN or (877) 673-6287*

Clean Water Act

Water pollution can negatively affect the use of water for drinking, household needs, recreation, fishing, transportation and commerce. The EPA enforces federal clean water and safe drinking water laws, provides support for municipal wastewater treatment plants, and takes part in pollution prevention efforts aimed at protecting watersheds and sources of drinking water.

The Clean Water Act establishes the basic structure for regulating discharges of pollutants into the waters of the United States. This includes:

✓ giving the EPA the authority to implement pollution control programs such as setting wastewater standards for industry;

✓ continuing requirements to set water quality standards for all contaminants in surface waters; and

✓ making it unlawful for any person to discharge any pollutant from a point source into navigable waters, unless a National Pollutant Discharge Elimination System (NPDES) permit was obtained under its provisions.

Stormwater Discharges and Construction Site Runoff: Before beginning any construction project, you must consider runoff and stormwater discharges that may originate from your site. These discharges often contain sediment and pollutants such as phosphorous and nitrogen (fertilizer), pesticides, oil and grease, concrete truck washout, construction chemicals, and solid wastes in quantities that could adversely affect water quality.

National Pollutant Discharge Elimination System (NPDES): The EPA has estimated that about 30 percent of known pollution to our nation's waters is attributable to stormwater runoff. In 1987, Congress directed the EPA to develop a regulatory program to address the stormwater problem. The EPA issued regulations in 1990 authorizing the creation of a NPDES permitting system for stormwater discharges from a select group, including construction activities disturbing five or more acres.

In 1999, the EPA expanded this program (called Phase II). This phase brought about two major new permittees:

✓ Construction sites that disturb one acre but less than five acres with possible exceptions allowing a waiver

✓ Small municipal separate storm sewer systems (MS4)

A "larger common plan of development or sale" is subject to stormwater permitting, even if the land is parceled off or sold, and construction occurs on plots that are less than one acre by separate, independent builders.

Assessing Stormwater Discharge: Listed below are questions that you need to consider when determining the need for a stormwater permit for your construction project:

✓ Will your construction project disturb one or more acres of land?

✓ Will your construction project disturb less than one acre of land, but is part of a larger common plan of development or sale that will disturb one or more acres?

✓ Will your construction project disturb less than one acre of land, but is designated by the NPDES (state agency or EPA) permitting authority as a regulated construction activity?

✓ Will stormwater from the construction site flow to a municipal separate storm sewer system or a water of the United States such as a lake, river, or wetland?

Municipal Technologies Agency: The EPA's Municipal Technologies Agency provides assistance in the area of municipal wastewater treatment technologies. Available assistance includes:

✓ consultation on design, operation, and maintenance of systems;

✓ identification and solution of problems;

✓ contributions in the development of regulations; and

✓ technical information, guidance, assessments, evaluation, and cost estimates for the design, construction, and operation and maintenance of municipal wastewater treatment facilities.

Division of Water Quality: The Division of Water Quality within the North Carolina Department of Environmental Quality is responsible for providing guidance and preparing several types of water permits, such as NPDES permits, stormwater general permits, wastewater general permits, and state stormwater management program permits.

This list of permits is not all-inclusive. Contact the permitting division for additional requirements.

    Water Quality Regional Offices:

    Asheville: (828) 296-4500
    Fayetteville: (910) 433-3300
    Mooresville: (704) 663-1699
    Raleigh: (919) 791-4200
    Washington: (252) 946-6481
    Wilmington: (910) 796-7215
    Winston-Salem: (336) 771-5000

Sedimentation and Erosion Control Measures

During a short period of time, construction sites can contribute more sediment to streams than can be deposited naturally during several decades. Excess sediment can quickly fill rivers and lakes, requiring dredging, and destroying aquatic habitats.

Measures can be taken to minimize erosion and sedimentation on construction sites:

✓ Sediment control measures include a silt fence or hay bales placed at the down gradient side of the construction site.

✓ Erosion control measures include placing mulch and vegetation as soon as feasible to permanently stabilize the site soil.

✓ A water misting system can control dust generated on the jobsite and loss of soil.

Erosion and sediment control minimizes pollution and contractor costs to rework eroded areas and replace lost soil. Individual states may have required sedimentation and erosion control measures.

Hazardous and Non-Hazardous Solid Waste

In general, construction sites generate more non-hazardous waste than hazardous waste. You should be aware of the regulations surrounding both.

Non-Hazardous Waste: Common non-hazardous waste generated at construction sites includes:

✓ scrap wood,

✓ drywall,

✓ bricks,

✓ concrete,

✓ plumbing fixtures and piping,

✓ roof coverings,

✓ metal scraps, and

✓ electrical wiring and components.

Non-hazardous waste is regulated at the state and local level and you should identify any requirements. For more information on state requirements, refer to the Construction Industry Compliance Assistance Center at www.cicacenter.org.

Hazardous Waste: Hazardous waste is regulated at the federal level and your state may have additional requirements.

Examples of hazardous waste are:

✓ lead-based paint,

✓ used oil,

✓ hydraulic fluid,

✓ gypsum drywall (due to sulfate), and

✓ mercury-containing demolition wastes such as batteries and thermostats.

Proper Notification: If you discover hazardous waste on your jobsite, you must notify your state and local authorities or the National Response Center Hotline at (800) 424-8802. Criminal charges may be filed if hazardous waste is present at the site and proper notification does not take place. If hazardous waste is produced through construction activities, the party that generated the waste is generally responsible for cleaning it up. Hazardous waste must be treated and disposed of at a facility permitted or licensed for that purpose by the state or federal government.

Hazardous Substances

Site Survey: Before beginning any construction or demolition activities at your construction site, you should evaluate the site for any hazardous substances.

Hazardous substances referred to in this section are chemicals that most likely induce serious acute reactions from short-term airborne exposure.

Notification: When you do a site survey, you should review historical records to determine previous uses of the site. A review of state and local files will help you identify past environmental concerns. If during construction you uncover hazardous substances, you must stop construction activities immediately and notify the owner and contact the National Response Hotline at (800) 424-8802.

Underground Storage Tanks (UST): An underground storage tank system (UST) is defined by the EPA as "a tank and any underground piping connected to the tank that has at least 10 percent of its combined volume underground." The federal UST regulations apply only to underground tanks and piping storing either petroleum or certain hazardous substances. Federal regulations do not apply to the following types of underground storage tanks:

✓ Farm and residential tanks of 1,100 gallons or less capacity holding motor fuel used for noncommercial purposes

✓ Tanks storing heating oil used on the premises where it is stored

✓ Tanks on or above the floor of underground areas, such as basements or tunnels

✓ Septic tanks and systems for collecting storm water and wastewater

✓ Flow-through process tanks

✓ Tanks of 110 gallons or less capacity

✓ Emergency spill and overfill tanks

Conduct a thorough site survey to anticipate any environmental hazards.

Lead

Exposure Hazards: Lead is considered a toxic and hazardous substance and can cause a serious risk of lead poisoning if overexposure occurs. OSHA regulates the amount of lead that workers can be exposed to (no more than 50 micrograms of lead per cubic meter of air averaged over an 8-hour day). Traditionally, the most over-exposure occurs in trades such as plumbing, welding, and painting.

Hazard Protection: The most effective way to protect workers is through good work practices and engineering controls. Respirators are not a substitute for these practices, but should be an additional measure of safety. Employers are required to supply respirators at no cost to employees who will potentially be exposed to lead and adopt a respirator program, including a written standard operating procedure, training, and regular equipment inspection.

Engineering controls to reduce worker exposure include:

✓ exhaust ventilation, such as power tools with dust collection shrouds or other attachments exhausted through a high-efficiency particulate air (HEPA) vacuum system;

✓ enclosure or encapsulation of lead particles (for example, lead-based paint can be made inaccessible by encapsulating it with a material that bonds to the surface such as epoxy coating);

✓ substituting lead-based products or products that create lead exposure with a comparable product;

✓ replacing lead components with non-lead components;

✓ process or equipment modifications that create less lead exposure from dust; and

✓ isolating the lead exposure area so other areas are not contaminated.

Construction Assistance: OSHA has downloadable software on its website designed to help small business owners understand the Lead in Construction standard. Users should still refer to OSHA standards for specific details as this represents the most up-to-date source.

Remodeling or Renovating a Home with Lead-Based Paint (Lead PRE)

In December 2008 (with amendments in 2010 and 2011), the EPA passed the Lead-Based Paint Renovation, Repair and Painting Program Rule that imposes additional lead-based paint regulations. Under this rule, only certified contractors can perform renovation, repair and painting projects that disturb lead-based paint in homes, child care facilities, and schools built before 1978. The EPA has authorized Alabama, Georgia, Iowa, Kansas, Massachusetts, Mississippi, North Carolina, Oregon, Rhode Island, Utah, Washington, and Wisconsin to administer their own Renovation, Repair and Painting Program. Contractors working in these states must follow the regulations put forth by the state program.

Contractors can become certified renovators by submitting an application and fee to the EPA or state-based program and taking an eight-hour training course from an EPA-accredited training provider. Certified contractors must follow specific work practices to prevent lead contamination. Three simple principles are applied when working with lead which includes:

✓ containing the work area to minimize lead contamination in other work areas;

✓ minimizing dust to prevent harmful airborne particles from being inhaled; and

✓ cleaning up the work area thoroughly.

Required Notification: Under Lead PRE, federal law requires that contractors provide lead information to residents before renovating pre-1978 housing. The EPA publishes a pamphlet titled Protect Your Family from Lead in Your Home which must be distributed to the owner and occupants before starting work. Confirmation of receipt of the lead pamphlet or a certificate of mailing must be kept for 3 years. For work in common areas of multi-family housing, renovation notices must be distributed to all tenants.

For renovations to child-occupied facilities, renovators must distribute the pamphlet titled Renovate Right: Important Lead Hazard Information for Families, Child Care Providers and Schools to owners, administrators, and parents or guardians of children under the age of six that attend these facilities.

Exemptions: This rule applies to nearly all remodeling or renovation work with the exception of the following circumstances:

✓ Housing for the elderly or disabled persons unless children will reside there

✓ Zero-bedroom dwellings

✓ Emergency renovations or repairs

✓ Minor repair and maintenance that disturb two square feet or less of paint per component

✓ Housing or components declared lead-free by a certified inspector or risk assessor

Lead Abatement: Work designed to permanently eliminate lead-based paint hazards is considered lead abatement and is not subject to the guidelines under Lead PRE. This does not include renovation, remodeling, landscaping, or other activities designed to repair, restore, and redesign a given building. The EPA outlines strict regulations for this type of work as discussed in the previous section on lead.

Renovation: Renovations under Lead PRE are modifications of all or part of any existing structure that disturbs a painted surface. This includes:

✓ removal/modification of painted surfaces, components or structures;

✓ surface preparation activities (sanding/scraping/ other activities that may create paint dust); and

✓ window replacement.

Penalties: Failure to comply with regulations concerning lead is a serious violation. Non-compliance carries substantial fines of up to $37,500 per day for each violation. Criminal penalties of imprisonment for up to one year also apply to willful or intentional violation of the regulation.

Assistance: You can obtain additional information by going online to the EPA website at www.epa.gov/lead or by contacting The National Lead Information Center (NLIC) at (800) 424-LEAD (5323).

Final Inspection...

Safety Standards: It is important to know the OSHA standards that pertain to the construction industry.

Safe Hiring and Training: Background checks can help you hire workers with good safety records. Regular training contributes to a safe working environment.

Substance Abuse Policies: Substance abuse compromises safety in the workplace. Clearly written and communicated policies are useful tools in reducing substance abuse.

Safety Equipment: Certain safety equipment may be required according to OSHA regulations, depending on the work being performed.

Emergency Action Plan: Either a written or an orally communicated emergency action plan is required by OSHA, depending on the number of employees you have.

OSHA Recordkeeping: Your company may be required to complete OSHA forms 300, 300A and 301.

OSHA Injury Decision Tree: The OSHA injury decision tree outlines the steps in making the determination for recording work-related injuries and illnesses.

Material Safety Data Sheets (MSDS): A material safety data sheet (MSDS) is required for all chemicals used.

Underground Utility Safety: Although laws on marking underground utilities vary from state to state, contractors should identify underground utilities before excavating.

Overhead Power Line Safety: Overhead power line safety should be considered when formulating a health and safety program and worksite planning. As a general rule, workers should a minimum distance of 10 feet from overhead power lines.

Benefits of Providing a Safe and Healthy Workplace: OSHA can assess citations for failing to provide a safe work environment. Ensuring workers are healthy and safe provides many direct and indirect benefits to employers.

Employee Rights: Employees are allowed to report OSHA violations without fear of retaliation.

Penalties: Penalties vary depending on the severity of OSHA violations. OSHA may conduct programmed or unprogrammed inspections.

Environmental Considerations: Environmental factors should be considered throughout all phases of construction. Obtaining proper permits is important for following environmental regulations.

U.S. Environmental Protection Agency (EPA): The EPA works to develop and enforce regulations that implement environmental laws enacted by Congress.

North Carolina Department of Environmental Quality: The North Carolina Department of Environmental Quality has several programs and activities that provide environmental and permitting assistance.

Environmental Law: Several laws exist to protect the environment. An assessment of environmental impacts should be done early on in the construction project.

Air Quality: Indoor and outdoor quality should be monitored throughout the construction project.

Asbestos: Before beginning remodeling or demolition of any project, assess whether you may encounter asbestos-releasing materials. Certain permitting and notification requirements may apply.

Clean Water Act: The Clean Water Act establishes the basic structure for regulating discharges of pollutants into the waters of the United States.

Sedimentation and Erosion Control Measures: Erosion and sediment control measures minimize pollution and contractor costs to rework eroded areas and replace lost soil.

Hazardous and Non-Hazardous Waste: Most construction waste is non-hazardous. Both hazardous and non-hazardous waste must be disposed of properly.

Hazardous Substances: Early identification of hazardous substances is important and proper notification is required.

Lead: Contact with lead can cause lead poisoning and you and your employees must follow specific regulations when working with it.

Remodeling or Renovating a Home with Lead-Based Paint: The Lead Pre-Renovation Education Rule (Lead PRE) is a federal regulation involving those performing renovations for compensation in residential housing that may contain lead paint.

Supplemental Forms

Supplemental forms and links are available at **NASCLAforms.org** using access code **NC129354**.

OSHA Forms for Recording Work-Related Injuries and Illnesses	OSHA forms 300, 300A and 301 with instructions
OSHA Compliance Assistance Employment Law Guide	OSHA guide summarizing employer responsibilities under the OSH Act
Managing Your Environmental Responsibilities: A Planning Guide for Construction and Development	EPA guide customized for the construction industry that outlines specific environmental responsibilities
Protect Your Family From Lead in Your Home	Mandatory brochure to distribute to the owner if you are doing renovations on pre-1978 housing

OSHA's Form 300 (Rev. 01/2004)

Log of Work-Related Injuries and Illnesses

Year 20____

U.S. Department of Labor
Occupational Safety and Health Administration

Form approved OMB no. 1218-0176.

You must record information about every work-related death and about every work-related injury or illness that involves loss of consciousness, restricted work activity or job transfer, days away from work, or medical treatment beyond first aid. You must also record significant work-related injuries and illnesses that are diagnosed by a physician or licensed health care professional. You must also record work-related injuries and illnesses that meet any of the specific recording criteria listed in 29 CFR Part 1904.8 through 1904.12. Feel free to use two lines for a single case if you need to. You must complete an injury and illness incident report (OSHA Form 301) or equivalent form for each injury or illness recorded on this form. If you're not sure whether a case is recordable, call your local OSHA office for help.

Identify the person

(A) Case no.	(B) Employee's name	(C) Job title (e.g. Welder)

Describe the case

(D) Date of injury or onset of illness	(E) Where the event occurred (e.g. Loading dock north end)	(F) Describe injury or illness, parts of body affected, and object/substance that directly injured or made person ill (e.g. Second degree burns on right forearm from acetylene torch)
month/day		
month/day		
month/day		
month/day		
month/day		
month/day		
month/day		
month/day		
month/day		
month/day		
month/day		
month/day		
month/day		

Classify the case

CHECK ONLY ONE box for each case based on the most serious outcome for that case:

(G) Death	(H) Days away from work	Remained at Work		Enter the number of days the injured or ill worker was:		Check the "injury" column or choose one type of illness:					
		(I) Job transfer or restriction	(J) Other recordable cases	(K) Away from work	(L) On job transfer or restriction	(M)(1) Injury	(2) Skin disorder	(3) Respiratory condition	(4) Poisoning	(5) Hearing loss	(6) All other illnesses
□	□	□	□	____ days	____ days	□	□	□	□	□	□
□	□	□	□	____ days	____ days	□	□	□	□	□	□
□	□	□	□	____ days	____ days	□	□	□	□	□	□
□	□	□	□	____ days	____ days	□	□	□	□	□	□
□	□	□	□	____ days	____ days	□	□	□	□	□	□
□	□	□	□	____ days	____ days	□	□	□	□	□	□
□	□	□	□	____ days	____ days	□	□	□	□	□	□
□	□	□	□	____ days	____ days	□	□	□	□	□	□
□	□	□	□	____ days	____ days	□	□	□	□	□	□
□	□	□	□	____ days	____ days	□	□	□	□	□	□
□	□	□	□	____ days	____ days	□	□	□	□	□	□
□	□	□	□	____ days	____ days	□	□	□	□	□	□
□	□	□	□	____ days	____ days	□	□	□	□	□	□

Page totals ▶

Be sure to transfer these totals to the Summary page (Form 300A) before you post it.

| | | | | | | (1) | (2) | (3) | (4) | (5) | (6) |

Establishment name _____

City _____ State _____

Page ____ of ____

OSHA's Form 300A (Rev. 01/2004)

Summary of Work-Related Injuries and Illnesses

Year 20____

U.S. Department of Labor
Occupational Safety and Health Administration

Form approved OMB no. 1218-0176

All establishments covered by Part 1904 must complete this Summary page, even if no work-related injuries or illnesses occurred during the year. Remember to review the Log to verify that the entries are complete and accurate before completing this summary.

Using the Log, count the individual entries you made for each category. Then write the totals below, making sure you've added the entries from every page of the Log. If you had no cases, write "0."

Employees, former employees, and their representatives have the right to review the OSHA Form 300 in its entirety. They also have limited access to the OSHA Form 301 or its equivalent. See 29 CFR Part 1904.35, in OSHA's recordkeeping rule, for further details on the access provisions for these forms.

Number of Cases

Total number of deaths

(G)

Total number of cases with days away from work

(H)

Total number of cases with job transfer or restriction

(I)

Total number of other recordable cases

(J)

Number of Days

Total number of days away from work

(K)

Total number of day-of-job transfer or restriction

(L)

Injury and Illness Types

Total number of . . .
(M)

(1) Injuries ____
(2) Skin disorders ____
(3) Respiratory conditions ____
(4) Poisonings ____
(5) Hearing loss ____
(6) All other illnesses ____

Post this Summary page from February 1 to April 30 of the year following the year covered by the form.

Public reporting burden for this collection of information is estimated to average 50 minutes per response, including time to review the instructions, search and gather the data needed, and complete and review the collection of information. Persons are not required to respond to the collection of information unless it displays a currently valid OMB control number. If you have any comments about these estimates or any other aspects of this data collection, contact: US Department of Labor, OSHA Office of Statistical Analysis, Room N-3644, 200 Constitution Avenue, NW, Washington, DC 20210. Do not send the completed forms to this office.

Establishment information

Your establishment name _____

Street _____

City _____ State _____ ZIP _____

Industry description (e.g., Manufacture of motor truck trailers) _____

Standard Industrial Classification (SIC), if known (e.g., 3715) __ __ __ __

OR

North American Industrial Classification (NAICS), if known (e.g., 336212) __ __ __ __ __ __

Employment information (If you don't have these figures, see the Worksheet on the back of this page to estimate.)

Annual average number of employees _____

Total hours worked by all employees last year _____

Sign here

Knowingly falsifying this document may result in a fine.

I certify that I have examined this document and that to the best of my knowledge the entries are true, accurate, and complete.

_____
Company executive

_____   Title _____
Phone   Date _____

OSHA's Form 301

Injury and Illness Incident Report

Form approved OMB no. 1218-0176

U.S. Department of Labor

Occupational Safety and Health Administration

Attention: This form contains information relating to employee health and must be used in a manner that protects the confidentiality of employees to the extent possible while the information is being used for occupational safety and health purposes.

This *Injury and Illness Incident Report* is one of the first forms you must fill out when a recordable work-related injury or illness has occurred. Together with the *Log of Work-Related Injuries and Illnesses* and the accompanying *Summary*, these forms help the employer and OSHA develop a picture of the extent and severity of work-related incidents.

Within 7 calendar days after you receive information that a recordable work-related injury or illness has occurred, you must fill out this form or an equivalent. Some state workers' compensation, insurance, or other reports may be acceptable substitutes. To be considered an equivalent form, any substitute must contain all the information asked for on this form.

According to Public Law 91-596 and 29 CFR 1904, OSHA's recordkeeping rule, you must keep this form on file for 5 years following the year to which it pertains.

If you need additional copies of this form, you may photocopy and use as many as you need.

Completed by _____

Title _____

Phone (____) ____ - ____   Date ____ / ____ / ____

Information about the employee

1) Full name _____

2) Street _____

City _____ State _____ ZIP _____

3) Date of birth ____ / ____ / ____

4) Date hired ____ / ____ / ____

5) ☐ Male
   ☐ Female

Information about the physician or other health care professional

6) Name of physician or other health care professional _____

7) If treatment was given away from the worksite, where was it given?

Facility _____

Street _____

City _____ State _____ ZIP _____

8) Was employee treated in an emergency room?
   ☐ Yes
   ☐ No

9) Was employee hospitalized overnight as an in-patient?
   ☐ Yes
   ☐ No

Information about the case

10) Case number from the *Log* _____ *(Transfer the case number from the Log after you record the case.)*

11) Date of injury or illness ____ / ____ / ____

12) Time employee began work _____ AM / PM

13) Time of event _____ AM / PM ☐ Check if time cannot be determined

14) **What was the employee doing just before the incident occurred?** Describe the activity, as well as the tools, equipment, or material the employee was using. Be specific. *Examples:* "climbing a ladder while carrying roofing materials"; "spraying chlorine from hand sprayer"; "daily computer key-entry."

15) **What happened?** Tell us how the injury occurred. *Examples:* "When ladder slipped on wet floor, worker fell 20 feet"; "Worker was sprayed with chlorine when gasket broke during replacement"; "Worker developed soreness in wrist over time."

16) **What was the injury or illness?** Tell us the part of the body that was affected and how it was affected; be more specific than "hurt," "pain," or sore." *Examples:* "strained back"; "chemical burn, hand"; "carpal tunnel syndrome."

17) **What object or substance directly harmed the employee?** *Examples:* "concrete floor"; "chlorine"; "radial arm saw." *If this question does not apply to the incident, leave it blank.*

18) **If the employee died, when did death occur?** Date of death ____ / ____ / ____

Public reporting burden for this collection of information is estimated to average 22 minutes per response, including time for reviewing instructions, searching existing data sources, gathering and maintaining the data needed, and completing and reviewing the collection of information. Persons are not required to respond to the collection of information unless it displays a current valid OMB control number. If you have any comments about this estimate or any other aspects of this data collection, including suggestions for reducing this burden, contact: US Department of Labor, OSHA's Office of Statistics Analysis, Room N-3644, 200 Constitution Avenue, NW, Washington, DC 20210. Do not send the completed forms to this office.

Chapter 13
WORKING WITH SUBCONTRACTORS

Chapter Survey...

⇨ *Sources for Finding the Right Subcontractor*

⇨ *Creating a Winning Partnership*

⇨ *Site Rules for Contractors*

⇨ *Employee or Independent Contractor: IRS Guidelines*

Subcontractors contract with the general contractor or other subcontractors to complete a portion of a larger project.

It is important to hire the right subcontractors because their work impacts your company's reputation. Just as you want employees who are easy to work with, the same applies to subcontractors.

There are basic criteria you can use to evaluate whether you want to hire a subcontractor:

✓ Do they sell or produce quality products?

✓ Are they reliable? Are they able to complete the project according to the schedule?

✓ Do they have good customer service skills?

✓ Are they able to effectively deal with problems?

✓ Do they give an overall impression of professionalism?

✓ Are they properly licensed and carry appropriate insurance coverage?

✓ Do they remedy situations that involve material defects or failures?

✓ How do they handle change orders?

✓ Are they competitively priced?

Now that you have established your requirements, it is time to find qualified leads.

Sources for Finding the Right Subcontractor

If you have a good reputation, the word travels fast. This also holds true for good subcontractors and suppliers. Some of your best subcontractors can come from referrals. Sources for these referrals might include:

✓ subcontractors in a different field who have worked with other subcontractors on other jobs;

✓ other contractors in your field;

✓ members of your local trade association;

✓ suppliers (for example, electrical supply firms can give referrals on electricians); and

✓ architects or engineers.

Once you come up with credible referrals, you want to make sure that you take extra steps to organize the process.

✓ Keep a list of qualified subcontractors.

✓ Allow sufficient lead time to line up subcontractors for jobs.

✓ Interview subcontractors for their qualifications, even when you are not scheduling them for a job.

✓ Check references if you have not worked with the subcontractor before.

✓ Ensure all subcontractors you work with have proper insurance coverage; request copies of insurance certificates and follow up to ensure coverage is current (as discussed in Chapter 4).

Creating a Winning Partnership

Once you have done all your homework and made your subcontractor selections, you'll want to create a relationship that will set both parties up for success.

✓ Provide an orientation on your policies and procedures.

✓ Be clear on all instructions and solicit questions.

✓ Be open to feedback and suggestions.

✓ Reward good work and provide constructive comments on improvements.

✓ Schedule trades so the job is ready for them and there are minimal barriers for them to complete their job.

✓ Visit the jobsite before the start of your portion of the project to tell other subcontractors your requirements (if it applies).

✓ Complete an IRS W-9 form prior to starting work.

Site Rules for Contractors

As part of an orientation with your subcontractors, you may want to review your site rules. Listed below are some rules to consider:

✓ Keep the jobsite clean and free of debris.

✓ All safety policies and OSHA regulations must be followed.

✓ You must provide your own tools and equipment.

✓ Work must be compliant with all applicable codes.

✓ Keep radios on the jobsite at a moderate listening level and free of offensive content.

✓ Behave professionally and do not use foul language.

✓ Salvage of items is prohibited without permission.

Site rules can be posted at the jobsite so they are visible to everyone and serve as a continual reminder.

Employee or Independent Contractor: IRS Guidelines

The IRS outlines specific guidelines regarding the difference between employees and independent contractors. Make sure you are working within an independent contractor relationship and not an employer-employee basis. If you do have an employer-employee relationship, your company is liable for payroll taxes, workers' compensation and employee benefits for that subcontractor.

To determine whether an individual is an employee or an independent contractor under common law, the relationship of the worker and your company

must be examined. In any employee-independent contractor determination, all information that provides evidence of the degree of control and the degree of independence must be considered.

Evidence of the degree of control and independence falls into three categories: **behavioral control, financial control and the type of relationship of the parties.**

Behavioral Control

Facts that show whether a business has a right to direct and control how the worker does the task for which the worker is hired include the type and degree of:

✓ **Instruction the business gives to the worker:** An employee is generally subject to the business' instructions about when, where, and how to work. In a subcontractor relationship, the business generally gives up the right to control the details of the worker's performance.

✓ **Training the business gives to the worker:** An employee may be trained to perform services in a particular manner. Independent contractors ordinarily use their own methods.

Financial Control

Facts that show whether the business has a right to control the business aspects of the worker's job include:

✓ **The extent to which the worker has un-reimbursed business expenses:** Independent contractors are more likely to have un-reimbursed expenses than are employees. Fixed ongoing costs that are incurred regardless of whether work is currently being performed are especially important.

✓ **The extent of the worker's investment:** An independent contractor often has a significant investment in the facilities he or she uses in performing services for someone else. However, a significant investment is not necessary for independent contractor status.

✓ **The extent to which the worker makes his or her services available to the relevant market:** An employee is generally guaranteed a regular wage amount for an hourly, weekly, or other period of time for one employer. An independent contractor is usually paid a flat fee by the business with which he or she has contracted. An independent contractor is free to manage multiple contracts.

✓ **The extent to which the worker can realize a profit or loss:** An independent contractor can make a profit or loss.

Type of Relationship

Facts that show the parties' type of relationship include:

✓ **Written contracts describing the relationship the parties intend to create**

✓ **Whether the business provides the worker with employee-type benefits, such as insurance, a pension plan, vacation pay, or sick pay**

✓ **The permanency of the relationship:** If you engage a worker with the expectation that the relationship will continue indefinitely rather than for a specific project or period, this is generally considered an employer-employee relationship.

✓ **The extent to which services performed by the worker are a key aspect of the regular business of the company:** If a worker provides services that are a key aspect of your regular business activity, it is more likely that you will have a right to direct and control his or her activities, indicating an employer-employee relationship.

Now that you know the rules, let's look at a few practical examples to demonstrate how classifications are made.

Example 1: Milton Manning, an experienced tile setter, orally agreed with a corporation to perform full-time services at construction sites. He uses his own tools and performs services in the order designated by the corporation and according to its specifications. The corporation supplies all materials, makes frequent inspections of his work, pays him on a piecework basis, and carries workers' compensation insurance on him. He does not have a place of business or hold himself out to perform similar services for others. Either party can end the services at any time. Milton Manning is an employee of the corporation.

Example 2: Vera Elm, an electrician, submitted a job estimate to a housing complex for electrical work at $16 per hour for 400 hours. She is to receive $1,280 every two weeks for the next 10 weeks. This is not considered payment by the hour. Even if she works more or less than 400 hours to complete the work, Vera Elm will receive $6,400. She also performs additional electrical installations under contracts with other companies that she obtained through advertisements. Vera is an independent contractor.

Assistance in Determining Status: If you are unable to determine whether the working relationship is on an employer-employee or employer-independent contractor basis, the IRS can assist by reviewing the circumstances of the working relationship and officially determining the individual's status. To request this review, a *Form SS-8, Determination of Worker Status for Purposes of Federal Employment Taxes and Income Tax Withholding*, is submitted to the IRS. This form and other assistance are available online at www.irs.gov.

Final Inspection...

Sources for Finding the Right Subcontractor: Referrals are a good way to find the right subcontractors. As you collect referrals, develop a process to organize and appropriately schedule them.

Creating a Winning Partnership: Establishing good communication and having clear policies in place set a solid foundation for positive subcontractor relationships.

Site Rules for Contractors: Subcontractors should receive an orientation on your site rules before starting work. Site rules should be posted at the jobsite so they are visible to everyone and serve as a continual reminder.

Employee or Independent Contractor: IRS Guidelines: The IRS uses behavioral control, financial control, and the type of relationship of the parties to make a determination whether someone is an employee or independent contractor.

PART 3
Office
Administration

Chapter 14
FINANCIAL MANAGEMENT

Chapter Survey...

⇨ Bookkeeping

⇨ The Accounting Cycle

⇨ Methods of Accounting

⇨ Contract Accounting

⇨ Cash Management

⇨ Equipment Records and Accounting

⇨ Accounting Process for Materials

⇨ Payroll Accounting

⇨ Technology Solutions for Accounting

Accounting is important to all businesses because it helps measure the financial fitness of the company. It is a process of collecting, analyzing, and reporting information to develop tools, such as financial statements, that are used to evaluate different financial aspects of the company.

Bookkeeping

The first step in the accounting process is bookkeeping. Bookkeeping involves the accurate recording of all financial transactions that occur in the business. Financial statements are derived from this information.

Here are a few tips to maintain accurate and timely bookkeeping:

✓ Open a separate business checking account and obtain a business credit card to keep business and personal finances separate.

✓ Keep track of all deductible expenses (discussed later in this chapter).

✓ Keep all receipts and identify the source of all receipts so you can separate business from personal receipts and taxable from non-taxable income.

✓ Update business records daily to have quick access to the daily financial position of your business.

✓ Accurately record all information in the checkbook ledger including date, who the check was written to, the amount, and the reason the check was written.

✓ Record expenses when they occur, so you have an accurate picture of your cash situation.

✓ Avoid paying with cash, so you have a "paper trail" of your expenditures.

✓ Balance your checking account monthly. You may want to request month-end bank statements to coordinate with other month-end records.

✓ Keep all financial records for the required amount of time as designated by the IRS.

Bookkeeping involves the clerical side of accounting and requires only minimal knowledge of the entire accounting cycle. You may want to consult with a professional accountant for the more complex financial decision-making of your business.

The Accounting Cycle

The accounting cycle is a series of events that is repeated each reporting period. The cycle begins with a transaction and ends with closing the books and preparing financial statements. Steps in the accounting cycle include:

1. **Classifying and recording transactions,**

2. **Posting transactions,**

3. **Preparing a trial balance,**

4. **Preparing an adjusted trial balance,**

5. **Preparing financial statements, and**

6. **Analyzing financial statements.**

Classify and Record Transactions

The accounting cycle begins with classifying and recording daily transactions. A **transaction** is an event that either increases or decreases an account balance. A **source document** is the proof that a transaction took place. Examples of source documents include:

- ✓ cash receipts,
- ✓ credit card receipts,
- ✓ customer invoices,
- ✓ purchase orders,
- ✓ materials invoices,
- ✓ deposit slips, and
- ✓ time cards.

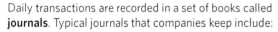

Daily transactions are recorded in a set of books called **journals**. Typical journals that companies keep include:

- ✓ **Cash receipts and sales journal:** This journal is used when cash comes in or a sale is charged to a customer.

- ✓ **Purchases journal:** This journal tracks all purchases made by the company.

- ✓ **Cash disbursements journal:** This journal is used when cash is paid out. Transactions such as loan payments and payments on vendor invoices are recorded here.

- ✓ **Payroll journal:** This journal is used to record a summary of payroll details, such as salaries and wages, deductions, and employer contributions.

- ✓ **General journal:** This journal is used for non-cash transactions.

Post Transactions

Posting is the process of transferring the transactions recorded in the journals to the appropriate accounts. An **account** is a register of value. Each account can be totaled to determine the balance. For example, cash is an asset account having a specific balance. Most companies use five basic types of accounts:

- ✓ Asset
- ✓ Liability
- ✓ Equity
- ✓ Income
- ✓ Expense

The **chart of accounts** is a numbering system that organizes these account types. A typical chart of accounts is listed below:

1000–1999: Assets

2000–2999: Liabilities

3000–3999: Equity

4000–4999: Revenue

5000–5999: Cost of Goods Sold

6000–6999: Expenses

7000–7999: Other Revenue (i.e., interest income)

8000–8999: Other Expenses (i.e., income taxes)

The accounts are located in the **general ledger**. When you post transactions, you are transferring them from the journal to the general ledger.

Prepare Trial Balance

When you tally the accounts, you prepare a **trial balance**. The trial balance is a total of all the ledger accounts.

At this point in the accounting cycle, you want to make sure the debits equal the credits.

*Understanding Debits and Credits: E*very accounting entry in the general ledger contains both a debit and a credit which must equal each other. Depending on what type of account you are dealing with, a debit or credit will either increase or decrease the account balance. The entries that increase or decrease each type of account are listed below.

Account Type	Debit	Credit
Assets	Increases	Decreases
Liabilities	Decreases	Increases
Equity	Decreases	Increases
Income	Decreases	Increases
Expenses	Increases	Decreases

For the accounts to balance, there must be a debit in one account and a credit in another. You may hear terms such as the left side or right side of the balance sheet. Something on the left side is simply a debit and the right side is a credit.

If you have any ledger account column totals that do not balance, look for math, posting, and recording errors.

Prepare Adjusted Trial Balance

There are six general types of adjusting entries:

- ✓ prepaid expense,
- ✓ accrued expense,
- ✓ accrued revenue,
- ✓ unearned revenue,
- ✓ estimated items, and
- ✓ inventory adjustment.

When you make adjusting entries, include an explanation as to why the change was made. Once adjusting entries are made, you must go back and tally the account balances where changes were made.

 Prepare Financial Statements

Now that you have posted transactions to your accounts and made adjusting entries, you can prepare your financial statements.

The three basic types of financial statements companies use are:

- ✓ **balance sheet,**
- ✓ **income statement, and**
- ✓ **statement of cash flows.**

Financial statements are tools that give insight into the financial health and activities of the company.

Balance Sheet

The balance sheet is one of the basic accounting financial statements. It gives the owner good insight into the growth and stability of the company at a particular point in time.

The balance sheet equation is comprised of assets, liabilities, and owners' equity:

Assets = Liabilities + Owners' Equity

Assets are items of value owned by the business. The cash in your bank account and other assets that can be converted into cash in less than one year are considered **current assets**. They are important because they are used to fund daily operations and can be liquidated easily.

Property and equipment (sometimes referred to as **capital** or **fixed assets**) are assets needed to carry on the business of a company and are not normally consumed in the operation of the business. Land, buildings, equipment, and furniture would all be considered fixed assets.

Other current assets consist of prepaid expenses, such as security deposits, and other miscellaneous assets, such as long-term investments.

Your company may also own **intangible assets**. Examples of these include patents, franchises, and goodwill from the acquisition of another company. It is not as easy to value these assets. Generally, the value of intangible assets is a value both parties agree to when the assets are created.

Liabilities are all debt and obligations owed by the business. Liabilities that will mature and must be paid within one year are called **current liabilities**. Trade credit is usually considered a current liability because it is a short-term debt.

Long-term liabilities are debt obligations that extend beyond one year. Examples of this type of liability include bank loans and deferred taxes.

Owners' equity is made up of the initial investment in the business, plus accumulated net profits not paid out to the owners.

Working capital can also be determined by looking at the balance sheet. The following equation is used to determine working capital.

Current Assets − Current Liabilities = Working Capital

Working capital measures the liquidity of the company's assets. Liquid assets are those that are easily converted to cash. Licensing agencies may look at working capital to determine license limitations.

The balance sheet is usually requested by potential lenders to determine credit limits. The following sample illustrates how the balance sheet equation and accounts are used in the balance sheet.

Quality Construction Company
Balance Sheet
December 31, 20XX

ASSETS

Current Assets:		
Cash	$ 1,200	
Accounts Receivable	25,200	
Total Current Assets		$ 26,400
Property and Equipment:		
Equipment	$ 53,200	
Building	120,000	
Land	75,000	
Total Property and Equipment		248,200
TOTAL ASSETS		$ 274,600

LIABILITIES AND OWNERS' EQUITY

Current Liabilities:		
Accounts Payable	$ 4,900	
Payroll Taxes Payable	3,300	
Total Current Liabilities		$ 8,200
Long-term Liabilities:		
Notes Payable	$ 6,700	
Mortgage Payable	195,000	
Total Long-term Liabilities		201,700
Owners' Equity		64,700
TOTAL LIABILITIES AND OWNERS' EQUITY		$ 274,600

Income Statement

The income statement, sometimes called the profit-and-loss statement, is a summary of the company's revenues and expenses over a given period of time.

The profit equation provides the basis for the income statement and is comprised of the following:

Income – Cost of Goods Sold = Gross Profit

Gross Profit – Expenses = Net Income

Revenues are the income received from the daily operations of the business. Most companies have only a few revenue accounts, but if you have several lines of business, you may want to create an account for each.

Expenses are the monies paid out or owed for goods or services over a given period of time. Most companies have separate accounts for the different types of expenses incurred.

Direct costs are those directly linked with a particular project. On a construction project, your direct costs might include materials, subcontractor fees, permit fees, and labor.

Operating expenses (sometimes called indirect expenses) are the general items that contribute to the cost of operating the business. These expenses can be put into two categories, **selling expenses** and **fixed overhead**. Selling expenses are the costs incurred to market the business. Fixed overhead expenses are those that cannot be linked to a specific project but are necessary for the operation of the business. For example, if you rent warehouse space to store your equipment year round, you would include this item in your bookkeeping under fixed overhead.

Tax provision expenses are the tax liabilities your company has for federal, state, and local taxes. Depending on your business structure, this section of the income statement will vary.

Net profit is the difference between revenues and expenses. Net profit directly contributes to the net worth of the company.

If net profit is on the positive side, those earnings are placed in a retained earnings or equity account.

If net profit is negative, it will reduce the net worth of the company.

The income statement is used by investors or lenders to determine the profitability of the company. The following sample illustrates how the income statement equation and accounts are used in the income statement.

Quality Construction Company
Income Statement
For the Period Ended December 31, 20XX

REVENUES:		
Construction Sales	$ 545,600	
Less Direct Labor	120,500	
Less Direct Materials	257,000	
Gross Profit		$ 168,100
EXPENSES:		
Selling Expenses:		
Advertising	$ 3,400	
Salaries - Sales	49,500	
Total Selling Expense	$ 52,900	
Administrative Expenses:		
Salaries - Office	$ 34,400	
Telephone	4,800	
Insurance Expense	29,700	
Total Administrative Expenses	$ 68,900	
Total Expenses		121,800
NET INCOME		$ 46,300

Quality Construction Company
Statement of Owners' Equity
For the Period Ended December 31, 20XX

Beginning Owners' Equity	$ 92,400
Add Net Income	46,300
Less Distributions to Owners	74,000
Ending Owners' Equity	$ 64,700

Statement of Cash Flows

The statement of cash flows summarizes your current cash position, your cash sources, and use of these funds over a given period of time. This financial statement lists changes in cash based on operating, investing, and financing activities.

The **operating activities** portion of the statement shows the performance of the company to generate a positive or negative cash flow from the operations.

The **investing activities** section lists the cash used or provided to purchase or sell revenue-producing assets.

The **financing activities** section measures the flow of cash between the owners and creditors.

If you want to finance a major project, the lender will likely want to look at your statement of cash flows. This financial statement provides good insight into the company's ability to meet its obligations. The company may appear profitable on other statements, but a lack of cash flow may indicate pending financial problems.

Notes to the Financial Statements

The notes to the financial statements contain important information that is relevant but have no specific place within the financial statement.

✓ **Accounting policies and procedures** important to the company's financial condition and results are disclosed in the notes section.

✓ Detailed information about **current and deferred income taxes** is broken down by federal, state, and local categories. The primary factors that affect the company's tax rate are described.

✓ Specific information about the assets and costs of a **pension plan and other retirement programs** are explained and indicate whether the plans are over- or underfunded.

Anything that affects the financial health of the company that cannot be reflected in the financial statements should be reported in this section.

STEP 6 — Analyze Financial Statements Using Financial Ratios

By using the basic concepts of the balance sheet and income statement, you can analyze them through financial ratios. Ratios can serve as a benchmark for the company's internal performance and as a comparison against industry averages.

Liquidity ratio

The liquidity ratio (sometimes called the **current ratio**) is calculated by dividing the current liabilities into the current assets.

Current Assets ÷ Current Liabilities = Liquidity (or Current) Ratio

The liquidity ratio determines if the company can pay its current debts. If the ratio is greater than one, the company is in a positive liquidity position. The higher the number, the better liquidity position the company has.

Quick ratio

The quick ratio (sometimes called the **acid test ratio**) is similar to the liquidity ratio. It is calculated by dividing the current liabilities into the current assets minus inventory.

(Current Assets − Inventory) ÷ Current Liabilities = Quick Ratio

A quick ratio of one or more is generally acceptable by most creditors. A higher number indicates a stronger financial position and a lower number a weaker position.

Activity Ratio

The activity ratio measures how effectively the company manages its credit. The formula for determining the average collection period is as follows:

Revenue ÷ Days in the Business Year = Sales per Day

Current Receivables ÷ Sales per Day = Average Collection Period

The company is in a better position when the average collection period is shorter (or the number is lower). This means that the company is converting credit accounts into cash faster.

Debt Ratio

The debt ratio measures the percent of total funds provided by creditors. The formula is as follows:

Total Debt ÷ Total Assets = Debt Ratio

Companies want to keep their debt ratio relatively low to avoid overextending debt.

Profitability Ratio

The profitability ratio is used to calculate the profit margin of the company. The formula is as follows:

$$\text{Net Income} \div \text{Revenues} = \text{Profit Margin}$$

The higher the profit margin percentage, the more profitably the company is performing.

Return on Total Assets Ratio

The return on total assets ratio is used to determine if the company's assets are being employed in the best manner. The formula is:

$$\text{Net Profit (after taxes)} \div \text{Total Assets} = \text{Return on Total Assets}$$

The company is in a favorable position when the percentage return on total assets is high.

Methods of Accounting

An accounting method is a set of rules used to determine when and how income and expenses are reported. There are two basic methods of accounting used to keep track of the company's income and expenses. These are:

- ✓ **Cash method**
- ✓ **Accrual method**

The primary difference between the methods is in when the transactions are recorded to your accounts.

Cash Method

Using the **cash method of accounting**, you report income in the year you receive it and deduct expenses in the year you paid them. This is the easier of the two accounting methods. Although it is a simpler method, it holds a significant disadvantage. The cash method does not match revenues with the expenses incurred related to that revenue. This gives an inaccurate picture of the company's overall financial situation.

Accrual Method

Using the **accrual method**, you recognize income when the services occur, not when you collect the money. The same principal is applied to expenses, which are recorded when they are incurred, not when you pay for them. Most construction businesses use the accrual method of accounting.

Changing Your Method of Accounting

Once you have set up your accounting method and file your first tax return, you must get IRS approval before you can change to another method. A change in accounting method not only includes a change in your overall system of accounting, but also a change in the treatment of any material item.

Contract Accounting

Most construction businesses use two tax accounting methods; one for their long-term contracts and one overall method for everything else. A long-term contract is defined as any contract that is not completed in the same year it was started.

The choice of your contract accounting method depends on:

- ✓ the type of contracts you have;
- ✓ your contracts' completion status at the end of your tax year; and
- ✓ your average annual gross receipts.

Each method discussed assumes that you use a calendar tax year from January 1 to December 31.

Completed Contract Method

Under the completed contract method, income or loss is reported in the year the contract is completed. Direct materials, labor costs, and all indirect costs associated with the contract must be allocated or capitalized to the same account as the income or loss. If the completed contract method is used for long-term contracts (contracts spanning over two calendar years), you may not allocate costs properly and you might overstate deductions.

The advantage of the completed contract method is that it normally achieves maximum deferral of taxes.

The disadvantages of the completed contract method are:

- ✓ the books and records do not show clear information on operations;
- ✓ income can be bunched into a year when a lot of jobs are completed; and
- ✓ losses on contracts are not deductible until the contracts are completed.

The completed contract method may be used only by small contractors whose average annual gross receipts do not exceed $10 million for the three tax years preceding the tax year of the contract.

Percentage of Completion Method

The percentage of completion method recognizes income as it is earned during the construction project.

The biggest advantage of using this method for long-term contracts is that it does a better job of matching revenue to the expenses incurred related to that revenue. Accurate matching of revenue to expenses gives you a better picture of your financial position.

The disadvantage of the percentage of completion method is that it relies on estimates. You are estimating the degree of completion on the project, the income and the expenses. The true numbers are not realized until the project is complete.

Percentage of completion is calculated individually by project. To determine the percentage of completion, use the following formula:

Project Costs Incurred ÷ Total Estimated Costs = Percentage of Completion

Once the percentage of completion is calculated, the cumulative earnings can be figured by using the following formula:

Percentage of Completion x Contract Amount = Cumulative Earnings

Adjustments must be made on the balance sheet for billings that are over or under the cumulative earnings. To figure the amount over or under cumulative earnings, use the following formula:

Cumulative Earnings - Amount Billed to Date = Billing Overage/Deficiency

Billings in excess of the cumulative earnings are considered a current liability. Billings less than cumulative earnings are considered a current asset.

Using these formulas, a percentage of completion worksheet example is shown below.

Project Name	Contract Amount	Estimated Cost	Project Cost to Date	Percent Complete	Cumulative Earnings	Amount Billed to Date	Billing Overage/ Deficiency
Project #1	70,000	62,350	35,500	56.94%	39,858	40,150	-292
Project #2	50,000	42,150	12,140	28.80%	14,400	13,500	900
Project #3	30,000	25,110	14,050	55.95%	16,785	15,220	1,565

Cost Comparison Method

The cost comparison method is an approach that combines the completed contract and percentage of completion methods. A 10 percent deferral election is allowed under the cost comparison method. This election allows you to defer recognized revenue on a contract until the total costs incurred equal 10 percent of the estimated contract costs. The initial project costs are capitalized and deferred until costs to date exceed 10 percent of total costs. After exceeding 10 percent, all costs incurred are treated as period costs. Revenue is also fully recognized in that period based on the level of project completion. From that point forward, revenue is calculated using the percentage of completion method until the project is finished.

Cash Management

Cash Flow

As discussed in Chapter 9, it is important to track your incoming cash and expenditures during the construction project to ensure you have enough working capital to complete the job. Balancing incoming progress payments and outgoing expenditures is important to managing the project effectively and should be a consideration when preparing your schedule.

Positive cash flow, meaning more cash is coming in than going out to pay expenses, is an important indicator of the health of your business. Without positive cash flow, your business cannot pay bills and employees. The business will eventually be unable to sustain itself and ultimately fail.

Two important aspects of maintaining a positive cash flow are collecting accounts receivable (money that is owed to your business) and billing and collecting for current projects.

Collecting Accounts Receivable: Collecting accounts receivable should be a systematic process:

✓ Correspondence should look professional, with the services rendered and amount due clearly displayed on the invoice.

✓ Follow-up invoices should be sent on a regular schedule. This will convey that you are serious about receiving prompt payment.

✓ If the account falls delinquent for more than three months, a stern letter outlining the consequences

for non-payment should accompany your follow-up invoices.

✓ If you find you are having problems collecting on accounts receivable, you may want to hire a professional collection agency.

Prompt pay and lien laws may also provide additional payment and collection tools.

Billing and Collecting for Current Projects: Prompt billing for current projects is important to receiving timely payments. Once you receive the approval for partial or final payment, you should immediately send an invoice requesting payment. The payment should clearly outline payment terms. For example, if your payment terms are "Net 30," this means that full payment of the invoice is due in 30 days. If amounts due for current projects are not collected in a prompt manner, you may run into cash flow problems.

Bad Debts: When you extend credit to your customers, this debt is recorded in your accounts receivable. Bad debts are uncollected accounts receivable. It is important to monitor accounts receivable regularly. If you notice that the amount of accounts receivable is increasing, you may need to adjust collection procedures. Bad debts affect cash flow and must be kept to a minimum.

According to IRS guidelines, a business deducts its bad debts from gross income when figuring taxable income. Bad debts may be deducted in part or in full. For more information on the specific IRS guidelines on business bad debts, refer to IRS Publication 535, Business Expenses. This publication can be downloaded from the IRS website at www.irs.gov.

Payments

Progress Payments: As discussed in Chapter 8, it is important to address the schedule of progress payments in the contract. Progress payments are partial payments made after specified phases of construction are complete.

To ensure adequate cash flow, it is important to monitor the progress payment schedule closely. You may be required to submit a partial payment estimate to the project architect or engineer prior to the payment due date. The partial payment estimate outlines the work performed and proof of materials and equipment delivery required for the next stage of construction. The architect or engineer certifies each progress payment by confirming the information in the partial payment estimate.

A retainage amount (commonly 10 percent) is usually withheld from progress payments. Retainage is released and paid out to the contractor after all final approvals are obtained at the end of a project.

Calculation of progress payments differs slightly, depending on the type of contract.

Payment for Lump Sum Contracts: Payments for lump sum contracts are calculated by the percentage of work completed. A schedule of estimated costs (sometimes called a schedule of values) is used as a basis to determine the degree of project completion.

Material and subcontractor invoices are compared against the schedule of values to support the degree of project completion.

Payment for Unit Price Contracts: Payments for unit price contracts are based on actual work units completed. The unit price payment request is more detailed and may take longer to complete, but it provides a more accurate picture of the degree of work completion.

Payment for Cost-Plus Contracts: Payments for cost-plus contracts are based on actual costs rather than a percentage of completed work. The schedule of payments should be clearly outlined in the contract. Cost-plus contracts generally include a markup in addition to costs. The payment request should include a markup proportionate to the costs. If payment estimates are required, reconciliation must be done once the actual costs occur to adjust for any amounts that fall over or under the estimate.

Final Payment: Final payment requests should include the final payment amount plus any retainages owed. Final payment is released after final inspection, acceptance by the owner, and submittal of proper documentation.

Prompt Payment Act: The Federal Prompt Payment Act ensures that federal contractors are paid in a timely manner. If late payment is made, interest penalties are charged on the amount due. Prime contractors must receive payment within 14 days after submitting a progress payment invoice. Prime contractors must pay subcontractors within seven days after receiving payment, or they must pay interest penalties.

North Carolina Prompt Pay Law: Payment guidelines for public contracts are outlined in North Carolina General Statute §143-134.1.

The following is a summary of these guidelines.

✓ **Prime Contractor Payment:** Payment to the prime contractor must be made within 45 days after completion of the project. Completion is defined as acceptance by the owner, certification by the architect, engineer or designer, or occupancy by the owner for the purpose in which the project was constructed.

✓ **Project Delays:** If the project is delayed by the fault of the contractor, the project may be occupied without payment or interest past the 45-day limit. Payment cannot be withheld because of a delay caused by another prime contractor.

✓ **Interest:** If final payment is delayed past the 45 days, the prime contractor is due 1 percent interest per month on the unpaid balance, unless a lower rate is agreed upon. Interest payments begin on the 46th day.

✓ **Subcontractor Payments**: Payment to subcontractors by the prime contractor must be made within seven days of a periodic or final payment receipt. Beginning on the eighth day, 1 percent interest per month on the unpaid balance is due.

✓ **Subcontractor Retainage:** Retainage for subcontractors cannot exceed the retainage percentage withheld from the prime contractors. Any retainage held in excess is subject to 1 percent interest per month.

Guidelines for payment of subcontractors on private projects are outlined in North Carolina General Statutes, Chapter 22C (found in Appendix L). Listed below is a summary of these guidelines.

✓ **Subcontractor Payments:** Payment to subcontractors by the prime contractor must be made within seven days of receiving a periodic or final payment.

✓ **Interest:** Beginning on the eighth day, 1 percent interest per month on the unpaid balance is due.

✓ **Grounds for Withholding Payment:** Payment may be withheld under certain conditions. These conditions include unsatisfactory job progress; defective construction not remedied; disputed work; third-party claims filed or reasonable evidence that a claim will be filed; failure of the subcontractor to make timely payments for labor, equipment, and materials; damage to the contractor or another subcontractor; reasonable evidence that the subcontract cannot be completed for the unpaid balance of the subcontract sum; or a reasonable amount for retainage not to exceed the initial percentage retained by the owner.

Petty Cash Fund

Small payments may sometimes be made without writing a check. A petty cash fund is used to make these payments. When you use the petty cash fund, it is important to document your expenditure. A voucher or petty cash disbursement slip should be completed and attached to your receipt as proof of payment.

The petty cash fund should be balanced and replenished monthly.

Equipment Records and Accounting

Options for owning, renting, and leasing equipment were discussed in Chapter 7. Equipment rates were then used to construct the equipment portion of the estimate. For accounting purposes, information on equipment must be tracked. Important information to record includes:

✓ use rate,

✓ use time,

✓ maintenance costs,

✓ repair costs, and

✓ operating costs (i.e., gas, oil, etc.).

A separate record should be prepared for each piece of equipment.

This information is also useful when analyzing the need for future equipment purchases or upgrades.

Depreciation Methods

Depreciation is the process of devaluing a fixed asset as a result of aging, wear and tear, or obsolescence. The asset is depreciated over the course of its "useful life." Depreciation is considered a non-cash expense. You can depreciate vehicles, office equipment,

buildings, and machinery. Land cannot be depreciated, because it does not "wear out" like depreciable items.

To determine the annual depreciation for an item, you must know the initial cost, how many years it will provide value for your business, and the salvage cost of the item when it is fully depreciated. There are two methods to depreciate fixed assets:

✓ **Straight line depreciation**

✓ **Accelerated depreciation**

Using **straight line depreciation**, you simply take the initial cost of the item and subtract the salvage cost. Then you take that total and divide it by the number of "useful life" years.

The calculation is as follows:

Initial Asset Cost – Salvage Cost = Depreciation Cost

Depreciation Cost ÷ Useful Life Years = Yearly Depreciation Amount

Using the **accelerated depreciation** method, the asset is depreciated at a higher rate during the early part of its useful life permitting larger tax deductions. This method is typically used for an asset that will probably be replaced before the end of its useful life. Depreciation percentages are based on the type of asset.

The **modified accelerated cost recovery system (MACRS)** is a depreciation method approved by the IRS. It allows for faster depreciation over longer periods. MACRS divides property into several different classes and takes into account the date the equipment was put in service, cost of equipment, cost recovery period, convention, and depreciation method that applies to your property. Given all these factors, a percentage rate is applied.

For further information, you may refer to the IRS website (www.irs.gov) on how to depreciate property, using MACRS and MACRS's percentage tables.

Accounting Process for Materials

As discussed in Chapter 9, purchase orders are an important project management tool. Purchase orders keep your expenses organized and document exactly what you ordered. They also facilitate the receiving process and timing of deliveries. Purchase orders help track material inventories and related expenses in the accounting system. Invoices should be matched with purchase orders to ensure that the billing is accurate.

Shipping and Delivery Expenses: In addition to the actual material costs, shipping and delivery expenses are factored into the final cost. Shipping and delivery expenses are charged in a few different ways. Two common shipping terms are:

✓ **FOB Freight Prepaid** requires the seller to pay for shipping charges.

✓ **FOB Freight Allowed** requires the buyer to pay shipping charges. A credit for the shipping amount is often given by the seller on the invoice.

It is important to understand the shipping terms ahead of time and note them on the purchase order.

Payment Terms: Payment terms depend on the payment agreement between the buyer and seller. They are generally listed on the seller's invoice. Terms can vary by seller. Listed below are some common terms you may see on your invoices.

✓ Net 10: Payment is due 10 days after receiving the invoice.

✓ Net 30: Payment is due 30 days after receiving the invoice.

✓ Net 60: Payment is due 60 days after receiving the invoice.

✓ COD: Cash payment is due on delivery.

✓ 1/10 Net 30: A 1 percent discount is given to payments received within 10 days; otherwise, payment is due 30 days after receiving the invoice.

✓ EOM: Payment is due at the end of the month.

✓ 1/10 EOM: A 1 percent discount is given to payments received by the 10th of the month following the shipment; otherwise, payment is due at the end of the month following the shipment.

Early payment discounts are a good way to cut costs. Depending on the contract arrangements, project cost savings may be given to the contractor or credited to the overall project budget.

Payroll Accounting

If you have employees, payroll distribution is done on a regular basis. Thorough payroll records are important for several reasons, such as calculating tax liabilities and tracking labor costs. The process for preparing payroll is as follows:

✓ calculate gross pay for each employee;

✓ calculate and deduct applicable taxes and other deductions;

✓ calculate net pay and issue checks; and

✓ update payroll journal.

Calculate Gross Pay

Gross pay is determined either by a salary that you set for the employee or based on an hourly wage multiplied by the number of hours worked. Salaried employees are generally paid the same amount each pay period, no matter how many hours they work. Hourly employees generally complete timecards that track the number of hours worked.

Time cards are important documentation if an unemployment benefit dispute arises. Many states require employers to keep timecards. If projects are tracked on the timecard, this information can be used for job costing purposes. The following is a sample time card.

Project Name or Number	Hours Worked								Work Completed	Supervisor Approval
	M	**Tu**	**W**	**Th**	**F**	**Sa**	**Su**	**Total**		
Total										

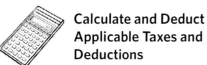

Calculate and Deduct Applicable Taxes and Deductions

Several types of taxes must be deducted from an employee's pay.

✓ **Federal income tax** is based on the information the employee provided on the W-4 form. Using IRS Publication: Circular E (sample below), you can determine the appropriate deduction.

Wage Bracket Method Tables for Income Tax Withholding

MARRIED Persons—**WEEKLY** Payroll Period

(For Wages Paid through December 2019)

And the wages are–		And the number of withholding allowances claimed is—										
At least	But less than	0	1	2	3	4	5	6	7	8	9	10
		The amount of income tax to be withheld is—										
$ 0	$227	$0	$0	$0	$0	$0	$0	$0	$0	$0	$0	$0
227	238	1	0	0	0	0	0	0	0	0	0	0
238	249	2	0	0	0	0	0	0	0	0	0	0
249	260	3	0	0	0	0	0	0	0	0	0	0
260	271	4	0	0	0	0	0	0	0	0	0	0
271	282	5	0	0	0	0	0	0	0	0	0	0
282	293	6	0	0	0	0	0	0	0	0	0	0
293	304	7	0	0	0	0	0	0	0	0	0	0
304	315	8	0	0	0	0	0	0	0	0	0	0
315	326	9	1	0	0	0	0	0	0	0	0	0
326	337	10	2	0	0	0	0	0	0	0	0	0
337	348	12	3	0	0	0	0	0	0	0	0	0
348	359	13	5	0	0	0	0	0	0	0	0	0
359	370	14	6	0	0	0	0	0	0	0	0	0
370	381	15	7	0	0	0	0	0	0	0	0	0
381	392	16	8	0	0	0	0	0	0	0	0	0
392	403	17	9	1	0	0	0	0	0	0	0	0
403	414	18	10	2	0	0	0	0	0	0	0	0
414	425	19	11	3	0	0	0	0	0	0	0	0
425	436	20	12	4	0	0	0	0	0	0	0	0
436	447	21	13	5	0	0	0	0	0	0	0	0
447	458	23	14	6	0	0	0	0	0	0	0	0
458	469	24	16	8	0	0	0	0	0	0	0	0
469	480	25	17	9	1	0	0	0	0	0	0	0
480	491	26	18	10	2	0	0	0	0	0	0	0
491	502	27	19	11	3	0	0	0	0	0	0	0
502	513	28	20	12	4	0	0	0	0	0	0	0
513	524	29	21	13	5	0	0	0	0	0	0	0
524	535	30	22	14	6	0	0	0	0	0	0	0
535	546	31	23	15	7	0	0	0	0	0	0	0
546	557	32	24	16	8	0	0	0	0	0	0	0
557	568	34	25	17	9	1	0	0	0	0	0	0
568	579	35	27	19	10	2	0	0	0	0	0	0
579	590	36	28	20	12	3	0	0	0	0	0	0
590	601	37	29	21	13	5	0	0	0	0	0	0
601	612	38	30	22	14	6	0	0	0	0	0	0
612	623	39	31	23	15	7	0	0	0	0	0	0
623	634	41	32	24	16	8	0	0	0	0	0	0
634	645	42	33	25	17	9	1	0	0	0	0	0
645	656	43	34	26	18	10	2	0	0	0	0	0
656	667	45	35	27	19	11	3	0	0	0	0	0
667	678	46	36	28	20	12	4	0	0	0	0	0
678	689	47	38	30	21	13	5	0	0	0	0	0
689	700	49	39	31	23	14	6	0	0	0	0	0
700	711	50	40	32	24	16	7	0	0	0	0	0
711	722	51	42	33	25	17	9	0	0	0	0	0
722	733	53	43	34	26	18	10	2	0	0	0	0
733	744	54	44	35	27	19	11	3	0	0	0	0
744	755	55	46	36	28	20	12	4	0	0	0	0
755	766	57	47	37	29	21	13	5	0	0	0	0
766	777	58	48	39	30	22	14	6	0	0	0	0
777	788	59	50	40	31	23	15	7	0	0	0	0
788	799	61	51	41	32	24	16	8	0	0	0	0
799	810	62	52	42	34	25	17	9	1	0	0	0
810	821	63	53	44	35	27	18	10	2	0	0	0
821	832	64	55	45	36	28	20	11	3	0	0	0
832	843	66	56	46	37	29	21	13	5	0	0	0
843	854	67	57	48	38	30	22	14	6	0	0	0
854	865	68	59	49	39	31	23	15	7	0	0	0
865	876	70	60	50	41	32	24	16	8	0	0	0
876	887	71	61	52	42	33	25	17	9	1	0	0
887	898	72	63	53	43	34	26	18	10	2	0	0
898	909	74	64	54	45	35	27	19	11	3	0	0
909	920	75	65	56	46	36	28	20	12	4	0	0
920	931	76	67	57	47	38	29	21	13	5	0	0
931	942	78	68	58	49	39	31	22	14	6	0	0
942	953	79	69	60	50	40	32	24	16	7	0	0
953	964	80	71	61	51	42	33	25	17	9	0	0
964	975	82	72	62	53	43	34	26	18	10	2	0
975	986	83	73	64	54	44	35	27	19	11	3	0

Wage Bracket Method Tables for Income Tax Withholding

MARRIED Persons—WEEKLY Payroll Period

(For Wages Paid through December 2019)

And the wages are—		And the number of withholding allowances claimed is—										
At least	But less than	0	1	2	3	4	5	6	7	8	9	10
		The amount of income tax to be withheld is—										
986	997	84	75	65	55	46	36	28	20	12	4	0
997	1,008	86	76	66	57	47	37	29	21	13	5	0
1,008	1,019	87	77	68	58	48	38	30	22	14	6	0
1,019	1,030	88	79	69	59	49	40	31	23	15	7	0
1,030	1,041	90	80	70	60	51	41	32	24	16	8	0
1,041	1,052	91	81	72	62	52	42	33	25	17	9	1
1,052	1,063	92	83	73	63	53	44	35	27	18	10	2
1,063	1,074	94	84	74	64	55	45	36	28	20	11	3
1,074	1,085	95	85	75	66	56	46	37	29	21	13	4
1,085	1,096	96	86	77	67	57	48	38	30	22	14	6
1,096	1,107	97	88	78	68	59	49	39	31	23	15	7
1,107	1,118	99	89	79	70	60	50	41	32	24	16	8
1,118	1,129	100	90	81	71	61	52	42	33	25	17	9
1,129	1,140	101	92	82	72	63	53	43	34	26	18	10
1,140	1,151	103	93	83	74	64	54	45	35	27	19	11
1,151	1,162	104	94	85	75	65	56	46	36	28	20	12
1,162	1,173	105	96	86	76	67	57	47	38	29	21	13
1,173	1,184	107	97	87	78	68	58	49	39	31	22	14
1,184	1,195	108	98	89	79	69	60	50	40	32	24	15
1,195	1,206	109	100	90	80	71	61	51	42	33	25	17
1,206	1,217	111	101	91	82	72	62	53	43	34	26	18
1,217	1,228	112	102	93	83	73	64	54	44	35	27	19
1,228	1,239	113	104	94	84	75	65	55	45	36	28	20
1,239	1,250	115	105	95	86	76	66	56	47	37	29	21
1,250	1,261	116	106	97	87	77	68	58	48	38	30	22
1,261	1,272	117	108	98	88	79	69	59	49	40	31	23
1,272	1,283	119	109	99	90	80	70	60	51	41	32	24
1,283	1,294	120	110	101	91	81	71	62	52	42	33	25
1,294	1,305	121	112	102	92	82	73	63	53	44	35	26
1,305	1,316	123	113	103	93	84	74	64	55	45	36	28
1,316	1,327	124	114	105	95	85	75	66	56	46	37	29
1,327	1,338	125	116	106	96	86	77	67	57	48	38	30
1,338	1,349	127	117	107	97	88	78	68	59	49	39	31
1,349	1,360	128	118	108	99	89	79	70	60	50	41	32
1,360	1,371	129	119	110	100	90	81	71	61	52	42	33
1,371	1,382	130	121	111	101	92	82	72	63	53	43	34
1,382	1,393	132	122	112	103	93	83	74	64	54	45	35
1,393	1,404	133	123	114	104	94	85	75	65	56	46	36
1,404	1,415	134	125	115	105	96	86	76	67	57	47	38
1,415	1,426	136	126	116	107	97	87	78	68	58	49	39
1,426	1,437	137	127	118	108	98	89	79	69	60	50	40
1,437	1,448	138	129	119	109	100	90	80	71	61	51	41
1,448	1,459	140	130	120	111	101	91	82	72	62	52	43
1,459	1,470	141	131	122	112	102	93	83	73	64	54	44
1,470	1,481	142	133	123	113	104	94	84	75	65	55	45
1,481	1,492	144	134	124	115	105	95	86	76	66	56	47
1,492	1,503	145	135	126	116	106	97	87	77	67	58	48
1,503	1,514	146	137	127	117	108	98	88	78	69	59	49
1,514	1,525	148	138	128	119	109	99	89	80	70	60	51
1,525	1,536	149	139	130	120	110	101	91	81	71	62	52
1,536	1,547	150	141	131	121	112	102	92	82	73	63	53
1,547	1,558	152	142	132	123	113	103	93	84	74	64	55
1,558	1,569	153	143	134	124	114	104	95	85	75	66	56
1,569	1,580	154	145	135	125	115	106	96	86	77	67	57
1,580	1,591	156	146	136	126	117	107	97	88	78	68	59
1,591	1,602	157	147	138	128	118	108	99	89	79	70	60
1,602	1,613	158	149	139	129	119	110	100	90	81	71	61
1,613	1,624	160	150	140	130	121	111	101	92	82	72	63
1,624	1,635	161	151	141	132	122	112	103	93	83	74	64
1,635	1,646	162	152	143	133	123	114	104	94	85	75	65
1,646	1,657	163	154	144	134	125	115	105	96	86	76	67
1,657	1,668	165	155	145	136	126	116	107	97	87	78	68
1,668	1,679	166	156	147	137	127	118	108	98	89	79	69
1,679	1,690	167	158	148	138	129	119	109	100	90	80	71
1,690	1,701	169	159	149	140	130	120	111	101	91	82	72
1,701	1,711	170	160	151	141	131	122	112	102	92	83	73

1,711 and over   Use Table 1(b) for a MARRIED person on page 46. Also see the instructions on page 44.

✓ **Social Security tax** is calculated at the current prevailing rate. The current tax rate is available online at www.ssa.gov. Employers must pay in an equal amount of Social Security tax but cannot deduct that amount from the employee's payroll.

✓ **Medicare tax** is calculated at the rate of 1.45 percent of gross pay. Employers must pay in an equal amount of Medicare tax but cannot deduct that amount from the employee's payroll.

✓ **State income tax** should be calculated as it applies to each individual state.

✓ **Other deductions** might include an employee's contribution for medical insurance, 401K, life insurance, etc.

Reporting of payroll taxes is covered in Chapter 15, Tax Basics.

Calculate Net Pay and Issue Checks

Net pay is the payroll amount the employee receives after deductions are taken. Net pay is calculated as:

Gross Pay – Taxes & Deductions = Net Pay

Employees should receive a statement of earnings with their paycheck. The statement of earnings shows how the net pay was calculated. The following is a sample statement of earnings.

Earnings				Current	Year to Date
Description	Rate	Hours	Overtime		
			Total Earnings		
			Taxes		
Employee Name:			Federal Withholding		
			Social Security		
Employee ID:			Medicare		
Pay Period:			State Withholding		
Check Date:			Insurance Deductions		
			Total Deductions		
			Net Pay		

Update Payroll Journal

Once checks are issued, the payroll journal must be updated to reflect the new account balance. The payroll journal should contain the same information as the employee statement of earnings. This topic is discussed in the previous section. This information is important to calculating your employer tax liabilities. Instructions on how to pay in employer taxes are covered in Chapter 15, Tax Basics.

Technology Solutions for Accounting

There are many accounting software programs on the market that can help make the accounting process easier.

As with all software, you still need to know the fundamentals, but it will help streamline the process and improve accuracy.

Accounting software can automate the process of posting transactions, creating financial statements, invoicing customers, creating purchase orders, and much more. Think of accounting software as an investment to make you more analytical and help you think strategically about your business.

When choosing the right software, consider what your needs are and how the technology can grow with your company. There are many options. You may want to look at programs that integrate job cost analysis with accounting that have been developed specifically for the construction industry.

Final Inspection...

Bookkeeping: The first step of the accounting process is bookkeeping. Bookkeeping is the accurate recording of all financial transactions that occur in the business.

The Accounting Cycle: The accounting cycle is a process that happens each reporting period, which starts with recording financial transactions and goes through analyzing financial statements.

Methods of Accounting: Cash and accrual are the two main methods of accounting. The primary difference between the two methods is the timing of when you record the transactions to your accounts.

Contract Accounting: The methods for contract accounting include completed contract, percentage of completion, and cost comparison.

Cash Management: Positive cash flow is an important indicator to the health of your business. Collecting on accounts receivable and billing and collecting on current accounts are important to the cash management process.

Equipment Records and Accounting: Depreciation is the process of devaluing a fixed asset as a result of aging, wear and tear, or obsolescence. The two primary methods of depreciation are straight line and accelerated.

Accounting Process for Materials: Purchase orders help track material inventories and related expenses in the accounting system. Invoices should be matched with purchase orders to ensure that the billing is accurate.

Payroll Accounting: Thorough payroll records are important for such reasons as calculating tax liabilities and tracking labor costs.

Technology Solutions for Accounting: Accounting software can automate the process of posting transactions, creating financial statements, invoicing customers, creating purchase orders, and much more.

Supplemental Forms

Supplemental forms and links are available at **NASCLAforms.org** using access code **NC129354**.

Balance Sheet	Example featured earlier in the chapter that can be modified in Excel
Income Statement	Example featured earlier in the chapter that can be modified in Excel
Time Card	Sample featured earlier in the chapter to track employee time
Earnings Statement	Sample featured earlier in the chapter as a summary to the employee's earnings

Chapter 15
TAX BASICS

Employer Identification Number

Before you become an employer and hire employees, you need a Federal Employer Identification Number (EIN) which is also referred to as a taxpayer identification number.

The only entities that do not need an EIN are:

✓ Sole proprietorships that have no employees and file no excise or pension tax returns; and

✓ LLCs with a single owner (where the owner will file employment tax returns).

In these instances, the owner uses his or her social security number as the taxpayer identification number.

All other types of business entities, including partnerships, are required to obtain an EIN.

The EIN is a 9-digit number that the IRS issues. The digits are arranged as follows: 00-0000000. It is used to identify the tax accounts of employers and certain others who have no employees. Use your EIN on all items you send to the Internal Revenue Service (IRS) and Social Security Administration (SSA).

There are several ways to obtain an EIN through the Internal Revenue Service (IRS).

✓ Call the Business and Specialty Tax Line at (800) 829-4933.

✓ Fax the completed Form SS-4 application to the fax number designated for your state.

✓ Mail the completed Form SS-4 application.

✓ Apply online at www.irs.gov.

Federal Business Taxes

The form of business you operate determines what taxes you must pay and how you pay them. The following are three general types of business taxes that you may be responsible for.

✓ **Income tax**

✓ **Self-employment tax**

✓ **Employment taxes**

The following table lists the tax responsibilities by business entity type and the corresponding forms to file with the IRS.

Summary of Federal Tax Forms

IF you are a...	Then you may be liable for...	Use Form...
Sole proprietor	Income tax	1040 and Schedule C [1] or C–EZ
	Self-employment tax	1040 and Schedule SE
	Estimated tax	1040–ES
	Employment taxes:	
	• Social security and Medicare taxes and income tax withholding	941
	• Federal unemployment (FUTA) tax	940 or 940–EZ
	• Depositing employment taxes	8109 [2]
	Excise taxes	See *Excise Taxes*
Partnership	Annual return of income	1065
	Employment taxes	Same as sole proprietor
	Excise taxes	See *Excise Taxes*
Partner in a partnership (individual)	Income tax	1040 and Schedule E [3]
	Self-employment tax	1040 and Schedule SE
	Estimated tax	1040–ES
Corporation or S corporation	Income tax	1120 or 1120–A (corporation) [3] 1120S (S corporation) [3]
	Estimated tax	1120–W (corporation only) and 8109 [2]
	Employment taxes	Same as sole proprietor
	Excise taxes	See *Excise Taxes*
S corporation shareholder	Income tax	1040 and Schedule E [3]
	Estimated tax	1040–ES

[1] File a separate schedule for each business.

[2] Do not use if you deposit taxes electronically.

[3] Various other schedules may be needed.

Income Tax

All businesses except partnerships must file an annual income tax return. Partnerships file an information return. The form you use depends on how your business is organized.

Estimated Tax

The federal income tax is a "pay-as-you-go" tax. You must pay the tax as you earn or receive income during the year. If you do not pay your tax through withholding, or do not pay enough tax that way, you might owe estimated tax. If you are not required to make estimated tax payments, you pay any tax due when you file your return.

Sole proprietors, partners, and S corporation shareholders generally have to make estimated tax payments if expected owed tax is $1,000 or more when the income tax return is filed. Form 1040-ES, Estimated Tax for Individuals, is available through the IRS to figure and pay estimated tax.

Corporations generally have to make estimated tax payments if expected owed tax is $500 or more when the income tax return is filed. Form 1120-W, Estimated Tax for Corporations, is available through the IRS to figure the estimated tax. You must deposit the payments electronically, through the mail, or delivery with a payment coupon.

Self-Employment Tax

Self-employment tax (SE tax) is a social security and Medicare tax primarily for individuals who work for themselves. Your payments of SE tax contribute to your coverage under the social security system. Social security coverage provides you with retirement benefits, disability benefits, survivor benefits, and hospital insurance (Medicare) benefits.

You must pay SE tax and file Schedule SE (Form 1040) if your net earnings from self-employment were $400 or more.

You must also pay SE tax on your share of certain partnership income and your guaranteed payments.

A Word About Deductible Expenses...

As defined by the IRS, to be deductible, a business expense must be both ordinary and necessary. An ordinary expense is one that is common and accepted in your industry. A necessary expense is one that is helpful and appropriate for your trade or business.

It is important to distinguish a business expense from a personal expense. Personal expenses would include living or family expenses which would not be considered deductible business expenses. A deductible business expense would include:

✓ Expenses used to figure cost of goods sold, such as cost of product, storage, direct labor, and project overhead; and

✓ Capital expenses, such as business assets and improvements (Although you generally cannot take a current deduction for a capital expense, you may be able to recover the amount you spend through depreciation, amortization, or depletion. These recovery methods allow you to deduct part of your cost each year.)

Federal Employment Taxes

When you have employees, you have certain employment tax responsibilities and forms you must file. Most employers must withhold (except FUTA), deposit, report and pay the following taxes:

✓ **Social security and Medicare taxes (FICA)**
✓ **Federal income tax withholding**
✓ **Federal unemployment (FUTA) tax**

Keep all records of employment taxes for at least four years.

Circular E

The IRS Publication Circular E: Employer's Tax Guide is a comprehensive reference providing thorough instructions on calculating, withholding and depositing employee taxes. The Circular E is found on the IRS website at www.irs.gov.

Social Security and Medicare Taxes (FICA)

 Social security and Medicare taxes pay for benefits that workers and families receive under the Federal Insurance Contributions Act (FICA). Social security tax pays for benefits under the old-age, survivors, and disability insurance part of FICA. Medicare tax pays for benefits under the hospital insurance part of FICA. Medicare is a part of the Social Security Program that provides hospital and medical insurance coverage to persons age 65 and over and those who have permanent kidney failure, or end stage renal disease, and people with other disabilities.

Social Security and Medicare tax is calculated at the current prevailing rate. The current tax rate is available online at www.ssa.gov.

Federal Income Tax Withholding

You generally must withhold federal income tax from your employees' wages. To figure how much to withhold from each wage payment, use the employee's form W-4, Employee's Withholding Allowance Certificate, and the methods described in the previous chapter. The W-4 deductions do not expire unless the employee gives you a new one or if the employee is claiming a tax exemption. A new W-4 form must be completed by February 15 each year from employees claiming a tax withholding exemption.

Form W-2: W-2, Wage and Tax Statement summarizes the employee's previous year's wages and withholding amounts. All employees must be furnished copies of the form W-2 by January 31 for the previous year's wages. Employees should receive copies B, C, and 2.

If employment ends before the end of the year, the W-2 form can be given to the employee at any time but no later than January 31. If an employee asks for the W-2 form, you must furnish copies within 30 days of the request or 30 days of the final payment, whichever is later.

Employers must send Copy A of the W-2 form with the entire page of the W-3 form to the Social Security Administration (SSA) by the last day of February (or last day of March if you file electronically). Send the forms to:

Social Security Administration
Data Operations Center
Wilkes-Barre, Pennsylvania 18769-0001

Deposit Schedule

There are three deposit schedules, monthly, semiweekly and daily, for determining when you deposit social security, Medicare and withheld income taxes. Prior to the beginning of the calendar year, you must determine which schedule you are required to use.

You are a monthly schedule depositor if your total payroll tax liability for the previous four quarters (July to June) was $50,000 or less. Payments are due on the fifteenth day of the following month after the payments were made. During your first year of business, you are a monthly schedule depositor.

If your total payroll tax liability from the previous four quarters (July to June) is greater than $50,000, you are a semiweekly schedule depositor. The semiweekly deposit schedule depends on your payroll date.

If your payday is on...	Then your deposit date is...
Wednesday, Thursday and/or Friday	Wednesday
Saturday, Sunday, Monday and/or Tuesday	Friday

If your accumulated tax liability is $100,000 or more on any day during a deposit period, you must deposit it on the next banking day. If you are a monthly schedule depositor and accumulate a $100,000 tax liability on any day, you automatically become a semiweekly depositor.

Form 941: If you report less than $2,500 for the quarter, you can use the IRS Form 941, Quarterly Employer's Tax Return to make payments by the due date of the return. If your tax obligation exceeds $2,500 for the quarter, you are subject to payments according to a deposit schedule.

Federal Unemployment Tax (FUTA)

The federal unemployment tax is part of the federal and state program under the Federal Unemployment Tax Act (FUTA) that pays unemployment compensation to workers who lose their jobs.

You report and pay FUTA tax separately from social security and Medicare taxes and withheld income tax. Employers are responsible for FUTA and cannot withhold this amount from the employees' payroll.

You are generally liable for both state and federal unemployment taxes if:

✓ you pay wages to employees totaling $1,500, or more, in any quarter of a calendar year, or

✓ you had at least one employee during any day of a week during 20 weeks in a calendar year, regardless of whether or not the weeks were consecutive.

Calculating FUTA: The FUTA base and tax rate is calculated at the current prevailing rate. Current tax information is available online at www.irs.gov. Employers who pay the state unemployment tax, on a timely basis, will receive an offset credit to the federal tax. State tax rates are based on requirements of state law.

Deposit Requirements: For deposit purposes, figure FUTA tax quarterly. If your FUTA tax liability is less than $500, you are not required to deposit the tax. Instead, carry it forward and add it to the liability figured in the next quarter to see if you must make a deposit. Use the following schedule to determine when to deposit FUTA taxes.

Quarter	Ending	Due Date
Jan-Feb-Mar	March 31	April 30
Apr-May-June	June 30	July 31
July-Aug-Sept	Sept. 30	Oct. 31
Oct-Nov-Dec	Dec. 31	Jan. 31

Form 940: Report FUTA taxes on Form 940, Employer's Annual Federal Unemployment (FUTA) Tax Return or if you qualify, you can use the simpler Form 940-EZ instead.

Penalties

Accurate and prompt deposits are required to avoid penalties which can range from 2 percent to 100 percent of your tax liability.

Penalties may apply if:

✓ you do not make payroll tax deposits on time;

✓ make deposits for less than the required amount; or

✓ do not use the Electronic Federal Tax Payment System (EFTPS) when required.

These penalties are as follows:

2%	Deposits made 1-5 days late.
5%	Deposits made 6-15 days late.
10%	Deposits made more than 16 days late. Also applies to amounts paid within 10 days of the date of the first notice the IRS sent asking for the tax due.
10%	Deposits made at an unauthorized financial institution, paid directly to the IRS, or paid with your tax return.
10%	Amounts subject to electronic deposit requirements but not deposited using EFTPS.
15%	Amounts still unpaid more than 10 days after the date of the first notice that the IRS sent asking for the tax due or the day on which you received notice and demand for immediate payment, whichever is earlier.
100%	Failure to pay "trust fund" taxes defined as withheld income, social security and Medicare taxes. The amount of the penalty is equal to the unpaid balance of the trust fund tax.

Information Returns – 1099-MISC

You may be required to file information returns to report certain types of payments made during the year to persons not treated as employees. Form 1099-MISC, Miscellaneous Income may be used to report payments of $600 or more to independent contractors. Form 1099-MISC must be filed by January 31 for the prior year's payments. Form 1096, Annual Summary and Transmittal of U.S. Information Returns, is used to transmit 1099 forms to the IRS. Form 1096 is due by February 28 for the previous year's 1099s.

Tax Calendar

Listed below are key employment tax deadlines as outlined in the IRS Publication Circular E. IRS Publication 509-Tax Calendar is also a good resource to keep track of other various tax due dates including income and employment taxes.

By January 31	Furnish Form W-2, Wage and Tax Statement to All Employees
	Furnish Form 1099 to Each Other Payee (for example, independent contractors with payments of $600 or more)
	File Form 940 or 940-EZ, Employer's Annual Federal Unemployment Tax (FUTA) Return
	File Form 945, Annual Return of Withheld Federal Income Tax
By February 15	Request a New W-4 Form from Employees Claiming a Tax Withholding Exemption
On February 16	Exempt Forms W-4 Expire
By February 28	File Copy A of All Forms 1099 with Form 1096, Annual Summary and Transmittal of U.S. Information Returns with the IRS
	File Copy A of W-2 Form, Wage and Tax Statement with W-3 Form, Transmittal of Wage and Tax Statements with the Social Security Administration
By March 31	File Electronic Forms 1099 and 8027 with IRS
	File Electronic W-2 Forms with the Social Security Administration
By April 30, July 31, October 31, and January 31	Deposit FUTA Taxes
	File Form 941, Employer's Quarterly Federal Tax Return and deposit any undeposited income, social security and Medicare taxes
Before December 1	Remind Employees to Submit New W-4 Forms if withholding allowances have changed

North Carolina State Tax Specifics

The North Carolina Department of Revenue is responsible for the administration of tax programs in the state. Activities include issuing sales tax licenses, assigning payroll and sales tax account numbers, and collecting various taxes. The department can be reached at the following address:

State of North Carolina
Department of Revenue
P.O. Box 25000
Raleigh, North Carolina 27640-0640

General Information:(877) 252-3052
Forms: (877) 252-3052

Website: www.ncdor.gov

The website contains many of the forms needed to conduct business with the department. Most of the forms include instructions to assist you.

Corporate Income Tax

Corporate Income Tax: The corporate income tax rate in North Carolina is 2.5 percent. Corporations with a taxable base in North Carolina and at least one other state are allowed to apportion their income. Apportionment is based on several factors, including a sales formula and property and payroll ratios.

Tax Credits: North Carolina provides several credits for new and expanding businesses that may be taken against corporate income tax. It is best to consult a tax professional when determining which credits apply to your business.

Estimated Tax: A declaration of estimated tax must be filed by a corporation for each taxable year in which it can reasonably expect a state income tax liability of $500 or more.

LLCs: An LLC is subject to taxation as a partnership or corporation depending on how it is classified for federal income tax purposes.

Franchise Tax

The franchise tax rate in North Carolina is $1.50 per $1,000. The minimum franchise tax is $35. Franchise tax is levied on the largest of 3 alternative tax bases. These bases are:

✓ the amount of the capital stock, surplus, and undivided profits apportionable to the state;

✓ 55 percent of the appraised value of property in the state subject to local taxation; or

✓ the book value of real and tangible personal property in the state less any debt outstanding which was created to acquire or improve the property.

Sales and Use Tax

Most property, such as construction materials and equipment rental and purchase, is subject to the 4.75 percent state and 2 percent local rate of tax (2.25% in Alexander, Buncombe, Cabarrus, Catawba, Cumberland, Duplin, Durham, Halifax, Haywood, Hertford, Lee, Martin, Montgomery, New Hanover, Onslow, Orange, Pitt, Randolph, Robeson, Rowan, Sampson, Surry, and Wilkes counties) for a combined 6.75 percent rate (7 percent in Alexander, Buncombe, Cabarrus, Catawba, Cumberland, Duplin, Durham, Halifax, Haywood, Hertford, Lee, Martin, Montgomery, New Hanover, Onslow, Orange, Pitt, Randolph, Robeson, Rowan, Sampson, Surry, and Wilkes counties). Sales tax is generally not due on services and is not charged to the final construction project.

Withholding Tax

North Carolina requires withholding from:

✓ wages;

✓ prizes;

✓ royalties;

✓ winnings;

✓ nonresident contractors on contracts exceeding $10,000;

✓ rental payments made to nonresidents who own five or more residential units or one or more commercial properties in North Carolina; and

✓ net proceeds going to nonresident sellers of real estate and associated tangible personal property located in North Carolina.

To register with the North Carolina Department of Revenue to withhold North Carolina income tax, use Form NC-BR.

North Carolina has adopted the use of the federal form W-4; therefore, it is not required that an employee file a separate form for state withholding purposes.

The withholding rate for North Carolina is 5.35 percent. Employers need a Withholding Booklet to calculate the amount. This booklet contains tax tables similar to the Circular E used to calculate federal withholding.

Withholding tax payments can be made online at the Department of Revenue website at www.ncdor.gov. Withholding payment due dates for North Carolina follow the federal withholding calendar.

Employers are required to withhold individual state income tax from the wages and salaries of their employees.

Registering to Withhold Tax: You must submit a completed business registration application, Form AS/RP1, to obtain a withholding tax identification number. After your application is processed, the Department of Revenue will mail information concerning your North Carolina withholding tax account number and pre-printed forms on which to report and submit your payment of the tax withheld.

Determining Withholding Amounts: Each employee must furnish you with a signed North Carolina Employee's Withholding Allowance Certificate, Form NC-4. You should use these forms along with the tax tables found in the publication, NC-30, to determine how much income tax should be withheld from each employee's paycheck.

Filing Withholding Tax Returns: Withholding tax returns are filed on a quarterly, monthly, or semi-weekly basis depending on the average amount of tax you withhold each month.

If you withhold an average of less than $250 from employee wages each month, you should file a return and pay the withheld taxes on a quarterly basis. The tax is due the last day of the month following the end of the quarter.

If you withhold an average of at least $250 but less than $2,000 from employee wages each month, you should file a return and pay the withheld taxes on a monthly basis. This tax is due on the fifteenth of the following month.

The December report is due by January 31 of the following year.

If you withhold an average of at least $2,000 or more from employee wages each month, you should file a return and pay the withheld taxes at the same time you are required to file the reports and pay the tax withheld on the same wages for federal income tax purposes. If payroll is made on Saturday, Sunday, Monday or Tuesday, it is due the following Friday of the same week. If payroll is made on Wednesday, Thursday, or Friday, it is due the following Wednesday.

Penalties: There is a 10 percent penalty for late payment of the tax due. There is also a penalty of 5 percent per month, with a maximum of 25 percent, for failure to file the report when due.

Income Tax Withholding Tables and Instructions: Publication NC-30 outlines the withholding process in detail and includes the withholding tables needed to withhold the proper amounts for each payroll. Listed below are key due dates included in the NC-30 publication.

At the Time a New Employee is Hired	Obtain Form NC-4, N.C. Employee's Withholding Allowance Certificate from each new employee when hired.
	Withhold North Carolina income tax upon each payment of wages to the employee.
On or Before January 31st and At the End of Employment	Give each employee a W-2, Wage and Tax Statement.
	Give each nonresident who received non-wage compensation for personal services performed in North Carolina a NC-1099PS, Personal Services Income Paid to a Nonresident, or Federal Form 1099-MISC.
	Give each recipient of distributions a completed Form 1099-R.

By February 15th	Ask for a new Form NC-4, Employee's Withholding Allowance Certificate from each employee who claimed total exemption from withholding during the prior year.
On February 16th	Begin withholding for each employee who previously claimed exemption from withholding but has not given you a Form NC-4 for the current year. If the new employee does not give you a new Form NC-4, withhold tax as if the employee is single with zero withholding allowances.
On or Before February 28th (Feb. 29th if a leap year)	File Annual Withholding Reconciliation (Form NC-3 or NC 3M) together with all N.C. Department of Revenue copies (copy 1) of the forms W-2, 1099-MISC, 1099-R or Form 1099PS.
Due Dates for Quarterly Returns	File Form NC-5, Withholding Return, and payment by the last day of the month following the end of the calendar quarter.
Due Dates for Monthly Returns	File Form NC-5, Withholding Return and payment by the 15th day of the month following the month in which the tax was withheld. The return and payment for the month of December are due by January 31.
Due Dates for Semiweekly Tax Payments	Pay tax with Form NC-5P, Withholding Payment Voucher, at the same time as required for federal purposes. Each time you are required to deposit federal employment taxes, you must remit North Carolina withholding. If you withhold $100,000 or more during any deposit period, you are required to deposit federal taxes by the next banking day. North Carolina did not adopt this rule and taxes are only submitted on or before the normal federal semiweekly schedule.
On or Before the Last Day of the Month Following the Quarter	File Form NC-5Q, North Carolina Quarterly Income Tax Withholding Return which reconciles the tax paid for the quarter against the actual tax withheld for the quarter for semiweekly filers.

Final Inspection...

Employer Identification Number: An employer identification number is used to identify the tax accounts of employers and certain others who have no employees.

Federal Business Taxes: The form of business you operate determines what taxes you must pay and how you pay them.

Summary of Federal Tax Forms: You must file the specific federal tax forms that correspond to your business entity type.

Income Tax: All businesses except partnerships must file an annual income tax return. Partnerships file an information return.

Self-Employment Tax: Self-employment tax (SE tax) is a social security and Medicare tax primarily for individuals who work for themselves.

Federal Employment Taxes: Federal employment taxes include social security and Medicare (FICA), federal income tax withholding, and federal unemployment tax (FUTA).

Penalties: Accurate and prompt deposits are required to avoid penalties which can range from 2 percent to 100 percent of your tax liability.

Information Returns-1099 MISC: Form 1099-MISC, Miscellaneous Income may be used to report payments of $600 or more to independent contractors.

Tax Calendar: IRS Publication Circular E and Publication 509 provide tax calendars for various taxes that may apply to your business.

North Carolina State Tax Specifics: Corporate income, franchise, sales and use, and withholding are a few state taxes that may apply to your business.

Supplemental Publications and Forms

Supplemental forms and links are available at **NASCLAforms.org** using access code **SCR129354**.

IRS Publication 334	Tax Guide for Small Business
IRS Publication 463	Travel, Entertainment and Gift Expenses
IRS Publication 505	Tax Withholding and Estimated Tax
IRS Publication 509	General Tax Calendar
IRS Publication 535	Business Expenses
IRS Publication 538	Accounting Periods and Methods
IRS Publication 541	Tax Information on Partnerships
IRS Publication 542	Tax Information on Corporations
IRS Publication 583	Taxpayers Starting a Business
IRS Publication 587	Business Use of Your Home
IRS Publication 946	How to Begin Depreciating Your Property
IRS Publication 1544	Reporting Cash Payments of Over $10,000
IRS Form W-2	Wage and Tax Statement
IRS Form W-3	Tax Reconciliation
IRS Form W-4	Employee Withholding
IRS Form SS-4	Application for Employer Identification Number

IRS Form 940	Employer Annual Federal Unemployment Tax Return
IRS Form 941	Employer's Quarterly Federal Tax Return
IRS Form 1040	U.S. Individual Income Tax Return
IRS Schedule C	Profit or Loss from Business
IRS Schedule-EZ	Net Profit from Business
IRS Schedule SE	Self-Employment Tax
IRS Form 1040-ES	Estimated Tax for Individuals
IRS Form 1065	U.S. Partnership Return of Income Schedule K-1, Partner's Share of Income, Credits, Deductions, etc.
IRS Form 1120	U.S. Corporation Income Tax Return
IRS Form 1120S	U.S. Income Tax Return for an S Corporation Schedule K-1
IRS Form 4562	Depreciation and Amortization
IRS Form 8300	Report of Cash Payments over $10,000 Received in a Trade or Business
Employer's Tax Guide (Circular E)	Publication used to determine federal income tax withholding for employees

Department of the Treasury
Internal Revenue Service

Publication 15
Cat. No. 10000W

(Circular E), Employer's Tax Guide

For use in **2019**

Get forms and other information faster and easier at:
- *IRS.gov* (English)
- *IRS.gov/Spanish* (Español)
- *IRS.gov/Chinese* (中文)
- *IRS.gov/Korean* (한국어)
- *IRS.gov/Russian* (Русский)
- *IRS.gov/Vietnamese* (TiếngViệt)

Dec 17, 2018

Contents

Future Developments

For the latest information about developments related to Pub. 15, such as legislation enacted after it was published, go to *IRS.gov/Pub15*.

What's New

Social security and Medicare tax for 2019. The social security tax rate is 6.2% each for the employee and employer, unchanged from 2018. The social security wage base limit is $132,900.

The Medicare tax rate is 1.45% each for the employee and employer, unchanged from 2018. There is no wage base limit for Medicare tax.

Social security and Medicare taxes apply to the wages of household workers you pay $2,100 or more in cash wages for 2019. Social security and Medicare taxes apply to election workers who are paid $1,800 or more in cash or an equivalent form of compensation in 2019.

2019 withholding tables. This publication includes the 2019 Percentage Method Tables and Wage Bracket Tables for Income Tax Withholding; see section 17.

2019 federal income tax withholding. Notice 2018-92, 2018-51 I.R.B. 1038, available at *IRS.gov/irb/ 2018-51 IRB#NOT-2018-92*, provides that until April 30, 2019, an employee who has a reduction in a claimed number of withholding allowances solely due to changes from the new tax legislation enacted on December 22, 2017 (P.L. 115-97, Tax Cuts and Jobs Act), isn't required to give his or her employer a new Form W-4 until May 10, 2019 (10 days after April 30, 2019). However, if an employee no longer reasonably expects to be entitled to a claimed number of withholding allowances because of a change in personal circumstances not solely related to changes made by P.L. 115-97 (for example, an employee's child no longer qualifies as the employee's dependent because of the child's change in residence), the employee must furnish his or her employer a new Form W-4 within 10 days after the change. In addition, if an employee who claimed married filing status on Form W-4 becomes divorced from his or her spouse, the employee must furnish his or her employer a new Form W-4 within 10 days after the change. An employee who has a reduction in a claimed number of withholding allowances after April 30, 2019, for any reason is required to give his or her employer a new Form W-4 within 10 days of the change in status resulting in the reduction in withholding allowances. See section 9 for more information about Form W-4.

Withholding allowance. The 2019 amount for one withholding allowance on an annual basis is $4,200.

Disaster tax relief. Disaster tax relief is available for those impacted by recent disasters. For more information about disaster relief, go to *IRS.gov/DisasterTaxRelief*.

Reminders

Moving expense reimbursement. P.L. 115-97 suspends the exclusion for qualified moving expense reimbursements from your employee's income for tax years beginning after 2017 and before 2026. However, the exclusion is still available in the case of a member of the U.S. Armed Forces on active duty who moves because of a permanent change of station. The exclusion applies only to reimbursement of moving expenses that the member could deduct if he or she had paid or incurred them without reimbursement. See *Moving Expenses* in Pub. 3, Armed Forces' Tax Guide, for the definition of what constitutes a permanent change of station and to learn which moving expenses are deductible.

Withholding on supplemental wages. P.L. 115-97 lowered the withholding rates on supplemental wages for tax years beginning after 2017 and before 2026. See section 7 for the new rates.

Backup withholding. P.L. 115-97 lowered the backup withholding rate to 24% for tax years beginning after 2017 and before 2026. For more information on backup withholding, see *Backup withholding*, later.

Qualified small business payroll tax credit for increasing research activities. For tax years beginning after 2015, a qualified small business may elect to claim up to $250,000 of its credit for increasing research activities as a payroll tax credit against the employer's share of social security tax. The payroll tax credit must be elected on an original income tax return that is timely filed (including extensions). The portion of the credit used against the employer's share of social security tax is allowed in the first calendar quarter beginning after the date that the qualified small business filed its income tax return. The election and determination of the credit amount that will be used against the employer's share of social security tax are made on Form 6765, Credit for Increasing Research Activities. The amount from Form 6765, line 44, must then be reported on Form 8974, Qualified Small Business Payroll Tax Credit for Increasing Research Activities. Form 8974 is used to determine the amount of the credit that can be used in the current quarter. The amount from Form 8974, line 12, is reported on Form 941 or 941-SS, line 11 (or Form 944, line 8). For more information about the payroll tax credit, see Notice 2017-23, 2017-16 I.R.B. 1100, available at *IRS.gov/irb/ 2017-16 IRB#NOT-2017-23*, and *IRS.gov/ ResearchPayrollTC*. Also see the line 16 instructions in the Instructions for Form 941 (line 13 instructions in the Instructions for Form 944).

Certification program for professional employer organizations (PEOs). The Tax Increase Prevention Act of 2014 required the IRS to establish a voluntary certification program for PEOs. PEOs handle various payroll administration and tax reporting responsibilities for their business clients and are typically paid a fee based on payroll costs. To become and remain certified under the certification program, certified professional employer organizations (CPEOs) must meet various requirements described in sections 3511 and 7705 and related published guidance. Certification as a CPEO may affect the employment tax liabilities of both the CPEO and its customers. A CPEO is generally treated for employment tax purposes as the employer of any individual who performs services for a customer of the CPEO and is covered by a contract described in section 7705(e)(2) between the CPEO and the customer (CPEO contract), but only for wages and other compensation paid to the individual by the CPEO. To become a CPEO, the organization must apply through the IRS Online Registration System. For more information or to apply to become a CPEO, go to *IRS.gov/CPEO*. Also see Revenue Procedure 2017-14, 2017-3 I.R.B. 426, available at *IRS.gov/irb/2017-03 IRB#RP-2017-14*.

Outsourcing payroll duties. Generally, as an employer, you're responsible to ensure that tax returns are filed and deposits and payments are made, even if you contract with a third party to perform these acts. You remain responsible if the third party fails to perform any required action. Before you choose to outsource any of your payroll and related tax duties (that is, withholding, reporting, and paying over social security, Medicare, FUTA, and income taxes) to a third-party payer, such as a payroll service provider or reporting agent, go to _IRS.gov/ OutsourcingPayrollDuties_ for helpful information on this topic. If a CPEO pays wages and other compensation to an individual performing services for you, and the services are covered by a contract described in section 7705(e)(2) between you and the CPEO (CPEO contract), then the CPEO is generally treated as the employer, but only for wages and other compensation paid to the individual by the CPEO. However, with respect to certain employees covered by a CPEO contract, you may also be treated as an employer of the employees and, consequently, may also be liable for federal employment taxes imposed on wages and other compensation paid by the CPEO to such employees. For more information on the different types of third-party payer arrangements, see section 16.

Aggregate Form 941 filers. Agents and CPEOs must complete Schedule R (Form 941), Allocation Schedule for Aggregate Form 941 Filers, when filing an aggregate Form 941. Aggregate Forms 941 are filed by agents approved by the IRS under section 3504 of the Internal Revenue Code. To request approval to act as an agent for an employer, the agent files Form 2678 with the IRS. Aggregate Forms 941 are also filed by CPEOs approved by the IRS under section 7705. CPEOs file Form 8973, Certified Professional Employer Organization/Customer Reporting Agreement, to notify the IRS that they've started or ended a service contract with a client or customer.

Aggregate Form 940 filers. Agents and CPEOs must complete Schedule R (Form 940), Allocation Schedule for Aggregate Form 940 Filers, when filing an aggregate Form 940, Employer's Annual Federal Unemployment (FUTA) Tax Return. Aggregate Forms 940 can be filed by agents acting on behalf of home care service recipients who receive home care services through a program administered by a federal, state, or local government. To request approval to act as an agent on behalf of home care service recipients, the agent files Form 2678 with the IRS. Aggregate Forms 940 are also filed by CPEOs approved by the IRS under section 7705. CPEOs file Form 8973 to notify the IRS that they've started or ended a service contract with a client or customer.

Work opportunity tax credit for qualified tax-exempt organizations hiring qualified veterans. The work opportunity tax credit is available for eligible unemployed veterans who begin work on or after November 22, 2011, and before January 1, 2020. Qualified tax-exempt organizations that hire eligible unemployed veterans can claim the work opportunity tax credit against their payroll tax liability using Form 5884-C. For more information, go to _IRS.gov/WOTC_.

COBRA premium assistance credit. Effective for tax periods beginning after 2013, the credit for COBRA premium assistance payments can't be claimed on Form 941, Employer's QUARTERLY Federal Tax Return (or Form 944, Employer's ANNUAL Federal Tax Return). Instead, after filing your Form 941 (or Form 944), file Form 941-X, Adjusted Employer's QUARTERLY Federal Tax Return or Claim for Refund (or Form 944-X, Adjusted Employer's

ANNUAL Federal Tax Return or Claim for Refund), respectively, to claim the COBRA premium assistance credit. Filing a Form 941-X (or Form 944-X) before filing a Form 941 (or Form 944) for the return period may result in errors or delays in processing your Form 941-X (or Form 944-X). For more information, see the Instructions for Form 941 (or the Instructions for Form 944), or go to _IRS.gov/COBRACredit_.

Medicaid waiver payments. Notice 2014-7 provides that certain Medicaid waiver payments are excludable from income for federal income tax purposes. See Notice 2014-7, 2014-4 I.R.B. 445, available at _IRS.gov/irb/ 2014-04_IRB#NOT-2014-7_. For more information, including questions and answers related to Notice 2014-7, go to _IRS.gov/MedicaidWaiverPayments_.

No federal income tax withholding on disability payments for injuries incurred as a direct result of a terrorist attack directed against the United States. Disability payments for injuries incurred as a direct result of a terrorist attack directed against the United States (or its allies) aren't included in income. Because federal income tax withholding is only required when a payment is includible in income, no federal income tax should be withheld from these payments.

Voluntary withholding on dividends and other distributions by an Alaska Native Corporation (ANC). A shareholder of an ANC may request voluntary income tax withholding on dividends and other distributions paid by an ANC. A shareholder may request voluntary withholding by giving the ANC a completed Form W-4V. For more information, see Notice 2013-77, 2013-50 I.R.B. 632, available at _IRS.gov/irb/2013-50_IRB#NOT-2013-77_.

Definition of marriage. A marriage of two individuals is recognized for federal tax purposes if the marriage is recognized by the state, possession, or territory of the United States in which the marriage is entered into, regardless of legal residence. Two individuals who enter into a relationship that is denominated as marriage under the laws of a foreign jurisdiction are recognized as married for federal tax purposes if the relationship would be recognized as marriage under the laws of at least one state, possession, or territory of the United States, regardless of legal residence. Individuals who have entered into a registered domestic partnership, civil union, or other similar relationship that isn't denominated as a marriage under the law of the state, possession, or territory of the United States where such relationship was entered into aren't lawfully married for federal tax purposes, regardless of legal residence.

Severance payments. Severance payments are wages subject to social security and Medicare taxes, income tax withholding, and FUTA tax.

You must receive written notice from the IRS to file Form 944. If you've been filing Forms 941 (or Forms 941-SS, Employer's QUARTERLY Federal Tax Return—American Samoa, Guam, the Commonwealth of the Northern Mariana Islands, and the U.S. Virgin Islands, or Formularios 941-PR, Planilla para la Declaración Federal TRIMESTRAL del Patrono), and believe your employment taxes for the calendar year will be $1,000 or less, and you would like to file Form 944 instead of Forms 941, you must contact the IRS during the first calendar quarter of the tax year to request to file Form 944. You must receive written notice from the IRS to file Form 944 instead of Forms 941 before you may file this form. For more information on requesting to file Form 944, including the methods and deadlines for making a request, see the Instructions for Form 944.

Employers can request to file Forms 941 instead of Form 944. If you received notice from the IRS to file Form 944 but would like to file Forms 941 instead, you must contact the IRS during the first calendar quarter of the tax year to request to file Forms 941. You must receive written notice from the IRS to file Forms 941 instead of Form 944 before you may file these forms. For more information on requesting to file Forms 941, including the methods and deadlines for making a request, see the Instructions for Form 944.

Federal tax deposits must be made by electronic funds transfer (EFT). You must use EFT to make all federal tax deposits. Generally, an EFT is made using the Electronic Federal Tax Payment System (EFTPS). If you don't want to use EFTPS, you can arrange for your tax professional, financial institution, payroll service, or other trusted third party to make electronic deposits on your behalf. Also, you may arrange for your financial institution to initiate a same-day wire payment on your behalf. EFTPS is a free service provided by the Department of the Treasury. Services provided by your tax professional, financial institution, payroll service, or other third party may have a fee.

For more information on making federal tax deposits, see *How To Deposit* in section 11. To get more information about EFTPS or to enroll in EFTPS, go to *EFTPS.gov*, or call 800-555-4477 or 800-733-4829 (TDD). Additional information about EFTPS is also available in Pub. 966.

Pub. 5146 explains employment tax examinations and appeal rights. Pub. 5146 provides employers with information on how the IRS selects employment tax returns to be examined, what happens during an exam, and what options an employer has in responding to the results of an exam, including how to appeal the results. Pub. 5146 also includes information on worker classification issues and tip exams.

- For electronic filing of Forms W-2, Wage and Tax Statement, go to *SSA.gov/employer*.

 If you're filing your tax return or paying your federal taxes electronically, a valid EIN is required at the time the return is filed or the payment is made. If a valid EIN isn't provided, the return or payment won't be processed. This may result in penalties. See section 1 for information about applying for an EIN.

Electronic funds withdrawal (EFW). If you file your employment tax return electronically, you can *e-file* and use EFW to pay the balance due in a single step using tax preparation software or through a tax professional. However, don't use EFW to make federal tax deposits. For more information on paying your taxes using EFW, go to *IRS.gov/EFW*.

Credit or debit card payments. You can pay the balance due shown on your employment tax return by credit or debit card. Your payment will be processed by a payment processor who will charge a processing fee. Don't use a credit or debit card to make federal tax deposits. For more information on paying your taxes with a credit or debit card, go to *IRS.gov/PayByCard*.

Online payment agreement. You may be eligible to apply for an installment agreement online if you can't pay the full amount of tax you owe when you file your employment tax return. For more information, see the instructions for your employment tax return or go to *IRS.gov/OPA*.

Forms in Spanish

You can provide Formulario W-4(SP), Certificado de Exención de Retenciones del Empleado, in place of Form W-4, Employee's Withholding Allowance Certificate, to your Spanish-speaking employees. For more information, see Pub. 17(SP), El Impuesto Federal sobre los Ingresos (Para Personas Físicas). For nonemployees, such as independent contractors, Formulario W-9(SP), Solicitud y Certificación del Número de Identificación del Contribuyente, may be used in place of Form W-9, Request for Taxpayer Identification Number and Certification.

Electronic Filing and Payment

Now, more than ever before, businesses can enjoy the benefits of filing and paying their federal taxes electronically. Whether you rely on a tax professional or handle your own taxes, the IRS offers you convenient programs to make filing and payment easier.

Spend less time and worry on taxes and more time running your business. Use *e-file* and EFTPS to your benefit.

- For *e-file,* go to *IRS.gov/EmploymentEfile* for additional information. A fee may be charged to file electronically.

- For EFTPS, go to *EFTPS.gov* or call EFTPS Customer Service at 800-555-4477 or 800-733-4829 (TDD).

Hiring New Employees

Eligibility for employment. You must verify that each new employee is legally eligible to work in the United States. This includes completing the U.S. Citizenship and Immigration Services (USCIS) Form I-9, Employment Eligibility Verification. You can get Form I-9 at *USCIS.gov/Forms*, USCIS offices, or by calling 800-870-3676. For more information, visit the USCIS website at *USCIS.gov/I-9-Central* or call 800-375-5283 or 800-767-1833 (TTY).

New hire reporting. You're required to report any new employee to a designated state new hire registry. A new employee is an employee who hasn't previously been employed by you or was previously employed by you but has been separated from such prior employment for at least 60 consecutive days.

Many states accept a copy of Form W-4 with employer information added. Visit the Office of Child Support Enforcement website at *acf.hhs.gov/programs/css/ employers* for more information.

W-4 request. Ask each new employee to complete the 2019 Form W-4. See section 9.

Name and social security number (SSN). Record each new employee's name and SSN from his or her social security card. Any employee without a social security card should apply for one. See section 4.

Paying Wages, Pensions, or Annuities

Correcting Form 941 or 944. If you discover an error on a previously filed Form 941, make the correction using Form 941-X. If you discover an error on a previously filed Form 944, make the correction using Form 944-X. Forms 941-X and 944-X are filed separately from Forms 941 and 944. Forms 941-X and 944-X are used by employers to claim refunds or abatements of employment taxes, rather than Form 843. See section 13 for more information.

Income tax withholding. Withhold federal income tax from each wage payment or supplemental unemployment compensation plan benefit payment according to the employee's Form W-4 and the correct withholding table. If you're paying supplemental wages to an employee, see

section 7. If you have nonresident alien employees, see *Withholding income taxes on the wages of nonresident alien employees* in section 9.

In 2019, withhold from periodic pension and annuity payments as if the recipient is married claiming three withholding allowances, unless he or she has provided Form W-4P, Withholding Certificate for Pension or Annuity Payments, either electing no withholding or giving a different number of allowances, marital status, or an additional amount to be withheld. Don't withhold on direct rollovers from qualified plans or governmental section 457(b) plans. See section 9 and Pub. 15-A, Employer's Supplemental Tax Guide. Pub. 15-A includes information about withholding on pensions and annuities.

Zero wage return. If you haven't filed a "final" Form 940 and "final" Form 941 or 944, or aren't a "seasonal" employer (Form 941 only), you must continue to file a Form 940 and Form 941 or 944, even for periods during which you paid no wages. The IRS encourages you to file your "Zero Wage" Form 940 and Form 941 or 944 electronically. Go to *IRS.gov/EmploymentEfile* for more information on electronic filing.

Information Returns

You may be required to file information returns to report certain types of payments made during the year. For example, you must file Form 1099-MISC, Miscellaneous

Employer Responsibilities

Employer Responsibilities: The following list provides a brief summary of your basic responsibilities. Because the individual circumstances for each employer can vary greatly, responsibilities for withholding, depositing, and reporting employment taxes can differ. Each item in this list has a page reference to a more detailed discussion in this publication.

New Employees:	Page
☐ Verify work eligibility of new employees	4
☐ Record employees' names and SSNs from social security cards	5
☐ Ask employees for Form W-4	5
Each Payday:	
☐ Withhold federal income tax based on each employee's Form W-4	20
☐ Withhold employee's share of social security and Medicare taxes	23
☐ Deposit:	
• Withheld income tax	
• Withheld and employer social security taxes	
• Withheld and employer Medicare taxes	25
Note: Due date of deposit generally depends on your deposit schedule (monthly or semiweekly).	
Quarterly (By April 30, July 31, October 31, and January 31):	
☐ Deposit FUTA tax if undeposited amount is over $500	36
☐ File Form 941 (pay tax with return if not required to deposit)	30

Annually (see *Calendar* for due dates):	Page
☐ File Form 944 if required (pay tax with return if not required to deposit)	30
☐ Remind employees to submit a new Form W-4 if they need to change their withholding	20
☐ Ask for a new Form W-4 from employees claiming exemption from income tax withholding	21
☐ Reconcile Forms 941 (or Form 944) with Forms W-2 and W-3	32
☐ Furnish each employee a Form W-2	8
☐ File Copy A of Forms W-2 and the transmittal Form W-3 with the SSA	8
☐ Furnish each other payee a Form 1099 (for example, Form 1099-MISC)	8
☐ File Forms 1099 and the transmittal Form 1096	8
☐ File Form 940	8
☐ File Form 945 for any nonpayroll income tax withholding	8

Income, to report payments of $600 or more to persons not treated as employees (for example, independent contractors) for services performed for your trade or business. For details about filing Forms 1099 and for information about required electronic filing, see the General Instructions for Certain Information Returns for general information, and the separate, specific instructions for each information return you file (for example, the Instructions for Form 1099-MISC). Generally, don't use Forms 1099 to report wages and other compensation you paid to employees; report these on Form W-2. See the General Instructions for Forms W-2 and W-3 for details about filing Form W-2 and for information about required electronic filing. If you file 250 or more Forms 1099-MISC, you must file them electronically. If you file 250 or more Forms W-2, you must file them electronically. Electronic filing is the only form of magnetic media that the IRS and the SSA will accept.

Information reporting customer service site. The IRS operates an information return customer service site to answer questions about reporting on Forms W-2, W-3, 1099, and other information returns. If you have questions related to reporting on information returns, call 866-455-7438 (toll free), 304-263-8700 (toll call), or 304-579-4827 (TDD/TTY for persons who are deaf, hard of hearing, or have a speech disability). The center can also be reached by email at mccirp@irs.gov. Don't include tax identification numbers (TINs) or attachments in email correspondence because electronic mail isn't secure.

Nonpayroll Income Tax Withholding

Nonpayroll federal income tax withholding (reported on Forms 1099 and Form W-2G, Certain Gambling Winnings) must be reported on Form 945, Annual Return of Withheld Federal Income Tax. Separate deposits are required for payroll (Form 941 or Form 944) and nonpayroll (Form 945) withholding. Nonpayroll items include the following.

- Pensions (including distributions from tax-favored retirement plans, for example, section 401(k), section 403(b), and governmental section 457(b) plans), annuities, and IRA distributions.

- Military retirement.

- Gambling winnings.

- Indian gaming profits.

- Certain government payments on which the recipient elected voluntary income tax withholding.

- Dividends and other distributions by an ANC on which the recipient elected voluntary income tax withholding.

- Payments subject to backup withholding.

For details on depositing and reporting nonpayroll income tax withholding, see the Instructions for Form 945.

Distributions from nonqualified pension plans and deferred compensation plans. Because distributions to participants from some nonqualified pension plans and deferred compensation plans (including section 457(b) plans of tax-exempt organizations) are treated as wages and are reported on Form W-2, income tax withheld must be reported on Form 941 or Form 944, not on Form 945. However, distributions from such plans to a beneficiary or estate of a deceased employee aren't wages and are reported on Forms 1099-R, Distributions From Pensions, Annuities, Retirement or Profit-Sharing Plans, IRAs, Insurance Contracts, etc.; income tax withheld must be reported on Form 945.

Backup withholding. You generally must withhold 24% of certain taxable payments if the payee fails to furnish you with his or her correct taxpayer identification number (TIN). This withholding is referred to as "backup withholding."

Payments subject to backup withholding include interest, dividends, patronage dividends, rents, royalties, commissions, nonemployee compensation, payments made in settlement of payment card or third-party network transactions, and certain other payments you make in the course of your trade or business. In addition, transactions by brokers and barter exchanges and certain payments made by fishing boat operators are subject to backup withholding.

 Backup withholding doesn't apply to wages, pensions, annuities, IRAs (including simplified employee pension (SEP) and SIMPLE retirement plans), section 404(k) distributions from an employee stock ownership plan (ESOP), medical savings accounts (MSAs), health savings accounts (HSAs), long-term-care benefits, or real estate transactions.

You can use Form W-9 or Formulario W-9(SP) to request payees to furnish a TIN. Form W-9 or Formulario W-9(SP) must be used when payees must certify that the number furnished is correct, or when payees must certify that they're not subject to backup withholding or are exempt from backup withholding. The Instructions for the Requester of Form W-9 or Formulario W-9(SP) includes a list of types of payees who are exempt from backup withholding. For more information, see Pub. 1281, Backup Withholding for Missing and Incorrect Name/TIN(s).

Recordkeeping

Keep all records of employment taxes for at least 4 years. These should be available for IRS review. Your records should include the following information.

- Your EIN.

- Amounts and dates of all wage, annuity, and pension payments.

- Amounts of tips reported to you by your employees.

- Records of allocated tips.

- The fair market value of in-kind wages paid.

- Names, addresses, SSNs, and occupations of employees and recipients.

- Any employee copies of Forms W-2 and W-2c returned to you as undeliverable.
- Dates of employment for each employee.
- Periods for which employees and recipients were paid while absent due to sickness or injury and the amount and weekly rate of payments you or third-party payers made to them.
- Copies of employees' and recipients' income tax withholding allowance certificates (Forms W-4, W-4P, W-4(SP), W-4S, and W-4V).
- Dates and amounts of tax deposits you made and acknowledgment numbers for deposits made by EFTPS.
- Copies of returns filed and confirmation numbers.
- Records of fringe benefits and expense reimbursements provided to your employees, including substantiation.

Change of Business Name

Notify the IRS immediately if you change your business name. Write to the IRS office where you file your returns, using the *Without a payment* address provided in the instructions for your employment tax return, to notify the IRS of any business name change. See Pub. 1635 to see if you need to apply for a new EIN.

Change of Business Address or Responsible Party

Notify the IRS immediately if you change your business address or responsible party. Complete and mail Form 8822-B to notify the IRS of a business address or responsible party change. For a definition of "responsible party," see the Instructions for Form SS-4.

Private Delivery Services

You can use certain private delivery services (PDSs) designated by the IRS to meet the "timely mailing as timely filing" rule for tax returns. Go to *IRS.gov/PDS* for the current list of PDSs.

The PDS can tell you how to get written proof of the mailing date.

For the IRS mailing address to use if you're using a PDS, go to *IRS.gov/PDSstreetAdresses*. Select the mailing address listed on the webpage that is in the same state as the address to which you would mail returns filed without a payment, as shown in the instructions for your employment tax return.

 PDSs can't deliver items to P.O. boxes. You must use the U.S. Postal Service to mail any item to an IRS P.O. box address.

Telephone Help

Tax questions. You can call the IRS Business and Specialty Tax Line with your employment tax questions at 800-829-4933.

Help for people with disabilities. You may call 800-829-4059 (TDD/TTY for persons who are deaf, hard of hearing, or have a speech disability) with any employment tax questions. You may also use this number for assistance with unresolved tax problems.

Additional employment tax information. Go to *IRS.gov/EmploymentTaxes* for additional employment tax information.

Ordering Employer Tax Forms and Publications

You can view, download, or print most of the forms, instructions, and publications you may need at *IRS.gov/Forms*. Otherwise, you can go to *IRS.gov/OrderForms* to place an order and have them mailed to you.

Instead of ordering paper Forms W-2 and W-3, consider filing them electronically using the SSA's free *e-file* service. Visit the SSA's Employer W-2 Filing Instructions & Information website at *SSA.gov/employer* to register for Business Services Online. You'll be able to create Forms W-2 online and submit them to the SSA by typing your wage information into easy-to-use fill-in fields. In addition, you can print out completed copies of Forms W-2 to file with state or local governments, distribute to your employees, and keep for your records. Form W-3 will be created for you based on your Forms W-2.

Filing Addresses

Generally, your filing address for Form 940, 941, 943, 944, 945, or CT-1 depends on the location of your residence or principal place of business and whether or not you're including a payment with your return. There are separate filing addresses for these returns if you're a tax-exempt organization or government entity. See the separate instructions for Forms 940, 941, 943, 944, 945, or CT-1 for the filing addresses.

Dishonored Payments

Any form of payment that is dishonored and returned from a financial institution is subject to a penalty. The penalty is $25 or 2% of the payment, whichever is more. However, the penalty on dishonored payments of $24.99 or less is an amount equal to the payment. For example, a dishonored payment of $18 is charged a penalty of $18.

Photographs of Missing Children

The IRS is a proud partner with the *National Center for Missing & Exploited Children® (NCMEC)*. Photographs of missing children selected by the Center may appear in this publication on pages that would otherwise be blank. You can help bring these children home by looking at the photographs and calling 1-800-THE-LOST (1-800-843-5678) if you recognize a child.

Calendar

The following is a list of important dates and responsibilities. See section 11 for information about depositing taxes reported on Forms 941, 944, and 945. See section 14 for information about depositing FUTA tax. Also see Pub. 509, Tax Calendars.

 If any date shown next for filing a return, furnishing a form, or depositing taxes falls on a Saturday, Sunday, or legal holiday, the due date is the next business day. The term "legal holiday" means any legal holiday in the District of Columbia. A statewide legal holiday delays a filing due date only if the IRS office where you're required to file is located in that state. However, a statewide legal holiday doesn't delay the due date of federal tax deposits. See Deposits Due on Business Days Only in section 11. For any filing due date, you'll meet the "file" or "furnish" requirement if the envelope containing the return or form is properly addressed, contains sufficient postage, and is postmarked by the U.S. Postal Service on or before the due date, or sent by an IRS-designated PDS on or before the due date. See Private Delivery Services under Reminders, earlier, for more information.

By January 31

File Form 941 or Form 944. File Form 941 for the fourth quarter of the previous calendar year and deposit any undeposited income, social security, and Medicare taxes. You may pay these taxes with Form 941 if your total tax liability for the quarter is less than $2,500. File Form 944 for the previous calendar year instead of Form 941 if the IRS has notified you in writing to file Form 944. Pay any undeposited income, social security, and Medicare taxes with your Form 944. You may pay these taxes with Form 944 if your total tax liability for the year is less than $2,500. For additional rules on when you can pay your taxes with your return, see *Payment with return* in section 11. If you timely deposited all taxes when due, you may file by February 10.

File Form 940. File Form 940 to report any FUTA tax. However, if you deposited all of the FUTA tax when due, you may file by February 10.

Furnish Forms 1099 and W-2. Furnish each employee a completed Form W-2. Furnish Form

1099-MISC to payees for nonemployee compensation. Most Forms 1099 must be furnished to payees by January 31, but some can be furnished by February 15. For more information, see *When to furnish forms or statements* in part M of the General Instructions for Certain Information Returns.

File Form W-2. File with the SSA Copy A of all 2018 paper and electronic Forms W-2 with Form W-3, Transmittal of Wage and Tax Statements. For more information on reporting Form W-2 information to the SSA electronically, visit the SSA's Employer W-2 Filing Instructions & Information webpage at *SSA.gov/employer*. If filing electronically, via the SSA's Form W-2 Online service, the SSA will generate Form W-3 data from the electronic submission of Form(s) W-2.

File Form 1099-MISC reporting nonemployee compensation. File with the IRS Copy A of all 2018 paper and electronic Forms 1099-MISC that report nonemployee compensation, with Form 1096, Annual Summary and Transmittal of U.S. Information Returns. For information on filing information returns electronically with the IRS, see Pub. 1220, Specifications for Electronic Filing of Forms 1097, 1098, 1099, 3921, 3922, 5498, and W-2G.

File Form 945. File Form 945 to report any nonpayroll federal income tax withheld. If you deposited all taxes when due, you may file by February 10. See *Nonpayroll Income Tax Withholding* under *Reminders*, earlier, for more information.

By February 15

Request a new Form W-4 from exempt employees. Ask for a new Form W-4 from each employee who claimed exemption from income tax withholding last year.

On February 16

Forms W-4 claiming exemption from withholding expire. Any Form W-4 claiming exemption from withholding for the previous year has now expired. Begin withholding for any employee who previously claimed exemption from withholding but hasn't given you a new Form W-4 for the current year. If the employee doesn't give you a new Form W-4, withhold tax based on the last valid Form W-4 you have for the employee that doesn't claim exemption from withholding or, if one doesn't exist, as if he or she is single with zero withholding allowances. See section 9 for more information. If the employee gives you a new Form W-4 claiming exemption from withholding after February 15, you may apply the exemption to future wages, but don't refund taxes withheld while the exempt status wasn't in place.

By February 28

File paper 2018 Forms 1099 and 1096. File Copy A of all paper 2018 Forms 1099, except Forms

1099-MISC reporting nonemployee compensation, with Form 1096 with the IRS. For electronically filed returns, see *By March 31* below.

File paper Form 8027. File paper Form 8027, Employer's Annual Information Return of Tip Income and Allocated Tips, with the IRS. See section 6. For electronically filed returns, see *By March 31* below.

By March 31

File electronic 2018 Forms 1099 and 8027. File electronic 2018 Forms 1099, except Forms 1099-MISC reporting nonemployee compensation, and 8027 with the IRS. For information on filing information returns electronically with the IRS, see Pub. 1220 and Pub. 1239, Specifications for Electronic Filing of Form 8027, Employer's Annual Information Return of Tip Income and Allocated Tips.

By April 30, July 31, October 31, and January 31

Deposit FUTA taxes. Deposit FUTA tax for the quarter (including any amount carried over from other quarters) if over $500. If $500 or less, carry it over to the next quarter. See section 14 for more information.

File Form 941. File Form 941 and deposit any undeposited income, social security, and Medicare taxes. You may pay these taxes with Form 941 if your total tax liability for the quarter is less than $2,500. If you timely deposited all taxes when due, you may file by May 10, August 10, November 10, or February 10, respectively. Don't file Form 941 for these quarters if you have been notified to file Form 944 and you didn't request and receive written notice from the IRS to file quarterly Forms 941.

Before December 1

New Forms W-4. Remind employees to submit a new Form W-4 if their marital status or withholding allowances have changed or will change for the next year.

Introduction

This publication explains your tax responsibilities as an employer. It explains the requirements for withholding, depositing, reporting, paying, and correcting employment taxes. It explains the forms you must give to your employees, those your employees must give to you, and those you must send to the IRS and the SSA. This guide also has tax tables you need to figure the taxes to withhold from each employee for 2019. References to "income tax" in this guide apply only to "federal" income tax. Contact your state or local tax department to determine their rules.

When you pay your employees, you don't pay them all the money they earned. As their employer, you have the added responsibility of withholding taxes from their paychecks. The federal income tax and employees' share of social security and Medicare taxes that you withhold from your employees' paychecks are part of their wages that you pay to the U.S. Treasury instead of to your employees. Your employees trust that you pay the withheld taxes to the U.S. Treasury by making federal tax deposits. This is the reason that these withheld taxes are called trust fund taxes. If federal income, social security, or Medicare taxes that must be withheld aren't withheld or aren't deposited or paid to the U.S. Treasury, the trust fund recovery penalty may apply. See section 11 for more information.

Additional employment tax information is available in Pub. 15-A. Pub. 15-A includes specialized information supplementing the basic employment tax information provided in this publication. Pub. 15-B, Employer's Tax Guide to Fringe Benefits, contains information about the employment tax treatment and valuation of various types of non-cash compensation.

Most employers must withhold (except FUTA), deposit, report, and pay the following employment taxes.

- Income tax.
- Social security tax.
- Medicare tax.
- FUTA tax.

There are exceptions to these requirements. See section 15 for guidance. Railroad retirement taxes are explained in the Instructions for Form CT-1. Employment taxes for agricultural employers are explained in Pub. 51.

Comments and suggestions. We welcome your comments about this publication and your suggestions for future editions.

You can send us comments from *IRS.gov/ FormComments*.

Or you can write to:

Internal Revenue Service
Tax Forms and Publications
1111 Constitution Ave. NW, IR-6526
Washington, DC 20224

Although we can't respond individually to each comment received, we do appreciate your feedback and will consider your comments as we revise our tax forms, instructions, and publications. We can't answer tax questions sent to the above address.

Federal government employers. The information in this publication, including the rules for making federal tax deposits, applies to federal agencies.

State and local government employers. Payments to employees for services in the employ of state and local government employers are generally subject to federal income tax withholding but not FUTA tax. Most elected and appointed public officials of state or local governments are employees under common law rules. See chapter 3 of Pub. 963, Federal-State Reference Guide. In addition, wages, with certain exceptions, are subject to social security and Medicare taxes. See section 15 for more information on the exceptions.

If an election worker is employed in another capacity with the same government entity, see Revenue Ruling 2000-6 on page 512 of Internal Revenue Bulletin 2000-6 at *IRS.gov/pub/irs-irbs/irb00-06.pdf*.

You can get information on reporting and social security coverage from your local IRS office. If you have any questions about coverage under a section 218 (Social Security Act) agreement, contact the appropriate state official. To find your State Social Security Administrator, visit the National Conference of State Social Security Administrators website at *NCSSSA.org*.

Indian tribal governments. See Pub. 4268 for employment tax information for Indian tribal governments.

Disregarded entities and qualified subchapter S subsidiaries (QSubs). Eligible single-owner disregarded entities and QSubs are treated as separate entities for employment tax purposes. Eligible single-member entities must report and pay employment taxes on wages paid to their employees using the entities' own names and EINs. See Regulations sections 1.1361-4(a)(7) and 301.7701-2(c)(2)(iv).

COBRA premium assistance credit. The Consolidated Omnibus Budget Reconciliation Act of 1985 (COBRA) provides certain former employees, retirees, spouses, former spouses, and dependent children the right to temporary continuation of health coverage at group rates. COBRA generally covers multiemployer health plans and health plans maintained by private-sector employers (other than churches) with 20 or more full- and part-time employees. Parallel requirements apply to these plans under the Employee Retirement Income Security Act of 1974 (ERISA). Under the Public Health Service Act, COBRA requirements apply also to health plans covering state or local government employees. Similar requirements apply under the Federal Employees Health Benefits Program and under some state laws. For the premium assistance (or subsidy) discussed below, these requirements are all referred to as COBRA requirements.

Under the American Recovery and Reinvestment Act of 2009 (ARRA), employers are allowed a credit against "payroll taxes" (referred to in this publication as "employment taxes") for providing COBRA premium assistance to assistance-eligible individuals. For periods of COBRA continuation coverage beginning after February 16, 2009, a group health plan must treat an assistance-eligible individual as having paid the required COBRA continuation coverage premium if the individual elects COBRA coverage and pays 35% of the amount of the premium.

An assistance-eligible individual is a qualified beneficiary of an employer's group health plan who is eligible for COBRA continuation coverage during the period beginning September 1, 2008, and ending May 31, 2010, due to the involuntary termination from employment of a covered employee during the period and elects continuation COBRA coverage. The assistance for the coverage can last up to 15 months.

The COBRA premium assistance credit was available to an employer for premiums paid on behalf of employees who were involuntarily terminated from employment between September 1, 2008, and May 31, 2010. The COBRA premium assistance credit isn't available for individuals who were involuntarily terminated after May 31, 2010. Therefore, only in rare circumstances will the credit still be available, such as instances where COBRA eligibility was delayed as a result of employer-provided health insurance coverage following termination. For more information about the credit, see Notice 2009-27, 2009-16 I.R.B. 838, available at *IRS.gov/irb/2009-16_IRB#NOT-2009-27*.

Administrators of the group health plans (or other entities) that provide or administer COBRA continuation coverage must provide notice to assistance-eligible individuals of the COBRA premium assistance.

The 65% of the premium not paid by the assistance-eligible individuals is reimbursed to the employer maintaining the group health plan. The reimbursement is made through a credit against the employer's employment tax liabilities. For information on how to claim the credit, see the Instructions for Form 941-X or the Instructions for Form 944-X. The credit is treated as a deposit made on the first day of the return period (quarter or year). In the case of a multiemployer plan, the credit is claimed by the plan, rather than the employer. In the case of an insured plan subject to state law continuation coverage requirements, the credit is claimed by the insurance company, rather than the employer.

Anyone claiming the credit for COBRA premium assistance payments must maintain the following information to support their claim.

- Information on the receipt of the assistance-eligible individuals' 35% share of the premium, including dates and amounts.

- In the case of an insurance plan, a copy of an invoice or other supporting statement from the insurance carrier and proof of timely payment of the full premium to the insurance carrier required under COBRA.

- In the case of a self-insured plan, proof of the premium amount and proof of the coverage provided to the assistance-eligible individuals.

- Attestation of involuntary termination, including the date of the involuntary termination for each covered employee whose involuntary termination is the basis for eligibility for the subsidy.

- Proof of each assistance-eligible individual's eligibility for COBRA coverage and the election of COBRA coverage.

- A record of the SSNs of all covered employees, the amount of the subsidy reimbursed with respect to each covered employee, and whether the subsidy was for one individual or two or more individuals.

For more information, go to *IRS.gov/COBRACredit*.

1. Employer Identification Number (EIN)

If you're required to report employment taxes or give tax statements to employees or annuitants, you need an EIN.

The EIN is a nine-digit number the IRS issues. The digits are arranged as follows: 00-0000000. It is used to identify the tax accounts of employers and certain others who have no employees. Use your EIN on all of the items you send to the IRS and the SSA. For more information, see Pub. 1635.

If you don't have an EIN, you may apply for one online by visiting the IRS website at *IRS.gov/EIN*. You may also apply for an EIN by faxing or mailing Form SS-4 to the IRS. If the principal business was created or organized outside of the United States or U.S. territories, you may also apply for an EIN by calling 267-941-1099 (toll call). Don't use an SSN in place of an EIN.

You should have only one EIN. If you have more than one and aren't sure which one to use, call 800-829-4933 or 800-829-4059 (TDD/TTY for persons who are deaf, hard of hearing, or have a speech disability). Give the numbers you have, the name and address to which each was assigned, and the address of your main place of business. The IRS will tell you which number to use. For more information, see Pub. 1635.

If you took over another employer's business (see *Successor employer* in section 9), don't use that employer's EIN. If you've applied for an EIN but don't have your EIN by the time a return is due, file a paper return and write "Applied For" and the date you applied for it in the space shown for the number.

2. Who Are Employees?

Generally, employees are defined either under common law or under statutes for certain situations. See Pub. 15-A for details on statutory employees and nonemployees.

Employee status under common law. Generally, a worker who performs services for you is your employee if you have the right to control what will be done and how it will be done. This is so even when you give the employee freedom of action. What matters is that you have the right to control the details of how the services are performed. See Pub. 15-A for more information on how to determine whether an individual providing services is an independent contractor or an employee.

Generally, people in business for themselves aren't employees. For example, doctors, lawyers, veterinarians, and others in an independent trade in which they offer their services to the public are usually not employees. However, if the business is incorporated, corporate officers who work in the business are employees of the corporation.

If an employer-employee relationship exists, it doesn't matter what it is called. The employee may be called an agent or independent contractor. It also doesn't matter how payments are measured or paid, what they're called, or if the employee works full or part time.

Statutory employees. If someone who works for you isn't an employee under the common law rules discussed earlier, don't withhold federal income tax from his or her pay, unless backup withholding applies. Although the following persons may not be common law employees, they're considered employees by statute for social security and Medicare tax purposes under certain conditions.

- An agent or commission driver who delivers meat, vegetable, fruit, or bakery products; beverages (other than milk); laundry; or dry cleaning for someone else.

- A full-time life insurance salesperson who sells primarily for one company.

- A homeworker who works at home or off premises according to guidelines of the person for whom the work is done, with materials or goods furnished by and returned to that person or to someone that person designates.

- A traveling or city salesperson (other than an agent or commission driver) who works full time (except for sideline sales activities) for one firm or person getting orders from customers. The orders must be for merchandise for resale or supplies for use in the customer's business. The customers must be retailers, wholesalers, contractors, or operators of hotels, restaurants, or other businesses dealing with food or lodging.

For FUTA tax, an agent or commission driver and a traveling or city salesperson are considered statutory employees; however, a full-time life insurance salesperson and a homeworker aren't considered statutory employees.

Statutory nonemployees. Direct sellers, qualified real estate agents, and certain companion sitters are, by law, considered nonemployees. They're generally treated as self-employed for all federal tax purposes, including income and employment taxes.

H-2A agricultural workers. On Form W-2, don't check box 13 (Statutory employee), as H-2A workers aren't statutory employees.

Treating employees as nonemployees. You'll generally be liable for social security and Medicare taxes and withheld income tax if you don't deduct and withhold these taxes because you treated an employee as a nonemployee. You may be able to figure your liability using special section 3509 rates for the employee share of social security and Medicare taxes and federal income tax withholding. The applicable rates depend on whether you filed required Forms 1099. You can't recover the employee share of social security tax, Medicare tax, or income tax withholding from the employee if the tax is paid under section 3509. You're liable for the income tax withholding regardless of whether the employee paid income tax on the wages. You continue to owe the full employer share of social security and Medicare taxes. The employee remains liable for the employee share of social security and Medicare taxes. See section 3509 for details. Also see the Instructions for Form 941-X.

Section 3509 rates aren't available if you intentionally disregard the requirement to withhold taxes from the employee or if you withheld income taxes but not social security or Medicare taxes. Section 3509 isn't available for reclassifying statutory employees. See *Statutory employees*, earlier.

If the employer issued required information returns, the section 3509 rates are the following.

- For social security taxes: employer rate of 6.2% plus 20% of the employee rate of 6.2%, for a total rate of 7.44% of wages.

- For Medicare taxes: employer rate of 1.45% plus 20% of the employee rate of 1.45%, for a total rate of 1.74% of wages.

- For Additional Medicare Tax: 0.18% (20% of the employee rate of 0.9%) of wages subject to Additional Medicare Tax.

- For income tax withholding, the rate is 1.5% of wages.

If the employer didn't issue required information returns, the section 3509 rates are the following.

- For social security taxes: employer rate of 6.2% plus 40% of the employee rate of 6.2%, for a total rate of 8.68% of wages.

- For Medicare taxes: employer rate of 1.45% plus 40% of the employee rate of 1.45%, for a total rate of 2.03% of wages.

- For Additional Medicare Tax: 0.36% (40% of the employee rate of 0.9%) of wages subject to Additional Medicare Tax.

- For income tax withholding, the rate is 3.0% of wages.

Relief provisions. If you have a reasonable basis for not treating a worker as an employee, you may be relieved from having to pay employment taxes for that worker. To get this relief, you must file all required federal tax returns, including information returns, on a basis consistent with your treatment of the worker. You (or your predecessor) must not have treated any worker holding a substantially similar position as an employee for any periods beginning after 1977. See Pub. 1976, Do You Qualify for Relief Under Section 530.

IRS help. If you want the IRS to determine whether a worker is an employee, file Form SS-8.

Voluntary Classification Settlement Program (VCSP). Employers who are currently treating their workers (or a class or group of workers) as independent contractors or other nonemployees and want to voluntarily reclassify their workers as employees for future tax periods may be eligible to participate in the VCSP if certain requirements are met. File Form 8952 to apply for the VCSP. For more information, go to *IRS.gov/VCSP*.

Business Owned and Operated by Spouses

If you and your spouse jointly own and operate a business and share in the profits and losses, you may be partners in a partnership, whether or not you have a formal partnership agreement. See Pub. 541 for more details. The partnership is considered the employer of any employees, and is liable for any employment taxes due on wages paid to its employees.

Exception—Qualified joint venture. For tax years beginning after 2006, the Small Business and Work Opportunity Tax Act of 2007 (Public Law 110-28) provides that a "qualified joint venture," whose only members are spouses filing a joint income tax return, can elect not to be treated as a partnership for federal tax purposes. A qualified joint venture conducts a trade or business where:

- The only members of the joint venture are spouses who file a joint income tax return,

- Both spouses materially participate (see *Material participation* in the Instructions for Schedule C (Form 1040), line G) in the trade or business (mere joint ownership of property isn't enough),

- Both spouses elect to not be treated as a partnership, and

- The business is co-owned by both spouses and isn't held in the name of a state law entity such as a partnership or limited liability company (LLC).

To make the election, all items of income, gain, loss, deduction, and credit must be divided between the spouses, in accordance with each spouse's interest in the venture, and reported on separate Schedules C or F as sole proprietors. Each spouse must also file a separate Schedule SE to pay self-employment taxes, as applicable.

Spouses using the qualified joint venture rules are treated as sole proprietors for federal tax purposes and generally don't need an EIN. If employment taxes are owed by the qualified joint venture, either spouse may report and pay the employment taxes due on the wages paid to the employees using the EIN of that spouse's sole proprietorship. Generally, filing as a qualified joint venture won't increase the spouses' total tax owed on the joint income tax return. However, it gives each spouse credit for social security earnings on which retirement benefits are based and for Medicare coverage without filing a partnership return.

Note. If your spouse is your employee, not your partner, see *One spouse employed by another* in section 3.

For more information on qualified joint ventures, go to *IRS.gov/QJV*.

Exception—Community income. If you and your spouse wholly own an unincorporated business as community property under the community property laws of a state, foreign country, or U.S. possession, you can treat the business either as a sole proprietorship (of the spouse who carried on the business) or a partnership. You may still make an election to be taxed as a qualified joint venture instead of a partnership. See *Exception—Qualified joint venture*, earlier.

---

3. Family Employees

Child employed by parents. Payments for the services of a child under age 18 who works for his or her parent in a trade or business aren't subject to social security and Medicare taxes if the trade or business is a sole proprietorship or a partnership in which each partner is a parent of the child. If these payments are for work other than in a trade or business, such as domestic work in the parent's private home, they're not subject to social security and Medicare taxes until the child reaches age 21. However, see *Covered services of a child or spouse*, later. Payments for the services of a child under age 21 who works for his or her parent, whether or not in a trade or business, aren't subject to FUTA tax. Payments for the services of a child of any age who works for his or her parent are generally subject to income tax withholding unless the payments are for domestic work in the parent's home, or unless the payments are for work other than in a trade or business and are less than $50 in the quarter or the child isn't regularly employed to do such work.

One spouse employed by another. The wages for the services of an individual who works for his or her spouse in a trade or business are subject to income tax withholding and social security and Medicare taxes, but not to FUTA tax. However, the payments for services of one spouse employed by another in other than a trade or business, such as domestic service in a private home, aren't subject to social security, Medicare, and FUTA taxes.

Covered services of a child or spouse. The wages for the services of a child or spouse are subject to income tax withholding as well as social security, Medicare, and FUTA taxes if he or she works for:

- A corporation, even if it is controlled by the child's parent or the individual's spouse;
- A partnership, even if the child's parent is a partner, unless each partner is a parent of the child;
- A partnership, even if the individual's spouse is a partner; or
- An estate, even if it is the estate of a deceased parent.

In these situations, the child or spouse is considered to work for the corporation, partnership, or estate, not you.

Parent employed by son or daughter. When the employer is a son or daughter employing his or her parent, the following rules apply.

- Payments for the services of a parent in the son's or daughter's (the employer's) trade or business are subject to income tax withholding and social security and Medicare taxes.
- Payments for the services of a parent not in the son's or daughter's (the employer's) trade or business are

generally not subject to social security and Medicare taxes.

 Social security and Medicare taxes do apply to payments made to a parent for domestic services if all of the following apply.

- *The parent is employed by his or her son or daughter.*
- *The son or daughter (the employer) has a child or stepchild (including an adopted child) living in the home.*
- *The son or daughter (the employer) is a widow or widower, divorced and not remarried, or living with a spouse who, because of a mental or physical condition, can't care for the child or stepchild for at least 4 continuous weeks in the calendar quarter in which the service is performed.*
- *The child or stepchild is either under age 18 or requires the personal care of an adult for at least 4 continuous weeks in the calendar quarter in which the service is performed due to a mental or physical condition.*

Payments made to a parent employed by his or her child aren't subject to FUTA tax, regardless of the type of services provided.

---

4. Employee's Social Security Number (SSN)

You're required to get each employee's name and SSN and to enter them on Form W-2. This requirement also applies to resident and nonresident alien employees. You should ask your employee to show you his or her social security card. The employee may show the card if it is available.

 Don't accept a social security card that says "Not valid for employment." A social security number issued with this legend doesn't permit employment.

You may, but aren't required to, photocopy the social security card if the employee provides it. If you don't provide the correct employee name and SSN on Form W-2, you may owe a penalty unless you have reasonable cause. See Pub. 1586, Reasonable Cause Regulations & Requirements for Missing and Incorrect Name/TINs, for information on the requirement to solicit the employee's SSN.

Applying for a social security card. Any employee who is legally eligible to work in the United States and doesn't have a social security card can get one by completing Form SS-5, Application for a Social Security Card, and submitting the necessary documentation. You can get Form SS-5 from the SSA website at *SSA.gov/forms/ss-5.pdf*, at SSA offices, or by calling 800-772-1213 or 800-325-0778 (TTY). The employee must complete and sign Form SS-5; it can't be filed by the employer. You may be asked to supply a letter to accompany Form SS-5 if the employee has exceeded his or her yearly or lifetime limit for the number of replacement cards allowed.

Applying for an SSN. If you file Form W-2 on paper and your employee applied for an SSN but doesn't have one when you must file Form W-2, enter "Applied For" on the form. If you're filing electronically, enter all zeros (000-00-0000 if creating forms online or 000000000 if uploading a file) in the SSN field. When the employee receives the SSN, file Copy A of Form W-2c, Corrected Wage and Tax Statement, with the SSA to show the employee's SSN. Furnish copies B, C, and 2 of Form W-2c to the employee. Up to 25 Forms W-2c for each Form W-3c, Transmittal of Corrected Wage and Tax Statements, may now be filed per session over the Internet, with no limit on the number of sessions. For more information, visit the SSA's Employer W-2 Filing Instructions & Information webpage at _SSA.gov/employer_. Advise your employee to correct the SSN on his or her original Form W-2.

Correctly record the employee's name and SSN. Record the name and SSN of each employee as they're shown on the employee's social security card. If the employee's name isn't correct as shown on the card (for example, because of marriage or divorce), the employee should request an updated card from the SSA. Continue to report the employee's wages under the old name until the employee shows you the updated social security card with the corrected name.

If the SSA issues the employee an updated card after a name change, or a new card with a different SSN after a change in alien work status, file a Form W-2c to correct the name/SSN reported for the most recently filed Form W-2. It isn't necessary to correct other years if the previous name and number were used for years before the most recent Form W-2.

IRS individual taxpayer identification numbers (ITINs) for aliens. Don't accept an ITIN in place of an SSN for employee identification or for work. An ITIN is only available to resident and nonresident aliens who aren't eligible for U.S. employment and need identification for other tax purposes. You can identify an ITIN because it is a nine-digit number, formatted like an SSN, that starts with the number "9" and has a range of numbers from "50–65," "70–88," "90–92," and "94–99" for the fourth and fifth digits (for example, 9NN-7N-NNNN). For more information about ITINs, see the Instructions for Form W-7 or go to _IRS.gov/ITIN_.

 An individual with an ITIN who later becomes eligible to work in the United States must obtain an SSN. If the individual is currently eligible to work in the United States, instruct the individual to apply for an SSN and follow the instructions under Applying for an SSN, earlier. Don't use an ITIN in place of an SSN on Form W-2.

Verification of SSNs. Employers and authorized reporting agents can use the Social Security Number Verification Service (SSNVS) to instantly verify up to 10 names

and SSNs (per screen) at a time, or submit an electronic file of up to 250,000 names and SSNs and usually receive the results the next business day. Go to _SSA.gov/employer/ssnv.htm_ for more information.

Registering for SSNVS. You must register online to use SSNVS. To register, visit the SSA's website at _SSA.gov/bso_ and click on the _Register_ link under _Business Services Online_. Follow the registration instructions to obtain a user identification (ID) and password. You'll need to provide the following information about yourself and your company.

- Name.
- SSN.
- Date of birth.
- Type of employer.
- EIN.
- Company name, address, and telephone number.
- Email address.

When you have completed the online registration process, the SSA will mail a one-time activation code to you. You must enter the activation code online to use SSNVS. Your employees must receive authorization from you to use SSNVS. If your employees register, the one-time activation code will be mailed to you.

5. Wages and Other Compensation

Wages subject to federal employment taxes generally include all pay you give to an employee for services performed. The pay may be in cash or in other forms. It includes salaries, vacation allowances, bonuses, commissions, and fringe benefits. It doesn't matter how you measure or make the payments. Amounts an employer pays as a bonus for signing or ratifying a contract in connection with the establishment of an employer-employee relationship and an amount paid to an employee for cancellation of an employment contract and relinquishment of contract rights are wages subject to social security, Medicare, and FUTA taxes and income tax withholding. Also, compensation paid to a former employee for services performed while still employed is wages subject to employment taxes.

More information. See section 6 for a discussion of tips and section 7 for a discussion of supplemental wages. Also, see section 15 for exceptions to the general rules for wages. Pub. 15-A provides additional information on wages, including nonqualified deferred compensation, and other compensation. Pub. 15-B provides information on other forms of compensation, including:

- Accident and health benefits,
- Achievement awards,
- Adoption assistance,

- Athletic facilities,
- De minimis (minimal) benefits,
- Dependent care assistance,
- Educational assistance,
- Employee discounts,
- Employee stock options,
- Employer-provided cell phones,
- Group-term life insurance coverage,
- Health savings accounts,
- Lodging on your business premises,
- Meals,
- No-additional-cost services,
- Retirement planning services,
- Transportation (commuting) benefits,
- Tuition reduction, and
- Working condition benefits.

Employee business expense reimbursements. A reimbursement or allowance arrangement is a system by which you pay the advances, reimbursements, and charges for your employees' business expenses. How you report a reimbursement or allowance amount depends on whether you have an accountable or a nonaccountable plan. If a single payment includes both wages and an expense reimbursement, you must specify the amount of the reimbursement.

These rules apply to all allowable ordinary and necessary employee business expenses.

Accountable plan. To be an accountable plan, your reimbursement or allowance arrangement must require your employees to meet all three of the following rules.

1. They must have paid or incurred allowable expenses while performing services as your employees. The reimbursement or advance must be payment for the expenses and must not be an amount that would have otherwise been paid to the employee as wages.

2. They must substantiate these expenses to you within a reasonable period of time.

3. They must return any amounts in excess of substantiated expenses within a reasonable period of time.

Amounts paid under an accountable plan aren't wages and aren't subject to income, social security, Medicare, and FUTA taxes.

If the expenses covered by this arrangement aren't substantiated (or amounts in excess of substantiated expenses aren't returned within a reasonable period of time), the amount paid under the arrangement in excess of the substantiated expenses is treated as paid under a nonaccountable plan. This amount is subject to income, social security, Medicare, and FUTA taxes for the first payroll period following the end of the reasonable period of time.

A reasonable period of time depends on the facts and circumstances. Generally, it is considered reasonable if

your employees receive their advance within 30 days of the time they pay or incur the expenses, adequately account for the expenses within 60 days after the expenses were paid or incurred, and return any amounts in excess of expenses within 120 days after the expenses were paid or incurred. Alternatively, it is considered reasonable if you give your employees a periodic statement (at least quarterly) that asks them to either return or adequately account for outstanding amounts and they do so within 120 days.

Nonaccountable plan. Payments to your employee for travel and other necessary expenses of your business under a nonaccountable plan are wages and are treated as supplemental wages and subject to income, social security, Medicare, and FUTA taxes. Your payments are treated as paid under a nonaccountable plan if:

- Your employee isn't required to or doesn't substantiate timely those expenses to you with receipts or other documentation,

- You advance an amount to your employee for business expenses and your employee isn't required to or doesn't return timely any amount he or she doesn't use for business expenses,

- You advance or pay an amount to your employee regardless of whether you reasonably expect the employee to have business expenses related to your business, or

- You pay an amount as a reimbursement you would have otherwise paid as wages.

See section 7 for more information on supplemental wages.

Per diem or other fixed allowance. You may reimburse your employees by travel days, miles, or some other fixed allowance under the applicable revenue procedure. In these cases, your employee is considered to have accounted to you if your reimbursement doesn't exceed rates established by the federal government. The 2018 standard mileage rate for auto expenses was 54.5 cents per mile. The rate for 2019 is 58 cents per mile.

The government per diem rates for meals and lodging in the continental United States can be found by visiting the U.S. General Services Administration website at GSA.gov/PerDiemRates. Other than the amount of these expenses, your employees' business expenses must be substantiated (for example, the business purpose of the travel or the number of business miles driven). For information on substantiation methods, see Pub. 463.

If the per diem or allowance paid exceeds the amounts substantiated, you must report the excess amount as wages. This excess amount is subject to income tax withholding and payment of social security, Medicare, and FUTA taxes. Show the amount equal to the substantiated amount (that is, the nontaxable portion) in box 12 of Form W-2 using code "L."

Wages not paid in money. If in the course of your trade or business you pay your employees in a medium that is neither cash nor a readily negotiable instrument, such as a check, you're said to pay them "in kind." Payments in kind may be in the form of goods, lodging, food, clothing, or services. Generally, the fair market value of such payments at the time they're provided is subject to federal income tax withholding and social security, Medicare, and FUTA taxes.

However, noncash payments for household work, agricultural labor, and service not in the employer's trade or business are exempt from social security, Medicare, and FUTA taxes. Withhold income tax on these payments only if you and the employee agree to do so. Nonetheless, noncash payments for agricultural labor, such as commodity wages, are treated as cash payments subject to employment taxes if the substance of the transaction is a cash payment.

Meals and lodging. The value of meals isn't taxable income and isn't subject to federal income tax withholding and social security, Medicare, and FUTA taxes if the meals are furnished for the employer's convenience and on the employer's premises. The value of lodging isn't subject to federal income tax withholding and social security, Medicare, and FUTA taxes if the lodging is furnished for the employer's convenience, on the employer's premises, and as a condition of employment.

"For the convenience of the employer" means you have a substantial business reason for providing the meals and lodging other than to provide additional compensation to the employee. For example, meals you provide at the place of work so that an employee is available for emergencies during his or her lunch period are generally considered to be for your convenience. You must be able to show these emergency calls have occurred or can reasonably be expected to occur, and that the calls have resulted, or will result, in you calling on your employees to perform their jobs during their meal period.

Whether meals or lodging are provided for the convenience of the employer depends on all of the facts and circumstances. A written statement that the meals or lodging are for your convenience isn't sufficient.

50% test. If over 50% of the employees who are provided meals on an employer's business premises receive these meals for the convenience of the employer, all meals provided on the premises are treated as furnished for the convenience of the employer. If this 50% test is met, the value of the meals is excludable from income for all employees and isn't subject to federal income tax withholding or employment taxes. For more information, see Pub. 15-B.

Health insurance plans. If you pay the cost of an accident or health insurance plan for your employees, including an employee's spouse and dependents, your payments aren't wages and aren't subject to social security, Medicare, and FUTA taxes, or federal income tax withholding. Generally, this exclusion also applies to qualified long-term care insurance contracts. However, for income tax withholding, the value of health insurance benefits must be included in the wages of S corporation employees who own more than 2% of the S corporation (2% shareholders). For social security, Medicare, and FUTA

taxes, the health insurance benefits are excluded from the wages only for employees and their dependents or for a class or classes of employees and their dependents. See Announcement 92-16 for more information. You can find Announcement 92-16 on page 53 of Internal Revenue Bulletin 1992-5.

Health savings accounts and medical savings accounts. Your contributions to an employee's health savings account (HSA) or Archer medical savings account (MSA) aren't subject to social security, Medicare, or FUTA taxes, or federal income tax withholding if it is reasonable to believe at the time of payment of the contributions they'll be excludable from the income of the employee. To the extent it isn't reasonable to believe they'll be excludable, your contributions are subject to these taxes. Employee contributions to their HSAs or MSAs through a payroll deduction plan must be included in wages and are subject to social security, Medicare, and FUTA taxes and income tax withholding. However, HSA contributions made under a salary reduction arrangement in a section 125 cafeteria plan aren't wages and aren't subject to employment taxes or withholding. For more information, see the Instructions for Form 8889.

Medical care reimbursements. Generally, medical care reimbursements paid for an employee under an employer's self-insured medical reimbursement plan aren't wages and aren't subject to social security, Medicare, and FUTA taxes, or income tax withholding. See Pub. 15-B for a rule regarding inclusion of certain reimbursements in the gross income of highly compensated individuals.

Differential wage payments. Differential wage payments are any payments made by an employer to an individual for a period during which the individual is performing service in the uniformed services while on active duty for a period of more than 30 days and represent all or a portion of the wages the individual would have received from the employer if the individual were performing services for the employer.

Differential wage payments are wages for income tax withholding, but aren't subject to social security, Medicare, or FUTA taxes. Employers should report differential wage payments in box 1 of Form W-2. For more information about the tax treatment of differential wage payments, see Revenue Ruling 2009-11, 2009-18 I.R.B. 896, available at IRS.gov/irb/2009-18_IRB#RR-2009-11.

Fringe benefits. You generally must include fringe benefits in an employee's wages (but see *Nontaxable fringe benefits* next). The benefits are subject to income tax withholding and employment taxes. Fringe benefits include cars you provide, flights on aircraft you provide, free or discounted commercial flights, vacations, discounts on property or services, memberships in country clubs or other social clubs, and tickets to entertainment or sporting events. In general, the amount you must include is the amount by which the fair market value of the benefit is more than the sum of what the employee paid for it plus any amount the law excludes. There are other special rules you and your employees may use to value certain fringe benefits. See Pub. 15-B for more information.

Nontaxable fringe benefits. Some fringe benefits aren't taxable (or are minimally taxable) if certain conditions are met. See Pub. 15-B for details. The following are some examples of nontaxable fringe benefits.

- Services provided to your employees at no additional cost to you.
- Qualified employee discounts.
- Working condition fringes that are property or services that would be allowable as a business expense or depreciation expense deduction to the employee if he or she had paid for them. Examples include a company car for business use and subscriptions to business magazines.
- Certain minimal value fringes (including an occasional cab ride when an employee must work overtime and meals you provide at eating places you run for your employees if the meals aren't furnished at below cost).
- Qualified transportation fringes subject to specified conditions and dollar limitations (including transportation in a commuter highway vehicle, any transit pass, and qualified parking).
- The use of on-premises athletic facilities operated by you if substantially all of the use is by employees, their spouses, and their dependent children.
- Qualified tuition reduction an educational organization provides to its employees for education. For more information, see Pub. 970.
- Employer-provided cell phones provided primarily for a noncompensatory business reason.

However, don't exclude the following fringe benefits from the wages of highly compensated employees unless the benefit is available to other employees on a nondiscriminatory basis.

- No-additional-cost services.
- Qualified employee discounts.
- Meals provided at an employer-operated eating facility.
- Reduced tuition for education.

For more information, including the definition of a highly compensated employee, see Pub. 15-B.

When fringe benefits are treated as paid. You may choose to treat certain noncash fringe benefits as paid by the pay period, by the quarter, or on any other basis you choose, as long as you treat the benefits as paid at least once a year. You don't have to make a formal choice of payment dates or notify the IRS of the dates you choose. You don't have to make this choice for all employees. You may change methods as often as you like, as long as you treat all benefits provided in a calendar year as paid by December 31 of the calendar year. See Pub. 15-B for more information, including a discussion of the special accounting rule for fringe benefits provided during November and December.

Valuation of fringe benefits. Generally, you must determine the value of fringe benefits no later than January 31 of the next year. Before January 31, you may reasonably estimate the value of the fringe benefits for purposes of withholding and depositing on time.

Withholding on fringe benefits. You may add the value of fringe benefits to regular wages for a payroll period and figure withholding taxes on the total, or you may withhold federal income tax on the value of the fringe benefits at the optional flat 22% supplemental wage rate. However, see *Withholding on supplemental wages when an employee receives more than $1 million of supplemental wages during the calendar year* in section 7.

You may choose not to withhold income tax on the value of an employee's personal use of a vehicle you provide. You must, however, withhold social security and Medicare taxes on the use of the vehicle. See Pub. 15-B for more information on this election.

Depositing taxes on fringe benefits. Once you choose when fringe benefits are paid, you must deposit taxes in the same deposit period you treat the fringe benefits as paid. To avoid a penalty, deposit the taxes following the general deposit rules for that deposit period.

If you determine by January 31 you overestimated the value of a fringe benefit at the time you withheld and deposited for it, you may claim a refund for the overpayment or have it applied to your next employment tax return. See *Valuation of fringe benefits*, earlier. If you underestimated the value and deposited too little, you may be subject to a failure-to-deposit (FTD) penalty. See section 11 for information on deposit penalties.

If you deposited the required amount of taxes but withheld a lesser amount from the employee, you can recover from the employee the social security, Medicare, or income taxes you deposited on his or her behalf, and included in the employee's Form W-2. However, you must recover the income taxes before April 1 of the following year.

Sick pay. In general, sick pay is any amount you pay under a plan to an employee who is unable to work because of sickness or injury. These amounts are sometimes paid by a third party, such as an insurance company or an employees' trust. In either case, these payments are subject to social security, Medicare, and FUTA taxes. These taxes don't apply to sick pay paid more than 6 calendar months after the last calendar month in which the employee worked for the employer. The payments are always subject to federal income tax. See Pub. 15-A for more information.

Identity protection services. The value of identity protection services provided by an employer to an employee isn't included in an employee's gross income and doesn't need to be reported on an information return (such as Form W-2) filed for employees. This includes identity protection services provided before a data breach occurs. This exception doesn't apply to cash received instead of identity protection services or to proceeds received under an identity theft insurance policy. For more information, see Announcement 2015-22, 2015-35 I.R.B. 288, available at *IRS.gov/irb/2015-35_IRB#ANN-2015-22*, and Announcement 2016-02, 2016-3 I.R.B. 283, available at *IRS.gov/irb/2016-03_IRB#ANN-2016-02*.

---

6. Tips

Tips your employee receives from customers are generally subject to withholding. Your employee must report cash tips to you by the 10th of the month after the month the tips are received. The report should include tips you paid over to the employee for charge customers, tips the employee received directly from customers, and tips received from other employees under any tip-sharing arrangement. Both directly and indirectly tipped employees must report tips to you. No report is required for months when tips are less than $20. Your employee reports the tips on Form 4070 or on a similar statement. The statement must be signed by the employee and must include:

* The employee's name, address, and SSN;
* Your name and address;
* The month and year (or the beginning and ending dates, if the statement is for a period of less than 1 calendar month) the report covers; and
* The total of tips received during the month or period.

Both Forms 4070 and 4070-A, Employee's Daily Record of Tips, are included in Pub. 1244, Employee's Daily Record of Tips and Report to Employer.

 You're permitted to establish a system for electronic tip reporting by employees. See Regulations section 31.6053-1(d).

Collecting taxes on tips. You must collect federal income tax, employee social security tax, and employee Medicare tax on the employee's tips. The withholding rules for withholding an employee's share of Medicare tax on tips also apply to withholding the Additional Medicare Tax once wages and tips exceed $200,000 in the calendar year.

You can collect these taxes from the employee's wages or from other funds he or she makes available. See *Tips treated as supplemental wages* in section 7 for more information. Stop collecting the employee social security tax when his or her wages and tips for tax year 2019 reach $132,900; collect the income and employee Medicare taxes for the whole year on all wages and tips. You're responsible for the employer social security tax on wages and tips until the wages (including tips) reach the limit. You're responsible for the employer Medicare tax for the whole year on all wages and tips. File Form 941 or Form 944 to report withholding and employment taxes on tips.

Ordering rule. If, by the 10th of the month after the month for which you received an employee's report on tips, you don't have enough employee funds available to deduct the employee tax, you no longer have to collect it. If there aren't enough funds available, withhold taxes in the following order.

1. Withhold on regular wages and other compensation.
2. Withhold social security and Medicare taxes on tips.
3. Withhold income tax on tips.

Reporting tips. Report tips and any collected and uncollected social security and Medicare taxes on Form W-2 and on Form 941, lines 5b, 5c, and, if applicable, 5d (Form 944, lines 4b, 4c, and, if applicable, 4d). Report an adjustment on Form 941, line 9 (Form 944, line 6), for the uncollected social security and Medicare taxes. Enter the amount of uncollected social security tax and Medicare tax on Form W-2, box 12, with codes "A" and "B." Don't include any uncollected Additional Medicare Tax in box 12 of Form W-2. For additional information on reporting tips, see section 13 and the General Instructions for Forms W-2 and W-3.

Revenue Ruling 2012-18 provides guidance for employers regarding social security and Medicare taxes imposed on tips, including information on the reporting of the employer share of social security and Medicare taxes under section 3121(q), the difference between tips and service charges, and the section 45B credit. See Revenue Ruling 2012-18, 2012-26 I.R.B. 1032, available at *IRS.gov/irb/2012-26_IRB#RR-2012-18*.

FUTA tax on tips. If an employee reports to you in writing $20 or more of tips in a month, the tips are also subject to FUTA tax.

Allocated tips. If you operate a large food or beverage establishment, you must report allocated tips under certain circumstances. However, don't withhold income, social security, or Medicare taxes on allocated tips.

A large food or beverage establishment is one that provides food or beverages for consumption on the premises, where tipping is customary, and where there were normally more than 10 employees on a typical business day during the preceding year.

The tips may be allocated by one of three methods—hours worked, gross receipts, or good faith agreement. For information about these allocation methods, including the requirement to file Forms 8027 electronically if 250 or more forms are filed, see the Instructions for Form 8027. For information on filing Form 8027 electronically with the IRS, see Pub. 1239.

Tip Rate Determination and Education Program. Employers may participate in the Tip Rate Determination and Education Program. The program primarily consists of two voluntary agreements developed to improve tip income reporting by helping taxpayers to understand and meet their tip reporting responsibilities. The two agreements are the Tip Rate Determination Agreement (TRDA) and the Tip Reporting Alternative Commitment (TRAC). A tip agreement, the Gaming Industry Tip Compliance Agreement (GITCA), is available for the gaming (casino) industry. To get more information about TRDA and TRAC agreements, see Pub. 3144. Additionally, visit IRS.gov and enter "MSU tips" in the search box to get more information about GITCA, TRDA, or TRAC agreements.

7. Supplemental Wages

Supplemental wages are wage payments to an employee that aren't regular wages. They include, but aren't limited to, bonuses, commissions, overtime pay, payments for accumulated sick leave, severance pay, awards, prizes, back pay, retroactive pay increases, and payments for nondeductible moving expenses. Other payments subject to the supplemental wage rules include taxable fringe benefits and expense allowances paid under a nonaccountable plan. How you withhold on supplemental wages depends on whether the supplemental payment is identified as a separate payment from regular wages. See Regulations section 31.3402(g)-1 for additional guidance for wages paid after January 1, 2007. Also see Revenue Ruling 2008-29, 2008-24 I.R.B. 1149, available at *IRS.gov/ irb/2008-24_IRB#RR-2008-29*.

Withholding on supplemental wages when an employee receives more than $1 million of supplemental wages from you during the calendar year. Special rules apply to the extent supplemental wages paid to any one employee during the calendar year exceed $1 million. If a supplemental wage payment, together with other supplemental wage payments made to the employee during the calendar year, exceeds $1 million, the excess is subject to withholding at 37% (or the highest rate of income tax for the year). Withhold using the 37% rate without regard to the employee's Form W-4. In determining supplemental wages paid to the employee during the year, include payments from all businesses under common control. For more information, see Treasury Decision 9276, 2006-37 I.R.B. 423, available at *IRS.gov/irb/ 2006-37_IRB#TD-9276*.

Withholding on supplemental wage payments to an employee who doesn't receive $1 million of supplemental wages during the calendar year. If the supplemental wages paid to the employee during the calendar year are less than or equal to $1 million, the following rules apply in determining the amount of income tax to be withheld.

Supplemental wages combined with regular wages. If you pay supplemental wages with regular wages but don't specify the amount of each, withhold federal income tax as if the total were a single payment for a regular payroll period.

Supplemental wages identified separately from regular wages. If you pay supplemental wages separately (or combine them in a single payment and specify the amount of each), the federal income tax withholding method depends partly on whether you withhold income tax from your employee's regular wages.

1. If you withheld income tax from an employee's regular wages in the current or immediately preceding calendar year, you can use one of the following methods for the supplemental wages.

a. Withhold a flat 22% (no other percentage allowed).

b. If the supplemental wages are paid concurrently with regular wages, add the supplemental wages to the concurrently paid regular wages. If there are no concurrently paid regular wages, add the supplemental wages to, alternatively, either the regular wages paid or to be paid for the current payroll period or the regular wages paid for the preceding payroll period. Figure the income tax withholding as if the total of the regular wages and supplemental wages is a single payment. Subtract the tax already withheld or to be withheld from the regular wages. Withhold the remaining tax from the supplemental wages. If there were other payments of supplemental wages paid during the payroll period made before the current payment of supplemental wages, aggregate all the payments of supplemental wages paid during the payroll period with the regular wages paid during the payroll period, figure the tax on the total, subtract the tax already withheld from the regular wages and the previous supplemental wage payments, and withhold the remaining tax.

2. If you didn't withhold income tax from the employee's regular wages in the current or immediately preceding calendar year, use method 1b. This would occur, for example, when the value of the employee's withholding allowances claimed on Form W-4 is more than the wages.

Regardless of the method you use to withhold income tax on supplemental wages, they're subject to social security, Medicare, and FUTA taxes.

Example 1. You pay John Peters a base salary on the 1st of each month. He is single and claims one withholding allowance. In January, he is paid $1,000. Using the wage bracket tables, you withhold $34 from this amount. In February, he receives salary of $1,000 plus a commission of $500, which you combine with regular wages and don't separately identify. You figure the withholding based on the total of $1,500. The correct withholding from the tables is $83.

Example 2. You pay Sharon Warren a base salary on the 1st of each month. She is single and claims one allowance. Her May 1 pay is $1,000. Using the wage bracket tables, you withhold $34. On May 15, she receives a bonus of $1,000. Electing to use supplemental wage withholding method 1b, you do the following.

1. Add the bonus amount to the amount of wages from the most recent base salary pay date (May 1) ($1,000 + $1,000 = $2,000).

2. Determine the amount of withholding on the combined $2,000 amount to be $143 using the wage bracket tables.

3. Subtract the amount withheld from wages on the most recent base salary pay date (May 1) from the combined withholding amount ($143 − $34 = $109).

4. Withhold $109 from the bonus payment.

Example 3. The facts are the same as in *Example 2*, except you elect to use the flat rate method of withholding on the bonus. You withhold 22% of $1,000, or $220, from Sharon's bonus payment.

Example 4. The facts are the same as in *Example 2*, except you elect to pay Sharon a second bonus of $500 on May 29. Using supplemental wage withholding method 1b, you do the following.

1. Add the first and second bonus amounts to the amount of wages from the most recent base salary pay date (May 1) ($1,000 + $1,000 + $500 = $2,500).

2. Determine the amount of withholding on the combined $2,500 amount to be $205 using the wage bracket tables.

3. Subtract the amounts withheld from wages on the most recent base salary pay date (May 1) and the amounts withheld from the first bonus payment from the combined withholding amount ($205 − $34 − $109 = $62).

4. Withhold $62 from the second bonus payment.

Tips treated as supplemental wages. Withhold income tax on tips from wages earned by the employee or from other funds the employee makes available. If an employee receives regular wages and reports tips, figure income tax withholding as if the tips were supplemental wages. If you haven't withheld income tax from the regular wages, add the tips to the regular wages. Then withhold income tax on the total. If you withheld income tax from the regular wages, you can withhold on the tips by method 1a or 1b discussed earlier in this section under *Supplemental wages identified separately from regular wages*.

Vacation pay. Vacation pay is subject to withholding as if it were a regular wage payment. When vacation pay is in addition to regular wages for the vacation period, treat it as a supplemental wage payment. If the vacation pay is for a time longer than your usual payroll period, spread it over the pay periods for which you pay it.

8. Payroll Period

Your payroll period is a period of service for which you usually pay wages. When you have a regular payroll period, withhold income tax for that time period even if your employee doesn't work the full period.

No regular payroll period. When you don't have a regular payroll period, withhold the tax as if you paid wages for a daily or miscellaneous payroll period. Figure the number of days (including Sundays and holidays) in the period covered by the wage payment. If the wages are unrelated to a specific length of time (for example, commis-

sions paid on completion of a sale), count back the number of days from the payment period to the latest of:

- The last wage payment made during the same calendar year;
- The date employment began, if during the same calendar year; or
- January 1 of the same year.

Employee paid for period less than 1 week. When you pay an employee for a period of less than 1 week, and the employee signs a statement under penalties of perjury indicating he or she isn't working for any other employer during the same week for wages subject to withholding, figure withholding based on a weekly payroll period. If the employee later begins to work for another employer for wages subject to withholding, the employee must notify you within 10 days. You then figure withholding based on the daily or miscellaneous period.

9. Withholding From Employees' Wages

Income Tax Withholding

Using Form W-4 to figure withholding. To know how much federal income tax to withhold from employees' wages, you should have a Form W-4 on file for each employee. Encourage your employees to file an updated Form W-4 for 2019, especially if they owed taxes or received a large refund when filing their 2018 tax return. Advise your employees to use the IRS Withholding Calculator available at *IRS.gov/W4App* for help in determining how many withholding allowances to claim on their Forms W-4.

Ask all new employees to give you a signed Form W-4 when they start work. Make the form effective with the first wage payment. If a new employee doesn't give you a completed Form W-4, withhold income tax as if he or she is single, with zero withholding allowances.

Form in Spanish. You can provide Formulario W-4(SP) in place of Form W-4 to your Spanish-speaking employees. For more information, see Pub. 17(SP). The rules discussed in this section that apply to Form W-4 also apply to Formulario W-4(SP).

Electronic system to receive Form W-4. You may establish a system to electronically receive Forms W-4 from your employees. See Regulations section 31.3402(f)(5)-1(c) for more information.

Effective date of Form W-4. A Form W-4 remains in effect until the employee gives you a new one. When you receive a new Form W-4 from an employee, don't adjust withholding for pay periods before the effective date of the new form. If an employee gives you a Form W-4 that replaces an existing Form W-4, begin withholding no later than the start of the first payroll period ending on or after the 30th day from the date when you received the replacement Form W-4. For exceptions, see *Exemption from federal income tax withholding*, *IRS review of requested Forms W-4*, and *Invalid Forms W-4*, later in this section.

 A Form W-4 that makes a change for the next calendar year won't take effect in the current calendar year.

Successor employer. If you're a successor employer (see *Successor employer*, later in this section), secure new Forms W-4 from the transferred employees unless the "Alternative Procedure" in section 5 of Revenue Procedure 2004-53 applies. See Revenue Procedure 2004-53, 2004-34 I.R.B. 320, available at *IRS.gov/irb/2004-34_IRB#RP-2004-53*.

Completing Form W-4. The amount of any federal income tax withholding must be based on marital status and withholding allowances. Your employees may not base their withholding amounts on a fixed dollar amount or percentage. However, an employee may specify a dollar amount to be withheld in addition to the amount of withholding based on filing status and withholding allowances claimed on Form W-4.

Employees may claim fewer withholding allowances than they're entitled to claim. They may wish to claim fewer allowances to ensure they have enough withholding or to offset the tax on other sources of taxable income not subject to withholding.

See Pub. 505 for more information about completing Form W-4. Along with Form W-4, you may wish to order Pub. 505 for use by your employees.

Don't accept any withholding or estimated tax payments from your employees in addition to withholding based on their Form W-4. If they require additional withholding, they should submit a new Form W-4 and, if necessary, pay estimated tax by filing Form 1040-ES or by using EFTPS to make estimated tax payments.

Exemption from federal income tax withholding. Generally, an employee may claim exemption from federal income tax withholding because he or she had no income tax liability last year and expects none this year. See the Form W-4 instructions for more information. However, the wages are still subject to social security and Medicare taxes. See also *Invalid Forms W-4*, later in this section.

A Form W-4 claiming exemption from withholding is effective when it is given to the employer and only for that calendar year. To continue to be exempt from withholding for 2019, an employee must give you a new Form W-4 by February 15. If the employee doesn't give you a new Form W-4 by February 15, begin withholding based on the last Form W-4 for the employee that didn't claim an exemption from withholding or, if one wasn't furnished, then withhold tax as if he or she is single with zero withholding allowances. If the employee provides a new Form W-4 claiming exemption from withholding on February 16 or later, you may apply it to future wages but don't refund any taxes withheld while the exempt status wasn't in place.

Withholding income taxes on the wages of nonresident alien employees. In general, you must withhold federal income taxes on the wages of nonresident alien employees. However, see Pub. 515 for exceptions to this general rule. Also see section 3 of Pub. 51 for guidance on H-2A visa workers.

Withholding adjustment for nonresident alien employees. Apply the procedure discussed next to figure the amount of income tax to withhold from the wages of nonresident alien employees performing services within the United States.

 Nonresident alien students from India and business apprentices from India aren't subject to this procedure.

Instructions. To figure how much income tax to withhold from the wages paid to a nonresident alien employee performing services in the United States, use the following steps.

Step 1. Add to the wages paid to the nonresident alien employee for the payroll period the amount shown in the chart next for the applicable payroll period.

Amount To Add to Nonresident Alien Employee's Wages for Calculating Income Tax Withholding Only

Payroll Period	Add Additional
Weekly	$ 153.80
Biweekly	307.70
Semimonthly	333.30
Monthly	666.70
Quarterly	2,000.00
Semiannually	4,000.00
Annually	8,000.00
Daily or Miscellaneous (each day of the payroll period)	30.80

Step 2. Use the amount figured in *Step 1* and the number of withholding allowances claimed (generally limited to one allowance) to figure income tax withholding. Determine the value of withholding allowances by multiplying the number of withholding allowances claimed by the appropriate amount from *Table 5* shown on page 45. If you're using the Percentage Method Tables for Income Tax Withholding, provided on pages 46–47, reduce the amount figured in *Step 1* by the value of withholding allowances and use that reduced amount to figure the income tax withholding. If you're using the Wage Bracket Method Tables for Income Tax Withholding, provided on pages 48–67, use the amount figured in *Step 1* and the number of withholding allowances to figure income tax withholding.

The amounts from the chart above are added to wages solely for calculating income tax withholding on the wages of the nonresident alien employee. The amounts from the chart shouldn't be included in any box on the employee's Form W-2 and don't increase the income tax liability of the employee. Also, the amounts from the chart don't increase the social security tax or Medicare tax liability of the employer or the employee, or the FUTA tax liability of the employer.

This procedure only applies to nonresident alien employees who have wages subject to income tax withholding.

Example. An employer using the percentage method of withholding pays wages of $500 for a biweekly payroll period to a married nonresident alien employee. The nonresident alien has properly completed Form W-4, entering marital status as "single" with one withholding allowance and indicating status as a nonresident alien on Form W-4, line 6 (see *Nonresident alien employee's Form W-4*, later in this section). The employer determines the wages to be used in the withholding tables by adding to the $500 amount of wages paid the amount of $307.70 from the chart under *Step 1* ($807.70 total). The employer then applies the applicable tables to determine the income tax withholding for nonresident aliens (see *Step 2*), earlier.

 If you use the Percentage Method Tables for Income Tax Withholding, reduce the amount figured in Step 1 *by the value of withholding allowances and use that reduced amount to figure income tax withholding.*

The $307.70 added to wages for calculating income tax withholding isn't reported on Form W-2, and doesn't increase the income tax liability of the employee. Also, the $307.70 added to wages doesn't affect the social security tax or Medicare tax liability of the employer or the employee, or the FUTA tax liability of the employer.

Supplemental wage payment. This procedure for determining the amount of income tax withholding doesn't apply to a supplemental wage payment (see section 7) if the 37% mandatory flat rate withholding applies or if the 22% optional flat rate withholding is being used to calculate income tax withholding on the supplemental wage payment.

Nonresident alien employee's Form W-4. When completing Forms W-4, nonresident aliens are required to:

- Not claim exemption from income tax withholding;

- Request withholding as if they're single, regardless of their actual marital status;

- Claim only one allowance (if the nonresident alien is a resident of Canada, Mexico, or South Korea, or a student or business apprentice from India, he or she may claim more than one allowance); and

- Write "Nonresident Alien" or "NRA" above the dotted line on line 6 of Form W-4.

If you maintain an electronic Form W-4 system, you should provide a field for nonresident aliens to enter nonresident alien status instead of writing "Nonresident Alien" or "NRA" above the dotted line on line 6.

 A nonresident alien employee may request additional withholding at his or her option for other purposes, although such additions shouldn't be necessary for withholding to cover federal income tax liability related to employment.

Form 8233. If a nonresident alien employee claims a tax treaty exemption from withholding, the employee must submit Form 8233 with respect to the income exempt under the treaty, instead of Form W-4. For more information, see *Pay for Personal Services Performed* in the *Withholding on Specific Income* section of Pub. 515 and the Instructions for Form 8233.

IRS review of requested Forms W-4. When requested by the IRS, you must make original Forms W-4 available for inspection by an IRS employee. You may also be directed to send certain Forms W-4 to the IRS. You may receive a notice from the IRS requiring you to submit a copy of Form W-4 for one or more of your named employees. Send the requested copy or copies of Form W-4 to the IRS at the address provided and in the manner directed by the notice. The IRS may also require you to submit copies of Form W-4 to the IRS as directed by Treasury Decision 9337, 2007-35 I.R.B. 455, which is available at *IRS.gov/irb/2007-35_IRB#TD-9337*. When we refer to Form W-4, the same rules apply to Formulario W-4(SP), its Spanish translation.

After submitting a copy of a requested Form W-4 to the IRS, continue to withhold federal income tax based on that Form W-4 if it is valid (see *Invalid Forms W-4*, later in this section). However, if the IRS later notifies you in writing that the employee isn't entitled to claim exemption from withholding or a claimed number of withholding allowances, withhold federal income tax based on the effective date, marital status, and maximum number of withholding allowances specified in the IRS notice (commonly referred to as a "lock-in letter").

Initial lock-in letter. The IRS uses information reported on Form W-2 to identify employees with withholding compliance problems. In some cases, if a serious underwithholding problem is found to exist for a particular employee, the IRS may issue a lock-in letter to the employer specifying the maximum number of withholding allowances and marital status permitted for a specific employee. You'll also receive a copy for the employee that identifies the maximum number of withholding allowances and marital status permitted and the process by which the employee can provide additional information to the IRS for purposes of determining the appropriate number of withholding allowances and/or modifying the specified marital status. You must furnish the employee copy to the employee within 10 business days of receipt if the employee is employed by you as of the date of the notice. Begin withholding based on the notice on the date specified in the notice.

Implementation of lock-in letter. When you receive the notice specifying the maximum number of withholding allowances and marital status permitted, you may not withhold immediately on the basis of the notice. You must begin withholding tax on the basis of the notice for any wages paid after the date specified in the notice. The delay between your receipt of the notice and the date to begin the withholding on the basis of the notice permits the employee time to contact the IRS.

Employee not performing services. If you receive a notice for an employee who isn't performing services for you, you must still furnish the employee copy to the employee and withhold based on the notice if any of the following apply.

- You're paying wages for the employee's prior services and the wages are subject to income tax withholding on or after the date specified in the notice.

- You reasonably expect the employee to resume services within 12 months of the date of the notice.

- The employee is on a leave of absence that doesn't exceed 12 months or the employee has a right to re-employment after the leave of absence.

Termination and re-hire of employees. If you must furnish and withhold based on the notice and the employment relationship is terminated after the date of the notice, you must continue to withhold based on the notice if you continue to pay any wages subject to income tax withholding. You must also withhold based on the notice or modification notice (explained next) if the employee resumes the employment relationship with you within 12 months after the termination of the employment relationship.

Modification notice. After issuing the notice specifying the maximum number of withholding allowances and marital status permitted, the IRS may issue a subsequent notice (modification notice) that modifies the original notice. The modification notice may change the marital status and/or the number of withholding allowances permitted. You must withhold federal income tax based on the effective date specified in the modification notice.

New Form W-4 after IRS notice. After the IRS issues a notice or modification notice, if the employee provides you with a new Form W-4 claiming complete exemption from withholding or claims a marital status, a number of withholding allowances, and any additional withholding that results in less withholding than would result under the IRS notice or modification notice, disregard the new Form W-4. You must withhold based on the notice or modification notice unless the IRS notifies you to withhold based on the new Form W-4. If the employee wants to put a new Form W-4 into effect that results in less withholding than required, the employee must contact the IRS.

If, after you receive an IRS notice or modification notice, your employee gives you a new Form W-4 that doesn't claim exemption from federal income tax withholding and claims a marital status, a number of withholding allowances, and any additional withholding that results in more withholding than would result under the notice or modification notice, you must withhold tax based on the new Form W-4. Otherwise, disregard any subsequent Forms W-4 provided by the employee and withhold based on the IRS notice or modification notice.

For additional information about these rules, see Treasury Decision 9337, 2007-35 I.R.B. 455, available at *IRS.gov/irb/2007-35_IRB#TD-9337*.

Substitute Forms W-4. You're encouraged to have your employees use the official version of Form W-4 to claim withholding allowances or exemption from withholding.

You may use a substitute version of Form W-4 to meet your business needs. However, your substitute Form W-4 must contain language that is identical to the official Form W-4 and your form must meet all current IRS rules for substitute forms. At the time you provide your substitute form to the employee, you must provide him or her with all tables, instructions, and worksheets from the current Form W-4.

You can't accept substitute Forms W-4 developed by employees. An employee who submits an employee-developed substitute Form W-4 after October 10, 2007, will be treated as failing to furnish a Form W-4. However, continue to honor any valid employee-developed Forms W-4 you accepted before October 11, 2007.

Invalid Forms W-4. Any unauthorized change or addition to Form W-4 makes it invalid. This includes taking out any language by which the employee certifies the form is correct. A Form W-4 is also invalid if, by the date an employee gives it to you, he or she clearly indicates it is false. An employee who submits a false Form W-4 may be subject to a $500 penalty. You may treat a Form W-4 as invalid if the employee wrote "exempt" on line 7 and also entered a number on line 5 or an amount on line 6.

When you get an invalid Form W-4, don't use it to figure federal income tax withholding. Tell the employee it is invalid and ask for another one. If the employee doesn't give you a valid one, withhold tax as if the employee is single with zero withholding allowances. However, if you have an earlier Form W-4 for this worker that is valid, withhold as you did before.

Amounts exempt from levy on wages, salary, and other income. If you receive a Notice of Levy on Wages, Salary, and Other Income (Forms 668-W(ACS), 668-W(c) (DO), or 668-W(ICS)), you must withhold amounts as described in the instructions for these forms. Pub. 1494 has tables to figure the amount exempt from levy. If a levy issued in a prior year is still in effect and the taxpayer submits a new Statement of Exemptions and Filing Status, use the current year Pub. 1494 to figure the exempt amount.

Social Security and Medicare Taxes

The Federal Insurance Contributions Act (FICA) provides for a federal system of old-age, survivors, disability, and hospital insurance. The old-age, survivors, and disability insurance part is financed by the social security tax. The hospital insurance part is financed by the Medicare tax. Each of these taxes is reported separately.

Generally, you're required to withhold social security and Medicare taxes from your employees' wages and pay the employer's share of these taxes. Certain types of wages and compensation aren't subject to social security and Medicare taxes. See section 5 and section 15 for details. Generally, employee wages are subject to social security and Medicare taxes regardless of the employee's age or whether he or she is receiving social security benefits. If the employee reported tips, see section 6.

Tax rates and the social security wage base limit. Social security and Medicare taxes have different rates and only the social security tax has a wage base limit. The wage base limit is the maximum wage subject to the tax for the year. Determine the amount of withholding for social security and Medicare taxes by multiplying each payment by the employee tax rate. There are no withholding allowances for social security and Medicare taxes.

For 2019, the social security tax rate is 6.2% (amount withheld) each for the employer and employee (12.4% total). The social security wage base limit is $132,900. The tax rate for Medicare is 1.45% (amount withheld) each for the employee and employer (2.9% total). There is no wage base limit for Medicare tax; all covered wages are subject to Medicare tax.

Additional Medicare Tax withholding. In addition to withholding Medicare tax at 1.45%, you must withhold a 0.9% Additional Medicare Tax from wages you pay to an employee in excess of $200,000 in a calendar year. You're required to begin withholding Additional Medicare Tax in the pay period in which you pay wages in excess of $200,000 to an employee and continue to withhold it each pay period until the end of the calendar year. Additional Medicare Tax is only imposed on the employee. There is no employer share of Additional Medicare Tax. All wages that are subject to Medicare tax are subject to Additional Medicare Tax withholding if paid in excess of the $200,000 withholding threshold.

For more information on what wages are subject to Medicare tax, see section 15. For more information on Additional Medicare Tax, go to IRS.gov/ADMT.

Successor employer. When corporate acquisitions meet certain requirements, wages paid by the predecessor are treated as if paid by the successor for purposes of applying the social security wage base and for applying the Additional Medicare Tax withholding threshold (that is, $200,000 in a calendar year). You should determine whether or not you should file Schedule D (Form 941), Report of Discrepancies Caused by Acquisitions, Statutory Mergers, or Consolidations, by reviewing the Instructions for Schedule D (Form 941). See Regulations section 31.3121(a)(1)-1(b) for more information. Also see Revenue Procedure 2004-53, 2004-34 I.R.B. 320, available at IRS.gov/irb/2004-34_IRB#RP-2004-53.

Example. Early in 2019, you bought all of the assets of a plumbing business from Mr. Martin. Mr. Brown, who had been employed by Mr. Martin and received $2,000 in wages before the date of purchase, continued to work for you. The wages you paid to Mr. Brown are subject to social security taxes on the first $130,900 ($132,900 minus $2,000). Medicare tax is due on all of the wages you pay him during the calendar year. You should include the $2,000 Mr. Brown received while employed by Mr. Martin in determining whether Mr. Brown's wages exceed the $200,000 for Additional Medicare Tax withholding threshold.

Motion picture project employers. All wages paid by a motion picture project employer to a motion picture project worker during a calendar year are subject to a single social security tax wage base ($132,900 for 2019) and a single FUTA tax wage base ($7,000 for 2019) regardless of the worker's status as a common law employee of multiple clients of the motion picture project employer. For more information, including the definition of a motion picture project employer and motion picture project worker, see section 3512.

Withholding social security and Medicare taxes on nonresident alien employees. In general, if you pay wages to nonresident alien employees, you must withhold social security and Medicare taxes as you would for a U.S. citizen or resident alien. However, see Pub. 515 for exceptions to this general rule.

International social security agreements. The United States has social security agreements, also known as totalization agreements, with many countries that eliminate dual taxation and dual coverage. Compensation subject to social security and Medicare taxes may be exempt under one of these agreements. You can get more information and a list of agreement countries from the SSA at SSA.gov/international. Also see Pub. 519, U.S. Tax Guide for Aliens.

Religious exemption. An exemption from social security and Medicare taxes is available to members of a recognized religious sect opposed to insurance. This exemption is available only if both the employee and the employer are members of the sect. For more information, see Pub. 517.

Foreign persons treated as American employers. Under section 3121(z), for services performed after July 31, 2008, a foreign person who meets both of the following conditions is generally treated as an American employer for purposes of paying FICA taxes on wages paid to an employee who is a U.S. citizen or resident.

1. The foreign person is a member of a domestically controlled group of entities.

2. The employee of the foreign person performs services in connection with a contract between the U.S. Government (or an instrumentality of the U.S. Government) and any member of the domestically controlled group of entities. Ownership of more than 50% constitutes control.

Part-Time Workers

Part-time workers and workers hired for short periods of time are treated the same as full-time employees for federal income tax withholding and social security, Medicare, and FUTA tax purposes.

Generally, it doesn't matter whether the part-time worker or worker hired for a short period of time has another job or has the maximum amount of social security tax withheld by another employer. See *Successor employer*, earlier, for an exception to this rule.

Income tax withholding may be figured the same way as for full-time workers or it may be figured by the part-year employment method explained in section 9 of Pub. 15-A.

10. Required Notice to Employees About the Earned Income Credit (EIC)

You must notify employees who have no federal income tax withheld that they may be able to claim a tax refund because of the EIC. Although you don't have to notify employees who claim exemption from withholding on Form W-4 about the EIC, you're encouraged to notify any employees whose wages for 2018 were less than $49,194 ($54,884 if married filing jointly) that they may be eligible to claim the credit for 2018. This is because eligible employees may get a refund of the amount of the EIC that is more than the tax they owe.

You'll meet this notification requirement if you issue the employee Form W-2 with the EIC notice on the back of Copy B, or a substitute Form W-2 with the same statement. You'll also meet the requirement by providing Notice 797, Possible Federal Tax Refund Due to the Earned Income Credit (EIC), or your own statement that contains the same wording.

If a substitute for Form W-2 is given to the employee on time but doesn't have the required statement, you must notify the employee within 1 week of the date the substitute for Form W-2 is given. If Form W-2 is required but isn't given on time, you must give the employee Notice 797 or your written statement by the date Form W-2 is required to be given. If Form W-2 isn't required, you must notify the employee by February 7, 2019.

11. Depositing Taxes

Generally, you must deposit federal income tax withheld and both the employer and employee social security and Medicare taxes. You must use EFT to make all federal tax deposits. See *How To Deposit*, later in this section, for information on electronic deposit requirements.

 The credit against employment taxes for COBRA assistance payments is treated as a deposit of taxes on the first day of your return period. See COBRA premium assistance credit under Introduction, earlier, for more information.

Payment with return. You may make a payment with a timely filed Form 941 or Form 944 instead of depositing, without incurring a penalty, if one of the following applies.

- Your Form 941 total tax liability for either the current quarter or the prior quarter is less than $2,500, and you didn't incur a $100,000 next-day deposit obligation during the current quarter. If you aren't sure your total tax liability for the current quarter will be less than $2,500 (and your liability for the prior quarter wasn't less than $2,500), make deposits using the semiweekly or monthly rules so you won't be subject to an FTD penalty.

- Your Form 944 net tax liability for the year is less than $2,500.

- You're a monthly schedule depositor (defined later) and make a payment in accordance with the *Accuracy of Deposits Rule*, discussed later in this section. This payment may be $2,500 or more.

Employers who have been notified to file Form 944 can pay their fourth quarter tax liability with Form 944 if the fourth quarter tax liability is less than $2,500. Employers must have deposited any tax liability due for the first, second, and third quarters according to the deposit rules to avoid an FTD penalty for deposits during those quarters.

Separate deposit requirements for nonpayroll (Form 945) tax liabilities. Separate deposits are required for nonpayroll and payroll income tax withholding. Don't combine deposits for Forms 941 (or Form 944) and Form 945 tax liabilities. Generally, the deposit rules for nonpayroll liabilities are the same as discussed next, except the rules apply to an annual rather than a quarterly return period. If the total amount of tax for the year reported on Form 945 is less than $2,500, you're not required to make deposits during the year. See the separate Instructions for Form 945 for more information.

When To Deposit

There are two deposit schedules—monthly and semiweekly—for determining when you deposit social security, Medicare, and withheld federal income taxes. These schedules tell you when a deposit is due after a tax liability arises (for example, when you have a payday). Before the beginning of each calendar year, you must determine which of the two deposit schedules you're required to use. The deposit schedule you must use is based on the total tax liability you reported on Form 941 during a lookback period, discussed next. Your deposit schedule isn't determined by how often you pay your employees or make deposits. See special rules for Forms 944 and 945, later. Also see *Application of Monthly and Semiweekly Schedules*, later in this section.

 These rules don't apply to FUTA tax. See section 14 for information on depositing FUTA tax.

Lookback period. If you're a Form 941 filer, your deposit schedule for a calendar year is determined from the total taxes reported on Forms 941, line 12, in a 4-quarter lookback period. The lookback period begins July 1 and ends June 30 as shown next in Table 1. If you reported $50,000 or less of taxes for the lookback period, you're a monthly schedule depositor; if you reported more than $50,000, you're a semiweekly schedule depositor.

Table 1. **Lookback Period for Calendar Year 2019**

July 1, 2017, through Sept. 30, 2017	Oct. 1, 2017, through Dec. 31, 2017	Jan. 1, 2018, through Mar. 31, 2018	Apr. 1, 2018, through June 30, 2018

 The lookback period for a 2019 Form 941 filer who filed Form 944 in either 2017 or 2018 is calendar year 2017.

If you're a Form 944 filer for the current year or either of the preceding 2 years, your deposit schedule for a calendar year is determined from the total taxes reported during the second preceding calendar year (either on your Form 941 for all 4 quarters of that year or your Form 944 for that year). The lookback period for 2019 for a Form 944 filer is calendar year 2017. If you reported $50,000 or less of taxes for the lookback period, you're a monthly schedule depositor; if you reported more than $50,000, you're a semiweekly schedule depositor.

If you're a Form 945 filer, your deposit schedule for a calendar year is determined from the total taxes reported on line 3 of your Form 945 for the second preceding calendar year. The lookback period for 2019 for a Form 945 filer is calendar year 2017.

Adjustments and the lookback rule. Adjustments made on Form 941-X, Form 944-X, and Form 945-X don't affect the amount of tax liability for previous periods for purposes of the lookback rule.

Example. An employer originally reported a tax liability of $45,000 for the lookback period. The employer discovered, during January 2019, that the tax reported for one of the lookback period quarters was understated by $10,000 and corrected this error by filing Form 941-X. This employer is a monthly schedule depositor for 2019 because the lookback period tax liabilities are based on the amounts originally reported, and they were $50,000 or less. The $10,000 adjustment is also not treated as part of the 2019 taxes.

Deposit period. The term "deposit period" refers to the period during which tax liabilities are accumulated for each required deposit due date. For monthly schedule depositors, the deposit period is a calendar month. The deposit periods for semiweekly schedule depositors are Wednesday through Friday and Saturday through Tuesday.

 If you're an agent with an approved Form 2678, the deposit rules apply to you based on the total employment taxes accumulated by you for your own employees and on behalf of all employers for whom you're authorized to act. For more information on an agent with an approved Form 2678, see Revenue Procedure 2013-39, 2013-52 I.R.B. 830, available at IRS.gov/irb/2013-52_IRB#RP-2013-39.

Monthly Deposit Schedule

You're a monthly schedule depositor for a calendar year if the total taxes on Form 941, line 12, for the 4 quarters in your lookback period were $50,000 or less. Under the monthly deposit schedule, deposit employment taxes on payments made during a month by the 15th day of the following month. See also *Deposits Due on Business Days Only* and the *$100,000 Next-Day Deposit Rule*, later in this section. Monthly schedule depositors shouldn't file Form 941 or Form 944 on a monthly basis.

New employers. Your tax liability for any quarter in the lookback period before you started or acquired your business is considered to be zero. Therefore, you're a monthly schedule depositor for the first calendar year of your business. However, see the *$100,000 Next-Day Deposit Rule*, later in this section.

Semiweekly Deposit Schedule

You're a semiweekly schedule depositor for a calendar year if the total taxes on Form 941, line 12, during your lookback period were more than $50,000. Under the semiweekly deposit schedule, deposit employment taxes for payments made on Wednesday, Thursday, and/or Friday by the following Wednesday. Deposit taxes for payments made on Saturday, Sunday, Monday, and/or Tuesday by the following Friday. See also *Deposits Due on Business Days Only*, later in this section.

 Semiweekly schedule depositors must complete Schedule B (Form 941), Report of Tax Liability for Semiweekly Schedule Depositors, and submit it with Form 941. If you file Form 944 and are a semiweekly schedule depositor, complete Form 945-A, Annual Record of Federal Tax Liability, and submit it with your return (instead of Schedule B).

Table 2. **Semiweekly Deposit Schedule**

IF the payday falls on a . . .	THEN deposit taxes by the following . . .
Wednesday, Thursday, and/or Friday	Wednesday
Saturday, Sunday, Monday, and/or Tuesday	Friday

Semiweekly deposit period spanning two quarters (Form 941 filers). If you have more than one pay date during a semiweekly period and the pay dates fall in different calendar quarters, you'll need to make **separate deposits** for the separate liabilities.

Example. If you have a pay date on Monday, September 30, 2019 (third quarter), and another pay date on Tuesday, October 1, 2019 (fourth quarter), two separate deposits would be required even though the pay dates fall within the same semiweekly period. Both deposits would be due Friday, October 4, 2019.

Semiweekly deposit period spanning two return periods (Form 944 or Form 945 filers). The period covered by a return is the return period. The return period for annual Forms 944 and 945 is a calendar year. If you have more than one pay date during a semiweekly period and the pay dates fall in different return periods, you'll need to make separate deposits for the separate liabilities. For example, if you have a pay date on Saturday, December 29, 2018, and another pay date on Tuesday, January 1, 2019, two separate deposits will be required even though the pay dates fall within the same semiweekly period. Both deposits will be due Friday, January 4, 2019 (3 business days from the end of the semiweekly deposit period).

> **Summary of Steps to Determine Your Deposit Schedule**
> 1. Identify your lookback period (see *Lookback period*, earlier in this section).
> 2. Add the total taxes you reported on Form 941, line 12, during the lookback period.
> 3. Determine if you're a monthly or semiweekly schedule depositor:

IF the total taxes you reported in the lookback period were	THEN you're a
$50,000 or less	Monthly Schedule Depositor
More than $50,000	Semiweekly Schedule Depositor

Example of Monthly and Semiweekly Schedules

Rose Co. reported Form 941 taxes as follows:

2018 Lookback Period		2019 Lookback Period	
3rd Quarter 2016	$12,000	3rd Quarter 2017	$12,000
4th Quarter 2016	12,000	4th Quarter 2017	12,000
1st Quarter 2017	12,000	1st Quarter 2018	12,000
2nd Quarter 2017	12,000	2nd Quarter 2018	15,000
	$48,000		$51,000

Rose Co. is a monthly schedule depositor for 2018 because its tax liability for the 4 quarters in its lookback period (third quarter 2016 through second quarter 2017) wasn't more than $50,000. However, for 2019, Rose Co. is a semiweekly schedule depositor because the total taxes exceeded $50,000 for the 4 quarters in its lookback period (third quarter 2017 through second quarter 2018).

Deposits Due on Business Days Only

If a deposit is required to be made on a day that isn't a business day, the deposit is considered timely if it is made by the close of the next business day. A business day is any day other than a Saturday, Sunday, or legal holiday. For example, if a deposit is required to be made on a Friday and Friday is a legal holiday, the deposit will be considered timely if it is made by the following Monday (if that Monday is a business day).

Semiweekly schedule depositors have at least 3 business days following the close of the semiweekly period to make a deposit. If any of the 3 weekdays after the end of a semiweekly period is a legal holiday, you'll have an additional day for each day that is a legal holiday to make the required deposit. For example, if a semiweekly schedule depositor accumulated taxes for payments made on Friday and the following Monday is a legal holiday, the deposit normally due on Wednesday may be made on Thursday (this allows 3 business days to make the deposit).

Legal holiday. The term "legal holiday" means any legal holiday in the District of Columbia. For purposes of the deposit rules, the term "legal holiday" doesn't include other statewide legal holidays. Legal holidays for 2019 are listed next.

- January 1—New Year's Day
- January 21—Birthday of Martin Luther King, Jr.
- February 18—Washington's Birthday
- April 16—District of Columbia Emancipation Day
- May 27—Memorial Day
- July 4—Independence Day
- September 2—Labor Day
- October 14—Columbus Day
- November 11—Veterans Day
- November 28—Thanksgiving Day
- December 25—Christmas Day

Application of Monthly and Semiweekly Schedules

The terms "monthly schedule depositor" and "semiweekly schedule depositor" don't refer to how often your business pays its employees or even how often you're required to make deposits. The terms identify which set of deposit rules you must follow when an employment tax liability arises. The deposit rules are based on the dates when wages are paid (cash basis), not on when tax liabilities are accrued for accounting purposes.

Monthly schedule example. Spruce Co. is a monthly schedule depositor with seasonal employees. It paid wages each Friday during June but didn't pay any wages during July. Under the monthly deposit schedule, Spruce Co. must deposit the combined tax liabilities for the June paydays by July 15. Spruce Co. doesn't have a deposit requirement for July (due by August 15) because no wages were paid and, therefore, it didn't have a tax liability for July.

Semiweekly schedule example. Green, Inc., is a semiweekly schedule depositor and pays wages once each month on the last Friday of the month. Although Green, Inc., has a semiweekly deposit schedule, it will deposit just once a month because it pays wages only once a month. The deposit, however, will be made under the semiweekly deposit schedule as follows: Green, Inc.'s tax liability for the April 26, 2019 (Friday), payday must be deposited by May 1, 2019 (Wednesday). Under the semiweekly deposit schedule, liabilities for wages paid on Wednesday through Friday must be deposited by the following Wednesday.

$100,000 Next-Day Deposit Rule

If you accumulate $100,000 or more in taxes on any day during a monthly or semiweekly deposit period (see *Deposit period*, earlier in this section), you must deposit the tax by the next business day, whether you're a monthly or semiweekly schedule depositor.

For purposes of the $100,000 rule, don't continue accumulating a tax liability after the end of a deposit period. For example, if a semiweekly schedule depositor has accumulated a liability of $95,000 on a Tuesday (of a Saturday-through-Tuesday deposit period) and accumulated a $10,000 liability on Wednesday, the $100,000 next-day deposit rule doesn't apply because the $10,000 is accumulated in the next deposit period. Thus, $95,000 must be deposited by Friday and $10,000 must be deposited by the following Wednesday.

However, once you accumulate at least $100,000 in a deposit period, stop accumulating at the end of that day and begin to accumulate anew on the next day. For example, Fir Co. is a semiweekly schedule depositor. On Monday, Fir Co. accumulates taxes of $110,000 and must deposit this amount on Tuesday, the next business day. On Tuesday, Fir Co. accumulates additional taxes of $30,000. Because the $30,000 isn't added to the previous $110,000 and is less than $100,000, Fir Co. must deposit the $30,000 by Friday (following the semiweekly deposit schedule).

 If you're a monthly schedule depositor and accumulate a $100,000 tax liability on any day during the deposit period, you become a semiweekly schedule depositor on the next day and remain so for at least the rest of the calendar year and for the following calendar year.

Example. Elm, Inc., started its business on May 6, 2019. On Wednesday, May 8, it paid wages for the first time and accumulated a tax liability of $40,000. On Friday, May 10, Elm, Inc., paid wages and accumulated a liability of $60,000, bringing its total accumulated tax liability to $100,000. Because this was the first year of its business,

the tax liability for its lookback period is considered to be zero, and it would be a monthly schedule depositor based on the lookback rules. However, since Elm, Inc., accumulated a $100,000 liability on May 10, it became a semiweekly schedule depositor on May 11. It will be a semiweekly schedule depositor for the remainder of 2019 and for 2020. Elm, Inc., is required to deposit the $100,000 by Monday, May 13, the next business day.

Accuracy of Deposits Rule

You're required to deposit 100% of your tax liability on or before the deposit due date. However, penalties won't be applied for depositing less than 100% if both of the following conditions are met.

- Any deposit shortfall doesn't exceed the greater of $100 or 2% of the amount of taxes otherwise required to be deposited.

- The deposit shortfall is paid or deposited by the shortfall makeup date as described next.

Makeup Date for Deposit Shortfall:

1. **Monthly schedule depositor.** Deposit the shortfall or pay it with your return by the due date of your return for the return period in which the shortfall occurred. You may pay the shortfall with your return even if the amount is $2,500 or more.

2. **Semiweekly schedule depositor.** Deposit by the earlier of:

   a. The first Wednesday or Friday (whichever comes first) that falls on or after the 15th day of the month following the month in which the shortfall occurred, or

   b. The due date of your return (for the return period of the tax liability).

For example, if a semiweekly schedule depositor has a deposit shortfall during June 2019, the shortfall makeup date is July 17, 2019 (Wednesday). However, if the shortfall occurred on the required April 3, 2019 (Wednesday), deposit due date for a March 29, 2019 (Friday), pay date, the return due date for the March 29, 2019, pay date (April 30, 2019) would come before the May 15, 2019 (Wednesday), shortfall makeup date. In this case, the shortfall must be deposited by April 30, 2019.

How To Deposit

You must deposit employment taxes, including Form 945 taxes, by EFT. See *Payment with return*, earlier in this section, for exceptions explaining when taxes may be paid with the tax return instead of being deposited.

Electronic deposit requirement. You must use EFT to make all federal tax deposits. Generally, an EFT is made using EFTPS. If you don't want to use EFTPS, you can arrange for your tax professional, financial institution, payroll service, or other trusted third party to make electronic deposits on your behalf. EFTPS is a free service provided by the Department of the Treasury. To get more information about EFTPS or to enroll in EFTPS, visit _EFTPS.gov_, or call 800-555-4477 or 800-733-4829 (TDD). Additional information about EFTPS is also available in Pub. 966.

When you receive your EIN. If you're a new employer that indicated a federal tax obligation when requesting an EIN, you'll be pre-enrolled in EFTPS. You'll receive information about Express Enrollment in your Employer Identification Number (EIN) Package and an additional mailing containing your EFTPS personal identification number (PIN) and instructions for activating your PIN. Call the toll-free number located in your "How to Activate Your Enrollment" brochure to activate your enrollment and begin making your payroll tax deposits. If you outsource any of your payroll and related tax duties to a third-party payer, such as a payroll service provider (PSP) or reporting agent, be sure to tell them about your EFTPS enrollment.

Deposit record. For your records, an EFT Trace Number will be provided with each successful payment. The number can be used as a receipt or to trace the payment.

Depositing on time. For deposits made by EFTPS to be on time, you must submit the deposit by 8 p.m. Eastern time the day before the date the deposit is due. If you use a third party to make a deposit on your behalf, they may have different cutoff times.

Same-day wire payment option. If you fail to submit a deposit transaction on EFTPS by 8 p.m. Eastern time the day before the date a deposit is due, you can still make your deposit on time by using the Federal Tax Collection Service (FTCS) to make a same-day wire payment. To use the same-day wire payment method, you'll need to make arrangements with your financial institution ahead of time. Please check with your financial institution regarding availability, deadlines, and costs. Your financial institution may charge you a fee for payments made this way. To learn more about the information you'll need to give to your financial institution to make a same-day wire payment, go to _IRS.gov/SameDayWire_.

How to claim credit for overpayments. If you deposited more than the right amount of taxes for a quarter, you can choose on Form 941 for that quarter (or on Form 944 for that year) to have the overpayment refunded or applied as a credit to your next return. Don't ask EFTPS to request a refund from the IRS for you.

Deposit Penalties

TIP *Although the deposit penalties information provided next refers specifically to Form 941, these rules also apply to Form 945 and Form 944. The penalties won't apply if the employer qualifies for the exceptions to the deposit requirements discussed under* Payment with return, *earlier in this section).*

Penalties may apply if you don't make required deposits on time or if you make deposits for less than the required

amount. The penalties don't apply if any failure to make a proper and timely deposit was due to reasonable cause and not to willful neglect. If you receive a penalty notice, you can provide an explanation of why you believe reasonable cause exists.

If you timely filed your employment tax return, the IRS may also waive deposit penalties if you inadvertently failed to deposit and it was the first quarter that you were required to deposit any employment tax, or if you inadvertently failed to deposit the first time after your deposit frequency changed. You must also meet the net worth and size limitations applicable to awards of administrative and litigation costs under section 7430; for individuals, this means that your net worth can't exceed $2 million, and for businesses, your net worth can't exceed $7 million and you also can't have more than 500 employees.

For amounts not properly or timely deposited, the penalty rates are as follows.

2% Deposits made 1 to 5 days late.

5% Deposits made 6 to 15 days late.

10% Deposits made 16 or more days late, but before 10 days from the date of the first notice the IRS sent asking for the tax due.

10% Amounts that should have been deposited, but instead were paid directly to the IRS, or paid with your tax return. But see _Payment with return_, earlier in this section, for exceptions.

15% Amounts still unpaid more than 10 days after the date of the first notice the IRS sent asking for the tax due or the day on which you received notice and demand for immediate payment, whichever is earlier.

Late deposit penalty amounts are determined using calendar days, starting from the due date of the liability.

Special rule for former Form 944 filers. If you filed Form 944 for the prior year and file Forms 941 for the current year, the FTD penalty won't apply to a late deposit of employment taxes for January of the current year if the taxes are deposited in full by March 15 of the current year.

Order in which deposits are applied. Deposits generally are applied to the most recent tax liability within the quarter. If you receive an FTD penalty notice, you may designate how your deposits are to be applied in order to minimize the amount of the penalty if you do so within 90 days of the date of the notice. Follow the instructions on the penalty notice you received. For more information on designating deposits, see Revenue Procedure 2001-58. You can find Revenue Procedure 2001-58 on page 579 of Internal Revenue Bulletin 2001-50 at _IRS.gov/pub/irs-irbs/irb01-50.pdf_.

Example. Cedar, Inc., is required to make a deposit of $1,000 on July 15 and $1,500 on August 15. It doesn't make the deposit on July 15. On August 15, Cedar, Inc., deposits $2,000. Under the deposits rule, which applies deposits to the most recent tax liability, $1,500 of the deposit is applied to the August 15 deposit and the remaining $500 is applied to the July deposit. Accordingly, $500 of the July 15 liability remains undeposited. The penalty on this underdeposit will apply as explained earlier.

Trust fund recovery penalty. If federal income, social security, or Medicare taxes that must be withheld (that is, trust fund taxes) aren't withheld or aren't deposited or paid to the U.S. Treasury, the trust fund recovery penalty may apply. The penalty is 100% of the unpaid trust fund tax. If these unpaid taxes can't be immediately collected from the employer or business, the trust fund recovery penalty may be imposed on all persons who are determined by the IRS to be responsible for collecting, accounting for, or paying over these taxes, and who acted willfully in not doing so.

A **responsible person** can be an officer or employee of a corporation, a partner or employee of a partnership, an accountant, a volunteer director/trustee, or an employee of a sole proprietorship, or any other person or entity that is responsible for collecting, accounting for, or paying over trust fund taxes. A responsible person also may include one who signs checks for the business or otherwise has authority to cause the spending of business funds.

Willfully means voluntarily, consciously, and intentionally. A responsible person acts willfully if the person knows the required actions of collecting, accounting for, or paying over trust fund taxes aren't taking place, or recklessly disregards obvious and known risks to the government's right to receive trust fund taxes.

Separate accounting when deposits aren't made or withheld taxes aren't paid. Separate accounting may be required if you don't pay over withheld employee social security, Medicare, or income taxes; deposit required taxes; make required payments; or file tax returns. In this case, you would receive written notice from the IRS requiring you to deposit taxes into a special trust account for the U.S. Government.

 You may be charged with criminal penalties if you don't comply with the special bank deposit requirements for the special trust account for the U.S. Government.

"Averaged" FTD penalty. The IRS may assess an "averaged" FTD penalty of 2% to 10% if you're a monthly schedule depositor and didn't properly complete Form 941, line 16, when your tax liability shown on Form 941, line 12, equaled or exceeded $2,500.

The IRS may also assess an "averaged" FTD penalty of 2% to 10% if you're a semiweekly schedule depositor and your tax liability shown on Form 941, line 12, equaled or exceeded $2,500 and you:

- Completed Form 941, line 16, instead of Schedule B (Form 941);
- Failed to attach a properly completed Schedule B (Form 941); or
- Improperly completed Schedule B (Form 941) by, for example, entering tax deposits instead of tax liabilities in the numbered spaces.

The FTD penalty is figured by distributing your total tax liability shown on Form 941, line 12, equally throughout the tax period. Then we apply your deposits and payments to the averaged liabilities in the date order we received your deposits. We figure the penalty on any tax not deposited, deposited late, or not deposited in the correct amounts. Your deposits and payments may not be counted as timely because the actual dates of your tax liabilities can't be accurately determined.

You can avoid an "averaged" FTD penalty by reviewing your return before you file it. Follow these steps before submitting your Form 941.

- If you're a monthly schedule depositor, report your tax liabilities (not your deposits) in the monthly entry spaces on Form 941, line 16.
- If you're a semiweekly schedule depositor, report your tax liabilities (not your deposits) on Schedule B (Form 941) in the lines that represent the dates your employees were paid.
- Verify your total liability shown on Form 941, line 16, or the bottom of Schedule B (Form 941) equals your tax liability shown on Form 941, line 12.
- Don't show negative amounts on Form 941, line 16, or Schedule B (Form 941).
- For prior period errors, don't adjust your tax liabilities reported on Form 941, line 16, or on Schedule B (Form 941). Instead, file an adjusted return (Form 941-X, 944-X, or 945-X) if you're also adjusting your tax liability. If you're only adjusting your deposits in response to an FTD penalty notice, see the Instructions for Schedule B (Form 941) or the Instructions for Form 945-A (for Forms 944 and 945).

12. Filing Form 941 or Form 944

Form 941. Each quarter, if you pay wages subject to income tax withholding (including withholding on sick pay and supplemental unemployment benefits) or social security and Medicare taxes, you must file Form 941 unless you receive an IRS notification that you're eligible to file Form 944 or the exceptions discussed later apply. Also, if you're required to file Forms 941 but believe your employment taxes for the calendar year will be $1,000 or less, and you would like to file Form 944 instead of Forms 941, you must contact the IRS during the first calendar quarter of the tax year to request to file Form 944. You must receive written notice from the IRS to file Form 944 instead of Forms 941 before you may file this form. For more information on requesting to file Form 944, including the methods and deadlines for making a request, see the Instructions for Form 944. Form 941 must be filed by the last day of the month that follows the end of the quarter. See the *Calendar*, earlier.

Form 944. If you receive written notification that you qualify for the Form 944 program, you must file Form 944 instead of Form 941. If you received this notification, but prefer to file Form 941, you can request to have your filing requirement changed to Form 941 during the first calendar quarter of the tax year. For more information on requesting to file Forms 941, including the methods and deadlines for making a request, see the Instructions for Form 944. File your 2018 Form 944 by January 31, 2019. However, if you timely deposited all taxes when due, you may file by February 11, 2019.

Exceptions. The following exceptions apply to the filing requirements for Forms 941 and 944.

- **Seasonal employers who don't have to file a Form 941 for quarters when they have no tax liability because they have paid no wages.** To alert the IRS you won't have to file a return for one or more quarters during the year, check the "Seasonal employer" box on Form 941, line 18. When you fill out Form 941, be sure to check the box on the top of the form that corresponds to the quarter reported. Generally, the IRS won't inquire about unfiled returns if at least one taxable return is filed each year. However, you must check the "Seasonal employer" box on **every** Form 941 you file. Otherwise, the IRS will expect a return to be filed for each quarter.

- **Household employers reporting social security and Medicare taxes and/or withheld income tax.** If you're a sole proprietor and file Form 941 or Form 944 for business employees, you may include taxes for household employees on your Form 941 or Form 944. Otherwise, report social security and Medicare taxes and income tax withholding for household employees on Schedule H (Form 1040). See Pub. 926 for more information.

- **Employers reporting wages for employees in American Samoa, Guam, the Commonwealth of the Northern Mariana Islands, the U.S. Virgin Islands, or Puerto Rico.** If your employees aren't subject to U.S. income tax withholding, use Forms 941-SS, 944, or Formulario 944(SP). Employers in Puerto Rico use Formularios 941-PR, 944(SP), or Form 944. If you have both employees who are subject to U.S. income tax withholding and employees who aren't subject to U.S. income tax withholding, you must file only Form 941 (or Form 944 or Formulario 944(SP)) and include all of your employees' wages on that form. For more information, see Pub. 80, Federal Tax Guide for Employers in U.S. Virgin Islands, Guam, American Samoa, and the Commonwealth of the Northern Mariana Islands, or Pub. 179, Guía Contributiva Federal para Patronos Puertorriqueños.

- **Agricultural employers reporting social security, Medicare, and withheld income taxes.** Report these taxes on Form 943. For more information, see Pub. 51.

Form 941 *e-file*. The Form 941 *e-file* program allows a taxpayer to electronically file Form 941 or Form 944 using a computer with an Internet connection and commercial tax preparation software. For more information, go to *IRS.gov/EmploymentEfile*, or call 866-255-0654.

Electronic filing by reporting agents. Reporting agents filing Forms 941 or Form 944 for groups of taxpayers can file them electronically. See *Reporting Agents* in section 7 of Pub. 15-A.

Electronic filing by CPEOs. With the exception of the first quarter for which a CPEO is certified, CPEOs are required to electronically file Form 941. Under certain circumstances, the IRS may waive the electronic filing requirement. To request a waiver, the CPEO must file a written request using the IRS Online Registration System for Professional Employer Organizations at least 45 days before the due date of the return for which the CPEO is unable to electronically file. For more information on filing a waiver request electronically, go to *IRS.gov/CPEO*.

Penalties. For each whole or part month a return isn't filed when required (disregarding any extensions of the filing deadline), there is a failure-to-file (FTF) penalty of 5% of the unpaid tax due with that return. The maximum penalty is generally 25% of the tax due. Also, for each whole or part month the tax is paid late (disregarding any extensions of the payment deadline), there is a failure-to-pay (FTP) penalty of 0.5% per month of the amount of tax. For individual filers only, the FTP penalty is reduced from 0.5% per month to 0.25% per month if an installment agreement is in effect. You must have filed your return on or before the due date of the return to qualify for the reduced penalty. The maximum amount of the FTP penalty is also 25% of the tax due. If both penalties apply in any month, the FTF penalty is reduced by the amount of the FTP penalty. The penalties won't be charged if you have a reasonable cause for failing to file or pay. If you receive a penalty notice, you can provide an explanation of why you believe reasonable cause exists.

Note. In addition to any penalties, interest accrues from the due date of the tax on any unpaid balance.

If income, social security, or Medicare taxes that must be withheld aren't withheld or aren't paid, you may be personally liable for the trust fund recovery penalty. See *Trust fund recovery penalty* in section 11.

Generally, the use of a third-party payer, such as a PSP or reporting agent, doesn't relieve an employer of the responsibility to ensure tax returns are filed and all taxes are paid or deposited correctly and on time. However, see *Certified professional employer organization (CPEO)*, later, for an exception.

Don't file more than one Form 941 per quarter or more than one Form 944 per year. Employers with multiple locations or divisions must file only one Form 941 per quarter or one Form 944 per year. Filing more than one return may result in processing delays and may require correspondence between you and the IRS. For information on making adjustments to previously filed returns, see section 13.

Reminders about filing.

- Don't report more than 1 calendar quarter on a Form 941.
- If you need Form 941 or Form 944, get one from the IRS in time to file the return when due. See *Ordering Employer Tax Forms and Publications*, earlier.
- Enter your name and EIN on Form 941 or Form 944. Be sure they're exactly as they appeared on earlier returns.
- See the Instructions for Form 941 or the Instructions for Form 944 for information on preparing the form.

Final return. If you go out of business, you must file a final return for the last quarter (last year for Form 944) in which wages are paid. If you continue to pay wages or other compensation for periods following termination of your business, you must file returns for those periods. See the Instructions for Form 941 or the Instructions for Form 944 for details on how to file a final return.

If you're required to file a final return, you're also required to furnish Forms W-2 to your employees and file Forms W-2 and W-3 with the SSA by the due date of your final return. Don't send an original or copy of your Form 941 or Form 944 to the SSA. See the General Instructions for Forms W-2 and W-3 for more information.

Filing late returns for previous years. If possible, get a copy of Form 941 or Form 944 (and separate instructions) with a revision date showing the year for which your delinquent return is being filed. See *Ordering Employer Tax Forms and Publications*, earlier. Contact the IRS at 800-829-4933 if you have any questions about filing late returns.

Table 3. **Social Security and Medicare Tax Rates** *(for 3 Prior Years)*

Calendar Year	Wage Base Limit (each employee)	Tax Rate on Taxable Wages and Tips
2018—Social Security	$128,400	12.4%
2018—Medicare	All Wages	2.9%
2017—Social Security	$127,200	12.4%
2017—Medicare	All Wages	2.9%
2016—Social Security	$118,500	12.4%
2016—Medicare	All Wages	2.9%

Reconciling Forms W-2, W-3, and 941 or 944. When there are discrepancies between Forms 941 or Form 944 filed with the IRS and Forms W-2 and W-3 filed with the SSA, the IRS or the SSA may contact you to resolve the discrepancies.

Take the following steps to help reduce discrepancies.

1. Report bonuses as wages and as social security and Medicare wages on Forms W-2 and on Form 941 or Form 944.

2. Report both social security and Medicare wages and taxes separately on Forms W-2, W-3, 941, and 944.

3. Report employee share of social security taxes on Form W-2 in the box for social security tax withheld (box 4), not as social security wages.

4. Report employee share of Medicare taxes on Form W-2 in the box for Medicare tax withheld (box 6), not as Medicare wages.

5. Make sure the social security wage amount for each employee doesn't exceed the annual social security wage base limit ($132,900 for 2019).

6. Don't report noncash wages that aren't subject to social security or Medicare taxes, as discussed earlier in *Wages not paid in money* in section 5, as social security or Medicare wages.

7. If you used an EIN on any Form 941 or Form 944 for the year that is different from the EIN reported on Form W-3, enter the other EIN on Form W-3 in the box for "Other EIN used this year" (box h).

8. Be sure the amounts on Form W-3 are the total of amounts from Forms W-2.

9. Reconcile Form W-3 with your four quarterly Forms 941 or annual Form 944 by comparing amounts reported for the following items.

   a. Federal income tax withheld.

   b. Social security and Medicare wages.

   c. Social security and Medicare taxes. Generally, the amounts shown on Forms 941 or annual Form 944, including current year adjustments, should be approximately twice the amounts shown on Form W-3.

Don't report backup withholding or withholding on nonpayroll payments, such as pensions, annuities, and gambling winnings, on Form 941 or Form 944. Withholding on nonpayroll payments is reported on Forms 1099 or W-2G and must be reported on Form 945. Only taxes and withholding reported on Form W-2 should be reported on Form 941 or Form 944.

Amounts reported on Forms W-2, W-3, and Forms 941 or Form 944 may not match for valid reasons. For example, if you withheld any Additional Medicare Tax from your employee's wages, the amount of Medicare tax that is reported on Forms 941, line 5c, column 2, or Form 944, line 4c, column 2, won't be twice the amount of the Medicare tax withheld that is reported in box 6 of Form W-3. Make sure there are valid reasons for any mismatch. Keep your reconciliation so you'll have a record of why amounts didn't match in case there are inquiries from the IRS or the SSA. See the Instructions for Schedule D (Form 941) if you need to explain any discrepancies that were caused by an acquisition, statutory merger, or consolidation.

13. Reporting Adjustments to Form 941 or Form 944

Current Period Adjustments

In certain cases, amounts reported as social security and Medicare taxes on Form 941, lines 5a–5d, column 2 (Form 944, lines 4a–4d, column 2), must be adjusted to arrive at your correct tax liability (for example, excluding amounts withheld by a third-party payer or amounts you weren't required to withhold). Current period adjustments are reported on Form 941, lines 7–9, or Form 944, line 6, and include the following types of adjustments.

Fractions-of-cents adjustment. If there is a small difference between total taxes after adjustments and credits (Form 941, line 12; Form 944, line 9) and total deposits (Form 941, line 13; Form 944, line 10), it may have been caused, all or in part, by rounding to the nearest cent each time you figured payroll. This rounding occurs when you figure the amount of social security and Medicare tax to be withheld and deposited from each employee's wages. The IRS refers to rounding differences relating to employee withholding of social security and Medicare taxes as "fractions-of-cents" adjustments. If you pay your taxes with Form 941 (or Form 944) instead of making deposits because your total taxes for the quarter (year for Form 944) are less than $2,500, you also may report a fractions-of-cents adjustment.

To determine if you have a fractions-of-cents adjustment for 2019, multiply the total wages and tips for the quarter subject to:

- Social security tax reported on Form 941 or Form 944 by 6.2% (0.062),
- Medicare tax reported on Form 941 or Form 944 by 1.45% (0.0145), and
- Additional Medicare Tax reported on Form 941 or Form 944 by 0.9% (0.009).

Compare these amounts (the employee share of social security and Medicare taxes) with the total social security and Medicare taxes actually withheld from employees and shown in your payroll records for the quarter (Form 941) or the year (Form 944). If there is a small difference, the amount, positive or negative, may be a fractions-of-cents adjustment. Fractions-of-cents adjustments are reported on Form 941, line 7, or Form 944, line 6. If the actual amount withheld is less, report a negative adjustment using a minus sign (if possible; otherwise, use parentheses) in the entry space. If the actual amount is more, report a positive adjustment.

 For the above adjustments, prepare and retain a brief supporting statement explaining the nature and amount of each. Don't attach the statement to Form 941 or Form 944.

Adjustment of tax on third-party sick pay. Report both the employer and employee share of social security and Medicare taxes for sick pay on Form 941, lines 5a and 5c (Form 944, lines 4a and 4c). If the aggregate wages paid for an employee by the employer and third-party payer exceed $200,000 for the calendar year, report the Additional Medicare Tax on Form 941, line 5d (Form 944, line 4d). Show as a negative adjustment on Form 941, line 8 (Form 944, line 6), the social security and Medicare taxes withheld on sick pay by a third-party payer. See section 6 of Pub. 15-A for more information.

Adjustment of tax on tips. If, by the 10th of the month after the month you received an employee's report on tips, you don't have enough employee funds available to withhold the employee's share of social security and Medicare taxes, you no longer have to collect it. However, report the entire amount of these tips on Form 941, lines 5b and 5c (Form 944, lines 4b and 4c). If the aggregate wages and tips paid for an employee exceed $200,000 for the calendar year, report the Additional Medicare Tax on Form 941, line 5d (Form 944, line 4d). Include as a negative adjustment on Form 941, line 9 (Form 944, line 6), the total uncollected employee share of the social security and Medicare taxes.

Adjustment of tax on group-term life insurance premiums paid for former employees. The employee share of social security and Medicare taxes for premiums on group-term life insurance over $50,000 for a former employee is paid by the former employee with his or her tax return and isn't collected by the employer. However, include all social security and Medicare taxes for such coverage on Form 941, lines 5a and 5c (Form 944, lines 4a and 4c). If the amount paid for an employee for premiums on group-term life insurance combined with other wages exceeds $200,000 for the calendar year, report the Additional Medicare Tax on Form 941, line 5d (Form 944, line 4d). Back out the amount of the employee share of these taxes as a negative adjustment on Form 941, line 9 (Form 944, line 6). See Pub. 15-B for more information on group-term life insurance.

Example. Cedar, Inc., was entitled to the following current period adjustments.

- **Fractions of cents.** Cedar, Inc., determined the amounts withheld and deposited for social security and Medicare taxes during the quarter were a net $1.44 more than the employee share of the amount figured on Form 941, lines 5a–5d, column 2 (social security and Medicare taxes). This difference was caused by adding or dropping fractions of cents when figuring social security and Medicare taxes for each wage payment. Cedar, Inc., must report a positive $1.44 fractions-of-cents adjustment on Form 941, line 7.

- **Third-party sick pay.** Cedar, Inc., included taxes of $2,000 for sick pay on Form 941, lines 5a and 5c, column 2, for social security and Medicare taxes. However, the third-party payer of the sick pay withheld and paid the employee share ($1,000) of these taxes.

Cedar, Inc., is entitled to a $1,000 sick pay adjustment (negative) on Form 941, line 8.

- **Life insurance premiums.** Cedar, Inc., paid group-term life insurance premiums for policies in excess of $50,000 for former employees. The former employees must pay the employee share of the social security and Medicare taxes ($200) on the policies. However, Cedar, Inc., must include the employee share of these taxes with the social security and Medicare taxes reported on Form 941, lines 5a and 5c, column 2. Therefore, Cedar, Inc., is entitled to a negative $200 adjustment on Form 941, line 9.

No change to record of federal tax liability. Don't make any changes to your record of federal tax liability reported on Form 941, line 16, or Schedule B (Form 941) (for Form 944 filers, Form 944, line 13, or Form 945-A) for current period adjustments. The amounts reported on the record reflect the actual amounts you withheld from employees' wages for social security and Medicare taxes. Because the current period adjustments make the amounts reported on Form 941, lines 5a–5d, column 2 (Form 944, lines 4a–4d, column 2), equal the actual amounts you withheld (the amounts reported on the record), no additional changes to the record of federal tax liability are necessary for these adjustments.

Prior Period Adjustments

Forms for prior period adjustments. Use Form 941-X or Form 944-X to make a correction after you discover an error on a previously filed Form 941 or Form 944. There are also Forms 943-X, 945-X, and CT-1 X to report corrections on the corresponding returns. Use Form 843 when requesting a refund or abatement of assessed interest or penalties.

 See Revenue Ruling 2009-39, 2009-52 I.R.B. 951, for examples of how the interest-free adjustment and claim for refund rules apply in 10 different situations. You can find Revenue Ruling 2009-39 at IRS.gov/irb/2009-52_IRB#RR-2009-39.

Background. Treasury Decision 9405 changed the process for making interest-free adjustments to employment taxes reported on Form 941 and Form 944 and for filing a claim for refund of employment taxes. Treasury Decision 9405, 2008-32 I.R.B. 293, is available at IRS.gov/irb/2008-32_IRB#TD-9405. You'll use the adjustment process if you underreported employment taxes and are making a payment, or if you overreported employment taxes and will be applying the credit to the Form 941 or Form 944 period during which you file Form 941-X or Form 944-X. You'll use the claim process if you overreported employment taxes and are requesting a refund or abatement of the overreported amount. We use the terms "correct" and "corrections" to include interest-free adjustments under sections 6205 and 6413, and claims for refund and abatement under sections 6402, 6414, and 6404.

Correcting employment taxes. When you discover an error on a previously filed Form 941 or Form 944, you must:

- Correct that error using Form 941-X or Form 944-X,
- File a separate Form 941-X or Form 944-X for each Form 941 or Form 944 you're correcting, and
- File Form 941-X or Form 944-X separately. Don't file with Form 941 or Form 944.

Continue to report current quarter adjustments for fractions of cents, third-party sick pay, tips, and group-term life insurance on Form 941 using lines 7–9, and on Form 944 using line 6.

Report the correction of underreported and overreported amounts for the same tax period on a single Form 941-X or Form 944-X unless you're requesting a refund. If you're requesting a refund and are correcting both underreported and overreported amounts, file one Form 941-X or Form 944-X correcting the underreported amounts only and a second Form 941-X or Form 944-X correcting the overreported amounts.

See the chart on the back of Form 941-X or Form 944-X for help in choosing whether to use the adjustment process or the claim process. See the Instructions for Form 941-X or the Instructions for Form 944-X for details on how to make the adjustment or claim for refund or abatement.

Income tax withholding adjustments. In a current calendar year, correct prior quarter income tax withholding errors by making the correction on Form 941-X when you discover the error.

You may make an adjustment only to correct income tax withholding errors discovered during the same calendar year in which you paid the wages. This is because the employee uses the amount shown on Form W-2 or, if applicable, Form W-2c, as a credit when filing his or her income tax return (Form 1040, etc.).

You can't adjust amounts reported as income tax withheld in a prior calendar year unless it is to correct an administrative error or section 3509 applies. An administrative error occurs if the amount you entered on Form 941 or Form 944 isn't the amount you actually withheld. For example, if the total income tax actually withheld was incorrectly reported on Form 941 or Form 944 due to a mathematical or transposition error, this would be an administrative error. The administrative error adjustment corrects the amount reported on Form 941 or Form 944 to agree with the amount actually withheld from employees and reported on their Forms W-2.

Additional Medicare Tax withholding adjustments. Generally, the rules discussed above under *Income tax withholding adjustments* apply to Additional Medicare Tax withholding adjustments. That is, you may make an adjustment to correct Additional Medicare Tax withholding errors discovered during the same calendar year in which you paid wages. You can't adjust amounts reported in a prior calendar year unless it is to correct an administrative error or section 3509 applies. If you have overpaid Additional Medicare Tax, you can't file a claim for refund for the amount of the overpayment unless the amount wasn't actually withheld from the employee's wages (which would be an administrative error).

If a prior year error was a nonadministrative error, you may correct only the **wages and tips** subject to Additional Medicare Tax withholding.

Collecting underwithheld taxes from employees. If you withheld no income, social security, or Medicare taxes or less than the correct amount from an employee's wages, you can make it up from later pay to that employee. But you're the one who owes the underpayment. Reimbursement is a matter for settlement between you and the employee. Underwithheld income tax and Additional Medicare Tax must be recovered from the employee on or before the last day of the calendar year. There are special rules for tax on tips (see section 6) and fringe benefits (see section 5).

Refunding amounts incorrectly withheld from employees. If you withheld more than the correct amount of income, social security, or Medicare taxes from wages paid, repay or reimburse the employee the excess. Any excess income tax or Additional Medicare Tax withholding must be repaid or reimbursed to the employee before the end of the calendar year in which it was withheld. Keep in your records the employee's written receipt showing the date and amount of the repayment or record of reimbursement. If you didn't repay or reimburse the employee, you must report and pay each excess amount when you file Form 941 for the quarter (or Form 944 for the year) in which you withheld too much tax.

Correcting filed Forms W-2 and W-3. When adjustments are made to correct wages and social security and Medicare taxes because of a change in the wage totals reported for a previous year, you also need to file Form W-2c and Form W-3c with the SSA. Up to 25 Forms W-2c per Form W-3c may now be filed per session over the Internet, with no limit on the number of sessions. For more information, visit the SSA's Employer W-2 Filing Instructions & Information webpage at SSA.gov/employer.

Exceptions to interest-free corrections of employment taxes. A correction won't be eligible for interest-free treatment if:

- The failure to report relates to an issue raised in an IRS examination of a prior return, or
- The employer knowingly underreported its employment tax liability.

A correction won't be eligible for interest-free treatment after the earlier of the following.

- Receipt of an IRS notice and demand for payment after assessment.
- Receipt of an IRS notice of determination under section 7436.

Wage Repayments

If an employee repays you for wages received in error, don't offset the repayments against current year wages unless the repayments are for amounts received in error in the current year.

Repayment of current year wages. If you receive repayments for wages paid during a prior quarter in the current year, report adjustments on Form 941-X to recover income tax withholding and social security and Medicare taxes for the repaid wages.

Repayment of prior year wages. If you receive repayments for wages paid during a prior year, report an adjustment on Form 941-X or Form 944-X to recover the social security and Medicare taxes. You can't make an adjustment for income tax withholding because the wages were income to the employee for the prior year. You can't make an adjustment for Additional Medicare Tax withholding because the employee determines liability for Additional Medicare Tax on the employee's income tax return for the prior year.

You also must file Forms W-2c and W-3c with the SSA to correct social security and Medicare wages and taxes. Don't correct wages (box 1) on Form W-2c for the amount paid in error. Give a copy of Form W-2c to the employee.

Employee reporting of repayment. The wages paid in error in the prior year remain taxable to the employee for that year. This is because the employee received and had use of those funds during that year. The employee isn't entitled to file an amended return (Form 1040X) to recover the income tax on these wages. Instead, the employee may be entitled to a deduction or credit for the repaid wages on his or her income tax return for the year of repayment. However, the employee should file an amended return (Form 1040X) to recover any Additional Medicare Tax paid on the wages paid in error in the prior year. See *Repayments* in the 2018 revision of Pub. 525 for more information. The IRS anticipates that the 2018 revision of Pub. 525 will be available in January 2019.

14. Federal Unemployment (FUTA) Tax

The Federal Unemployment Tax Act (FUTA), with state unemployment systems, provides for payments of unemployment compensation to workers who have lost their jobs. Most employers pay both a federal and a state unemployment tax. For a list of state unemployment agencies, visit the U.S. Department of Labor's website at oui.doleta.gov/unemploy/agencies.asp. Only the employer pays FUTA tax; it isn't withheld from the employee's wages. For more information, see the Instructions for Form 940.

Services rendered to a federally recognized Indian tribal government (or any subdivision, subsidiary, or business wholly owned by such an Indian tribe) are exempt from FUTA tax, subject to the tribe's compliance with state law. For more information, see section 3309(d) and Pub. 4268.

Who must pay? Use the following three tests to determine whether you must pay FUTA tax. Each test applies to a different category of employee, and each is independent of the others. If a test describes your situation, you're subject to FUTA tax on the wages you pay to employees in that category during the current calendar year.

1. **General test.**

    You're subject to FUTA tax in 2019 on the wages you pay employees who aren't farmworkers or household workers if:

    a. You paid wages of $1,500 or more in any calendar quarter in 2018 or 2019, or

    b. You had one or more employees for at least some part of a day in any 20 or more different weeks in 2018 or 20 or more different weeks in 2019.

2. **Household employees test.**

    You're subject to FUTA tax if you paid total cash wages of $1,000 or more to household employees in any calendar quarter in 2018 or 2019. A household employee is an employee who performs household work in a private home, local college club, or local fraternity or sorority chapter.

3. **Farmworkers test.**

    You're subject to FUTA tax on the wages you pay to farmworkers if:

    a. You paid cash wages of $20,000 or more to farmworkers during any calendar quarter in 2018 or 2019, or

    b. You employed 10 or more farmworkers during at least some part of a day (whether or not at the same time) during any 20 or more different weeks in 2018 or 20 or more different weeks in 2019.

Figuring FUTA tax. For 2019, the FUTA tax rate is 6.0%. The tax applies to the first $7,000 you pay to each employee as wages during the year. The $7,000 is the federal wage base. Your state wage base may be different.

Generally, you can take a credit against your FUTA tax for amounts you paid into state unemployment funds. The credit may be as much as 5.4% of FUTA taxable wages. If you're entitled to the maximum 5.4% credit, the FUTA tax rate after credit is 0.6%. You're entitled to the maximum credit if you paid your state unemployment taxes in full, on time, and on all the same wages as are subject to FUTA tax, and as long as the state isn't determined to be a credit reduction state. See the Instructions for Form 940 to determine the credit.

In some states, the wages subject to state unemployment tax are the same as the wages subject to FUTA tax. However, certain states exclude some types of wages from state unemployment tax, even though they're subject to FUTA tax (for example, wages paid to corporate officers, certain payments of sick pay by unions, and certain fringe benefits). In such a case, you may be required to deposit more than 0.6% FUTA tax on those wages. See the Instructions for Form 940 for further guidance.

 In years when there are credit reduction states, you must include liabilities owed for credit reduction with your fourth quarter deposit. You may deposit the anticipated extra liability throughout the year, but it isn't due until the due date for the deposit for the fourth quarter, and the associated liability should be recorded as being incurred in the fourth quarter. See the Instructions for Form 940 for more information.

Successor employer. If you acquired a business from an employer who was liable for FUTA tax, you may be able to count the wages that employer paid to the employees who continue to work for you when you figure the $7,000 FUTA tax wage base. See the Instructions for Form 940.

Depositing FUTA tax. For deposit purposes, figure FUTA tax quarterly. Determine your FUTA tax liability by multiplying the amount of taxable wages paid during the quarter by 0.6%. Stop depositing FUTA tax on an employee's wages when he or she reaches $7,000 in taxable wages for the calendar year.

If your FUTA tax liability for any calendar quarter is $500 or less, you don't have to deposit the tax. Instead, you may carry it forward and add it to the liability figured in the next quarter to see if you must make a deposit. If your FUTA tax liability for any calendar quarter is over $500 (including any FUTA tax carried forward from an earlier quarter), you must deposit the tax by EFT. See section 11 for more information on EFT.

Household employees. You're not required to deposit FUTA taxes for household employees unless you report their wages on Form 941, 943, or 944. See Pub. 926 for more information.

When to deposit. Deposit the FUTA tax by the last day of the first month that follows the end of the quarter. If the due date for making your deposit falls on a Saturday, Sunday, or legal holiday, you may make your deposit on the next business day. See Legal holiday, earlier, for a list of the legal holidays for 2019.

If your liability for the fourth quarter (plus any undeposited amount from any earlier quarter) is over $500, deposit the entire amount by the due date of Form 940 (January 31). If it is $500 or less, you can make a deposit, pay the tax with a credit or debit card, or pay the tax with your 2018 Form 940 by January 31, 2019. If you file Form 940 electronically, you can e-file and use EFW to pay the balance due. For more information on paying your taxes with a credit or debit card or using EFW, go to IRS.gov/ Payments.

Table 4. **When To Deposit FUTA Taxes**

Quarter	Ending	Due Date
Jan.–Feb.–Mar.	Mar. 31	Apr. 30
Apr.–May–June	June 30	July 31
July–Aug.–Sept.	Sept. 30	Oct. 31
Oct.–Nov.–Dec.	Dec. 31	Jan. 31

Reporting FUTA tax. Use Form 940 to report FUTA tax. File your 2018 Form 940 by January 31, 2019. However, if you deposited all FUTA tax when due, you may file on or before February 11, 2019.

Form 940 e-file. The Form 940 *e-file* program allows a taxpayer to electronically file Form 940 using a computer with an Internet connection and commercial tax preparation software. For more information, visit the IRS website at *IRS.gov/EmploymentEfile,* or call 866-255-0654.

Household employees. If you didn't report employment taxes for household employees on Form 941, 943, or 944, report FUTA tax for these employees on Schedule H (Form 1040). See Pub. 926 for more information. You must have an EIN to file Schedule H (Form 1040).

Electronic filing by reporting agents. Reporting agents filing Forms 940 for groups of taxpayers can file them electronically. See the *Reporting Agent* discussion in section 7 of Pub. 15-A.

Electronic filing by CPEOs. CPEOs are required to electronically file Form 940. Under certain circumstances, the IRS may waive the electronic filing requirement. To request a waiver, the CPEO must file a written request using the IRS Online Registration System for Professional Employer Organizations at least 45 days before the due date of the return for which the CPEO is unable to electronically file. For more information on filing a waiver request electronically, go to *IRS.gov/CPEO*.

15. Special Rules for Various Types of Services and Payments

Section references are to the Internal Revenue Code unless otherwise noted.

Special Classes of Employment and Special Types of Payments	Treatment Under Employment Taxes		
	Income Tax Withholding	Social Security and Medicare (including Additional Medicare Tax when wages are paid in excess of $200,000)	FUTA
Aliens, nonresident.	See Pub. 515 and Pub. 519.		
Aliens, resident:			
1. Service performed in the U.S.	Same as U.S. citizen.	Same as U.S. citizen. (Exempt if any part of service as crew member of foreign vessel or aircraft is performed outside U.S.)	Same as U.S. citizen.
2. Service performed outside the U.S.	Withhold	Taxable if (1) working for an American employer, or (2) an American employer by agreement covers U.S. citizens and residents employed by its foreign affiliates.	Exempt unless on or in connection with an American vessel or aircraft and either performed under contract made in U.S., or alien is employed on such vessel or aircraft when it touches U.S. port.
Cafeteria plan benefits under section 125.	If employee chooses cash, subject to all employment taxes. If employee chooses another benefit, the treatment is the same as if the benefit was provided outside the plan. See Pub. 15-B for more information.		
Deceased worker:			
1. Wages paid to beneficiary or estate in same calendar year as worker's death. See the Instructions for Forms W-2 and W-3 for details.	Exempt	Taxable	Taxable
2. Wages paid to beneficiary or estate after calendar year of worker's death.	Exempt	Exempt	Exempt
Dependent care assistance programs.	Exempt to the extent it is reasonable to believe amounts are excludable from gross income under section 129.		
Disabled worker's wages paid after year in which worker became entitled to disability insurance benefits under the Social Security Act.	Withhold	Exempt if worker didn't perform any service for employer during the period for which payment is made.	Taxable
Employee business expense reimbursement:			
1. Accountable plan.			
a. Amounts not exceeding specified government rate for per diem or standard mileage.	Exempt	Exempt	Exempt
b. Amounts in excess of specified government rate for per diem or standard mileage.	Withhold	Taxable	Taxable
2. Nonaccountable plan. See section 5 for details.	Withhold	Taxable	Taxable
Family employees:			
1. Child employed by parent (or partnership in which each partner is a parent of the child).	Withhold	Exempt until age 18; age 21 for domestic service.	Exempt until age 21
2. Parent employed by child.	Withhold	Taxable if in course of the son's or daughter's business. For domestic services, see section 3.	Exempt
3. Spouse employed by spouse. See section 3 for more information.	Withhold	Taxable if in course of spouse's business.	Exempt
Fishing and related activities.	See Pub. 334.		
Foreign governments and international organizations.	Exempt	Exempt	Exempt

Special Classes of Employment and Special Types of Payments	Treatment Under Employment Taxes		
	Income Tax Withholding	Social Security and Medicare (including Additional Medicare Tax when wages are paid in excess of $200,000)	FUTA
Foreign service by U.S. citizens:			
1. As U.S. government employees.	Withhold	Same as within U.S.	Exempt
2. For foreign affiliates of American employers and other private employers.	Exempt if at time of payment (1) it is reasonable to believe employee is entitled to exclusion from income under section 911, or (2) the employer is required by law of the foreign country to withhold income tax on such payment.	Exempt unless (1) an American employer by agreement covers U.S. citizens employed by its foreign affiliates, or (2) U.S. citizen works for American employer.	Exempt unless (1) on American vessel or aircraft and work is performed under contract made in U.S. or worker is employed on vessel when it touches U.S. port, or (2) U.S. citizen works for American employer (except in a contiguous country with which the U.S. has an agreement for unemployment compensation) or in the U.S. Virgin Islands.
Fringe benefits.	Taxable on excess of fair market value of the benefit over the sum of an amount paid for it by the employee and any amount excludable by law. However, special valuation rules may apply. Benefits provided under cafeteria plans may qualify for exclusion from wages for social security, Medicare, and FUTA taxes. See Pub. 15-B for details.		
Government employment:			
State/local governments and political subdivisions, employees of:			
1. Salaries and wages (includes payments to most elected and appointed officials). See chapter 3 of Pub. 963.	Withhold	Generally, taxable for (1) services performed by employees who are either (a) covered under a section 218 agreement, or (b) not covered under a section 218 agreement and not a member of a public retirement system (mandatory social security and Medicare coverage); and (2) (for Medicare tax only) for services performed by employees hired or rehired after March 31, 1986, who aren't covered under a section 218 agreement or the mandatory social security provisions, unless specifically excluded by law. See Pub. 963.	Exempt
2. Election workers. Election individuals are workers who are employed to perform services for state or local governments at election booths in connection with national, state, or local elections. **Note.** File Form W-2 for payments of $600 or more even if no social security or Medicare taxes were withheld.	Exempt	Taxable if paid $1,800 or more in 2019 (lesser amount if specified by a section 218 social security agreement). See Revenue Ruling 2000-6.	Exempt
3. Emergency workers. Emergency workers who were hired on a temporary basis in response to a specific unforeseen emergency and aren't intended to become permanent employees.	Withhold	Exempt if serving on a temporary basis in case of fire, storm, snow, earthquake, flood, or similar emergency.	Exempt
U.S. federal government employees.	Withhold	Taxable for Medicare. Taxable for social security unless hired before 1984. See section 3121(b)(5).	Exempt

Special Classes of Employment and Special Types of Payments	Treatment Under Employment Taxes		
	Income Tax Withholding	Social Security and Medicare (including Additional Medicare Tax when wages are paid in excess of $200,000)	FUTA
Homeworkers (industrial, cottage industry):			
1. Common law employees.	Withhold	Taxable	Taxable
2. Statutory employees. See section 2 for details.	Exempt	Taxable if paid $100 or more in cash in a year.	Exempt
Hospital employees:			
1. Interns.	Withhold	Taxable	Exempt
2. Patients.	Withhold	Taxable (Exempt for state or local government hospitals.)	Exempt
Household employees:			
1. Domestic service in private homes. Farmers, see Pub. 51.	Exempt (withhold if both employer and employee agree).	Taxable if paid $2,100 or more in cash in 2019. Exempt if performed by an individual under age 18 during any portion of the calendar year and isn't the principal occupation of the employee.	Taxable if employer paid total cash wages of $1,000 or more in any quarter in the current or preceding calendar year.
2. Domestic service in college clubs, fraternities, and sororities.	Exempt (withhold if both employer and employee agree).	Exempt if paid to regular student; also exempt if employee is paid less than $100 in a year by an income-tax-exempt employer.	Taxable if employer paid total cash wages of $1,000 or more in any quarter in the current or preceding calendar year.
Insurance for employees:			
1. Accident and health insurance premiums under a plan or system for employees and their dependents generally or for a class or classes of employees and their dependents.	Exempt (except 2% shareholder-employees of S corporations).	Exempt	Exempt
2. Group-term life insurance costs. See Pub. 15-B for details.	Exempt	Exempt, except for the cost of group-term life insurance includible in the employee's gross income. Special rules apply for former employees.	Exempt
Insurance agents or solicitors:			
1. Full-time life insurance salesperson.	Withhold only if employee under common law. See section 2.	Taxable	Taxable if (1) employee under common law, and (2) not paid solely by commissions.
2. Other salesperson of life, casualty, etc., insurance.	Withhold only if employee under common law.	Taxable only if employee under common law.	Taxable if (1) employee under common law, and (2) not paid solely by commissions.
Interest on loans with below-market interest rates (foregone interest and deemed original issue discount).	See Pub. 15-A.		
Leave-sharing plans: Amounts paid to an employee under a leave-sharing plan.	Withhold	Taxable	Taxable
Newspaper carriers and vendors: Newspaper carriers under age 18; newspaper and magazine vendors buying at fixed prices and retaining receipts from sales to customers. See Pub. 15-A for information on statutory nonemployee status.	Exempt (withhold if both employer and employee voluntarily agree).	Exempt	Exempt

Special Classes of Employment and Special Types of Payments	Treatment Under Employment Taxes		
	Income Tax Withholding	Social Security and Medicare (including Additional Medicare Tax when wages are paid in excess of $200,000)	FUTA
Noncash payments:			
1. For household work, agricultural labor, and service not in the course of the employer's trade or business.	Exempt (withhold if both employer and employee voluntarily agree).	Exempt	Exempt
2. To certain retail commission salespersons ordinarily paid solely on a cash commission basis.	Optional with employer, except to the extent employee's supplemental wages during the year exceed $1 million.	Taxable	Taxable
Nonprofit organizations.	See Pub. 15-A.		
Officers or shareholders of an S corporation: Distributions and other payments by an S corporation to a corporate officer or shareholder must be treated as wages to the extent the amounts are reasonable compensation for services to the corporation by an employee. See the Instructions for Form 1120S.	Withhold	Taxable	Taxable
Partners: Payments to general or limited partners of a partnership. See Pub. 541 for partner reporting rules.	Exempt	Exempt	Exempt
Railroads: Payments subject to the Railroad Retirement Act. See Pub. 915 for more details.	Withhold	Exempt	Exempt
Religious exemptions.	See Pub. 15-A and Pub. 517.		
Retirement and pension plans:			
1. Employer contributions to a qualified plan.	Exempt	Exempt	Exempt
2. Elective employee contributions and deferrals to a plan containing a qualified cash or deferred compensation arrangement (401(k)).	Generally exempt, but see section 402(g) for limitation.	Taxable	Taxable
3. Employer contributions to individual retirement accounts under simplified employee pension plan (SEP).	Generally exempt, but see section 402(g) for salary reduction SEP limitation.	Exempt, except for amounts contributed under a salary reduction SEP agreement.	
4. Employer contributions to section 403(b) annuities including salary reduction contributions.	Generally exempt, but see section 402(g) for limitation.	Taxable if paid through a salary reduction agreement (written or otherwise).	
5. Employee salary reduction contributions to a SIMPLE retirement account.	Exempt	Taxable	Taxable
6. Distributions from qualified retirement and pension plans and section 403(b) annuities. See Pub. 15-A for information on pensions, annuities, and employer contributions to nonqualified deferred compensation arrangements.	Withhold, but recipient may elect exemption on Form W-4P in certain cases; mandatory 20% withholding applies to an eligible rollover distribution that isn't a direct rollover; exempt for direct rollover. See Pub. 15-A.	Exempt	Exempt
7. Employer contributions to a section 457(b) plan.	Generally exempt, but see section 402(g) limitation.	Taxable	Taxable
8. Employee salary reduction contributions to a section 457(b) plan.	Generally exempt, but see section 402(g) salary reduction limitation.	Taxable	Taxable
Salespersons:			
1. Common law employees.	Withhold	Taxable	Taxable
2. Statutory employees.	Exempt	Taxable	Taxable, except for full-time life insurance sales agents.
3. Statutory nonemployees (qualified real estate agents, direct sellers, and certain companion sitters). See Pub. 15-A for details.	Exempt	Exempt	Exempt

Special Classes of Employment and Special Types of Payments	Treatment Under Employment Taxes		
	Income Tax Withholding	Social Security and Medicare (including Additional Medicare Tax when wages are paid in excess of $200,000)	FUTA
Scholarships and fellowship grants (includible in income under section 117(c)).	Withhold	Taxability depends on the nature of the employment and the status of the organization. See *Students, scholars, trainees, teachers, etc.* below.	
Severance or dismissal pay.	Withhold	Taxable	Taxable
Service not in the course of the employer's trade or business (other than on a farm operated for profit or for household employment in private homes).	Withhold only if employee earns $50 or more in cash in a quarter and works on 24 or more different days in that quarter or in the preceding quarter.	Taxable if employee receives $100 or more in cash in a calendar year.	Taxable only if employee earns $50 or more in cash in a quarter and works on 24 or more different days in that quarter or in the preceding quarter.
Sick pay. See Pub. 15-A for more information.	Withhold	Exempt after end of 6 calendar months after the calendar month employee last worked for employer.	
Students, scholars, trainees, teachers, etc.:			
1. Student enrolled and regularly attending classes, performing services for the following.			
a. Private school, college, or university.	Withhold	Exempt	Exempt
b. Auxiliary nonprofit organization operated for and controlled by school, college, or university.	Withhold	Exempt unless services are covered by a section 218 (Social Security Act) agreement.	Exempt
c. Public school, college, or university.	Withhold	Exempt unless services are covered by a section 218 (Social Security Act) agreement.	Exempt
2. Full-time student performing service for academic credit, combining instruction with work experience as an integral part of the program.	Withhold	Taxable	Exempt unless program was established for or on behalf of an employer or group of employers.
3. Student nurse performing part-time services for nominal earnings at hospital as incidental part of training.	Withhold	Exempt	Exempt
4. Student employed by organized camps.	Withhold	Taxable	Exempt
5. Student, scholar, trainee, teacher, etc., as nonimmigrant alien under section 101(a)(15)(F), (J), (M), or (Q) of Immigration and Nationality Act (that is, aliens holding F-1, J-1, M-1, or Q-1 visas).	Withhold unless excepted by regulations.	Exempt if service is performed for purpose specified in section 101(a)(15)(F), (J), (M), or (Q) of Immigration and Nationality Act. However, these taxes may apply if the employee becomes a resident alien. See the special residency tests for exempt individuals in chapter 1 of Pub. 519.	
Supplemental unemployment compensation plan benefits.	Withhold	Exempt under certain conditions. See Pub. 15-A.	
Tips:			
1. If $20 or more in a month.	Withhold	Taxable	Taxable for all tips reported in writing to employer.
2. If less than $20 in a month. See section 6 for more information.	Exempt	Exempt	Exempt
Worker's compensation.	Exempt	Exempt	Exempt

16. Third-Party Payer Arrangements

An employer may outsource some or all of its federal employment tax withholding, reporting, and payment obligations. An employer who outsources payroll and related tax duties (that is, withholding, reporting, and paying over social security, Medicare, FUTA, and income taxes) to a third-party payer, generally will remain responsible for those duties, including liability for the taxes. However, see *Certified professional employer organization (CPEO)*, later, for an exception.

If an employer outsources some or all of its payroll responsibilities, the employer should consider the following information.

- The employer remains responsible for federal tax deposits and other federal tax payments even though the employer may forward the tax amounts to the third-party payer to make the deposits and payments. If the third party fails to make the deposits and payments, the IRS may assess penalties and interest on the employer's account. As the employer, you may be liable for all taxes, penalties, and interest due. The employer may also be held personally liable for certain unpaid federal taxes.

- If the employer's account has any issues, the IRS will send correspondence to the employer at the address of record. We strongly recommend that the employer maintain its address as the address of record with the IRS. Having correspondence sent to the address of the third-party payer may significantly limit the employer's ability to be informed about tax matters involving the employer's business.

- When a third party enrolls an employer in EFTPS for federal tax deposits, the employer will receive an Inquiry PIN. Employers should activate and use this Inquiry PIN to monitor their account and ensure the third party is making the required tax deposits.

The following are common third-party payers who an employer may contract with to perform payroll and related tax duties.

- Payroll service provider (PSP).
- Reporting agent.
- Agent with approved Form 2678.
- Payer designated under section 3504.
- Certified professional employer organization (CPEO).

Payroll service provider (PSP). A PSP helps administer payroll and payroll-related tax duties on behalf of the employer. A PSP may prepare paychecks for employees, prepare and file employment tax returns, prepare Form W-2, and make federal tax deposits and other federal tax payments. A PSP performs these functions using the EIN of the employer. A PSP isn't liable as either an employer or an agent of the employer for the employer's employ-

ment taxes. If an employer is using a PSP to perform its tax duties, the employer remains liable for its employment tax obligations, including liability for employment taxes.

An employer who uses a PSP should ensure the PSP is using EFTPS to make federal tax deposits on behalf of the employer so the employer can confirm that the payments are being made on its behalf.

Reporting agent. A reporting agent is a type of PSP. A reporting agent helps administer payroll and payroll-related tax duties on behalf of the employer, including authorization to electronically sign and file forms set forth on Form 8655. An employer uses Form 8655 to authorize a reporting agent to perform functions on behalf of the employer. A reporting agent performs these functions using the EIN of the employer. A reporting agent isn't liable as either an employer or an agent of the employer for the employer's employment taxes. If an employer is using a reporting agent to perform its tax duties, the employer remains liable for its employment obligations, including liability for employment taxes.

A reporting agent must use EFTPS to make federal tax deposits on behalf of an employer. The employer has access to EFTPS to confirm federal tax deposits were made on its behalf.

For more information on reporting agents, see Revenue Procedure 2012-32, 2012-34 I.R.B. 267, at *IRS.gov/irb/2012-34_IRB#RP-2012-32*, and Pub. 1474, Technical Specifications Guide for Reporting Agent Authorization and Federal Tax Depositors.

Agent with an approved Form 2678. An agent with an approved Form 2678 helps administer payroll and related tax duties on behalf of the employer. An agent authorized under section 3504 may pay wages or compensation to some or all of the employees of an employer, prepare and file employment tax returns as set forth on Form 2678, prepare Form W-2, and make federal tax deposits and other federal tax payments. An employer uses Form 2678 to request authorization to appoint an agent to perform functions on behalf of the employer. An agent with an approved Form 2678 is authorized to perform these functions using its own EIN. The agent files a Schedule R (Form 941) or, if applicable, Schedule R (Form 943) to allocate wages and taxes to the employers it represents as an agent.

If an employer is using an agent with an approved Form 2678 to perform its tax duties, the agent and the employer are jointly liable for the employment taxes and related tax duties for which the agent is authorized to perform.

Form 2678 doesn't apply to FUTA taxes reportable on Form 940 unless the employer is a home care service recipient receiving home care services through a program administered by a federal, state, or local government agency.

For more information on an agent with an approved Form 2678, see Revenue Procedure 2013-39, 2013-52 I.R.B. 830, at *IRS.gov/irb/2013-52_IRB#RP-2013-39*.

Payer designated under section 3504. In certain circumstances, the IRS may designate a third-party payer to perform the acts of an employer. The IRS will designate a third-party payer on behalf of an employer if the third party has a service agreement with the employer. A service agreement is an agreement between the third-party payer and an employer in which the third-party payer (1) asserts it is the employer of individuals performing services for the employer; (2) pays wages to the individuals that perform services for the employer; and (3) assumes responsibility to withhold, report, and pay federal employment taxes for the wages it pays to the individuals that perform services for the employer.

A payer designated under section 3504 performs tax duties under the service agreement using its own EIN. If the IRS designates a third-party payer under section 3504, the designated payer and the employer are jointly liable for the employment taxes and related tax duties for which the third-party payer is designated.

For more information on a payer designated under section 3504, see Regulations section 31.3504-2.

Certified professional employer organization (CPEO). The Tax Increase Prevention Act of 2014 required the IRS to establish a voluntary certification program for professional employer organizations (PEOs). PEOs handle various payroll administration and tax reporting responsibilities for their business clients and are typically paid a fee based on payroll costs. To become and remain certified under the certification program, certified professional employer organizations (CPEOs) must meet various requirements described in sections 3511 and 7705 and related published guidance. Certification as a CPEO may affect the employment tax liabilities of both the CPEO and its customers. A CPEO is generally treated as the employer of any individual who performs services for a customer of the CPEO and is covered by a contract described in section 7705(e)(2) between the CPEO and the customer (CPEO contract), but only for wages and other compensation paid to the individual by the CPEO. However, with respect to certain employees covered by a CPEO contract, you may also be treated as an employer of the employees and, consequently, may also be liable for federal employment taxes imposed on wages and other compensation paid by the CPEO to such employees. For more information, go to *IRS.gov/CPEO*.

17. Federal Income Tax Withholding Methods

There are several ways to figure income tax withholding. The following methods of withholding are based on the information you get from your employees on Form W-4. You must first reduce the amount you pay your employees by nontaxable payments before figuring the tax to withhold on taxable wages. See section 5 and Pub. 15-B for more information about nontaxable amounts of pay. See section 9 for more information on Form W-4.

 Adjustments aren't required when there will be more than the usual number of pay periods, for example, 27 biweekly pay dates instead of 26.

Wage Bracket Method

Under the wage bracket method, find the proper table (on pages 48–67) for your payroll period and the employee's marital status as shown on his or her Form W-4. Then, based on the number of withholding allowances claimed on the Form W-4 and the amount of taxable wages, find the amount of income tax to withhold. If your employee is claiming more than 10 withholding allowances, see below.

If you can't use the wage bracket tables because taxable wages exceed the amount shown in the last bracket of the table, use the percentage method of withholding described below. Be sure to reduce taxable wages by the amount of total withholding allowances in Table 5 before using the percentage method tables (pages 46–47).

Adjusting wage bracket withholding for employees claiming more than 10 withholding allowances. The wage bracket tables can be used if an employee claims up to 10 allowances. More than 10 allowances may be claimed because of the special withholding allowance, additional allowances for deductions and credits, and the system itself.

Adapt the tables to more than 10 allowances as follows.

1. Multiply the number of withholding allowances over 10 by the allowance value for the payroll period. The allowance values are in Table 5.

2. Subtract the result from the employee's taxable wages.

3. On this amount, find and withhold the tax in the column for 10 allowances.

This is a voluntary method. If you use the wage bracket tables, you may continue to withhold the amount in the "10" column when your employee has more than 10 allowances, using the method above. You can also use any other method described next.

Percentage Method

If you don't want to use the wage bracket tables on pages 48–67 to figure how much income tax to withhold, you can use a percentage computation based on Table 5 and the appropriate rate table. This method works for any number of withholding allowances the employee claims and any amount of wages.

Use these steps to figure the income tax to withhold under the percentage method.

1. Multiply one withholding allowance for your payroll period (see Table 5) by the number of allowances the employee claims.

2. Subtract that amount from the employee's taxable wages.

3. Determine the amount to withhold from the appropriate table on pages 46–47.

Table 5. Percentage Method—2019 Amount for One Withholding Allowance

Payroll Period	One Withholding Allowance
Weekly	$ 80.80
Biweekly	161.50
Semimonthly	175.00
Monthly	350.00
Quarterly	1,050.00
Semiannually	2,100.00
Annually	4,200.00
Daily or miscellaneous (each day of the payroll period)	16.20

Example. An unmarried employee is paid $800 weekly. This employee has in effect a Form W-4 claiming two withholding allowances. Using the percentage method, figure the income tax to withhold as follows:

1.	Total wage payment	$800.00
2.	One allowance $80.80	
3.	Allowances claimed on Form W-4 . .	2
4.	Multiply line 2 by line 3	$161.60
5.	Amount subject to withholding (subtract line 4 from line 1)	$638.40
6.	Tax to be withheld on $638.40 from Table 1—single person, page 46 . . .	$64.11

Rounding. To figure the income tax to withhold, you may reduce the last digit of the wages to zero, or figure the wages to the nearest dollar. You may also round the tax for the pay period to the nearest dollar. If rounding is used, it must be used consistently. Withheld tax amounts should be rounded to the nearest whole dollar by dropping amounts under 50 cents and increasing amounts from 50 to 99 cents to the next dollar. For example, $2.30 becomes $2 and $2.50 becomes $3. This rounding meets the tolerances under section 3402(h)(4).

Annual income tax withholding. Figure the income tax to withhold on annual wages under the percentage method for an annual payroll period. Then prorate the tax back to the payroll period.

Example. A married person claims four withholding allowances. She is paid $1,000 a week. Multiply the weekly wages by 52 weeks to figure the annual wage of $52,000. Subtract $16,800 (the value of four withholding allowances for 2019) for a balance of $35,200. Using Table 7(b) on page 47, $2,420 is withheld. Divide the annual tax by 52. The weekly income tax to withhold is $46.54.

Alternative Methods of Income Tax Withholding

Rather than the wage bracket method or percentage method described in this section, you can use an alternative method to withhold income tax. Pub. 15-A describes these alternative methods and contains:

- Formula tables for percentage method withholding (for automated payroll systems);

- Wage bracket percentage method tables (for automated payroll systems); and

- Combined income, social security, and Medicare tax withholding tables.

Some of the alternative methods explained in Pub. 15-A are annualized wages, average estimated wages, cumulative wages, and part-year employment.

Percentage Method Tables for Income Tax Withholding

(For Wages Paid in 2019)

TABLE 1—WEEKLY Payroll Period

(a) SINGLE person (including head of household)—

If the amount of wages (after subtracting withholding allowances) is:
Not over $73 . . . . $0

The amount of income tax to withhold is:

Over—	But not over—		of excess over—
$73	—$260	$0.00 plus 10%	—$73
$260	—$832	$18.70 plus 12%	—$260
$832	—$1,692	$87.34 plus 22%	—$832
$1,692	—$3,164	$276.54 plus 24%	—$1,692
$3,164	—$3,998	$629.82 plus 32%	—$3,164
$3,998	—$9,887	$896.70 plus 35%	—$3,998
$9,887	. . . .	$2,957.85 plus 37%	—$9,887

(b) MARRIED person—

If the amount of wages (after subtracting withholding allowances) is:
Not over $227 . . . . $0

The amount of income tax to withhold is:

Over—	But not over—		of excess over—
$227	—$600	$0.00 plus 10%	—$227
$600	—$1,745	$37.30 plus 12%	—$600
$1,745	—$3,465	$174.70 plus 22%	—$1,745
$3,465	—$6,409	$553.10 plus 24%	—$3,465
$6,409	—$8,077	$1,259.66 plus 32%	—$6,409
$8,077	—$12,003	$1,793.42 plus 35%	—$8,077
$12,003	. . . .	$3,167.52 plus 37%	—$12,003

TABLE 2—BIWEEKLY Payroll Period

(a) SINGLE person (including head of household)—

If the amount of wages (after subtracting withholding allowances) is:
Not over $146 . . . . $0

The amount of income tax to withhold is:

Over—	But not over—		of excess over—
$146	—$519	$0.00 plus 10%	—$146
$519	—$1,664	$37.30 plus 12%	—$519
$1,664	—$3,385	$174.70 plus 22%	—$1,664
$3,385	—$6,328	$553.32 plus 24%	—$3,385
$6,328	—$7,996	$1,259.64 plus 32%	—$6,328
$7,996	—$19,773	$1,793.40 plus 35%	—$7,996
$19,773	. . . .	$5,915.35 plus 37%	—$19,773

(b) MARRIED person—

If the amount of wages (after subtracting withholding allowances) is:
Not over $454 . . . . $0

The amount of income tax to withhold is:

Over—	But not over—		of excess over—
$454	—$1,200	$0.00 plus 10%	—$454
$1,200	—$3,490	$74.60 plus 12%	—$1,200
$3,490	—$6,931	$349.40 plus 22%	—$3,490
$6,931	—$12,817	$1,106.42 plus 24%	—$6,931
$12,817	—$16,154	$2,519.06 plus 32%	—$12,817
$16,154	—$24,006	$3,586.90 plus 35%	—$16,154
$24,006	. . . .	$6,335.10 plus 37%	—$24,006

TABLE 3—SEMIMONTHLY Payroll Period

(a) SINGLE person (including head of household)—

If the amount of wages (after subtracting withholding allowances) is:
Not over $158 . . . . $0

The amount of income tax to withhold is:

Over—	But not over—		of excess over—
$158	—$563	$0.00 plus 10%	—$158
$563	—$1,803	$40.50 plus 12%	—$563
$1,803	—$3,667	$189.30 plus 22%	—$1,803
$3,667	—$6,855	$599.38 plus 24%	—$3,667
$6,855	—$8,663	$1,364.50 plus 32%	—$6,855
$8,663	—$21,421	$1,943.06 plus 35%	—$8,663
$21,421	. . . .	$6,408.36 plus 37%	—$21,421

(b) MARRIED person—

If the amount of wages (after subtracting withholding allowances) is:
Not over $492 . . . . $0

The amount of income tax to withhold is:

Over—	But not over—		of excess over—
$492	—$1,300	$0.00 plus 10%	—$492
$1,300	—$3,781	$80.80 plus 12%	—$1,300
$3,781	—$7,508	$378.52 plus 22%	—$3,781
$7,508	—$13,885	$1,198.46 plus 24%	—$7,508
$13,885	—$17,500	$2,728.94 plus 32%	—$13,885
$17,500	—$26,006	$3,885.74 plus 35%	—$17,500
$26,006	. . . .	$6,862.84 plus 37%	—$26,006

TABLE 4—MONTHLY Payroll Period

(a) SINGLE person (including head of household)—

If the amount of wages (after subtracting withholding allowances) is:
Not over $317 . . . . $0

The amount of income tax to withhold is:

Over—	But not over—		of excess over—
$317	—$1,125	$0.00 plus 10%	—$317
$1,125	—$3,606	$80.80 plus 12%	—$1,125
$3,606	—$7,333	$378.52 plus 22%	—$3,606
$7,333	—$13,710	$1,198.46 plus 24%	—$7,333
$13,710	—$17,325	$2,728.94 plus 32%	—$13,710
$17,325	—$42,842	$3,885.74 plus 35%	—$17,325
$42,842	. . . .	$12,816.69 plus 37%	—$42,842

(b) MARRIED person—

If the amount of wages (after subtracting withholding allowances) is:
Not over $983 . . . . $0

The amount of income tax to withhold is:

Over—	But not over—		of excess over—
$983	—$2,600	$0.00 plus 10%	—$983
$2,600	—$7,563	$161.70 plus 12%	—$2,600
$7,563	—$15,017	$757.26 plus 22%	—$7,563
$15,017	—$27,771	$2,397.14 plus 24%	—$15,017
$27,771	—$35,000	$5,458.10 plus 32%	—$27,771
$35,000	—$52,013	$7,771.38 plus 35%	—$35,000
$52,013	. . . .	$13,725.93 plus 37%	—$52,013

Percentage Method Tables for Income Tax Withholding (continued)

(For Wages Paid in 2019)

TABLE 5—QUARTERLY Payroll Period

(a) SINGLE person (including head of household)—

If the amount of wages (after subtracting withholding allowances) is: Not over $950 . . . . The amount of income tax to withhold is: $0

Over—	But not over—		of excess over—
$950	—$3,375	$0.00 plus 10%	—$950
$3,375	—$10,819	$242.50 plus 12%	—$3,375
$10,819	—$22,000	$1,135.78 plus 22%	—$10,819
$22,000	—$41,131	$3,595.60 plus 24%	—$22,000
$41,131	—$51,975	$8,187.04 plus 32%	—$41,131
$51,975	—$128,525	$11,657.12 plus 35%	—$51,975
$128,525	. . . .	$38,449.62 plus 37%	—$128,525

(b) MARRIED person—

If the amount of wages (after subtracting withholding allowances) is: Not over $2,950 . . . . The amount of income tax to withhold is: $0

Over—	But not over—		of excess over—
$2,950	—$7,800	$0.00 plus 10%	—$2,950
$7,800	—$22,688	$485.00 plus 12%	—$7,800
$22,688	—$45,050	$2,271.56 plus 22%	—$22,688
$45,050	—$83,313	$7,191.20 plus 24%	—$45,050
$83,313	—$105,000	$16,374.32 plus 32%	—$83,313
$105,000	—$156,038	$23,314.16 plus 35%	—$105,000
$156,038	. . . .	$41,177.46 plus 37%	—$156,038

TABLE 6—SEMIANNUAL Payroll Period

(a) SINGLE person (including head of household)—

If the amount of wages (after subtracting withholding allowances) is: Not over $1,900 . . . . The amount of income tax to withhold is: $0

Over—	But not over—		of excess over—
$1,900	—$6,750	$0.00 plus 10%	—$1,900
$6,750	—$21,638	$485.00 plus 12%	—$6,750
$21,638	—$44,000	$2,271.56 plus 22%	—$21,638
$44,000	—$82,263	$7,191.20 plus 24%	—$44,000
$82,263	—$103,950	$16,374.32 plus 32%	—$82,263
$103,950	—$257,050	$23,314.16 plus 35%	—$103,950
$257,050	. . . .	$76,899.16 plus 37%	—$257,050

(b) MARRIED person—

If the amount of wages (after subtracting withholding allowances) is: Not over $5,900 . . . . The amount of income tax to withhold is: $0

Over—	But not over—		of excess over—
$5,900	—$15,600	$0.00 plus 10%	—$5,900
$15,600	—$45,375	$970.00 plus 12%	—$15,600
$45,375	—$90,100	$4,543.00 plus 22%	—$45,375
$90,100	—$166,625	$14,382.50 plus 24%	—$90,100
$166,625	—$210,000	$32,748.50 plus 32%	—$166,625
$210,000	—$312,075	$46,628.50 plus 35%	—$210,000
$312,075	. . . .	$82,354.75 plus 37%	—$312,075

TABLE 7—ANNUAL Payroll Period

(a) SINGLE person (including head of household)—

If the amount of wages (after subtracting withholding allowances) is: Not over $3,800 . . . . The amount of income tax to withhold is: $0

Over—	But not over—		of excess over—
$3,800	—$13,500	$0.00 plus 10%	—$3,800
$13,500	—$43,275	$970.00 plus 12%	—$13,500
$43,275	—$88,000	$4,543.00 plus 22%	—$43,275
$88,000	—$164,525	$14,382.50 plus 24%	—$88,000
$164,525	—$207,900	$32,748.50 plus 32%	—$164,525
$207,900	—$514,100	$46,628.50 plus 35%	—$207,900
$514,100	. . . .	$153,798.50 plus 37%	—$514,100

(b) MARRIED person—

If the amount of wages (after subtracting withholding allowances) is: Not over $11,800 . . . . . . The amount of income tax to withhold is: $0

Over—	But not over—		of excess over—
$11,800	—$31,200	$0.00 plus 10%	—$11,800
$31,200	—$90,750	$1,940.00 plus 12%	—$31,200
$90,750	—$180,200	$9,086.00 plus 22%	—$90,750
$180,200	—$333,250	$28,765.00 plus 24%	—$180,200
$333,250	—$420,000	$65,497.00 plus 32%	—$333,250
$420,000	—$624,150	$93,257.00 plus 35%	—$420,000
$624,150	. . . .	$164,709.50 plus 37%	—$624,150

TABLE 8—DAILY or MISCELLANEOUS Payroll Period

(a) SINGLE person (including head of household)—

If the amount of wages (after subtracting withholding allowances) divided by the number of days in the payroll period is: Not over $14.60 . . . . The amount of income tax to withhold per day is: $0

Over—	But not over—		of excess over—
$14.60	—$51.90	$0.00 plus 10%	—$14.60
$51.90	—$166.40	$3.73 plus 12%	—$51.90
$166.40	—$338.50	$17.47 plus 22%	—$166.40
$338.50	—$632.80	$55.33 plus 24%	—$338.50
$632.80	—$799.60	$125.96 plus 32%	—$632.80
$799.60	—$1,977.30	$179.34 plus 35%	—$799.60
$1,977.30	. . . .	$591.54 plus 37%	—$1,977.30

(b) MARRIED person—

If the amount of wages (after subtracting withholding allowances) divided by the number of days in the payroll period is: Not over $45.40 . . . . The amount of income tax to withhold per day is: $0

Over—	But not over—		of excess over—
$45.40	—$120.00	$0.00 plus 10%	—$45.40
$120.00	—$349.00	$7.46 plus 12%	—$120.00
$349.00	—$693.10	$34.94 plus 22%	—$349.00
$693.10	—$1,281.70	$110.64 plus 24%	—$693.10
$1,281.70	—$1,615.40	$251.90 plus 32%	—$1,281.70
$1,615.40	—$2,400.60	$358.68 plus 35%	—$1,615.40
$2,400.60	. . . .	$633.50 plus 37%	—$2,400.60

Wage Bracket Method Tables for Income Tax Withholding

SINGLE Persons—WEEKLY Payroll Period

(For Wages Paid through December 2019)

And the wages are–		And the number of withholding allowances claimed is—										
At least	But less than	0	1	2	3	4	5	6	7	8	9	10
		The amount of income tax to be withheld is—										
$ 0	$73	$0	$0	$0	$0	$0	$0	$0	$0	$0	$0	$0
73	84	1	0	0	0	0	0	0	0	0	0	0
84	95	2	0	0	0	0	0	0	0	0	0	0
95	106	3	0	0	0	0	0	0	0	0	0	0
106	117	4	0	0	0	0	0	0	0	0	0	0
117	128	5	0	0	0	0	0	0	0	0	0	0
128	139	6	0	0	0	0	0	0	0	0	0	0
139	150	7	0	0	0	0	0	0	0	0	0	0
150	161	8	0	0	0	0	0	0	0	0	0	0
161	172	9	1	0	0	0	0	0	0	0	0	0
172	183	10	2	0	0	0	0	0	0	0	0	0
183	194	12	3	0	0	0	0	0	0	0	0	0
194	205	13	5	0	0	0	0	0	0	0	0	0
205	216	14	6	0	0	0	0	0	0	0	0	0
216	227	15	7	0	0	0	0	0	0	0	0	0
227	238	16	8	0	0	0	0	0	0	0	0	0
238	249	17	9	1	0	0	0	0	0	0	0	0
249	260	18	10	2	0	0	0	0	0	0	0	0
260	271	19	11	3	0	0	0	0	0	0	0	0
271	282	21	12	4	0	0	0	0	0	0	0	0
282	293	22	13	5	0	0	0	0	0	0	0	0
293	304	23	14	6	0	0	0	0	0	0	0	0
304	315	25	16	7	0	0	0	0	0	0	0	0
315	326	26	17	9	1	0	0	0	0	0	0	0
326	337	27	18	10	2	0	0	0	0	0	0	0
337	348	29	19	11	3	0	0	0	0	0	0	0
348	359	30	20	12	4	0	0	0	0	0	0	0
359	370	31	22	13	5	0	0	0	0	0	0	0
370	381	33	23	14	6	0	0	0	0	0	0	0
381	392	34	24	15	7	0	0	0	0	0	0	0
392	403	35	26	16	8	0	0	0	0	0	0	0
403	414	37	27	17	9	1	0	0	0	0	0	0
414	425	38	28	18	10	2	0	0	0	0	0	0
425	436	39	29	20	12	3	0	0	0	0	0	0
436	447	40	31	21	13	5	0	0	0	0	0	0
447	458	42	32	22	14	6	0	0	0	0	0	0
458	469	43	33	24	15	7	0	0	0	0	0	0
469	480	44	35	25	16	8	0	0	0	0	0	0
480	491	46	36	26	17	9	1	0	0	0	0	0
491	502	47	37	28	18	10	2	0	0	0	0	0
502	513	48	39	29	19	11	3	0	0	0	0	0
513	524	50	40	30	21	12	4	0	0	0	0	0
524	535	51	41	32	22	13	5	0	0	0	0	0
535	546	52	43	33	23	14	6	0	0	0	0	0
546	557	54	44	34	25	16	7	0	0	0	0	0
557	568	55	45	36	26	17	9	0	0	0	0	0
568	579	56	47	37	27	18	10	2	0	0	0	0
579	590	58	48	38	29	19	11	3	0	0	0	0
590	601	59	49	40	30	20	12	4	0	0	0	0
601	612	60	51	41	31	22	13	5	0	0	0	0
612	623	62	52	42	33	23	14	6	0	0	0	0
623	634	63	53	44	34	24	15	7	0	0	0	0
634	645	64	55	45	35	25	16	8	0	0	0	0
645	656	66	56	46	36	27	17	9	1	0	0	0
656	667	67	57	47	38	28	18	10	2	0	0	0
667	678	68	59	49	39	29	20	11	3	0	0	0
678	689	70	60	50	40	31	21	13	5	0	0	0
689	700	71	61	51	42	32	22	14	6	0	0	0
700	711	72	62	53	43	33	24	15	7	0	0	0
711	722	73	64	54	44	35	25	16	8	0	0	0
722	733	75	65	55	46	36	26	17	9	1	0	0
733	744	76	66	57	47	37	28	18	10	2	0	0
744	755	77	68	58	48	39	29	19	11	3	0	0
755	766	79	69	59	50	40	30	21	12	4	0	0
766	777	80	70	61	51	41	32	22	13	5	0	0
777	788	81	72	62	52	43	33	23	14	6	0	0
788	799	83	73	63	54	44	34	25	16	7	0	0
799	810	84	74	65	55	45	36	26	17	9	0	0
810	821	85	76	66	56	47	37	27	18	10	2	0
821	832	87	77	67	58	48	38	29	19	11	3	0

Wage Bracket Method Tables for Income Tax Withholding

SINGLE Persons—WEEKLY Payroll Period

(For Wages Paid through December 2019)

And the wages are–		And the number of withholding allowances claimed is—										
At least	But less than	0	1	2	3	4	5	6	7	8	9	10
		The amount of income tax to be withheld is—										
832	843	89	78	69	59	49	40	30	20	12	4	0
843	854	91	80	70	60	51	41	31	21	13	5	0
854	865	93	81	71	62	52	42	32	23	14	6	0
865	876	96	82	73	63	53	43	34	24	15	7	0
876	887	98	84	74	64	55	45	35	25	16	8	0
887	898	101	85	75	66	56	46	36	27	17	9	1
898	909	103	86	77	67	57	47	38	28	18	10	2
909	920	105	88	78	68	58	49	39	29	20	11	3
920	931	108	90	79	69	60	50	40	31	21	13	4
931	942	110	93	80	71	61	51	42	32	22	14	6
942	953	113	95	82	72	62	53	43	33	24	15	7
953	964	115	97	83	73	64	54	44	35	25	16	8
964	975	118	100	84	75	65	55	46	36	26	17	9
975	986	120	102	86	76	66	57	47	37	28	18	10
986	997	122	105	87	77	68	58	48	39	29	19	11
997	1,008	125	107	89	79	69	59	50	40	30	21	12
1,008	1,019	127	109	92	80	70	61	51	41	32	22	13
1,019	1,030	130	112	94	81	72	62	52	43	33	23	14
1,030	1,041	132	114	97	83	73	63	54	44	34	25	15
1,041	1,052	135	117	99	84	74	65	55	45	36	26	17
1,052	1,063	137	119	101	85	76	66	56	47	37	27	18
1,063	1,074	139	122	104	87	77	67	58	48	38	28	19
1,074	1,085	142	124	106	88	78	69	59	49	40	30	20
1,085	1,096	144	126	109	91	80	70	60	51	41	31	21
1,096	1,107	147	129	111	93	81	71	62	52	42	32	23
1,107	1,118	149	131	113	96	82	73	63	53	43	34	24
1,118	1,129	151	134	116	98	84	74	64	54	45	35	25
1,129	1,140	154	136	118	101	85	75	65	56	46	36	27
1,140	1,151	156	139	121	103	86	76	67	57	47	38	28
1,151	1,162	159	141	123	105	88	78	68	58	49	39	29
1,162	1,173	161	143	126	108	90	79	69	60	50	40	31
1,173	1,184	164	146	128	110	92	80	71	61	51	42	32
1,184	1,195	166	148	130	113	95	82	72	62	53	43	33
1,195	1,206	168	151	133	115	97	83	73	64	54	44	35
1,206	1,217	171	153	135	118	100	84	75	65	55	46	36
1,217	1,228	173	155	138	120	102	86	76	66	57	47	37
1,228	1,239	176	158	140	122	105	87	77	68	58	48	39
1,239	1,250	178	160	143	125	107	89	79	69	59	50	40
1,250	1,261	180	163	145	127	109	92	80	70	61	51	41
1,261	1,272	183	165	147	130	112	94	81	72	62	52	43
1,272	1,283	185	168	150	132	114	96	83	73	63	54	44
1,283	1,294	188	170	152	134	117	99	84	74	65	55	45
1,294	1,305	190	172	155	137	119	101	85	76	66	56	47
1,305	1,316	193	175	157	139	122	104	87	77	67	58	48
1,316	1,327	195	177	159	142	124	106	88	78	69	59	49
1,327	1,338	197	180	162	144	126	109	91	80	70	60	50
1,338	1,349	200	182	164	147	129	111	93	81	71	61	52
1,349	1,360	202	184	167	149	131	113	96	82	73	63	53
1,360	1,371	205	187	169	151	134	116	98	84	74	64	54
1,371	1,382	207	189	172	154	136	118	100	85	75	65	56
1,382	1,393	210	192	174	156	138	121	103	86	76	67	57
1,393	1,404	212	194	176	159	141	123	105	88	78	68	58
1,404	1,415	214	197	179	161	143	126	108	90	79	69	60
1,415	1,426	217	199	181	163	146	128	110	92	80	71	61
1,426	1,437	219	201	184	166	148	130	113	95	82	72	62
1,437	1,448	222	204	186	168	151	133	115	97	83	73	64
1,448	1,459	224	206	189	171	153	135	117	100	84	75	65
1,459	1,470	226	209	191	173	155	138	120	102	86	76	66
1,470	1,481	229	211	193	176	158	140	122	105	87	77	68
1,481	1,492	231	214	196	178	160	142	125	107	89	79	69
1,492	1,503	234	216	198	180	163	145	127	109	92	80	70
1,503	1,514	236	218	201	183	165	147	130	112	94	81	72
1,514	1,525	239	221	203	185	167	150	132	114	96	83	73
1,525	1,536	241	223	205	188	170	152	134	117	99	84	74
1,536	1,547	243	226	208	190	172	155	137	119	101	85	76

1,547 and over   Use Table 1(a) for a SINGLE person on page 46. Also see the instructions on page 44.

Wage Bracket Method Tables for Income Tax Withholding

MARRIED Persons—**WEEKLY** Payroll Period

(For Wages Paid through December 2019)

And the wages are–		And the number of withholding allowances claimed is—										
At least	But less than	0	1	2	3	4	5	6	7	8	9	10
		The amount of income tax to be withheld is—										
$ 0	$227	$0	$0	$0	$0	$0	$0	$0	$0	$0	$0	$0
227	238	1	0	0	0	0	0	0	0	0	0	0
238	249	2	0	0	0	0	0	0	0	0	0	0
249	260	3	0	0	0	0	0	0	0	0	0	0
260	271	4	0	0	0	0	0	0	0	0	0	0
271	282	5	0	0	0	0	0	0	0	0	0	0
282	293	6	0	0	0	0	0	0	0	0	0	0
293	304	7	0	0	0	0	0	0	0	0	0	0
304	315	8	0	0	0	0	0	0	0	0	0	0
315	326	9	1	0	0	0	0	0	0	0	0	0
326	337	10	2	0	0	0	0	0	0	0	0	0
337	348	12	3	0	0	0	0	0	0	0	0	0
348	359	13	5	0	0	0	0	0	0	0	0	0
359	370	14	6	0	0	0	0	0	0	0	0	0
370	381	15	7	0	0	0	0	0	0	0	0	0
381	392	16	8	0	0	0	0	0	0	0	0	0
392	403	17	9	1	0	0	0	0	0	0	0	0
403	414	18	10	2	0	0	0	0	0	0	0	0
414	425	19	11	3	0	0	0	0	0	0	0	0
425	436	20	12	4	0	0	0	0	0	0	0	0
436	447	21	13	5	0	0	0	0	0	0	0	0
447	458	23	14	6	0	0	0	0	0	0	0	0
458	469	24	16	8	0	0	0	0	0	0	0	0
469	480	25	17	9	1	0	0	0	0	0	0	0
480	491	26	18	10	2	0	0	0	0	0	0	0
491	502	27	19	11	3	0	0	0	0	0	0	0
502	513	28	20	12	4	0	0	0	0	0	0	0
513	524	29	21	13	5	0	0	0	0	0	0	0
524	535	30	22	14	6	0	0	0	0	0	0	0
535	546	31	23	15	7	0	0	0	0	0	0	0
546	557	32	24	16	8	0	0	0	0	0	0	0
557	568	34	25	17	9	1	0	0	0	0	0	0
568	579	35	27	19	10	2	0	0	0	0	0	0
579	590	36	28	20	12	3	0	0	0	0	0	0
590	601	37	29	21	13	5	0	0	0	0	0	0
601	612	38	30	22	14	6	0	0	0	0	0	0
612	623	39	31	23	15	7	0	0	0	0	0	0
623	634	41	32	24	16	8	0	0	0	0	0	0
634	645	42	33	25	17	9	1	0	0	0	0	0
645	656	43	34	26	18	10	2	0	0	0	0	0
656	667	45	35	27	19	11	3	0	0	0	0	0
667	678	46	36	28	20	12	4	0	0	0	0	0
678	689	47	38	30	21	13	5	0	0	0	0	0
689	700	49	39	31	23	14	6	0	0	0	0	0
700	711	50	40	32	24	16	7	0	0	0	0	0
711	722	51	42	33	25	17	9	0	0	0	0	0
722	733	53	43	34	26	18	10	2	0	0	0	0
733	744	54	44	35	27	19	11	3	0	0	0	0
744	755	55	46	36	28	20	12	4	0	0	0	0
755	766	57	47	37	29	21	13	5	0	0	0	0
766	777	58	48	39	30	22	14	6	0	0	0	0
777	788	59	50	40	31	23	15	7	0	0	0	0
788	799	61	51	41	32	24	16	8	0	0	0	0
799	810	62	52	42	34	25	17	9	1	0	0	0
810	821	63	53	44	35	27	18	10	2	0	0	0
821	832	64	55	45	36	28	20	11	3	0	0	0
832	843	66	56	46	37	29	21	13	5	0	0	0
843	854	67	57	48	38	30	22	14	6	0	0	0
854	865	68	59	49	39	31	23	15	7	0	0	0
865	876	70	60	50	41	32	24	16	8	0	0	0
876	887	71	61	52	42	33	25	17	9	1	0	0
887	898	72	63	53	43	34	26	18	10	2	0	0
898	909	74	64	54	45	35	27	19	11	3	0	0
909	920	75	65	56	46	36	28	20	12	4	0	0
920	931	76	67	57	47	38	29	21	13	5	0	0
931	942	78	68	58	49	39	31	22	14	6	0	0
942	953	79	69	60	50	40	32	24	16	7	0	0
953	964	80	71	61	51	42	33	25	17	9	0	0
964	975	82	72	62	53	43	34	26	18	10	2	0
975	986	83	73	64	54	44	35	27	19	11	3	0

Wage Bracket Method Tables for Income Tax Withholding

MARRIED Persons—WEEKLY Payroll Period

(For Wages Paid through December 2019)

And the wages are–		And the number of withholding allowances claimed is—										
At least	But less than	0	1	2	3	4	5	6	7	8	9	10
		The amount of income tax to be withheld is—										
986	997	84	75	65	55	46	36	28	20	12	4	0
997	1,008	86	76	66	57	47	37	29	21	13	5	0
1,008	1,019	87	77	68	58	48	38	30	22	14	6	0
1,019	1,030	88	79	69	59	49	40	31	23	15	7	0
1,030	1,041	90	80	70	60	51	41	32	24	16	8	0
1,041	1,052	91	81	72	62	52	42	33	25	17	9	1
1,052	1,063	92	83	73	63	53	44	35	27	18	10	2
1,063	1,074	94	84	74	64	55	45	36	28	20	11	3
1,074	1,085	95	85	75	66	56	46	37	29	21	13	4
1,085	1,096	96	86	77	67	57	48	38	30	22	14	6
1,096	1,107	97	88	78	68	59	49	39	31	23	15	7
1,107	1,118	99	89	79	70	60	50	41	32	24	16	8
1,118	1,129	100	90	81	71	61	52	42	33	25	17	9
1,129	1,140	101	92	82	72	63	53	43	34	26	18	10
1,140	1,151	103	93	83	74	64	54	45	35	27	19	11
1,151	1,162	104	94	85	75	65	56	46	36	28	20	12
1,162	1,173	105	96	86	76	67	57	47	38	29	21	13
1,173	1,184	107	97	87	78	68	58	49	39	31	22	14
1,184	1,195	108	98	89	79	69	60	50	40	32	24	15
1,195	1,206	109	100	90	80	71	61	51	42	33	25	17
1,206	1,217	111	101	91	82	72	62	53	43	34	26	18
1,217	1,228	112	102	93	83	73	64	54	44	35	27	19
1,228	1,239	113	104	94	84	75	65	55	45	36	28	20
1,239	1,250	115	105	95	86	76	66	56	47	37	29	21
1,250	1,261	116	106	97	87	77	68	58	48	38	30	22
1,261	1,272	117	108	98	88	79	69	59	49	40	31	23
1,272	1,283	119	109	99	90	80	70	60	51	41	32	24
1,283	1,294	120	110	101	91	81	71	62	52	42	33	25
1,294	1,305	121	112	102	92	82	73	63	53	44	34	26
1,305	1,316	123	113	103	93	84	74	64	55	45	36	28
1,316	1,327	124	114	105	95	85	75	66	56	46	37	29
1,327	1,338	125	116	106	96	86	77	67	57	48	38	30
1,338	1,349	127	117	107	97	88	78	68	59	49	39	31
1,349	1,360	128	118	108	99	89	79	70	60	50	41	32
1,360	1,371	129	119	110	100	90	81	71	61	52	42	33
1,371	1,382	130	121	111	101	92	82	72	63	53	43	34
1,382	1,393	132	122	112	103	93	83	74	64	54	45	35
1,393	1,404	133	123	114	104	94	85	75	65	56	46	36
1,404	1,415	134	125	115	105	96	86	76	67	57	47	38
1,415	1,426	136	126	116	107	97	87	78	68	58	49	39
1,426	1,437	137	127	118	108	98	89	79	69	60	50	40
1,437	1,448	138	129	119	109	100	90	80	71	61	51	41
1,448	1,459	140	130	120	111	101	91	82	72	62	52	43
1,459	1,470	141	131	122	112	102	93	83	73	64	54	44
1,470	1,481	142	133	123	113	104	94	84	75	65	55	45
1,481	1,492	144	134	124	115	105	95	86	76	66	56	47
1,492	1,503	145	135	126	116	106	97	87	77	67	58	48
1,503	1,514	146	137	127	117	108	98	88	78	69	59	49
1,514	1,525	148	138	128	119	109	99	89	80	70	60	51
1,525	1,536	149	139	130	120	110	101	91	81	71	62	52
1,536	1,547	150	141	131	121	112	102	92	82	73	63	53
1,547	1,558	152	142	132	123	113	103	93	84	74	64	55
1,558	1,569	153	143	134	124	114	104	95	85	75	66	56
1,569	1,580	154	145	135	125	115	106	96	86	77	67	57
1,580	1,591	156	146	136	126	117	107	97	88	78	68	59
1,591	1,602	157	147	138	128	118	108	99	89	79	70	60
1,602	1,613	158	149	139	129	119	110	100	90	81	71	61
1,613	1,624	160	150	140	130	121	111	101	92	82	72	63
1,624	1,635	161	151	141	132	122	112	103	93	83	74	64
1,635	1,646	162	152	143	133	123	114	104	94	85	75	65
1,646	1,657	163	154	144	134	125	115	105	96	86	76	67
1,657	1,668	165	155	145	136	126	116	107	97	87	78	68
1,668	1,679	166	156	147	137	127	118	108	98	89	79	69
1,679	1,690	167	158	148	138	129	119	109	100	90	80	71
1,690	1,701	169	159	149	140	130	120	111	101	91	82	72
1,701	1,711	170	160	151	141	131	122	112	102	92	83	73

1,711 and over — Use Table 1(b) for a MARRIED person on page 46. Also see the instructions on page 44.

Wage Bracket Method Tables for Income Tax Withholding

SINGLE Persons—**BIWEEKLY** Payroll Period

(For Wages Paid through December 2019)

And the wages are-		And the number of withholding allowances claimed is—										
At least	But less than	0	1	2	3	4	5	6	7	8	9	10
		The amount of income tax to be withheld is—										
$ 0	$146	$0	$0	$0	$0	$0	$0	$0	$0	$0	$0	$0
146	157	1	0	0	0	0	0	0	0	0	0	0
157	168	2	0	0	0	0	0	0	0	0	0	0
168	179	3	0	0	0	0	0	0	0	0	0	0
179	190	4	0	0	0	0	0	0	0	0	0	0
190	201	5	0	0	0	0	0	0	0	0	0	0
201	212	6	0	0	0	0	0	0	0	0	0	0
212	223	7	0	0	0	0	0	0	0	0	0	0
223	234	8	0	0	0	0	0	0	0	0	0	0
234	245	9	0	0	0	0	0	0	0	0	0	0
245	256	10	0	0	0	0	0	0	0	0	0	0
256	267	12	0	0	0	0	0	0	0	0	0	0
267	278	13	0	0	0	0	0	0	0	0	0	0
278	289	14	0	0	0	0	0	0	0	0	0	0
289	300	15	0	0	0	0	0	0	0	0	0	0
300	311	16	0	0	0	0	0	0	0	0	0	0
311	322	17	1	0	0	0	0	0	0	0	0	0
322	333	18	2	0	0	0	0	0	0	0	0	0
333	344	19	3	0	0	0	0	0	0	0	0	0
344	355	20	4	0	0	0	0	0	0	0	0	0
355	366	21	5	0	0	0	0	0	0	0	0	0
366	377	23	6	0	0	0	0	0	0	0	0	0
377	388	24	7	0	0	0	0	0	0	0	0	0
388	399	25	9	0	0	0	0	0	0	0	0	0
399	410	26	10	0	0	0	0	0	0	0	0	0
410	421	27	11	0	0	0	0	0	0	0	0	0
421	432	28	12	0	0	0	0	0	0	0	0	0
432	443	29	13	0	0	0	0	0	0	0	0	0
443	454	30	14	0	0	0	0	0	0	0	0	0
454	465	31	15	0	0	0	0	0	0	0	0	0
465	476	32	16	0	0	0	0	0	0	0	0	0
476	487	34	17	1	0	0	0	0	0	0	0	0
487	498	35	18	2	0	0	0	0	0	0	0	0
498	509	36	20	3	0	0	0	0	0	0	0	0
509	529	37	21	5	0	0	0	0	0	0	0	0
529	549	40	23	7	0	0	0	0	0	0	0	0
549	569	42	25	9	0	0	0	0	0	0	0	0
569	589	44	27	11	0	0	0	0	0	0	0	0
589	609	47	29	13	0	0	0	0	0	0	0	0
609	629	49	31	15	0	0	0	0	0	0	0	0
629	649	52	33	17	1	0	0	0	0	0	0	0
649	669	54	35	19	3	0	0	0	0	0	0	0
669	689	56	37	21	5	0	0	0	0	0	0	0
689	709	59	39	23	7	0	0	0	0	0	0	0
709	729	61	42	25	9	0	0	0	0	0	0	0
729	749	64	44	27	11	0	0	0	0	0	0	0
749	769	66	47	29	13	0	0	0	0	0	0	0
769	789	68	49	31	15	0	0	0	0	0	0	0
789	809	71	51	33	17	1	0	0	0	0	0	0
809	829	73	54	35	19	3	0	0	0	0	0	0
829	849	76	56	37	21	5	0	0	0	0	0	0
849	869	78	59	39	23	7	0	0	0	0	0	0
869	889	80	61	42	25	9	0	0	0	0	0	0
889	909	83	63	44	27	11	0	0	0	0	0	0
909	929	85	66	47	29	13	0	0	0	0	0	0
929	949	88	68	49	31	15	0	0	0	0	0	0
949	969	90	71	51	33	17	1	0	0	0	0	0
969	989	92	73	54	35	19	3	0	0	0	0	0
989	1,009	95	75	56	37	21	5	0	0	0	0	0
1,009	1,029	97	78	59	39	23	7	0	0	0	0	0
1,029	1,049	100	80	61	42	25	9	0	0	0	0	0
1,049	1,069	102	83	63	44	27	11	0	0	0	0	0
1,069	1,089	104	85	66	46	29	13	0	0	0	0	0
1,089	1,109	107	87	68	49	31	15	0	0	0	0	0
1,109	1,129	109	90	71	51	33	17	0	0	0	0	0
1,129	1,149	112	92	73	54	35	19	2	0	0	0	0
1,149	1,169	114	95	75	56	37	21	4	0	0	0	0
1,169	1,189	116	97	78	58	39	23	6	0	0	0	0
1,189	1,209	119	99	80	61	41	25	8	0	0	0	0
1,209	1,229	121	102	83	63	44	27	10	0	0	0	0

Wage Bracket Method Tables for Income Tax Withholding

SINGLE Persons—BIWEEKLY Payroll Period

(For Wages Paid through December 2019)

And the wages are–		And the number of withholding allowances claimed is—										
At least	But less than	0	1	2	3	4	5	6	7	8	9	10
		The amount of income tax to be withheld is—										
1,229	1,249	124	104	85	66	46	29	12	0	0	0	0
1,249	1,269	126	107	87	68	49	31	14	0	0	0	0
1,269	1,289	128	109	90	70	51	33	16	0	0	0	0
1,289	1,309	131	111	92	73	53	35	18	2	0	0	0
1,309	1,329	133	114	95	75	56	37	20	4	0	0	0
1,329	1,349	136	116	97	78	58	39	22	6	0	0	0
1,349	1,369	138	119	99	80	61	41	24	8	0	0	0
1,369	1,389	140	121	102	82	63	44	26	10	0	0	0
1,389	1,409	143	123	104	85	65	46	28	12	0	0	0
1,409	1,429	145	126	107	87	68	48	30	14	0	0	0
1,429	1,449	148	128	109	90	70	51	32	16	0	0	0
1,449	1,469	150	131	111	92	73	53	34	18	2	0	0
1,469	1,489	152	133	114	94	75	56	36	20	4	0	0
1,489	1,509	155	135	116	97	77	58	39	22	6	0	0
1,509	1,529	157	138	119	99	80	60	41	24	8	0	0
1,529	1,549	160	140	121	102	82	63	43	26	10	0	0
1,549	1,569	162	143	123	104	85	65	46	28	12	0	0
1,569	1,589	164	145	126	106	87	68	48	30	14	0	0
1,589	1,609	167	147	128	109	89	70	51	32	16	0	0
1,609	1,629	169	150	131	111	92	72	53	34	18	2	0
1,629	1,649	172	152	133	114	94	75	55	36	20	4	0
1,649	1,669	174	155	135	116	97	77	58	38	22	6	0
1,669	1,689	178	157	138	118	99	80	60	41	24	8	0
1,689	1,709	182	159	140	121	101	82	63	43	26	10	0
1,709	1,729	187	162	143	123	104	84	65	46	28	12	0
1,729	1,749	191	164	145	126	106	87	67	48	30	14	0
1,749	1,769	196	167	147	128	109	89	70	50	32	16	0
1,769	1,789	200	169	150	130	111	92	72	53	34	18	2
1,789	1,809	204	171	152	133	113	94	75	55	36	20	4
1,809	1,829	209	174	155	135	116	96	77	58	38	22	6
1,829	1,849	213	178	157	138	118	99	79	60	41	24	8
1,849	1,869	218	182	159	140	121	101	82	62	43	26	10
1,869	1,889	222	186	162	142	123	104	84	65	45	28	12
1,889	1,909	226	191	164	145	125	106	87	67	48	30	14
1,909	1,929	231	195	167	147	128	108	89	70	50	32	16
1,929	1,949	235	200	169	150	130	111	91	72	53	34	18
1,949	1,969	240	204	171	152	133	113	94	74	55	36	20
1,969	1,989	244	208	174	154	135	116	96	77	57	38	22
1,989	2,009	248	213	177	157	137	118	99	79	60	40	24
2,009	2,029	253	217	182	159	140	120	101	82	62	43	26
2,029	2,049	257	222	186	162	142	123	103	84	65	45	28
2,049	2,069	262	226	190	164	145	125	106	86	67	48	30
2,069	2,089	266	230	195	166	147	128	108	89	69	50	32
2,089	2,109	270	235	199	169	149	130	111	91	72	52	34
2,109	2,129	275	239	204	171	152	132	113	94	74	55	36
2,129	2,149	279	244	208	174	154	135	115	96	77	57	38
2,149	2,169	284	248	212	177	157	137	118	98	79	60	40
2,169	2,189	288	252	217	181	159	140	120	101	81	62	43
2,189	2,209	292	257	221	186	161	142	123	103	84	64	45
2,209	2,229	297	261	226	190	164	144	125	106	86	67	47
2,229	2,249	301	266	230	195	166	147	127	108	89	69	50
2,249	2,269	306	270	234	199	169	149	130	110	91	72	52
2,269	2,289	310	274	239	203	171	152	132	113	93	74	55
2,289	2,309	314	279	243	208	173	154	135	115	96	76	57
2,309	2,329	319	283	248	212	177	156	137	118	98	79	59
2,329	2,349	323	288	252	217	181	159	139	120	101	81	62
2,349	2,369	328	292	256	221	185	161	142	122	103	84	64
2,369	2,389	332	296	261	225	190	164	144	125	105	86	67
2,389	2,409	336	301	265	230	194	166	147	127	108	88	69
2,409	2,429	341	305	270	234	199	168	149	130	110	91	71
2,429	2,449	345	310	274	239	203	171	151	132	113	93	74
2,449	2,469	350	314	278	243	207	173	154	134	115	96	76
2,469	2,489	354	318	283	247	212	176	156	137	117	98	79
2,489	2,509	358	323	287	252	216	181	159	139	120	100	81
2,509	2,529	363	327	292	256	221	185	161	142	122	103	83

2,529 and over   Use Table 2(a) for a SINGLE person on page 46. Also see the instructions on page 44.

Wage Bracket Method Tables for Income Tax Withholding

MARRIED Persons—BIWEEKLY Payroll Period

(For Wages Paid through December 2019)

And the wages are–		And the number of withholding allowances claimed is—										
At least	But less than	0	1	2	3	4	5	6	7	8	9	10
		The amount of income tax to be withheld is—										
$ 0	$454	$0	$0	$0	$0	$0	$0	$0	$0	$0	$0	$0
454	464	1	0	0	0	0	0	0	0	0	0	0
464	474	2	0	0	0	0	0	0	0	0	0	0
474	484	3	0	0	0	0	0	0	0	0	0	0
484	494	4	0	0	0	0	0	0	0	0	0	0
494	504	5	0	0	0	0	0	0	0	0	0	0
504	524	6	0	0	0	0	0	0	0	0	0	0
524	544	8	0	0	0	0	0	0	0	0	0	0
544	564	10	0	0	0	0	0	0	0	0	0	0
564	584	12	0	0	0	0	0	0	0	0	0	0
584	604	14	0	0	0	0	0	0	0	0	0	0
604	624	16	0	0	0	0	0	0	0	0	0	0
624	644	18	2	0	0	0	0	0	0	0	0	0
644	664	20	4	0	0	0	0	0	0	0	0	0
664	684	22	6	0	0	0	0	0	0	0	0	0
684	704	24	8	0	0	0	0	0	0	0	0	0
704	724	26	10	0	0	0	0	0	0	0	0	0
724	744	28	12	0	0	0	0	0	0	0	0	0
744	764	30	14	0	0	0	0	0	0	0	0	0
764	784	32	16	0	0	0	0	0	0	0	0	0
784	804	34	18	2	0	0	0	0	0	0	0	0
804	824	36	20	4	0	0	0	0	0	0	0	0
824	844	38	22	6	0	0	0	0	0	0	0	0
844	864	40	24	8	0	0	0	0	0	0	0	0
864	884	42	26	10	0	0	0	0	0	0	0	0
884	904	44	28	12	0	0	0	0	0	0	0	0
904	924	46	30	14	0	0	0	0	0	0	0	0
924	944	48	32	16	0	0	0	0	0	0	0	0
944	964	50	34	18	2	0	0	0	0	0	0	0
964	984	52	36	20	4	0	0	0	0	0	0	0
984	1,004	54	38	22	6	0	0	0	0	0	0	0
1,004	1,024	56	40	24	8	0	0	0	0	0	0	0
1,024	1,044	58	42	26	10	0	0	0	0	0	0	0
1,044	1,064	60	44	28	12	0	0	0	0	0	0	0
1,064	1,084	62	46	30	14	0	0	0	0	0	0	0
1,084	1,104	64	48	32	16	0	0	0	0	0	0	0
1,104	1,124	66	50	34	18	1	0	0	0	0	0	0
1,124	1,144	68	52	36	20	3	0	0	0	0	0	0
1,144	1,164	70	54	38	22	5	0	0	0	0	0	0
1,164	1,184	72	56	40	24	7	0	0	0	0	0	0
1,184	1,204	74	58	42	26	9	0	0	0	0	0	0
1,204	1,224	76	60	44	28	11	0	0	0	0	0	0
1,224	1,244	79	62	46	30	13	0	0	0	0	0	0
1,244	1,264	81	64	48	32	15	0	0	0	0	0	0
1,264	1,284	83	66	50	34	17	1	0	0	0	0	0
1,284	1,304	86	68	52	36	19	3	0	0	0	0	0
1,304	1,324	88	70	54	38	21	5	0	0	0	0	0
1,324	1,344	91	72	56	40	23	7	0	0	0	0	0
1,344	1,364	93	74	58	42	25	9	0	0	0	0	0
1,364	1,384	95	76	60	44	27	11	0	0	0	0	0
1,384	1,404	98	79	62	46	29	13	0	0	0	0	0
1,404	1,424	100	81	64	48	31	15	0	0	0	0	0
1,424	1,444	103	83	66	50	33	17	1	0	0	0	0
1,444	1,464	105	86	68	52	35	19	3	0	0	0	0
1,464	1,484	107	88	70	54	37	21	5	0	0	0	0
1,484	1,504	110	91	72	56	39	23	7	0	0	0	0
1,504	1,524	112	93	74	58	41	25	9	0	0	0	0
1,524	1,544	115	95	76	60	43	27	11	0	0	0	0
1,544	1,564	117	98	78	62	45	29	13	0	0	0	0
1,564	1,584	119	100	81	64	47	31	15	0	0	0	0
1,584	1,604	122	103	83	66	49	33	17	1	0	0	0
1,604	1,624	124	105	86	68	51	35	19	3	0	0	0
1,624	1,644	127	107	88	70	53	37	21	5	0	0	0
1,644	1,664	129	110	90	72	55	39	23	7	0	0	0
1,664	1,684	131	112	93	74	57	41	25	9	0	0	0
1,684	1,704	134	115	95	76	59	43	27	11	0	0	0
1,704	1,724	136	117	98	78	61	45	29	13	0	0	0
1,724	1,744	139	119	100	81	63	47	31	15	0	0	0
1,744	1,764	141	122	102	83	65	49	33	17	1	0	0
1,764	1,784	143	124	105	85	67	51	35	19	3	0	0

Wage Bracket Method Tables for Income Tax Withholding

MARRIED Persons—**BIWEEKLY** Payroll Period

(For Wages Paid through December 2019)

And the wages are–		And the number of withholding allowances claimed is—										
At least	But less than	0	1	2	3	4	5	6	7	8	9	10
		The amount of income tax to be withheld is—										
1,784	1,804	146	127	107	88	69	53	37	21	5	0	0
1,804	1,824	148	129	110	90	71	55	39	23	7	0	0
1,824	1,844	151	131	112	93	73	57	41	25	9	0	0
1,844	1,864	153	134	114	95	76	59	43	27	11	0	0
1,864	1,884	155	136	117	97	78	61	45	29	13	0	0
1,884	1,904	158	139	119	100	80	63	47	31	15	0	0
1,904	1,924	160	141	122	102	83	65	49	33	17	1	0
1,924	1,944	163	143	124	105	85	67	51	35	19	3	0
1,944	1,964	165	146	126	107	88	69	53	37	21	5	0
1,964	1,984	167	148	129	109	90	71	55	39	23	7	0
1,984	2,004	170	151	131	112	92	73	57	41	25	9	0
2,004	2,024	172	153	134	114	95	75	59	43	27	11	0
2,024	2,044	175	155	136	117	97	78	61	45	29	13	0
2,044	2,064	177	158	138	119	100	80	63	47	31	15	0
2,064	2,084	179	160	141	121	102	83	65	49	33	17	0
2,084	2,104	182	163	143	124	104	85	67	51	35	19	2
2,104	2,124	184	165	146	126	107	87	69	53	37	21	4
2,124	2,144	187	167	148	129	109	90	71	55	39	23	6
2,144	2,164	189	170	150	131	112	92	73	57	41	25	8
2,164	2,184	191	172	153	133	114	95	75	59	43	27	10
2,184	2,204	194	175	155	136	116	97	78	61	45	29	12
2,204	2,224	196	177	158	138	119	99	80	63	47	31	14
2,224	2,244	199	179	160	141	121	102	82	65	49	33	16
2,244	2,264	201	182	162	143	124	104	85	67	51	35	18
2,264	2,284	203	184	165	145	126	107	87	69	53	37	20
2,284	2,304	206	187	167	148	128	109	90	71	55	39	22
2,304	2,324	208	189	170	150	131	111	92	73	57	41	24
2,324	2,344	211	191	172	153	133	114	94	75	59	43	26
2,344	2,364	213	194	174	155	136	116	97	77	61	45	28
2,364	2,384	215	196	177	157	138	119	99	80	63	47	30
2,384	2,404	218	199	179	160	140	121	102	82	65	49	32
2,404	2,424	220	201	182	162	143	123	104	85	67	51	34
2,424	2,444	223	203	184	165	145	126	106	87	69	53	36
2,444	2,464	225	206	186	167	148	128	109	89	71	55	38
2,464	2,484	227	208	189	169	150	131	111	92	73	57	40
2,484	2,504	230	211	191	172	152	133	114	94	75	59	42
2,504	2,524	232	213	194	174	155	135	116	97	77	61	44
2,524	2,544	235	215	196	177	157	138	118	99	80	63	46
2,544	2,564	237	218	198	179	160	140	121	101	82	65	48
2,564	2,584	239	220	201	181	162	143	123	104	84	67	50
2,584	2,604	242	223	203	184	164	145	126	106	87	69	52
2,604	2,624	244	225	206	186	167	147	128	109	89	71	54
2,624	2,644	247	227	208	189	169	150	130	111	92	73	56
2,644	2,664	249	230	210	191	172	152	133	113	94	75	58
2,664	2,684	251	232	213	193	174	155	135	116	96	77	60
2,684	2,704	254	235	215	196	176	157	138	118	99	79	62
2,704	2,724	256	237	218	198	179	159	140	121	101	82	64
2,724	2,744	259	239	220	201	181	162	142	123	104	84	66
2,744	2,764	261	242	222	203	184	164	145	125	106	87	68
2,764	2,784	263	244	225	205	186	167	147	128	108	89	70
2,784	2,804	266	247	227	208	188	169	150	130	111	91	72
2,804	2,824	268	249	230	210	191	171	152	133	113	94	74
2,824	2,844	271	251	232	213	193	174	154	135	116	96	77
2,844	2,864	273	254	234	215	196	176	157	137	118	99	79
2,864	2,884	275	256	237	217	198	179	159	140	120	101	82
2,884	2,904	278	259	239	220	200	181	162	142	123	103	84
2,904	2,924	280	261	242	222	203	183	164	145	125	106	86
2,924	2,944	283	263	244	225	205	186	166	147	128	108	89
2,944	2,964	285	266	246	227	208	188	169	149	130	111	91
2,964	2,984	287	268	249	229	210	191	171	152	132	113	94
2,984	3,004	290	271	251	232	212	193	174	154	135	115	96
3,004	3,024	292	273	254	234	215	195	176	157	137	118	98
3,024	3,044	295	275	256	237	217	198	178	159	140	120	101
3,044	3,064	297	278	258	239	220	200	181	161	142	123	103
3,064	3,084	299	280	261	241	222	203	183	164	144	125	106
3,084	3,104	302	283	263	244	224	205	186	166	147	127	108

3,104 and over   Use Table 2(b) for a MARRIED person on page 46. Also see the instructions on page 44.

Wage Bracket Method Tables for Income Tax Withholding

SINGLE Persons—**SEMIMONTHLY** Payroll Period

(For Wages Paid through December 2019)

And the wages are–		And the number of withholding allowances claimed is—										
At least	But less than	0	1	2	3	4	5	6	7	8	9	10
		The amount of income tax to be withheld is—										
$ 0	$158	$0	$0	$0	$0	$0	$0	$0	$0	$0	$0	$0
158	169	1	0	0	0	0	0	0	0	0	0	0
169	180	2	0	0	0	0	0	0	0	0	0	0
180	191	3	0	0	0	0	0	0	0	0	0	0
191	202	4	0	0	0	0	0	0	0	0	0	0
202	213	5	0	0	0	0	0	0	0	0	0	0
213	224	6	0	0	0	0	0	0	0	0	0	0
224	235	7	0	0	0	0	0	0	0	0	0	0
235	246	8	0	0	0	0	0	0	0	0	0	0
246	257	9	0	0	0	0	0	0	0	0	0	0
257	268	10	0	0	0	0	0	0	0	0	0	0
268	279	12	0	0	0	0	0	0	0	0	0	0
279	290	13	0	0	0	0	0	0	0	0	0	0
290	301	14	0	0	0	0	0	0	0	0	0	0
301	312	15	0	0	0	0	0	0	0	0	0	0
312	323	16	0	0	0	0	0	0	0	0	0	0
323	334	17	0	0	0	0	0	0	0	0	0	0
334	345	18	1	0	0	0	0	0	0	0	0	0
345	356	19	2	0	0	0	0	0	0	0	0	0
356	367	20	3	0	0	0	0	0	0	0	0	0
367	378	21	4	0	0	0	0	0	0	0	0	0
378	389	23	5	0	0	0	0	0	0	0	0	0
389	400	24	6	0	0	0	0	0	0	0	0	0
400	411	25	7	0	0	0	0	0	0	0	0	0
411	422	26	8	0	0	0	0	0	0	0	0	0
422	433	27	9	0	0	0	0	0	0	0	0	0
433	444	28	11	0	0	0	0	0	0	0	0	0
444	455	29	12	0	0	0	0	0	0	0	0	0
455	466	30	13	0	0	0	0	0	0	0	0	0
466	477	31	14	0	0	0	0	0	0	0	0	0
477	488	32	15	0	0	0	0	0	0	0	0	0
488	499	34	16	0	0	0	0	0	0	0	0	0
499	510	35	17	0	0	0	0	0	0	0	0	0
510	530	36	19	1	0	0	0	0	0	0	0	0
530	550	38	21	3	0	0	0	0	0	0	0	0
550	570	40	23	5	0	0	0	0	0	0	0	0
570	590	43	25	7	0	0	0	0	0	0	0	0
590	610	45	27	9	0	0	0	0	0	0	0	0
610	630	47	29	11	0	0	0	0	0	0	0	0
630	650	50	31	13	0	0	0	0	0	0	0	0
650	670	52	33	15	0	0	0	0	0	0	0	0
670	690	55	35	17	0	0	0	0	0	0	0	0
690	710	57	37	19	2	0	0	0	0	0	0	0
710	730	59	39	21	4	0	0	0	0	0	0	0
730	750	62	41	23	6	0	0	0	0	0	0	0
750	770	64	43	25	8	0	0	0	0	0	0	0
770	790	67	46	27	10	0	0	0	0	0	0	0
790	810	69	48	29	12	0	0	0	0	0	0	0
810	830	71	50	31	14	0	0	0	0	0	0	0
830	850	74	53	33	16	0	0	0	0	0	0	0
850	870	76	55	35	18	0	0	0	0	0	0	0
870	890	79	58	37	20	2	0	0	0	0	0	0
890	910	81	60	39	22	4	0	0	0	0	0	0
910	930	83	62	41	24	6	0	0	0	0	0	0
930	950	86	65	44	26	8	0	0	0	0	0	0
950	970	88	67	46	28	10	0	0	0	0	0	0
970	990	91	70	49	30	12	0	0	0	0	0	0
990	1,010	93	72	51	32	14	0	0	0	0	0	0
1,010	1,030	95	74	53	34	16	0	0	0	0	0	0
1,030	1,050	98	77	56	36	18	1	0	0	0	0	0
1,050	1,070	100	79	58	38	20	3	0	0	0	0	0
1,070	1,090	103	82	61	40	22	5	0	0	0	0	0
1,090	1,110	105	84	63	42	24	7	0	0	0	0	0
1,110	1,130	107	86	65	44	26	9	0	0	0	0	0
1,130	1,150	110	89	68	47	28	11	0	0	0	0	0
1,150	1,170	112	91	70	49	30	13	0	0	0	0	0
1,170	1,190	115	94	73	52	32	15	0	0	0	0	0
1,190	1,210	117	96	75	54	34	17	0	0	0	0	0
1,210	1,230	119	98	77	56	36	19	1	0	0	0	0
1,230	1,250	122	101	80	59	38	21	3	0	0	0	0

Wage Bracket Method Tables for Income Tax Withholding

SINGLE Persons—SEMIMONTHLY Payroll Period

(For Wages Paid through December 2019)

And the wages are–		And the number of withholding allowances claimed is—										
At least	But less than	0	1	2	3	4	5	6	7	8	9	10
		The amount of income tax to be withheld is—										
1,250	1,270	124	103	82	61	40	23	5	0	0	0	0
1,270	1,290	127	106	85	64	43	25	7	0	0	0	0
1,290	1,310	129	108	87	66	45	27	9	0	0	0	0
1,310	1,330	131	110	89	68	47	29	11	0	0	0	0
1,330	1,350	134	113	92	71	50	31	13	0	0	0	0
1,350	1,370	136	115	94	73	52	33	15	0	0	0	0
1,370	1,390	139	118	97	76	55	35	17	0	0	0	0
1,390	1,410	141	120	99	78	57	37	19	2	0	0	0
1,410	1,430	143	122	101	80	59	39	21	4	0	0	0
1,430	1,450	146	125	104	83	62	41	23	6	0	0	0
1,450	1,470	148	127	106	85	64	43	25	8	0	0	0
1,470	1,490	151	130	109	88	67	46	27	10	0	0	0
1,490	1,510	153	132	111	90	69	48	29	12	0	0	0
1,510	1,530	155	134	113	92	71	50	31	14	0	0	0
1,530	1,550	158	137	116	95	74	53	33	16	0	0	0
1,550	1,570	160	139	118	97	76	55	35	18	0	0	0
1,570	1,590	163	142	121	100	79	58	37	20	2	0	0
1,590	1,610	165	144	123	102	81	60	39	22	4	0	0
1,610	1,630	167	146	125	104	83	62	41	24	6	0	0
1,630	1,650	170	149	128	107	86	65	44	26	8	0	0
1,650	1,670	172	151	130	109	88	67	46	28	10	0	0
1,670	1,690	175	154	133	112	91	70	49	30	12	0	0
1,690	1,710	177	156	135	114	93	72	51	32	14	0	0
1,710	1,730	179	158	137	116	95	74	53	34	16	0	0
1,730	1,750	182	161	140	119	98	77	56	36	18	1	0
1,750	1,770	184	163	142	121	100	79	58	38	20	3	0
1,770	1,790	187	166	145	124	103	82	61	40	22	5	0
1,790	1,810	189	168	147	126	105	84	63	42	24	7	0
1,810	1,830	193	170	149	128	107	86	65	44	26	9	0
1,830	1,850	197	173	152	131	110	89	68	47	28	11	0
1,850	1,870	202	175	154	133	112	91	70	49	30	13	0
1,870	1,890	206	178	157	136	115	94	73	52	32	15	0
1,890	1,910	211	180	159	138	117	96	75	54	34	17	0
1,910	1,930	215	182	161	140	119	98	77	56	36	19	1
1,930	1,950	219	185	164	143	122	101	80	59	38	21	3
1,950	1,970	224	187	166	145	124	103	82	61	40	23	5
1,970	1,990	228	190	169	148	127	106	85	64	43	25	7
1,990	2,010	233	194	171	150	129	108	87	66	45	27	9
2,010	2,030	237	199	173	152	131	110	89	68	47	29	11
2,030	2,050	241	203	176	155	134	113	92	71	50	31	13
2,050	2,070	246	207	178	157	136	115	94	73	52	33	15
2,070	2,090	250	212	181	160	139	118	97	76	55	35	17
2,090	2,110	255	216	183	162	141	120	99	78	57	37	19
2,110	2,130	259	221	185	164	143	122	101	80	59	39	21
2,130	2,150	263	225	188	167	146	125	104	83	62	41	23
2,150	2,170	268	229	191	169	148	127	106	85	64	43	25
2,170	2,190	272	234	195	172	151	130	109	88	67	46	27
2,190	2,210	277	238	200	174	153	132	111	90	69	48	29
2,210	2,230	281	243	204	176	155	134	113	92	71	50	31
2,230	2,250	285	247	208	179	158	137	116	95	74	53	33
2,250	2,270	290	251	213	181	160	139	118	97	76	55	35
2,270	2,290	294	256	217	184	163	142	121	100	79	58	37
2,290	2,310	299	260	222	186	165	144	123	102	81	60	39
2,310	2,330	303	265	226	188	167	146	125	104	83	62	41
2,330	2,350	307	269	230	192	170	149	128	107	86	65	44
2,350	2,370	312	273	235	196	172	151	130	109	88	67	46
2,370	2,390	316	278	239	201	175	154	133	112	91	70	49
2,390	2,410	321	282	244	205	177	156	135	114	93	72	51
2,410	2,430	325	287	248	210	179	158	137	116	95	74	53
2,430	2,450	329	291	252	214	182	161	140	119	98	77	56
2,450	2,470	334	295	257	218	184	163	142	121	100	79	58
2,470	2,490	338	300	261	223	187	166	145	124	103	82	61
2,490	2,510	343	304	266	227	189	168	147	126	105	84	63
2,510	2,530	347	309	270	232	193	170	149	128	107	86	65
2,530	2,550	351	313	274	236	197	173	152	131	110	89	68

2,550 and over	Use Table 3(a) for a SINGLE person on page 46. Also see the instructions on page 44.

Wage Bracket Method Tables for Income Tax Withholding

MARRIED Persons—SEMIMONTHLY Payroll Period

(For Wages Paid through December 2019)

And the wages are—		And the number of withholding allowances claimed is—										
At least	But less than	0	1	2	3	4	5	6	7	8	9	10
		The amount of income tax to be withheld is—										
$ 0	$492	$0	$0	$0	$0	$0	$0	$0	$0	$0	$0	$0
492	502	1	0	0	0	0	0	0	0	0	0	0
502	512	2	0	0	0	0	0	0	0	0	0	0
512	522	3	0	0	0	0	0	0	0	0	0	0
522	532	4	0	0	0	0	0	0	0	0	0	0
532	542	5	0	0	0	0	0	0	0	0	0	0
542	552	6	0	0	0	0	0	0	0	0	0	0
552	562	7	0	0	0	0	0	0	0	0	0	0
562	572	8	0	0	0	0	0	0	0	0	0	0
572	582	9	0	0	0	0	0	0	0	0	0	0
582	592	10	0	0	0	0	0	0	0	0	0	0
592	602	11	0	0	0	0	0	0	0	0	0	0
602	612	12	0	0	0	0	0	0	0	0	0	0
612	622	13	0	0	0	0	0	0	0	0	0	0
622	632	14	0	0	0	0	0	0	0	0	0	0
632	642	15	0	0	0	0	0	0	0	0	0	0
642	652	16	0	0	0	0	0	0	0	0	0	0
652	662	17	0	0	0	0	0	0	0	0	0	0
662	672	18	0	0	0	0	0	0	0	0	0	0
672	682	19	1	0	0	0	0	0	0	0	0	0
682	692	20	2	0	0	0	0	0	0	0	0	0
692	702	21	3	0	0	0	0	0	0	0	0	0
702	712	22	4	0	0	0	0	0	0	0	0	0
712	722	23	5	0	0	0	0	0	0	0	0	0
722	732	24	6	0	0	0	0	0	0	0	0	0
732	742	25	7	0	0	0	0	0	0	0	0	0
742	752	26	8	0	0	0	0	0	0	0	0	0
752	762	27	9	0	0	0	0	0	0	0	0	0
762	772	28	10	0	0	0	0	0	0	0	0	0
772	782	29	11	0	0	0	0	0	0	0	0	0
782	792	30	12	0	0	0	0	0	0	0	0	0
792	802	31	13	0	0	0	0	0	0	0	0	0
802	812	32	14	0	0	0	0	0	0	0	0	0
812	822	33	15	0	0	0	0	0	0	0	0	0
822	832	34	16	0	0	0	0	0	0	0	0	0
832	842	35	17	0	0	0	0	0	0	0	0	0
842	852	36	18	1	0	0	0	0	0	0	0	0
852	862	37	19	2	0	0	0	0	0	0	0	0
862	872	38	20	3	0	0	0	0	0	0	0	0
872	882	39	21	4	0	0	0	0	0	0	0	0
882	892	40	22	5	0	0	0	0	0	0	0	0
892	902	41	23	6	0	0	0	0	0	0	0	0
902	912	42	24	7	0	0	0	0	0	0	0	0
912	922	43	25	8	0	0	0	0	0	0	0	0
922	932	44	26	9	0	0	0	0	0	0	0	0
932	942	45	27	10	0	0	0	0	0	0	0	0
942	952	46	28	11	0	0	0	0	0	0	0	0
952	962	47	29	12	0	0	0	0	0	0	0	0
962	972	48	30	13	0	0	0	0	0	0	0	0
972	982	49	31	14	0	0	0	0	0	0	0	0
982	992	50	32	15	0	0	0	0	0	0	0	0
992	1,002	51	33	16	0	0	0	0	0	0	0	0
1,002	1,022	52	35	17	0	0	0	0	0	0	0	0
1,022	1,042	54	37	19	2	0	0	0	0	0	0	0
1,042	1,062	56	39	21	4	0	0	0	0	0	0	0
1,062	1,082	58	41	23	6	0	0	0	0	0	0	0
1,082	1,102	60	43	25	8	0	0	0	0	0	0	0
1,102	1,122	62	45	27	10	0	0	0	0	0	0	0
1,122	1,142	64	47	29	12	0	0	0	0	0	0	0
1,142	1,162	66	49	31	14	0	0	0	0	0	0	0
1,162	1,182	68	51	33	16	0	0	0	0	0	0	0
1,182	1,202	70	53	35	18	0	0	0	0	0	0	0
1,202	1,222	72	55	37	20	2	0	0	0	0	0	0
1,222	1,242	74	57	39	22	4	0	0	0	0	0	0
1,242	1,262	76	59	41	24	6	0	0	0	0	0	0
1,262	1,282	78	61	43	26	8	0	0	0	0	0	0
1,282	1,302	80	63	45	28	10	0	0	0	0	0	0
1,302	1,322	82	65	47	30	12	0	0	0	0	0	0
1,322	1,342	85	67	49	32	14	0	0	0	0	0	0
1,342	1,362	87	69	51	34	16	0	0	0	0	0	0

Wage Bracket Method Tables for Income Tax Withholding

MARRIED Persons—SEMIMONTHLY Payroll Period

(For Wages Paid through December 2019)

And the wages are—		And the number of withholding allowances claimed is—										
At least	But less than	0	1	2	3	4	5	6	7	8	9	10
		The amount of income tax to be withheld is—										
1,362	1,382	89	71	53	36	18	1	0	0	0	0	0
1,382	1,402	92	73	55	38	20	3	0	0	0	0	0
1,402	1,422	94	75	57	40	22	5	0	0	0	0	0
1,422	1,442	97	77	59	42	24	7	0	0	0	0	0
1,442	1,462	99	79	61	44	26	9	0	0	0	0	0
1,462	1,482	101	81	63	46	28	11	0	0	0	0	0
1,482	1,502	104	83	65	48	30	13	0	0	0	0	0
1,502	1,522	106	85	67	50	32	15	0	0	0	0	0
1,522	1,542	109	88	69	52	34	17	0	0	0	0	0
1,542	1,562	111	90	71	54	36	19	1	0	0	0	0
1,562	1,582	113	92	73	56	38	21	3	0	0	0	0
1,582	1,602	116	95	75	58	40	23	5	0	0	0	0
1,602	1,622	118	97	77	60	42	25	7	0	0	0	0
1,622	1,642	121	100	79	62	44	27	9	0	0	0	0
1,642	1,662	123	102	81	64	46	29	11	0	0	0	0
1,662	1,682	125	104	83	66	48	31	13	0	0	0	0
1,682	1,702	128	107	86	68	50	33	15	0	0	0	0
1,702	1,722	130	109	88	70	52	35	17	0	0	0	0
1,722	1,742	133	112	91	72	54	37	19	2	0	0	0
1,742	1,762	135	114	93	74	56	39	21	4	0	0	0
1,762	1,782	137	116	95	76	58	41	23	6	0	0	0
1,782	1,802	140	119	98	78	60	43	25	8	0	0	0
1,802	1,822	142	121	100	80	62	45	27	10	0	0	0
1,822	1,842	145	124	103	82	64	47	29	12	0	0	0
1,842	1,862	147	126	105	84	66	49	31	14	0	0	0
1,862	1,882	149	128	107	86	68	51	33	16	0	0	0
1,882	1,902	152	131	110	89	70	53	35	18	0	0	0
1,902	1,922	154	133	112	91	72	55	37	20	2	0	0
1,922	1,942	157	136	115	94	74	57	39	22	4	0	0
1,942	1,962	159	138	117	96	76	59	41	24	6	0	0
1,962	1,982	161	140	119	98	78	61	43	26	8	0	0
1,982	2,002	164	143	122	101	80	63	45	28	10	0	0
2,002	2,022	166	145	124	103	82	65	47	30	12	0	0
2,022	2,042	169	148	127	106	85	67	49	32	14	0	0
2,042	2,062	171	150	129	108	87	69	51	34	16	0	0
2,062	2,082	173	152	131	110	89	71	53	36	18	1	0
2,082	2,102	176	155	134	113	92	73	55	38	20	3	0
2,102	2,122	178	157	136	115	94	75	57	40	22	5	0
2,122	2,142	181	160	139	118	97	77	59	42	24	7	0
2,142	2,162	183	162	141	120	99	79	61	44	26	9	0
2,162	2,182	185	164	143	122	101	81	63	46	28	11	0
2,182	2,202	188	167	146	125	104	83	65	48	30	13	0
2,202	2,222	190	169	148	127	106	85	67	50	32	15	0
2,222	2,242	193	172	151	130	109	88	69	52	34	17	0
2,242	2,262	195	174	153	132	111	90	71	54	36	19	1
2,262	2,282	197	176	155	134	113	92	73	56	38	21	3
2,282	2,302	200	179	158	137	116	95	75	58	40	23	5
2,302	2,322	202	181	160	139	118	97	77	60	42	25	7
2,322	2,342	205	184	163	142	121	100	79	62	44	27	9
2,342	2,362	207	186	165	144	123	102	81	64	46	29	11
2,362	2,382	209	188	167	146	125	104	83	66	48	31	13
2,382	2,402	212	191	170	149	128	107	86	68	50	33	15
2,402	2,422	214	193	172	151	130	109	88	70	52	35	17
2,422	2,442	217	196	175	154	133	112	91	72	54	37	19
2,442	2,462	219	198	177	156	135	114	93	74	56	39	21
2,462	2,482	221	200	179	158	137	116	95	76	58	41	23
2,482	2,502	224	203	182	161	140	119	98	78	60	43	25
2,502	2,522	226	205	184	163	142	121	100	80	62	45	27
2,522	2,542	229	208	187	166	145	124	103	82	64	47	29
2,542	2,562	231	210	189	168	147	126	105	84	66	49	31
2,562	2,582	233	212	191	170	149	128	107	86	68	51	33
2,582	2,602	236	215	194	173	152	131	110	89	70	53	35
2,602	2,622	238	217	196	175	154	133	112	91	72	55	37
2,622	2,642	241	220	199	178	157	136	115	94	74	57	39
2,642	2,662	243	222	201	180	159	138	117	96	76	59	41
2,662	2,682	245	224	203	182	161	140	119	98	78	61	43

| 2,682 and over | | Use Table 3(b) for a MARRIED person on page 46. Also see the instructions on page 44. |

Wage Bracket Method Tables for Income Tax Withholding

SINGLE Persons—**MONTHLY** Payroll Period

(For Wages Paid through December 2019)

And the wages are–		And the number of withholding allowances claimed is—										
At least	But less than	0	1	2	3	4	5	6	7	8	9	10
		The amount of income tax to be withheld is—										
$ 0	$317	$0	$0	$0	$0	$0	$0	$0	$0	$0	$0	$0
317	327	1	0	0	0	0	0	0	0	0	0	0
327	337	2	0	0	0	0	0	0	0	0	0	0
337	347	3	0	0	0	0	0	0	0	0	0	0
347	357	4	0	0	0	0	0	0	0	0	0	0
357	367	5	0	0	0	0	0	0	0	0	0	0
367	377	6	0	0	0	0	0	0	0	0	0	0
377	387	7	0	0	0	0	0	0	0	0	0	0
387	397	8	0	0	0	0	0	0	0	0	0	0
397	407	9	0	0	0	0	0	0	0	0	0	0
407	417	10	0	0	0	0	0	0	0	0	0	0
417	427	11	0	0	0	0	0	0	0	0	0	0
427	437	12	0	0	0	0	0	0	0	0	0	0
437	447	13	0	0	0	0	0	0	0	0	0	0
447	457	14	0	0	0	0	0	0	0	0	0	0
457	467	15	0	0	0	0	0	0	0	0	0	0
467	477	16	0	0	0	0	0	0	0	0	0	0
477	487	17	0	0	0	0	0	0	0	0	0	0
487	497	18	0	0	0	0	0	0	0	0	0	0
497	507	19	0	0	0	0	0	0	0	0	0	0
507	517	20	0	0	0	0	0	0	0	0	0	0
517	527	21	0	0	0	0	0	0	0	0	0	0
527	537	22	0	0	0	0	0	0	0	0	0	0
537	547	23	0	0	0	0	0	0	0	0	0	0
547	557	24	0	0	0	0	0	0	0	0	0	0
557	567	25	0	0	0	0	0	0	0	0	0	0
567	577	26	0	0	0	0	0	0	0	0	0	0
577	587	27	0	0	0	0	0	0	0	0	0	0
587	597	28	0	0	0	0	0	0	0	0	0	0
597	607	29	0	0	0	0	0	0	0	0	0	0
607	617	30	0	0	0	0	0	0	0	0	0	0
617	627	31	0	0	0	0	0	0	0	0	0	0
627	637	32	0	0	0	0	0	0	0	0	0	0
637	647	33	0	0	0	0	0	0	0	0	0	0
647	657	34	0	0	0	0	0	0	0	0	0	0
657	667	35	0	0	0	0	0	0	0	0	0	0
667	677	36	1	0	0	0	0	0	0	0	0	0
677	687	37	2	0	0	0	0	0	0	0	0	0
687	697	38	3	0	0	0	0	0	0	0	0	0
697	707	39	4	0	0	0	0	0	0	0	0	0
707	717	40	5	0	0	0	0	0	0	0	0	0
717	727	41	6	0	0	0	0	0	0	0	0	0
727	737	42	7	0	0	0	0	0	0	0	0	0
737	747	43	8	0	0	0	0	0	0	0	0	0
747	757	44	9	0	0	0	0	0	0	0	0	0
757	767	45	10	0	0	0	0	0	0	0	0	0
767	777	46	11	0	0	0	0	0	0	0	0	0
777	787	47	12	0	0	0	0	0	0	0	0	0
787	797	48	13	0	0	0	0	0	0	0	0	0
797	807	49	14	0	0	0	0	0	0	0	0	0
807	817	50	15	0	0	0	0	0	0	0	0	0
817	827	51	16	0	0	0	0	0	0	0	0	0
827	837	52	17	0	0	0	0	0	0	0	0	0
837	847	53	18	0	0	0	0	0	0	0	0	0
847	857	54	19	0	0	0	0	0	0	0	0	0
857	867	55	20	0	0	0	0	0	0	0	0	0
867	877	56	21	0	0	0	0	0	0	0	0	0
877	887	57	22	0	0	0	0	0	0	0	0	0
887	897	58	23	0	0	0	0	0	0	0	0	0
897	907	59	24	0	0	0	0	0	0	0	0	0
907	917	60	25	0	0	0	0	0	0	0	0	0
917	927	61	26	0	0	0	0	0	0	0	0	0
927	937	62	27	0	0	0	0	0	0	0	0	0
937	947	63	28	0	0	0	0	0	0	0	0	0
947	957	64	29	0	0	0	0	0	0	0	0	0
957	967	65	30	0	0	0	0	0	0	0	0	0
967	977	66	31	0	0	0	0	0	0	0	0	0
977	987	67	32	0	0	0	0	0	0	0	0	0
987	997	68	33	0	0	0	0	0	0	0	0	0
997	1,007	69	34	0	0	0	0	0	0	0	0	0

Wage Bracket Method Tables for Income Tax Withholding

SINGLE Persons—MONTHLY Payroll Period

(For Wages Paid through December 2019)

And the wages are–		And the number of withholding allowances claimed is—										
At least	But less than	0	1	2	3	4	5	6	7	8	9	10
		The amount of income tax to be withheld is—										
1,007	1,027	70	35	0	0	0	0	0	0	0	0	0
1,027	1,047	72	37	2	0	0	0	0	0	0	0	0
1,047	1,067	74	39	4	0	0	0	0	0	0	0	0
1,067	1,087	76	41	6	0	0	0	0	0	0	0	0
1,087	1,107	78	43	8	0	0	0	0	0	0	0	0
1,107	1,127	80	45	10	0	0	0	0	0	0	0	0
1,127	1,147	82	47	12	0	0	0	0	0	0	0	0
1,147	1,167	85	49	14	0	0	0	0	0	0	0	0
1,167	1,187	87	51	16	0	0	0	0	0	0	0	0
1,187	1,207	89	53	18	0	0	0	0	0	0	0	0
1,207	1,227	92	55	20	0	0	0	0	0	0	0	0
1,227	1,247	94	57	22	0	0	0	0	0	0	0	0
1,247	1,267	97	59	24	0	0	0	0	0	0	0	0
1,267	1,287	99	61	26	0	0	0	0	0	0	0	0
1,287	1,307	101	63	28	0	0	0	0	0	0	0	0
1,307	1,327	104	65	30	0	0	0	0	0	0	0	0
1,327	1,347	106	67	32	0	0	0	0	0	0	0	0
1,347	1,367	109	69	34	0	0	0	0	0	0	0	0
1,367	1,387	111	71	36	1	0	0	0	0	0	0	0
1,387	1,407	113	73	38	3	0	0	0	0	0	0	0
1,407	1,427	116	75	40	5	0	0	0	0	0	0	0
1,427	1,447	118	77	42	7	0	0	0	0	0	0	0
1,447	1,467	121	79	44	9	0	0	0	0	0	0	0
1,467	1,487	123	81	46	11	0	0	0	0	0	0	0
1,487	1,507	125	83	48	13	0	0	0	0	0	0	0
1,507	1,527	128	86	50	15	0	0	0	0	0	0	0
1,527	1,547	130	88	52	17	0	0	0	0	0	0	0
1,547	1,567	133	91	54	19	0	0	0	0	0	0	0
1,567	1,587	135	93	56	21	0	0	0	0	0	0	0
1,587	1,607	137	95	58	23	0	0	0	0	0	0	0
1,607	1,627	140	98	60	25	0	0	0	0	0	0	0
1,627	1,647	142	100	62	27	0	0	0	0	0	0	0
1,647	1,667	145	103	64	29	0	0	0	0	0	0	0
1,667	1,687	147	105	66	31	0	0	0	0	0	0	0
1,687	1,707	149	107	68	33	0	0	0	0	0	0	0
1,707	1,727	152	110	70	35	0	0	0	0	0	0	0
1,727	1,747	154	112	72	37	2	0	0	0	0	0	0
1,747	1,767	157	115	74	39	4	0	0	0	0	0	0
1,767	1,787	159	117	76	41	6	0	0	0	0	0	0
1,787	1,807	161	119	78	43	8	0	0	0	0	0	0
1,807	1,827	164	122	80	45	10	0	0	0	0	0	0
1,827	1,847	166	124	82	47	12	0	0	0	0	0	0
1,847	1,867	169	127	85	49	14	0	0	0	0	0	0
1,867	1,887	171	129	87	51	16	0	0	0	0	0	0
1,887	1,907	173	131	89	53	18	0	0	0	0	0	0
1,907	1,927	176	134	92	55	20	0	0	0	0	0	0
1,927	1,947	178	136	94	57	22	0	0	0	0	0	0
1,947	1,967	181	139	97	59	24	0	0	0	0	0	0
1,967	1,987	183	141	99	61	26	0	0	0	0	0	0
1,987	2,007	185	143	101	63	28	0	0	0	0	0	0
2,007	2,047	189	147	105	66	31	0	0	0	0	0	0
2,047	2,087	194	152	110	70	35	0	0	0	0	0	0
2,087	2,127	199	157	115	74	39	4	0	0	0	0	0
2,127	2,167	203	161	119	78	43	8	0	0	0	0	0
2,167	2,207	208	166	124	82	47	12	0	0	0	0	0
2,207	2,247	213	171	129	87	51	16	0	0	0	0	0
2,247	2,287	218	176	134	92	55	20	0	0	0	0	0
2,287	2,327	223	181	139	97	59	24	0	0	0	0	0
2,327	2,367	227	185	143	101	63	28	0	0	0	0	0
2,367	2,407	232	190	148	106	67	32	0	0	0	0	0
2,407	2,447	237	195	153	111	71	36	1	0	0	0	0
2,447	2,487	242	200	158	116	75	40	5	0	0	0	0
2,487	2,527	247	205	163	121	79	44	9	0	0	0	0
2,527	2,567	251	209	167	125	83	48	13	0	0	0	0
2,567	2,607	256	214	172	130	88	52	17	0	0	0	0
2,607	2,647	261	219	177	135	93	56	21	0	0	0	0

2,647 and over — Use Table 4(a) for a SINGLE person on page 46. Also see the instructions on page 44.

Wage Bracket Method Tables for Income Tax Withholding

MARRIED Persons—**MONTHLY** Payroll Period

(For Wages Paid through December 2019)

And the wages are—		And the number of withholding allowances claimed is—										
At least	But less than	0	1	2	3	4	5	6	7	8	9	10
		The amount of income tax to be withheld is—										
$ 0	$983	$0	$0	$0	$0	$0	$0	$0	$0	$0	$0	$0
983	994	1	0	0	0	0	0	0	0	0	0	0
994	1,005	2	0	0	0	0	0	0	0	0	0	0
1,005	1,016	3	0	0	0	0	0	0	0	0	0	0
1,016	1,027	4	0	0	0	0	0	0	0	0	0	0
1,027	1,038	5	0	0	0	0	0	0	0	0	0	0
1,038	1,049	6	0	0	0	0	0	0	0	0	0	0
1,049	1,060	7	0	0	0	0	0	0	0	0	0	0
1,060	1,071	8	0	0	0	0	0	0	0	0	0	0
1,071	1,082	9	0	0	0	0	0	0	0	0	0	0
1,082	1,093	10	0	0	0	0	0	0	0	0	0	0
1,093	1,104	12	0	0	0	0	0	0	0	0	0	0
1,104	1,115	13	0	0	0	0	0	0	0	0	0	0
1,115	1,126	14	0	0	0	0	0	0	0	0	0	0
1,126	1,137	15	0	0	0	0	0	0	0	0	0	0
1,137	1,148	16	0	0	0	0	0	0	0	0	0	0
1,148	1,159	17	0	0	0	0	0	0	0	0	0	0
1,159	1,170	18	0	0	0	0	0	0	0	0	0	0
1,170	1,181	19	0	0	0	0	0	0	0	0	0	0
1,181	1,192	20	0	0	0	0	0	0	0	0	0	0
1,192	1,203	21	0	0	0	0	0	0	0	0	0	0
1,203	1,214	23	0	0	0	0	0	0	0	0	0	0
1,214	1,225	24	0	0	0	0	0	0	0	0	0	0
1,225	1,236	25	0	0	0	0	0	0	0	0	0	0
1,236	1,247	26	0	0	0	0	0	0	0	0	0	0
1,247	1,258	27	0	0	0	0	0	0	0	0	0	0
1,258	1,269	28	0	0	0	0	0	0	0	0	0	0
1,269	1,280	29	0	0	0	0	0	0	0	0	0	0
1,280	1,291	30	0	0	0	0	0	0	0	0	0	0
1,291	1,302	31	0	0	0	0	0	0	0	0	0	0
1,302	1,313	32	0	0	0	0	0	0	0	0	0	0
1,313	1,324	34	0	0	0	0	0	0	0	0	0	0
1,324	1,335	35	0	0	0	0	0	0	0	0	0	0
1,335	1,346	36	1	0	0	0	0	0	0	0	0	0
1,346	1,357	37	2	0	0	0	0	0	0	0	0	0
1,357	1,368	38	3	0	0	0	0	0	0	0	0	0
1,368	1,379	39	4	0	0	0	0	0	0	0	0	0
1,379	1,390	40	5	0	0	0	0	0	0	0	0	0
1,390	1,401	41	6	0	0	0	0	0	0	0	0	0
1,401	1,412	42	7	0	0	0	0	0	0	0	0	0
1,412	1,423	43	8	0	0	0	0	0	0	0	0	0
1,423	1,434	45	10	0	0	0	0	0	0	0	0	0
1,434	1,445	46	11	0	0	0	0	0	0	0	0	0
1,445	1,456	47	12	0	0	0	0	0	0	0	0	0
1,456	1,467	48	13	0	0	0	0	0	0	0	0	0
1,467	1,478	49	14	0	0	0	0	0	0	0	0	0
1,478	1,489	50	15	0	0	0	0	0	0	0	0	0
1,489	1,500	51	16	0	0	0	0	0	0	0	0	0
1,500	1,511	52	17	0	0	0	0	0	0	0	0	0
1,511	1,522	53	18	0	0	0	0	0	0	0	0	0
1,522	1,533	54	19	0	0	0	0	0	0	0	0	0
1,533	1,544	56	21	0	0	0	0	0	0	0	0	0
1,544	1,555	57	22	0	0	0	0	0	0	0	0	0
1,555	1,566	58	23	0	0	0	0	0	0	0	0	0
1,566	1,577	59	24	0	0	0	0	0	0	0	0	0
1,577	1,588	60	25	0	0	0	0	0	0	0	0	0
1,588	1,599	61	26	0	0	0	0	0	0	0	0	0
1,599	1,610	62	27	0	0	0	0	0	0	0	0	0
1,610	1,621	63	28	0	0	0	0	0	0	0	0	0
1,621	1,632	64	29	0	0	0	0	0	0	0	0	0
1,632	1,643	65	30	0	0	0	0	0	0	0	0	0
1,643	1,654	67	32	0	0	0	0	0	0	0	0	0
1,654	1,665	68	33	0	0	0	0	0	0	0	0	0
1,665	1,676	69	34	0	0	0	0	0	0	0	0	0
1,676	1,687	70	35	0	0	0	0	0	0	0	0	0
1,687	1,698	71	36	1	0	0	0	0	0	0	0	0
1,698	1,709	72	37	2	0	0	0	0	0	0	0	0
1,709	1,720	73	38	3	0	0	0	0	0	0	0	0
1,720	1,731	74	39	4	0	0	0	0	0	0	0	0
1,731	1,742	75	40	5	0	0	0	0	0	0	0	0

Publication 15 (2019)

Wage Bracket Method Tables for Income Tax Withholding

MARRIED Persons—**MONTHLY** Payroll Period

(For Wages Paid through December 2019)

And the wages are–		And the number of withholding allowances claimed is—										
At least	But less than	0	1	2	3	4	5	6	7	8	9	10
		The amount of income tax to be withheld is—										
1,742	1,753	76	41	6	0	0	0	0	0	0	0	0
1,753	1,773	78	43	8	0	0	0	0	0	0	0	0
1,773	1,793	80	45	10	0	0	0	0	0	0	0	0
1,793	1,813	82	47	12	0	0	0	0	0	0	0	0
1,813	1,833	84	49	14	0	0	0	0	0	0	0	0
1,833	1,853	86	51	16	0	0	0	0	0	0	0	0
1,853	1,873	88	53	18	0	0	0	0	0	0	0	0
1,873	1,893	90	55	20	0	0	0	0	0	0	0	0
1,893	1,913	92	57	22	0	0	0	0	0	0	0	0
1,913	1,933	94	59	24	0	0	0	0	0	0	0	0
1,933	1,953	96	61	26	0	0	0	0	0	0	0	0
1,953	1,973	98	63	28	0	0	0	0	0	0	0	0
1,973	1,993	100	65	30	0	0	0	0	0	0	0	0
1,993	2,013	102	67	32	0	0	0	0	0	0	0	0
2,013	2,033	104	69	34	0	0	0	0	0	0	0	0
2,033	2,053	106	71	36	1	0	0	0	0	0	0	0
2,053	2,073	108	73	38	3	0	0	0	0	0	0	0
2,073	2,093	110	75	40	5	0	0	0	0	0	0	0
2,093	2,113	112	77	42	7	0	0	0	0	0	0	0
2,113	2,133	114	79	44	9	0	0	0	0	0	0	0
2,133	2,153	116	81	46	11	0	0	0	0	0	0	0
2,153	2,173	118	83	48	13	0	0	0	0	0	0	0
2,173	2,193	120	85	50	15	0	0	0	0	0	0	0
2,193	2,213	122	87	52	17	0	0	0	0	0	0	0
2,213	2,233	124	89	54	19	0	0	0	0	0	0	0
2,233	2,253	126	91	56	21	0	0	0	0	0	0	0
2,253	2,273	128	93	58	23	0	0	0	0	0	0	0
2,273	2,293	130	95	60	25	0	0	0	0	0	0	0
2,293	2,313	132	97	62	27	0	0	0	0	0	0	0
2,313	2,333	134	99	64	29	0	0	0	0	0	0	0
2,333	2,353	136	101	66	31	0	0	0	0	0	0	0
2,353	2,373	138	103	68	33	0	0	0	0	0	0	0
2,373	2,393	140	105	70	35	0	0	0	0	0	0	0
2,393	2,413	142	107	72	37	2	0	0	0	0	0	0
2,413	2,433	144	109	74	39	4	0	0	0	0	0	0
2,433	2,453	146	111	76	41	6	0	0	0	0	0	0
2,453	2,473	148	113	78	43	8	0	0	0	0	0	0
2,473	2,493	150	115	80	45	10	0	0	0	0	0	0
2,493	2,513	152	117	82	47	12	0	0	0	0	0	0
2,513	2,553	155	120	85	50	15	0	0	0	0	0	0
2,553	2,593	159	124	89	54	19	0	0	0	0	0	0
2,593	2,633	163	128	93	58	23	0	0	0	0	0	0
2,633	2,673	168	132	97	62	27	0	0	0	0	0	0
2,673	2,713	173	136	101	66	31	0	0	0	0	0	0
2,713	2,753	178	140	105	70	35	0	0	0	0	0	0
2,753	2,793	182	144	109	74	39	4	0	0	0	0	0
2,793	2,833	187	148	113	78	43	8	0	0	0	0	0
2,833	2,873	192	152	117	82	47	12	0	0	0	0	0
2,873	2,913	197	156	121	86	51	16	0	0	0	0	0
2,913	2,953	202	160	125	90	55	20	0	0	0	0	0
2,953	2,993	206	164	129	94	59	24	0	0	0	0	0
2,993	3,033	211	169	133	98	63	28	0	0	0	0	0
3,033	3,073	216	174	137	102	67	32	0	0	0	0	0
3,073	3,113	221	179	141	106	71	36	1	0	0	0	0
3,113	3,153	226	184	145	110	75	40	5	0	0	0	0
3,153	3,193	230	188	149	114	79	44	9	0	0	0	0
3,193	3,233	235	193	153	118	83	48	13	0	0	0	0
3,233	3,273	240	198	157	122	87	52	17	0	0	0	0
3,273	3,313	245	203	161	126	91	56	21	0	0	0	0
3,313	3,353	250	208	166	130	95	60	25	0	0	0	0
3,353	3,393	254	212	170	134	99	64	29	0	0	0	0
3,393	3,433	259	217	175	138	103	68	33	0	0	0	0
3,433	3,473	264	222	180	142	107	72	37	2	0	0	0
3,473	3,513	269	227	185	146	111	76	41	6	0	0	0
3,513	3,553	274	232	190	150	115	80	45	10	0	0	0
3,553	3,593	278	236	194	154	119	84	49	14	0	0	0

3,593 and over   Use Table 4(b) for a MARRIED person on page 46. Also see the instructions on page 44.

Wage Bracket Method Tables for Income Tax Withholding

SINGLE Persons—DAILY Payroll Period

(For Wages Paid through December 2019)

And the wages are–		And the number of withholding allowances claimed is—										
At least	But less than	0	1	2	3	4	5	6	7	8	9	10
		The amount of income tax to be withheld is—										
$ 0	$15	$0	$0	$0	$0	$0	$0	$0	$0	$0	$0	$0
15	25	1	0	0	0	0	0	0	0	0	0	0
25	35	2	0	0	0	0	0	0	0	0	0	0
35	45	3	1	0	0	0	0	0	0	0	0	0
45	55	4	2	0	0	0	0	0	0	0	0	0
55	65	5	3	1	0	0	0	0	0	0	0	0
65	75	6	4	2	1	0	0	0	0	0	0	0
75	85	7	5	3	2	0	0	0	0	0	0	0
85	95	8	6	4	3	1	0	0	0	0	0	0
95	105	10	8	6	4	2	0	0	0	0	0	0
105	115	11	9	7	5	3	1	0	0	0	0	0
115	125	12	10	8	6	4	2	1	0	0	0	0
125	135	13	11	9	7	5	3	2	0	0	0	0
135	145	14	12	10	8	7	5	3	1	0	0	0
145	155	16	14	12	10	8	6	4	2	1	0	0
155	165	17	15	13	11	9	7	5	3	2	0	0
165	175	18	16	14	12	10	8	6	4	3	1	0
175	185	20	17	15	13	11	9	7	6	4	2	0
185	195	23	19	16	14	13	11	9	7	5	3	1
195	205	25	21	18	16	14	12	10	8	6	4	2
205	215	27	24	20	17	15	13	11	9	7	5	3
215	225	29	26	22	19	16	14	12	10	8	6	5
225	235	31	28	24	21	17	15	13	12	10	8	6
235	245	34	30	27	23	19	17	15	13	11	9	7
245	255	36	32	29	25	22	18	16	14	12	10	8
255	265	38	35	31	27	24	20	17	15	13	11	9
265	275	40	37	33	30	26	22	19	16	14	12	11
275	285	42	39	35	32	28	25	21	18	16	14	12
285	295	45	41	38	34	30	27	23	20	17	15	13
295	305	47	43	40	36	33	29	26	22	18	16	14
305	315	49	46	42	38	35	31	28	24	21	17	15
315	325	51	48	44	41	37	33	30	26	23	19	17
325	335	53	50	46	43	39	36	32	29	25	21	18
335	345	56	52	49	45	41	38	34	31	27	24	20
345	360	59	55	51	48	44	41	37	34	30	26	23
360	375	62	58	55	51	47	44	40	37	33	30	26
375	390	66	62	58	54	51	47	44	40	37	33	29
390	405	69	66	62	58	54	51	47	43	40	36	33
405	420	73	69	65	61	58	54	50	47	43	40	36
420	435	77	73	69	65	61	57	54	50	46	43	39
435	450	80	76	73	69	65	61	57	53	50	46	43
450	465	84	80	76	72	68	65	61	57	53	50	46
465	480	87	84	80	76	72	68	64	60	56	53	49
480	495	91	87	83	79	76	72	68	64	60	56	53
495	510	95	91	87	83	79	75	71	68	64	60	56
510	525	98	94	91	87	83	79	75	71	67	63	60
525	540	102	98	94	90	86	83	79	75	71	67	63
540	555	105	102	98	94	90	86	82	78	74	71	67
555	570	109	105	101	97	94	90	86	82	78	74	70
570	585	113	109	105	101	97	93	89	86	82	78	74
585	600	116	112	109	105	101	97	93	89	85	81	78
600	615	120	116	112	108	104	101	97	93	89	85	81
615	630	123	120	116	112	108	104	100	96	92	89	85
630	645	127	123	119	115	112	108	104	100	96	92	88
645	660	132	127	123	119	115	111	107	104	100	96	92
660	675	137	132	127	123	119	115	111	107	103	99	96
675	690	142	137	132	126	122	119	115	111	107	103	99
690	705	147	141	136	131	126	122	118	114	110	107	103
705	720	151	146	141	136	131	126	122	118	114	110	106
720	735	156	151	146	141	136	130	125	122	118	114	110
735	750	161	156	151	146	140	135	130	125	121	117	114
750	765	166	161	156	150	145	140	135	130	125	121	117
765	780	171	165	160	155	150	145	140	134	129	125	121
780	795	175	170	165	160	155	150	144	139	134	129	124
795	810	180	175	170	165	160	154	149	144	139	134	129
810	825	186	180	175	170	164	159	154	149	144	139	133
825	840	191	185	180	174	169	164	159	154	149	143	138
840	855	196	190	185	179	174	169	164	158	153	148	143
855	870	201	196	190	184	179	174	168	163	158	153	148
870	885	207	201	195	190	184	178	173	168	163	158	153

Publication 15 (2019)

Wage Bracket Method Tables for Income Tax Withholding

SINGLE Persons—DAILY Payroll Period

(For Wages Paid through December 2019)

And the wages are–		And the number of withholding allowances claimed is—										
At least	But less than	0	1	2	3	4	5	6	7	8	9	10
		The amount of income tax to be withheld is—										
885	900	212	206	201	195	189	184	178	173	168	163	157
900	915	217	211	206	200	194	189	183	178	173	167	162
915	930	222	217	211	205	200	194	188	183	177	172	167
930	945	228	222	216	211	205	199	194	188	182	177	172
945	960	233	227	222	216	210	205	199	193	188	182	177
960	975	238	232	227	221	215	210	204	199	193	187	182
975	990	243	238	232	226	221	215	209	204	198	192	187
990	1,005	249	243	237	232	226	220	215	209	203	198	192
1,005	1,020	254	248	243	237	231	226	220	214	209	203	197
1,020	1,035	259	253	248	242	236	231	225	220	214	208	203
1,035	1,050	264	259	253	247	242	236	230	225	219	213	208
1,050	1,065	270	264	258	253	247	241	236	230	224	219	213
1,065	1,080	275	269	264	258	252	247	241	235	230	224	218
1,080	1,095	280	274	269	263	257	252	246	241	235	229	224
1,095	1,110	285	280	274	268	263	257	251	246	240	234	229
1,110	1,125	291	285	279	274	268	262	257	251	245	240	234
1,125	1,140	296	290	285	279	273	268	262	256	251	245	239
1,140	1,155	301	295	290	284	278	273	267	262	256	250	245
1,155	1,170	306	301	295	289	284	278	272	267	261	255	250
1,170	1,185	312	306	300	295	289	283	278	272	266	261	255
1,185	1,200	317	311	306	300	294	289	283	277	272	266	260
1,200	1,215	322	316	311	305	299	294	288	283	277	271	266
1,215	1,230	327	322	316	310	305	299	293	288	282	276	271
1,230	1,245	333	327	321	316	310	304	299	293	287	282	276
1,245	1,260	338	332	327	321	315	310	304	298	293	287	281
1,260	1,275	343	337	332	326	320	315	309	304	298	292	287
1,275	1,290	348	343	337	331	326	320	314	309	303	297	292
1,290	1,305	354	348	342	337	331	325	320	314	308	303	297
1,305	1,320	359	353	348	342	336	331	325	319	314	308	302
1,320	1,335	364	358	353	347	341	336	330	325	319	313	308
1,335	1,350	369	364	358	352	347	341	335	330	324	318	313
1,350	1,365	375	369	363	358	352	346	341	335	329	324	318
1,365	1,380	380	374	369	363	357	352	346	340	335	329	323
1,380	1,395	385	379	374	368	362	357	351	346	340	334	329
1,395	1,410	390	385	379	373	368	362	356	351	345	339	334
1,410	1,425	396	390	384	379	373	367	362	356	350	345	339
1,425	1,440	401	395	390	384	378	373	367	361	356	350	344
1,440	1,455	406	400	395	389	383	378	372	367	361	355	350
1,455	1,470	411	406	400	394	389	383	377	372	366	360	355
1,470	1,485	417	411	405	400	394	388	383	377	371	366	360
1,485	1,500	422	416	411	405	399	394	388	382	377	371	365
1,500	1,515	427	421	416	410	404	399	393	388	382	376	371
1,515	1,530	432	427	421	415	410	404	398	393	387	381	376
1,530	1,545	438	432	426	421	415	409	404	398	392	387	381
1,545	1,560	443	437	432	426	420	415	409	403	398	392	386
1,560	1,575	448	442	437	431	425	420	414	409	403	397	392
1,575	1,590	453	448	442	436	431	425	419	414	408	402	397
1,590	1,605	459	453	447	442	436	430	425	419	413	408	402
1,605	1,620	464	458	453	447	441	436	430	424	419	413	407
1,620	1,635	469	463	458	452	446	441	435	430	424	418	413
1,635	1,650	474	469	463	457	452	446	440	435	429	423	418
1,650	1,665	480	474	468	463	457	451	446	440	434	429	423
1,665	1,680	485	479	474	468	462	457	451	445	440	434	428
1,680	1,695	490	484	479	473	467	462	456	451	445	439	434
1,695	1,710	495	490	484	478	473	467	461	456	450	444	439
1,710	1,725	501	495	489	484	478	472	467	461	455	450	444
1,725	1,740	506	500	495	489	483	478	472	466	461	455	449
1,740	1,755	511	505	500	494	488	483	477	472	466	460	455
1,755	1,770	516	511	505	499	494	488	482	477	471	465	460
1,770	1,785	522	516	510	505	499	493	488	482	476	471	465
1,785	1,800	527	521	516	510	504	499	493	487	482	476	470
1,800	1,815	532	526	521	515	509	504	498	493	487	481	476
1,815	1,830	537	532	526	520	515	509	503	498	492	486	481
1,830	1,845	543	537	531	526	520	514	509	503	497	492	486
1,845	1,860	548	542	537	531	525	520	514	508	503	497	491
1,860	1,862	551	545	540	534	528	523	517	511	506	500	494

1,862 and over	Use Table 8(a) for a SINGLE person on page 47. Also see the instructions on page 44.

Wage Bracket Method Tables for Income Tax Withholding

MARRIED Persons—DAILY Payroll Period

(For Wages Paid through December 2019)

And the wages are–		And the number of withholding allowances claimed is—										
At least	But less than	0	1	2	3	4	5	6	7	8	9	10
		The amount of income tax to be withheld is—										
$ 0	$46	$0	$0	$0	$0	$0	$0	$0	$0	$0	$0	$0
46	56	1	0	0	0	0	0	0	0	0	0	0
56	66	2	0	0	0	0	0	0	0	0	0	0
66	76	3	1	0	0	0	0	0	0	0	0	0
76	86	4	2	0	0	0	0	0	0	0	0	0
86	96	5	3	1	0	0	0	0	0	0	0	0
96	106	6	4	2	1	0	0	0	0	0	0	0
106	116	7	5	3	2	0	0	0	0	0	0	0
116	126	8	6	4	3	1	0	0	0	0	0	0
126	136	9	7	5	4	2	0	0	0	0	0	0
136	146	10	8	6	5	3	1	0	0	0	0	0
146	156	11	9	7	6	4	2	1	0	0	0	0
156	166	12	10	9	7	5	3	2	0	0	0	0
166	176	14	12	10	8	6	4	3	1	0	0	0
176	186	15	13	11	9	7	5	4	2	1	0	0
186	196	16	14	12	10	8	6	5	3	2	0	0
196	206	17	15	13	11	9	7	6	4	3	1	0
206	216	18	16	15	13	11	9	7	5	4	2	0
216	226	20	18	16	14	12	10	8	6	5	3	1
226	236	21	19	17	15	13	11	9	7	6	4	2
236	246	22	20	18	16	14	12	10	8	7	5	3
246	256	23	21	19	17	15	13	12	10	8	6	4
256	266	24	22	21	19	17	15	13	11	9	7	5
266	276	26	24	22	20	18	16	14	12	10	8	6
276	286	27	25	23	21	19	17	15	13	11	9	7
286	296	28	26	24	22	20	18	16	14	12	11	9
296	306	29	27	25	23	21	19	18	16	14	12	10
306	316	30	28	27	25	23	21	19	17	15	13	11
316	326	32	30	28	26	24	22	20	18	16	14	12
326	336	33	31	29	27	25	23	21	19	17	15	13
336	346	34	32	30	28	26	24	22	20	18	17	15
346	361	36	34	32	30	28	26	24	22	20	18	16
361	376	39	36	33	31	30	28	26	24	22	20	18
376	391	43	39	35	33	31	29	27	26	24	22	20
391	406	46	42	39	35	33	31	29	27	25	23	21
406	421	49	46	42	38	35	33	31	29	27	25	23
421	436	52	49	45	42	38	35	33	31	29	27	25
436	451	56	52	49	45	42	38	35	33	31	29	27
451	466	59	55	52	48	45	41	38	35	33	31	29
466	481	62	59	55	52	48	45	41	37	34	32	30
481	496	66	62	59	55	51	48	44	41	37	34	32
496	511	69	65	62	58	55	51	48	44	40	37	34
511	526	72	69	65	62	58	54	51	47	44	40	37
526	541	76	72	68	65	61	58	54	51	47	44	40
541	556	79	75	72	68	65	61	58	54	50	47	43
556	571	82	79	75	71	68	64	61	57	54	50	47
571	586	85	82	78	75	71	68	64	61	57	53	50
586	601	89	85	82	78	75	71	67	64	60	57	53
601	616	92	88	85	81	78	74	71	67	64	60	56
616	631	95	92	88	85	81	78	74	70	67	63	60
631	646	99	95	92	88	84	81	77	74	70	67	63
646	661	102	98	95	91	88	84	81	77	73	70	66
661	676	105	102	98	95	91	87	84	80	77	73	70
676	691	109	105	101	98	94	91	87	84	80	77	73
691	706	112	108	105	101	98	94	91	87	83	80	76
706	721	116	112	108	104	101	97	94	90	87	83	80
721	736	119	115	111	108	104	101	97	94	90	86	83
736	751	123	119	115	111	108	104	100	97	93	90	86
751	766	126	122	119	115	111	107	104	100	97	93	89
766	781	130	126	122	118	114	111	107	103	100	96	93
781	796	134	130	126	122	118	114	110	107	103	100	96
796	811	137	133	129	126	122	118	114	110	106	103	99
811	826	141	137	133	129	125	121	117	114	110	106	103
826	841	144	140	137	133	129	125	121	117	113	110	106
841	856	148	144	140	136	132	129	125	121	117	113	109
856	871	152	148	144	140	136	132	128	124	121	117	113
871	886	155	151	147	144	140	136	132	128	124	120	116
886	901	159	155	151	147	143	139	135	132	128	124	120
901	916	162	158	155	151	147	143	139	135	131	127	124
916	931	166	162	158	154	150	147	143	139	135	131	127

Publication 15 (2019)

Wage Bracket Method Tables for Income Tax Withholding

MARRIED Persons—DAILY Payroll Period

(For Wages Paid through December 2019)

And the wages are–		And the number of withholding allowances claimed is—										
At least	But less than	0	1	2	3	4	5	6	7	8	9	10
		The amount of income tax to be withheld is—										
931	946	170	166	162	158	154	150	146	142	139	135	131
946	961	173	169	165	162	158	154	150	146	142	138	134
961	976	177	173	169	165	161	157	153	150	146	142	138
976	991	180	176	173	169	165	161	157	153	149	145	142
991	1,006	184	180	176	172	168	165	161	157	153	149	145
1,006	1,021	188	184	180	176	172	168	164	160	157	153	149
1,021	1,036	191	187	183	180	176	172	168	164	160	156	152
1,036	1,051	195	191	187	183	179	175	171	168	164	160	156
1,051	1,066	198	194	191	187	183	179	175	171	167	163	160
1,066	1,081	202	198	194	190	186	183	179	175	171	167	163
1,081	1,096	206	202	198	194	190	186	182	178	175	171	167
1,096	1,111	209	205	201	198	194	190	186	182	178	174	170
1,111	1,126	213	209	205	201	197	193	189	186	182	178	174
1,126	1,141	216	212	209	205	201	197	193	189	185	181	178
1,141	1,156	220	216	212	208	204	201	197	193	189	185	181
1,156	1,171	224	220	216	212	208	204	200	196	193	189	185
1,171	1,186	227	223	219	216	212	208	204	200	196	192	188
1,186	1,201	231	227	223	219	215	211	207	204	200	196	192
1,201	1,216	234	230	227	223	219	215	211	207	203	199	196
1,216	1,231	238	234	230	226	222	219	215	211	207	203	199
1,231	1,246	242	238	234	230	226	222	218	214	211	207	203
1,246	1,261	245	241	237	234	230	226	222	218	214	210	206
1,261	1,276	249	245	241	237	233	229	225	222	218	214	210
1,276	1,291	252	248	245	241	237	233	229	225	221	217	214
1,291	1,306	257	252	248	244	240	237	233	229	225	221	217
1,306	1,321	262	257	252	248	244	240	236	232	229	225	221
1,321	1,336	267	262	257	252	248	244	240	236	232	228	224
1,336	1,351	272	267	261	256	251	247	243	240	236	232	228
1,351	1,366	276	271	266	261	256	251	247	243	239	235	232
1,366	1,381	281	276	271	266	261	255	251	247	243	239	235
1,381	1,396	286	281	276	271	265	260	255	250	247	243	239
1,396	1,411	291	286	281	275	270	265	260	255	250	246	242
1,411	1,426	296	291	285	280	275	270	265	259	254	250	246
1,426	1,441	300	295	290	285	280	275	269	264	259	254	250
1,441	1,456	305	300	295	290	285	279	274	269	264	259	254
1,456	1,471	310	305	300	295	289	284	279	274	269	264	258
1,471	1,486	315	310	305	299	294	289	284	279	274	268	263
1,486	1,501	320	315	309	304	299	294	289	283	278	273	268
1,501	1,516	324	319	314	309	304	299	293	288	283	278	273
1,516	1,531	329	324	319	314	309	303	298	293	288	283	278
1,531	1,546	334	329	324	319	313	308	303	298	293	288	282
1,546	1,561	339	334	329	323	318	313	308	303	298	292	287
1,561	1,576	344	339	333	328	323	318	313	307	302	297	292
1,576	1,591	348	343	338	333	328	323	317	312	307	302	297
1,591	1,606	353	348	343	338	333	327	322	317	312	307	302
1,606	1,621	358	353	348	343	337	332	327	322	317	312	306
1,621	1,636	363	358	353	347	342	337	332	327	322	316	311
1,636	1,651	369	363	357	352	347	342	337	331	326	321	316
1,651	1,666	374	368	362	357	352	347	341	336	331	326	321
1,666	1,681	379	373	368	362	357	351	346	341	336	331	326
1,681	1,696	384	379	373	367	362	356	351	346	341	336	330
1,696	1,711	390	384	378	373	367	361	356	351	346	340	335
1,711	1,726	395	389	383	378	372	367	361	355	350	345	340
1,726	1,741	400	394	389	383	377	372	366	360	355	350	345
1,741	1,756	405	400	394	388	383	377	371	366	360	355	350
1,756	1,771	411	405	399	394	388	382	377	371	365	360	354
1,771	1,786	416	410	404	399	393	388	382	376	371	365	359
1,786	1,801	421	415	410	404	398	393	387	381	376	370	364
1,801	1,816	426	421	415	409	404	398	392	387	381	375	370
1,816	1,831	432	426	420	415	409	403	398	392	386	381	375
1,831	1,846	437	431	425	420	414	409	403	397	392	386	380
1,846	1,861	442	436	431	425	419	414	408	402	397	391	385
1,861	1,876	447	442	436	430	425	419	413	408	402	396	391
1,876	1,891	453	447	441	436	430	424	419	413	407	402	396
1,891	1,906	458	452	446	441	435	430	424	418	413	407	401
1,906	1,908	461	455	449	444	438	432	427	421	416	410	404

1,908 and over — Use Table 8(b) for a MARRIED person on page 47. Also see the instructions on page 44.

How To Get Tax Help

If you have questions about a tax issue, need help preparing your tax return, or want to download free publications, forms, or instructions, go to IRS.gov and find resources that can help you right away.

Tax reform. Major tax reform legislation impacting individuals, businesses, and tax-exempt entities was enacted in the Tax Cuts and Jobs Act on December 22, 2017. Go to *IRS.gov/TaxReform* for information and updates on how this legislation affects your taxes.

Preparing and filing your tax return. Go to *IRS.gov/EmploymentEfile* for more information on filing your employment tax returns electronically.

 Getting answers to your tax questions. On IRS.gov, get answers to your tax questions anytime, anywhere.

- Go to *IRS.gov/Help* for a variety of tools that will help you get answers to some of the most common tax questions.

- You may also be able to access tax law information in your electronic filing software.

Getting tax forms and publications. Go to *IRS.gov/Forms* to view, download, or print most of the forms and publications you may need. You can also download and view popular tax publications and instructions (including Pub. 15) on mobile devices as an eBook at no charge. Or you can go to *IRS.gov/OrderForms* to place an order and have forms mailed to you within 10 business days.

Getting a transcript or copy of a return. You can get a copy of your tax transcript or a copy of your return by calling 800-829-4933 or by mailing Form 4506-T (transcript request) or Form 4506 (copy of return) to the IRS.

Resolving tax-related identity theft issues.

- The IRS doesn't initiate contact with taxpayers by email or telephone to request personal or financial information. This includes any type of electronic communication, such as text messages and social media channels.

- Go to *IRS.gov/IDProtection* for information.

- If your EIN has been lost or stolen or you suspect you're a victim of tax-related identity theft, visit *IRS.gov/IdentityTheft* to learn what steps you should take.

Making a tax payment. The IRS uses the latest encryption technology to ensure your electronic payments are safe and secure. You can make electronic payments online, by phone, and from a mobile device using the IRS2Go app. Paying electronically is quick, easy, and faster than mailing in a check or money order. Go to

IRS.gov/Payments to make a payment using any of the following options.

- **Debit or credit card:** Choose an approved payment processor to pay online, by phone, and by mobile device.

- **Electronic Funds Withdrawal:** Offered only when filing your federal taxes using tax return preparation software or through a tax professional.

- **Electronic Federal Tax Payment System:** Best option for businesses. Enrollment is required.

- **Check or money order:** Mail your payment to the address listed on the notice or instructions.

- **Cash:** You may be able to pay your taxes with cash at a participating retail store.

What if I can't pay now? Go to *IRS.gov/Payments* for more information about your options.

- Apply for an *online payment agreement* (*IRS.gov/OPA*) to meet your tax obligation in monthly installments if you can't pay your taxes in full today. Once you complete the online process, you will receive immediate notification of whether your agreement has been approved.

- Use the *Offer in Compromise Pre-Qualifier* (*IRS.gov/OIC*) to see if you can settle your tax debt for less than the full amount you owe.

Understanding an IRS notice or letter. Go to *IRS.gov/Notices* to find additional information about responding to an IRS notice or letter.

Contacting your local IRS office. Keep in mind, many questions can be answered on IRS.gov without visiting an IRS Tax Assistance Center (TAC). Go to *IRS.gov/LetUsHelp* for the topics people ask about most. If you still need help, IRS TACs provide tax help when a tax issue can't be handled online or by phone. All TACs now provide service by appointment so you'll know in advance that you can get the service you need without long wait times. Before you visit, go to *IRS.gov/TACLocator* to find the nearest TAC, check hours, available services, and appointment options. Or, on the IRS2Go app, under the Stay Connected tab, choose the Contact Us option and click on "Local Offices."

Watching IRS videos. The IRS Video portal (*IRSVideos.gov*) contains video and audio presentations for individuals, small businesses, and tax professionals.

Getting tax information in other languages. For taxpayers whose native language isn't English, we have the following resources available. Taxpayers can find information on IRS.gov in the following languages.

- *Spanish* (*IRS.gov/Spanish*).

- *Chinese* (*IRS.gov/Chinese*).

- *Vietnamese* (*IRS.gov/Vietnamese*).

- *Korean* (*IRS.gov/Korean*).

- *Russian* (*IRS.gov/Russian*).

The IRS TACs provide over-the-phone interpreter service in over 170 languages, and the service is available free to taxpayers.

The Taxpayer Advocate Service (TAS) Is Here To Help You
What is TAS?

TAS is an **independent** organization within the IRS that helps taxpayers and protects taxpayer rights. Their job is to ensure that every taxpayer is treated fairly and that you know and understand your rights under the *Taxpayer Bill of Rights*.

How Can You Learn About Your Taxpayer Rights?

The Taxpayer Bill of Rights describes 10 basic rights that all taxpayers have when dealing with the IRS. Go to *TaxpayerAdvocate.IRS.gov* to help you understand *what these rights mean to you* and how they apply. These are **your** rights. Know them. Use them.

What Can TAS Do For You?

TAS can help you resolve problems that you can't resolve with the IRS. And their service is free. If you qualify for their assistance, you will be assigned to one advocate who will work with you throughout the process and will do everything possible to resolve your issue. TAS can help you if:

- Your problem is causing financial difficulty for you, your family, or your business;
- You face (or your business is facing) an immediate threat of adverse action; or
- You've tried repeatedly to contact the IRS but no one has responded, or the IRS hasn't responded by the date promised.

How Can You Reach TAS?

TAS has offices *in every state, the District of Columbia, and Puerto Rico*. Your local advocate's number is in your local directory and at *TaxpayerAdvocate.IRS.gov/Contact-Us*. You can also call them at 877-777-4778.

How Else Does TAS Help Taxpayers?

TAS works to resolve large-scale problems that affect many taxpayers. If you know of one of these broad issues, please report it to them at *IRS.gov/SAMS*.

TAS also has a website, *Tax Reform Changes*, which shows you how the new tax law may change your future tax filings and helps you plan for these changes. The information is categorized by tax topic in the order of the IRS Form 1040. Go to *TaxChanges.us* for more information.

Index

To help us develop a more useful index, please let us know if you have ideas for index entries. See "Comments and Suggestions" in the "Introduction" for the ways you can reach us.

Chapter 16
NORTH CAROLINA MECHANICS'
LIEN LAW

Chapter Survey...

⇨ *What is a Lien?*

⇨ *Who is Entitled to a Mechanics' Lien?*

⇨ *North Carolina's Lien Agent System*

⇨ *Notice of Contract*

⇨ *Notice of Subcontract*

⇨ *Filing a Notice of Claim of Lien*

⇨ *Filing a Claim of Lien*

⇨ *Monetary Awards*

⇨ *Time in Which to File a Lien Foreclosure Petition*

⇨ *Sale of Land to Satisfy Lien*

What is a Lien?

Mechanics' and materialmen's liens "cloud" the title to real property but can be an effective method (and sometimes the only method) for securing payment for labor or materials used in the improvement of real property. The lien stops the owner from selling the property with a clear title. The lien may be foreclosed in a lawsuit. The court can order that property be sold and the proceeds used to pay the contractor, subcontractor, laborer, or material supplier. This may be true even if the owner has already paid a general contractor, meaning that the owner may have to pay twice. This is one of the reasons that a lien can be such a powerful collection tool.

The law governing mechanics' liens is found in Chapter 44A of the General Statutes of North Carolina. The state statutes and court opinions establish a strict procedure to perfect and foreclose a lien. It is strongly recommended that a professional be routinely used to record and foreclose on construction liens.

Who is Entitled to a Mechanics' Lien?

Contracts with the Owner: The state statutes specify that "any person who performs or furnishes labor or professional design or surveying services or furnishes materials or furnishes rental equipment" and who contracted directly with the owner has lien rights against the property where the construction project was performed.

Contracts with the General Contractor: First-tier subcontractors are those who contract with the general contractor. First-tier subcontractors have lien rights against the money owed to the contractor by the owner.

Contracts with First-Tier Subcontractors: Second-tier contractors are those who contract with first-tier contractors. Second-tier subcontractors have lien rights against the money owed to the first-tier contractor by the general contractor.

Contracts with Second-Tier Subcontractors: Third-tier contractors are those who contract with second-tier contractors. Third-tier subcontractors have lien rights against the money owed to the second-tier contractor by the first-tier contractor.

Remote Contracts: Contracts more remote than third-tier have lien rights against the funds owed to the party with whom they contracted with to perform the work.

North Carolina's Lien Agent System

North Carolina mechanics' lien agent system allows (but does not require) potential lien claimants to give notice they are working on a project. Then closing attorneys, lenders and purchasers will have the ability to address those known potential lien claimants at closing. The mechanics' lien agent system became effective on April 1, 2013 to facilitate Chapter 44-A, Article 2, of the NC General Statutes.

The online system involves a simple 3-step process:

✓ Register the project by filing an Appointment of Lien Agent,

✓ Include potential lien claimants' contact information by filing Notice(s) to Lien Agent, and

✓ Perform a search to see all NC construction projects.

To register a project, file a notice, or search the system for project details visit www.liensnc.com.

Notice of Contract

Within 30 days of the building permit issuance, the general contractor can file a notice of contract with the office of the clerk of superior court. The notice must be posted on the property in a visible location adjacent to the posted building permit.

The notice of contract must follow a similar format to the following form:

NOTICE OF CONTRACT

(1) Name and address of the Contractor:

(2) Name and address of the owner of the real property at the time this Notice of Contract is recorded:

(3) General description of the real property to be improved (street address, tax map lot and block number, reference to recorded instrument, or any other description that reasonably identifies the real property):

(4) Name and address of the person, firm or corporation filing this Notice of Contract:

Dated: _____

_____
Contractor

Filed this the ____ day of _____, ____.

_____
Clerk of Superior Court

Notice of Subcontract

To preserve lien rights, the second- or third-tier subcontractor must serve upon the contractor who has filed a notice of contract with a completed and signed notice of subcontract form.

The notice of subcontract must follow a similar format to the following form:

NOTICE OF SUBCONTRACT

(1) Name and address of the subcontractor:

(2) General description of the real property where the labor was performed or the material was furnished (street address, tax map lot and block number, reference to recorded instrument, or any description that reasonably identifies the real property):

(3)   (i)   General description of the subcontractor's contract, including the names of the parties thereto:

        (ii)   General description of the labor and material performed and furnished thereunder:

(4) Request is hereby made by the undersigned subcontractor that he be notified in writing by the contractor of, and within five days following, each subsequent payment by the contractor to the first-tier subcontractor for labor performed or material furnished at the improved real property within the above descriptions of such in paragraph (2) and subparagraph (3)(ii), respectively, the date payment was made and the period for which payment is made.

Dated: _____

_____
Subcontractor

Filing a Notice of Claim of Lien

Prior to filing a claim of lien, first-tier, second-tier, third-tier, and remote contractors must file a notice of claim of lien.

Required Information: This notice must contain the following information:

✓ name and address of the person claiming the lien upon funds;

✓ general description of the real property improved;

✓ name and address of the person with whom the lien claimant contracted to improve real property;

✓ name and address of each person against or through whom subrogation rights are claimed;

✓ general description of the contract and the person against whose interest the lien upon funds is claimed; and

✓ amount of the lien upon funds claimed by the lien claimant under the contract.

First, Second and Third-Tier Notice Format: The notice for first, second and third-tier contractors must follow a similar format to the following form:

NOTICE OF CLAIM OF LIEN UPON FUNDS BY FIRST, SECOND, OR THIRD-TIER SUBCONTRACTOR

To:

1. _____, owner of property involved.

(Name and address)

2. _____, general contractor.

(Name and address)

3. _____, first-tier subcontractor against or through

(Name and address)   whom subrogation is claimed, if any.

4. _____, second-tier subcontractor against or through

(Name and address)   whom subrogation is claimed, if any.

General description of real property where labor performed or material furnished:

_____

General description of undersigned lien claimant's contract including the names of the parties thereto:

_____

The amount of lien upon funds claimed pursuant to the above described contract:

$ _____

The undersigned lien claimant gives this notice of claim of lien upon funds pursuant to North Carolina law and claims all rights of subrogation to which he is entitled under Part 2 of Article 2 of Chapter 44A of the General Statutes of North Carolina.

Dated _____

_____, Lien Claimant

_____(Address)

Remote Contractors Notice Format: The notice for contractors more remote than third-tier must follow a similar format to the following form:

NOTICE OF CLAIM OF LIEN UPON FUNDS BY SUBCONTRACTOR
MORE REMOTE THAN THE THIRD TIER

To:

_____, person holding funds against which lien

(Name and Address)

upon funds is claimed.

General description of real property where labor performed or material furnished:

_____

_____

General description of undersigned lien claimant's contract including the names of the parties thereto:

_____

_____

The amount of lien upon funds claimed pursuant to the above described contract:

$ _____

The undersigned lien claimant gives this notice of claim of lien upon funds pursuant to North Carolina law and claims all rights to which he or she is entitled under Part 2 of Article 2 of Chapter 44A of the General Statutes of North Carolina.

Dated: _____

_____, Lien Claimant

_____ (Address)

Filing a Claim of Lien

Time in Which to File: A claim of lien must be filed within 120 days of the last date that labor or materials were furnished.

Required Information: The claim of lien must contain the following information:

✓ name and address of the person claiming the claim of lien on real property;

✓ name and address of the record owner of the real property claimed to be subject to the claim of lien on real property at the time the claim of lien on real property is filed;

✓ description of the real property upon which the claim of lien on real property is claimed: (Street address, tax lot and block number, reference to recorded instrument, or any other description of real property is sufficient, whether or not it is specific, if it reasonably identifies what is described.);

✓ name and address of the person with whom the claimant contracted for the furnishing of labor or materials;

✓ date upon which labor or materials were first furnished upon said property by the claimant;

✓ date upon which labor or materials were last furnished upon said property by the claimant;

✓ general description of the labor performed or materials furnished and the amount claimed; and

✓ signature of the lien claimant.

Where to File: All claims of lien must be filed in the office of the clerk of the superior court in each county where the property subject to the claim of lien is located.

Lien Waiver: A waiver of lien rights as part of a contract's provisions is unenforceable.

Monetary Awards

Prorating Liens: If the amount due to the contractor is not sufficient to pay all the lienors, the owner will prorate the amount due to all of those claiming a lien.

If the amount due to the lower-tier contractor is not sufficient, the party claiming the lien will prorate the amount due to all of those claiming a lien.

Time in Which to File a Lien Foreclosure Petition

A lawsuit to foreclose on the lien must be filed within 180 days after the lienor last provided materials or labor for the construction project.

Sale of Land to Satisfy Lien

A judge can order the sale of the land to pay the lien or can remove the lien if it is not valid. An owner can also bond around the lien. This allows the sale of the land with a clear title but also makes the bond available to pay the lien-holder and any of the lower-tier contractors if the lawsuit is successful.

Summary of Lien Process

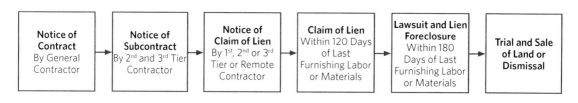

Final Inspection...

What is a Lien? A lien can be a useful tool in securing payment for labor or materials for improvement on real property.

Who is Entitled to a Mechanics' Lien? State statutes give those who contract with the owner and first-tier, second-tier, third-tier, and remote contractors lien rights.

North Carolina's Lien Agent System: North Carolina mechanics' lien agent system allows (but does not require) potential lien claimants to give notice they are working on a project.

Notice of Contract: The general contractor can file a notice of contract within 30 days of receiving a building permit.

Notice of Subcontract: If the general contractor filed a notice of contract, the second- and third-tier contractors must file a notice of subcontract.

Filing a Notice of Claim of Lien: Before filing a claim of lien, the notice of claim of lien must be filed.

Filing a Claim of Lien: A claim of lien must contain all the required information and be filed within 120 days of last furnishing labor or materials.

Monetary Awards: Monetary awards are prorated if the amount due is not sufficient to pay the lienors.

Time in Which to File a Lien Foreclosure Petition: A lawsuit to foreclose on a lien must be filed within 180 days of last furnishing labor or materials.

Sale of Land to Satisfy Lien: A judge can order the sale of land or remove a lien if it is not valid.

Appendix A: Glossary

A

Accelerated Depreciation: A method of depreciation where an asset is depreciated at a higher rate during the early part of its useful life permitting larger tax deductions.

Acceptance (Legal): An agreement to an offer made and generally is done by signing the offer. In some cases, a counteroffer is made. A counteroffer is not considered acceptance. It is only when both parties agree to the contract terms that you obtain acceptance.

Accounting Cycle: A process that happens each financial reporting period which starts with recording financial transactions and goes through analysis of financial statements.

Accounts Receivable: Monies that are owed to a business for products and/or services provided.

Accrual Method of Accounting: A method of accounting where income is recognized when the services occur, not when the money is collected. Expenses are recorded when they are incurred, not when they are paid.

Acid Test Ratio: See *Quick Ratio*.

Activity Ratio: A formula that measures how effectively a company manages its credit. It is calculated by dividing sales per day into current receivables.

Addenda or Addendum: Changes made to bid documents after they are issued but before they are due. Addenda ultimately become part of the contract after the bid is accepted.

ADA: The abbreviation for the Americans with Disabilities Act. See *Americans with Disabilities Act*.

AGC: The abbreviation for the Associated General Contractors of America.

Age Discrimination in Employment Act (ADEA): A federal law that prohibits discrimination against individuals who are age 40 or older.

AIA: The abbreviation for the American Institute of Architects.

All-Risk Builders' Risk Insurance: A form of property insurance that covers property owners and builders for buildings under construction typically covering machinery, equipment, materials, supplies, and fixtures that are part of the structure or will become part of the structure. Additional coverage can be added for items, such as temporary structures and scaffolding, used during construction. In general, major construction defects such as poor workmanship and faulty design are not covered.

Allowance: A specified amount designated in an estimate for items that are not specified in the project plans, such as finish materials (carpeting, fixtures, lighting, etc.).

Americans with Disabilities Act (ADA): The Americans with Disabilities Act (ADA) makes it unlawful to discriminate in employment against a qualified individual with a disability.

Arbitration: Arbitration uses a third-party arbitrator or arbitrators to act as a judge or judges to render a decision by which all parties are legally bound. Arbitration is held in a format less formal than a trial.

Asbestos: These naturally occurring, fibrous materials are woven together to create a product with high tensile strength. This material is commonly found in thermal insulation and fireproofing, roofing, and flooring materials.

When these fibers become airborne, they cause a hazard due to their ability to enter the lungs. Diseases associated with asbestos include asbestosis, lung cancer, and mesothelioma.

Asset: Items of value owned by a business.

At-Will Employment: An employment agreement where either the employer or the employee may terminate employment at any time without notice or cause.

Automobile Insurance: A type of insurance providing coverage for liability and physical damage associated with a company vehicle or a fleet of vehicles. All states require vehicle owners to carry some level of liability insurance covering bodily injury and property damage incurred in a vehicle accident.

B

Bad Debt: Uncollectible accounts receivable which is deducted from gross income when figuring taxable income.

Balance Sheet: One of the basic accounting financial statements that shows a company's assets, liabilities, and owners' equity.

Bank Letter of Credit: A cash guarantee that can be converted to a payment to the owner by a bank or lending institution.

Bid: A formal offer to complete a project according to the terms and conditions of the contract for a specified price.

Bid Bond: *A type of bond that* guarantees the contractor, if awarded the job, will do work at the submitted bid price, enter into a contract with the owner, and furnish the required performance and payment bonds.

Bid Documents: A bid package put together in a competitive bid situation. It may include an invitation to bid, bid instructions, bid sheet, bid schedule, bidder's questionnaire on experience, financial responsibility and capability, copy of the contract, and supplements.

Bid Peddling: An unethical situation where the subcontractor approaches the general contractor after the project is awarded with the intent of lowering the original price submitted on bid day.

Bid Rigging: A form of collusion where contractors coordinate their bids to fix the award outcome of a project.

Bid Shopping: An unethical situation where the general contractor approaches subcontractors other than those who have submitted bids to seek a lower offer than what was quoted in the original bids.

Boilerplate Provisions: Standard language or clauses used in a legal contract that generally appear at the end of the contract. Their purpose is to protect the business in the event of a lawsuit.

Bond: A risk transfer mechanism between a surety bonding company, the contractor, and the project owner. The agreement binds the contractor to comply with the terms and conditions of a contract. If the contractor cannot perform the contract, the surety bonding company assumes the contractor's responsibilities and ensures that the project is completed.

Breach of Contract: When one of the parties involved fails to perform in accordance with any of the terms and conditions of a contract.

Burglary and Theft Insurance: A type of insurance covering loss or damage caused by burglary, theft, larceny, robbery, forgery, fraud, and vandalism.

Business Owner's Policies (BOPs): A type of insurance that bundles property and liability coverage together to eliminate policy gaps or overlaps.

Business Plan: A planning document that outlines business strategies and goals. It is particularly useful for newly-formed or early-stage businesses and companies making major strategic changes. Typical contents are an executive and company summary, products and services description, market analysis, marketing plan, and financial plan.

C

Capital Assets: See *Fixed Assets*.

Cash Method of Accounting: A method of accounting where income is reported in the year it is received and expenses are deducted in the year they are paid.

Certificate of Occupancy: A certificate issued by a building inspector that deems a structure meets all applicable codes and is safe for occupancy.

Certificate of Substantial Completion: A certificate issued by the architect that deems a structure can be used for its intended purpose.

CFR: The abbreviation for Code of Federal Regulations.

Change Order: A written agreement between the owner and contractor to change the contract. Change orders add to, delete from, or otherwise alter the work set forth in the construction documents.

Circular E: An IRS Publication that provides instructions on calculating, withholding and depositing employee taxes and tax tables.

Clean Air Act: A federal law that allows the EPA to set limits on how much of a pollutant is allowed in the air anywhere in the United States.

Clean Water Act: A federal law that establishes the basic structure for regulating discharges of pollutants into the waters of the United States. This act gives the EPA authority to implement pollution control programs, such as setting wastewater standards for the industry and water quality standards for all contaminants in surface waters.

Collaborative Law: A facilitative process wherein all parties agree at the onset to work to identify a solution that is beneficial to all parties involved. In collaborative law, the parties use their advocates, most often their lawyers, to facilitate a mutually beneficial result through the process of negotiation.

Commercial General Liability Insurance (CGL): A basic liability insurance covering bodily injury that results in actual physical damage or loss for individuals who are not employees, damage or loss to property not belonging to the business, personal injury, including slander or damage to reputation, and advertising injury, including charges of negligence that result from promotion of goods or services.

Company Overhead: The expenses that are necessary to keep business operations running but not directly associated with a project (e.g. taxes, legal fees, etc.).

Completed Contract Method: A method of contract accounting where income or loss is reported in the year the contract is completed.

Completed Operations Liability Insurance: A type of liability insurance that provides coverage for loss arising out of completed projects.

Completion Bond: A type of bond that provides assurance to the financial backers of a construction project that it will be completed on time.

Conceptual Estimate: An estimate prepared by the architect using cost models from previous projects.

Consideration (Legal): When both parties give up something of value, typically, services and products in exchange for monetary compensation.

Consolidated Omnibus Budget Act of 1985 (COBRA): A federal law that gives "qualified beneficiaries" (a covered employee's spouse and dependent children) the right to maintain, at their own expense, coverage under their health plan that would be lost due to a "qualifying event," such as termination of employment, at a cost comparable to what it would be if they were still members of the employer's group.

Construction Management (Contracting): A type of contracting where the project owner contracts with a professional construction manager to coordinate and manage a construction project.

Construction Safety Act: See *Contract Work Hours and Safety Standards Act.*

Construction Wrap-Up Liability Insurance: A type of insurance that bundles liability and workers' compensation insurance for general contractors and subcontractors on large construction projects to eliminate gaps in coverage. To qualify for this type of insurance, certain contract cost requirements must be met. These requirements vary by state.

Contingency: A specified amount added to an estimate to protect the contractor if an unanticipated problem or condition arises during the course of the project.

Contract: Legally binding agreement between two or more parties with the main purpose of preventing disputes between parties entering into the agreement. A legally binding contract must have offer and acceptance, consideration, competent parties, and legal purpose.

Contract Work Hours and Safety Standards Act: A federal law that sets overtime standards for service and construction contracts on federal projects. Commonly referred to as the Construction Safety Act.

Contractor's Protective Public and Property Damage Liability Insurance: A type of liability insurance that protects contractors who supervise and subsequently are held liable for actions of subcontractors from claims for personal injury and property damage.

Contractual Liability Insurance: A type of liability insurance that provides contractors with protection for damages that result from their negligence while under written contract.

Corporation (sometimes referred to as C Corporation): A legal business entity that has independent ownership of assets and liabilities from its shareholders. Its existence continues even if one or more shareholders leave.

Cost Comparison Method: A method of contract accounting that combines the completed contract and percentage of completion methods.

Cost-Plus Contract: A type of contract where the contractor is reimbursed for the actual cost of labor and materials and is paid a markup fee for overhead and profit.

Critical Path: The sequence of tasks that determines the duration of the project. Subsequent project tasks cannot begin until a critical path item is complete.

Current Assets: Cash and other assets that can be converted into cash in less than one year.

Current Liabilities: Liabilities that will mature and must be paid within one year.

Current Ratio: See *Liquidity Ratio.*

D

Davis-Bacon Act: The federal law that requires payment of prevailing wage rates and fringe benefits on federally-financed or assisted construction.

Debt Ratio: A formula that measures the percent of total funds provided by creditors. It is calculated by dividing total assets into total debt.

De Minimis Violation: A violation of standards which have no direct or immediate relationship to safety or health.

Depreciation: The process of devaluing a fixed asset as a result of aging, wear and tear, or obsolescence.

Design/Build: A type of contracting where the owner contracts with one company to complete a construction project from start to finish. The company awarded the design/build contract puts together a team of construction professionals, which may include designers, architects, engineers, and contractors.

Direct Costs: Costs directly linked with a particular project.

E

EEOC: Abbreviation for the Equal Employment Opportunity Commission.

Employee Polygraph Protection Act: A federal law that prohibits most private employers from using any type of lie detector test, either for pre-employment screening of job applicants or for testing current employees during the course of employment.

Endangered Species Act (ESA): A federal law that protects threatened or endangered species from further harm.

Entrepreneur: A person engaged in strategic activities that involve the initiation and development of a new business, created to build long-term value and steady cash flow streams.

Equal Pay Act of 1963: A federal law that prohibits employers from paying different wages to men and women who perform essentially the same work under similar working conditions.

Equipment Floater Policy: A type of inland marine insurance covering direct physical loss to equipment and mobile equipment while it is stored on premises, in transit, or at temporary locations or jobsites.

Errors and Omissions Insurance: See *Professional Liability Insurance*.

Expenses: Monies paid out or owed for goods or services.

F

Failure to Abate Prior Violation: A safety violation given when a previous violation has not been corrected.

Fair Labor Standards Act (FLSA): The federal law which prescribes standards for the basic minimum wage and overtime pay and affects most private and public employment. It applies to employers who have one or more employees. FLSA is administered by the Employment Standards Administration's Wage and Hour Division within the U.S. Department of Labor.

Family and Medical Leave Act (FMLA): A federal law that entitles eligible employees of covered employers to take up to 12 weeks of unpaid job-protected leave each year, with the maintenance of group health insurance, for the birth and care of a child, for the placement of a child for adoption or foster care, for the care of a child, spouse, or parent with a serious health condition, or for the employee's serious health condition.

Fast Track Construction: A phased approach where the construction process begins before completion of the contract documents. Generally, the cost is not fixed until after construction documents are complete and some construction commitments have already been made.

Federal Employer Identification Number (EIN): A 9-digit number issued by the IRS, which is used to identify the tax accounts of employers and certain others who have no employees (also referred to as a taxpayer identification number).

Federal Unemployment Tax Act (FUTA): The federal unemployment tax that is part of the federal and state program under which unemployment compensation is paid to workers who lose their jobs.

Fidelity Bond: A type of bond that covers business owners for losses due to dishonest acts by their employees.

Fixed Assets: Assets needed to carry on the business of a company, which are not normally consumed in the operation of the business (sometimes referred to as capital assets).

Foreign Entity: A business originally established in another state or another country.

Foreman: An individual who assists the superintendent with daily project operations and usually supervises specific areas by trade.

For Profit Corporation: A corporation in existence to make a profit for its owners or shareholders. Corporate tax status is determined by the Internal Revenue Service.

FUTA: An abbreviation for Federal Unemployment Tax Act.

H

Health Insurance Portability and Accountability Act of 1996 (HIPAA): A federal law that provides for improved portability and continuity of health insurance coverage connected with employment.

I

I-9 Form: The form required for employers to complete to verify employment eligibility under the Immigration and Nationality Act. I-9 forms must be kept on file for at least three years after the date of hire or for one year after the date employment ends, whichever is later.

Immaterial Breach (Partial Breach): A less serious violation of a contract that usually does not result in termination of the contract. The injured party may only sue for the value of the damages.

Immigration and Nationality Act (INA): A federal law that outlines the conditions for the temporary and permanent employment of aliens in the United States. It includes provisions for all employers that address employment eligibility and employment verification.

Income Statement: A financial statement that provides a summary of the company's revenues and expenses over a given period of time (sometimes called the profit-and-loss statement).

Indemnification: A way to transfer risk and exemption from loss that absolves the indemnified party from any payment for losses and damages incurred by a third party.

Indemnity: A way to transfer risk and exemption from loss incurred by any course of action. Sometimes an insurance payout is called an indemnity.

Indirect Expenses: See *Operating Expenses.*

Inland Marine Insurance (Equipment Theft Insurance): A type of property insurance for your tools and equipment that provides coverage for goods in transit and projects under construction.

Insurance: A protective measure in which coverage is obtained for a specific risk (or set of risks) through a contract. In this contract or policy, one party indemnifies another against specified loss in return for premiums paid.

K

Key Man Insurance: A type of insurance coverage for a specific individual necessary for the continuing success of a business. Key man insurance is available as life insurance, disability insurance, or both.

L

Lead-Based Paint Renovation, Repair and Painting Program: This federal regulation involves those who perform renovations for compensation in residential housing that may contain lead paint. It requires for additional provisions to the Lead PRE regulations. Under the Lead-Based Paint Renovation, Repair and

Painting Program, contractors must be certified to perform renovation work that disturbs lead-based paint in homes, child care facilities, and schools built before 1978.

Lead PRE: This federal regulation involves those who perform renovations for compensation in residential housing built before 1978 that may contain lead paint. It requires mandatory notification for owners and occupants of the building being renovated.

Liabilities: All debt and obligations owed by a business.

Liability Insurance: A type of insurance designed to protect against third-party claims that arise from alleged negligence resulting in bodily injury or property damage.

Lien Bond: A type of bond that guarantees liens cannot be placed against the owner's property by contractors for payment of services.

Limited Liability Company (LLC): A legal business entity that has characteristics of both sole proprietorships and corporations. Federal income taxes are paid only on income distributed to members as ordinary income. Members have protection from liability for actions taken by the company or by other members of your company but are not protected from liability for personal actions.

Liquid Assets: Assets that are easily converted to cash.

Liquidity Ratio: A calculation used to determine if a company can pay its current debts. Calculated by dividing current liabilities into the current assets (sometimes called current ratio).

Little Miller Acts: Laws enacted by individual states and local governments regarding required bonds to bid and perform public works projects.

Long-Term Liabilities: Debt obligations that extend beyond one year.

Lump Sum Contract: A contract where the contractor agrees to complete the project for a predetermined, specified price. The contractor essentially assumes all of the risk under this contract agreement because the contractor is responsible for additional costs associated with unforeseen circumstances.

M

Maintenance Bond: A type of bond that guarantees for a stated period, typically for one year, no defective workmanship or material will appear in the completed project.

Marketing: Strategies and techniques used to bring in new customers and retain current customers to ensure a steady flow of leads and customers. This process includes advertising and promotion, pricing strategies, timely distribution, and product design and attributes to meet customer needs.

Marketing Plan: A formal document focusing on a company's marketing strategy by outlining the company's vision, customer base, methods of promotion (e.g. advertising, public relations, online marketing, direct sales, etc.), marketing budget, individual responsible for executing the plan, and industry opportunities and challenges.

MasterFormat: A classification system published by the Construction Specifications Institute that includes numbers and job tasks grouped by major construction activities.

Material Breach: A serious violation of a contract that may void the contract and will most likely end up in litigation.

Material Safety Data Sheet (MSDS): A form that accompanies chemicals and is important to workplace safety. The MSDS contains information such as first aid when contact occurs, disposal, storage, protective equipment required, and spill handling procedures.

Materials Expediter: An individual who supervises the materials procurement process to ensure accurate and timely delivery of materials.

Mechanics' Lien: A legal action that "clouds" the title to real property and serves as an effective method (and sometimes the only method) for securing payment for labor or materials used in the improvement of real property. The lien stops the owner from selling the property with a clear title.

Medicare: Social Security and Medicare taxes pay for benefits that workers and families receive under the Federal Insurance Contributions Act (FICA). Medicare tax pays for benefits under the hospital insurance part of FICA.

Miller Act: The Miller Act requires performance and payment bonds on all federal construction projects valued at greater than $100,000.

Minimum Wage: The minimum amount an employer can pay employees. FLSA and individual state laws designate the minimum pay rate.

Minor: An individual under 18 years of age.

Modified Accelerated Cost Recovery System (MACRS): A depreciation method approved by the IRS that allows for faster depreciation over longer periods.

Motor Truck Cargo Insurance: A type of inland marine insurance protecting the transporter in the event of damaged or lost freight.

N

Named Peril Builders' Risk Insurance: An insurance policy with narrower coverage than all-risk insurance that specifies which perils are covered.

National Environmental Policy Act (NEPA): A federal law that ensures that federal agencies consider environmental impacts in federal planning and decision making and covers construction and post-construction activities.

National Historic Preservation Act (NHPA): A federal law that protects property that is eligible for or included on the National Register of Historic Places (NRHP).

Negotiation (Alternative Dispute Resolution): A dialogue entered into for the purpose of resolving disputes or producing an agreed upon course or courses of action.

Negotiation (Contract): The process where the owner and contractor come to an agreement on the price and terms of the contract.

Net Pay: The payroll amount an employee receives after taxes and deductions are taken out.

Net Profit: The difference between revenues and expenses. Net profit directly contributes to the net worth of the company.

NPDES: The abbreviation for the National Pollutant Discharge Elimination System.

O

Occupational Safety and Health Act (OSHA): Federal law governing safe and healthy working conditions by developing standards, providing assistance, information and training, and conducting research.

Offer: An offer specifically outlines the obligations of the contract, including the work to be done and compensation for this work (e.g. estimate or bid).

Operating Expenses: General items that contribute to the cost of operating the business. These expenses can be put into two categories, selling expenses and fixed overhead (sometimes called indirect expenses).

OSHA: An abbreviation for Occupational Safety and Health Administration; Occupational Safety and Health Act.

OSHA Form 300: An OSHA form that serves as an injury/illness log, with a separate line entry for each recordable injury or illness.

OSHA Form 300A: An OSHA form that includes a summary of the previous year's work-related injuries and illnesses.

OSHA Form 301: An OSHA form that serves as an individual incident report providing details about each specific recordable injury or illness.

Other Than Serious Violation: A safety violation that has a direct relationship to workplace safety and health, but probably would not cause death or serious physical harm.

Overhead: See *company overhead; project overhead.*

Overtime: The hours an employee works when it exceeds more than 40 hours in a workweek. FLSA designates that eligible employees are paid one-and-one-half-times the regular rate for overtime hours.

Owners' Equity: Consists of the initial investment in a business, plus accumulated net profits not paid out to the owners.

Owner's Representative (Owner's Agent): An appointed representative designated to oversee a project and serve as a liaison to the owner. The owner's representative (agent) may have legal authority to make certain legal decisions on behalf of the owner.

P

Partnership: A business relationship between two or more persons who join to carry on a trade or business. Each person contributes money, property, labor, or skill, and each partner expects to share in the profits and losses of the business.

Payment Bond: A type of bond that guarantees subcontractors and suppliers will be paid for work if they perform properly under the contract.

Percentage of Completion Method: A method of contract accounting that recognizes income as it is earned during the construction project.

Performance Bond: A type of bond that guarantees the contractor will complete a contract within its time frame and conditions.

Petty Cash Fund: A cash fund used to make small payments instead of writing a check.

Positive Cash Flow: A term used to describe when more cash is received than is going out to pay expenses.

Professional Liability Insurance (sometimes called Errors and Omissions Insurance): A type of liability insurance that protects contractors from negligence resulting from errors or omissions of designers and architects.

Profitability Ratio: A formula used to calculate the profit margin of a company. It is calculated by dividing revenues into net income.

Profit-and-Loss Statement: See *Income Statement.*

Progressive Discipline: A method of corrective action where the consequences of the improper behavior become more significant if it continues.

Progress Payments: Partial payments made after completion of specified phases of construction. Payments are generally calculated by taking the difference between the completed work and materials delivered and a predetermined schedule of unit costs.

Project Manager: An individual who plans and coordinates a construction project to meet the overall goals of the project and serves as the main contact with the owner.

Project Overhead: Items necessary to complete the project but not directly associated with labor and materials (e.g. temporary storage, dumpsters, etc.).

Property Insurance: An insurance policy covering property when damage, theft, or loss occurs. Specific risk provisions are often available for occurrences such as fire or theft. Broad-based policies cover a variety of risks (including fire, theft, vandalism, and "acts of God" such as lightning strikes).

Q

Quick Ratio: Similar to the liquidity ratio, it is calculated by dividing the current liabilities into the current assets minus inventory (sometimes called the acid test ratio).

R

Recitals (Legal): Language at the beginning of a contract that provides background to the contract.

Repeated Violation: A safety violation of any standard, regulation, rule, or order where, upon reinspection, a substantially similar violation is found.

Retainage: A specified amount withheld from each progress payment as protection for the owner to ensure completion of the construction project and provide protection against liens, claims, and defaults.

Return on Total Assets Ratio: A formula used to determine if the company's assets are being employed in the best manner. It is calculated by dividing total assets into net profit (after taxes).

Revenues: The income received from the daily operations of the business.

Right-to-Work Laws: Laws passed at the state-level that secure the right of employees to decide for themselves whether or not to join or financially support a union.

Risk Management: An assessment of all areas of a business from operations to administrative functions for the risk of financial loss, lower profit margins, and unnecessary liabilities.

S

S Corporation: A legal business entity formed under the rules of Subchapter S of the Internal Revenue Code. It is taxed like a partnership by passing items of income, loss, deduction, and credits through to its shareholders to be included on their separate returns.

Self-Employment Tax: A social security and Medicare tax primarily for individuals who work for themselves.

Serious Violation: A violation where there is substantial probability that death or serious physical harm could result and that the employer knew, or should have known, of the hazard.

Service Contract Act: The federal act that requires payment of prevailing wage rates and fringe benefits on contracts to provide services to the federal government.

Single Prime Contracting: Traditional form of contracting where the project owner typically hires an architectural firm to design the project and the contractor then performs the work according to the specifications of the project and is responsible for the costs of all materials and labor to obtain project completion.

Social Security Tax: Social Security and Medicare taxes pay for benefits that workers and families receive under the Federal Insurance Contributions Act (FICA). Social Security tax pays for benefits under the old-age, survivors, and disability insurance part of FICA.

Sole Proprietorship: A business that has one individual as the owner (proprietor) who is responsible for 100% of the decisions made on behalf of the business and owns all of the business assets. It can employ others but may just be the owner who works for the business.

Square-Foot Method Estimate: An estimate based on a calculation of the square footage of the project multiplied by a unit cost.

Statement of Cash Flows: A financial statement that summarizes current cash position, cash sources, and use of these funds over a given period of time.

Statute of Limitations: Laws that set a maximum period of time within which a lawsuit or claim may be filed.

Straight Line Depreciation: A method of depreciation where the salvage cost is subtracted from the initial cost of the item.

Subcontractor: An individual or business that contracts with the general contractor or other subcontractors to complete a portion of a larger project.

Subcontractor's Bond: A type of bond that protects the general contractor in the event that the subcontractor does not fully perform the contract and/or pay for labor and materials.

Superintendent: An onsite supervisor responsible for the daily operations.

SUTA Dumping: The transfer of employees between businesses for the purpose of obtaining a lower unemployment compensation tax rate. SUTA dumping is illegal and subject to criminal and/or civil penalties.

T

Taxpayer Identification Number: See *Federal Employer Identification Number*.

Tax Provision Expenses: Tax liabilities owed for federal, state, and local taxes.

Title III of the Consumer Credit Protection Act (CCPA): A federal law that protects employees from being discharged by their employers because their wages have been garnished for any one debt and limits the amount of employees' earnings that may be garnished in any one week.

Title VII of the Civil Rights Act of 1964: A federal law that prohibits discrimination on the basis of race, color, religion, national origin, and sex.

Transportation Floater Insurance: A type of inland marine insurance protecting the transporter against damage that occurs to freight during transport.

Turnkey Construction: Similar to the design/build model, the contractor puts together and manages the construction and design team but also obtains financing and land.

U

Unemployment Insurance: A type of insurance that provides unemployment benefits to eligible workers who become unemployed through no fault of their own and meet certain other eligibility requirements. This program is jointly financed through federal and state employer payroll taxes.

Uniformed Services Employment and Reemployment Rights Act (USERRA): A federal law that protects service members' reemployment rights when returning from a period of service in the uniformed services, including those called up from the reserves or National Guard, and prohibits employer discrimination based on military service or obligation.

Unit-Price Contract: A type of contract where a price per unit is calculated for each item and the contractor is paid according to the actual quantities used.

Unit Price Estimating Method: A method of estimating that bundles all of the cost factors such as labor, materials, equipment, and subcontractors to come up with a unit price for the entire task.

V

Value Engineering: A project management approach with the primary objective of understanding the owner's cost, quality, and time priorities to deliver a product of the highest value.

W

Wage Garnishment Law: A federal law that limits the amount an individual's income may be legally garnished and prohibits firing an employee whose pay is garnished for payment of a single debt.

Walsh-Healey Public Contracts Act: A federal law that requires payment of minimum wage rates and overtime pay on contracts that provide goods to the federal government.

Willful Violation: A safety violation that the employer knowingly commits or commits with plain indifference to the law.

Work Hours: As defined under FLSA, hours that ordinarily include all time during which an employee is required to be on the employer's premises, on duty, or at a prescribed work place.

Worker Adjustment and Retraining Notification Act (WARN): A federal law that offers protection to workers, their families, and communities by requiring employers to provide notice 60 days in advance of covered plant closings and covered mass layoffs.

Workers' Compensation Insurance: A type of insurance providing monetary compensation to employees who are injured or disabled on the job and benefits for dependents of those workers who are killed because of work-related accidents or illnesses. The insurance is purchased by the employer; no part of it should be paid for by employees or deducted from their pay.

Working Capital: The amount of cash available after liabilities or debts are paid. Working capital measures the liquidity of the company's assets.

Workweek: As defined under FLSA, it is a period of 168 hours during seven consecutive 24-hour periods. It may begin on any day of the week and at any hour of the day established by the employer.

Appendix B: Business Plan Template

The following business plan template can be customized for your company. These forms are also located on the accompanying disc in case you need to modify them on your computer. You may want to work through this plan as you review each chapter, as some of the business plan section topics are covered in more depth.

Business Plan Outline	

Section 1: Cover Sheet
 	
  1a. Name of Business
  1b. Contact Information
 	
Section 2: Executive Summary
 	
  2a. Plan Highlights
  2b. Keys to Success
 	
Section 3: Company Summary
 	
  3a. Vision
  3b. Mission
  3c. Legal Structure
  3d. Management and Personnel Plan
  3e. Proposed Location
  3f. Facilities Requirements
  3g. Operational Hours
 	
Section 4: Products and/or Service
 	
  4a. Product and/or Service Description
  4b. Vendors
  4c. Technology
  4d. Expansion Opportunities
	Section 5: Market Analysis
	
	  5a. Target Market Definition
	  5b. Market Needs
	  5c. Market Trends
	  5d. Market Growth
	  5e. Competitive Comparison
	
	Section 6: Marketing Strategy
	
	  6a. Value Proposition
	  6b. Competitive Edge
	  6c. Pricing Strategy
	  6d. Promotion Strategy
	  6e. Marketing Programs
	
	Section 7: Financial Plan
	
	  7a. Sales Forecast and Assumptions
	  7b. Profit and Loss Pro Forma
	  7c. Source of Financing

Note: You may also refer to the Financial Management chapter for additional financial documents such as a balance sheet, income statement, and statement of cash flows. The profit and loss pro forma is a good tool for newly-established businesses to determine how much revenue is needed to break even.

Section 1: Cover Sheet

The cover sheet should contain the name of the business, address, phone number, fax number, email address, and contact name. Some cover sheets also contain a confidentiality statement.

Section 2: Executive Summary

A business plan normally starts with an executive summary, which should be concise and interesting. This summary includes the highlights of your plan and serves as an introduction to the rest of your plan. Topics in your executive summary should include, but not be limited to, the following:

- ✓ Business name
- ✓ Business location
- ✓ Product or service offered
- ✓ Purpose of the plan
- ✓ Projected sales
- ✓ Profitability
- ✓ Keys to success

The executive summary should only be a page or two long. Although the executive summary appears first in the printed document, most business plan developers do not write it until after the plan is complete.

Section 3: Company Summary

1. **Vision and Mission:** Include a vision and mission statement for your company. The vision should be a short statement about the company's aspirations for the future. The mission describes the company's primary business purpose or goal. These statements outline the business concept and provide a concise definition of where your company fits in the market.

2. **Legal Structure:** Define the legal structure of your company (i.e., sole proprietorship, partnership, corporation, or limited liability company). Explain why you chose this structure and the benefits it will provide to you and your company. Legal structure is covered in Chapter 2.

3. **Management:** Outline the key management personnel needed to run your business. Can you run the business yourself or do you need to hire managers to help run the operations? What are the job responsibilities of these managers?

4. **Employees:** How many employees do you require? What are the job responsibilities of the employees?

5. **Location:** Describe the location of your business. You do not need to provide a specific address if you do not have one, but identify the area (e.g., downtown location, at home, in a rural area). Explain why this location will provide you with the best opportunity for success.

6. **Facility Requirements:** Identify your facility requirements. Do you need office space, a production area, storage space, or mobile storage? You may want to draw a diagram of the space.

7. **Hours of Operation:** What are your hours of operation? Explain how these hours will provide the maximum benefit to your customer. How will you handle emergency situations that arise outside of normal working hours?

Section 4: Product or Service Description

Defining your product or service (or both) may seem simple. You must describe not only your product or service but how you will provide it to your customers. For example, you may be a general contractor, but without reliable subcontractors and suppliers, you may not be able to complete your projects in the time frame promised to the customer.

1. **Product or Service Description:** Write a summary explaining your specialty. For example, are you a general contractor, plumbing contractor, etc.?

2. **Legal Requirements:** Do you have any licensing or registration requirements? Are there any legal requirements for practicing your trade or running your business?

3. **Subcontractors and Suppliers:** Who will be your primary subcontractors and suppliers? What process will you use to evaluate subcontractors and suppliers?

4. **Technology Trends:** Summarize how technology will affect your business. Are there efficiencies that can be gained through technology? For example, can you integrate scheduling or estimating systems into your business processes?

5. **Growth Opportunities:** What expansion opportunities exist in the future after your company is established? Can you offer additional products or services, or expand your customer base to other locations?

Section 5: Market Analysis

A market analysis is often performed as one of the first tasks in researching and formulating a business plan. Understanding your customers, the demand for your work, and your competition is important to the future success of your business.

1. **Target Market:** Define the target market for your product or service. Describe the key characteristics of your customers. For example, do your primary customers include families, retired adults, or businesses?

2. **Product or Service Description:** Describe the need your product or service will be filling for your customers. If you will provide both products and services, describe how these will benefit your customers.

3. **Trends:** Describe how your product or service aligns with the consumer trends of your customers. What are the construction trends for your trade and how do these fit your customer's needs?

4. **Growth Opportunities:** Outline growth opportunities that exist within your target market. For example, if you are a pool builder and your target market is young families, you may want to concentrate on single-family homes rather than commercial projects.

5. **Competition:** List your major competitors. Are they local, regional, or national?

Section 6: Marketing Strategy

A marketing strategy is easily formulated by using the "4 P's:" Product, Price, Promotion, and Place. Product is not just your product or service, but how it will benefit your customer. Price refers to your pricing strategy, which can vary based on the market, your goals, and your competition. Promotion deals with marketing in a traditional sense. Your customers will find out about your business through your promotional efforts. Place defines your distribution strategy. In the construction industry, distribution defines the type of customers you want to target. For example, you may decide to differentiate yourself by specializing in certain types of construction.

1. **Value Proposition:** Describe the value that your company will provide your customers. What benefits of using your company will you promote to your customers? For example, you may promote your level of quality or service.

2. **Competitive Edge:** Describe what makes your product or service unique and how you have differentiated yourself from your competitors.

3. **Pricing Strategy:** What pricing strategy will you use? Some options include:
    ✓ Cost-plus pricing, where you determine a markup percentage and add it to the cost of the job.
    ✓ Consistency with competition, where your pricing reflects what the competition is charging.
    ✓ Value pricing, where you try to undercut your competition with lower prices.

4. **Promotion:** How will you familiarize potential customers with your business? Will you promote your product in special venues (i.e., trade shows or special events)? Are there any businesses you can build a co-op relationship with so you can cross-promote each other? For example, you might partner with another trade or supplier to promote each other.

5. **Advertising:** How will you advertise? Will you use media such as radio, TV, newspapers, and the Internet? How often will you advertise?

6. **Sales:** Will you hire sales representatives to promote your company? If so, how many? How will the sales force be divided up? By area or region?

Section 7: Financial Plan

A financial plan can include several aspects of the potential financial health of the company. At a minimum, it should include projected profits over a specific period. This template, for example, shows the first three years of operation. The financial plan should also explain projected cash flow and identify any additional capital required from outside investors or loans.

The profit-and-loss statement is a tabulation of the gross sales income for the company from which all attributed costs must be deducted. A *pro forma* is a "best guess" at these sales numbers and the associated costs. From this pro forma, you can see your profit or loss based on the numbers you projected and adjust your budget accordingly. A blank profit-and-loss form is located at the end of this section, if you are unable to use the form on the disc. IIf you use the spreadsheet located on the disc, it will automatically calculate gross profit and net income. These calculations were derived from the following formulas:

Income - Cost of Goods Sold = Gross Profit
Gross Profit - Expenses = Net Income

You will learn more about financial calculations in the financial management chapter 14.

Sales/Income

Use the following points to help you make your sales and expense projections.

You need to determine the average price of the jobs you perform and the number of customers you are projecting for the year. This is your "best guess," but if you have any historical sales data, you may want to use this information in your calculations to determine how your business sales will grow over time.

However you determine your sales, you must list your assumptions so the person reviewing your business plan will understand the numbers presented in your plan.

Projected sales numbers

	Sales (in dollars)
Year 1	
Year 2	
Year 3	

Transfer sales numbers into the profit-and-loss worksheet.

Cost of Goods Sold (COGS)

Cost of goods sold shows the cost of materials and production of the goods a business sells. For each year, enter your inventory cost and the cost to produce the final product for the customer and add together to show the totals. This total represents the cost of goods sold.

	Year 1	Year 2	Year 3
Inventory			
Production Payroll			
Total			

Transfer COGS numbers into the profit-and-loss worksheet.

Management Salaries

Determine how many managers or supervisors you will need to operate your business. A published salary survey will help you estimate what they earn in your type of business and in your region. Determine if you will need to add managers or supervisors in years two and three if you have an increase in business.

	Number of Managers	Manager Annual Salary	Total Management Salaries
Year 1			
Year 2			
Year 3			

Enter the total management salaries in the respective boxes on your spreadsheet.

Payroll Taxes

Payroll taxes are calculated at approximately 13% of the salaries listed on your spreadsheet. A formula has been entered to calculate that amount automatically.

Payroll taxes include the following items:

✓ Social Security, also known as FICA (a set percentage deducted from an employee's check and EMPLOYER MATCHED)

✓ Medicare, also called FICA Medicare (a set percentage deducted from an employee's check and EMPLOYER MATCHED)

✓ FUTA - Federal Unemployment Tax Act, authorizes the IRS to use monies for job service and training funded through the federal employment agency; EMPLOYER PAID ONLY

✓ SUTA - State Unemployment Tax Act, authorizes the state to use monies for job service/training and retraining of displaced workers; EMPLOYER-PAID ONLY

✓ FUI - Federal Unemployment Insurance; EMPLOYER-PAID ONLY

✓ SUI - State Unemployment Insurance; EMPLOYER-PAID ONLY

More details on payroll taxes are provided in Chapter 14.

Outside Services

These services apply to people or businesses who provide services to your company not directly related to the sales or income of the company. They would not appear on your payroll. Estimate your annual expenses for the following outside services. Keep in mind that the cost may be higher in the first year due to start-up needs. The cost may drop in the second year and then level off in the third year.

	Year 1	Year 2	Year 3
Lawyer			
Accountant			
Technology Consultant			
Total			

Enter the year totals into the spreadsheet.

Advertising and Promotion

Consider the type of marketing you will need. If you are creating a radio, newspaper or TV ad, get an estimate on what that would cost. Don't forget to calculate the frequency of advertising you will do. For example, let's say a magazine ad costs $1,000 for a quarter-page ad and the magazine comes out monthly. Your advertising cost would be $12,000 a year. You may want to advertise by printing flyers and mailing them out. Calculate the printing costs as well as the postage to send out the flyers.

	Year 1	Year 2	Year 3
Radio			
TV			
Newspaper			
Magazine			
Flyers			
Direct Mail			
Special Events			
Online Ads			
Other (i.e., social media) Please Specify:			
Total			

Enter the year totals into the spreadsheet.

Rent

If you rent a facility, determine the rental costs per year. If you have not decided on a location, you may want to look at a few locations and calculate an average rent cost to determine a figure for this category. Keep in mind the square footage requirements that you have set out.

	Annual Rent
Location #1	
Location #2	
Location #3	
Average of all three locations	

If you are going to stay in one location, your rent should remain fixed over three years. If you plan on expanding in years two and three, you may want to increase rent accordingly.

Enter the average of all three locations in the rent column on your spreadsheet.

Office Supplies

Office supplies include items such as paper, pens, printer cartridges, tape, and other materials as well as cleaning supplies. As your business increases, the consumption of these supplies may increase accordingly.

	Year 1	Year 2	Year 3
Office Supplies			
Cleaning Supplies			
Total			

Enter the year totals into the spreadsheet.

Dues, Subscriptions, and Licenses

You may want to join a Chamber of Commerce or trade group or subscribe to trade publications. Your business may also need a license to operate. For example, if you are starting a plumbing company, you may be required to get a contractor's license.

	Year 1	Year 2	Year 3
Chamber of Commerce Membership			
Business Organization Membership (i.e., National Homebuilders Association)			
Magazine/Newspaper Subscriptions			
Business License Fees			
Total			

Enter the year totals into the spreadsheet.

Travel

Does your business require you to travel to meet with customers? Will you travel locally, regionally, or nationally? What are the air travel, rental car, and hotel costs for this travel requirement? Note that the spreadsheet has a separate section for automobile expenses, where you enter costs such as gasoline or repairs. Use the automobile expense section for trips that will be taken in a company or personal vehicle.

	Year 1	Year 2	Year 3
Air Travel			
Rental Cars			
Hotel			
Other Please Specify:			
Total			

Enter the year totals into the spreadsheet.

Meals and Entertainment

Determine if you will be providing meals or taking your clients and vendors out for entertainment.

Keep in mind that the IRS allows you to take only a 50 percent deduction on meals and entertainment. It is not considered a 100 percent business expense. Although you enter the full amount on your profit-and-loss statement, your tax accountant will make the proper adjustments on your tax return at the end of the year.

	Year 1	Year 2	Year 3
Meals			
Entertainment			
Total			

Enter the year totals into the spreadsheet.

Automobile Expense

Determine if you will need one or more automobiles or trucks to operate your business. The cost to purchase each vehicle appears under "Assets" on your balance sheet, and the cost to operate the vehicles appears under automobile expense on the profit-and-loss statement.

	Year 1	Year 2	Year 3
Gasoline			
Oil Changes			
Car Washes			
Other (Repairs) Please Specify:			
Total			

Enter the annual totals into the spreadsheet.

Utilities and Telephone

Determine what your utilities and telephone costs will be for the first three years your business is operational. To arrive at this estimate, you will need to determine how many telephone lines and cell phones you need. You should also itemize Internet service and record these totals under this line item.

	Year 1	Year 2	Year 3
Electric			
Water			
Garbage			
Telephone			
Internet Service			
Other Please Specify:			
Total			

Enter the annual totals into the spreadsheet.

Auto Insurance

If you have business vehicles, you will need to carry insurance on them. If you increase the number of vehicles in years two and three, insurance expenses will increase as well. Certain vehicles may also cost more to insure than others. For example, if you have delivery trucks, the insurance will probably be more expensive than a mid-size car.

	Year 1	Year 2	Year 3
Vehicle #1			
Vehicle #2			
Vehicle #3			
Total			

Enter the annual totals into the spreadsheet.

Group Medical Insurance

You may want to carry medical, dental, or life insurance for your employees as a benefit and to increase employee retention.

	Year 1	Year 2	Year 3
Medical			
Dental			
Life			
Total			

Enter the annual totals into the spreadsheet.

Business Insurance

By law, businesses are required to carry workers' compensation insurance. Business liability insurance protects your business against accidents such as fire, flooding, burglary, etc. Business liability insurance is not required by law but by contract. For example, most landlords require you to carry business liability insurance, as do banks and governmental agencies with which you have a contract. Insurance and risk management are covered in more detail in the managing risk chapter 4.

	Year 1	Year 2	Year 3
Workers' Compensation			
Business Liability			
Total			

Enter the annual totals into the spreadsheet.

Worksheet

This is a scratch sheet for entering estimates and data that can then be entered in the spreadsheet.

	Year 1	Year 2	Year 3
Income			
Sales			
Total Income	0.00	0.00	0.00
Cost of Goods Sold			
Inventory Cost			
Production Payroll Cost			
Total COGS	0.00	0.00	0.00
Gross Profit	0.00	0.00	0.00
Expense			
Management Salaries			
Payroll Taxes	0.00	0.00	0.00
Outside Services			
Advertising and Promotion			
Rent			
Office Supplies			
Dues, Subscriptions, and Licenses			
Travel			
Meals and Entertainment			
Automobile Expense			
Utilities/Telephone			
Insurance Auto			
Insurance Group Medical			
Business Insurance			
Total Expense	0.00	0.00	0.00
Net Income	0.00	0.00	0.00

Appendix C: Useful Links

Listed below are website links that relate to each of the chapters. These websites are provided for your reference for more in-depth searches of the topic areas contained in this book.

Chapter 1 - The Plan

American Express Small Business	American Express offers business planning links and an area where you can post questions for a small business advisor.	www.americanexpress.com/en-us/business/trends-and-insights/
Business Plan Pro	This site offers tools on how to write a business plan including samples and tips to starting a business.	www.bplans.com
Sample Business Plans	These sites provide sample business plans and other valuable business management materials.	www.allbusiness.com
		www.inc.com
		www.bizmove.com/starting/m1e2.htm
SBA Business Planning	The SBA has several different links on writing and using your business plan.	www.sba.gov/business-guide/plan-your-business/write-your-business-plan

Chapter 2 - Choosing Your Business Structure

IRS Business Structures	The IRS provides a summary of tax considerations by business structure.	www.irs.gov/businesses/small-businesses-self-employed
North Carolina Secretary of State	The North Carolina Secretary of State Business Registration Division has information on business filings and forms.	www.sosnc.gov
SBA Legal Aspects	The SBA has several different links on forms of ownership and licenses.	www.sba.gov/business-guide/launch-your-business/apply-licenses-permits

Chapter 3 - Becoming a Licensed Contractor

North Carolina Licensing Board for General Contractors	The North Carolina Licensing Board for General Contractors regulates general contractor licensing. Their website has useful information on the licensing process and licensing laws and regulations.	nclbgc.org
PSI Exams Online	Licensing candidates can register online for exams and download the Candidate Information Bulletin.	candidate.psiexams.com

Chapter 4 – Managing Risk

Entrepreneur. Com	Entrepreneur.com has links to insurance resources.	www.entrepreneur.com/topic/insurance
North Carolina Industrial Commission	This site has information on the rules, practice and procedures involved with workers' compensation.	www.ic.nc.gov
Surety Information Office	This site has resources related to bonding, bank letters of credit and publishes the "Construction Project Owners Guide to Surety Bond Claims."	www.sio.org

Chapter 5 – Your Business Toolbox

North Carolina Department of Commerce	The North Carolina Department of Commerce website has information on starting and operating your business in North Carolina and a new business checklist.	www.nccommerce.com
North Carolina Community College, Economic and Workforce Development Division	The community college site has information on the Small Business Center Network that provides business counseling, training and resource centers.	www.nccommunitycolleges.edu/small-business-center-network
The North Carolina Institute	The North Carolina Institute (formerly the North Carolina Institute of Minority Economic Development) site has information on financial and technical assistance available to minority businesses.	theinstitutenc.org
SBA Special Interests	The SBA has several different links for women and minority entrepreneurs.	www.sba.gov/federal-contracting/contracting-assistance-programs/8a-business-development-program
Service Corps of Retired Executives (SCORE)	The SCORE website has useful links for small business and a listing of local SCORE centers.	www.score.org
Small Business Administration (SBA)	The SBA website has resources for small businesses and a link to the North Carolina District Office website.	www.sba.gov/offices/district/nc/charlotte
U.S. Minority Business Development Agency (MBDA)	The U.S. MBDA website has links on starting, managing, and financing your business.	www.mbda.gov
U.S. Department of Commerce, Economic Development Administration (EDA)	The U.S. Department of Commerce, EDA division, has information on funding opportunities and additional resources.	www.eda.gov

Chapter 6 – Marketing and Sales

Entrepreneur.com Marketing	Entrepreneur.com has several articles on small business marketing.	www.entrepreneur.com/topic/marketing
KnowThis.com Sample Marketing Plans	KnowThis.com has information on writing marketing plans and sample plans.	www.knowthis.com/how-to-write-a-marketing-plan/marketing-plan-intro/

| **SBA Marketing Basics** | The SBA has several different links on marketing research and writing your marketing plan. | www.sba.gov/business-guide/manage-your-business/marketing-sales |

Chapter 7 – Bidding and Estimating

| **U.S. Department of Labor, Bureau of Labor Statistics** | The Bureau of Labor Statistics site has helpful information on wages, earnings, and business costs. | www.bls.gov |
| **DMOZ.com Estimating Software** | This site gives a comprehensive list of estimating software. | dmoztools.net/Business/Construction_and_Maintenance/Estimating/ |

Chapter 8 – Contract Management

B4UBuild.com	B4UBuild.com has articles on contract law for residential builders.	www.b4ubuild.com
Free Advice.com	FreeAdvice.com has links to different contract topics.	www.law.freeadvice.com/general_practice/contract_law
Nolo.com	Nolo.com has articles about contract law.	www.nolo.com

Chapter 9 – Scheduling and Project Management

| **Construction place.com** | Constructionplace.com has an informative glossary of terms focused on construction management. | www.constructionplace.com/Glossary |
| **FreeDownload Center.com** | FreeDownloadCenter.com has project management software downloads. | www.freedownloadscenter.com/Business/Project_Management |

Chapter 10 – Customer Relations

| **Microsoft Small Business Center** | The Microsoft site offers helpful customer relations links | business.microsoft.com |
| **Quicken Small Business Center** | The Quicken site offers articles on building excellent customer relations. | www.quicken.com/personal-finance/home-business |

Chapter 11 – Employee Management

| **DOL Employment Compliance Guide** | The Department of Labor has several links on employment law compliance, a compliance guide, and a compliance advisor. | webapps.dol.gov/elaws/elg/index.htm webapps.dol.gov/elaws/ |

IRS Forms	This site contains IRS forms, such as the W-4, that you can download.	www.irs.gov/forms-instructions
North Carolina Department of Labor (DOL)	The North Carolina DOL site gives information on employment laws and resources for employers	www.labor.nc.gov
North Carolina Division of Employment Security	The North Carolina Division of Employment Security website gives information on the state unemployment program.	des.nc.gov
North Carolina Industrial Commission	The North Carolina Industrial Commission website provides information on the state workers' compensation program.	www.ic.nc.gov
North Carolina New Hire Reporting	The North Carolina new hire link has information on reporting requirements for new hires.	www.ncnewhires.com
U.S. Citizenship and Immigration Services	The I-9 form can be downloaded from this site.	www.uscis.gov
U.S. Equal Employment Opportunity Commission (EEOC)	The EEOC website has information about the Americans with Disabilities Act (ADA).	www.eeoc.gov

Chapter 12 – Jobsite Safety and Environmental Factors

Common Ground Alliance (CGA)	The Common Ground Alliance is available by calling 811. CGA can connect contractors to One Call Centers to locate underground utilities.	www.call811.com
Construction Industry Compliance Center	The Construction Industry Compliance Center website has information available on environmental regulations including hazardous and non-hazardous waste.	www.cicacenter.org
Energy Star	The Energy Star website has eco-friendly resources for home improvement and residential and commercial construction.	www.energystar.gov
Environmental Protection Agency	The Environmental Protection Agency provides a publication called *Managing Your Environmental Responsibilities*.	archive.epa.gov/compliance/resources/publications/assistance/sectors/web/html/
Environmental Protection Agency-Asbestos-Containing Materials List	The Environmental Protection Agency website provides a list of asbestos-containing materials.	www.epa.gov/asbestos
Environmental Protection Agency-Green Building	The Environmental Protection Agency website provides information on components of green building, national, state and local funding opportunities, and publications on various environmental topics.	www.epa.gov/greenbuilding
Environmental Protection Agency: Lead in Paint, Dust, and Soil	The Environmental Protection Agency website provides information on lead hazards.	www.epa.gov/lead

North Carolina Department of Environmental Quality (NCDEQ)	The NCDEQ website has information on environmental regulations and permits.	deq.nc.gov
North Carolina Industrial Commission-Health Hazards Control Unit	The Health Hazards Control Unit website has information on asbestos regulations and permits.	epi.dph.ncdhhs.gov/asbestos/ahmp.html
North Carolina Department of Labor, Occupational Health and Safety Division	The Occupational Health and Safety Division is responsible for assisting employers in complying with federal OSHA requirements.	www.labor.nc.gov/safety-and-health/occupational-safety-and-health
OSHA	The OSHA website has links regarding safety on the job and safety laws and programs.	www.osha.gov
OSHA Compliance Assistance for Construction	The OSHA website has a page with numerous construction compliance assistance links.	www.osha.gov/doc
U.S. Green Building Council	The USGBC is committed to transforming the way buildings are designed, constructed, and operated through LEED—the top third-party verification system for sustainable structures around the world.	www.usgbc.org.

Chapter 13 - Working with Subcontractors

IRS Publication 1779	This IRS publication provides criteria to determine employee versus independent contractor status.	www.irs.gov/pub/irs-pdf/p1779.pdf

Chapter 14 - Financial Management

IRS Publication 15: Circular E	Circular E, used for federal income tax withholding, is available on the IRS website.	www.irs.gov/publications/p15
SBA Balance Sheet Template	The SBA has a balance sheet template that you can customize.	www.sba.gov/sites/default/files/balance_sheet.xlt
SBA Income Statement Template	The SBA has an income statement template that you can customize.	www.sba.gov/sites/default/files/income_statement.xlt
SBA Financing Basics	The SBA has several different links on financing and financial statements.	www.sba.gov/category/navigation-structure/starting-managing-business/starting-business/preparing-your-finances
Social Security Administration	The Social Security Administration website has information on the current social security tax rate.	www.ssa.gov

Chapter 15 – Tax Basics

How to Apply for an EIN	There are several ways to apply for an EIN. The IRS outlines the procedure on their website.	www.irs.gov/businesses/small-businesses-self-employed/how-to-apply-for-an-ein
IRS Service	The IRS site has tax forms, publications, and useful information for small businesses.	www.irs.gov
North Carolina Department of Revenue	The North Carolina Department of Revenue site provides helpful information on state taxes.	www.ncdor.gov
Tax Basics	The SBA has several different links on federal, state, and local taxes.	www.sba.gov/business-guide/manage-your-business/pay-taxes

Chapter 16 – North Carolina Mechanics' Lien Law

North Carolina General Assembly	You can search for legislation including mechanics' lien law on the North Carolina General Assembly site.	www.ncleg.gov

Trade Links

American Institute of Architects (AIA)	This site has information about the organization and contract documents for purchase.	www.aia.org
American National Standards Institute (ANSI)	The ANSI website has information on membership, accreditation services, and educational resources.	www.ansi.org
American Society of Plumbing Engineers (ASPE)	The ASPE website has information on membership, certifications, and useful resources.	www.aspe.org
American Society of Civil Engineers (ASCE)	The ASCE website has information on membership, conferences, publications, and continuing education.	www.asce.org
American Subcontractors Association (ASA)	This site has information for subcontractors and suppliers in the construction industry.	www.asaonline.com
American Water Works Association (AWWA)	The AWWA website has information on membership, accreditation services, and educational resources.	www.awwa.org

Associated Builders and Contractors (ABC)	The ABC website has information on membership, training, a list of contractors, and links to business development, safety, insurance, and legal resources.	www.abc.org
Associated General Contractors (AGC)	This site has information for construction contractors and industry related companies.	www.agc.org
International Association of Plumbing and Mechanical Officials (IAPMO)	The IAPMO website has information on membership, certification, and educational resources.	www.iapmo.org
National Association of Home Builders (NAHB)	This site is for people interested in homebuilding and the industry.	www.nahb.org
National Association of the Remodeling Industry (NARI)	This site is for people interested in the remodeling industry.	www.nari.org
National Association of State Contractor Licensing Agencies (NASCLA)	This site contains useful information about state licensing agencies and information about the organization.	www.nascla.org
National Association of Women in Construction (NAWIC)	This site has information for women in the construction industry.	www.nawic.org
National Electrical Contractors Association (NECA)	The NECA website has information on membership, codes and standards, industry news, and educational resources.	www.necanet.org
North Carolina Home Builders Association	The NCHBA website contains important information on state-specific building codes, councils, careers, general guidance, and builders' events.	www.nchba.org
Plumbing, Heating and Cooling Contractors Association (PHCC)	The PHCC website has information on membership, educational resources, and a list of contractors.	www.phccweb.org
Water Quality Association (WQA)	The WQA website has information on membership, certifications, educational resources, and a list of contractors.	www.wqa.org

Appendix D: New Business Checklist

The following is a checklist of steps to starting your business. These steps provide a general overview, but you should check with a professional to determine the legal, financial, and tax obligations specific to your business.

Complete Your Business Plan (covered in Chapter 1 and Appendix B)

✓ Establish your business vision and mission.

✓ Determine your management structure.

✓ Identify your facility requirements and location.

✓ Research your market and identify your competitors.

✓ Establish a marketing plan and expansion goals.

✓ Determine your break-even point and your financial goals.

Choose Your Form of Organization (covered in Chapter 2)

✓ Hire a lawyer to prepare organization documents and give legal advice on business issues.

✓ Choose a form of organization (i.e., sole proprietorship, partnership, or corporation).

✓ Prepare and file business organization documents (i.e., Partnership Agreement, Articles of Organization, Articles of Incorporation, etc.).

✓ Register any fictitious names with the proper state and local municipalities.

✓ Obtain the required business licenses from state and local municipalities.

Set Up Business Finances

✓ Select an accountant to prepare financial documents and give business financial advice.

✓ Select a banker and open a business checking account.

✓ Apply for business loans (if applicable).

✓ Apply for business credit cards and establish a line of credit.

Obtain the Proper Contractor's Licensure (covered in Chapter 3)

✓ Obtain the proper application materials and review the process for obtaining licensure.

✓ Complete application materials with required documentation.

✓ Understand the requirements for maintaining proper licensure.

Assess Your Areas of Risk and Obtain the Proper Insurance Coverage (covered in Chapter 4)

✓ Select an insurance company and agent to help assess your risk and coverage requirements.

✓ Obtain business insurance (liability, workers' compensation, automobile, etc.).

✓ Obtain required bonds.

✓ Obtain unemployment insurance registration materials from the proper state agency.

Obtain the Proper Tax Documentation (covered in Chapter 15)

✓   Apply for a federal employer identification number (if applicable).

✓   Obtain a state employer identification number (if applicable).

✓   Obtain the proper federal and state tax forms (i.e., sales and use tax, withholding tax, etc.).

Appendix E: General Contractor

LIMITATIONS

LIMITED – Up to $500,000.00 on any single project

INTERMEDIATE – Up to $1,000,000.00 on any single project

UNLIMITED – Not restricted as to the value of any single project

CLASSIFICATIONS

Building
Residential
Highway
Public Utilities
Specialty
Unclassified – (includes all of the above classifications)

EXAMINATIONS and LICENSURE (N.C. G.S. 87-10)

A qualifying examination is not an occupational license, and does not grant the holder of such examination the authority to practice general contracting. Individuals may be licensed by their personal examinations or the examination of a responsible managing employee. Partnerships and corporations are licensed by examination of a responsible managing officer or member of the personnel of the applicant. If the qualifying party leaves, however, the licensee must replace the qualifying party within ninety (90) days or the license becomes invalid.

Licensees should not allow unlicensed persons, firms or corporations to use the general contractor's license with the licensee's permission. Although licensed general contractors may have an ownership interest in an unlicensed entity, the unlicensed contractor may not use a general contractor's license for any reason. Violators of the general contractor laws and regulations may be disciplined by the Licensing Board for General Contractors for allowing the use of a license by an unlicensed person or other entities. Appropriate sanctions may include suspension or revocation of license.

Licenses must be renewed annually by December 31 for the following year, or the license expires. If a license is not renewed within sixty (60) days following expiration, then it becomes "invalid," and the contractor becomes, in effect, unlicensed. Reexamination is required if a license is not renewed for four (4) years following expiration. After a lapse of four years, no renewal shall be effected and all requirements for a new license must be fulfilled, in accordance with G.S. 87-10.

Published September 2019

AN ACT TO REGULATE THE
PRACTICE OF GENERAL CONTRACTING

§87-1.   "General contractor" defined; exceptions.

(a) For the purpose of this Article any person or firm or corporation who for a fixed price, commission, fee, or wage, undertakes to bid upon or to construct or who undertakes to superintend or manage, on his own behalf or for any person, firm, or corporation that is not licensed as a general contractor pursuant to this Article, the construction of any building, highway, public utilities, grading or any improvement or structure where the cost of the undertaking is thirty thousand dollars ($30,000) or more, or undertakes to erect a North Carolina labeled manufactured modular building meeting the North Carolina State Building Code, shall be deemed to be a "general contractor" engaged in the business of general contracting in the State of North Carolina.

(b) This section shall not apply to the following:

(1) Persons, firms, or corporations furnishing or erecting industrial equipment, power plant equipment, radial brick chimneys, and monuments.

(2) Any person, firm, or corporation who constructs or alters a building on land owned by that person, firm, or corporation provided (i) the building is intended solely for occupancy by that person and his family, firm, or corporation after completion; and (ii) the person, firm, or corporation complies with G.S. 87-14. If the building is not occupied solely by the person and his family, firm, or corporation for at least 12 months following completion, it shall be presumed that the person, firm, or corporation did not intend the building solely for occupancy by that person and his family, firm, or corporation.

(3) Any person engaged in the business of farming who constructs or alters a building on land owned by that person and used in the business of farming, when the building is intended for use by that person after completion.

§87-1.1   Exception for licensees under Article 2 or 4.

G.S. 87-1 shall not apply to a licensee under Article 2 or 4 of this Chapter of the General Statutes, G.S. 87-43 shall not apply to a licensee under Article 2 of this Chapter of the General Statutes, and G.S. 87-21(a)(5) shall not apply to a licensee under Article 4 of this Chapter of the General Statutes when the licensee is bidding and contracting directly with the owner of a public building project if: (i) a licensed general contractor performs all work that falls within the classifications in G.S. 87-10(b) and the State Licensing Board of General Contractor's rules; and (ii) the total amount of the general contracting work so classified does not exceed a percentage of the total bid price pursuant to rules established by the Board; and (iii) a licensee with the appropriate license under Article 2 or Article 4 of this Chapter performs all work that falls within the classifications in Article 2 and Article 4 of this Chapter.

§87-1.2   Exception for specified Department of Transportation contractors.

The letting of contracts for the types of projects specified in G.S. 136-28.14 shall not be subject to the licensing requirement of this Article.

§87-2.   Licensing Board; organization.

There is created the State Licensing Board for General Contractors consisting of nine members appointed by the Governor for staggered five-year terms. Five of the members shall be general contractors, one member shall be a registered engineer who practices structural engineering, and three shall be public members. Of the general contractor members, one shall have as the larger part of his business the construction of highways; one shall have as the larger part of his business the construction of public utilities; one shall have as the larger part of his business the construction of buildings; and two shall have as a larger part of their businesses the construction of residences, one of whom shall be the holder of an unlimited general contractor's license. The public members shall have no ties with the construction industry and shall represent the interests of the public at large. Members shall serve until the expiration of their respective terms and until their successors are appointed and qualified. Vacancies occurring during a term shall be filled by appointment of the Governor for the remainder of the unexpired term. The Governor may remove any member of the Board for misconduct, incompetency, or neglect of duty. No Board member shall serve more than two complete consecutive terms.

§87-3. Members of the Board to take oath.

Each member of the Board shall, before entering upon the discharge of the duties of his office, take and file with the Secretary of State an oath in writing to properly perform the duties of his office as a member of said Board and to uphold the Constitution of North Carolina and the Constitution of the United States.

§87-4. First meeting of the Board; officers; secretary-treasurer and assistants.

The said Board shall, within 30 days after its appointment by the Governor, meet in the City of Raleigh, at a time and place to be designated by the Governor, and organize by electing a chairman, a vice-chairman, and a secretary-treasurer, each to serve for one year. Said Board shall have power to make such bylaws, rules and regulations as it shall deem best, provided the same are not in conflict with the laws of North Carolina. The secretary-treasurer shall give bond in such sum as the Board shall determine, with such security as shall be approved by the Board, said bond to be conditioned for the faithful performance of the duties of his office and for the faithful accounting of all moneys and other property as shall come into his hands. The secretary-treasurer need not be a member of the Board, and the Board is hereby authorized to employ a full-time secretary-treasurer, and such other assistants and make such other expenditures as may be necessary to the proper carrying out of the provisions of this Article. Payment of compensation and reimbursement of expenses of Board members shall be governed by G.S. 93B-5.

§87-5. Seal of the Board

The Board shall adopt a seal for its own use. The seal shall have the words "North Carolina Licensing Board for General Contractors" and the secretary shall have charge, care and custody thereof.

§87-6. Meetings; notice; quorum.

The Board shall meet twice each year, once in April and once in October, for the purpose of transacting such business as may properly come before it. At the April meeting in each year the Board shall elect officers. Special meetings may be held at such times as the Board may provide in the bylaws it shall adopt. Due notice of each meeting and the time and place thereof shall be given to each member in such manner as the bylaws may provide. Five members of the Board shall constitute a quorum.

§87-7. Records of Board; disposition of funds.

The secretary-treasurer shall keep a record of the proceedings of the said Board and shall receive and account for all moneys derived from the operation of this Article. Any funds remaining in the hands of the secretary-treasurer to the credit of the Board after the expenses of the Board for the current year have been paid shall be paid over to the Greater University of North Carolina for the use of the School of Engineering through the North Carolina Engineering Foundation. The Board has the right, however, to retain at least ten percent (10%) of the total expense it incurs for a year's operation to meet any emergency that may arise. As an expense of the Board, said Board is authorized to expend such funds as it deems necessary to provide retirement and disability compensation for its employees.

§87-8.   Records; roster of licensed contractors; report to Governor.

The secretary-treasurer shall keep a record of the proceedings of the Board and a register of all applicants for license showing for each the date of application, name, qualifications, place of business, place of residence, and whether license was granted or refused. The books and register of this Board shall be prima facie evidence of all matters recorded therein. A roster showing the names and places of business and of residence of all licensed general contractors shall be prepared by the secretary of the Board during the month of March of each year; the roster shall be printed by the Board out of funds of the Board as provided in G.S. 87-7, with copies being made available to contractors and members of the public, at cost, upon request, or furnished without cost, as directed by the Board. On or before the last day of March of each year the Board shall submit to the Governor a report of its transactions for the preceding year, and shall file with the Secretary of State a copy of the report, together with a complete statement of the receipts and expenditures of the Board, attested by the affidavits of the chairman and the secretary, and a copy of the roster of licensed general contractors.

§87-9.   Compliance with Federal Highway Act, etc.; contracts financed by federal road funds; contracts concerning water or waste water systems.

Nothing in this Article shall operate to prevent the Department of Transportation from complying with any act of Congress and any rules and regulations pursuant thereto for carrying out the provisions of the Federal Highway Act, or shall apply to any person, firm or corporation proposing to submit a bid or enter into contract for any work to be financed in whole or in part with federal aid road funds in such a manner as will conflict with any act of Congress or any such rules and regulations promulgated pursuant thereto.

Neither shall anything in this Article prevent the State of North Carolina or any of its political subdivisions or their contractors from complying with any act of Congress and any rules and regulations promulgated pursuant thereto for carrying out the provisions of any federal program to assist in the planning, financing, or construction of drinking water or waste water processing, collection, and disposal systems and facilities.

§87-9.1.   Ownership of real property: equipment; liability insurance.

(a) The Board shall have the power to acquire, hold, rent, encumber, alienate, and otherwise deal with real property in the same manner as a private person or corporation, subject only to approval of the Governor and the Council of State as to the acquisition, rental, encumbering, leasing, and sale of real property. Collateral pledged by the Board for an encumbrance is limited to the assets, income, and revenues of the Board.

(b) The Board may purchase or rent equipment and supplies and purchase liability insurance or other insurance to cover the activities of the Board, its operations, or its employees.

§87-10.   Application for license; examination; certificate; renewal.

(a) Anyone seeking to be licensed as a general contractor in this State shall submit an application. Before being entitled to an examination. An applicant shall:

(1)   Be at least 18 years of age.

(2)   Possess good moral character as determined by the Board.

(3)   Provide evidence of financial responsibility as determined by the Board.

(4)   Submit the appropriate application fee.

(a1) The Board shall require an applicant to pay the Board or a provider contracted by the Board an examination fee not to exceed one hundred ($100.00). In addition, the Board shall require an applicant to pay the Board a fee not to exceed one hundred twenty-five dollars ($125.00) if the application is for an unlimited license, one hundred dollars ($100.00) if the application is for an intermediate license, or seventy-five dollars ($75.00) if the application is for a limited license. The fees accompanying any application or examination shall be nonrefundable. The holder of an unlimited license shall be entitled to act as general contractor without restriction as to value of any single project; the holder of an intermediate license shall be entitled to act as general contractor for any single project with a value of up to one million dollars ($1,000,000), excluding the cost of land and any ancillary costs to improve the land: the holder of a limited license shall be entitled to act as general contractor for any single project with a value of up to five hundred thousand dollars ($500.000), excluding the cost of land and any ancillary costs to improve the land. The license certificate shall be classified in accordance with this section.

(b) An applicant shall identify an individual who has successfully passed an examination approved by the Board who, for purposes of this section, shall be known as the "qualifier" or the "qualifying party" of the applicant. If the qualifier or the qualifying party seeks to take an examination the examination shall establish (i) the ability of the applicant to make a practical application of the applicant's knowledge of the profession of contracting; (ii) the qualifications of the applicant in reading plans and specifications, knowledge of relevant matters contained in the North Carolina State Building Code, knowledge of estimating costs, construction , ethics, and other similar matters pertaining to the contracting business; (iii) the knowledge of the applicant as to the responsibilities of a contractor to the public and of the requirements of the laws of the State of North Carolina relating to contractors, construction, and liens; and (iv) the applicant's knowledge of requirements of the Sedimentation Pollution Control Act of 1973, Article 4 of Chapter 113A of the General Statutes, and the rules adopted pursuant to that Article. If the qualifier or qualifying party passes the examination, upon review of the application and all relevant information, the Board shall issue a license to the applicant to engage in general contracting in the State of North Carolina, which may be limited as follows:

(1) Building contractor, which shall include private, public, commercial, industrial and residential buildings of all types.

(1a) Residential contractor, which shall include any general contractor constructing only residences which are required to conform to the residential building code adopted by the Building Code Council pursuant to G.S. 143-138.

(2) Highway contractor.

(3) Public utilities contractors, which shall include those whose operations are the performance of construction work on the following subclassifications of facilities:

a. Water and sewer mains, water service lines, and house and building sewer lines as defined in the North Carolina State Building Code, and water storage tanks, lift stations, pumping stations, and appurtenances to water storage tanks, lift stations, and pumping stations.

b. Water and wastewater treatment facilities and appurtenances thereto.

c. Electrical power transmission facilities, and primary and secondary distribution facilities ahead of the point of delivery of electric service to the customer.

      d.   Public communication distribution facilities.

      e.   Natural gas and other petroleum products distribution facilities; provided the General Contractors Licensing Board may issue license to a public utilities contractor limited to any of the above subclassifications for which the general contractor qualifies.

  (4) Specialty contractor, which shall include those whose operations as such are the performance of construction work requiring special skill and involving the use of specialized building trades or crafts, but which shall not include any operations now or hereafter under the jurisdiction, for the issuance of license by any board or commission pursuant to the laws of the State of North Carolina.

(b1) Public utilities contractors constructing house and building sewer lines as provided in sub-subdivision a. of subdivision (3) of subsection (b) of this section shall, at the junction of the public sewer line and the house or building sewer line, install as an extension of the public sewer line a cleanout at or near the property line that terminates at or above the finished grade. Public utilities contractors constructing water service lines as provided in sub-subdivision a. of subdivision (3) of subsection (b) of this section shall terminate the water service lines at a valve, box, or meter at which the facilities from the building may be connected. Public utilities contractors constructing fire service mains for connection to fire sprinkler systems shall terminate those lines at a flange, cap, plug, or valve inside the building one foot above the finished floor. All fire service mains shall comply with the NFPA standards for fire service mains as incorporated into and made applicable by Volume V of the North Carolina Building Code.

(c) If an applicant is an individual, examination may be taken by his personal appearance for examination, or by the appearance for examination of one or more of his responsible managing employees. If an applicant is a copartnership, a corporation, or any other combination or organization, the examination may be taken by one or more of the responsible managing officers or members of the personnel of the applicant.

(c1) If the qualifier or qualifying party shall cease to be connected with the licensee, then the license shall remain in full force and effect for a period of 90 days. After 90 days, the license shall be invalidated, however the licensee shall be entitled to return to active status pursuant to all relevant statutes and rules promulgated by the Board. However, during the 90-day period described in this subsection, the licensee shall not bid on or undertake any additional contracts from the time such qualifier or qualifying part v ceased to be connected with the licensee until the license is reinstated as provided in this Article.

(d) The Board may require a new application if a qualifier or qualifying party requests to take an examination a third or subsequent time.

(e) A license shall expire on the first day of January following its issuance or renewal and shall become invalid 60 days from that date unless renewed, subject to the approval of the Board. Renewal applications shall be submitted with a fee not to exceed one hundred twenty-five dollars ($125.00) for an unlimited license, one hundred dollars ($100.00) for an intermediate license, and seventy-five dollars ($75.00) for a limited license. Renewal applications shall be accompanied by evidence of continued financial responsibility and evidence of satisfactory completion of continuing education as required by G.S. 87-10.2. Renewal applications received by the Board on or after the first day of January shall be accompanied by a late payment of ten dollars ($10.00) for each month or part after January.

(f) After a license has been invalid for four years, a licensee shall not be permitted to renew the license, and the license shall be deemed archived. If a licensee wishes to be relicensed subsequent to the archival of the license, the licensee shall fulfill all requirements of a new applicant as set forth in this section. Archived license numbers shall not be renewed.

§87-10.1. Licensing of nonresidents.

(a) Definitions. The following definitions apply in this section:

(1) Delinquent income tax debt. The amount of income tax due as stated in a final notice of assessment issued to a taxpayer by the Secretary of Revenue when the taxpayer no longer has the right to contest the amount.

(2) Foreign corporation—Defined in G.S. 55 1-40.

(3) Foreign entity—A foreign corporation, a foreign limited liability company, or a foreign partnership.

(4) Foreign limited liability company—Defined in G.S. 57C 1-03.

(5) Foreign partnership—Either of the following that does not have a permanent place of business in this State:

a. A foreign limited partnership as defined in G.S. 59-102.

b. A general partnership formed under the laws of a jurisdiction other than this State.

(b) Licensing. The Board shall not issue a certificate of license for a foreign corporation unless the corporation has obtained a certificate of authority from the Secretary of State pursuant to Article 15 of Chapter 55 of the General Statutes. The Board shall not issue a certificate of license for a foreign limited liability company unless the company has obtained a certificate of authority from the Secretary of State pursuant to Article 7 of Chapter 57C of the General Statutes.

(c) Information. Upon request, the Board shall provide the Secretary of Revenue on an annual basis the name, address, and tax identification number of every nonresident individual and foreign entity licensed by the Board. The information shall be provided in the format required by the Secretary of Revenue.

(d) Delinquents. If the Secretary of Revenue determines that any nonresident individual or foreign corporation licensed by the Board, a member of any foreign limited liability company licensed by the Board, or a partner in any foreign partnership licensed by the Board, owes a delinquent income tax debt, the Secretary of Revenue may notify the Board of these nonresident individuals and foreign entities and instruct the Board not to renew their certificates of license. The Board shall not renew the certificate of license of such nonresident individual or foreign entity identified by the Secretary of Revenue unless the Board receives a written statement from the Secretary that the debt either has been paid or is being paid pursuant to an installment agreement.

§87-10.2. Continuing Education.

(a) As a condition of license renewal, at least one qualifier or qualifying party of a licensee holding a building contractor, residential contractor, or unclassified contractor license classification shall complete, on an annual basis, eight hours of continuing education approved in accordance with this section. Where an entity holding a building contractor, residential contractor, or unclassified contractor license classification has multiple qualifiers or qualifying parties, at least one qualifier or qualifying party of the licensee shall complete this requirement for the license to remain valid.

(b) Of the eight hours of annual continuing education required by this section, two hours shall be a mandatory course approved by the Board and the remaining six hours shall be elective courses approved by the Board. Each qualifier or qualifying party shall complete the mandatory course each year. Each qualifier or qualifying party may accumulate and carry forward up to four hours of elective course credit to the next calendar year. The Board shall evaluate and approve:

(1)   The content of continuing education courses.

(2)   Accreditation of continuing education sponsors and programs.

(3)   Computation of credit.

(4)   General compliance procedures.

(c) All prospective providers of the mandatory course shall attend a training program established, approved, and administered by the Board to ensure the quality and consistency of mandatory course information. All prospective providers of elective courses shall submit course materials and instructor qualifications for Board evaluation, approval, and accreditation.

(d) Continuing education credit hours may only be given for courses that are taught live by an instructor approved by the Board. To receive credit, a qualifier or qualifying party shall attend and view the live teaching of the course and shall certify this requirement in the manner required by the Board. Only the period of live instruction shall apply to the satisfaction of the continuing education requirement established by this section. Continuing education providers shall certify the attendance of course attendees and shall transmit the qualifier or qualifying party's certification to the Board. For the purposes of this subsection, "live instruction" includes credit hours presented by video or by Internet transmission of a previously recorded and approved presentation by an approved instructor or instructors provided the presentation is either proctored by the approved sponsor or contains safeguards as approved by the Board that allow the approved sponsor to certify that the qualifier or qualifying party has viewed the presentation. The Board shall implement procedures to ensure that qualifiers and qualifying parties may satisfy all of the continuing education requirements of this section through approved courses offered by approved providers by Internet transmission.

(e) False certification of attendance shall be grounds for the suspension or revocation of the course provider's privilege to provide courses in this State. The Board may take disciplinary action against any licensee on account of a false certification of attendance by that licensee's qualifier or qualifying party at any continuing education course.

(f) The Board shall maintain and distribute to licensees and qualifiers, as appropriate, records of the educational coursework successfully completed by each qualifier or qualifying party, including the subject matter and the number of hours of each course.

(g) Continuing education requirements shall begin on January 1 of any calendar year and shall be completed by November 30 of that calendar year. The Board shall establish a 90-day grace period following November 30 of each calendar year for any qualifier or qualifying party who has failed to complete the continuing education requirement. Failure of the qualifier or qualifying party of the entity holding a building contractor, residential contractor, or unclassified contractor license classification to satisfy the annual continuing education requirement by the expiration of the grace period shall result in the license of the entity being invalidated until such time that continuing education and all other licensing requirements have been met.

(h) Any licensee who chooses not to complete the annual continuing education as required by this section may request that the Board place the licensee's license in an inactive status and the license shall become invalid. However, in order for the license to be maintained as inactive, the licensee shall pay the same annual renewal fee paid by active licensees. Should the licensee desire to return to active status, the qualifier or qualifying party of the licensee shall satisfactorily complete the following continuing education requirements prior to seeking reinstatement:

(1)   If the licensee seeks reinstatement during the first two years after the license becomes inactive, the qualifier or qualifying party shall complete eight hours of continuing education, including the mandatory course offered during the year of reinstatement.

(2)   If the licensee seeks reinstatement more than two years after the license becomes inactive, the qualifier or qualifying party shall complete 16 hours of continuing education, including the mandatory course offered during the year of reinstatement.

(i) The Board shall establish nonrefundable fees for the purpose of administering the continuing education program. The Board may charge the sponsor of a proposed course a nonrefundable fee not to exceed twenty-five dollars ($25.00) per credit hour for the initial review of the course and a nonrefundable fee of twelve dollars and fifty cents ($12.50) per credit hour for the annual renewal of a course previously approved. The Board shall require an approved course provider to pay a fee, not to exceed five dollars ($5.00) per credit hour per qualifier or qualifying party, for each qualifier or qualifying party completing an approved continuing education course conducted by that provider.

(j) The Board may modify the continuing education requirements set forth in this Article in cases of certified illness or undue hardship as provided for in the rules of the Board.

(k) The Board may adopt rules to implement the requirements of this section.

§87-11.   Revocation of license; charges of fraud, negligence, incompetency, etc.; hearing thereon; reissuance of certificate.

(a) The Board shall have the power to refuse to issue or renew or revoke, suspend, or restrict a certificate of license or to issue a reprimand or take other disciplinary action if a general contractor licensed under this Article is found guilty of any fraud or deceit in obtaining a license, or gross negligence, incompetency, or misconduct in the practice of his or her profession, or willful violation of any provision of this Article. The Board shall also have the power to revoke, suspend, or otherwise restrict the ability of any person to act as a qualifying party for a license to practice general contracting, as provided in G.S.. 87-10(c), for any copartnership, corporation or any other organization or combination, if that person committed any act in violation of the provisions of this section and the Board may take disciplinary action against the individual license held by that person.

(a1) Any person may prefer charges of fraud, deceit, negligence, or misconduct against any general contractor licensed under this Article. The charges shall be in writing and sworn to by the complainant and submitted to the Board. The charges, unless dismissed without hearing by the Board as unfounded or trivial, shall be heard and determined by the Board in accordance with the provisions of Chapter 150B of the General Statutes.

(b) The Board shall adopt and publish guidelines, consistent with the provisions of this Article, governing the suspension and revocation of licenses.

(c) The Board shall establish and maintain a system whereby detailed records are kept regarding complaints against each licensee. This record shall include, for each licensee, the date and nature of each complaint, investigatory action taken by the Board, any findings by the Board, and the disposition of the matter.

(d) The Board may reissue a license to any person, firm, or corporation whose license has been revoked: Provided, five or more members of the Board vote in favor of such reissuance for reasons the Board may deem sufficient.

The Board shall immediately notify the Secretary of State of its findings in the case of the revocation of a license or of the reissuance of a revoked license.

A certificate of license to replace any certificate lost, destroyed or mutilated may be issued subject to the rules and regulations of the Board.

(e) The Board shall be entitled to recover its reasonable administrative costs associated with the investigation and prosecution of a violation of this Article or rules or regulations of the Board up to a maximum of five thousand dollars ($5,000) for any licensee or qualifying party found to have committed any of the following:

(1)   Fraud or deceit in obtaining a license.

(2)   Gross negligence, incompetency, or misconduct in the practice of general contracting.

(3)   Willful violation of any provision of this Article.

§87-12. Certificate evidence of license.
The issuance of a certificate of license or limited license by this Board shall be evidence that the person, firm, or corporation named therein is entitled to all the rights and privileges of a licensed or limited licensed general contractor while said license remains unrevoked or unexpired. A licensed general contractor holding a license which qualifies him for work as described in G.S. 87-10 shall be authorized to perform the said work without any additional occupational license, notwithstanding the provisions of any other occupational licensing statute. A license issued by another occupational licensing board having jurisdiction over any work described in G.S. 87-10 shall qualify such licensee to perform the work for which the license qualifies him without obtaining the license from the General Contractors Licensing Board. Nothing contained herein shall operate to relieve any general contractor from the necessity of compliance with other provisions of the law requiring building permits and construction in accordance with appropriate provisions of the North Carolina State Building Code.

§87-13. Unauthorized practice of contracting; impersonating contractor; false certificate; giving false evidence to Board; penalties.
Any person, firm, or corporation not being duly authorized who shall contract for or bid upon the construction of any of the projects or works enumerated in G.S. 87-1, without having first complied with the provisions hereof, or who shall attempt to practice general contracting in the State, except as provided for in this Article, and any person, firm, or corporation presenting or attempting to file as his own the licensed certificate of another or who shall give false or forged evidence of any kind to the Board or to any member thereof in maintaining a certificate of license or who falsely shall impersonate another or who shall use an expired or revoked certificate of license, or who falsely claims or suggests in connection with any business activities regulated by the Board that a person, firm, or corporation is licensed under this Chapter, and any architect or engineer who recommends to any project owner the award of a contract to anyone not properly licensed under this Article, shall be deemed guilty of a Class 2 misdemeanor. And the Board may, in its discretion, use its funds to defray the expense, legal or otherwise, in the prosecution of any violations of this Article. No architect or engineer shall be guilty of

a violation of this section if his recommendation to award a contract is made in reliance upon current written information received by him from the appropriate Contractor Licensing Board of this State which information erroneously indicates that the contractor being recommended for contract award is properly licensed.

§87-13.1. Board may seek injunctive relief.

Whenever the Board determines that any person, firm or corporation has violated or is violating any of the provisions of this Article or rules and regulations of the Board promulgated under this Article, the Board may apply to the superior court for a restraining order and injunction to restrain the violation; and the superior courts have jurisdiction to grant the requested relief, irrespective of whether or not criminal prosecution has been instituted or administrative sanctions imposed by reason of the violation. The court may award the Board its reasonable costs associated with the investigation and prosecution of the violation.

§87-14. Regulations as to issue of building permits.

(a) Any person, firm, or corporation, upon making application to the building inspector or such other authority of any incorporated city, town, or county in North Carolina charged with the duty of issuing building or other permits for the construction of any building, highway, sewer, grading, or any improvement or structure where the cost thereof is to be thirty thousand dollars ($30,000) or more, shall, before being entitled to the issuance of a permit, satisfy the following:

(1) Furnish satisfactory proof to the inspector or authority that the person seeking the permit or another person contracting to superintend or manage the construction is duly licensed under the terms of this Article to carry out or superintend the construction or is exempt from licensure under G.S. 87-1(b). If an applicant claims an exemption from licensure pursuant to G.S.87-1(b)(2), the applicant for the building permit shall execute a verified affidavit attesting to the following:

a. That the person is the owner of the property on which the building is being constructed or, in the case of a firm or corporation, is legally authorized to act on behalf of the firm or corporation.

b. That the person will personally superintend and manage all aspects of the construction of the building and that the duty will not be delegated to any other person not duly licensed under the terms of this Article.

c. That the person will be personally present for all inspections required by the North Carolina State Building Code, unless the plans for the building were drawn and sealed by an architect licensed pursuant to Chapter 83A of the General Statutes.

The building inspector or other authority shall transmit a copy of the affidavit to the Board, who shall verify that the applicant was validly entitled to claim the exemption under G.S. 87-1(b)(2). If the Board determines that the applicant was not entitled to claim the exemption under G.S. 87-1(b)(2), the building permit shall be revoked pursuant to G.S. 153A-362 or G.S.160A-422.

(2) Furnish proof that the person has in effect Workers' Compensation insurance as required by Chapter 97 of the General Statutes.

(3) Any person, firm, or corporation, upon making application to the building inspector or such other authority of any incorporated city, town, or county in North Carolina charged with the duty of issuing building permits pursuant to G.S. 160A-417(a)(1) or G.S. 153A-357(a)(1) for any improvements for which the combined cost is to be thirty thousand

dollars ($30,000) or more, other than for improvements to an existing single-family residential dwelling unit as defined in G.S. 87-15.5(7) that the owner occupies as a residence, or for the addition of an accessory building or accessory structure as defined in the North Carolina Uniform Residential Building Code, the use of which is incidental to that residential dwelling unit, shall be required to provide to the building inspector or other authority the name, physical and mailing address, telephone number, facsimile number, and electronic mail address of the lien agent designated by the owner pursuant to G.S. 44A-11.1(a).

(b) It shall be unlawful for the building inspector or other authority to issue or allow the issuance of a building permit pursuant to this section unless and until the applicant has furnished evidence that the applicant is either exempt from the provisions of this Article and, if applicable, fully complied with the provisions of subdivision (a)(1) of this section, or is duly licensed under this Article to carry out or superintend the work for which permit has been applied; and further, that the applicant has in effect Workers' Compensation insurance as required by Chapter 97 of the General Statutes. Any building inspector or other authority who is subject to and violates the terms of this section shall be guilty of a Class 3 misdemeanor and subject only to a fine of not more than fifty dollars ($50.00).

§87-15. Copy of Article included in specifications, bid not considered unless contractor licensed.

All architects and engineers preparing plans and specifications for work to be contracted in the State of North Carolina shall include in their invitations to bidders and in the specifications a copy of this Article or such portions thereof as are deemed necessary to convey to the invited bidder, whether he be a resident or nonresident of this State and whether a license has been issued to him or not, the information that it will be necessary for him to show evidence of a license before his bid is considered.

§87-15.1. Reciprocity of licensing.

To the extent that other states which provide for the licensing of general contractors provide for similar action, the Board in its discretion may grant licenses of the same or equivalent classification to general contractors licensed by other states, without written examination upon satisfactory proof furnished to the Board that the qualifications of such applicants are equal to the qualifications of holders of similar licenses in North Carolina and upon payment of the required fee.

§87-15.2. Public awareness program.

The Board shall establish and implement a public awareness program to inform the general public of the purpose and function of the Board.

§87-15.3. Identity of complaining party confidential.

Once a complaint has been filed with the Board against a licensee or an unlicensed general contractor, the Board may, in its discretion, keep the identity of a complaining party confidential and not a public record within the meaning of Chapter 132 of the General Statutes until a time no later than the receipt of the complaint by the full Board for a disciplinary hearing or injunctive action.

§87-15.4. Builder designations created.

(a) A licensee who successfully completes the educational requirements for accredited builder or accredited master builder, as established by the North Carolina Builders Institute (Institute), shall be designated by the Board as a "North Carolina Certified Accredited Residential Builder" or "North Carolina Certified Accredited Master Residential Builder," respectively. The Institute shall provide to the Board written certification of those licensees who have successfully completed the requirements for the designations. The certification shall remain in effect as long as: (i) the licensee's license is in effect pursuant to G.S. 87-10; and (ii) the licensee completes at least eight hours of continuing education each calendar year as certified by the Institute.

(b) The Board shall approve for designation a licensee who has successfully completed a course of study, deemed by the Board to be equivalent to the educational requirements under subsection (a) of this section, offered by a community college or by another provider, and who completes the requisite number of hours of continuing education required by the Board.

(c) The Board may use all powers granted to it under this Article to enforce the provisions of this section and ensure that the designations created by this section are conferred upon and used only by a licensee who complies with the provisions of this section and any rules adopted by the Board.

SECTION 2. Any individual currently licensed by the State Licensing Board of General Contractors (Board) who has successfully completed the requirements of G.S. 87-15.4, as enacted by Section 1 of this act, before the effective date of this act may be designated by the Board as a "North Carolina Certified Accredited Residential Builder" or "North Carolina Certified Accredited Master Residential Builder" upon submitting to the Board certification from the North Carolina Builders Institute of successful completion of the requirements of G.S. 87-15.4.

ARTICLE 1A. HOMEOWNERS RECOVERY FUND

§87-15.5. Definitions

The following definitions apply in this Article:

(1)   Applicant.—The owner or former owner of a single-family residential dwelling unit who has suffered a reimbursable loss and has filed an application for reimbursement from the Fund.

(2)   Board.—The State Licensing Board for General Contractors.

(3)   Dishonest conduct.—Fraud or deceit in either of the following:

(a)   Obtaining a license under Article 1 of Chapter 87 of the General Statutes.

(b)   The practice of general contracting by a general contractor.

(4)   Fund.—The Homeowners Recovery Fund.

(5)   General contractor.—A person or other entity who meets any of the following descriptions:

(a)   Is licensed under Article 1 of Chapter 87 of the General Statutes

(b)   Fraudulently procures any building permit by presenting the license certificate of a general contractor.

(c)   Fraudulently procures any building permit by falsely impersonating a licensed general contractor.

(6)   Reimbursable loss.—A monetary loss that meets all of the following requirements:

(a)   Results from dishonest or incompetent conduct by a general contractor in constructing or altering a single-family residential dwelling unit.

(b)   Is not paid, in whole or in part, by or on behalf of the general contractor whose conduct caused the loss.

(c)   Is not covered by a bond, a surety agreement, or an insurance contract.

(7)   Single-family residential dwelling unit.—A separately owned residence for use of one or more persons as a housekeeping unit with space for eating,

living, and permanent provisions for cooking and sanitation, whether or not attached to other such residences.

§87-15.6. Homeowners
           Recovery Fund

(a) The Homeowners Recovery Fund is established as a special account of the Board. The Board shall administer the Fund. The purpose of the Fund is to reimburse homeowners who have suffered a reimbursable loss in constructing or altering a single-family residential dwelling unit.

(b) Whenever a general contractor applies for the issuance of a permit for the construction of any single-family residential dwelling unit or for the alteration of an existing single-family residential dwelling unit, a city or county building inspector shall collect from the general contractor a fee in the amount of ten dollars ($10.00) for each dwelling unit to be constructed or altered under the permit. The city or county inspector shall forward nine dollars ($9.00) of each fee collected to the Board on a quarterly basis and the city or county may retain one dollar ($1.00) of each fee collected. The Board shall deposit the fees received into the Fund. The Board may accept donations and appropriations to the Fund. G.S. 87-7 shall not apply to the Fund.

The Board may suspend collection of this fee for any year upon a determination that the amount in the Fund is sufficient to meet likely disbursements from the Fund for that year. The Board shall notify city and county building inspectors when it suspends collection of the fee.

(c) The Board may adopt rules to implement this Article.

§87-15.7. Fund
           Administration

(a) The Board shall determine the procedure for applying to the Board for reimbursement from the Fund, for processing applications, for granting requests for reimbursement, and for the subrogation or assignment of the rights of any reimbursed applicant. The Board shall submit annually a report to the State Treasurer accounting for all monies credited to and expended from the Fund.

(b) The Board may use monies in the Fund only for the following purposes:

(1)   To reimburse an applicant's reimbursable loss after approval by the Board.

(2)   To purchase insurance to cover reimbursable losses when the Board finds it appropriate to do so.

(3)   To invest amounts in the Fund that are not currently needed to reimburse losses and maintain adequate reserves in the manner in which State law allows fiduciaries to invest funds.

(4)   To pay the expenses of the Board to administer the Fund, including employment of counsel to prosecute subrogation claims.

§87-15.8. Application for
           reimbursement

(a) The Board shall prepare a form to be used to apply for reimbursement from the Fund. Only a person whom the Board determines to meet all of the following requirements may be reimbursed from the Fund:

(1)   Has suffered a reimbursable loss in the construction or alteration of a single-
      family residential dwelling unit owned or previously owned by that person.

(2)   Did not, directly or indirectly, obtain the building permit in the person's own name or did use a general contractor.

(3)   Has exhausted all civil remedies against the general contractor whose conduct caused the loss and, if applicable, the general contractor's estate, and has obtained a judgment against the general contractor that remains unsatisfied. This requirement is waived if the person is prevented from

filing suit or obtaining a judgment against the contractor due to the automatic stay provision of section 362 of the U.S. Bankruptcy Code.

(4)   Has complied with the applicable rules of the Board.

(b) The Board shall investigate all applications for reimbursement and may reject or allow part or all of a claim based on the amount of money in the Fund. The Board shall have complete discretion to determine the order, amount, and manner of payment of approved applications. All payments are a matter of privilege and not of right and no person has a right to reimbursement from the Fund as a third party beneficiary or otherwise. No attorney shall be compensated by the Board for prosecuting an application before it.

§87-15.9.   Subrogation for reimbursement made

The Board is subrogated to an applicant who is reimbursed from the Fund in the amount reimbursed and may bring an action against the general contractor whose conduct caused the reimbursable loss, the general contractor's assets, or the general contractor's estate. The Board may enforce any claims it may have for restitution or otherwise, and may employ and compensate consultants, agents, legal counsel, and others it finds necessary and appropriate to carry out its authority under this section.

Sec. 2 This act becomes effective October 1, 1991, and applies to reimbursable losses caused by the dishonest or incompetent conduct of a general contractor that occurs on or after that date.

OTHER GENERAL STATUTES

§14-401.1.   Misdemeanor to tamper with examination questions

Any person who, without authority of the entity who prepares or administers the examination, purloins, steals, buys, receives, or sells, gives or offers to buy, give, or sell any examination questions or copies thereof of any examination provided and prepared by law shall be guilty of a Class 2 misdemeanor. (1917, C. 146, s. 10; C.S., s. 5658; 1969, c. 1224, s. 3; 1991, c.360, s. 2; 1993, c. 539, s. 271; 1994, Ex. Sess., C. 24, s. 14(c).)

§22C-2.   Performance by subcontractor

Performance by a subcontractor in accordance with the provisions of its contract shall entitle it to payment from the party with whom it contracts. Payment by the owner to a contractor is not a condition precedent for payment to a subcontractor and payment by a contractor to a subcontractor is not a condition precedent for payment to any other subcontractor, and an agreement to the contrary is unenforceable. (1987 (Reg. Sess., 1988), c. 946; 1991, c. 620.)

§93B-3.   Register of Persons licensed; information as to licensed status of individuals

Each occupational licensing board shall prepare a register of all persons currently licensed by the board and shall supplement said register annually by listing the changes made in it by reason of new licenses issued, licenses revoked or suspended, death, or any other cause. The board shall, upon request of any citizen of the State, inform the requesting person as to the licensed status of any individual.

§93B-4.   Audit of occupational licensing boards; payment of costs

(a) The State Auditor shall audit occupational licensing boards from time to time to ensure their proper operation. The books, records, and operations of each occupational licensing board shall be subject to the oversight of the State Auditor pursuant to Article 5A of Chapter 147 of the General Statutes. In accordance with G.S. 147-64.7

(b) The State Auditor may contract with independent professionals to meet the requirements of this section. (b) Each occupational licensing board with a budget of at least fifty thousand dollars ($50,000) shall conduct an annual financial audit of its operations and provide a copy to the State Auditor.

§93B-8. Examination
          Procedures

(a) Each applicant for an examination given by any occupational licensing board shall be informed in writing or print of the required grade for passing the examination prior to the taking of such examination.

(b) Each applicant for an examination given by any occupational licensing board shall be identified, for purposes of the examination, only by number rather than by name.

(c) Each applicant who takes an examination given by any occupational licensing board, and does not pass such examination, shall have the privilege to review his examination in the presence of the board or a representative of the board. Except as provided in this subsection, an occupational licensing board shall not be required to disclose the contents of any examination or of any questions which have appeared thereon, or which may appear thereon in the future.

(d) Notwithstanding the provisions of this section, under no circumstances shall an occupational licensing board be required to disclose to an applicant questions or answers to tests provided by recognized testing organizations pursuant to contracts which prohibit such disclosures.

§93B-8.1 Use of Criminal
          History Records

(a) The following definitions apply in this section:

(1) Applicant.—A person who makes application for licensure from an occupational licensing board.

(2) Board.—An occupational licensing board as defined in G.S. 93B-1.

(3) Criminal history record.—A State or federal history of conviction of a crime, whether a misdemeanor or felony, that bears upon an applicant's or a licensee's fitness to be licensed or disciplined.

(4) Licensee.—A person who has obtained a license to engage in or represent himself or herself to be a member of a particular profession or occupation.

(b) Unless federal law governing a particular board provides otherwise, a board may deny an applicant on the basis of a conviction of a crime only if the board finds that the applicant's criminal conviction history is directly related to the duties and responsibilities for the licensed occupation or the conviction is for a crime that is violent or sexual in nature. Notwithstanding any other provision of law, a board shall not automatically deny licensure on the basis of an applicant's criminal history, and no board may deny an applicant a license based on a determination that a conviction is for a crime of moral turpitude. The board shall make its determination based on the factors specified in subsection (b1).

(b1) Before a board may deny an applicant a license due to a criminal conviction under subsection (b) of this section, the board must specifically consider all of the following factors:

(1) The level and seriousness of the crime.

(2) The date of the crime.

(3) The age of the person at the time of the crime.

(4) The circumstances surrounding the commission of the crime, if known.

(5) The nexus between the criminal conduct and the prospective duties of the applicant as a licensee.

(6) The prison, jail, probation, parole, rehabilitation, and employment records of the applicant since the date the crime was committed.

(6a) The completion of, or active participation in, rehabilitative drug or alcohol treatment.

(6b) A Certificate of Relief granted pursuant to G.S. 15A-173.2.

(7)   The subsequent commission of a crime by the applicant.

(8)   Any affidavits or other written documents, including character references.

(b2) If the board denies an applicant a license under this section, the board shall:

(1)   Make written findings specifying the factors in subsection (b1) of this section the board deemed relevant to the applicant and explaining the reason for the denial. The board's presiding officer must sign the findings.

(2)   Provide or serve a signed copy of the written findings to the applicant within 60 days of the denial.

(3)   Retain a signed copy of the written findings for no less than five years.

(b3) Each board shall include in its application for licensure and on its public Web site all of the following information:

(1)   Whether the board requires applicants to consent to a criminal history record check.

(2)   The factors under subsection (b1) of this section which the board shall consider when making a determination of licensure.

(3)   The appeals process pursuant to Chapter 150B of the General Statutes if the board denies an applicant licensure in whole or in part because of a criminal conviction.

(b4) If a board requires an applicant to submit a criminal history record, the board shall require the provider of the criminal history record to provide the applicant with access to the applicant's criminal history record or otherwise deliver a copy of the criminal history record to the applicant. If an applicant's criminal history includes matters that will or may prevent the board from issuing a license to the applicant, the board shall notify the applicant in writing of the specific issues in sufficient time for the applicant to provide additional documentation supporting the application for consideration by the board prior to any final decision to deny the application. After being notified of any potential issue with licensure due to criminal conviction(s), an applicant shall have 30 days to respond by either correcting any inaccuracy in the criminal history record or submitting evidence of mitigation or rehabilitation for consideration by the board.

(b5) If, following a hearing, a board denies an application for licensure, the board's written order shall include specific reference to any criminal conviction(s) considered as part or all of any basis for the denial and the rationale for the denial, as well as a reference to the appeal process and the applicant's ability to reapply. No applicant shall be restricted from reapplying for licensure for more than two years from the date of the most recent application.

(b6) Notwithstanding any other provisions in the law, an individual with a criminal history may petition a board at any time, including before an individual starts or completes any mandatory education or training requirements, for a predetermination of whether the individual's criminal history will likely disqualify the individual from obtaining a license. This petition shall include a criminal history record report obtained by the individual from a reporting service designated by the board, the cost of which shall be borne by the applicant. Criminal history records relating to a predetermination petition shall not be considered public records under

Chapter 132 of the General Statutes. A board may predetermine that the petitioner's criminal history is likely grounds for denial of a license only after the board has applied the requirements of subsection (b) of this section. Each board shall delegate authority for such a predetermination to its Executive Director or their equivalent, or a committee of the board, so that the predeterminations can be made in a timely manner. No board member having served on a predetermination committee for an individual shall be required to recuse in any later determinations or hearings involving the same applicant. The board shall inform the individual of the board's determination within 45 days of receiving the petition from the individual. The board may charge a fee to recoup its costs not to exceed forty-five dollars ($45.00) for each petition. If the board determines an applicant would likely be denied licensure based on their criminal history, the board shall notify the individual in writing of the following:

(1)   The grounds and reasons for the predetermination.

(2)   That the petitioner has the right to complete any requirements for licensure and apply to the board and have their application considered by the board under its application process.

(3)   That further evidence of rehabilitation will be considered upon application.

(b7)   A predetermination made under this section that a petitioner's criminal history would likely prevent them from licensure is not a final agency decision and shall not entitle the individual to any right to judicial review under Article 4 of Chapter 150B of the General Statutes.

(b8)   A predetermination made under subsection (b6) of this section that a petitioner is eligible for a license shall be binding if the petitioner applies for licensure and fulfills all other requirements for the occupational license and the applicant's submitted criminal history was correct and remains unchanged at the time of application for a license.

(c)   The board may deny licensure to an applicant who refuses to consent to a criminal history record check or use of fingerprints or other identifying information required by the State or National Repositories of Criminal Histories.

(d)   This section does not apply to The North Carolina Criminal Justice Education and Training Standards Commission and the North Carolina Sheriffs' Education and Training Standards Commission."

§93B-8.2. Prohibit licensees from serving as investigators

No occupational licensing board shall contract with or employ a person licensed by the board to serve as an investigator or inspector if the licensee is actively practicing in the profession or occupation and is in competition with other members of the profession or occupation over which the board has jurisdiction. Nothing in this section shall prevent a board from (i) employing licensees who are not otherwise employed in the same profession or occupation as investigators or inspectors or for other purposes or (ii) contracting with licensees of the board to serve as expert witnesses or consultants in cases where special knowledge and experience is required, provided that the board limits the duties and authority of the expert witness or consultant to serving as an information resource to the board and board personnel.

§93B-9. Age Requirement

Except certifications issued by the North Carolina Criminal Justice Education and Training Standards Commission and the North Carolina Sheriffs' Education and Training Standards Commission pursuant to Chapters 17C, 17E, 74E, and 74G of the General Statutes, no occupational licensing board may require that an individual be more than 18 years of age as a requirement for receiving a license with the following exceptions: the North Carolina Criminal Justice Education and Training Standards Commission and the North Carolina Sheriffs' Education and Training Standards Commission may establish a higher age as a requirement for holding certification through either Commission.

§93B-13. Revocation when licensing privilege forfeited for nonpayment of child support or for failure to comply with subpoena

(a) Upon receipt of a court order, pursuant to G.S. 50-13.12 and G.S. 110-142.1, revoking the occupational license of a licensee under its jurisdiction, an occupational licensing board shall note the revocation in its records, report the action within 30 days to the Department of Health and Human Services, and follow the normal post revocation rules and procedures of the board as if the revocation had been ordered by the board. The revocation shall remain in effect until the board receives certification by the clerk of superior court or the Department of Health and Human Services in an IV-D case that the licensee is no longer delinquent in child support payments, or, as applicable, that the licensee is in compliance with or is no longer subject to the subpoena that was the basis for the revocation.

(b) Upon receipt of notification from the Department of Health and Human Services that a licensee under an occupational licensing board's jurisdiction has forfeited the licensee's occupational license pursuant to G.S. 110-142.1, then the occupational licensing board shall send a notice of intent to revoke or suspend the occupational license of that licensee as provided by G.S. 110-142.1(d). If the license is revoked as provided by the provisions of G.S. 110-142.1, the revocation shall remain in effect until the board receives certification by the designated representative or the child support enforcement agency that the licensee is no longer delinquent in child support payments, or, as applicable, that the licensee is in compliance with or no longer subject to a subpoena that was the basis for the revocation.

(c) If at the time the court revokes a license pursuant to subsection (a) of this section, or if at the time the occupational licensing board revokes a license pursuant to subsection (b) of this section, the occupational licensing board has revoked the same license under the licensing board's disciplinary authority over licensees under its jurisdiction, and that revocation period is greater than the revocation period resulting from forfeiture pursuant to G.S. 50-13.12 or G.S. 110-142.1 then the revocation period imposed by the occupational licensing board applies.

(d) Immediately upon certification by the clerk of superior court or the child support enforcement agency that the licensee whose license was revoked pursuant to subsection (a) or (b) of this section is no longer delinquent in child support payments, the occupational licensing board shall reinstate the license. Immediately upon certification by the clerk of superior court or the child support enforcement agency that the licensee whose license was revoked because of failure to comply with a subpoena is in compliance with or no longer subject to the subpoena, the occupational licensing board shall reinstate the license. Reinstatement of a license pursuant to this section shall be made at no additional cost to the licensee.

§93B-14. Information on applicants for licensure

Every occupational licensing board shall require applicants for licensure to provide to the Board the applicant's social security number. This information shall be treated as confidential and may be released only as follows:

(1) To the State Child Support Enforcement Program of the Department of Health and Human Services upon its request and for the purpose of enforcing a child support order.

(2) To the Department of Revenue for the purpose of administering the State's tax laws.

§93B-15 Payment of License fees by members of the Armed Forces; board waiver rules

(a) An individual who is serving in the Armed Forces of the United States and to whom G.S. 105-249.2 grants an extension of time to file a tax return is granted an extension of time to pay any license fee charged by an occupational licensing board as a condition of retaining a license granted by the board. The extension is for the same period that would apply if the license fee were a tax.

(b) Occupational licensing boards shall adopt rules to postpone or waive continuing education, payment of renewal and other fees, and any other requirements or conditions relating to the maintenance of licensure by an individual who is currently licensed by and in good standing with the board, is serving in the Armed Forces of the United States, and to whom G.S. 105-249.2 grants an extension of time to file a tax return.

§93B-15.1. Licensure for individuals with military training and experience; proficiency examination; licensure by endorsement for military spouses; temporary license

(a) Except as provided by subsection (a2) of this section, and notwithstanding any other provision of law, an occupational licensing board, as defined in G.S. 93B-I, shall issue a license, certification, or registration to a military-trained applicant to allow the applicant to lawfully practice the applicant's occupation in this State if, upon application to an occupational licensing board, the applicant satisfies the following conditions:

(1) Has been awarded a military occupational specialty and has done all of the following at a level that is substantially equivalent to or exceeds the requirements for licensure, certification, or registration of the occupational licensing board from which the applicant is seeking licensure, certification, or registration in this State: completed a military program of training, completed testing or equivalent training and experience as determined by the board, and performed in the occupational specialty.

(2) Has engaged in the active practice of the occupation for which the person is seeking a license, certification, or permit from the occupational licensing board in this State for at least two of the five years preceding the date of the application under this section.

(3) Has not committed any act in any jurisdiction that would have constituted grounds for refusal, suspension, or revocation of a license to practice that occupation in this State at the time the act was committed.

(4) Pays any fees required by the occupational licensing board for which the applicant is seeking licensure, certification, or registration in this State.

(a1) No later than 30 days following receipt of an application, an occupational licensing board shall notify an applicant when the applicant's military training or experience does not satisfy the requirements for licensure, certification, or registration and shall specify the criteria or requirements that the board determined that the applicant failed to meet and the basis for that determination.

(a2) An occupational licensing board, as defined in G.S. 93B-1, shall issue a license, certification, or registration to a military-trained applicant to allow the applicant to lawfully practice the applicant's occupation in this State if the military-trained applicant, upon application to the occupational licensing board:

(1) Presents official, notarized documentation, such as a U.S. Department of Defense Form 214 (DD-214), or similar substantiation, attesting to the applicant's military occupational specialty certification and experience in an occupational field within the board's purview: and

(2) Passes a proficiency examination offered by the board to military-trained applicants in lieu of satisfying the conditions set forth in subsection (a) of

this section: however, if an applicant fails the proficiency examination, then the applicant may be required by the board to satisfy those conditions.

In any case where a proficiency examination is not offered routinely by an occupational licensing board, the board shall design a fair proficiency examination for military-trained applicants to obtain licensure, certification, or registration under this section. If a proficiency examination is offered routinely by an occupational licensing board, that examination shall satisfy the requirements of this section.

(b) Notwithstanding any other provision of law, an occupational licensing board, as defined in G.S. 93B-1, shall issue a license, certification, or registration to a military spouse to allow the military spouse to lawfully practice the military spouse's occupation in this State if, upon application to an occupational licensing board, the military spouse satisfies the following conditions:

(1) Holds a current license, certification, or registration from another jurisdiction, and that jurisdiction's requirements for licensure, certification, or registration are substantially equivalent to or exceed the requirements for licensure, certification, or registration of the occupational licensing board for which the applicant is seeking licensure, certification, or registration in this State.

(2) Can demonstrate competency in the occupation through methods as determined by the Board, such as having completed continuing education units or having had recent experience for at least two of the five years preceding the date of the application under this section.

(3) Has not committed any act in any jurisdiction that would have constituted grounds for refusal, suspension, or revocation of a license to practice that occupation in this State at the time the act was committed.

(4) Is in good standing and has not been disciplined by the agency that had jurisdiction to issue the license, certification, or permit.

(5) Pays any fees required by the occupational licensing board for which the applicant is seeking licensure, certification, or registration in this State.

(c) All relevant experience of a military service member in the discharge of official duties or, for a military spouse, all relevant experience, including fulltime and part-time experience, regardless of whether in a paid or volunteer capacity, shall be credited in the calculation of years of practice in an occupation as required under subsection (a) or (b) of this section.

(c1) Each occupational licensing board shall publish a document that lists the specific criteria or requirements for licensure, registration, or certification by the board, with a description of the criteria or requirements that are satisfied by military training or experience as provided in this section, and any necessary documentation needed for obtaining the credit or satisfying the requirement. The information required by this subsection shall be published on the occupational licensing board's Web site and the Web site of the North Carolina Division of Veterans Affairs.

(d) A nonresident licensed, certified, or registered under this section shall be entitled to the same rights and subject to the same obligations as required of a resident licensed, certified, or registered by an occupational licensing board in this State.

(e) Nothing in this section shall be construed to apply to the practice of law as regulated under Chapter 84 of the General Statutes.

(f) An occupational licensing board may issue a temporary practice permit to a military-trained applicant or a military spouse licensed, certified, or registered in another jurisdiction while the military-trained applicant or military spouse is satisfying the requirements for licensure under subsection (a) or (b) of this section if that jurisdiction has licensure, certification, or registration standards substantially equivalent to the standards for licensure, certification, or registration of an occupational licensing board in this State. The military-trained applicant or military spouse may practice under the temporary permit until a license, certification, or registration is granted or until a notice to deny a license, certification, or registration is issued in accordance with rules adopted by the occupational licensing board.

(g) An occupational licensing board may adopt rules necessary to implement this section. Nothing in this section shall be construed to prohibit a military-trained applicant or military spouse from proceeding under the existing licensure, certification, or registration requirements established by an occupational licensing board in this State.

(h) For the purposes of this section, the State Board of Education shall be considered an occupational licensing board when issuing teacher licenses under G.S.115C-296.

(i) For the purposes of this section, the North Carolina Medical Board shall not be considered an occupational licensing board.

(j) For the purposes of this section, the North Carolina Medical Board shall not be considered an occupational licensing board.

§136-28.14. Project contractor licensing requirements

(See also Exception at G.S. §87-1.2)

The letting of contracts under this Chapter for the following types of projects shall not be subject to the licensing requirements of Article 1 of Chapter 87 of the General Statutes:

(1) Routine maintenance and minor repair of pavements, bridges, roadside vegetation and plantings, drainage systems, concrete sidewalks, curbs, gutters, and rest areas.

(2) Installation and maintenance of pavement markings and markers, ground mounted signs, guardrail, fencing, and roadside vegetation and plantings.

§153A-360. Inspections of work in progress

Subject to the limitation imposed by G.S. 153A-352(b), as the work pursuant to a permit progresses, local inspectors shall make as many inspections of the work as may be necessary to satisfy them that it is being done according to the provisions of the applicable State and local laws and local ordinances and regulations and of the terms of the permit. In exercising this power, each member of the inspection department has a right, upon presentation of proper credentials, to enter on any premises within the territorial jurisdiction of the department at any reasonable hour for the purposes of inspection or other enforcement action. If a permit has been obtained by an owner exempt from licensure under G.S. 87-1(b)(2), no inspection shall be conducted without the owner being personally present, unless the plans for the building were drawn and sealed by an architect licensed pursuant to Chapter 83A of the General Statutes. (1969, c. 1066, s. 1; 1973, c. 822, s. 1; 2011-376, s. 3; 2015-145, s. 1(a).)

§160A-420. Inspections of work in progress

Subject to the limitation imposed by G.S. 160A-412(b), as the work pursuant to a permit progresses, local inspectors shall make as many inspections thereof as may be necessary to satisfy them that the work is being done according to the provisions of any applicable State and local laws and of the terms of the permit. In exercising this power, members of the inspection department shall have a right to enter on any premises within the jurisdiction of the department at all reasonable hours for the purposes of inspection or other enforcement action, upon presentation of proper credentials. If a permit has been obtained by an owner exempt from licensure under G.S. 87-1(b)(2), no inspection shall be conducted without the owner being personally present, unless the plans for the building were drawn and sealed by an architect licensed pursuant to Chapter 83A of the General Statutes. (1969, c. 1065, s. 1; 1971, c. 698, s. 1; 2011-376, s. 4; 2015-145, s. 1(b).)

Appendix F: Rules and Regulations

North Carolina Licensing Board for General Contractors
NORTH CAROLINA ADMINISTRATIVE CODE
Title 21; Chapter 12

Statutory Authority;
Chapter 87,
Section 1-15.9,
and Chapter 150B(3)
of theGeneral Statutes
of North Carolina

SECTION .0100 — ORGANIZATION OF BOARD

.0101   Identification   The State Licensing Board for General Contractors, hereinafter referred to as the "North Carolina Licensing Board for General Contractors" or "the Board," is located in Raleigh, North Carolina; its mailing address is 5400 Creedmoor Road, Raleigh, North Carolina 27612. The Board website is www.nclbgc.org.

History Note: Authority G.S. 87 2; Eff. February 1, 1976; Amended Eff. June 23, 1977; Readopted Eff. September 26, 1977; Amended Eff. December 1, 1985; January 1, 1983; Pursuant to G.S. 150B-21.3A, rule is necessary without substantive public interest Eff. July 23, 2016; Amended Eff. April 1, 2018.

.0102   General Purpose of Board   (a) The purpose of the Board is to regulate persons who engage in activities which constitute the practice of general contracting as defined in G.S. 87-1 in order to safeguard the life, health and property of the people of North Carolina as well as promote the public welfare.

(b) The Board regulates the practice of general contracting by:

(1)   determining the qualifications of persons seeking to enter the practice of general contracting and granting to those persons who have met the statutory requirements the privilege of entering the practice of general contracting;

(2)   enforcing the provisions of the North Carolina General Statutes pertaining to general contractors; and

(3)   enforcing the Board's Rules, which are designed to ensure a high degree of competence in the practice of general contracting.

History Note: Authority G.S. 87-1; 87-2; Eff. February 1, 1976; Readopted Eff. September 26, 1977; Amended Eff. May 1, 1989.

.0103   Structure of Board   (a) Officers. Annually, during the April meeting, the Board shall elect from its members a Chairman and Vice-Chairman. The Chairman shall preside over all meetings of the Board and perform other duties as he or she may be directed to do by the Board. The Vice-Chairman shall function as Chairman if the Chairman is unavailable.

(b) Secretary-Treasurer. In addition to those duties and responsibilities required of him or her by G.S. 87-8, the Secretary-Treasurer, referred to as "Secretary-Treasurer" or "Executive Director," as the Board's Chief Administrative Officer, has the responsibility and power to:

(1)   employ the clerical and legal services necessary to assist the Board in carrying out the requirements of the North Carolina General Statutes;

(2)   purchase or rent whatever office equipment, stationery, or other miscellaneous articles as are necessary to keep the records of the Board;

(3)   make expenditures from the funds of the Board by signing checks, or authorizing the designee of the Secretary-Treasurer to sign checks, for expenditures after the checks are signed by the Chairman or Vice-Chairman; and

(4)   do such other acts as may be required of him or her by the Board.

(c) Official Meetings of the Board.

(1) Regular Meetings. Regular meetings shall be held during January, April, July and October of each year at the Board's office or at any other place so designated by the Board.

(2) Special Meetings. Special meetings shall be called and conducted in accordance with Article 33C of Chapter 143 of the North Carolina General Statutes.

(3) Notice of Meetings. Notice of all official meetings of the Board shall be given pursuant to Article 33C of Chapter 143 of the North Carolina General Statutes.

History Note: Authority G.S. 87-2; 87-4; 87-6; 87-7; Eff. February 1, 1976; Readopted Eff. September 26, 1977; Amended Eff. April 1, 2014; August 1, 2002; January 1, 1992; May 1, 1989; January 1, 1983; Pursuant to G.S. 150B-21.3A, rule is necessary without substantive public interest Eff. July 23, 2016; Amended Eff. April 1, 2018.

SECTION .0200 — LICENSING REQUIREMENTS

.0201   Definitions

The following definitions shall apply to the Rules in this Chapter:

(1) Completion: As used in G.S. 87-1(b), occurs upon issuance of a certificate of occupancy by the permitting authority with jurisdiction over the project.

(2) Cost of the undertaking: As used in G.S. 87-1(a), means the final price of a project, excluding the cost of land, as evidenced by the contract, or in the absence of a contract, permit records, invoices, and cancelled checks.

(3) Personally: As used in G.S. 87-14(a)(1), "personally" means the physical presence of the owner of the property and excludes the use of a power of attorney.

(4) Solely for occupancy: As used in G.S. 87-1(b), "solely for occupancy" is restricted to the family of a person, the officers and shareholders of a firm or corporation, and guests and social invitees where no consideration is received. For purposes of G.S. 87-1(b)(2), "family" is defined as a spouse or other family member living in the same household.

(5) Value: As used in G.S. 87-10(a1), means the same as "cost of the undertaking."

History Note: Authority G.S. 87-1, 87-10, and 87-14; Eff. February 1, 1976; Readopted Eff. September 26, 1977; Amended Eff. January 1, 1983; Repealed Eff. May 1, 1989; Codifier approved agency's waiver request to reuse rule number; Eff. September 1, 2019.

.0202   Classification

(a) A general contractor shall be certified in one of the following five classifications:

(1) Building Contractor. This classification covers all building construction and demolition activity including: commercial, industrial, institutional, and all residential building construction. It includes parking decks; all site work, grading and paving of parking lots, driveways, sidewalks, and gutters; storm drainage, retaining or screen walls, and hardware and accessory structures; and indoor and outdoor recreational facilities including natural and artificial surface athletic fields, running tracks, bleachers, and seating. It also covers work done under the specialty classifications of S(Concrete Construction), S(Insulation), S(Interior Construction), S(Marine Construction), S(Masonry Construction), S(Roofing), S(Metal Erection), S(Swimming Pools), and S(Asbestos), and S(Wind Turbine).

(2)   Residential Contractor. This classification covers all construction and demolition activity pertaining to the construction of residential units that are required to conform to the residential building code adopted by the Building Code Council pursuant to G.S. 143-138; all site work, driveways, sidewalks, and water and wastewater systems ancillary to the aforementioned structures and improvements; and the work done as part of such residential units under the specialty classifications of S(Insulation), S(Interior Construction), S(Masonry Construction), S(Roofing), S(Swimming Pools), and S(Asbestos).

(3)   Highway Contractor. This classification covers all highway construction activity including: grading, paving of all types, installation of exterior artificial athletic surfaces, relocation of public and private utility lines ancillary to a principal project, bridge construction and repair, culvert construction and repair, parking decks, sidewalks, curbs, gutters and storm drainage. It also includes installation and erection of guard rails, fencing, signage and ancillary highway hardware; covers paving and grading of airport and airfield runways, taxiways, and aprons, including the installation of fencing, signage, runway lighting and marking; and work done under the specialty classifications of S(Boring and Tunneling), S(Concrete Construction), S(Marine Construction), S(Railroad Construction), and H(Grading and Excavating).

(4)   Public Utilities Contractor. This classification includes operations that are the performance of construction work on water and wastewater systems and on the subclassifications of facilities set forth in G.S. 87-10(b)(3). The Board shall issue a license to a public utilities contractor that is limited to any of the subclassifications set forth in G.S. 87-10(b)(3) for which the contractor qualifies. A public utilities contractor license covers work done under the specialty classifications of S(Boring and Tunneling), PU(Communications), PU(Fuel Distribution), PU(Electrical-Ahead of Point of Delivery), PU(Water Lines and Sewer Lines), PU(Water Purification and Sewage Disposal), and S(Swimming Pools).

(5)   Specialty Contractor. This classification covers all construction operation and performance of contract work outlined as follows:

(A)   H(Grading and Excavating). This classification covers the digging, moving, and placing of materials forming the surface of the earth, excluding air and water, in such a manner that the cut, fill, excavation, grade, trench, backfill, or any similar operation may be executed with the use of hand and power tools and machines used for these types of digging, moving, and material placing. It covers work on earthen dams and the use of explosives used in connection with all or any part of the activities described in this Subparagraph. It also includes clearing and grubbing, and erosion control activities.

(B)   S(Boring and Tunneling). This classification covers the construction of underground or underwater passageways by digging or boring through and under the earth's surface, including the bracing and compacting of such passageways to make them safe for the purpose intended. It includes preparation of the ground surfaces at points of ingress and egress.

(C)   PU (Communications). This classification covers the installation of the following:

      (i)   all types of pole lines, and aerial and underground distribution cable for telephone systems;

      (ii)   aerial and underground distribution cable for cable TV and master antenna TV systems capable of transmitting R.F. signals;

      (iii)   underground conduit and communication cable including fiber optic cable; and

      (iv)   microwave systems and towers, including foundations and excavations where required, when the microwave systems are being used for the purpose of transmitting R.F. signals; and installation of PCS or cellular telephone towers and sites.

(D)   S(Concrete Construction). This classification covers the construction, demolition, and installation of foundations, pre-cast silos, and other concrete tanks or receptacles, prestressed components, and gunite applications, but excludes bridges, streets, sidewalks, curbs, gutters, driveways, parking lots, and highways.

(E)   PU(Electrical-Ahead of Point of Delivery). This classification covers the construction, installation, alteration, maintenance, or repair of an electrical wiring system, including sub-stations or components thereof, which is or is intended to be owned, operated, and maintained by an electric power supplier, such as a public or private utility, a utility cooperative, or any other properly franchised electric power supplier, for the purpose of furnishing electrical services to one or more customers.

(F)   PU(Fuel Distribution). This classification covers the construction, installation, alteration, maintenance, or repair of systems for distribution of petroleum fuels, petroleum distillates, natural gas, chemicals, and slurries through pipeline from one station to another. It includes all excavating, trenching, and backfilling in connection therewith. It covers the installation, replacement, and removal of above ground and below ground fuel storage tanks.

(G)   PU(Water Lines and Sewer Lines). This classification covers construction work on water and sewer mains, water service lines, and house and building sewer lines, as defined in the North Carolina State Building Code, and covers water storage tanks, lift stations, pumping stations, and appurtenances to water storage tanks, lift stations and pumping stations. It includes pavement patching, backfill, and erosion control as part of construction.

(H)   PU(Water Purification and Sewage Disposal). This classification covers the performance of construction work on water and wastewater systems; water and wastewater treatment facilities; and all site work, grading, and paving of parking lots, driveways, sidewalks, and curbs and gutters that are ancillary to such construction of water and wastewater treatment facilities. It covers the work done under the specialty classifications of S(Concrete Construction), S(Insulation), S(Interior Construction), S(Masonry Construction), S(Roofing), and S(Metal Erection) as part of the work on water and wastewater treatment facilities.

(I)   S(Insulation). This classification covers the installation, alteration, or repair of materials classified as insulating media used for the non-mechanical control of temperatures in the construction of residential and commercial buildings. It does not include the insulation of mechanical equipment, and ancillary lines and piping.

(J) S(Interior Construction). This classification covers the installation and demolition of acoustical ceiling systems and panels, load bearing and non-load bearing partitions, lathing and plastering, flooring and finishing, interior recreational surfaces, window and door installation, and installation of fixtures, cabinets, and millwork. It includes the removal of asbestos and replacement with non-toxic substances.

(K) S(Marine Construction). This classification covers all marine construction and repair activities and all types of marine construction and demolition in deep-water installations and in harbors, inlets, sounds, bays, and channels; it covers dredging, construction, and installation of pilings, piers, decks, slips, docks, and bulkheads. It does not include structures required on docks, slips, and piers.

(L) S(Masonry Construction). This classification covers the demolition and installation, with or without the use of mortar or adhesives, of the following:

(i) brick, concrete block, gypsum partition tile, pumice block, or other lightweight and facsimile units and products common to the masonry industry;

(ii) installation of fire clay products and refractory construction; and

(iii) installation of rough cut and dressed stone, marble panels and slate units, and installation of structural glazed tile or block, glass brick or block, and solar screen tile or block.

(M) S(Railroad Construction). This classification covers the building, construction, and repair of railroad lines including:

(i) the clearing and filling of rights-of-way;

(ii) shaping, compacting, setting, and stabilizing of road beds;

(iii) setting ties, tie plates, rails, rail connectors, frogs, switch plates, switches, signal markers, retaining walls, dikes, fences, and gates; and

(iv) construction and repair of tool sheds and platforms.

(N) S(Roofing). This classification covers the installation, demolition, and repair of roofs and decks on residential, commercial, industrial, and institutional structures requiring materials that form a water-tight and weather-resistant surface. The term "materials" for purposes of this Subparagraph includes cedar, cement, asbestos, clay tile and composition shingles, all types of metal coverings, wood shakes, single ply and built-up roofing, protective and reflective roof and deck coatings, sheet metal valleys, flashings, gravel stops, gutters and downspouts, and bituminous waterproofing.

(O) S(Metal Erection). This classification covers:

(i) the field fabrication, demolition, erection, repair, and alteration of architectural and structural shapes, plates, tubing, pipe and bars, not limited to steel or aluminum, that are or may be used as structural members for buildings, equipment, and structure; and

(ii) the layout, assembly and erection by welding, bolting, riveting, or fastening in any manner metal products as curtain walls, tanks of all types, hoppers, structural members for buildings, towers, stairs, conveyor frames, cranes and crane runways, canopies, carports, guard rails, signs, steel scaffolding as a permanent structure, rigging, flagpoles, fences, steel and aluminum siding, bleachers, fire escapes, and seating for stadiums, arenas, and auditoriums.

(P) S(Swimming Pools). This classification covers the construction, demolition, service, and repair of all swimming pools. It includes:

(i) excavation and grading;

(ii) construction of concrete, gunite, and plastic-type pools, pool decks, and walkways, and tiling and coping; and

(iii) installation of all equipment including pumps, filters, and chemical feeders. It does not include direct connections to a sanitary sewer system or to portable water lines, nor the grounding and bonding of any metal surfaces or the making of any electrical connections.

(Q) S(Asbestos). This classification covers renovation or demolition activities involving the repair, maintenance, removal, isolation, encapsulation, or enclosure of Regulated Asbestos Containing Materials (RACM) for any commercial, industrial, or institutional building, whether public or private. It also covers all types of residential building construction involving RACM during renovation or demolition activities. This specialty is required only when the cost of asbestos activities as described herein are equal to or exceed thirty thousand dollars ($30,000).

(R) S(Wind Turbine). This classification covers the construction, demolition, installation, and repair of wind turbines, wind generators, and wind power units. It includes assembly of blades, generator, turbine structures, and towers. It also includes ancillary foundation work, field fabrication of metal equipment, and structural support components.

(b) An applicant may be licensed in more than one classification of general contracting provided the applicant meets the qualifications for the classifications, which includes passing the examinations for the classifications requested by the applicant. The license granted to an applicant who meets the qualifications for all of the classifications set forth in the rules of this Section shall be designated "unclassified."

History Note: *Authority G.S. 87-1; 87-4; 87-10; Eff. February 1, 1976; Readopted Eff. September 26, 1977; Amended Eff. June 1, 1994; June 1, 1992; May 1, 1989; January 1, 1983; Temporary Amendment Eff. February 18, 1997; Amended Eff. April 1, 2014; June 1, 2011; September 1, 2009; April 1, 2004; April 1, 2003; August 1, 2002; April 1, 2001; August 1, 2000; August 1, 1998; Pursuant to G.S. 150B-21.3A, rule is necessary without substantive public interest Eff. July 23, 2016; Amended Eff. September 1, 2019; April 1, 2018.*

.0203   Limitaton of License   *History Note:* *Authority G.S. 87-1; 87-10; Eff. February 1, 1976; Readopted Eff. September 26, 1977; Amended Eff. January 1, 1983; Repealed Eff. May 1, 1989.*

.0204   License Limitations; Eligibility.

(a) All licenses shall have an appropriate limitation as set forth in this Rule.

(b) Limited License. The applicant for a limited license shall:

(1)   meet the requirements set out in G.S. 87-10 and Section .0400 of this Chapter;

(2)   have current assets that exceed the total current liabilities by at least seventeen thousand dollars ($17,000) or have a total net worth of at least eighty thousand dollars ($80,000);

(3)   pass the examination which shall contain subject matter related to the specific contracting classification chosen by the applicant with a score as set out in Rule .0404 of this Chapter; and

(4)   if the applicant or any owner, principal, or qualifier is in bankruptcy or has been in bankruptcy within five years prior to the filing of the application, provide to the Board an agreed-upon procedures report on a form provided by the Board or an audited financial statement with a classified balance sheet as part of the application. This requirement shall not apply to shareholders of an applicant that is a publicly traded corporation.

(c) Intermediate License. The applicant for an intermediate license shall:

(1)   meet the requirements set out in G.S. 87-10 and Section .0400 of this Chapter;

(2)   have current assets that exceed the total current liabilities by at least seventy-five thousand dollars ($75,000), as reflected in an agreed-upon procedures report on a form provided by the Board or an audited financial statement prepared by a certified public accountant or an independent accountant who is engaged in the public practice of accountancy; and

(3)   pass the examination which shall contain subject matter related to the specific contracting classification chosen by the applicant with a score as set out in Rule .0404 of this Chapter.

(d) Unlimited License. The applicant for an unlimited license shall:

(1)   meet the requirements set out in G.S. 87-10 and Section .0400 of this Chapter;

(2)   have current assets that exceed the total current liabilities by at least one hundred fifty thousand dollars ($150,000), as reflected in an agreed-upon procedures report on a form provided by the Board or an audited financial statement prepared by a certified public accountant or an independent accountant who is engaged in the public practice of accountancy;

(3)   pass the examination which shall contain subject matter related to the specific contracting classification chosen by the applicant with a score as set out in Rule .0404 of this Chapter.

(e) Surety Bonds. In lieu of demonstrating the level of working capital as required in Subparagraphs (c)(2) and (d)(2) of this Rule or net worth under Subparagraph (b)(2) of this Rule, an applicant may obtain a surety bond from a surety authorized to transact surety business in North Carolina pursuant to G.S. 58 Articles 7, 16, 21, or 22. The surety shall maintain a rating from A.M. Best, or its successor rating organization, of either Superior (A++ or A+) or Excellent (A or A-). The bond shall be continuous in form and shall be maintained in effect for as long as the applicant maintains a license to practice general contracting in North Carolina or until the applicant demonstrates the required level of working capital as required by Subparagraphs (c)(2) and (d)(2) of this Rule. The applicant shall submit proof of a surety bond meeting the requirements of this Rule with the application form and subsequent annual license renewal forms. The applicant shall maintain the bond in the amount of one hundred seventy-five thousand dollars ($175,000) for a limited license, five hundred thousand dollars ($500,000) for an intermediate license, and one million dollars ($1,000,000) for an unlimited license. The bond shall list the State of North Carolina as obligee and be for the benefit of any person who is damaged by an act or omission of the applicant constituting breach of a construction contract, breach of a contract for the furnishing of labor, materials, or professional services to construction undertaken by the applicant, or by an unlawful act or omission of the applicant in the performance of a construction contract. The bond required by this Rule shall be in addition to and not in lieu of any other bond required of the applicant by law, regulation, or any party to a contract with the applicant. Should the surety cancel the bond, the surety and the applicant both shall notify the Board within 30 days in writing. If the applicant fails to provide written proof of financial responsibility in compliance with this Rule within 30 days of the bond's cancellation, then the applicant's license shall be suspended until written proof of compliance is provided.

(f) Financial statements, accounting, and reporting standards. Financial statements submitted by applicants to the Board shall be no older than twelve months from the date of submission. Financial statements shall conform to United States "generally accepted accounting principles" (GAAP). The Board may require non-GAAP financial statements from applicants wherein the only exception to GAAP is that such presentation is necessary to ascertain the working capital or net worth of the particular applicant. Examples of the circumstances when non-GAAP presentation may be necessary to ascertain the working capital or net worth of the applicant shall be when the only exception to GAAP is that assets and liabilities are classified as "current" and "noncurrent" on personal financial statements and when the only exception to GAAP is that the particular applicant is not combined with a related entity into one financial statement pursuant to AICPA Financial Interpretation 46R (ASC 810). The terminologies, working capital, balance sheet with current and fixed assets, current and long term liabilities, and any other accounting terminologies, used herein shall be construed in accordance with GAAP Standards as promulgated by the Financial Accounting Standards Board (FASB). The terminologies, audited financial statement, unqualified opinion, and any other auditing terminologies used herein shall be construed in accordance with those standards referred to as "generally accepted auditing standards" (GAAS) as promulgated by the American Institute of Certified Public Accountants (AICPA).

History Note: Authority G.S. 87-1; 87-4; 87-10; 87-15.1; Eff. February 1, 1976; Readopted Eff. September 26, 1977; Amended Eff. January 1, 1983; ARRC Objection March 19, 1987; Amended Eff. May 1, 1989; August 1, 1987; Temporary Amendment Eff. June 28, 1989 for a Period of 155 Days to Expire on December 1, 1989; Amended Eff. December 1, 1989; Temporary Amendment Eff. May 31, 1996; RRC Removed Objection Eff. October 17, 1996; Amended Eff. August 1, 1998; April 1, 1997; Temporary Amendment Eff. August 24, 1998; Amended Eff. April 1, 2014; April 1, 2013; August 1, 2008; April 1, 2006; March 1, 2005; August 1, 2002; April 1, 2001; August 1, 2000; Pursuant to G.S. 150B-21.3A, rule is necessary without substantive public interest Eff. July 23, 2016; Ammended Eff. September 1, 2019; April 1, 2018.

.0205   Qualifier

(a) The qualifier for the applicant shall be a responsible managing employee, officer, or member of the personnel of the applicant. A person may serve as a qualifier for no more than two licenses. A qualifier's examination credentials shall archive if the qualifier does not serve as a qualifier for an active licensee for a period of four consecutive years. Once a qualifier's examination credentials archive, he or she shall retake the examination and earn a passing grade in accordance with Rule .0404 of this Chapter to serve as a qualifier.

(b) Subject to the provisions of G.S. 150B and Section .0800 of these Rules, the Board may reject the application of an applicant seeking qualification by employment of a person who has already passed an examination if such person has previously served as qualifier for a licensee that has been disciplined by the Board.

(c) A licensee shall notify the Board in writing in the event a qualifier ceases to be connected with the licensee. The notice shall include the date on which the qualifier was last connected with the licensee and shall be submitted no later than 10 days after the date of separation. A qualifier shall also be required to notify the Board in writing in such circumstances. After such notice is filed with the Board in writing, or the Board determines that the qualifier is no longer connected with the licensee, and if there are no additional qualifiers for the licensee, the license shall be invalidated in accordance with G.S. 87-10.

(d) Persons associated with a firm or corporation may take the required examination on behalf of the firm or corporation as described in G.S. 87-10. A partner may take an examination on behalf of a partnership.

(e) "Responsible managing" as used in G.S. 87-10 means a person who is engaged in the work of the applicant a minimum of 20 hours per week or a majority of the hours operated by the applicant, whichever is less. If the person described herein is not an owner, officer, or partner of the applicant or licensee, the person must be a W-2 employee.

(f) "Members of the personnel" as used in G.S. 87-10 means a person who is a responsible managing employee of the applicant or licensee. A member of the personnel must be a W-2 employee and shall not be an independent contractor. contractor of the applicant or licensee.

(g) An applicant or licensee may have more than one qualifier. If one person associated with the applicant fails, and another passes, the license shall be granted to that applicant. A license shall be issued only in the classification held by a qualifier who has passed an examination in that classification.

History Note: *Authority G.S. 87-1; 87-4; 87-10; 87-11(a); Eff. February 1, 1976; Readopted Eff. September 26, 1977; Amended Eff. April 1, 2014; July 1, 2008; April 1, 2006; August 1, 2000; June 1, 1994; June 1, 1992; May 1, 1989; July 1, 1987; Pursuant to G.S. 150B-21.3A, rule is necessary without substantive public interest Eff. July 23, 2016; Amended Eff. September 1, 2019; September 1, 2018; April 1, 2018.*

.0206   Joint Venture

History Note: *Authority G.S. 87-1; 87-10; Eff. February 1, 1976; Readopted Eff. September 26, 1977; Repealed Eff. May 1, 1989.*

.0207   Joint Venture

A joint venture may practice general contracting in North Carolina if every principal or member of the joint venture is licensed to practice general contracting in North Carolina with the appropriate classification and at least one principal has the appropriate limitation, or if the joint venture obtains a general contracting license in its own name in accordance with G.S. 87 10 and these Rules. If an LLC is a joint venturer, all members and managers of the LLC shall be licensed to practice general contracting in North Carolina with the appropriate classification and limitation.

History Note: Authority G.S. 87 1; 87 10; Eff. June 1, 1992; Pursuant to
                G.S. 150B-21.3A, rule is necessary without substantive public interest
                Eff. July 23, 2016; Amended Eff. April 1, 2018.

.0208   Construction   (a) The phrase "undertakes to superintend or manage" as used in G.S. 87-1 to
         Management   describe a person, firm, or corporation deemed to be a general contractor means that the person, firm, or corporation shall be responsible for superintending or managing the construction of an entire project, and either contracts directly with subcontractors to perform the construction for the project or is compensated for superintending or managing the project based upon the cost of the project or the time taken to complete the project. The person, firm, or corporation shall hold a general contracting license in the classifications and limitation applicable to the construction of the project.

(b) The phrase "undertakes to superintend or manage" described in Paragraph (a) of this Rule shall not include the following:

(1)   an architect or engineer licensed in North Carolina who is supervising the execution of design plans for the project owner and who does not contract directly with subcontractors to perform the construction for the project; or

(2)   subject to the conditions stated within this Subparagraph and Paragraph (c), any person, firm, or corporation retained by an owner of real property as a consultant, agent, or advisor to perform development-related functions, including:

(A)   assisting with site planning and design;

(B)   formulating a development scheme;

(C)   obtaining zoning and other entitlements;

(D)   tenant selection and negotiation;

(E)   interfacing and negotiating with the general contractor, engineer, architect, other construction and design professionals, and other development consultants with whom the land owner separately contracts, including, negotiating contracts on the owner's behalf, assisting with scheduling issues, ensuring that any disputes between such parties are resolved to the owner's satisfaction, and otherwise ensuring that such parties are proceeding in an efficient, coordinated manner to complete the project;

(F)   providing cost estimates, bids, and budgeting;

(G)   monitoring the progress of development activities performed by other parties;

(H)   arranging and negotiating governmental incentives and entitlements; and

(I)   selecting and sequencing sites for development.

(c) The exclusions set forth in Subparagraph (b)(2) shall not apply, however, unless the following conditions are satisfied:

(1)   the owner has retained a licensed general contractor or licensed general contractors to construct the entire project or to directly superintend and manage all construction work in which the person, firm, or corporation has any involvement and that would otherwise require the use of a licensed general contractor; and

(2)   the use of the person, firm, or corporation will not impair the general contractor's ability to communicate directly with the owner and to verify the owner's informed consent and ratification of the directions and decisions made by the person, firm, or corporation to the extent that such directions or decisions affect the construction activities otherwise requiring the use of a licensed general contractor. For the purposes of this Subparagraph, the general contractor shall be entitled to make a written demand for written verification from the owner of any directions given or decisions made by such a person, firm, or corporation on the owner's behalf. In that regard, if the general contractor delivers a written request directly to the owner asking that the owner confirm in writing that the owner desires that the general contractor perform consistent with a direction or decision made by such person, firm, or corporation:

(A)   the general contractor shall not be obligated to follow such direction or decision in question until such time as the owner provides written verification of the direction or decision; and

(B)   if the third party person, firm, or corporation whose direction or decision is being questioned by the general contractor attempts to itself provide the confirmation requested from the owner by the general contractor as provided above, such person, firm, or corporation shall be deemed to be "undertaking to superintend or manage" as described in Paragraph (a) of this Rule.

History Note: Authority G.S. 87-1; 87-4; Eff. May 1, 1995; Amended Eff. June 1, 2010; Pursuant to G.S. 150B-21.3A, rule is necessary without substantive public interest Eff. July 23, 2016; Amended Eff. April 1, 2018.

.0209   Application

(a) Any application made pursuant to G.S. 87-10 shall be accompanied by a Certificate of Assumed Name filed in accordance with Chapter 66, Article 14A of the General Statutes. Applications submitted to the Board on behalf of corporations, limited liability companies and partnerships shall be accompanied by a copy of any documents required to be filed with the North Carolina Secretary of State's office, such as Articles of Incorporation or Certificate of Authority.

(b) All licensees shall comply with the requirements of G.S. 66-71.4 and shall notify the Board within 30 days of any change in the name in which the licensee is conducting business in the State of North Carolina.

(c) No applicant or licensee shall use or adopt an assumed name used by any other licensee, or any name so similar to an assumed name used by another licensee that could confuse or mislead the public.

History Note: Authority G.S. 66-71.4; 87-1; 87-4; 87-10; Eff. August 1, 2000; Amended Eff. April 1, 2014; Pursuant to G.S. 150B-21.3A, rule is necessary without substantive public interest Eff. July 23, 2016; Amended Eff. September 1, 2018

| .0210 | Public Building Projects | If a public building project is performed pursuant to G.S. 87-1.1, the total amount of work to be performed by all licensed general contractors shall not exceed 25% of the total bid price. A licensed general contractor shall hold the applicable classifications and limitation for the work undertaken by such licensed general contractor. For the purpose of this Rule, a public building project is a building project that is governed by G.S. 143, Article8. |

History Note: Authority G.S. 87-1.1; 87-4; Eff. April 1, 2004.

| .0211 | Multiunit Buildings | (a) If a project consists of the construction or alteration of one or more buildings that fall under the requirements of the North Carolina Building Code, all structures and units on the same parcel of land shall be considered as a single project. |

(b) If a project consists of the construction or alteration of one or more buildings that fall under the requirements of the North Carolina Residential Code, only structures and units on the same parcel of land shall be considered as one project.

(c) The North Carolina State Building Code standards are hereby incorporated by reference, including subsequent amendments and editions. The current Code may be found online at http://www.ncdoi.com/OSFM/Engineering_and_Codes/Default.aspx?field1=Codes_-_Current_and_Past&user=State_Building_Codes.

History Note: Authority G.S. 87-1; 87-4; 87-10; Eff. August 11, 2009; Amended Eff. April 1, 2010; Pursuant to G.S. 150B-21.3A, rule is necessary without substantive public interest Eff. July 23, 2016; Amended Eff. April 1, 2018.

SECTION .0300 — APPLICATION PROCEDURE

| .0301 | General | *History Note: Authority G.S. 87 1; 87 10; Eff. February 1, 1976; Readopted Eff. September 26, 1977; Amended Eff. May 1, 1989; Pursuant to G.S.150B-21.3A, rule is necessary without substantive public interest Eff. July 23, 2016; Repealed Eff. April 1, 2018.* |

| .0302 | Request | *History Note: Authority G.S. 87 1; 87 10; 150B-19(5); Eff. February 1, 1976; Amended Eff. June 23, 1977; Readopted Eff. September 26, 1977; Amended Eff. May 1, 2006; December 1, 1995; June 1, 1992; Pursuant to G.S. 150B-21.3A, rule is necessary without substantive public interest Eff. July 23, 2016; Repealed Eff. April 1, 2018.* |

| .0303 | Application for Licensure | (a) General. Applications for licensure shall contain the following: |

    (1) the Social Security Number of examinee(s) and qualifier(s) and tax identification numbers for corporate applicants;

    (2) the applicant's contact information;

    (3) the name of business under which the licensee will be operating, if any;

    (4) requested designation of license limitation and classifications;

    (5) information about all crimes of which the applicant has been convicted;

    (6) certified copies of court records reflecting information regarding all crimes of which the applicant and qualifier(s) have been convicted;

    (7) information indicating whether the applicant or qualifier(s) has any disciplinary history with the Board or any other occupational licensing, registration, or certification agency;

(8)   information establishing financial responsibility as required by
G.S. 87-10(a) and Rule .0204 of this Chapter;

(9)   letters of reference as prescribed in Rule .0308 of this Chapter; and

(10) the application fee as set forth in Rule .0304 of this Chapter.

(b) Reciprocity. Applicants based on reciprocity shall submit with the application
form a copy of the applicant's license in the other state, certified by the other state
licensing board as being a copy of a valid license. Applicants shall have taken and
passed the exam offered in the state from which they are seeking reciprocity, or an
examination offered by the National Association of State Contractors Licensing
Agencies (NASCLA). Applicants shall also be required to take and pass the Board's
North Carolina law, rule, and building code examination prior to licensure.

*History Note: Authority G.S. 87 1; 87 10; Eff. February 1, 1976; Readopted Eff.
September 26, 1977; Amended Eff. May 1, 1989; Pursuant to
G.S. 150B-21.3A, rule is necessary without substantive public interest
Eff. July 23, 2016; Amended Eff. September 1, 2019; April 1, 2018.*

.0304   Fees   (a) The Board shall charge the following fees:

(1)   Application for limited license: $75.00;

(2)   Application for intermediate license: $100.00;

(3)   Application for unlimited license: $125.00;

(4)   Application for increase in limitation: $100.00 for increase to intermedi-
ate license and $125.00 for increase to unlimited license;

(5)   Late renewal: $10.00 per month for every month or part after the first day
of January.

(b) All fees charged by the Board shall be non-refundable.

*History Note: Authority G.S. 87 1; 87 10; Eff. February 1, 1976; Readopted Eff.
September 26, 1977; Amended Eff. January 1, 1983; Repealed Eff.
May 1, 1989; Codifier approved agency's waiver request to reuse rule
number; Eff. April 1, 2018.*

.0305   Filing Address   *History Note: Authority G.S. 87 1; 87 10; Eff. February 1, 1976; Amended Eff.
June 23, 1977; Readopted Eff. September 26, 1977; Amended Eff.
May 1, 1989; Pursuant to G.S. 150B-21.3A, rule is necessary without
substantive public interest Eff. July 23, 2016, Repealed Eff. April 1, 2018.*

.0306   Filing Deadline   *History Note: Authority G.S. 87-1; 87-10; Eff. February 1, 1976; Readopted Eff.
September 26, 1977; Amended Eff. June 1, 1994; June 1, 1992;
Repealed Eff. April 1, 2001.*

.0307   Notice of Approval   *History Note: Authority G.S. 87-1; 87-10; Eff. February 1, 1976; Readopted Eff.
September 26, 1977; Amended Eff. May 1, 1989; Repealed Eff.
August 1, 2000.*

.0308   Character References   (a) Each applicant shall submit to the Board three written evaluations of the
applicant as to the character reference's knowledge of and experience with the
applicant. If the applicant is a legal entity, character references shall be submitted
for all individ-uals who sign the application on behalf of the applicant. If the
applicant is a sole proprietorship, character references shall be for the applicant
itself.

(b) All character references shall include:

(1) name of the person submitting the reference;

(2) mailing address, phone number, and email address of the person submitting the reference;

(3) date of the reference; and

(4) information regarding the reference's knowledge of and experience with the applicant or person about whom the reference is being provided.

(c) Character references shall be completed and dated no more than 12 months prior to the date the reference is submitted to the Board.

History Note: Authority G.S. 87-1; 87-10; Eff. February 1, 1976; Readopted Eff. September 26, 1977; Amended Eff. May 1, 1989; Pursuant to G.S. 150-B-21.3A, rule is necessary without substantive public interest Eff. July 23, 2016; Amended Eff. September 1, 2019.

.0309 Licensure for Military-Trained Applicant; Licensure for Military Spouse

(a) Licensure for a military-trained applicant. Upon receipt of a request for licensure pursuant to G.S. 93B-15.1 from a military trained applicant, the Board shall issue a license to the applicant who satisfies the following conditions:

(1) submission of a complete Application for License to Practice General Contracting;

(2) submission of a license fee in accordance with G.S. 87-10;

(3) providing documentation to satisfy the conditions set out in G.S. 93B-15.1(a)(1)and (2); and

(4) providing documentation that the applicant has not committed any act in any jurisdiction that would constitute grounds for refusal, suspension, or revocation of a license in North Carolina at the time the act was committed.

(b) Licensure for a military spouse. Upon receipt of a request for licensure pursuant to G.S. 93B-15.1 from a military spouse, the Board shall issue a license to the applicant who satisfies the following conditions:

(1) submission of a complete Application for License to Practice General Contracting;

(2) submission of a license fee in accordance with G.S. 87-10;

(3) submission of written documentation demonstrating that the applicant is married to an active member of the U.S. military;

(4) providing documentation to satisfy conditions set out in G.S. 93B-15.1(b)(1)and (2);

(5) providing documentation that the applicant has not committed any act in any jurisdiction that would constitute grounds for refusal, suspension, or revocation of a license in North Carolina at the time the act was committed; and

(6) is in good standing and has not been disciplined by any agency that had jurisdiction to issue the license, certification, or permit.

History Note: Authority G.S. 87-4; 93B-15.1; Eff. April 1, 2014

SECTION .0400 — EXAMINATION

| .0401 | General | *History Note:* | Authority G.S. 87-1; 87-10; 87-15.1; Eff. February 1, 1976; Readopted Eff. September 26, 1977; Repealed Eff. May 1, 1989. |

.0402 Subject Matter

(a) Examinations for licensure shall ascertain the following:

    (1)   The criteria set out in G.S. 87-10(b); and

    (2)   The qualifiers's knowledge of the practice of general contracting within the specific classification(s) he or she is seeking to be qualified as described in Rule .0202 of this Chapter.

(b) As a part of the Board's examination process, all applicants, including those seeking reciprocity from other jurisdictions, shall be tested on the Board's laws and rules.

History Note: Authority G.S. 87 1; 87 10; Eff. February 1, 1976; Readopted Eff. September 26, 1977; Amended Eff. August 1, 2000; June 1, 1994; May 1, 1989; Pursuant to G.S. 150B-21.3A, rule is necessary without substantive public interest Eff. July 23, 2016; Repealed Eff. April 1, 2018; Codifier approved agency's waiver request to reuse rule number; Eff. September 1, 2019.

.0403 Number of Examinations Taken

An applicant must take one different examination for each classification of general contracting for which the applicant seeks licensure.

History Note: Authority G.S. 87-1; 87-10; Eff. February 1, 1976; Readopted Eff. September 26, 1977; Amended Eff. May 1, 1989.

.0404 Passing Grade

Persons taking the examination shall receive a score of at least 70 in order to pass the examination.

History Note: Authority G.S. 87 1; 87 10; Eff. February 1, 1976; Readopted Eff. September 26, 1977; Amended Eff. January 1, 1983; Repealed Eff. May 1, 1989; Codifier approved agency's waiver request to reuse rule number; Eff. April 1, 2018.

.0405 Examination Schedule

Upon approval of the application by the Board, applicants will be notified as to the instructions for scheduling the required examination or examinations. Applicants may receive details from the examinations provider concerning the actual date, time and location to report for the examination or examinations requested.

History Note: Authority G.S. 87-1; 87-10; Eff. February 1, 1976; Readopted Eff. September 26, 1977; Amended Eff. August 1, 2000; May 1, 1989.

.0406 Filing Deadline
.0407 Re-Examination

History Note: Authority G.S. 87-1; 87-10; Eff. February 1, 1976; Readopted Eff. September 26, 1977; Amended Eff. January 1, 1993; Repealed Eff. May 1, 1989.

.0408 Person Taking Examination

History Note: Authority G.S. 87 1; 87 10; Eff. February 1, 1976; Readopted Eff. September 26, 1977; Amended Eff. April 1, 2006; September 1, 1992; May 1, 1989; Pursuant to G.S. 150B-21.3A, rule is necessary without substantive public interest Eff. July 23, 2016; Repealed Eff. April 1, 2018.

.0409 Review Workshop Charge

History Note: Authority G.S. 87-10; 150B-19(5)d; Eff. June 1, 1992; Repealed Eff. April 1, 2004.

.0410   Failing   *History Note:*   *Authority G.S. 87-10; Eff. December 1, 1995; Amended Eff.*
        Examination   *August 1, 2000; Pursuant to G.S. 150B-21.3A, rule is necessary*
                                           without substantive public interest Eff. July 23, 2016; Repealed
                                           Eff. April 1, 2018.

SECTION .0500 — LICENSE

.0501   License Granted   (a) License numbers shall be included on all contracts and bids.

                          (b) If a licensee files Articles of Dissolution or the N.C. Department of the
                          Secretary of State withdraws the licensee's Certificate of Authority, the Board shall
                          archive the license.

                          History Note: *Authority G.S. 87 1; 87 10; 87 12; Eff. February 1, 1976; Readopted*
                                            Eff. September 26, 1977; Amended Eff. May 1, 1989; Pursuant to
                                            G.S. 150B-21.3A, rule is necessary without substantive public interest
                                            Eff. July 23, 2016; Amended Eff. September 1, 2019; April 1, 2018.

.0502   Temporary License   The Board shall issue a temporary license only as required by G.S. 93B-15.1.

                          History Note: *Authority G.S. 87 1; 87 10; Eff. February 1, 1976; Readopted Eff.*
                                            September 26, 1977; Pursuant to G.S. 150B-21.3A, rule is necessary
                                            without substantive public interest Eff. July 23, 2016; Amended
                                            Eff. April 1, 2018.

.0503   Renewal of   (a) Applications for renewal of license shall contain the following:
        License
                          (1) the Social Security Number of the applicant and qualifier(s) and tax iden-
                               tification number for corporations, LLCs, or partnerships;
                          (2) the applicant's contact information;
                          (3) the name of business under which licensee will be operating, if any;
                          (4) information regarding any changes made in the status of the licensee's
                               business, since the initial application or last renewal was submitted to the
                               Board, whichever is later;
                          (5) confirmation of license limitation and classifications;
                          (6) information about all crimes of which the applicant has been convicted
                               since the initial application or last renewal was submitted to the Board,
                               whichever is later;
                          (7) documentation regarding all crimes referenced above;
                          (8) information indicating whether the applicant has any disciplinary his-
                               tory with any other occupational licensing, registration, or certification
                               agency since the initial application or last renewal was submitted to the
                               Board, whichever is later;
                          (9) an attestation that the applicant maintains continued financial responsi-
                               bility pursuant to Rule .0204 of this Chapter;
                          (10) if applicable, proof that the surety bond is maintained in compliance with
                               Rule .0204 of this Chapter; and
                          (11) the application fee and any accrued late fees as set forth in Rule .0304 of
                               this Chapter.

                          (b) A licensee shall submit an audited financial statement as evidence of continued
                          financial responsibility in accordance with Rule .0204 of this Chapter if the Board

finds that the licensee is insolvent, financially unstable, or unable to meet its financial responsibilities based upon the information provided in the renewal application.

(c) A licensee shall provide the Board with a copy of any bankruptcy petition filed by the licensee within 30 days of its filing. A licensee in bankruptcy shall provide to the Board an agreed-upon procedures report on a form provided by the Board or an audited financial statement with a classified balance sheet as part of any application for renewal.

(d) A corporate license shall not be renewed unless it is in good standing with the N.C. Department of the Secretary of State.

(e) Upon receipt of a written request by or on behalf of a licensee who is currently in good standing with the Board, is serving in the armed forces of the United States, and to whom G.S. 105-249.2 grants an extension of time to file a tax return, the Board shall grant that same extension of time for complying with renewal application deadlines, for paying renewal fees, and for meeting any other requirement or conditions related to the maintenance or renewal of the license issued by the Board. The applicant shall furnish to the Board a copy of the military orders or the extension approval by the Internal Revenue Service or by the North Carolina Department of Revenue.

History Note: Authority G.S. 87-1; 87-4;87-10; 87-12; 87-13; 93B-15;
               Eff. February 1, 1976; Readopted Eff. September 26, 1977; ARRC
               Objection March 19, 1987; Amended Eff. May 1, 1989; August 1,
               1987; Temporary Amendment Eff. June 28, 1989 for a period of 155
               Days to Expire on December 1, 1989; Amended Eff. December 1, 1989;
               RRC Removed Objection of March 19, 1987 Eff. August 20, 1992
               based on subsequent amendment; Amended Eff. September 1, 1992;
               Temporary Amendment Eff. May 31, 1996; Amended Eff. April 1,
               2014; June 1, 2011; June 1, 2003; April 1, 2003; August 1, 2002;
               April 1, 1997; Pursuant to G.S. 150B-21.3A, rule is necessary without
               substantive public interest Eff. July 23, 2016; Amended Eff. September 1,
               2019; April 1, 2018.

.0504   Increase in   (a) General. A person, firm, or corporation holding a valid license to engage in
        Limitation   the practice of general contracting in North Carolina may apply for a different
                           limitation by making application for such different limitation with the Board. The
                           application shall contain the following:

                           (1)   the Social Security Number of individual applicant, qualifier(s), and tax
                                 identification number for corporations, LLCs, or partnerships;

                           (2)   the applicant's contact information;

                           (3)   the exact name of the business as reflected on the previously issued
                                 license that is subject to the limitation increase application;

                           (4)   information regarding any changes made in the status of the licensee's
                                 business since the initial application or last renewal was submitted to the
                                 Board, whichever is later;

                           (5)   confirmation of license limitation and classifications;

                           (6)   requested limitation;

                           (7)   an audited financial statement prepared in accordance with Rule .0204 of
                                 this Chapter;

(8) if applicable, proof that the surety bond is maintained in compliance with Rule .0204 of this Chapter; and

(9) the application fee as set forth in Rule .0304 of this Chapter.

(b) Eligibility. An applicant shall be eligible for a new limitation if he or she possesses the qualifications necessary in accordance with Rule .0204 of this Chapter, except that he or she shall not be required to take a written exam.

History Note: Authority G.S. 87 1; 87-4; 87 10; Eff. February 1, 1976; Amended Eff. June 23, 1977; Readopted Eff. September 26, 1977; Amended Eff. May 1, 1989; January 1, 1983; Temporary Amendment Eff. June 28, 1989, for a period of 155 days to expire on December 1, 1989; Amended Eff. August 1, 2000; December 1, 1989; Pursuant to G.S. 150B-21.3A, rule is necessary without substantive public interest Eff. July 23, 2016; Amended Eff. April 1, 2018.

.0505   Maintaining Current Address; Notification

(a) All licensees, applicants, and qualifiers shall notify the Board of any change in mailing address, phone number, or email address within 30 days from the date of the change. Notice shall be given in writing or through the Board's website portal for licensees.

(b) Notification from the Board shall be deemed received if mailed to the address provided by the licensee and shown in the records of the Board.

History Note: Authority G.S. 87 8; Eff. June 1, 1992; Pursuant to G.S. 150B-21.3A, rule is necessary without substantive public interest Eff. July 23, 2016; Amended Eff. April 1, 2018.

.0506   Charge for Status of Licensure

The Board shall charge persons requesting a verified copy of all or part of its roster of licensed contractors a fee to cover the cost of copying and mailing.

History Note: Authority G.S. 87 8; 87 13; 150B-19(5); Eff. June 1, 1992; Amended Eff. May 1, 2006; May 1, 1995; Pursuant to G.S. 150B-21.3A, rule is necessary without substantive public interest Eff. July 23, 2016; Amended Eff. April 1, 2018.

.0507   Fund Suspension

In the event the Board's authority to expend funds is suspended pursuant to G.S. 93B-2, the Board shall continue to issue and renew licenses and all fees tendered shall be placed in an escrow account maintained by the Board for this purpose. Once the Board's authority is restored, the funds shall be moved from the escrow account into the general operating account.

History Note: Authority G.S. 87-4; 93B-2; Eff. June 1, 2011.

SECTION .0600 — RULE-MAKING PROCEDURES

.0601   Petitions
.0602   Notice
.0603   Hearings
.0604   Emergency Rules
.0605   Declaratory Rulings

History Note: Authority G.S. 150A-12; 150A-12(d); 150A-13; 150A-16; 150A-17; Eff. February 1, 1976; Amended Eff. June 23, 1977; Readopted Eff. September 26, 1977; Repealed Eff. January 1, 1983.

.0606   Rule-Making

History Note: Authority G.S. 150A-11; 150A-14; Eff. January 1, 1983; Amended Eff. December 1, 1985; Repealed Eff. September 1, 1988.

SECTION .0700 — BOARD DISCIPLINARY PROCEDURES

.0701   Improper Practice

(a) Complaint. Any person who believes that a licensed general contractor is in violation of the provisions of G.S. 87-11 may file a complaint with the Board against a licensee, qualifier, or both by setting forth in writing those charges and swearing to their authenticity. The complaint shall be submitted to the Board and include the complainant's contact information, project location, and name of the licensee, qualifier, or both.

(b) Preliminary or Threshold Determination:

(1) A complaint filed in accordance with G.S. 87-11(a1) shall be forwarded to a staff investigator for investigation. Within 30 days, the Board shall forward a written notice of the complaint to the licensee and qualifier(s) against whom the charge is made. The notice shall request a response from the licensee and qualifier(s). The Board shall send notice of the charge and of the alleged facts or alleged conduct by first class mail to the last known address and by email to the address of the licensee and qualifier(s).

(2) After the investigation is complete, the charge shall be referred to the review committee. The review committee shall consist of the following individuals:

(A) one member of the Board;

(B) the Secretary-Treasurer or his designee; and

(C) a staff person agreed upon by the individuals listed above.

(3) Based upon the complaint and investigation, the review committee shall recommend to the Board that:

(A) The charge be dismissed;

(B) When the charge is admitted as true by the licensee and qualifier(s), the Board accept the licensee's and qualifier(s') admission of guilt and order the licensee and qualifier(s) not to commit in the future the act or acts admitted by him to have been violated and not to violate any of the acts of misconduct specified in G.S. 87-11 at any time in the future; or

(C) The charge, whether admitted or denied, be presented to the full Board for a hearing and determination by the Board on the merits of the charge in accordance with the substantive and procedural requirements of the provisions of Section .0800 of this Chapter and the provisions of G.S. 87-11. Prior to the charges being heard and determined by the Board, it may be resolved by consent order.

History Note: Authority G.S. 87-4; 87-11; 150B-3; 150B-38; Eff. February 1, 1976; Readopted Eff. September 26, 1977; Amended Eff. April 1, 2014; June 1, 2011; April 1, 2006; April 1, 2003; May 1, 1989; Pursuant to G.S. 150B-21.3A, rule is necessary without substantive public interest Eff. July 23, 2016; Amended Eff. April 1, 2018.

.0702   Unlicensed Practice

(a) Complaint. Any person who believes that a person, firm, or corporation is in violation of the acts specified in G.S. 87-13 may file a complaint against that person, firm, or corporation. The complaint shall be filed with the Board and include the complainant's contact information, project location, and name of alleged violator.

(b) Preliminary or Threshold Determination:

    (1)   A complaint filed in accordance with G.S. 87-13 shall be forwarded to a staff investigator for investigation. Board staff shall investigate the charge to determine whether there is probable cause to believe that a party against whom a charge has been brought violated the provisions of G.S. 87-13.

    (2)   After the investigation is complete, the charge shall be referred to the review committee. The review committee shall consist of the following individuals:

        (A) one member of the Board;

        (B) the Secretary-Treasurer or his designee; and

        (C) a staff person agreed upon by the individuals listed above.

    (3)   Based upon the complaint and investigation, if the review committee determines that probable cause exists that a person, firm, or corporation is practicing general contracting without a license, it shall recommend to the Board that injunctive relief be sought. If the Board concurs with the review committee's recommendation, the investigation shall be forwarded to Board counsel to seek injunctive relief. If the review committee does not believe that the person, firm, or corporation is practicing general contracting without a license, it shall recommend to the Board dismissal of the complaint. Once dismissed, the Board shall notify the complainant.

History Note: *Authority G.S. 87-1; 87-4; 87-13; 87-13.1; Eff. February 1, 1976; Readopted Eff. September 26, 1977; Amended Eff. April 1, 2014; June 1, 2011; May 1, 1989; Pursuant to G.S. 150B-21.3A, rule is necessary without substantive public interest Eff. July 23, 2016; Amended Eff. April 1, 2018.*

.0703   Fee for Submittal of Bad Check

(a) The Board shall charge the maximum processing fee allowed by G.S. 25-3-506 if a check submitted to the Board is returned by a financial institution because of insufficient funds or because the drawer did not have an account at that bank.

(b) Until such time as the drawer of the bad check has paid the prescribed fee, the drawer shall not be eligible to take an examination, review an examination, obtain a license, or have the license renewed. For the purpose of this Rule, "prescribed fee" shall mean the sum of:

    (1)   the maximum processing fee allowed by G.S. 25-3-506;

    (2)   the renewal or application fee, whichever is applicable; and

    (3)   the late payment fee described in G.S. 87-10(e).

(c) Any license that has been issued or renewed based on a check which is returned to the Board shall be invalid until such time as the drawer has paid the prescribed fee. The invalidity of the license or renewal shall commence on the date of the issuance of the license or renewal.

(d) Payment of the prescribed fee to the Board shall be made in the form of a cashier's check, money order, credit card, or debit card.

(e) In the event the drawer of the bad check fails to pay the prescribed fee, during which time the license or renewal lapses for four years, the license shall not be renewed and the licensee for whom the check was to benefit shall fulfill all requirements of a new applicant set forth in G.S. 87-10 and Rules .0303 and .0503 of this Chapter.

History Note: *Authority G.S. 25-3-506; 87-4; 87-10; Eff. January 1, 1983;*
Amended Eff. April 1, 2014; April 1, 2003; May 1, 1989; Pursuant to
G.S. 150B-21.3A, rule is necessary without substantive public interest
Eff. July 23, 2016; Amended Eff. April 1, 2018.

SECTION .0800 — CONTESTED CASES

History Note: *Authority G.S. 1A-1; Rule 24; 1A-1; Rules 26 through 33; 87-10;*
87-11; 87-15.1; 150A-3; 150A-23; 150A-23(a); 150A-24 through;
150A-33; 150A-36; 150A-37; Eff. February 1, 1976; Amended Eff.
June 23, 1977; Readopted Eff. September 26, 1977; Repealed
Eff. January 1, 1983.

History Note: *Authority G.S. 150A-11; 150A-14; Eff. January 1, 1983; Amended Eff.*
December 1, 1985; Repealed Eff. September 1, 1988.

History Note: *Authority G.S. 87 11(b); 150B 11; 150B 38; Eff. September 1, 1988;*
Pursuant to G.S. 150B-21.3A, rule is necessary without substantive
public interest Eff. July 23, 2016; Repealed Eff. April 1, 2018.

.0818   Request for Hearing

(a) A person aggrieved as defined by G.S. 150B-2 may submit a request for a hearing pursuant to G.S. 150B-38 before the Board in writing to the Board's office, with the request bearing the notation: REQUEST FOR ADMINISTRATIVE HEARING. The request shall contain the following information:

    (1) name and address of the aggrieved person;

    (2) a statement of the action taken by the Board that is challenged; and

(3)   a statement of the way in which the aggrieved person has been aggrieved.

(b) Upon receipt of a request for a hearing, the Board shall acknowledge the request and schedule a hearing.

History Note: Authority G.S. 87-4; 87-11; 150B-38; Eff. September 1, 1988; Amended Eff. June 1, 2011; August 1, 2002; Pursuant to G.S. 150B-21.3A, rule is necessary without substantive public interest Eff. July 23, 2016; Amended Eff. April 1, 2018.

.0819   Granting or Denying Hearing Request

(a) The Board shall decide whether to grant a request for a hearing.

(b) The denial of request for a hearing shall be issued immediately upon decision, and in no case later than 60 days after the submission of the request. Such denial shall contain a statement of the reasons leading the Board to deny the request.

(c) Approval of a request for a hearing shall be signified by the issuing of a notice as required by G.S. 150B-38(b).

History Note: Authority G.S. 87-11(b); 150B-38; Eff. September 1, 1988; Amended Eff. July 1, 2008.

.0820   Notice of Hearing

(a) The Board shall give the party or parties in a contested case a notice of hearing not less than 15 days before the hearing. Said notice shall comply with G.S. 150B-38(b).

(b) Based upon information received, if the Board determines that the public health, safety, or welfare requires emergency action, it may issue an order summarily suspending a license or exam credentials. Upon service of the order, the licensee or qualifier to whom the order is directed shall cease the practice of general contracting in North Carolina. The Board shall give notice of hearing pursuant to G.S. 150B 38 following service of the order. The suspension shall remain in effect pending issuance by the Board of a final agency decision pursuant to G.S. 150B 42.

History Note: Authority G.S. 87-4; 87 11(b); 150B 3(c); 150B 38; Eff. October 1, 1988; Pursuant to G.S. 150B-21.3A, rule is necessary without substantive public interest Eff. July 23, 2016; Amended Eff. April 1, 2018.

.0821   Who Shall Hear Contested Cases

All administrative hearings will be conducted by the Board, a panel consisting of a majority of the members of the Board, or an administrative law judge designated to hear the case pursuant to G.S. 150B-40(e).

History Note: Authority G.S. 87-11(b); 150B-11; 150B-38; 150B-40; Eff. October 1, 1988. Pursuant to G.S. 150B-21.3A, rule is necessary without substantive public interest Eff. July 23, 2016

.0822   Informal Procedures

The Board and the party or parties may agree in advance to simplify the hearing by: decreasing the number of issues to be contested at the hearing; accepting the validity of certain proposed evidence; accepting the findings in some other case with relevance to the case at hand; or agreeing to such other matters as may expedite the hearing.

History Note: Authority G.S. 87-11(b); 150B-11; 150B-41; Eff. October 1, 1988. Pursuant to G.S. 150B-21.3A, rule is necessary without substantive public interest Eff. July 23, 2016

| .0823 | Petition for Intervention | (a) A person desiring to intervene in a contested case must file a written petition with the Board's office. The request should bear the notation: PETITION TO INTERVENE IN THE CASE OF (Name of case). |

(b) The petition must include the following information:

(1) The name and address of petitioner;

(2) The business or occupation of petitioner, where relevant;

(3) A full identification of the hearing in which petitioner is seeking to intervene;

(4) The statutory or non-statutory grounds for intervention;

(5) Any claim or defense in respect of which intervention is sought; and

(6) A summary of the arguments of evidence petitioner seeks to present.

(c) The person desiring to intervene shall serve copies of the petition on all parties to the case.

(d) If the Board determines to allow intervention, notice of that decision will be issued promptly to all parties, and to the petitioner. In cases of discretionary intervention, such notification will include a statement of any limitations of time, subject matter, evidence or whatever else is deemed necessary, which are imposed on the intervenor.

(e) If the Board's decision is to deny intervention, the petitioner will be notified promptly. Such notice will be in writing, identifying the reasons for the denial, and will be issued to the petitioner and all parties.

*History Note: Authority G.S. 87-11(b); 150B-11; 150B-38; Eff. October 1, 1988.
Pursuant to G.S. 150B-21.3A, rule is necessary without substantive
public interest Eff. July 23, 2016*

.0824   Types of Intervention   (a) Intervention of Right. A petition to intervene as of right, as provided in the North Carolina Rules of Civil Procedure, Rule 24, will be granted if the petitioner meets the criteria of that rule and the petition is timely.

(b) Permissive Intervention. A petition to intervene permissibly as provided in the North Carolina Rules of Civil Procedure, Rule 24, will be granted if the petitioner meets the criteria of that rule and the Board determines that:

(1) There is sufficient legal or factual similarity between the petitioner's claimed rights, privileges, or duties and those of the parties to the hearing; and

(2) Permitting intervention by the petitioner as a party would aid the purpose of the hearing.

(c) The Board may allow discretionary intervention, with whatever limits and restrictions are deemed appropriate.

*History Note: Authority G.S. 87-11(b); 150B-11; 150B-38; Eff. September 1, 1988.
Pursuant to G.S. 150B-21.3A, rule is necessary without substantive
public interest Eff. July 23, 2016*

.0825   Disqualification of Board Members   *History Note: Authority G.S. 87-11(b); 150B-11; 150B-38; 150B-40; Eff. October 1,
1988; Expired effective August 1, 2016 pursuant to G.S. 150B-21.3A*

.0826   Failure to Appear   Should a party fail to appear at a scheduled hearing, the Board may proceed with the hearing and make its decision in the absence of the party, provided that the party has been given notice in accordance with G.S. 150B-38 and unless otherwise directed by law. The Board may order a continuance in order to give the party another opportunity to appear as determined on a case by case basis and upon good cause shown.

History Note: Authority G.S. 87-4; 87 11(b); 150B 38; 150B 40; Eff. October 1, 1988; Pursuant to G.S. 150B-21.3A, rule is necessary without substantive public interest Eff. July 23, 2016; Amended Eff. April 1, 2018.

.0827   Subpoenas   (a) Requests for subpoenas for the attendance and testimony of witnesses or for the production of documents, either at a hearing or for the purposes of discovery, shall:

(1)   be made in writing to the Board;

(2)   identify any document sought;

(3)   include the full name and home or business address of all persons to be subpoenaed; and

(4)   if known, the date, time, and place for responding to the subpoena.

The Board shall issue the requested subpoenas within three days of receipt of the request.

(b) Subpoenas shall contain the following:

(1)   the caption of the case;

(2)   the name and address of the person subpoenaed;

(3)   the date, hour, and location of the hearing in which the witness is commanded to appear;

(4)   a particularized description of the books, papers, records, or objects the witness is directed to bring with him to the hearing, if any;

(5)   the identity of the party on whose application the subpoena was issued;

(6)   the date of issue;

(7)   the signature of the presiding officer or his designee; and

(8)   a "return of service." The "return of service" form as filled out, shall show:

(A) the name and capacity of the person serving the subpoena;

(B) the date on which the subpoena was delivered to the person directed to make service;

(C) the date on which service was made;

(D) the person on whom service was made;

(E) the manner in which service was made; and

(F) the signature of the person making service.

(c) Subpoenas shall be served in a manner set forth in Rule 45 of the N.C. Rules of Civil Procedure.

(d) Any person receiving a subpoena from the Board may object thereto by filing a written objection to the subpoena with the Board's office. Written objections shall comply with Rule 45 of the N.C. Rules of Civil Procedure.

(e) The party who requested the subpoena may file a written response to the objection. The written response shall be served by the requesting party on the objecting witness with filing the response with the Board.

(f) After receipt of the objection and response thereto, if any, the Board shall issue a notice to the party who requested the subpoena and the party challenging the subpoena to be scheduled as soon as practicable, at which time evidence and testimony may be presented, limited to the narrow questions raised by the objection and response.

(g) Promptly after the close of such hearing, a majority of the Board members with voting authority will rule on the challenge and issue a written decision. A copy of the decision will be issued to all parties and made a part of the record.

History Note: Authority G.S. 87 11(b); 150B 38; 150B-39; 150B 40; Eff. October 1, 1988; Pursuant to G.S. 150B-21.3A, rule is necessary without substantive public interest Eff. July 23, 2016; Amended Eff. April 1, 2018.

.0828   Witnesses

Any party may be a witness and may present witnesses on the party's behalf at the hearing. All oral testimony at the hearing shall be under oath or affirmation and shall be recorded. At the request of a party or upon the Board's own motion, the presiding officer may exclude witnesses from the hearing room so that they cannot hear the testimony of other witnesses.

History Note: Authority G.S. 87-11(b); 150B-11; 150B-38; 150B-40; Eff. September 1, 1988. Pursuant to G.S. 150B-21.3A, rule is necessary without substantive public interest Eff. July 23, 2016

.0829   Final Decision

In all cases heard by the Board, the Board shall issue a final written decision within 60 days following the close of the hearing. This decision will be the prerequisite "final agency decision" for the right to judicial review.

History Note: Authority G.S. 87-4; 87 11(b); 150B 38; 150B 42; Eff. September 1, 1988; Pursuant to G.S. 150B-21.3A, rule is necessary without substantive public interest Eff. July 23, 2016; Amended Eff. April 1, 2018.

.0830   Proposals for Decisions

(a) If an administrative law judge hears a contested case pursuant to G.S. 150B-40(e), a party may file written exception and alternative finding of facts and conclusions of law to the "proposal for decision" issued by the administrative law judge. The written exceptions and alternative findings of facts and conclusions of law shall be received by the Board within 10 days after the party has received the "proposal for decision" as drafted by the administrative law judge.

(b) Any exceptions shall be written and refer specifically to pages of the record or otherwise identify the occurrence to which exception is taken. The exceptions must be filed with the Board within ten days of the receipt of the proposal for decision. The written exceptions shall bear the notation: EXCEPTIONS TO THE PROCEEDINGS IN THE CASE OF (Name of case).

(c) Pursuant to G.S. 150B-40(e), any party may present oral argument to the Board upon request. The request must be included with the written exceptions.

(d) Upon receipt of request for further oral argument, Board staff shall issue notice to all parties designating time and place for such oral argument.

(e) The Board's final decision shall be a part of the record, a copy shall be given to all parties, and shall be the "final agency decision" for the right to judicial review.

The final written decision shall be issued by the Board within 60 days from the date oral arguments were presented to the Board. If there are no oral arguments presented, the final written decision shall be issued within 60 days of the date on which the Board rendered its decision.

History Note: Authority G.S. 87-4; 87 11(b); 150B 38; 150B 40; Eff. September 1, 1988; Amended Eff. July 1, 2008; Pursuant to G.S. 150B-21.3A, rule is necessary without substantive public interest Eff. July 23, 2016; Amended Eff. April 1, 2018.

SECTION .0900 — HOMEOWNERS RECOVERY FUND

.0901   Definitions

The following definitions apply to the Board's administration of the Homeowners Recovery Fund established pursuant to Article 1A, Chapter 87 of the General Statutes:

(1)   "Constructing or altering" means contracting for the construction or alteration of a single-family residential dwelling unit.

(2)   "Dishonest conduct" means conduct described in G.S. 87-15.5(3).

(3)   "Incompetent conduct" means conduct which demonstrates a lack of ability or fitness to discharge a duty associated with undertaking to construct or alter a single-family residential dwelling or the supervision of such construction or alteration.

(4)   "Owner or former owner" means a person who contracted with a general contractor for the construction or purchase of a single-family residential dwelling unit. "Owner or former owner" does not include a person who is a spouse, child, parent, grandparent, sibling, partner, associate, officer, or employee of a general contractor whose conduct caused a reimbursable loss. In addition, the term does not include general contractors or any financial or lending institution, or any owner or former owner of a single-family residential dwelling unit that has been the subject of an award from the Homeowners Recovery Fund resulting from the same dishonest or incompetent conduct. "Owner or former owner" does not include the owner of real property who purchased, owned, constructed, altered, or contracted for construction or alteration of a single-family residential dwelling unit without intending to occupy the single-family residential dwelling unit as a residence.

(5)   "Substantial completion" means that degree of completion of a project, improvement or specified area or portion thereof whereupon the owner can use the same for its intended use.

(6)   "Separately owned residence" means a building whose construction is governed by the Building Code Council pursuant to G.S. 143-138.

History Note: Authority G.S. 87-15.6; Eff. January 4, 1993; Amended Eff. April 1, 2014; July 1, 2008; April 1, 2007; April 1, 2001; August 1, 2000; August 1, 1998.

.0902   Management of Fund

(a) The Secretary-Treasurer, as the Board's Chief Administrative Officer, shall:

(1)   Establish a special account of the Board for those monies collected pursuant to G.S. 87-15.6(b);

(2)   Make expenditures from the fund as authorized by G.S. 87-15.7(b) by signing checks for expenditures after the checks are signed by the Chairman.

(b) Until such time as the fund initially reaches two hundred fifty thousand dollars ($250,000.00),or at any time thereafter that the fund has insufficient assets in excess of two hundred fifty thousand dollars ($250,000.00) to pay outstanding claims, the Secretary-Treasurer shall not disburse any payments to an applicant for recovery. Any applicant who is awarded payment from the fund, however, shall hold a vested right for payment once the fund reaches a sufficient level. Authorized payments which cannot be made due to lack of funds will be paid as funds become available, beginning with those payments which have been unsatisfied for the longest period of time.

(c) Monies forwarded to the Board pursuant to G.S. 87-15.6(b) for deposit into the fund shall be accompanied by a verified statement signed by the city or county inspector on a form provided by the Board. The form shall require information concerning the number of permits issued by the reporting inspections department from which the recovery fund fee was collected and the total dollar amount due to the fund for that particular quarter.

History Note: Authority G.S. 87-15.6; 87-15.7; 87-15.8; Eff. January 4, 1993.

.0903   Application for Payment

(a) Homeowners meeting the requirements of G.S. 87-15.8 who wish to file for reimbursement from the Homeowners Recovery Fund shall provide the following information on an application prescribed by the Board:

1)   the applicant's name and address,

2)   the amount of the claim,

3)   a description of the acts of the general contractor which constitute the grounds for the claim claim, and

4)   a statement that the applicant has exhausted all civil remedies or the general contractor has filed for bankruptcy.

Requests for the application form shall be directed to the Board at the address shown in Rule .0101 of this Chapter.

(b) If the applicant has exhausted all civil remedies pursuant to G.S. 87-15.8(3)(a), the application shall include certified copies of the complaint, judgment, and return of execution marked as unsatisfied."

(c) If the applicant is claiming against a general contractor that was a corporation dissolved no later than one year after the date of discovery by the applicant of the facts constituting the dishonest or incompetent conduct, then the applicant shall include certified copies of documents evidencing the dissolution.

(d) If the applicant has been precluded from filing suit, obtaining a judgment, or otherwise proceeding due to the bankruptcy of the general contractor, then the applicant shall submit a certified copy of the bankruptcy petition, any proof of claim, and documents from the bankruptcy court or trustee certifying that the applicant has not and will not receive any payment from the bankruptcy proceeding.

(e) If the applicant is claiming against the estate of a deceased general contractor, then the applicant shall submit a statement from the administrator of the estate certifying that the applicant has not and will not receive any payment from the estate.

(f) If the applicant includes copies of a judgment and return of execution marked as unsatisfied, the applicant must demonstrate that the writ of execution was filed in the following counties:

(1) where the project at issue was located;

(2) where the contractor's last known principal place of business was located; and

(3) if the contractor was a licensee of the Board, the county in which the last address provided to the Board was located.

History Note: Authority G.S. 87-15.6; 87-15.7; 87-15.8; Eff. January 4, 1993; Amended Eff. March 1, 2005; August 1, 1998; Pursuant to G.S. 150-B-21.3A, rule is necessary without substantive public interest Eff. July 23, 2016; Amended Eff. September 1, 2019.

.0904   Filing Deadline and Service

(a) Applicants seeking recovery from the fund shall be forever barred unless application is made within one year after termination of all proceedings, including appeals, in connection with an unsatisfied judgment obtained against a general contractor. Claims based upon the bankruptcy, death, or dissolution of the general contractor shall be forever barred unless application is made within three years from the date of discovery by the applicant of the facts constituting the dishonest or incompetent conduct or within six years of substantial completion of the construction or alteration of the residence in question, whichever comes first.

(b) Applications shall be filed at the address shown in Rule .0101 of this Chapter. The Board shall serve a copy of the application upon the general contractor who allegedly caused the loss. Service shall be accomplished by certified mail, return receipt requested, or other methods authorized by G.S. 150B-38(c).

History Note: Authority G.S. 87-15.6; 87-15.7; 87-15.8; Eff. January 4, 1993; Amended Eff. April 1, 2007; August 1, 1998.

.0905   Multiple Claims

(a) Any time the Board has notice of more than one application or potential claim for payment from the fund arising out of the conduct of a single general contractor, the Board may, in its discretion, direct that all applications filed before a date determined by the Board, be consolidated for hearing.

(b) When consolidation is appropriate, the Board shall issue to the general contractor, the applicants and potential claimants, an Order of Consolidation setting forth the deadline for filing all applications to be consolidated. On or before the deadline, the Board may, in its discretion, either extend the deadline or issue to the general contractor and all applicants notice of the time, date and place set for a hearing on the consolidated applications.

(c) Claims for which the Board has received no notice or for which no application has been filed prior to the deadline set forth in the Order of Consolidation shall not be considered by the Board until after the completion of all proceedings relating to the consolidated applications and payment thereon.

History Note: Authority G.S. 87-15.6; 87-15.7; Eff. January 4, 1993.

.0906   Processing of Claim Application

(a) Staff shall refer a filed application to the Recovery Fund Review Committee.

The Recovery Fund Review Committee is a committee made up of the following individuals:

(1)   one member of the Board;

(2)   the legal counsel of the Board; and

(3)   the Secretary-Treasurer.

(b) Within 30 days after service of a copy of the application upon the general contractor, the general contractor may file a response to the application setting forth answers and defenses. Responses shall be filed with the Board and copies shall be served on the applicant.

(c) The Committee shall dismiss a claim if an applicant fails to respond to an inquiry from the Committee or its representative within six months of receipt of the inquiry.

(d) After all preliminary evidence has been received, the Committee shall make a recommendation regarding the disposition of the application. From the evidence, it shall recommend to the Board that:

(1)   the application be dismissed as meritless; or

(2)   the application and charges contained therein be presented to the Board for a hearing and determination by the Board on the merits of the application.

(e) The Committee shall give notice of the recommendation to the applicant and the general contractor within 10 days of the Committee's decision. The Committee is not required to notify the parties of the reasons for its recommendation. The decision of the Board is final.

History Note: Authority G.S. 87-4; 87-15.6; 87-15.7; 87-15.8; Eff. January 4, 1993; Amended Eff. April 1, 2007.

.0907   Homeowners Recovery Fund Hearing

(a) If it is determined by the Recovery Fund Review Committee that the Board should conduct a hearing on an application, the Board shall give the applicant and general contractor notice of hearing not less than 15 days before the hearing. Notice of hearing to the general contractor shall be sufficient if mailed to the last known address of the general contractor at least 15 days prior to the date of the hearing. The notice shall contain the following information:

(1)   The name, position, address and telephone number of a person at the offices of the Board to contact for further information or discussion;

(2)   The date, time, and place for a pre-hearing conference, if any, and

(3)   Any other information being relevant to informing the parties as to the procedure of the hearing.

(b) All homeowners recovery fund hearings shall be conducted by the Board or a panel consisting of a majority of the members of the Board.

(c) The provisions of 21 NCAC 12 .0825 governing disqualification of Board members shall also govern hearings conducted pursuant to this Section.

(d) Should a party fail to appear at a hearing, the Board may proceed with the hearing and make its decision in the absence of the party, provided that the party has been given proper notice.

(e) Any party may be a witness and may present witnesses on the party's behalf at the hearing. The Board staff may also present evidence and participate at the hearing. All oral testimony at the hearing shall be under oath or affirmation. At the request of a party, the presiding officer may exclude witnesses from the hearing room so that they cannot hear the testimony of other witnesses.

(f) At the hearing, the applicant shall be required to show:

    (1) He has suffered a reimbursable loss as defined in G.S. 87-15.5(6) and Rule .0901(c) of this Chapter in the construction or alteration of a single-family dwelling unit owned or previously owned by that person, provided, that if there have been findings entered in a contested civil action relevant to the issue of whether the applicant has suffered a reimbursable loss, then such findings shall be presumed as established for purposes of this Section subject to rebuttal by the general contractor;

    (2) He did not, directly or indirectly, obtain the building permit in his own name or did use a general contractor;

    (3) He has made application within one year after the termination of all judicial proceedings, including appeals, in connection with the unsatisfied judgment or within the period prescribed in Rule .0904(a) of this Chapter for claims based upon the automatic stay provisions of Section 362 of the U.S. Bankruptcy Code;

    (4) He has diligently pursued his remedies against the general contractor and on any applicable bond, surety agreement or insurance contract, and attempted execution on the judgments against all judgment debtors without success.

(g) The general contractor shall be permitted to participate in the hearing as a party and shall have recourse to all appropriate means of defense, including the examination of witnesses.

History Note: Authority G.S. 87-15.5; 87-15.6; 87-15.7; 87-15.8; Eff. January 4, 1993; Amended Eff. August 1, 2000.

.0908   Order Directing Payment From Fund

After any hearing, the Board may find that an applicant should be paid from the fund and the Board may enter an Order requiring payment from the fund in whatever sum the Board deems appropriate in accordance with the limitations contained in Rule .0910 of this Chapter. All payments are a matter of privilege and not of right.

History Note: Authority G.S. 87-15.5; 87-15.6; 87-15.7; 87-15.8; Eff. January 4, 1993.

.0909   Settlement of Claims

The claim or claims forming the basis of an application for recovery from the fund may be compromised and settled by the applicant and the general contractor after the filing of the application. The parties shall notify the Board immediately of any such settlement. Payment of the claim, in whole or in part, by the general contractor as part of a settlement will result in the claim no longer being a "reimbursable loss" as defined by G.S. 87-15.5(6)(b), and the claim will be dismissed by the Board.

History Note: Authority G.S. 87-15.6; 87-15.7; 87-15.8; Eff. January 4, 1993.

.0910   Limitations; Pro Rata Distribution

(a) Payments from the fund for an approved application shall not exceed an amount equal to 10 percent of the total amount in the fund at the time the application is approved by the Board. All applications considered by the Board at the same meeting shall be subject to the same limitation.

(b) Consequential damages, multiple or punitive damages, civil or criminal penalties or fines, incidental damages, special damages, interest, and court costs shall not constitute monetary losses.

History Note: Authority G.S. 87-15.6; 87-15.7; 87-15.8; Eff. March 1, 1993.

.0911   Subrogation of Rights   When the Board has paid from the fund any sum to the applicant, the Board shall be subrogated to the rights of the applicant and the applicant shall assign to the Board all of his rights, title, and interest in the claim to the extent of the amount paid from the fund.

History Note: Authority G.S. 87-15.6; 87-15.7; 87-15.9; Eff. January 4, 1993.

.0912   Actions Against General Contractor   Nothing contained in these Rules shall prohibit or limit the authority of the Board to take disciplinary action against its licensees or to seek injunctive relief against those persons who have engaged in the unauthorized practice of general contracting. Stipulations made between the general contractor and the applicant as part of settlement or compromise of any claim shall not be binding on the Board in any disciplinary proceeding or action for injunction.

History Note: Authority G.S. 87-11; 87-13; 87-13.1; 87-15.6;
Eff. January 4, 1993.

Appendix G: Model Payment and Performance Bond

§ 44A25. Definitions.

Unless the context otherwise requires in this Article:

(1) "Claimant" includes any individual, firm, partnership, association or corporation entitled to maintain an action on a bond described in this Article and shall include the "contracting body" in a suit to enforce the performance bond.

(2) "Construction contract" means any contract for the construction, reconstruction, alteration or repair of any public building or other public work or public improvement, including highways.

(3) "Contracting body" means any department, agency, or political subdivision of the State of North Carolina which has authority to enter into construction contracts.

(4) "Contractor" means any person who has entered into a construction contract with a contracting body.

(5) "Labor or materials" shall include all materials furnished or labor performed in the prosecution of the work called for by the construction contract regardless of whether or not the labor or materials enter into or become a component part of the public improvement, and further shall include gas, power, light, heat, oil, gasoline, telephone services and rental of equipment or the reasonable value of the use of equipment directly utilized in the performance of the work called for in the construction contract.

(6) "Subcontractor" means any person who has contracted to furnish labor or materials to, or who has performed labor for, a contractor or another subcontractor in connection with a construction contract. (1973, c. 1194, s. 1.)

§ 44A26. Bonds required.

(a) When the total amount of construction contracts awarded for any one project exceeds three hundred thousand dollars ($300,000), a performance and payment bond as set forth in (1) and (2) is required by the contracting body from any contractor or construction manager at risk with a contract more than fifty thousand dollars ($50,000); provided that, for State departments, State agencies, and The University of North Carolina and its constituent institutions, a performance and payment bond is required in accordance with this subsection if the total amount of construction contracts awarded for any one project exceeds five hundred thousand dollars ($500,000). In the discretion of the contracting body, a performance and payment bond may be required on any construction contract as follows:

(1) A performance bond in the amount of one hundred percent (100%) of the construction contract amount, conditioned upon the faithful performance of the contract in accordance with the plans,

specifications and conditions of the contract. Such bond shall be solely for the protection of the contracting body that is constructing the project.

(2)   A payment bond in the amount of one hundred percent (100%) of the construction contract amount, conditioned upon the prompt payment for all labor or materials for which a contractor or subcontractor is liable. The payment bond shall be solely for the protection of the persons furnishing materials or performing labor for which a contractor, subcontractor, or construction manager at risk is liable.

(b)   The performance bond and the payment bond shall be executed by one or more surety companies legally authorized to do business in the State of North Carolina and shall become effective upon the awarding of the construction contract. (1973, c. 1194, s. 1; 1983, c. 818; 1987 (Reg. Sess., 1988), c. 1108, s. 10; 1995, c. 367, s. 3; 2001496, s. 7; 2010148, s. 1.)

§ 44A27. Actions on payment bonds; service of notice.

(a)   Subject to the provision of subsection (b) hereof, any claimant who has performed labor or furnished materials in the prosecution of the work required by any contract for which a payment bond has been given pursuant to the provisions of this Article, and who has not been paid in full therefor before the expiration of 90 days after the day on which the claimant performed the last such labor or furnished the last such materials for which he claims payment, may bring an action on such payment bond in his own name, to recover any amount due him for such labor or materials and may prosecute such action to final judgment and have execution on the judgment.

(b)   Any claimant who has a direct contractual relationship with any subcontractor but has no contractual relationship, express or implied, with the contractor may bring an action on the payment bond only if he has given written notice to the contractor within 120 days from the date on which the claimant performed the last of the labor or furnished the last of the materials for which he claims payment, stating with substantial accuracy the amount claimed and the name of the person for whom the work was performed or to whom the material was furnished.

(c)   The notice required by subsection (b), above, shall be served by registered or certified mail, postage prepaid, in an envelope addressed to such contractor at any place where his office is regularly maintained for the transaction of business or served in any manner provided by law for the service of summons. (1973, c. 1194, s. 1; 1987, c. 569; 2001177, s. 1; 2001487, s. 100.)

§ 44A28. Actions on payment bonds; venue and limitations.

(c)   Every action on a payment bond as provided in G.S. 44A 27 shall be brought in a court of appropriate jurisdiction in a county where the construction contract or any part thereof is to be or has been performed.

(d)   No action on a payment bond shall be commenced after the expiration of the longer period of one year from the day on which the last of the labor was performed or material was furnished by the claimant, or one year from the day on which final settlement was made with the contractor. (1973, c. 1194, s. 1.)

§ 44A29. Limitation of liability of a surety.

No surety shall be liable under a payment bond for a total amount greater than the face amount of the payment bond. A judgment against any surety may be reduced or set aside upon motion by the surety and a showing that the total amount of claims paid and judgments previously rendered under such payment bond, together with the amount of the judgment to be reduced or set aside, exceeds the face amount of the bond. (1973, c. 1194, s. 1.)

§ 44A30. Variance of liability; contents of bond.

(a)   No act of or agreement between à contracting body, a contractor or a surety shall reduce the period of time for giving notice under G.S. 44A27(b) or commencing action under G.S. 44A28(b) or otherwise reduce or limit the liability of the contractor or surety as prescribed in this Article.

(b)   Every bond given by a contractor to a contracting body pursuant to this Article shall be conclusively presumed to have been given in accordance herewith, whether or not such bond be so drawn as to conform to this Article. This Article shall be conclusively presumed to have been written into every bond given pursuant thereto. (1973, c. 1194, s. 1.)

§ 44A31. Certified copy of bond and contract.

(a)   Any person entitled to bring an action or any defendant in an action on a payment bond shall have a right to require the contracting body to certify and furnish a copy of the payment bond and of the construction contract covered by the bond. It shall be the duty of such contracting body to give any such person a certified copy of the payment bond and the construction contract upon not less than 10 days' notice and request. The contracting body may require a reasonable payment for the actual cost of furnishing the certified copy.

(b)   A copy of any payment bond and of the construction contract covered by the bond certified by the contracting body shall constitute prima facie evidence of the contents, execution and delivery of such bond and construction contract. (1973, c. 1194, s. 1.)

§ 44A32. Designation of official; violation a misdemeanor.

 Each contracting body shall designate an official thereof to require the bonds described by this Article. If the official so designated shall fail to require said bond, he shall be guilty of a Class 1 misdemeanor. (1973, c. 1194, s. 1; 1993, c. 539, s. 407; 1994, Ex. Sess., c. 24, s. 14(c).)

§ 44A33. Form.

(a)   A performance bond form containing the following provisions shall comply with this Article: the date the bond is executed; the name of the principal; the name of the surety; the name of the contracting body; the amount of the bond; the contract number; and the following conditions:

"KNOW ALL MEN BY THESE PRESENTS, That we, the PRINCIPAL AND SURETY above named, are held and firmly bound unto the above named Contracting Body, hereinafter called the Contracting Body, in the penal sum of the amount stated above for the payment of which sum well and truly to be made, we bind ourselves, our heirs, executors, administrators, and successors, jointly and severally, firmly by these presents.

"THE CONDITION OF THIS OBLIGATION IS SUCH, that whereas the Principal entered into a certain contract with the Contracting Body, numbered as shown above and hereto attached:

"NOW THEREFORE, if the Principal shall well and truly perform and fulfill all the undertakings, covenants, terms, conditions, and agreements of said contract during the original term of said contract and any extensions thereof that may be granted by the Contracting Body, with or without notice to the Surety, and during the life of any guaranty required under the contract, and shall also well and truly perform and fulfill all the undertakings, covenants, terms, conditions, and agreements of any and all duly authorized modifications of said contract that may hereafter be made, notice of which modifications to the Surety being hereby waived, then, this obligation to be void; otherwise to remain in full force and virtue.

"IN WITNESS WHEREOF, the abovebounden parties have executed this instrument under their several seals on the date indicated above, the name and corporate seal of each corporate party being hereto affixed and these presents duly signed by its undersigned representative, pursuant to authority of its governing body."

 Appropriate places for execution by the surety and principal shall be provided.

(b)   A payment bond form containing the following provisions shall comply with this Article: the date the bond is executed; the name of the principal; the name of the surety; the name of the contracting body; the contract number; and the following conditions:

"KNOW ALL MEN BY THESE PRESENTS, That we, the PRINCIPAL and SURETY above named, are held and firmly bound unto the above named Contracting Body, hereinafter called the Contracting Body, in the penal sum of the amount stated above, for the payment of which sum well and truly to be made, we bind ourselves, our heirs, executors, administrators, and successors, jointly and severally, firmly by these presents.

"THE CONDITION OF THIS OBLIGATION IS SUCH, that whereas the Principal entered into a certain contract with the Contracting Body, numbered as shown above and hereto attached;

"NOW THEREFORE, if the Principal shall promptly make payment to all persons supplying labor and material in the prosecution of the work provided for in said contract, and any and all duly authorized modifications of said contract that may hereafter be made, notice of which modifications to the Surety being hereby waived, then this obligation to be void; otherwise to remain in full force and virtue.

"IN WITNESS WHEREOF, the abovebounden parties have executed this instrument under their several seals on the date indicated above, the name and corporate seal of each corporate party being hereto affixed and these presents duly signed by its undersigned representative, pursuant to authority of its governing body."

Appropriate places for execution by the surety and principal shall be provided. (1973, c. 1194, s. 1.)

§ 44A34. Construction of Article.

The addition of this Article shall not be construed as making the provisions of Articles 1 and 2 of Chapter 44A of the General Statutes apply to public bodies or public buildings. (1973, c. 1194, s. 3.)

§ 44A35. Attorneys' fees.

In any suit brought or defended under the provisions of Article 2 or Article 3 of this Chapter, the presiding judge may allow a reasonable attorneys' fee to the attorney representing the prevailing party. This attorneys' fee is to be taxed as part of the court costs and be payable by the losing party upon a finding that there was an unreasonable refusal by the losing party to fully resolve the matter which constituted the basis of the suit or the basis of the defense. For purposes of this section, "prevailing party" is a party plaintiff or third party plaintiff who obtains a judgment of at least fifty percent (50%) of the monetary amount sought in a claim or is a party defendant or third party defendant against whom a claim is asserted which results in a judgment of less than fifty percent (50%) of the amount sought in the claim defended. Notwithstanding the foregoing, in the event an offer of judgment is served in accordance with G.S. 1A1, Rule 68, a "prevailing party" is an offeree who obtains judgment in an amount more favorable than the last offer or is an offeror against whom judgment is rendered in an amount less favorable than the last offer. (1991 (Reg. Sess., 1992), c. 1010, s. 3; 1993 (Reg. Sess., 1994), c. 763, s. 1.)

§§ 44A36 through 44A39. Reserved for future codification purposes.

Appendix H: Public Contracts

EXCERPTS FROM CHAPTER 143, ARTICLE 8

§ 143128. Requirements for certain building contracts.

(a)   Preparation of specifications. – Every officer, board, department, commission or commissions charged with responsibility of preparation of specifications or awarding or entering into contracts for the erection, construction, alteration or repair of any buildings for the State, or for any county, municipality, or other public body, shall have prepared separate specifications for each of the following subdivisions or branches of work to be performed:

(1)   Heating, ventilating, air conditioning and accessories (separately or combined into one conductive system), refrigeration for cold storage (where the cold storage cooling load is 15 tons or more of refrigeration), and all related work.

(2)   Plumbing and gas fittings and accessories, and all related work.

(3)   Electrical wiring and installations, and all related work.

(4)   General work not included in subdivisions (1), (2), and (3) of this subsection relating to the erection, construction, alteration, or repair of any building.

Specifications for contracts that will be bid under the separateprime system or dual bidding system shall be drawn as to permit separate and independent bidding upon each of the subdivisions of work enumerated in this subsection. The above enumeration of subdivisions or branches of work shall not be construed to prevent any officer, board, department, commission or commissions from preparing additional separate specifications for any other category of work.

(a1)   Construction methods. – The State, a county, municipality, or other public body shall award contracts to erect, construct, alter, or repair buildings pursuant to any of the following methods:

(1)   Separateprime bidding.

(2)   Singleprime bidding.

(3)   Dual bidding pursuant to subsection (d1) of this section.

(4)   Construction management at risk contracts pursuant to G.S. 143128.1.

(5)   Alternative contracting methods authorized pursuant to G.S. 143135.26(9).

(a2)   Annually, on or before April 1st, beginning April 1, 2003, The University of North Carolina and all other public entities shall report to the Secretary of the Department of Administration on the effectiveness and costbenefit of utilization of each of the construction methods authorized in G.S. 143128(a1) that are used by the public entity.

The reports, which shall be initially filed in the year in which the project is completed, shall be in the format and contain the data prescribed by the Secretary of Administration and shall include at least the following:

(1)   The type of construction method used on the project.

(2)   The total dollar value of building projects by specific project with costs.

(3)   The bid costs and relevant postbid costs.

(4)   A detailed listing of all contractors and subcontractors used on the project indicating whether the contractor or subcontractor was an outofstate contractor or subcontractor.

(5)   If any contractor or subcontractor was an outofstate contractor or subcontractor, the reasons why the contractor or subcontractor was selected.

The Secretary of the Department of Administration shall report to the General Assembly on or before May 1st each year on the information collected pursuant to this subsection.

(b)   Separateprime contracts. – When the State, county, municipality, or other public body uses the separateprime contract system, it shall accept bids for each subdivision of work for which specifications are required to be prepared under subsection (a) of this section and shall award the respective work specified separately to responsible and reliable persons, firms or corporations regularly engaged in their respective lines of work. When the estimated cost of work to be performed in any single subdivision or branch for which separate bids are required by this subsection is less than twentyfive thousand dollars ($25,000), the same may be included in the contract for one of the other subdivisions or branches of the work, irrespective of total project cost. The contracts shall be awarded to the lowest responsible, responsive bidders, taking into consideration quality, performance, the time specified in the bids for performance of the contract, and compliance with G.S. 143128.2. Bids may also be accepted from and awards made to separate contractors for other categories of work.

Each separate contractor shall be directly liable to the State of North Carolina, or to the county, municipality, or other public body and to the other separate contractors for the full performance of all duties and obligations due respectively under the terms of the separate contracts and in accordance with the plans and specifications, which shall specifically set forth the duties and obligations of each separate contractor. For the purpose of this section, "separate contractor" means any person, firm or corporation who shall enter into a contract with the State, or with any county, municipality, or other public entity to erect, construct, alter or repair any building or buildings, or parts of any building or buildings.

(c)   Repealed by Session Laws 2001496, s. 3, effective January 1, 2001.

(d)   Singleprime contracts. – All bidders in a singleprime project shall identify on their bid the contractors they have selected for the subdivisions or branches of work for:

(1)   Heating, ventilating, and air conditioning;

(2)   Plumbing;

(3)   Electrical; and

(4)   General.

The contract shall be awarded to the lowest responsible, responsive bidder, taking into consideration quality, performance, the time specified in the bids for performance of the contract, and compliance with G.S. 143128.2. A contractor whose bid is accepted shall not substitute any person as subcontractor in the place of the subcontractor listed in the original bid, except (i) if the listed subcontractor's bid is later determined by the contractor to be nonresponsible or nonresponsive or the listed subcontractor refuses to enter into a contract for the complete performance of the bid work, or (ii) with the approval of the awarding authority for good cause shown by the contractor. The terms, conditions, and requirements of each contract between the contractor and a subcontractor performing work under a subdivision or branch of work listed in this subsection shall incorporate by reference the terms, conditions, and requirements of the contract between the contractor and the State, county, municipality, or other public body.

When contracts are awarded pursuant to this section, the public body shall make available to subcontractors the dispute resolution process as provided for in subsection (f1) of this section.

(d1)   Dual bidding. – The State, a county, municipality, or other public entity may accept bids to erect, construct, alter, or repair a building under both the singleprime and separateprime contracting systems and shall award the contract to the lowest responsible, responsive bidder under the singleprime system or to the lowest responsible, responsive bidder under the separateprime system, taking into consideration quality, performance, compliance with G.S. 143128.2, and time specified in the bids to perform the contract. In determining the system under which the contract will be awarded to the lowest responsible, responsive bidder, the public entity may consider cost of construction oversight, time for completion, and other factors it considers appropriate. The bids received as separateprime bids shall be received, but not opened, one hour prior to the deadline for the submission of singleprime bids. The amount of a bid submitted by a subcontractor to the general contractor under the singleprime system shall not exceed the amount bid, if any, for the same work by that subcontractor to the public entity under the separateprime system. The provisions of subsection (b) of this section shall apply to separateprime contracts awarded pursuant to this section and the provisions of subsection (d) of this section shall apply to singleprime contracts awarded pursuant to this section.

(e)   Project expediter; scheduling; public body to resolve project disputes. – The State, county, municipality, or other public body may, if specified in the bid documents, provide for assignment of responsibility for expediting the work on a project to a single responsible and reliable person, firm or corporation, which may be a prime contractor. In executing this responsibility, the designated project expediter may recommend to the State, county, municipality, or other public body whether payment to a contractor should be approved. The project expediter, if required by the contract documents, shall be responsible for preparing the project schedule and shall allow all contractors and subcontractors performing any of the branches of work listed in subsection (d) of this section equal input into the preparation of the initial schedule. Whenever separate contracts are awarded and separate contractors engaged for a project pursuant to this section, the public body may provide in the contract documents for resolution of project disputes through alternative dispute resolution processes as provided for in subsection (f1) of this section.

(f)   Repealed by Session Laws 2001496, s. 3, effective January 1, 2001.

(f1)   Dispute resolution. – A public entity shall use the dispute resolution process adopted by the State Building Commission pursuant to G.S. 143135.26(11), or shall adopt another dispute resolution process, which shall include mediation, to be used as an alterative to the dispute resolution process adopted by the State Building Commission. This dispute resolution process will be available to all the parties involved in the public entity's construction project including the public entity, the architect, the construction manager, the contractors, and the firsttier and lowertier subcontractors and shall be available for any issues arising out of the contract or construction process. The public entity may set a reasonable threshold, not to exceed fifteen thousand dollars ($15,000), concerning the amount in controversy that must be at issue before a party may require other parties to participate in the dispute resolution process. The public entity may require that the costs of the process be divided between the parties to the dispute with at least onethird of the cost to be paid by the public entity, if the public entity is a party to the dispute. The public entity may require in its contracts that a party participate in mediation concerning a dispute as a precondition to initiating litigation concerning the dispute.

(g)   Exceptions. – This section shall not apply to:

(1)   The purchase and erection of prefabricated or relocatable buildings or portions thereof, except that portion of the work which must be performed at the construction site.

(2)   The erection, construction, alteration, or repair of a building when the cost thereof is three hundred thousand dollars ($300,000) or less.

(3)   The erection, construction, alteration, or repair of a building by The University of North Carolina or its constituent institutions when the cost thereof is five hundred thousand dollars ($500,000) or less.

Notwithstanding the other provisions of this subsection, subsection (f1) of this section shall apply to any erection, construction, alteration, or repair of a building by a public entity.

(1925, c. 141, s. 2; 1929, c. 339, s. 2; 1931, c. 46; 1943, c. 387; 1945, c. 851; 1949, c. 1137, s. 1; 1963, c. 406, ss. 27; 1967, c. 860; 1973, c. 1419; 1977, c. 620; 1987 (Reg. Sess., 1988), c. 1108, ss. 4, 5; 1989, c. 480, s. 1; 1995, c. 358, s. 4; c. 367, ss. 1, 4, 5; c. 509, s. 79; 1998137, s. 1; 1998193, s. 1; 2001496, ss. 3, 13; 2002159, s. 42; 2007322, s. 3.)

§ 143128.1. Construction management at risk contracts.

(a)   For purposes of this section and G.S. 14364.31:

(1)   "Construction management services" means services provided by a construction manager, which may include preparation and coordination of bid packages, scheduling, cost control, value engineering, evaluation, preconstruction services, and construction administration.

(2)   "Construction management at risk services" means services provided by a person, corporation, or entity that (i) provides construction management services for a project throughout the preconstruction and construction phases, (ii) who is licensed as a general contractor, and (iii) who guarantees the cost of the project.

(3)   "Construction manager at risk" means a person, corporation, or entity that provides construction management at risk services.

(4)   "Firsttier subcontractor" means a subcontractor who contracts directly with the construction manager at risk.

(b)   The construction manager at risk shall be selected in accordance with Article 3D of this Chapter. Design services for a project shall be performed by a licensed architect or engineer. The public owner shall contract directly with the architect or engineer.

(c)   The construction manager at risk shall contract directly with the public entity for all construction; shall publicly advertise as prescribed in G.S. 143129; and shall prequalify and accept bids from firsttier subcontractors for all construction work under this section. The prequalification criteria shall be determined by the public entity and the construction manager at risk to address quality, performance, the time specified in the bids for performance of the contract, the cost of construction oversight, time for completion, capacity to perform, and other factors deemed appropriate by the public entity. The public entity shall require the construction manager at risk to submit its plan for compliance with G.S. 143128.2 for approval by the public entity prior to soliciting bids for the project's firsttier subcontractors. A construction manager at risk and firsttier subcontractors shall make a good faith effort to recruit and select minority businesses for participation in contracts pursuant to G.S. 143128.2. A construction manager at risk may perform a portion of the work only if (i) bidding produces no responsible, responsive bidder for that portion of the work, the lowest responsible, responsive bidder will not execute a contract for the bid portion of the work, or the subcontractor defaults and a prequalified replacement cannot be obtained in a timely manner, and (ii) the public entity approves of the construction manager at risk's performance of the work. All bids shall be opened publicly, and once they are opened, shall be public records under Chapter 132 of the General Statutes. The construction manager at risk shall act as the fiduciary of the public entity in handling and opening bids. The construction manager at risk shall award the contract to the lowest responsible, responsive bidder, taking into consideration quality, performance, the time specified in the bids for performance of the contract, the cost of construction oversight, time for completion, compliance with G.S. 143128.2, and other factors deemed appropriate by the public entity and advertised as part of the bid solicitation. The public entity may require the selection of a different firsttier subcontractor for any portion of the work, consistent with this section, provided that the construction manager at risk is compensated for any additional cost incurred.

When contracts are awarded pursuant to this section, the public entity shall provide for a dispute resolution procedure as provided in G.S. 143128(g).

(d)   The construction manager at risk shall provide a performance and payment bond to the public entity in accordance with the provisions of Article 3 of Chapter 44A of the General Statutes. (2001496, s. 2.)

§ 143128.2. Minority business participation goals.

(a)   The State shall have a verifiable ten percent (10%) goal for participation by minority businesses in the total value of work for each State building project, including building projects done by a private entity on a facility to be leased or purchased by the State. A local government unit or other public or private entity that receives State appropriations for a building project or other State grant funds for a building project, including a building project done by a private entity on a facility to be leased or purchased by the local government unit, where the project cost is one hundred thousand dollars ($100,000) or more, shall have a verifiable ten percent (10%) goal for participation by minority businesses in the total value of the work; provided, however, a local government unit may apply a different verifiable goal that was adopted prior to December 1, 2001, if the local government unit had and continues to have a sufficiently strong basis in evidence to justify the use of that goal. On State building projects and building projects subject to the State goal requirement, the Secretary shall identify the appropriate percentage goal, based on adequate data, for each category of minority business as defined in G.S. 143128.2(g)(1) based on the specific contract type.

Except as otherwise provided for in this subsection, each city, county, or other local public entity shall adopt, after a notice and public hearing, an appropriate verifiable percentage goal for participation by minority businesses in the total value of work for building projects.

Each entity required to have verifiable percentage goals under this subsection shall make a good faith effort to recruit minority participation in accordance with this section or G.S. 143131(b), as applicable.

(b)   A public entity shall establish prior to solicitation of bids the good faith efforts that it will take to make it feasible for minority businesses to submit successful bids or proposals for the contracts for building projects. Public entities shall make good faith efforts as set forth in subsection (e) of this section. Public entities shall require contractors to make good faith efforts pursuant to subsection (f) of this section. Each firsttier subcontractor on a construction management at risk project shall comply with the requirements applicable to contractors under this subsection.

(c)   Each bidder, which shall mean firsttier subcontractor for construction manager at risk projects for purposes of this subsection, on a project bid under any of the methods authorized under G.S. 143128(a1) shall identify on its bid the minority businesses that it will use on the project and an affidavit listing the good faith efforts it has made pursuant to subsection (f) of this section and the total dollar value of the bid that will be performed by the minority businesses. A contractor, including a firsttier subcontractor on a construction manager at risk project, that performs all of the work under a contract with its own workforce may submit an affidavit to that effect in lieu of the affidavit otherwise required under this subsection. The apparent lowest responsible, responsive bidder shall also file the following:

(1)   Within the time specified in the bid documents, either:

a.   An affidavit that includes a description of the portion of work to be executed by minority businesses, expressed as a percentage of the total contract price, which is equal to or more than the applicable goal. An affidavit under this subsubdivision shall give rise to a presumption that the bidder has made the required good faith or effort; or

b.   Documentation of its good faith effort to meet the goal. The documentation must include evidence of all good faith efforts that were implemented, including any advertisements, solicitations, and evidence of other specific actions demonstrating recruitment and selection of minority businesses for participation in the contract.

(2)   Within 30 days after award of the contract, a list of all identified subcontractors that the contractor will use on the project.

Failure to file a required affidavit or documentation that demonstrates that the contractor made the required good faith effort is grounds for rejection of the bid.

(d)   No subcontractor who is identified and listed pursuant to subsection (c) of this section may be replaced with a different subcontractor except:

(1)   If the subcontractor's bid is later determined by the contractor or construction manager at risk to be nonresponsible or nonresponsive, or the listed subcontractor refuses to enter into a contract for the complete performance of the bid work, or

(2)   With the approval of the public entity for good cause.

Good faith efforts as set forth in G.S. 143131(b) shall apply to the selection of a substitute subcontractor. Prior to substituting a subcontractor, the contractor shall identify the substitute subcontractor and inform the public entity of its good faith efforts pursuant to G.S. 143131(b).

(e)   Before awarding a contract, a public entity shall do the following:

(1)   Develop and implement a minority business participation outreach plan to identify minority businesses that can perform public building projects and to implement outreach efforts to encourage minority business participation in these projects to include education, recruitment, and interaction between minority businesses and nonminority businesses.

(2)   Attend the scheduled prebid conference.

(3)   At least 10 days prior to the scheduled day of bid opening, notify minority businesses that have requested notices from the public entity for public construction or repair work and minority businesses that otherwise indicated to the Office of Historically Underutilized Businesses an interest in the type of work being bid or the potential contracting opportunities listed in the proposal. The notification shall include the following:

a.   A description of the work for which the bid is being solicited.

b.   The date, time, and location where bids are to be submitted.

c.   The name of the individual within the public entity who will be available to answer questions about the project.

        d.   Where bid documents may be reviewed.

        e.   Any special requirements that may exist.

   (4)   Utilize other media, as appropriate, likely to inform potential minority businesses of the bid being sought.

(f)   A public entity shall require bidders to undertake the following good faith efforts to the extent required by the Secretary on projects subject to this section. The Secretary shall adopt rules establishing points to be awarded for taking each effort and the minimum number of points required, depending on project size, cost, type, and other factors considered relevant by the Secretary. In establishing the point system, the Secretary may not require a contractor to earn more than fifty (50) points, and the Secretary must assign each of the efforts listed in subdivisions (1) through (10) of this subsection at least 10 points. The public entity may require that additional good faith efforts be taken, as indicated in its bid specifications. Good faith efforts include:

   (1)   Contacting minority businesses that reasonably could have been expected to submit a quote and that were known to the contractor or available on State or local government maintained lists at least 10 days before the bid or proposal date and notifying them of the nature and scope of the work to be performed.

   (2)   Making the construction plans, specifications and requirements available for review by prospective minority businesses, or providing these documents to them at least 10 days before the bid or proposals are due.

   (3)   Breaking down or combining elements of work into economically feasible units to facilitate minority participation.

   (4)   Working with minority trade, community, or contractor organizations identified by the Office of Historically Underutilized Businesses and included in the bid documents that provide assistance in recruitment of minority businesses.

   (5)   Attending any prebid meetings scheduled by the public owner.

   (6)   Providing assistance in getting required bonding or insurance or providing alternatives to bonding or insurance for subcontractors.

   (7)   Negotiating in good faith with interested minority businesses and not rejecting them as unqualified without sound reasons based on their capabilities. Any rejection of a minority business based on lack of qualification should have the reasons documented in writing.

   (8)   Providing assistance to an otherwise qualified minority business in need of equipment, loan capital, lines of credit, or joint pay agreements to secure loans, supplies, or letters of credit, including waiving credit that is ordinarily required. Assisting minority businesses in obtaining the same unit pricing with the bidder's suppliers in order to help minority businesses in establishing credit.

   (9)   Negotiating joint venture and partnership arrangements with minority businesses in order to increase opportunities for minority business participation on a public construction or repair project when possible.

 (10)   Providing quick pay agreements and policies to enable minority contractors and suppliers to meet cashflow demands.

(g)   As used in this section:

   (1)   The term "minority business" means a business:

      a.   In which at least fiftyone percent (51%) is owned by one or more minority persons or socially and economically disadvantaged individuals, or in the case of a corporation, in which at least fiftyone percent (51%) of the stock is owned by one or more minority persons or socially and economically disadvantaged individuals; and

      b.   Of which the management and daily business operations are controlled by one or more of the minority persons or socially and economically disadvantaged individuals who own it.

   (2)   The term "minority person" means a person who is a citizen or lawful permanent resident of the United States and who is:

      a.   Black, that is, a person having origins in any of the black racial groups in Africa;

      b.   Hispanic, that is, a person of Spanish or Portuguese culture with origins in Mexico, South or Central America, or the Caribbean Islands, regardless of race;

      c.   Asian American, that is, a person having origins in any of the original peoples of the Far East, Southeast Asia and Asia, the Indian subcontinent, or the Pacific Islands;

      d.   American Indian, that is, a person having origins in any of the original Indian peoples of North America; or

      e.   Female.

   (3)   The term "socially and economically disadvantaged individual" means the same as defined in 15 U.S.C. 637.

(h)   The State, counties, municipalities, and all other public bodies shall award public building contracts, including those awarded under G.S. 143128.1, 143129, and 143131, without regard to race, religion, color, creed, national origin, sex, age, or handicapping condition, as defined in G.S. 168A3. Nothing in this section shall be construed to require contractors or awarding authorities to award contracts or subcontracts to or to make purchases of materials or equipment from minoritybusiness contractors or minoritybusiness subcontractors who do not submit the lowest responsible, responsive bid or bids.

(i)   Notwithstanding G.S. 1323 and G.S. 1215, all public records created pursuant to this section shall be maintained by the public entity for a period of not less than three years from the date of the completion of the building project.

(j)   Except as provided in subsections (a), (g), (h) and (i) of this section, this section shall only apply to building projects costing three hundred thousand dollars ($300,000) or more. This section shall not apply to the purchase and erection of prefabricated or relocatable buildings or portions thereof, except that portion of the work which must be performed at the construction site. (2001496, s. 3.1.)

§ 143128.3. Minority business participation administration.

(a)   All public entities subject to G.S. 143128.2 shall report to the Department of Administration, Office of Historically Underutilized Business, the following with respect to each building project:

   (1)   The verifiable percentage goal.

(2)   The type and total dollar value of the project, minority business utilization by minority business category, trade, total dollar value of contracts awarded to each minority group for each project, the applicable good faith effort guidelines or rules used to recruit minority business participation, and good faith documentation accepted by the public entity from the successful bidder.

(3)   The utilization of minority businesses under the various construction methods under G.S. 143128(a1).

The reports shall be in the format and contain the data prescribed by the Secretary of Administration. The University of North Carolina and the State Board of Community Colleges shall report quarterly and all other public entities shall report semiannually. The Secretary of the Department of Administration shall make reports every six months to the Joint Legislative Committee on Governmental Operations on information reported pursuant to this subsection.

(b)   A public entity that has been notified by the Secretary of its failure to comply with G.S. 143128.2 on a project shall develop a plan of compliance that addresses the deficiencies identified by the Secretary. The corrective plan shall apply to the current project or to subsequent projects under G.S. 143128, as appropriate, provided that the plan must be implemented, at a minimum, on the current project to the extent feasible. If the public entity, after notification from the Secretary, fails to file a corrective plan, or if the public entity does not implement the corrective plan in accordance with its terms, the Secretary shall require one or both of the following:

(1)   That the public entity consult with the Department of Administration, Office of Historically Underutilized Businesses on the development of a new corrective plan, subject to the approval of the Department and the Attorney General. The public entity may designate a representative to appear on its behalf, provided that the representative has managerial responsibility for the construction project.

(2)   That the public entity not bid another contract under G.S. 143128 without prior review by the Department and the Attorney General of a good faith compliance plan developed pursuant to subdivision (1) of this subsection. The public entity shall be subject to the review and approval of its good faith compliance plan under this subdivision with respect to any projects bid pursuant to G.S. 143128 during a period of time determined by the Secretary, not to exceed one year.

A public entity aggrieved by the decision of the Secretary may file a contested case proceeding under Chapter 150B of the General Statutes.

(c)   The Secretary shall study and recommend to the General Assembly and other State agencies ways to improve the effectiveness and efficiency of the State capital facilities development, minority business participation program and good faith efforts in utilizing minority businesses as set forth in G.S. 143128.2, and other appropriate good faith efforts that may result in the increased utilization of minority businesses.

(d)   The Secretary shall appoint an advisory board to develop recommendations to improve the recruitment and utilization of minority businesses. The Secretary, with the input of its advisory board, shall review the State's programs for promoting the recruitment and utilization of minority businesses involved in State capital projects and shall recommend to the General Assembly, the State Construction Office, The University of North Carolina, and the community colleges system changes in the terms and conditions of State laws, rules, and policies that will enhance opportunities for utilization of minority businesses on these projects. The Secretary shall provide guidance to these agencies on identifying types of projects likely to attract increased participation by minority businesses and breaking down or combining elements of work into economically feasible units to facilitate minority business participation.

(e)   The Secretary shall adopt rules for State entities, The University of North Carolina, and community colleges and shall adopt guidelines for local government units to implement the provisions of G.S. 143128.2.

(e1)   *Repealed by Session Laws 2007392, s. 3, effective October 1, 2007.*

(f)   The Secretary shall provide the following information to the Attorney General:

    (1)   Failure by a public entity to report data to the Secretary in accordance with this section.

    (2)   Upon the request of the Attorney General, any data or other information collected under this section.

    (3)   False statements knowingly provided in any affidavit or documentation under G.S. 143128.2 to the State or other public entity. Public entities shall provide to the Secretary information concerning any false information knowingly provided to the public entity pursuant to G.S. 143128.2.

(g)   The Secretary shall report findings and recommendations as required under this section to the Joint Legislative Committee on Governmental Operations annually on or before June 1, beginning June 1, 2002. (2001496, s. 3.6; 2005270, s. 2; 2007392, s. 3.)

§ 143128.4. Historically underutilized business defined.

(a)   As used in this Chapter, the term "historically underutilized business" means a business that meets all of the following conditions:

    (1) At least fiftyone percent (51%) of the business is owned by one or more persons who are members of at least one of the groups set forth in subsection (b) of this section, or in the case of a corporation, at least fiftyone percent (51%) of the stock is owned by one or more persons who are members of at least one of the groups set forth in subsection (b) of this section.

    (2) The management and daily business operations are controlled by one or more owners of the business who are members of at least one of the groups set forth in subsection (b) of this section.

(a1)   As used in this Chapter, the term "minority business" means a historically underutilized business.

(b)   To qualify as a historically underutilized business under this section, a business must be owned and controlled as set forth in subsection (a) of this section by one or more citizens or lawful permanent residents of the United States who are members of one or more of the following groups:

    (1)   Black. – A person having origins in any of the black racial groups of Africa.

    (2)   Hispanic. – A person of Spanish or Portuguese culture having origins in Mexico, South or Central America, or the Caribbean islands, regardless of race.

    (3)   Asian American. – A person having origins in any of the original peoples of the Far East, Southeast Asia, Asia, Indian continent, or Pacific islands.

    (4)   American Indian. – A person having origins in any of the original Indian peoples of North America.

    (5)   Female.

    (6)   Disabled. – A person with a disability as defined in G.S. 1681 or G.S. 168A3.

(7)   Disadvantaged. – A person who is socially and economically disadvantaged as defined in 15 U.S.C. § 637.

(c)   In addition to the powers and duties provided in G.S. 14349, the Secretary of Administration shall have the power, authority, and duty to:

(1)   Develop and administer a statewide uniform program for: (i) the certification of a historically underutilized business, as defined in this section, for use by State departments, agencies, and institutions, and political subdivisions of the State; and (ii) the creation and maintenance of a database of the businesses certified as historically underutilized businesses.

(2)   Adopt rules and procedures for the statewide uniform certification of historically underutilized businesses.

(3)   Provide for the certification of all businesses designated as historically underutilized businesses to be used by State departments, agencies, and institutions, and political subdivisions of the State.

(d)   The Secretary of Administration shall seek input from State departments, agencies, and institutions, political subdivisions of the State, and any other entity deemed appropriate to determine the qualifications and criteria for statewide uniform certification of historically underutilized businesses.

(e)   Only businesses certified in accordance with this section shall be considered by State departments, agencies, and institutions, and political subdivisions of the State as historically underutilized businesses for minority business participation purposes under this Chapter. (2005270, s. 3; 2007392, s. 4; 2009243, s. 3.)

§ 143129. Procedure for letting of public contracts.

(a)   Bidding Required. – No construction or repair work requiring the estimated expenditure of public money in an amount equal to or more than five hundred thousand dollars ($500,000) or purchase of apparatus, supplies, materials, or equipment requiring an estimated expenditure of public money in an amount equal to or more than ninety thousand dollars ($90,000) may be performed, nor may any contract be awarded therefor, by any board or governing body of the State, or of any institution of the State government, or of any political subdivision of the State, unless the provisions of this section are complied with; provided that The University of North Carolina and its constituent institutions may award contracts for construction or repair work that requires an estimated expenditure of less than five hundred thousand dollars ($500,000) without complying with the provisions of this section.

For purchases of apparatus, supplies, materials, or equipment, the governing body of any political subdivision of the State may, subject to any restriction as to dollar amount, or other conditions that the governing body elects to impose, delegate to the manager, school superintendent, chief purchasing official, or other employee the authority to award contracts, reject bids, or readvertise to receive bids on behalf of the unit. Any person to whom authority is delegated under this subsection shall comply with the requirements of this Article that would otherwise apply to the governing body.

(b)   Advertisement and Letting of Contracts. – Where the contract is to be let by a board or governing body of the State government or of a State institution, proposals shall be invited by advertisement in a newspaper having general circulation in the State of North Carolina. Where the contract is to be let by a political subdivision of the State, proposals shall be invited by advertisement in a newspaper having general circulation in the political subdivision or by electronic means, or both. A decision to advertise solely by electronic means, whether for particular contracts or generally for all contracts that are subject to this Article, shall be approved by the governing board of the political subdivision of the State at a regular meeting of the board.

The advertisements for bidders required by this section shall appear at a time where at least seven full days shall lapse between the date on which the notice appears and the date of the opening of bids. The advertisement shall: (i) state the time and place where plans and specifications of proposed work or a complete description of the apparatus, supplies, materials, or equipment may be had; (ii) state the time and place for opening of the proposals; and (iii) reserve to the board or governing body the right to reject any or all proposals.

Proposals may be rejected for any reason determined by the board or governing body to be in the best interest of the unit. However, the proposal shall not be rejected for the purpose of evading the provisions of this Article. No board or governing body of the State or political subdivision thereof may assume responsibility for construction or purchase contracts, or guarantee the payments of labor or materials therefor except under provisions of this Article.

All proposals shall be opened in public and the board or governing body shall award the contract to the lowest responsible bidder or bidders, taking into consideration quality, performance and the time specified in the proposals for the performance of the contract.

In the event the lowest responsible bids are in excess of the funds available for the project or purchase, the responsible board or governing body is authorized to enter into negotiations with the lowest responsible bidder above mentioned, making reasonable changes in the plans and specifications as may be necessary to bring the contract price within the funds available, and may award a contract to such bidder upon recommendation of the Department of Administration in the case of the State government or of a State institution or agency, or upon recommendation of the responsible commission, council or board in the case of a subdivision of the State, if such bidder will agree to perform the work or provide the apparatus, supplies, materials, or equipment at the negotiated price within the funds available therefor. If a contract cannot be let under the above conditions, the board or governing body is authorized to readvertise, as herein provided, after having made such changes in plans and specifications as may be necessary to bring the cost of the project or purchase within the funds available therefor. The procedure above specified may be repeated if necessary in order to secure an acceptable contract within the funds available therefor.

No proposal for construction or repair work may be considered or accepted by said board or governing body unless at the time of its filing the same shall be accompanied by a deposit with said board or governing body of cash, or a cashier's check, or a certified check on some bank or trust company insured by the Federal Deposit Insurance Corporation in an amount equal to not less than five percent (5%) of the proposal. In lieu of making the cash deposit as above provided, such bidder may file a bid bond executed by a corporate surety licensed under the laws of North Carolina to execute such bonds, conditioned that the surety will upon demand forthwith make payment to the obligee upon said bond if the bidder fails to execute the contract in accordance with the bid bond. This deposit shall be retained if the successful bidder fails to execute the contract within 10 days after the award or fails to give satisfactory surety as required herein.

Bids shall be sealed and the opening of an envelope or package with knowledge that it contains a bid or the disclosure or exhibition of the contents of any bid by anyone without the permission of the bidder prior to the time set for opening in the invitation to bid shall constitute a Class 1 misdemeanor.

(c)   Contract Execution and Security. – All contracts to which this section applies shall be executed in writing. The board or governing body shall require the person to whom the award of a contract for construction or repair work is made to furnish bond as required by Article 3 of Chapter 44A; or require a deposit of money, certified check or government securities for the full amount of said contract to secure the faithful performance of the terms of said contract and the payment of all sums due for labor and materials in a manner consistent with Article 3 of Chapter 44A; and the contract shall not be altered except by written agreement of the contractor and the board or governing body. The surety bond or deposit required herein shall be deposited with the board or governing body for which the work is to be performed. When a deposit, other than a surety bond, is made with the board or governing body, the board or governing body assumes all the liabilities, obligations and duties of a surety as provided in Article 3 of Chapter 44A to the extent of said deposit.

The owning agency or the Department of Administration, in contracts involving a State agency, and the owning agency or the governing board, in contracts involving a political subdivision of the State, may reject the bonds of any surety company against which there is pending any unsettled claim or complaint made by a State agency or the owning agency or governing board of any political subdivision of the State arising out of any contract under which State funds, in contracts with the State, or funds of political subdivisions of the State, in contracts with such political subdivision, were expended, provided such claim or complaint has been pending more than 180 days.

(d)   Use of Unemployment Relief Labor. – Nothing in this section shall operate so as to require any public agency to enter into a contract which will prevent the use of unemployment relief labor paid for in whole or in part by appropriations or funds furnished by the State or federal government.

(e)   Exceptions. – The requirements of this Article do not apply to:

(1)   The purchase, lease, or other acquisition of any apparatus, supplies, materials, or equipment from: (i) the United States of America or any agency thereof; or (ii) any other government unit or agency thereof within the United States. The Secretary of Administration or the governing board of any political subdivision of the State may designate any officer or employee of the State or political subdivision to enter a bid or bids in its behalf at any sale of apparatus, supplies, materials, equipment, or other property owned by: (i) the United States of America or any agency thereof; or (ii) any other governmental unit or agency thereof within the United States. The Secretary of Administration or the governing board of any political subdivision of the State may authorize the officer or employee to make any partial or down payment or payment in full that may be required by regulations of the governmental unit or agency disposing of the property.

(2)   Cases of special emergency involving the health and safety of the people or their property.

(3)   Purchases made through a competitive bidding group purchasing program, which is a formally organized program that offers competitively obtained purchasing services at discount prices to two or more public agencies.

(4)   Construction or repair work undertaken during the progress of a construction or repair project initially begun pursuant to this section.

(5)   Purchase of gasoline, diesel fuel, alcohol fuel, motor oil, fuel oil, or natural gas. These purchases are subject to G.S. 143131.

(6)   Purchases of apparatus, supplies, materials, or equipment when: (i) performance or price competition for a product are not available; (ii) a needed product is available from only one source of supply; or (iii) standardization or compatibility is the overriding consideration. Notwithstanding any other provision of this section, the governing board of a political subdivision of the State shall approve the purchases listed in the preceding sentence prior to the award of the contract.

    In the case of purchases by hospitals, in addition to the other exceptions in this subsection, the provisions of this Article shall not apply when: (i) a particular medical item or prosthetic appliance is needed; (ii) a particular product is ordered by an attending physician for his patients; (iii) additional products are needed to complete an ongoing job or task; (iv) products are purchased for "overthecounter" resale; (v) a particular product is needed or desired for experimental, developmental, or research work; or (vi) equipment is already installed, connected, and in service under a lease or other agreement and the governing body of the hospital determines that the equipment should be purchased. The governing body of a hospital shall keep a record of all purchases made pursuant to this subdivision. These records are subject to public inspection.

(7)   Purchases of information technology through contracts established by the State Office of Information Technology Services as provided in G.S. 14733.82(b) and G.S. 14733.92(b).

(8)   Guaranteed energy savings contracts, which are governed by Article 3B of Chapter 143 of the General Statutes.

(9)   Purchases from contracts established by the State or any agency of the State, if the contractor is willing to extend to a political subdivision of the State the same or more favorable prices, terms, and conditions as established in the State contract.

(9a)   Purchases of apparatus, supplies, materials, or equipment from contracts established by the United States of America or any federal agency, if the contractor is willing to extend to a political subdivision of the State the same or more favorable prices, terms, and conditions as established in the federal contract.

(10)   Purchase of used apparatus, supplies, materials, or equipment. For purposes of this subdivision, remanufactured, refabricated or demo apparatus, supplies, materials, or equipment are not included in the exception. A demo item is one that is used for demonstration and is sold by the manufacturer or retailer at a discount.

(11)   Contracts by a public entity with a construction manager at risk executed pursuant to G.S. 143128.1.

(12)   (Repealed effective July 1, 2015) Buildtosuit capital leases with a private developer under G.S. 115C532.

(f)   Repealed by Session Laws 2001328, s. 1, effective August 2, 2001.

(g)   Waiver of Bidding for Previously Bid Contracts. – When the governing board of any political subdivision of the State, or the person to whom authority has been delegated under subsection (a) of this section, determines that it is in the best interest of the unit, the requirements of this section may be waived for the purchase of apparatus, supplies, materials, or equipment from any person or entity that has, within the previous 12 months, after having completed a public, formal bid process substantially similar to that required by this Article, contracted to furnish the apparatus, supplies, materials, or equipment to:

(1)   The United States of America or any federal agency;

(2)   The State of North Carolina or any agency or political subdivision of the State; or

(3)   Any other state or any agency or political subdivision of that state, if the person or entity is willing to furnish the items at the same or more favorable prices, terms, and conditions as those provided under the contract with the other unit or agency. Notwithstanding any other provision of this section, any purchase made under this subsection shall be approved by the governing body of the purchasing political subdivision of the State at a regularly scheduled meeting of the governing body no fewer than 10 days after publication of notice that a waiver of the bid procedure will be considered in order to contract with a qualified supplier pursuant to this section. Notice may be published in a newspaper having general circulation in the political subdivision or by electronic means, or both. A decision to publish notice solely by electronic means for a particular contract or for all contracts under this subsection shall be approved by the governing board of the political subdivision. Rules issued by the Secretary of Administration pursuant to G.S. 14349(6) shall apply with respect to participation in State term contracts.

(h)   Transportation Authority Purchases. – Notwithstanding any other provision of this section, any board or governing body of any regional public transportation authority, hereafter referred to as a "RPTA," created pursuant to Article 26 of Chapter 160A of the General Statutes, or a regional transportation authority, hereafter referred to as a "RTA," created pursuant to Article 27 of Chapter 160A of the General Statutes, may approve the entering into of any contract for the purchase, lease, or other acquisition of any apparatus, supplies, materials, or equipment without competitive bidding and without meeting the requirements of subsection (b) of this section if the following procurement by competitive proposal (Request for Proposal) method is followed.

The competitive proposal method of procurement is normally conducted with more than one source submitting an offer or proposal. Either a fixed price or cost reimbursement type contract is awarded. This method of procurement is generally used when conditions are not appropriate for the use of sealed bids. If this procurement method is used, all of the following requirements apply:

(1)   Requests for proposals shall be publicized. All evaluation factors shall be identified along with their relative importance.

(2)   Proposals shall be solicited from an adequate number of qualified sources.

(3)   RPTAs or RTAs shall have a method in place for conducting technical evaluations of proposals received and selecting awardees, with the goal of promoting fairness and competition without requiring strict adherence to specifications or price in determining the most advantageous proposal.

(4)   The award may be based upon initial proposals without further discussion or negotiation or, in the discretion of the evaluators, discussions or negotiations may be conducted either with all offerors or with those offerors determined to be within the competitive range, and one or more revised proposals or a best and final offer may be requested of all remaining offerors. The details and deficiencies of an offeror's proposal may not be disclosed to other offerors during any period of negotiation or discussion.

(5)   The award shall be made to the responsible firm whose proposal is most advantageous to the RPTA's or the RTA's program with price and other factors considered.

The contents of the proposals shall not be public records until 14 days before the award of the contract.

The board or governing body of the RPTA or the RTA shall, at the regularly scheduled meeting, by formal motion make findings of fact that the procurement by competitive proposal (Request for Proposals) method of procuring the particular apparatus, supplies, materials, or equipment is the most appropriate acquisition method prior to the issuance of the requests for proposals and shall by formal motion certify that the requirements of this subsection have been followed before approving the contract.

Nothing in this subsection subjects a procurement by competitive proposal under this subsection to G.S. 14349, 14352, or 14353.

RPTAs and RTAs may adopt regulations to implement this subsection.

(i)   Procedure for Letting of Public Contracts. – The Department of Transportation ("DOT"), The University of North Carolina and its constituent institutions ("UNC"), and the Department of Administration ("DOA") shall monitor all projects in those agencies and institutions that are let without a performance or payment bond to determine the number of defaults on those projects, the cost to complete each defaulted project, and each project's contract price. Beginning March 1, 2011, and annually thereafter, DOT, UNC, and DOA shall report this information to the Joint Legislative Committee on Governmental Operations. (1931, c. 338, s. 1; 1933, c. 50; c. 400, s. 1; 1937, c.

355; 1945, c. 144; 1949, c. 257; 1951, c. 1104, ss. 1, 2; 1953, c. 1268; 1955, c. 1049; 1957, c. 269, s. 3; c. 391; c. 862, ss. 14; 1959, c. 392, s. 1; c. 910, s. 1; 1961, c. 1226; 1965, c. 841, s. 2; 1967, c. 860; 1971, c. 847; 1973, c. 1194, s. 2; 1975, c. 879, s. 46; 1977, c. 619, ss. 1, 2; 1979, c. 182, s. 1; 1979, 2nd Sess., c. 1081; 1981, c. 346, s. 1; c. 754, s. 1; 1985, c. 145, ss. 1, 2; 1987, c. 590; 1987 (Reg. Sess., 1988), c. 1108, ss. 7, 8; 1989, c. 350; 1993, c. 539, s. 1007; 1994, Ex. Sess., c. 24, s. 14(c); 1995, c. 367, s. 6; 1997174, ss. 14; 1998185, s. 1; 1998217, s. 16; 2001328, s. 1; 2001487, s. 88; 2001496, ss. 4, 5; 2005227, s. 1; 2006232, s. 2; 200794, s. 1; 2007322, s. 4; 2007446, s. 6; 2010148, s. 1.2; 2011234, s. 1.)

§ 143129.1. Withdrawal of bid.

A public agency may allow a bidder submitting a bid pursuant to G.S. 143129 for construction or repair work or for the purchase of apparatus, supplies, materials, or equipment to withdraw his bid from consideration after the bid opening without forfeiture of his bid security if the price bid was based upon a mistake, which constituted a substantial error, provided the bid was submitted in good faith, and the bidder submits credible evidence that the mistake was clerical in nature as opposed to a judgment error, and was actually due to an unintentional and substantial arithmetic error or an unintentional omission of a substantial quantity of work, labor, apparatus, supplies, materials, equipment, or services made directly in the compilation of the bid, which unintentional arithmetic error or unintentional omission can be clearly shown by objective evidence drawn from inspection of the original work papers, documents or materials used in the preparation of the bid sought to be withdrawn. A request to withdraw a bid must be made in writing to the public agency which invited the proposals for the work prior to the award of the contract, but not later than 72 hours after the opening of bids, or for a longer period as may be specified in the instructions to bidders provided prior to the opening of bids.

If a request to withdraw a bid has been made in accordance with the provisions of this section, action on the remaining bids shall be considered, in accordance with North Carolina G.S. 143129, as though said bid had not been received. Notwithstanding the foregoing, such bid shall be deemed to have been received for the purpose of complying with the requirements of G.S. 143132. If the work or purchase is relet for bids, under no circumstances may the bidder who has filed a request to withdraw be permitted to rebid the work or purchase.

If a bidder files a request to withdraw his bid, the agency shall promptly hold a hearing thereon. The agency shall give to the withdrawing bidder reasonable notice of the time and place of any such hearing. The bidder, either in person or through counsel, may appear at the hearing and present any additional facts and arguments in support of his request to withdraw his bid. The agency shall issue a written ruling allowing or denying the request to withdraw within five days after the hearing. If the agency finds that the price bid was based upon a mistake of the type described in the first paragraph of this section, then the agency shall issue a ruling permitting the bidder to withdraw without forfeiture of the bidder's security. If the agency finds that the price bid was based upon a mistake not of the type described in the first paragraph of this section, then the agency shall issue a ruling denying the request to withdraw and requiring the forfeiture of the bidder's security. A denial by the agency of the request to withdraw a bid shall have the same effect as if an award had been made to the bidder and a refusal by the bidder to accept had been made, or as if there had been a refusal to enter into the contract, and the bidder's bid deposit or bid bond shall be forfeited.

In the event said ruling denies the request to withdraw the bid, the bidder shall have the right, within 20 days after receipt of said ruling, to contest the matter by the filing of a civil action in any court of competent jurisdiction of the State of North Carolina. The procedure shall be the same as in all civil actions except all issues of law and fact and every other issue shall be tried de novo by the judge without jury; provided that the matter may be referred in the instances and in the manner provided for by North Carolina G.S. 1A1, Rule 53, as amended. Notwithstanding the foregoing, if the public agency involved is the Department of Administration, it may follow its normal rules and regulations with respect to contested matters, as opposed to following the administrative procedures set forth herein. If it is finally determined that the bidder did not have the right to withdraw his bid pursuant to the provisions of this section, the bidder's security shall be forfeited. Every bid bond or bid deposit given by a bidder to a public agency pursuant to G.S. 143129 shall be conclusively presumed to have been given in accordance with this section, whether or not it be so drawn as to conform to this section. This section shall be conclusively presumed to have been written into every bid bond given pursuant to G.S. 143129.

Neither the agency nor any elected or appointed official, employee, representative or agent of such agency shall incur any liability or surcharge, in the absence of fraud or collusion, by permitting the withdrawal of a bid pursuant to the provisions of this section.

No withdrawal of the bid which would result in the award of the contract on another bid of the same bidder, his partner, or to a corporation or business venture owned by or in which he has an interest shall be permitted. No bidder who is permitted to withdraw a bid shall supply any material or labor to, or perform any subcontract or work agreement for, any person to whom a contract or subcontract is awarded in the performance of the contract for which the withdrawn bid was submitted, without the prior written approval of the agency. Whoever violates the provisions of the foregoing sentence shall be guilty of a Class 1 misdemeanor. (1977, c. 617, s. 1; 1993, c. 539, s. 1008; 1994, Ex. Sess., c. 24, s. 14(c); 2001328, s. 2.)

§ 143129.2. Construction, design, and operation of solid waste management and sludge management facilities.

(a)   All terms relating to solid waste management and disposal as used in this section shall be defined as set forth in G.S. 130A290, except that the term "unit of local government" also includes a sanitary district created under Part 2 of Article 2 of Chapter 130A of the General Statutes, an authority created under Article 1 of Chapter 162A of the General Statutes, a metropolitan sewerage district created under Article 5 of Chapter 162A of the General Statutes, and a county water and sewer district created under Article 6 of Chapter 162A of the General Statutes. As used in this section, the term "sludge management facility" means a facility that processes sludge that has been generated by a municipal wastewater treatment plant for final end use or disposal but does not include any component of a wastewater treatment process or facility that generates sludge.

(b)   To acknowledge the highly complex and innovative nature of solid waste and sludge management technologies for processing mixed solid waste and sludge generated by water and wastewater treatment facilities, the relatively limited availability of existing and proven proprietary technology involving solid waste and sludge management facilities, the desirability of a single point of responsibility for the development of facilities and the economic and technical utility of contracts for solid waste and sludge management which include in their scope combinations of design, construction, operation, management and maintenance responsibilities over prolonged periods of time and that in some instances it may be beneficial to a unit of local government to award a contract on the basis of factors other than cost alone, including but not limited to facility design, operational experience, system reliability, energy production efficiency, longterm operational costs, compatibility with source separation and other recycling systems, environmental impact and operational guarantees. Accordingly, and notwithstanding other provisions of this Article or any local law, a contract entered into between a unit of local government and any person pursuant to this section may be awarded in accordance with the following provisions for the award of a contract based upon an evaluation of proposals submitted in response to a request for proposals prepared by or for a unit of local government.

(c)   The unit of local government shall require in its request for proposals that each proposal to be submitted shall include all of the following:

(1)   Information relating to the experience of the proposer on the basis of which said proposer purports to be qualified to carry out all work required by a proposed contract; the ability of the proposer to secure adequate financing; and proposals for project staffing, implementation of work tasks, and the carrying out of all responsibilities required by a proposed contract.

(2)   A proposal clearly identifying and specifying all elements of cost which would become charges to the unit of local government, in whatever form, in return for the fulfillment by the proposer of all tasks and responsibilities established by the request for the proposal for the full lifetime of

a proposed contract, including, as appropriate, but not limited to, the cost of planning, design, construction, operation, management and/or maintenance of any facility; provided, that the unit of local government may prescribe the form and content of the proposal and that, in any event, the proposer must submit sufficiently detailed information to permit a fair and equitable evaluation of the proposal.

(3)   Any other information as the unit of local government may determine to have a material bearing on its ability to evaluate any proposal in accordance with this section.

(d)   Proposals received in response to a request for proposals may be evaluated on the basis of a technical analysis of facility design, operational experience of the technology to be utilized in the proposed facility, system reliability and availability, energy production balance and efficiency, environmental impact and protection, recovery of materials, required staffing level during operation, projection of anticipated revenues from the sale of energy and materials recovered by the facility, net cost to the unit of local government for operation and maintenance of the facility for the duration of time to be established in the request for proposals and upon any other factors and information that the unit of local government determined to have a material bearing on its ability to evaluate any proposal, which factors were set forth in said request for proposal.

(e)   The unit of local government may make a contract award to any responsible proposer selected pursuant to this section based upon a determination that the selected proposal is more responsive to the request for proposals and may thereupon negotiate a contract with said proposer for the performance of the services set forth in the request for proposals and the response thereto, the determination shall be deemed to be conclusive. Notwithstanding other provisions of this Article or any local law, a contract may be negotiated and entered into between a unit of local government and any person selected as a responsible proposer hereunder which may provide for, but not be limited to, the following:

(1)   A contract, lease, rental, license, permit or other authorization to design, construct, operate and maintain a solid waste or sludge management facility upon such terms and conditions, for such consideration, and for such duration, not to exceed 40 years, as may be agreed upon by the unit of local government and the person.

(2)   Payment by the unit of local government of a fee or other charge to the person for acceptance, processing, recycling, management and disposal of solid waste or sludge.

(3)   An obligation on the part of a unit of local government to deliver or cause to be delivered to a solid waste or sludge management facility guaranteed quantities of solid wastes or sludge.

(4)   The sale, utilization or disposal of any form of energy, recovered material or residue resulting from the operation of any solid waste or sludge management facility.

(f)   Except for authorities created pursuant to Article 22 of Chapter 153A of the General Statutes, the construction work for any facility or structure that is ancillary to a solid waste or sludge management facility and that does not involve storage and processing of solid waste or sludge or the separation, extraction, and recovery of useful or marketable forms of energy and materials from solid waste at a solid waste management facility shall be procured through competitive bidding procedures described by G.S. 143128 through 143129.1. Ancillary facilities include but are not limited to roads, water and sewer lines to the facility limits, transfer stations, scale houses, administration buildings, and residue and bypass disposal sites. (1983, c. 795, ss. 4, 8.1; 2005176, s. 1; 2007131, s. 3.)

§ 143129.3. Exemption of General Assembly from certain purchasing requirements.

(a)   The Legislative Services Commission may provide that the provisions of G.S. 143129 and Article 3 of this Chapter do not apply to purchases by the General Assembly of data processing and data communications equipment, supplies, and services. Such exemption may vary according to the type or amount of purchase, and may vary as to whether the exemption is from some or all of those statutory provisions.

(b)   The Legislative Services Commission must give specific approval to any purchase in excess of five thousand dollars ($5,000) made under an exemption provided by subsection (a) of this section. (1989, c. 82.)

§ 143129.4. Guaranteed energy savings contracts.

The solicitation and evaluation of proposals for guaranteed energy savings contracts, as defined in Part 2 of Article 3B of this Chapter, and the letting of contracts for these proposals are not governed by this Article but instead are governed by the provisions of that Part; except that guaranteed energy savings contracts are subject to the requirements of G.S. 143128.2 and G.S. 143135.3. (1993 (Reg. Sess., 1994), c. 775, s. 4; 1995, c. 509, s. 135.2(k); 2001496, s. 3.3; 2002161, s. 11.)

§ 143129.5. Purchases from nonprofit work centers for the blind and severely disabled.

Notwithstanding G.S. 143129, a city, county, or other governmental entity subject to this Article may purchase goods and services directly from a nonprofit work center for the blind and severely disabled, as defined in G.S. 14348.

The Department of Administration shall report annually to the Joint Legislative Commission on Governmental Operations on its administration of this program. (1995, c. 265, s. 4; 199920, s. 1.)

§ 143129.6. Reserved for future codification purposes.

§ 143129.7. Purchase with tradein of apparatus, supplies, materials, and equipment.

Notwithstanding the provisions of Article 12 of Chapter 160A of the General Statutes, municipalities, counties, and other political subdivisions of the State may include in specifications for the purchase of apparatus, supplies, materials, or equipment an opportunity for bidders to purchase as "tradein" specified personal property owned by the municipality, county, or other political subdivision, and the awarding authority may award a contract for both the purchase of the apparatus, supplies, materials, or equipment and the sale of tradein property, taking into consideration the amount offered on the tradein when applying the criteria for award established in this Article. (1997174, s. 7.)

§ 143129.8. Purchase of information technology goods and services.

(a)   In recognition of the complex and innovative nature of information technology goods and services and of the desirability of a single point of responsibility for contracts that include combinations of purchase of goods, design, installation, training, operation, maintenance, and related services, a political subdivision of the State may contract for information technology, as defined in G.S. 14733.81(2), using the procedure set forth in this section, in addition to or instead of any other procedure available under North Carolina law.

(b)   Contracts for information technology may be entered into under a request for proposals procedure that satisfies the following minimum requirements:

(1)   Notice of the request for proposals shall be given in accordance with G.S. 143129(b).

(2)   Contracts shall be awarded to the person or entity that submits the best overall proposal as determined by the awarding authority. Factors to be considered in awarding contracts shall be identified in the request for proposals.

(c)   The awarding authority may use procurement methods set forth in G.S. 143135.9 in developing and evaluating requests for proposals under this section. The awarding authority may negotiate with any proposer in order to obtain a final contract that best meets the needs of the awarding authority. Negotiations allowed under this section shall not alter the contract beyond the scope of the original request for proposals in a manner that: (i) deprives the proposers or potential proposers of a fair opportunity to compete for the contract; and (ii) would have resulted in the award of the contract to a different person or entity if the alterations had been included in the request for proposals.

(d)   Proposals submitted under this section shall not be subject to public inspection until a contract is awarded. (2001328, s. 3; 2004199, s. 36(b); 2004203, s. 10.)

§ 143129.8A. Purchase of certain goods and services for the North Carolina Zoological Park.

(a)   Exemption. - The North Carolina Zoological Park is a State entity whose primary purpose is the attraction of, interaction with, and education of the public regarding issues of global conservation, ecological preservation, and scientific exploration, and that purpose presents unique challenges requiring greater flexibility and faster responsiveness in meeting the needs of and creating the attractions for the Park. Accordingly, the Department of Environment and Natural Resources may use the procedure set forth in this section, in addition to or instead of any other procedure available under North Carolina law, to contract with a nonState entity on behalf of the Park for the acquisition of goods and services where: (i) the contract directly results in the generation of revenue for the State of North Carolina or (ii) the use of the acquired goods and services by the Park results in increased revenue or decreased expenditures for the State of North Carolina.

(b)   Limitation. - Contracts executed pursuant to the exemption of subsection (a) of this section may be entered into under a request for proposals procedure that satisfies the following minimum requirements:

(1)   Notice of the request for proposals shall be given in accordance with G.S. 143129(b).

(2)   Contracts shall be awarded to the person or entity that submits the best overall proposal as determined by the awarding authority. Factors to be considered in awarding contracts shall be identified in the request for proposals.

(c)   Procurement Methods. - The Department may use procurement methods set forth in G.S. 143135.9 in developing and evaluating requests for proposals under this section. The Department may negotiate with any proposer in order to obtain a final contract that best meets the needs of the awarding authority. Negotiations allowed under this section shall not alter the contract beyond the scope of the original request for proposals in a manner that: (i) deprives the proposers or potential proposers of a fair opportunity to compete for the contract; and (ii) would have resulted in the award of the contract to a different person or entity if the alterations had been included in the request for proposals.

(d)   Promotional Rights. - Subject to the approval of the Department, a nonState entity awarded a contract that results in increased revenue or decreased expenditures for the Park may advertise, announce, or otherwise publicize the provision of services pursuant to award of the contract. (2009329, s. 1.1.)

§ 143129.9. Alternative competitive bidding methods.

(a)   A political subdivision of the State may use any of the following methods to obtain competitive bids for the purchase of apparatus, supplies, materials, or equipment as an alternative to the otherwise applicable requirements in this Article:

(1)   Reverse auction. - For purposes of this section, "reverse auction" means a realtime purchasing process in which bidders compete to provide goods at the lowest selling price in an open and interactive environment. The bidders' prices may be revealed during the reverse auction. A reverse

auction may be conducted by the political subdivision or by a third party under contract with the political subdivision. A political subdivision may also conduct a reverse auction through the State electronic procurement system, and compliance with the procedures and requirements of the State's reverse auction process satisfies the political subdivision's obligations under this Article.

(2)   Electronic bidding. – A political subdivision may receive bids electronically in addition to or instead of paper bids. Procedures for receipt of electronic bids for contracts that are subject to the requirements of G.S. 143129 shall be designed to ensure the security, authenticity, and confidentiality of the bids to at least the same extent as is provided for with sealed paper bids.

(b)   The requirements for advertisement of bidding opportunities, timeliness of the receipt of bids, the standard for the award of contracts, and all other requirements in this Article that are not inconsistent with the methods authorized in this section shall apply to contracts awarded under this section.

(c)   Reverse auctions shall not be utilized for the purchase or acquisition of construction aggregates, including, but not limited to, crushed stone, sand, and gravel. (2002107, s. 1.)

§ 143130. Allowance for convict labor must be specified.

In cases where the board or governing body of a State agency or of any political subdivision of the State may furnish convict or other labor to the contractor, manufacturer, or others entering into contracts for the performance of construction work, installation of apparatus, supplies, materials or equipment, the specifications covering such projects shall carry full information as to what wages shall be paid for such labor or the amount of allowance for same. (1933, c. 400, s. 2; 1967, c. 860.)

§ 143131. When counties, cities, towns and other subdivisions may let contracts on informal bids.

(a)   All contracts for construction or repair work or for the purchase of apparatus, supplies, materials, or equipment, involving the expenditure of public money in the amount of thirty thousand dollars ($30,000) or more, but less than the limits prescribed in G.S. 143129, made by any officer, department, board, local school administrative unit, or commission of any county, city, town, or other subdivision of this State shall be made after informal bids have been secured. All such contracts shall be awarded to the lowest responsible, responsive bidder, taking into consideration quality, performance, and the time specified in the bids for the performance of the contract. It shall be the duty of any officer, department, board, local school administrative unit, or commission entering into such contract to keep a record of all bids submitted, and such record shall not be subject to public inspection until the contract has been awarded.

(b)   All public entities shall solicit minority participation in contracts for the erection, construction, alteration or repair of any building awarded pursuant to this section. The public entity shall maintain a record of contractors solicited and shall document efforts to recruit minority business participation in those contracts. Nothing in this section shall be construed to require formal advertisement of bids. All data, including the type of project, total dollar value of the project, dollar value of minority business participation on each project, and documentation of efforts to recruit minority participation shall be reported to the Department of Administration, Office for Historically Underutilized Business, upon the completion of the project. (1931, c. 338, s. 2; 1957, c. 862, s. 5; 1959, c. 406; 1963, c. 172; 1967, c. 860; 1971, c. 593; 1981, c. 719, s. 1; 1987 (Reg. Sess., 1988), c. 1108, s. 6; 1997174, s. 5; 2001496, s. 5.1; 2005227, s. 2.)

§ 143132. Minimum number of bids for public contracts.

(a)   No contract to which G.S. 143129 applies for construction or repairs shall be awarded by any board or governing body of the State, or any subdivision thereof, unless at least three competitive bids have been received from reputable and qualified contractors regularly engaged in their respective lines of endeavor; however, this section shall not apply to contracts which are negotiated as provided for in G.S. 143129. Provided that if after advertisement for bids as required by G.S. 143129, not as many as three competitive bids have been received from reputable and qualified contractors regularly engaged in their respective lines of endeavor, said board or governing body of the State agency or of a county, city, town or other subdivision of the State shall again advertise for bids; and if as a result of such second advertisement, not as many as three competitive bids from reputable and qualified contractors are received, such board or governing body may then let the contract to the lowest responsible bidder submitting a bid for such project, even though only one bid is received.

(b)   For purposes of contracts bid in the alternative between the separateprime and singleprime contracts, pursuant to G.S. 143128(d1) each singleprime bid shall constitute a competitive bid in each of the four subdivisions or branches of work listed in G.S. 143128(a), and each full set of separateprime bids shall constitute a competitive singleprime bid in meeting the requirements of subsection (a) of this section. If there are at least three singleprime bids but there is not at least one full set of separateprime bids, no separateprime bids shall be opened.

(c)   The State Building Commission shall develop guidelines no later than January 1, 1991, governing the opening of bids pursuant to this Article. These guidelines shall be distributed to all public bodies subject to this Article. The guidelines shall not be subject to the provisions of Chapter 150B of the General Statutes. (1931, c. 291, s. 3; 1951, c. 1104, s. 3; 1959, c. 392, s. 2; 1963, c. 289; 1967, c. 860; 1977, c. 644; 1979, c. 182, s. 2; 1989, c. 480, s. 2; 1989 (Reg. Sess., 1990), c. 1051, s. 4; 1991 (Reg. Sess., 1992), c. 985, s. 1; 1995, c. 358, s. 4; c. 367, ss. 1, 7; 2001496, s. 9.)

§ 143133. No evasion permitted.

No bill or contract shall be divided for the purpose of evading the provisions of this Article. (1933, c. 400, s. 3; 1967, c. 860.)

§ 143134. Applicable to Department of Transportation and Department of Correction; exceptions.

(a)   This Article shall apply to the Department of Transportation and the Division of Adult Correction of the Department of Public Safety except in the construction of roads, bridges and their approaches; provided however, that whenever the Director of the Budget determines that the repair or construction of a building by the Department of Transportation or by the Division of Adult Correction of the Department of Public Safety can be done more economically through use of employees of the Department of Transportation and/or prison inmates than by letting such repair or building construction to contract, the provisions of this Article shall not apply to such repair or construction.

(b)   Notwithstanding the provisions of subsection (a) of this section, the Department of Transportation and the Division of Adult Correction of the Department of Public Safety shall: (i) submit all proposed contracts for supplies, materials, printing, equipment, and contractual services that exceed one million dollars ($1,000,000) to the Attorney General or the Attorney General's designee for review as provided in G.S. 1148.3; and (ii) include in all contracts to be awarded by the Department of Transportation or the Division of Adult Correction of the Department of Public Safety a standard clause which provides that the State Auditor and internal auditors of the Department of Transportation or the Division of Adult Correction of the Department of Public Safety may audit the records of the contractor during and after the term of the contract to verify accounts and data affecting fees and performance. Neither the Department of Transportation nor the Division of Adult Correction of the Department of Public Safety shall award a cost plus percentage of cost agreement or contract for any purpose. (1933, c. 400, s. 3A; 1955, c. 572; 1957, c. 65, s. 11; 1967, c. 860; c. 996, s. 13; 1973, c. 507, s. 5; 1977, c. 464, s. 34; 2010194, s. 24; 2011145, s. 19.1(h); 2011326, s. 15(y).)

§ 143134.1. Interest on final payments due to prime contractors; payments to subcontractors.

(a)   On all public construction contracts which are let by a board or governing body of the State government or any political subdivision thereof, except contracts let by the Department of Transportation pursuant to G.S. 13628.1, the balance due prime contractors shall be paid in full within 45 days after respective prime contracts of the project have been accepted by the owner, certified by the architect, engineer or designer to be completed in accordance with terms of the plans and specifications, or occupied by the owner and used for the purpose for which the project was constructed, whichever occurs first. However, when the architect or consulting engineer in charge of the project determines that delay in completion of the project in accordance with terms of the plans and specifications is the fault of the contractor, the project may be occupied and used for the purposes for which it was constructed without payment of any interest on amounts withheld past the 45 day limit.

No payment shall be delayed because of the failure of another prime contractor on the project to complete his contract. Should final payment to any prime contractor beyond the date the contracts have been certified to be completed by the designer or architect, accepted by the owner, or occupied by the owner and used for the purposes for which the project was constructed, be delayed by more than 45 days, the prime contractor shall be paid interest, beginning on the 46th day, at the rate of one percent (1%) per month or fraction thereof unless a lower rate is agreed upon on the unpaid balance as may be due. In addition to the above final payment provisions, periodic payments due a prime contractor during construction shall be paid in accordance with the provisions of this section and the payment provisions of the contract documents that do not conflict with this section, or the prime contractor shall be paid interest on any unpaid amount at the rate stipulated above for delayed final payments. The interest shall begin on the date the payment is due and continue until the date on which payment is made. The due date may be established by the terms of the contract. Funds for payment of the interest on stateowned projects shall be obtained from the current budget of the owning department, institution, or agency. Where a conditional acceptance of a contract exists, and where the owner is retaining a reasonable sum pending correction of the conditions, interest on the reasonable sum shall not apply.

(b)   Within seven days of receipt by the prime contractor of each periodic or final payment, the prime contractor shall pay the subcontractor based on work completed or service provided under the subcontract. If any periodic or final payment to the subcontractor is delayed by more than seven days after receipt of periodic or final payment by the prime contractor, the prime contractor shall pay the subcontractor interest, beginning on the eighth day, at the rate of one percent (1%) per month or fraction thereof on the unpaid balance as may be due.

(b1)   No retainage on periodic or final payments made by the owner or prime contractor shall be allowed on public construction contracts in which the total project costs are less than one hundred thousand dollars ($100,000). Retainage on periodic or final payments on public construction contracts in which the total project costs are equal to or greater than one hundred thousand dollars ($100,000) is allowed as follows:

(1)   The owner shall not retain more than five percent (5%) of any periodic payment due a prime contractor.

(2)   When the project is fifty percent (50%) complete, the owner, with written consent of the surety, shall not retain any further retainage from periodic payments due the contractor if the contractor continues to perform satisfactorily and any nonconforming work identified in writing prior to that time by the architect, engineer, or owner has been corrected by the contractor and accepted by the architect, engineer, or owner. If the owner determines the contractor's performance is unsatisfactory, the owner may reinstate retainage for each subsequent periodic payment application as authorized in this subsection up to the maximum amount of five percent (5%). The project shall be deemed fifty percent (50%) complete when the contractor's gross project invoices, excluding the value of materials stored offsite, equal or exceed fifty percent (50%) of the value of the contract, except the value of materials stored onsite shall not exceed twenty percent (20%) of the contractor's gross project invoices for the purpose of determining whether the project is fifty percent (50%) complete.

(3)   A subcontract on a contract governed by this section may include a provision for the retainage on periodic payments made by the prime contractor to the subcontractor. However, the percentage

of the payment retained: (i) shall be paid to the subcontractor under the same terms and conditions as provided in subdivision (2) of this subsection and (ii) subject to subsection (b3) of this section, shall not exceed the percentage of retainage on payments made by the owner to the prime contractor. Subject to subsection (b3) of this section, any percentage of retainage on payments made by the prime contractor to the subcontractor that exceeds the percentage of retainage on payments made by the owner to the prime contractor shall be subject to interest to be paid by the prime contractor to the subcontractor at the rate of one percent (1%) per month or fraction thereof.

(4)   Within 60 days after the submission of a pay request and one of the following occurs, as specified in the contract documents, the owner with written consent of the surety shall release to the contractor all retainage on payments held by the owner: (i) the owner receives a certificate of substantial completion from the architect, engineer, or designer in charge of the project; or (ii) the owner receives beneficial occupancy or use of the project. However, the owner may retain sufficient funds to secure completion of the project or corrections on any work. If the owner retains funds, the amount retained shall not exceed two and onehalf times the estimated value of the work to be completed or corrected. Any reduction in the amount of the retainage on payments shall be with the consent of the contractor's surety.

(5)   The existence of any thirdparty claims against the contractor or any additive change orders to the construction contract shall not be a basis for delaying the release of any retainage on payments.

(b2)   Full payment, less authorized deductions, shall also be made for those trades that have reached one hundred percent (100%) completion of their contract by or before the project is fifty percent (50%) complete if the contractor has performed satisfactorily. However, payment to the early finishing trades is contingent upon the owner's receipt of an approval or certification from the architect of record or applicable engineer that the work performed by the subcontractor is acceptable and in accordance with the contract documents. At that time, the owner shall reduce the retainage for such trades to fivetenths percent (0.5%) of the contract. Payments under this subsection shall be made no later than 60 days following receipt of the subcontractor's request or immediately upon receipt of the surety's consent, whichever occurs later. Early finishing trades under this subsection shall include structural steel, piling, caisson, and demolition. The early finishing trades for which lineitem release of retained funds is required shall not be construed to prevent an owner or an owner's representative from identifying any other trades not listed in this subsection that are also allowed lineitem release of retained funds. Should the owner or owner's representative identify any other trades to be afforded lineitem release of retainage, the trade shall be listed in the original bid documents. Each bid document shall list the inspections required by the owner before accepting the work, and any financial information required by the owner to release payment to the trades, except the failure of the bid documents to contain this information shall not obligate the owner to release the retainage if it has not received the required certification from the architect of record or applicable engineer.

(b3)   Notwithstanding subdivisions (2) and (3) of subsection (b1) of this section, and subsection (b2) of this section, following fifty percent (50%) completion of the project, the owner shall be authorized to withhold additional retainage from a subsequent periodic payment, not to exceed five percent (5%) as set forth in subdivision (1) of subsection (b1) of this section, in order to allow the owner to retain two and onehalf percent (2.5%) total retainage through the completion of the project. In the event that the owner elects to withhold additional retainage on any periodic payment subsequent to release of retainage pursuant to subsection (b2) of this section, the general contractor may also withhold from the subcontractors remaining on the project sufficient retainage to offset the additional retainage held by the owner, notwithstanding the actual percentage of retainage withheld by the owner of the project as a whole.

(b4)   Neither the owner's nor contractor's release of retainage on payments as part of a payment in full on a lineitem of work under subsection (b2) of this section shall affect any applicable warranties on work done by the contractor or subcontractor, and the warranties shall not begin to run any earlier than either the owner's receipt of a certificate of substantial completion from the architect, engineer, or designer in charge of the project or the owner receives beneficial occupancy.

(b5)   The State or any political subdivision of the State may allow contractors to bid on bonded projects with and without retainage on payments.

(b6)   Nothing in subsections (b1), (b2), (b3), and (b4) of this section shall operate to prevent any agency or any political subdivision of the State from complying with the requirements of a federal contract or grant when the requirements of the federal contract or grant conflict with subsections (b1), (b2), (b3), or (b4) of this section. Each bid document must specify when federal preemption of this section shall apply.

(c)   Repealed by Session Laws 2007365, s. 1, effective January 1, 2008.

(d)   Nothing in this section shall prevent the prime contractor at the time of application and certification to the owner from withholding application and certification to the owner for payment to the subcontractor for unsatisfactory job progress; defective construction not remedied; disputed work; third party claims filed or reasonable evidence that claim will be filed; failure of subcontractor to make timely payments for labor, equipment, and materials; damage to prime contractor or another subcontractor; reasonable evidence that subcontract cannot be completed for the unpaid balance of the subcontract sum; or a reasonable amount for retainage not to exceed the initial percentage retained by the owner.

(e)   Nothing in this section shall prevent the owner from withholding payment to the contractor in addition to the amounts authorized by this section for unsatisfactory job progress, defective construction not remedied, disputed work, or thirdparty claims filed against the owner or reasonable evidence that a thirdparty claim will be filed. (1959, c. 1328; 1967, c. 860; 1979, c. 778; 1983, c. 804, ss. 1, 2; 2007365, s. 1.)

§ 143134.2. Actions by contractor on behalf of subcontractor.

(a)   A contractor may, on behalf of a subcontractor of any tier under the contractor, file an action against an owner regarding a claim arising out of or relating to labor, materials, or services furnished by the subcontractor to the contractor pursuant to a contract between the subcontractor and the contractor for the same project that is the subject of the contract between the contractor and the owner.

(b)   In any action filed by a contractor against an owner under subsection (a) of this section, it shall not be a defense that the costs and damages at issue were incurred by a subcontractor and that subcontractor has not been paid for these costs and damages. The owner shall not be required to pay the contractor for the costs and damages incurred by a subcontractor, unless the subcontractor submits proof to the court that the contractor has paid these costs and damages to the subcontractor. (1997489, s. 1.)

§ 143134.3. No damage for delay clause.

No contractual language forbidding or limiting compensable damages for delays caused solely by the owner or its agent may be enforced in any construction contract let by any board or governing body of the State, or of any institution of State government, or of any county, city, town, or other political subdivision thereof. For purposes of this section, the phrase "owner or its agent" does not include prime contractors or their subcontractors. (1997489, s. 1.)

§ 143135. Limitation of application of Article.

Except for the provisions of G.S. 143129 requiring bids for the purchase of apparatus, supplies, materials or equipment, this Article shall not apply to construction or repair work undertaken by the State or by subdivisions of the State of North Carolina (i) when the work is performed by duly elected officers or agents using force account qualified labor on the permanent payroll of the agency concerned and (ii) when either the total cost of the project, including without limitation all direct and indirect costs of labor, services, materials, supplies and equipment, does not exceed one hundred twentyfive thousand dollars ($125,000) or the total cost of labor on the project does not exceed fifty thousand dollars ($50,000); provided that, for The University of North Carolina and its constituent institutions, force account qualified labor may be used (i) when the work is performed by duly elected officers or agents using force account qualified labor on the permanent payroll of the university and (ii) when either the total cost of the project, including, without limitation, all direct and indirect costs of labor, services, materials, supplies, and equipment, does not exceed two hundred thousand dollars ($200,000) or the total cost of labor on the project does not exceed one hundred thousand dollars ($100,000). This force account work shall be subject to the approval of the Director of the Budget in the case of State agencies, of the responsible commission, council, or board in the case of subdivisions of the State. Complete and accurate records of the entire cost of such work, including without limitation, all direct and indirect costs of labor, services, materials, supplies and equipment performed and furnished in the prosecution and completion thereof, shall be maintained by such agency, commission, council or board for the inspection by the general public. Construction or repair work undertaken pursuant to this section shall not be divided for the purposes of evading the provisions of this Article. (1933, c. 552, ss. 1, 2; 1949, c. 1137, s. 2; 1951, c. 1104, s. 6; 1967, c. 860; 1975, c. 292, ss. 1, 2; c. 879, s. 46; 1979, 2nd Sess., c. 1248; 1981, c. 860, s. 13; 1995, c. 274, s. 1; 2007322, s. 5.)

§ 143135.1.   State buildings exempt from county and municipal building requirements; consideration of recommendations by counties and municipalities.

(a)   Buildings constructed by the State of North Carolina or by any agency or institution of the State in accordance with plans and specifications approved by the Department of Administration or by The University of North Carolina or one of its affiliated or constituent institutions pursuant to G.S. 11631.11 shall not be subject to inspection by any county or municipal authorities and shall not be subject to county or municipal building codes and requirements.

(b)   Inspection fees fixed by counties and municipalities shall not be applicable to such construction by the State of North Carolina. County and municipal authorities may inspect any plans or specifications upon their request to the Department of Administration or, with respect to projects under G.S. 11631.11, The University of North Carolina, and any and all recommendations made by them shall be given consideration. Requests by county and municipal authorities to inspect plans and specifications for State projects shall be on the basis of a specific project. Should any agency or institution of the State require the services of county or municipal authorities, notice shall be given for the need of such services, and appropriate fees for such services shall be paid to the county or municipality; provided, however, that the application for such services to be rendered by any county or municipality shall have prior written approval of the Department of Administration, or with respect to projects under G.S. 11631.11, The University of North Carolina.

(c)   Notwithstanding any law to the contrary, including any local act, no county or municipality may impose requirements that exceed the North Carolina State Building Code regarding the design or construction of buildings constructed by the State of North Carolina. (1951, c. 1104, s. 4; 1967, c. 860; 1971, c. 563; 1985, c. 757, s. 170(a); 1997412, s. 10; 2001496, s. 8(c); 2005300, s. 1.)

§ 143135.2. Contracts for restoration of historic buildings with private donations.

This Article shall not apply to building contracts let by a State agency for restoration of a historic building or structure where the funds for the restoration of such building or structure are provided entirely by funds donated from private sources. (1955, c. 27; 1967, c. 860.)

§ 143135.3. Adjustment and resolution of State board construction contract claim.

(a)   The word "board" as used in this section shall mean the State of North Carolina or any board, bureau, commission, institution, or other agency of the State, as distinguished from a board or governing body of a subdivision of the State. "A contract for construction or repair work," as used in this section, is defined as any contract for the construction of buildings and appurtenances thereto, including, but not by way of limitation, utilities, plumbing, heating, electrical, air conditioning, elevator, excavation, grading, paving, roofing, masonry work, tile work and painting, and repair work as well as any contract for the construction of airport runways, taxiways and parking aprons, sewer and water mains, power lines, docks, wharves, dams, drainage canals, telephone lines, streets, site preparation, parking areas and other types of construction on which the Department of Administration or The University of North Carolina enters into contracts.

"Contractor" as used in this section includes any person, firm, association or corporation which has contracted with a State board for architectural, engineering or other professional services in connection with construction or repair work as well as those persons who have contracted to perform such construction or repair work.

(b)   A contractor who has not completed a contract with a board for construction or repair work and who has not received the amount he claims is due under the contract may submit a verified written claim to the Director of the Office of State Construction of the Department of Administration for the amount the contractor claims is due. The Director may deny, allow, or compromise the claim, in whole or in part. A claim under this subsection is not a contested case under Chapter 150B of the General Statutes.

(c)   A contractor who has completed a contract with a board for construction or repair work and who has not received the amount he claims is due under the contract may submit a verified written claim to the Director of the Office of State Construction of the Department of Administration for the amount the contractor claims is due. The claim shall be submitted within 60 days after the contractor receives a final statement of the board's disposition of his claim and shall state the factual basis for the claim.

The Director shall investigate a submitted claim within 90 days of receiving the claim, or within any longer time period upon which the Director and the contractor agree. The contractor may appear before the Director, either in person or through counsel, to present facts and arguments in support of his claim. The Director may allow, deny, or compromise the claim, in whole or in part. The Director shall give the contractor a written statement of the Director's decision on the contractor's claim.

A contractor who is dissatisfied with the Director's decision on a claim submitted under this subsection may commence a contested case on the claim under Chapter 150B of the General Statutes. The contested case shall be commenced within 60 days of receiving the Director's written statement of the decision.

(c1)   A contractor who is dissatisfied with the Director's decision on a claim submitted under subsection (c) of this section may commence a contested case on the claim under Chapter 150B of the General Statutes. The contested case shall be commenced within 60 days of receiving the Director's written statement of the decision.

(d)   As to any portion of a claim that is denied by the Director, the contractor may, in lieu of the procedures set forth in the preceding subsection of this section, within six months of receipt of the Director's final decision, institute a civil action for the sum he claims to be entitled to under the contract by filing a verified complaint and the issuance of a summons in the Superior Court of Wake County or in the superior court of any county where the work under the contract was performed. The procedure shall be the same as in all civil actions except that all issues shall be tried by the judge, without a jury.

(e)   The provisions of this section are part of every contract for construction or repair work made by a board and a contractor. A provision in a contract that conflicts with this section is invalid. (1965, c. 1022; 1967, c. 860; 1969, c. 950, s. 1; 1973, c. 1423; 1975, c. 879, s. 46; 1981, c. 577; 1983, c. 761, s. 190; 1985, c. 746, s. 18; 1987, c. 847, s. 4; 1989, c. 40, s. 1; 1991, c. 103, s. 1; 1997412, s. 7; 2001496, s. 8(c); 2005300, s. 1.)

§ 143135.4. Authority of Department of Administration not repealed.

Nothing contained in this Article shall be construed as contravening or repealing any authorities given by statute to the Department of Administration. (1967, c. 860; 1975, c. 879, s. 46.)

§ 143135.5. State policy; cooperation in promoting the use of small, minority, physically handicapped and women contractors; purpose.

(a)   It is the policy of this State to encourage and promote the use of small, minority, physically handicapped and women contractors in State construction projects. All State agencies, institutions and political subdivisions shall cooperate with the Department of Administration and all other State agencies, institutions and political subdivisions in efforts to encourage and promote the use of small, minority, physically handicapped and women contractors in achieving the purpose of this Article, which is the effective and economical construction of public buildings.

(b)   It is the policy of this State not to accept bids or proposals from, nor to engage in business with, any business that, within the last two years, has been finally found by a court or an administrative agency of competent jurisdiction to have unlawfully discriminated on the basis of race, gender, religion, national origin, age, physical disability, or any other unlawful basis in its solicitation, selection, hiring, or treatment of another business. (1983, c. 692, s. 1; 2001496, s. 5.2.)

§ 143135.6. Adjustment and resolution of community college board construction contract claim.

(a)   A contractor who has not completed a contract with a board of a community college for construction or repair work and who has not received the amount he claims is due under the contract may follow the claims procedure in G.S. 143135.3(b) that is available to a contractor who has contracted with a State board.

(b)   A contractor who has completed a contract with a board of a community college for construction or repair work and who has not received the amount he claims is due under the contract may follow the same claims procedure in G.S. 143135.3(c) that is available to a contractor who has contracted with a State board.

(c)   A contractor who is dissatisfied with the Director's decision on any portion of a claim submitted pursuant to subsection (b) of this section may, within six months of receipt of the Director's final decision, institute a civil action for the sum he claims to be entitled to under the contract in the Superior Court of Wake County or in the superior court of any county where the work under the contract was performed. The procedure shall be the same as in all civil actions except that all issues shall be tried by the judge, without a jury. A contractor may not commence an action under Chapter 150B of the General Statutes.

(d)   ' The provisions of this section are part of every contract for construction or repair work made by a board of a community college and a contractor. A provision in a contract that conflicts with this section is invalid.

(e)   For the purposes of this section, the following definitions shall apply, unless the context indicates otherwise:

   (1)   "Community college" has the same meaning as in G.S. 115D2(2).

   (2)   "Contract for construction or repair work" has the same meaning as in G.S. 143135.3(a).

   (3)   "Contractor" means any person, firm, association, or corporation which has contracted for architectural, engineering, or other professional services in connection with construction or repair work, as well as those persons who have contracted to perform the construction or repair work.

(f)   The provisions of this section are applicable only to community college buildings subject to G.S. 143341(3). (1989, c. 40, s. 2.)

§ 143135.7. Safety officers.

(a)   Each contract for a State capital improvement project, as defined in Article 8B of this Chapter, shall require the contractor to designate a responsible person as safety officer to inspect the project site for unsafe health and safety hazards, to report these hazards to the contractor for correction, and to provide other safety and health measures on the project site as required by the terms and conditions of the contract. (1991 (Reg. Sess., 1992), c. 893, s. 3.)

§ 143135.8. Prequalification.

(a)   Bidders may be prequalified for any public construction project. (1995, c. 367, s. 8.)

§ 143135.9. Best Value procurements.

(a)   Definitions. - The following definitions apply in this section:

　　　(1)   Best Value procurement. - The selection of a contractor based on a determination of which proposal offers the best tradeoff between price and performance, where quality is considered an integral performance factor. The award decision is made based on multiple factors, including: total cost of ownership, meaning the cost of acquiring, operating, maintaining, and supporting a product or service over its projected lifetime; the evaluated technical merit of the vendor's proposal; the vendor's past performance; and the evaluated probability of performing the requirements stated in the solicitation on time, with high quality, and in a manner that accomplishes the stated business objectives and maintains industry standards compliance.

　　　(2)   GovernmentVendor partnership. - A mutually beneficial contractual relationship between State government and a contractor, wherein the two share risk and reward, and value is added to the procurement of needed goods or services.

　　　(3)   Information technology. - Electronic data processing and telecommunications goods and services, microelectronics, software, information processing, office systems, any services related to the foregoing, and consulting or other services for design and/or redesign of business processes.

　　　(4)   SolutionBased solicitation. - A solicitation in which the requirements are stated in terms of how the product or service being purchased should accomplish the business objectives, rather than in terms of the technical design of the product or service.

(b)   Intent. - The intent of Best Value procurement is to enable contractors to offer and the agency to select the most appropriate solution to meet the business objectives defined in the solicitation and to keep all parties focused on the desired outcome of a procurement.

(c)   Information Technology. - The acquisition of information technology by the State of North Carolina shall be conducted using the Best Value procurement method. For purposes of this section, business process reengineering, system design, and technology implementation may be combined into a single solicitation. For acquisitions which the procuring agency and the Division of Purchase and Contracts or the Office of Information Technology Services, as applicable, deem to be highly complex or determine that the optimal solution to the business problem at hand is not known, the use of SolutionBased Solicitation and GovernmentVendor Partnership is authorized and encouraged. Any county, city, town, or subdivision of the State may acquire information technology pursuant to this section.

(d)   Repealed by Session Laws 2009320, s. 1, effective July 24, 2009.

(e)   North Carolina Zoological Park. - The acquisition of goods and services under a contract entered pursuant to the exemption of G.S. 143129.8A(a) by the Department of Environment and Natural Resources on behalf of the North Carolina Zoological Park may be conducted using the Best Value procurement method. For acquisitions which the procuring agency deems to be highly complex, the use of GovernmentVendor partnership is authorized. (1998189, s. 1; 1999434, s. 15; 1999456, s. 39; 2009329, s. 1.2.)

REGULATION OF CONTRACTORS FOR PUBLIC WORKS

EXCERPTS FROM CHAPTER 133, ARTICLE 3

§ 13323. Definition.

(a)   The term "governmental agency" shall include the State of North Carolina, its agencies, institutions, and political subdivisions, all municipal corporations and all other public units, agencies and authorities which are authorized to enter into public contracts for construction or repair or for procurement of goods or services.

(b)   The term "person" shall mean any individual, partnership, corporation, association, or other entity formed for the purpose of doing business as a contractor, subcontractor, or supplier.

(c)   The term "subsidiary" shall mean a corporation with respect to which another corporation by virtue of its shareholdings alone has legal power, either directly or indirectly through another corporation or series of other corporations, domestic or foreign, to elect a majority of the directors. A corporation is a subsidiary of each such corporation, including any corporation through which this legal power may be indirectly exercised. (1981, c. 764, s. 1; 1991 (Reg. Sess., 1992), c. 1030, s. 38.)

§ 13324. Government contracts; violation of G.S. 751 and 752.

Every person who shall engage in any conspiracy, combination, or any other act in restraint of trade or commerce declared to be unlawful by the provisions of G.S. 751 and 752 shall be guilty of a felony under this section where the combination, conspiracy, or other unlawful act in restraint of trade involves:

(1)   A contract for the purchase of equipment, goods, services or materials or for construction or repair let or to be let by a governmental agency;

(2)   A subcontract for the purchase of equipment, goods, services or materials or for construction or repair with a prime contractor or proposed prime contractor for a governmental agency. (1981, c. 764, s. 1.)

§ 13325. Conviction; punishment.

(a)   Upon conviction of violating G.S. 13324, any person shall be punished as a Class H felon. The court may also impose a fine of up to one hundred thousand dollars ($100,000) on any convicted individual and a fine of up to one million dollars ($1,000,000) on any convicted corporation. Any fine imposed pursuant to this section shall not be deductible on a State income tax return for any purpose.

(b)   For a period of up to three years from the date of conviction, said period to be determined in the discretion of the court, no person shall be eligible to enter into a contract with any governmental agency, either directly as a contractor or indirectly as a subcontractor, if that person has been convicted of violating G.S. 133 24.

(c)   In the event an individual is convicted of violating G.S. 133 24, the court may, in its discretion, for a period of up to three years from the date of conviction, provide that the individual shall not be employed by a corporation as an officer, director, employee or agent, if that corporation engages in public construction or repair contracts with a governmental agency, either directly as a contractor or indirectly as a subcontractor.

(d)   The court shall also have authority to direct the appropriate contractor's licensing board to suspend the license of any contractor convicted of violating G.S. 13324 for a period of up to three years from the date of conviction. (1981, c. 764, s. 1.)

§ 13326. Individuals convicted may not serve on licensing boards.

No individual shall be eligible to serve as a member of any contractor's licensing board who has been convicted of criminal charges involving either:

(1)   A conspiracy in restraint of trade in the courts of this State in violation of G.S. 751, 752, or 13324, or similar charges in any federal court or in any other state court; or

(2)   Bribery or commercial bribery in violation of G.S. 14218 or 14353 in the courts of this State, or of similar charges in any federal court or the court of any other state. (1981, c. 764, s. 1.)

§ 13327. Suspension from bidding.

Any governmental agency shall have the authority to suspend for a period of up to three years from the date of conviction any person and any subsidiary or affiliate of any person from further bidding to the agency and from being a subcontractor to a contractor for the agency and from being a supplier to the agency if that person or any officer, director, employee or agent of that person has been convicted of charges of engaging in any conspiracy, combination, or other unlawful act in restraint of trade or of similar charges in any federal court or a court of any other state.

A governmental agency may order a temporary suspension of any contractor, subcontractor, or supplier or subsidiary or affiliate thereof charged in an indictment or an information with engaging in any conspiracy, combination, or other unlawful act in restraint of trade or of similar charges in any federal court or a court of this or any other state until the charges are resolved.

The provisions of this section are in addition to and not in derogation of any other powers and authority of any governmental agency. (1981, c. 764, s. 1.)

§ 13328. Civil damages; liability; statute of limitations.

(a)   Any governmental agency entering into a contract which is or has been the subject of a conspiracy prohibited by G.S. 751 or 752 shall have a right of action against the participants in the conspiracy to recover damages, as provided herein. The governmental agency shall have the option to proceed jointly and severally in a civil action against any one or more of the participants for recovery of the full amount of the damages. There shall be no right to contribution among participants not named defendants by the governmental agency.

(b)   At the election of the governmental agency, the measure of damages recoverable under this section shall be either the actual damages or ten percent (10%) of the contract price which shall be trebled as provided in G.S. 7516.

(c)   The cause of action shall accrue at the time of discovery of the conspiracy by the governmental agency which entered into the contract. The action shall be brought within six years of the date of accrual of the cause of action. (1981, c. 764, s. 1; 1993, c. 441.)

§ 13329. Reporting of violations of G.S. 751 or 752.

Any person having knowledge of acts committed in violation of G.S. 751 or 752 involving a contract with a governmental agency who reports the same to that governmental agency and assists in any resulting proceedings may receive a reward as set forth herein. The governmental agency is authorized to pay to the informant up to twenty five percent (25%) of any civil damages that it collects from the violator named by the informant by reason of the information furnished by the informant. The information and knowledge to be reported includes but is not limited to any agreement or proposed agreement or offer or request for agreement among contractors, subcontractors or suppliers to rotate bids, to share the profits with a contractor not the low bidder, to sublet work in advance of bidding as a means of preventing competition, to refrain from bidding, to submit prearranged bids, to submit complimentary bids, to set up territories to restrict competition, or to alternate bidding. (1981, c. 764, s. 1.)

§ 13330. Noncollusion affidavits.

Noncollusion affidavits may be required by rule of any governmental agency from all prime bidders. Any such requirement shall be set forth in the invitation to bid. Failure of any bidder to provide a required affidavit to the governmental agency shall be grounds for disqualification of his bid. The provisions of this section are in addition to and not in derogation of any other powers and authority of any governmental agency. (1981, c. 764, s. 1.)

§ 13331. Perjury; punishment.

Any person who shall willfully commit perjury in any affidavit taken pursuant to this Article or rules pursuant thereto shall be guilty of a felony and shall be punished as a Class I felon. (1981, c. 764, s. 1; 1993, c. 539, s. 1307; 1994, Ex. Sess., c. 24, s. 14(c).)

§ 13332. Gifts and favors regulated.

(a)   It shall be unlawful for any contractor, subcontractor, or supplier who:

   (1)   Has a contract with a governmental agency; or

   (2)   Has performed under such a contract within the past year; or

   (3)   Anticipates bidding on such a contract in the future

to make gifts or to give favors to any officer or employee of a governmental agency who is charged with the duty of:

   (1)   Preparing plans, specifications, or estimates for public contract; or

   (2)   Awarding or administering public contracts; or

   (3)   Inspecting or supervising construction.

It shall also be unlawful for any officer or employee of a governmental agency who is charged with the duty of:

   (1)   Preparing plans, specifications, or estimates for public contracts; or

   (2)   Awarding or administering public contracts; or

   (3)   Inspecting or supervising construction willfully to receive or accept any such gift or favor.

(b)   A violation of subsection (a) shall be a Class 1 misdemeanor.

(c)   Gifts or favors made unlawful by this section shall not be allowed as a deduction for North Carolina tax purposes by any contractor, subcontractor or supplier or officers or employees thereof.

(d)   This section is not intended to prevent a gift a public servant would be permitted to accept under G.S. 138A32, or the gift and receipt of honorariums for participating in meetings, advertising items or souvenirs of nominal value, or meals furnished at banquets. This section is not intended to prevent any contractor, subcontractor, or supplier from making donations to professional organizations to defray meeting expenses where governmental employees are members of such professional organizations, nor is it intended to prevent governmental employees who are members of professional organizations from participation in all scheduled meeting functions available to all members of the professional organization attending the meeting. This section is also not intended to prohibit customary gifts or favors between employees or officers and their friends and relatives or the friends and relatives of their spouses, minor children, or members of their household where it is clear that it is that relationship rather than the business of the individual concerned which is the motivating factor for the gift or favor. However, all such gifts knowingly made or received are required to be reported by the donee to the agency head if the gifts are made by a contractor, subcontractor, or supplier doing business directly or indirectly with the governmental agency employing the recipient of such a gift. (1981, c. 764, s. 1; 1987, c. 399; 1993, c. 539, s. 970; 1994, Ex. Sess., c. 24, s. 14(c); 2007348, s. 18.)

§ 13333. Cost estimates; bidders' lists.

Any governmental agency responsible for letting public contracts may promulgate rules concerning the confidentiality of:

(1)   The agency's cost estimate for any public contracts prior to bidding; and

(2)   The identity of contractors who have obtained proposals for bid purposes for a public contract.

If the agency's rules require that such information be kept confidential, an employee or officer of the agency who divulges such information to any unauthorized person shall be subject to disciplinary action. This section shall not be construed to require that cost estimates or bidders' lists be kept confidential. (1981, c. 764, s. 1.)

Appendix I: Electrical Materials, Devices, Appliances, and Equipment

CHAPTER 66, ARTICLE 4

66-23. Sale of electrical goods regulated.

66-24. Identification marks required.

66-25. Acceptable listings as to safety of goods.

66-26. Legal responsibility of proper installations unaffected.

66-27.Violation made misdemeanor.

66-27.01. Enforcement.

66-23. Sale of electrical goods regulated.

Every person, firm or corporation before selling, offering for sale, assigning, or disposing of by gift, as premiums or in any similar manner any electrical material, devices, appliances or equipment shall first determine if such electrical materials, devices, appliances and equipment comply with the provision of this Article. (1933, c. 555, s. 1; 1989, c. 681, s. 1.)

66-24. Identification marks required.

All electrical materials, devices, appliances and equipment shall have the maker's name, trademark, or other identification symbol placed thereon, together with such other markings giving voltage, current, wattage, or other appropriate ratings as may be necessary to determine the character of the material, device, appliance or equipment and the use for which it is intended; and it shall be unlawful for any person, firm or corporation to remove, alter, change or deface the maker's name, trademark or other identification symbol. (1933, c. 555, s. 2; 1989, c. 681, s. 1.)

66-25.Acceptable listings as to safety of goods.

All electrical materials, devices, appliances, and equipment shall be evaluated for safety and suitability for intended use. This evaluation shall be conducted in accordance with nationally recognized standards and shall be conducted by a qualified testing laboratory. The Commissioner of Insurance, through the Engineering Division of the Department of Insurance, shall implement the procedures necessary to approve suitable national standards and to approve suitable qualified testing laboratories. The Commissioner may assign his authority to implement the procedures for specific materials, devices, appliances, or equipment to other agencies or bodies when they would be uniquely qualified to implement those procedures.

In the event that the Commissioner determines that electrical materials, devices, appliances, or equipment in question cannot be adequately evaluated through the use of approved national standards or by approved qualified testing laboratories, the Engineering Division of the Department of Insurance shall specify any alternative evaluations which safety requires.

The Engineering Division of the Department of Insurance shall keep in file, where practical, copies of all approved national standards and resumes of approved qualified testing laboratories. (1933, c. 555, s. 3; 1989, c. 681, s. 1.)

66-26. Legal responsibility of proper installations unaffected.

This Article shall not be construed to relieve from or to lessen the responsibility or liability of any party owning, operating, controlling or installing any electrical materials, devices, appliances or equipment for damages to persons or property caused by any defect therein, nor shall the electrical inspector, the Commissioner, or agents of the Commissioner be held as assuming any such liability by reason of the approval of any material, device, appliance or equipment authorized herein. (1933, c. 555, s. 4; 1989, c. 681, s. 1.)

66-27. Violation made misdemeanor.

Any person, firm or corporation who shall violate any of the provisions of this Article shall be guilty of a Class 2 misdemeanor. (1933, c. 555, s. 5; 1989, c. 681, s. 1; 1993, c. 539, s. 509; 1994, Ex. Sess., c. 24, s. 14(c).)

66-27.01. Enforcement.

The Commissioner or his designee or the electrical inspector of any State or local governing agency may initiate any appropriate action or proceedings to prevent, restrain, or correct any violation of this Article. The Commissioner or his designee, upon showing proper credentials and in discharge of his duties pursuant to this Article may, at reasonable times and without advance notice, enter and inspect any facility within the State in which there is reasonable cause to suspect that electrical materials, devices, appliances, or equipment not in conformance with the requirements of this Article are being sold, offered for sale, assigned, or disposed of by gift, as premiums, or in any other similar manner. (1989, c. 681, s. 1.; 1997-456, s. 27.)

Appendix J: Building Inspection (Counties)

CHAPTER 153A, PART 4

153A-350. "Building" defined.

153A-350.1. Tribal lands

153A-351. Inspection department; certification of electrical inspectors.

153A-351.1. Qualifications of inspectors.

153A-352. Duties and responsibilities.

153A-353. Joint inspection department; other arrangements.

153A-354. Financial support.

153A-355. Conflicts of interest.

153A-356. Failure to perform duties.

153A-357. Permits.

153A-358. Time limitations on validity of permits.

153A-359. Changes in work.

153A-360. Inspections of work in progress.

153A-361. Stop orders.

153A-362. Revocation of permits.

153A-363. Certificates of compliance.

153A-364. Periodic inspections for hazardous or unlawful conditions.

153A-365. Defects in buildings to be corrected.

153A-366. Unsafe buildings condemned.

153A-367. Removing notice from condemned building.

153A-368. Action in event of failure to take corrective action.

153A-369. Order to take corrective action.

153A-370. Appeal; finality of order not appealed.

153A-371. Failure to comply with order.

153A-372. Equitable enforcement.

153A-373. Records and reports.

153A-374. Appeals.

153A-375. Establishment of fire limits.

153A-350."Building"defined.

As used in this Part, the words "building" or "buildings" include other structures. (1973, c. 822, s. 1.)

153A-350.1. Tribal lands.

As used in this Part, the term:

(1)   "Board of commissioners" includes the Tribal Council of such tribe.

(2)   "County" or "counties" also means a federally recognized Indian Tribe, and as to such tribe includes lands held in trust for the tribe. (1999-78, s. 1.)

153A-351. Inspection department; certification of electrical inspectors.

(a)   A county may create an inspection department, consisting of one or more inspectors who may be given the titles of building inspector, electrical inspector, plumbing inspector, housing inspector, zoning inspector, heating and air-conditioning inspector, fire prevention inspector, deputy or assistant inspector, or any other title that is generally descriptive of the duties assigned. The department may be headed by a superintendent or director of inspections.

(a1)   Every county shall perform the duties and responsibilities set forth in G.S. 153A-352 either by:

(1)   Creating its own inspection department;

(2)   Creating a joint inspection department in cooperation with one or more other units of local government, pursuant to G.S. 153A-353 or Part 1 of Article 20 of Chapter 160A; or,

(3)   Contracting with another unit of local government for the provision of inspection services pursuant to Part 1 of Article 20 of Chapter 160A.

Such action shall be taken no later than the applicable date in the schedule below, according to the county's population as published in the 1970 United States Census:

Counties over 75,000 population - July 1, 1979

Counties between 50,001 and 75,000 - July 1, 1981

Counties between 25,001 and 50,000 - July 1, 1983

Counties 25,000 and under - July 1, 1985.

In the event that any county shall fail to provide inspection services by the date specified above or shall cease to provide such services at any time thereafter, the Commissioner of Insurance shall arrange for the provision of such services, either through personnel employed by his Department or through an arrangement with other units of government. In either event, the Commissioner shall have and may exercise within the county's jurisdiction all powers made available to the board of county commissioners with respect to building inspection under Part 4 of Article 18 of this Chapter and Part 1 of Article 20 of Chapter 160A.Whenever the Commissioner has intervened in this manner, the county may assume provision of inspection services only after giving the Commissioner two years' written notice of its intention to do so; provided, however, that the Commissioner may waive this requirement or permit assumption at an earlier date if he finds that such earlier assumption will not unduly interfere with arrangements he has made for the provision of those services.

(b)   No person may perform electrical inspections pursuant to this Part unless he has been certified as qualified by the Commissioner of Insurance. To be certified a person must pass a written examination based on the electrical regulations included in the latest edition of the State Building Code as filed with the Secretary of State. The examination shall be under the supervision of and conducted according to rules and regulations prescribed by the Chief State Electrical Inspector or Engineer of the State Department of Insurance and the Board of Examiners of Electrical Contractors. It shall be held quarterly, in Raleigh or any other place designated by the Chief State Electrical Inspector or Engineer.

The rules and regulations may provide for the certification of class I, class II, and class III inspectors, according to the results of the examination. The examination shall be based on the type and character of electrical installations being made in the territory in which the applicant wishes to serve as an electrical inspector. A class I inspector may serve anywhere in the State, but class II and class III inspectors shall be limited to service in the territory for which they have qualified.

The Commissioner of Insurance shall issue a certificate to each person who passes the examination, approving the person for service in a designated territory. To remain valid, a certificate must be renewed each January by payment of an annual renewal fee of one dollar ($1.00). The examination fee shall be five dollars ($5.00).

If the person appointed by a county as electrical inspector fails to pass the examination, the county shall continue to make appointments until an appointee has passed the examination. For the interim the Commissioner of Insurance may authorize the county to use a temporary inspector.

The provisions of this subsection shall become void and ineffective on such date as the North Carolina Code Officials Qualification Board certifies to the Secretary of State that it has placed in effect a certification system for electrical inspectors pursuant to its authority granted by Article 9C of Chapter 143 of the General Statutes. (1937, c. 57; 1941, c. 105; 1947, c. 719; 1951, c. 651; 1953, c. 984; 1955, cc. 144, 942, 1171; 1957, cc. 415, 456, 1286, 1294; 1959, cc. 399, 940, 1031; 1961, cc. 763, 884, 1036; 1963, cc. 639, 868; 1965, cc. 243, 371, 453, 494, 846; 1967, cc. 45, 73, 113; c. 495, ss. 1, 3; 1969, cc. 675, 918; c. 1003, s. 7; c. 1010, s. 4; c. 1064, ss. 1, 4, 5; c. 1066, s. 1; 1973, c. 822, s. 1; 1977, c. 531, ss. 2, 3; 1991, c. 720, s. 77.)

153A-351.1. Qualifications of inspectors.

On and after the applicable date set forth in the schedule in G.S. 153A-351, no county shall employ an inspector to enforce the State Building Code as a member of a county or joint inspection department who does not have one of the following types of certificates issued by the North Carolina Code Officials Qualification Board attesting to his qualifications to hold such position: (i) a probationary certificate, valid for one year only; (ii) a standard certificate; or (iii) a limited certificate, which shall be valid only as an authorization for him to continue in the position held on the date specified in G.S. 143-151.10(c) and which shall become invalid if he does not successfully complete in-service training prescribed by the Qualification Board within the period specified in G.S. 143-151.10(c). An inspector holding one of the above certificates can be promoted to a position requiring a higher level certificate only upon issuance by the Board of a standard certificate or probationary certificate appropriate for such new position. (1977, c. 531, s. 4.)

153A-352. Duties and responsibilities.

The duties and responsibilities of an inspection department and of the inspectors in it are to enforce within the county's territorial jurisdiction State and local laws and local ordinances and regulations relating to:

(1)   The construction of buildings;

(2)   The installation of such facilities as plumbing systems, electrical systems, heating systems, refrigeration systems, and air-conditioning systems;

(3)   The maintenance of buildings in a safe, sanitary, and healthful condition;

(4)   Other matters that may be specified by the board of commissioners.

These duties and responsibilities include receiving applications for permits and issuing or denying permits, making necessary inspections, issuing or denying certificates of compliance, issuing orders to correct violations, bringing judicial actions against actual or threatened violations, keeping adequate records, and taking any other actions that may be required to adequately enforce the laws and ordinances and regulations. The board of commissioners may enact reasonable and appropriate provisions governing the enforcement of the laws and ordinances and regulations. (1937, c. 57; 1941, c. 105; 1947, c. 719; 1951, c. 651; 1953, c. 984; 1955, cc. 144, 942, 1171; 1957, cc. 415, 456, 1286, 1294; 1959, cc. 399, 940, 1031; 1961, cc. 763, 884, 1036; 1963, cc. 639, 868; 1965, cc. 243, 371, 453, 494, 846; 1967, cc. 45, 73, 113; c. 495, ss. 1, 3; 1969, cc. 675, 918; c. 1003, s. 7; c. 1010, s. 4; c. 1064, ss. 1, 4, 5; c. 1066, s. 1; 1973, c. 822, s. 1.)

153A-353. Joint inspection department; other arrangements.

A county may enter into and carry out contracts with one or more other counties or cities under which the parties agree to create and support a joint inspection department for enforcing those State and local laws and local ordinances and regulations specified in the agreement. The governing bodies of the contracting units may make any necessary appropriations for this purpose.

In lieu of a joint inspection department, a county may designate an inspector from another county or from a city to serve as a member of the county inspection department, with the approval of the governing body of the other county or city. A county may also contract with an individual who is not a city or county employee but who holds one of the applicable certificates as provided in G.S. 153A351.1 or G.S. 160A411.1 or with the employer of an individual who holds one of the applicable certificates as provided in G.S. 153A351.1 or G.S. 160A411.1. The inspector, if designated from another county or city under this section, while exercising the duties of the position, is a county employee. The county shall have the same potential liability, if any, for inspections conducted by an individual who is not an employee of the county as it does for an individual who is an employee of the county. The company or individual with whom the county contracts shall have errors and omissions and other insurance coverage acceptable to the county. (1937, c. 57; 1941, c. 105; 1947, c. 719; 1951, c. 651; 1959, c. 940; 1963, c. 639; 1965, c. 371; 1967, c. 495, s. 1; 1969, c. 918; c. 1010, s. 4; c. 1064, ss. 1, 5; c. 1066, s. 1; 1973, c. 822, s. 1; 1993, c. 232, s. 1; 1999372, s. 1; 2001278, s. 1.)

153A-354. Financial support.

A county may appropriate any available funds for the support of its inspection department. It may provide for paying inspectors fixed salaries, or it may reimburse them for their services by paying over part or all of any fees collected. It may fix reasonable fees for issuing permits, for inspections, and for other services of the inspection department. (1937, c. 57; 1941, c. 105; 1947, c. 719; 1951, c. 651; 1953, c. 984; 1955, cc. 144, 942, 1171; 1957, cc. 415, 456, 1286, 1294; 1959, cc. 399, 940, 1031; 1961, cc. 763, 884, 1036; 1963, cc. 639, 868; 1965, cc. 243, 371, 453, 494, 846; 1967, cc. 45, 73, 113; c. 495, ss. 1, 3; 1969, cc. 675, 918; c. 1003, s. 7; c. 1010, s. 4; c. 1064, ss. 1, 4, 5; c. 1066, s. 1; 1973, c. 822, s. 1.)

153A-355.Conflicts of interest.

Unless he or she is the owner of the building, no member of an inspection department shall be financially interested or employed by a business that is financially interested in furnishing labor, material, or appliances for the construction, alteration, or maintenance of any building within the county's territorial jurisdiction or any part or system thereof, or in making plans or specifications therefor. No member of any inspection department or other individual or an employee of a company contracting with a county to conduct inspections may engage in any work that is inconsistent with his or her duties or with the interest of the county, as determined by the county.

The county must find a conflict of interest if any of the following is the case:

(1)   If the individual, company, or employee of a company contracting to perform inspections for the county has worked for the owner, developer, contractor, or project manager of the project to be inspected within the last two years.

(2)   If the individual, company, or employee of a company contracting to perform inspections for the county is closely related to the owner, developer, contractor, or project manager of the project to be inspected.

(3)   If the individual, company, or employee of a company contracting to perform inspections for the county has a financial or business interest in the project to be inspected. (1937, c. 57; 1941, c. 105; 1947, c. 719; 1951, c. 651; 1953, c. 984; 1955, cc. 144, 942, 1171; 1957, cc. 415, 456, 1286, 1294; 1959, cc. 399, 1031; 1961, cc. 763, 884, 1036; 1963, c. 868; 1965, cc. 243, 453, 494, 846; 1967, cc. 45, 73, 113; c. 495, s. 3; 1969, cc. 675, 918; c. 1003, s. 7; c. 1064, ss. 1, 4; c. 1066, s. 1; 1973, c. 822, s. 1; 1993, c. 232, s. 2; 1999-372, s. 2.)

153A-356. Failure to perform duties.

If a member of an inspection department willfully fails to perform the duties required of him by law, or willfully improperly issues a permit, or gives a certificate of compliance without first making the inspections required by law, or willfully improperly gives a certificate of compliance, he is guilty of a Class 1 misdemeanor. (1969, c. 1066, s. 1; 1973, c. 822, s. 1; 1993, c. 539, s. 1064; 1994, Ex. Sess., c. 24, s. 14(c).)

153A-357. Permits.

(a)   No person may commence or proceed with any of the following without first securing from the inspection department with jurisdiction over the site of the work each permit required by the State Building Code and any other State or local law or local ordinance or regulation applicable to the work:

(1)   The construction, reconstruction, alteration, repair, movement to another site, removal, or demolition of any building.

(2)   The installation, extension, or general repair of any plumbing system except that in any one or twofamily dwelling unit a permit shall not be required for the connection of a water heater that is being replaced, provided that the work is performed by a person licensed under G.S. 8721, who personally examines the work at completion and ensures that a leak test has been performed on the gas piping, and provided the energy use rate or thermal input is not greater than that of the water heater which is being replaced, there is no change in fuel, energy source, location, capacity, or routing or sizing of venting and piping, and the replacement is installed in accordance with the current edition of the State Building Code.

(3)   The installation, extension, alteration, or general repair of any heating or cooling equipment system.

(4)   The installation, extension, alteration, or general repair of any electrical wiring, devices, appliances, or equipment except that in any one or twofamily dwelling unit a permit shall not be required for repair or replacement of electrical lighting fixtures or devices, such as receptacles and lighting switches, or for the connection of an existing branch circuit to an electric water heater that is being replaced, provided that all of the following requirements are met:

    a.   With respect to electric water heaters, the replacement water heater is placed in the same location and is of the same or less capacity and electrical rating as the original.

    b.   With respect to electrical lighting fixtures and devices, the replacement is with a fixture or device having the same voltage and the same or less amperage.

    c.   The work is performed by a person licensed under G.S. 8743.

    d.   The repair or replacement installation meets the current edition of the State Building Code, including the State Electrical Code.

A permit shall be in writing and shall contain a provision that the work done shall comply with the State Building Code and all other applicable State and local laws and local ordinances and regulations. Nothing in this section shall require a county to review and approve residential building plans submitted to the county pursuant to Section R110 of Volume VII of the North Carolina State Building Code; provided that the county may review and approve such residential building plans as it deems necessary. No permit may be issued unless the plans and specifications are identified by the name and address of the author thereof; and if the General Statutes of North Carolina require that plans for certain types of work be prepared only by a registered architect or registered engineer, no permit may be issued unless the plans and specifications bear the North Carolina seal of a registered architect or of a registered engineer. If a provision of the General Statutes of North Carolina or of any ordinance requires that work be done by a licensed specialty contractor of any kind, no permit for the work may be issued unless the work is to be performed by such a duly licensed contractor. No permit issued under Articles 9 or 9C of G.S. Chapter 143 shall be required for any construction, installation, repair, replacement, or alteration costing five thousand dollars ($5,000) or less in any singlefamily residence or farm building unless the work involves: the addition, repair or replacement of load bearing structures; the addition (excluding replacement of same size and capacity) or change in the design of plumbing; the addition, replacement or change in the design of heating, air conditioning, or electrical wiring, devices, appliances, or equipment; the use of materials not permitted by the North Carolina Uniform Residential Building Code; or the addition (excluding replacement of like grade of fire resistance) of roofing. Violation of this section constitutes a Class 1 misdemeanor.

(b)   No permit shall be issued pursuant to subsection (a) for any landdisturbing activity, as defined in G.S. 113A52(6), for any activity covered by G.S. 113A57, unless an erosion and sedimentation control plan has been approved by the Sedimentation Pollution Control Commission pursuant to G.S. 113A54(d)(4) or by a local government pursuant to G.S. 113A61 for the site of the activity or a tract of land including the site of the activity.

(c)   (1)   A county may by ordinance provide that a permit may not be issued under subsection (a) of this section to a person who owes delinquent property taxes, determined under G.S. 105360, on property owned by the person. Such ordinance may provide that a building permit may be issued to a person protesting the assessment or collection of property taxes.

(2)   This subsection applies to Alexander, Alleghany, Anson, Bertie, Catawba, Chowan, Currituck, Davie, Gates, Greene, Lenoir, Lincoln, Iredell, Stokes, Surry, Tyrrell, Wayne, and Yadkin Counties only.

(d)   No permit shall be issued pursuant to subsection (a) of this section for any landdisturbing activity that is subject to, but does not comply with, the requirements of G.S. 113A71. (1969, c. 1066, s. 1; 1973, c. 822, s. 1; 1981, c. 677, s. 2; 1983, c. 377, s. 2; c. 614, s. 2; 1987 (Reg. Sess., 1988), c. 1000, s. 1; 1993, c. 539, s. 1065; 1994, Ex. Sess., c. 24, s. 14(c); 1993 (Reg. Sess., 1994), c. 741, s. 1; 2002165, s. 2.19; 2005433, s. 3; 2006150, s. 2; 200758, s. 1; 2008198, s. 8(c); 2009117, s. 1; 2009532, s. 2; 201030, s. 3.)

153A-358. Time limitations on validity of permits.

A permit issued pursuant to G.S. 153A-357 expires six months, or any lesser time fixed by ordinance of the county, after the date of issuance if the work authorized by the permit has not commenced. If after commencement the work is discontinued for a period of 12 months, the permit therefor immediately expires. No work authorized by a permit that has expired may thereafter be performed until a new permit has been secured. (1969, c. 1066, s. 1; 1973, c. 822, s. 1.)

153A-359. Changes in work.

After a permit has been issued, no change or deviation from the terms of the application, the plans and specifications, or the permit, except if the change or deviation is clearly permissible under the State Building Code, may be made until specific written approval of the proposed change or deviation has been obtained from the inspection department. (1969, c. 1066, s. 1; 1973, c. 822, s. 1.)

153A-360. Inspections of work in progress.

As the work pursuant to a permit progresses, local inspectors shall make as many inspections of the work as may be necessary to satisfy them that it is being done according to the provisions of the applicable State and local laws and local ordinances and regulations and of the terms of the permit. In exercising this power, each member of the inspection department has a right, upon presentation of proper credentials, to enter on any premises within the territorial jurisdiction of the department at any reasonable hour for the purposes of inspection or other enforcement action. If a permit has been obtained by an owner exempt from licensure under G.S. 871(b)(2), no inspection shall be conducted without the owner being personally present, unless the plans for the building were drawn and sealed by an architect licensed pursuant to Chapter 83A of the General Statutes. (1969, c. 1066, s. 1; 1973, c. 822, s. 1; 2011376, s. 3.)

153A-361. Stop orders.

Whenever a building or part thereof is being demolished, constructed, reconstructed, altered, or repaired in a hazardous manner, or in substantial violation of a State or local building law or local building ordinance or regulation, or in a manner that endangers life or property, the appropriate inspector may order the specific part of the work that is in violation or that presents such a hazard to be immediately stopped. The stop order shall be in writing and directed to the person doing the work, and shall state the specific work to be stopped, the specific reasons for the stoppage, and the conditions under which the work may be resumed. The owner or builder may appeal from a stop order involving alleged violation of the State Building Code or any approved local modification thereof to the North Carolina Commissioner of Insurance or his designee within five days after the day the order is issued. The owner or builder shall give to the Commissioner of Insurance or his designee written notice of appeal, with a copy to the local inspector. The Commissioner or his designee shall promptly conduct an investigation and the appellant and the inspector shall be permitted to submit relevant evidence. The Commissioner or his designee shall as expeditiously as possible provide a written statement of the decision setting forth the facts found, the decision reached, and the reasons for the decision. Pending the ruling by the Commissioner of Insurance or his designee on an appeal, no further work may take place in violation of a stop order. In the event of dissatisfaction with the decision, the person affected shall have the options of:

      (1)   Appealing to the Building Code Council, or

      (2)   Appealing to the Superior Court as provided in G.S. 143-141.

Violation of a stop order constitutes a Class 1 misdemeanor. (1969, c. 1066, s. 1; 1973, c. 822, s. 1; 1983, c. 377, s. 4; 1989, c. 681, s. 5; 1993, c. 539, s. 1066; 1994, Ex. Sess., c. 24, s. 14(c).)

153A-362. Revocation of permits.

The appropriate inspector may revoke and require the return of any permit by giving written notice to the permit holder, stating the reason for the revocation. Permits shall be revoked for any substantial departure from the approved application or plans and specifications, for refusal or failure to comply with the requirements of any applicable State or local laws or local ordinances or regulations, or for false statements or misrepresentations made in securing the permit. A permit mistakenly issued in violation of an applicable State or local law or local ordinance or regulation also may be revoked. (1969, c. 1066, s. 1; 1973, c. 822, s. 1.)

153A-363. Certificates of compliance.

At the conclusion of all work done under a permit, the appropriate inspector shall make a final inspection. If he finds that the completed work complies with all applicable State and local laws and local ordinances and regulations and with the terms of the permit, he shall issue a certificate of compliance. No new building or part thereof may be occupied, no addition or enlargement of an existing building may be occupied, and no existing building that has been altered or removed may be occupied until the inspection department has issued a certificate of compliance. A temporary certificate of compliance may be issued permitting occupancy for a stated period of specified portions of the building that the inspector finds may safely be occupied before completion of the entire building. Violation of this section constitutes a Class 1 misdemeanor. (1973, c. 822, s. 1; 1993, c. 539, s. 1067; 1994, Ex. Sess., c. 24, s. 14(c).)

153A-364. Periodic inspections for hazardous or unlawful conditions.

      (a)   The inspection department may make periodic inspections, subject to the board of commissioners' directions, for unsafe, unsanitary, or otherwise hazardous and unlawful conditions in buildings or structures within its territorial jurisdiction. Except as provided in subsection (b) of this section, the inspection department may make periodic inspections only when there is reasonable cause to believe that unsafe, unsanitary, or otherwise hazardous or unlawful conditions may exist in a residential building or structure. For purposes of this section, the term "reasonable cause" means any of the following: (i) the landlord or owner has a history of more than two verified violations of the housing ordinances or codes within a 12month period; (ii) there has been a complaint that substandard conditions exist within the building or there has been a request that the building be inspected; (iii) the inspection department has actual knowledge of an unsafe condition within the building; or (iv) violations of the local ordinances or codes are visible from the outside of the property. In conducting inspections authorized under this section, the inspection department shall not discriminate between singlefamily and multifamily buildings. In exercising these powers, each member of the inspection department has a right, upon presentation of proper credentials, to enter on any premises within the territorial jurisdiction of the department at any reasonable hour for the purposes of inspection or other enforcement action. Nothing in this section shall be construed to prohibit periodic inspections in accordance with State fire prevention code or as otherwise required by State law.

      (b)   A county may require periodic inspections as part of a targeted effort within a geographic area that has been designated by the county commissioners. The county shall not discriminate in its selection of areas or housing types to be targeted and shall (i) provide notice to all owners and residents of properties in the affected area about the periodic inspections plan and information regarding a public hearing regarding the plan; (ii) hold a public hearing regarding the plan; and (iii) establish a plan to address the ability of lowincome residential property owners to comply with minimum housing code standards.

(c)   In no event may a county do any of the following: (i) adopt or enforce any ordinance that would require any owner or manager of rental property to obtain any permit or permission from the county to lease or rent residential real property, except for those rental units that have more than three verified violations of housing ordinances or codes in a 12month period or upon the property being identified within the top 10% of properties with crime or disorder problems as set forth in a local ordinance; (ii) require that an owner or manager of residential rental property enroll or participate in any governmental program as a condition of obtaining a certificate of occupancy; or (iii) except as provided in subsection (d) of this section, levy a special fee or tax on residential rental property that is not also levied against other commercial and residential properties.

(d)   A county may levy a fee for residential rental property registration under subsection (c) of this section for those rental units which have been found with more than two verified violations of housing ordinances or codes within the previous 12 months or upon the property being identified within the top 10% of properties with crime or disorder problems as set forth in a local ordinance. The fee shall be an amount that covers the cost of operating a residential registration program and shall not be used to supplant revenue in other areas. Counties using registration programs that charge registration fees for all residential rental properties as of June 1, 2011, may continue levying a fee on all residential rental properties as follows:

(1)   For properties with 20 or more residential rental units, the fee shall be no more than fifty dollars ($50.00) per year.

(2)   For properties with fewer than 20 but more than three residential rental units, the fee shall be no more than twentyfive dollars ($25.00) per year.

(3)   For properties with three or fewer residential rental units, the fee shall be no more than fifteen dollars ($15.00) per year. (1969, c. 1066, s. 1; 1973, c. 822, s. 1; 2011281, s. 1.)

153A-365. Defects in buildings to be corrected.

If a local inspector finds any defect in a building, or finds that the building has not been constructed in accordance with the applicable State and local laws and local ordinances and regulations, or finds that a building because of its condition is dangerous or contains fire-hazardous conditions, he shall notify the owner or occupant of the building of its defects, hazardous conditions, or failure to comply with law. The owner and the occupant shall each immediately remedy the defects, hazardous conditions, or violations of law in the property each owns. (1969, c. 1066, s. 1; 1973, c. 822, s. 1.)

153A-366. Unsafe buildings condemned.

The inspector shall condemn as unsafe each building that appears to him to be especially dangerous to life because of its liability to fire, bad conditions of walls, overloaded floors, defective construction, decay, unsafe wiring or heating system, inadequate means of egress, or other causes; and he shall affix a notice of the dangerous character of the building to a conspicuous place on its exterior wall. (1969, c. 1066, s. 1; 1973, c. 822, s. 1.)

153A-367. Removing notice from condemned building.

If a person removes a notice that has been affixed to a building by a local inspector and that states the dangerous character of the building, he is guilty of a Class 1 misdemeanor. (1969, c. 1066, s. 1; 1973, c. 822, s. 1; 1993, c. 539, s. 1068; 1994, Ex. Sess., c. 24, s. 14(c).)

153A-368. Action in event of failure to take corrective action.

If the owner of a building that has been condemned as unsafe pursuant to G.S. 153A-366 fails to take prompt corrective action, the local inspector shall by certified or registered mail to his last known address or by personal service give him written notice:

(1)   That the building is in a condition that appears to constitute a fire or safety hazard or to be dangerous to life, health, or other property;

(2)   That a hearing will be held before the inspector at a designated place and time, not later than 10 days after the date of the notice, at which time the owner is entitled to be heard in person or by counsel and to present arguments and evidence pertaining to the matter; and

(3)   That following the hearing, the inspector may issue any order to repair, close, vacate, or demolish the building that appears appropriate.

If the name or whereabouts of the owner cannot after due diligence be discovered, the notice shall be considered properly and adequately served if a copy thereof is posted on the outside of the building in question at least 10 days before the day of the hearing and a notice of the hearing is published at least once not later than one week before the hearing. (1969, c. 1066, s. 1; 1973, c. 822, s. 1.)

153A-369. Order to take corrective action.

If, upon a hearing held pursuant to G.S. 153A-368, the inspector finds that the building is in a condition that constitutes a fire or safety hazard or renders it dangerous to life, health, or other property, he shall issue a written order, directed to the owner of the building, requiring the owner to remedy the defective conditions by repairing, closing, vacating, or demolishing the building or taking other necessary steps, within such period, not less than 60 days, as the inspector may prescribe; provided, that where the inspector finds that there is imminent danger to life or other property, he may order that corrective action be taken in such lesser period as may be feasible. (1969, c. 1066, s. 1; 1973, c. 822, s. 1; 1979, c. 611, s. 5.)

153A-370.Appeal; finality of order not appealed.

An owner who has received an order under G.S. 153A-369 may appeal from the order to the board of commissioners by giving written notice of appeal to the inspector and to the clerk within 10 days following the day the order is issued. In the absence of an appeal, the order of the inspector is final. The board of commissioners shall hear any appeal within a reasonable time and may affirm, modify and affirm, or revoke the order. (1969, c. 1066, s. 1; 1973, c. 822, s. 1.)

153A-371. Failure to comply with order.

If the owner of a building fails to comply with an order issued pursuant to G.S. 153A- 369 from which no appeal has been taken, or fails to comply with an order of the board of commissioners following an appeal, he is guilty of a Class 1 misdemeanor. (1969, c. 1066, s. 1; 1973, c. 822, s. 1; 1993, c. 539, s. 1069; 1994, Ex. Sess., c. 24, s. 14(c).)

153A-372. Equitable enforcement.

Whenever a violation is denominated a misdemeanor under the provisions of this Part, the county, either in addition to or in lieu of other remedies, may initiate any appropriate action or proceeding to prevent, restrain, correct, or abate the violation or to prevent the occupancy of the building involved. (1969, c. 1066, s. 1; 1973, c. 822, s. 1.)

153A372.1. Ordinance authorized as to repair, closing, and demolition of nonresidential buildings or structures; order of public officer.

The provisions of G.S. 160A439 shall apply to counties. (2007414, s. 2.)

153A-373. Records and reports.

The inspection department shall keep complete and accurate records in convenient form of each application received, each permit issued, each inspection and reinspection made, and each defect found, each certificate of compliance granted, and all other work and activities of the department. These records shall be kept in the manner and for the periods prescribed by the North Carolina Department of Cultural Resources. The department shall submit periodic reports to the board of commissioners and to the Commissioner of Insurance as the board or the Commissioner may require. (1969, c. 1066, s. 1; 1973, c. 822, s. 1; 1983, c. 377, s. 6.)

153A-374. Appeals.

Unless otherwise provided by law, any appeal from an order, decision, or determination of a member of a local inspection department pertaining to the State Building Code or any other State building law shall be taken to the Commissioner of Insurance or his designee or other official specified in G.S. 143-139, by filing a written notice with him and with the inspection department within 10 days after the day of the order, decision, or determination. Further appeals may be taken to the State Building Code Council or to the courts as provided by law. (1969, c. 1066, s. 1; 1973, c. 822, s. 1; 1989, c. 681, s. 7.)

153A-375. Establishment of fire limits.

A county may by ordinance establish and define fire limits in any area within the county and not within a city. The limits may include only business and industrial areas. Within any fire limits, no frame or wooden building or addition thereto may be erected, altered, repaired, or moved (either into the fire limits or from one place to another within the limits) except upon the permit of the inspection department and approval of the Commissioner of Insurance. The board of commissioners may make additional regulations necessary for the prevention, extinguishment, or mitigation of fires within the fire limits. (1969, c. 1066, s. 1; 1973, c. 822, s. 1.)

Appendix K: Building Inspection (Cities)

CHAPTER 160A, PART 5

160A-411. Inspection department.

Every city in the State is hereby authorized to create an inspection department, and may appoint one or more inspectors who may be given the titles of building inspector, electrical inspector, plumbing inspector, housing inspector, zoning inspector, heating and air-conditioning inspector, fire prevention inspector, or deputy or assistant inspector, or such other titles as may be generally descriptive of the duties assigned. The department may be headed by a superintendent or director of inspections. Every city shall perform the duties and responsibilities set forth in G.S. 160A-412 either by: (i) creating its own inspection department; (ii) creating a joint inspection department in cooperation with one or more other units of local government, pursuant to G.S. 160A-413 or Part 1 of Article 20 of this Chapter; (iii) contracting with another unit of local government for the provision of inspection services pursuant to Part 1 of Article 20 of this Chapter; or (iv) arranging for the county in which it is located to perform inspection services within the city's jurisdiction as authorized by G.S. 160A-413 and G.S. 160A-360. Such action shall be taken no later than the applicable date in the schedule below, according to the city's population as published in the 1970 United States Census:

Cities over 75,000 population - July 1, 1979

Cities between 50,001 and 75,000 - July 1, 1981

Cities between 25,001 and 50,000 - July 1, 1983

Cities 25,000 and under - July 1, 1985.

In the event that any city shall fail to provide inspection services by the date specified above or shall cease to provide such services at any time thereafter, the Commissioner of Insurance shall arrange for the provision of such services, either through personnel employed by his department or through an arrangement with other units of government. In either event, the Commissioner shall have and may exercise within the city's jurisdiction all powers made available to the city council with respect to building inspection under Part 5 of Article 19, and Part 1 of Article 20 of this Chapter. Whenever the Commissioner has intervened in this manner, the city may assume provision of inspection services only after giving the Commissioner two years' written notice of its intention to do so; provided, however, that the Commissioner may waive this requirement or permit assumption at an earlier date if he finds that such earlier assumption will not unduly interfere with arrangements he has made for the provision of those services. (1969, c. 1065, s. 1; 1971, c. 698, s. 1; 1977, c. 531, s. 5.)

160A-411.1. Qualifications of inspectors.

On and after the applicable date set forth in the schedule in G.S. 160A-411, no city shall employ an inspector to enforce the State Building Code as a member of a city or joint inspection department who does not have one of the following types of certificates issued by the North Carolina Code Officials Qualification Board attesting to his qualifications to hold such position: (i) a probationary certificate, valid for one year only; (ii) a standard certificate; or (iii) a limited certificate which shall be valid only as an authorization for him to continue in the position held on the date specified in G.S. 143-151.13(c) and which shall become invalid if he does not successfully complete in-service training specified by the Qualification Board within the period specified in G.S. 143-151.13(c). An inspector holding one of the above certificates can be promoted to a position requiring a higher level certificate only upon issuance by the Board of a standard certificate or probationary certificate appropriate for such new position. (1977, c. 531, s. 6.)

160A-412. Duties and responsibilities.

The duties and responsibilities of an inspection department and of the inspectors therein shall be to enforce within their territorial jurisdiction State and local laws relating to:

(1) The construction of buildings and other structures;

(2) The installation of such facilities as plumbing systems, electrical systems, heating systems, refrigeration systems, and air-conditioning systems;

(3) The maintenance of buildings and other structures in a safe, sanitary, and healthful condition;

(4) Other matters that may be specified by the city council.

These duties shall include the receipt of applications for permits and the issuance or denial of permits, the making of any necessary inspections, the issuance or denial of certificates of compliance, the issuance of orders to correct violations, the bringing of judicial actions against actual or threatened violations, the keeping of adequate records, and any other actions that may be required in order adequately to enforce those laws. The city council shall have the authority to enact reasonable and appropriate provisions governing the enforcement of those laws. (1969, c. 1065, s. 1; 1971, c. 698, s. 1.)

160A-413. Joint inspection department; other arrangements.

A city council may enter into and carry out contracts with another city, county, or combination thereof under which the parties agree to create and support a joint inspection department for the enforcement of State and local laws specified in the agreement. The governing boards of the contracting parties are authorized to make any necessary appropriations for this purpose.

In lieu of a joint inspection department, a city council may designate an inspector from any other city or county to serve as a member of its inspection department with the approval of the governing body of the other city or county. A city may also contract with an individual who is not a city or county employee but who holds one of the applicable certificates as provided in G.S. 160A411.1 or G.S. 153A351.1 or with the employer of an individual who holds one of the applicable certificates as provided in G.S. 160A411.1 or G.S. 153A351.1. The inspector, if designated from another city or county under this section, shall, while exercising the duties of the position, be considered a municipal employee. The city shall have the same potential liability, if any, for inspections conducted by an individual who is not an employee of the city as it does for an individual who is an employee of the city. The company or individual with whom the city contracts shall have errors and omissions and other insurance coverage acceptable to the city.

The city council of any city may request the board of county commissioners of the county in which the city is located to direct one or more county building inspectors to exercise their powers within part or all of the city's jurisdiction, and they shall thereupon be empowered to do so until the city council officially withdraws its request in the manner provided in G.S. 160A360(g). (1969, c. 1065, s. 1; 1971, c. 698, s. 1; 1973, c. 426, s. 64; 1993, c. 232, s. 3; 1999372, s. 3; 2001278, s. 2.)

160A-414. Financial support.

The city council may appropriate for the support of the inspection department any funds that it deems necessary. It may provide for paying inspectors fixed salaries or it may reimburse them for their services by paying over part or all of any fees collected. It shall have power to fix reasonable fees for issuance of permits, inspections, and other services of the inspection department. (1969, c. 1065, s. 1; 1971, c. 698, s. 1.)

160A-415. Conflicts of interest.

No member of an inspection department shall be financially interested or employed by a business that is financially interested in the furnishing of labor, material, or appliances for the construction, alteration, or maintenance of any building within the city's jurisdiction or any part or system thereof, or in the making of plans or specifications therefor, unless he is the owner of the building. No member of an inspection department or other individual or an employee of a company contracting with a city to conduct inspections shall engage in any work that is inconsistent with his or her duties or with the interest of the city, as determined by the city. The city must find a conflict of interest if any of the following is the case:

(1)   If the individual, company, or employee of a company contracting to perform inspections for the city has worked for the owner, developer, contractor, or project manager of the project to be inspected within the last two years.

(2)   If the individual, company, or employee of a company contracting to perform inspections for the city is closely related to the owner, developer, contractor, or project manager of the project to be inspected.

(3)   If the individual, company, or employee of a company contracting to perform inspections for the city has a financial or business interest in the project to be inspected.

The provisions of this section do not apply to a firefighter whose primary duties are fire suppression and rescue, but who engages in some fire inspection activities as a secondary responsibility of the firefighter's employment as a firefighter, except no firefighter may inspect any work actually done, or materials or appliances supplied, by the firefighter or the firefighter's business within the preceding six years. (1969, c. 1065, s. 1; 1971, c. 698, s. 1; 1993, c. 232, s. 4; 1998-122, s. 1; 1999-372, s. 4.)

160A-416. Failure to perform duties.

If any member of an inspection department shall willfully fail to perform the duties required of him by law, or willfully shall improperly issue a permit, or shall give a certificate of compliance without first making the inspections required by law, or willfully shall improperly give a certificate of compliance, he shall be guilty of a Class 1 misdemeanor. (1969, c. 1065, s. 1; 1971, c. 698, s. 1; 1993, c. 539, s. 1089; 1994, Ex. Sess., c. 24, s. 14(c).)

160A-417. Permits.

(a)   No person shall commence or proceed with any of the following without first securing from the inspection department with jurisdiction over the site of the work any and all permits required by the State Building Code and any other State or local laws applicable to the work:

(1)   The construction, reconstruction, alteration, repair, movement to another site, removal, or demolition of any building or structure.

(2)   The installation, extension, or general repair of any plumbing system except that in any one or twofamily dwelling unit a permit shall not be required for the connection of a water heater that is being replaced, provided that the work is performed by a person licensed under G.S. 8721, who personally examines the work at completion and ensures that a leak test has been performed on the gas piping, and provided the energy use rate or thermal input is not greater than that of the water heater which is being replaced, there is no change in fuel, energy source, location, capacity, or routing or sizing of venting and piping, and the replacement is installed in accordance with the current edition of the State Building Code.

(3)   The installation, extension, alteration, or general repair of any heating or cooling equipment system.

(4)   The installation, extension, alteration, or general repair of any electrical wiring, devices, appliances, or equipment except that in any one or twofamily dwelling unit a permit shall not be required for repair or replacement of electrical lighting fixtures or devices, such as receptacles and lighting switches, or for the connection of an existing branch circuit to an electric water heater that is being replaced, provided that all of the following requirements are met:

  a.   With respect to electric water heaters, the replacement water heater is placed in the same location and is of the same or less capacity and electrical rating as the original.

  b.   With respect to electrical lighting fixtures and devices, the replacement is with a fixture or device having the same voltage and the same or less amperage.

  c.   The work is performed by a person licensed under G.S. 8743.

  d.   The repair or replacement installation meets the current edition of the State Building Code, including the State Electrical Code.

A permit shall be in writing and shall contain a provision that the work done shall comply with the State Building Code and all other applicable State and local laws. Nothing in this section shall require a city to review and approve residential building plans submitted to the city pursuant to Section R110 of Volume VII of the North Carolina State Building Code; provided that the city may review and approve such residential building plans as it deems necessary. No permits shall be issued unless the plans and specifications are identified by the name and address of the author thereof, and if the General Statutes of North Carolina require that plans for certain types of work be prepared only by a registered architect or registered engineer, no permit shall be issued unless the plans and specifications bear the North Carolina seal of a registered architect or of a registered engineer. When any provision of the General Statutes of North Carolina or of any ordinance requires that work be done by a licensed specialty contractor of any kind, no permit for the work shall be issued unless the work is to be performed by such a duly licensed contractor. No permit issued under Articles 9 or 9C of Chapter 143 shall be required for any construction, installation, repair, replacement, or alteration costing five thousand dollars ($5,000) or less in any single family residence or farm building unless the work involves: the addition, repair or replacement of load bearing structures; the addition (excluding replacement of same size and capacity) or change in the design of plumbing; the addition, replacement or change in the design of heating, air conditioning, or electrical wiring, devices, appliances, or equipment; the use of materials not permitted by the North Carolina Uniform Residential Building Code; or the addition (excluding replacement of like grade of fire resistance) of roofing. Violation of this section shall constitute a Class 1 misdemeanor.

(b)   No permit shall be issued pursuant to subsection (a) for any landdisturbing activity, as defined in G.S. 113A52(6), for any activity covered by G.S. 113A57, unless an erosion and sedimentation control plan has been approved by the Sedimentation Pollution Control Commission pursuant to G.S. 113A54(d)(4) or by a local government pursuant to G.S. 113A61 for the site of the activity or a tract of land including the site of the activity.

(c)   No permit shall be issued pursuant to subsection (a) of this section for any landdisturbing activity that is subject to, but does not comply with, the requirements of G.S. 113A71. (1905, c. 506, s. 26; Rev., s. 2986; 1915, c. 192, s. 3; C.S., s. 2748; 1957, c. 817; 1969, c. 1065, s. 1; 1971, c. 698, s. 1; 1973, c. 426, s. 65; 1981, c. 677, s. 1; 1983, c. 377, s. 3; c. 614, s. 1; 1987 (Reg. Sess., 1988), c. 1000, s. 2; 1993, c. 539, s. 1090; 1994, Ex. Sess., c. 24, s. 14(c); 1993 (Reg. Sess., 1994), c. 741, s. 2; 2002165, s. 2.20; 2008198, s. 8(d); 2009532, s. 3.)

160A-418. Time limitations on validity of permits.

A permit issued pursuant to G.S. 160A-417 shall expire by limitation six months, or any lesser time fixed by ordinance of the city council, after the date of issuance if the work authorized by the permit has not been commenced. If after commencement the work is discontinued for a period of 12 months, the permit therefor shall immediately expire. No work authorized by any permit that has expired shall thereafter be performed until a new permit has been secured. (1969, c. 1065, s. 1; 1971, c. 698, s. 1.)

160A-419. Changes in work.

After a permit has been issued, no changes or deviations from the terms of the application, plans and specifications, or the permit, except where changes or deviations are clearly permissible under the State Building Code, shall be made until specific written approval of proposed changes or deviations has been obtained from the inspection department. (1969, c. 1065, s. 1; 1971, c. 698, s. 1.)

160A-420. Inspections of work in progress.

As the work pursuant to a permit progresses, local inspectors shall make as many inspections thereof as may be necessary to satisfy them that the work is being done according to the provisions of any applicable State and local laws and of the terms of the permit. In exercising this power, members of the inspection department shall have a right to enter on any premises within the jurisdiction of the department at all reasonable hours for the purposes of inspection or other enforcement action, upon presentation of proper credentials. If a permit has been obtained by an owner exempt from licensure under G.S. 871(b)(2), no inspection shall be conducted without the owner being personally present, unless the plans for the building were drawn and sealed by an architect licensed pursuant to Chapter 83A of the General Statutes. (1969, c. 1065, s. 1; 1971, c. 698, s. 1; 2011376, s. 4.)

160A-421. Stop orders.

(a) Whenever any building or structure or part thereof is being demolished, constructed, reconstructed, altered, or repaired in a hazardous manner, or in substantial violation of any State or local building law, or in a manner that endangers life or property, the appropriate inspector may order the specific part of the work that is in violation or presents such a hazard to be immediately stopped. The stop order shall be in writing, directed to the person doing the work, and shall state the specific work to be stopped, the specific reasons therefor, and the conditions under which the work may be resumed.

(b) The owner or builder may appeal from a stop order involving alleged violation of the State Building Code or any approved local modification thereof to the North Carolina Commissioner of Insurance or his designee within a period of five days after the order is issued. Notice of appeal shall be given in writing to the Commissioner of Insurance or his designee, with a copy to the local inspector. The Commissioner of Insurance or his designee shall promptly conduct an investigation and the appellant and the inspector shall be permitted to submit relevant evidence. The Commissioner of Insurance or his designee shall as expeditiously as possible provide a written statement of the decision setting forth the facts found, the decision reached, and the reasons for the decision. Pending the ruling by the Commissioner of Insurance or his designee on an appeal no further work shall take place in violation of a stop order. In the event of dissatisfaction with the decision, the person affected shall have the options of:

(1) Appealing to the Building Code Council, or

(2) Appealing to the Superior Court as provided in G.S. 143-141.

(c) The owner or builder may appeal from a stop order involving alleged violation of a local zoning ordinance by giving notice of appeal in writing to the board of adjustment. The appeal shall be heard and decided within the period established by the ordinance, or if none is specified, within a reasonable time. No further work shall take place in violation of a stop order pending a ruling.

(d)   Violation of a stop order shall constitute a Class 1 misdemeanor. (1969, c. 1065, s. 1; 1971, c. 698, s. 1; 1983, c. 377, s. 5; 1989, c. 681, s. 6; 1991, c. 512, s. 3; 1993, c. 539, s. 1091; 1994, Ex. Sess., c. 24, s. 14(c).)

160A-422. Revocation of permits.

The appropriate inspector may revoke and require the return of any permit by notifying the permit holder in writing stating the reason for the revocation. Permits shall be revoked for any substantial departure from the approved application, plans, or specifications; for refusal or failure to comply with the requirements of any applicable State or local laws; or for false statements or misrepresentations made in securing the permit. Any permit mistakenly issued in violation of an applicable State or local law may also be revoked. (1969, c. 1065, s. 1; 1971, c. 698, s. 1.)

160A-423. Certificates of compliance.

At the conclusion of all work done under a permit, the appropriate inspector shall make a final inspection, and if he finds that the completed work complies with all applicable State and local laws and with the terms of the permit, he shall issue a certificate of compliance. No new building or part thereof may be occupied, and no addition or enlargement of an existing building may be occupied, and no existing building that has been altered or moved may be occupied, until the inspection department has issued a certificate of compliance. A temporary certificate of compliance may be issued permitting occupancy for a stated period of specified portions of the building that the inspector finds may safely be occupied prior to final completion of the entire building. Violation of this section shall constitute a Class 1 misdemeanor. (1969, c. 1065, s. 1; 1971, c. 698, s. 1; 1973, c. 426, s. 66; 1993, c. 539, s. 1092; 1994, Ex. Sess., c. 24, s. 14(c).)

160A-424. Periodic inspections.

(a)   The inspection department may make periodic inspections, subject to the council's directions, for unsafe, unsanitary, or otherwise hazardous and unlawful conditions in buildings or structures within its territorial jurisdiction. Except as provided in subsection (b) of this section, the inspection department may make periodic inspections only when there is reasonable cause to believe that unsafe, unsanitary, or otherwise hazardous or unlawful conditions may exist in a residential building or structure. For purposes of this section, the term "reasonable cause" means any of the following: (i) the landlord or owner has a history of more than two verified violations of the housing ordinances or codes within a 12month period; (ii) there has been a complaint that substandard conditions exist within the building or there has been a request that the building be inspected; (iii) the inspection department has actual knowledge of an unsafe condition within the building; or (iv) violations of the local ordinances or codes are visible from the outside of the property. In conducting inspections authorized under this section, the inspection department shall not discriminate between singlefamily and multifamily buildings. In exercising this power, members of the department shall have a right to enter on any premises within the jurisdiction of the department at all reasonable hours for the purposes of inspection or other enforcement action, upon presentation of proper credentials. Nothing in this section shall be construed to prohibit periodic inspections in accordance with State fire prevention code or as otherwise required by State law.

(b)   A city may require periodic inspections as part of a targeted effort within a geographic area that has been designated by the city council. The municipality shall not discriminate in its selection of areas or housing types to be targeted and shall (i) provide notice to all owners and residents of properties in the affected area about the periodic inspections plan and information regarding a public hearing regarding the plan; (ii) hold a public hearing regarding the plan; and (iii) establish a plan to address the ability of lowincome residential property owners to comply with minimum housing code standards.

(c)   In no event may a city do any of the following: (i) adopt or enforce any ordinance that would require any owner or manager of rental property to obtain any permit or permission from the city to lease or rent residential real property, except for those properties that have more than three verified violations in a 12month period or upon the property being identified within the top 10% of properties with crime or disorder problems as set forth in a local ordinance; (ii) require that an owner or manager of residential rental property enroll or participate in any governmental program as a condition of obtaining a certificate of occupancy; or (iii) except as provided in subsection (d) of this section, levy a special fee or tax on residential rental property that is not also levied against other commercial and residential properties.

(d)   A city may levy a fee for residential rental property registration under subsection (c) of this section for those rental units which have been found with more than two verified violations of local ordinances within the previous 12 months or upon the property being identified within the top 10% of properties with crime or disorder problems as set forth in a local ordinance. The fee shall be an amount that covers the cost of operating a residential registration program and shall not be used to supplant revenue in other areas. Cities using registration programs that charge registration fees for all residential rental properties as of June 1, 2011, may continue levying a fee on all residential rental properties as follows:

    (1)   For properties with 20 or more residential rental units, the fee shall be no more than fifty dollars ($50.00) per year.

    (2)   For properties with fewer than 20 but more than three residential rental units, the fee shall be no more than twentyfive dollars ($25.00) per year.

    (3)   For properties with three or fewer residential rental units, the fee shall be no more than fifteen dollars ($15.00) per year. (1969, c. 1065, s. 1; 1971, c. 698, s. 1; 2011281, s. 2.)

160A-425. Defects in buildings to be corrected.

When a local inspector finds any defects in a building, or finds that the building has not been constructed in accordance with the applicable State and local laws, or that a building because of its condition is dangerous or contains fire hazardous conditions, it shall be his duty to notify the owner or occupant of the building of its defects, hazardous conditions, or failure to comply with law. The owner or occupant shall each immediately remedy the defects, hazardous conditions, or violations of law in the property he owns. (1905, c. 506, s. 28; Rev., s. 3009; 1915, c. 192, s. 14; C.S., s. 2771; 1969, c. 1065, s. 1; 1971, c. 698, s. 1; 1973, c. 426, s. 67.)

160A-425.1. Repealed by Session Laws 2009263, s. 1, effective October 1, 2009.

160A-426.Unsafe buildings condemned in localities.

(a)   Residential Building and Nonresidential Building or Structure. – Every building that shall appear to the inspector to be especially dangerous to life because of its liability to fire or because of bad condition of walls, overloaded floors, defective construction, decay, unsafe wiring or heating system, inadequate means of egress, or other causes, shall be held to be unsafe, and the inspector shall affix a notice of the dangerous character of the structure to a conspicuous place on the exterior wall of the building.

(b)   Nonresidential Building or Structure. – In addition to the authority granted in subsection (a) of this section, an inspector may declare a nonresidential building or structure within a community development target area to be unsafe if it meets both of the following conditions:

    (1)   It appears to the inspector to be vacant or abandoned.

(2)   It appears to the inspector to be in such dilapidated condition as to cause or contribute to blight, disease, vagrancy, fire or safety hazard, to be a danger to children, or to tend to attract persons intent on criminal activities or other activities that would constitute a public nuisance.

(c)   If an inspector declares a nonresidential building or structure to be unsafe under subsection (b) of this section, the inspector must affix a notice of the unsafe character of the structure to a conspicuous place on the exterior wall of the building. For the purposes of this section, the term "community development target area" means an area that has characteristics of an urban progress zone under G.S. 143B437.09, a "nonresidential redevelopment area" under G.S. 160A503(10), or an area with similar characteristics designated by the city council as being in special need of revitalization for the benefit and welfare of its citizens.

(d)   A municipality may expand subsections (b) and (c) of this section to apply to residential buildings by adopting an ordinance. Before adopting such an ordinance, a municipality shall hold a public hearing and shall provide notice of the hearing at least 10 days in advance of the hearing. (1905, c. 506, s. 15; Rev., s. 3010; 1915, c. 192, s. 15; C.S., s. 2773; 1929, c. 199, s. 1; 1969, c. 1065, s. 1; 1971, c. 698, s. 1; 2000-164, s. 1; 2001386, s. 1; 2006252, s. 2.19; 2009263, s. 2.)

160A-427. Removing notice from condemned building.

If any person shall remove any notice that has been affixed to any building or structure by a local inspector of any municipality and that states the dangerous character of the building or structure, he shall be guilty of a Class 1 misdemeanor. (1905, c. 50-6, s. 15; Rev., s. 3799; C.S., s. 2775; 1969, c. 1065, s. 1; 1971, c. 698, s. 1; 1993, c. 539, s. 1093; 1994, Ex. Sess., c. 24, s. 14(c).)

160A-428.Action in event of failure to take corrective action.

If the owner of a building or structure that has been condemned as unsafe pursuant to G.S. 160A426 shall fail to take prompt corrective action, the local inspector shall give him written notice, by certified or registered mail to his last known address or by personal service:

(1)   That the building or structure is in a condition that appears to meet one or more of the following conditions:

    a.   Constitutes a fire or safety hazard.

    b.   Is dangerous to life, health, or other property.

    c.   Is likely to cause or contribute to blight, disease, vagrancy, or danger to children.

    d.   Has a tendency to attract persons intent on criminal activities or other activities which would constitute a public nuisance.

(2)   That a hearing will be held before the inspector at a designated place and time, not later than 10 days after the date of the notice, at which time the owner shall be entitled to be heard in person or by counsel and to present arguments and evidence pertaining to the matter; and

(3)   That following the hearing, the inspector may issue such order to repair, close, vacate, or demolish the building or structure as appears appropriate.

If the name or whereabouts of the owner cannot after due diligence be discovered, the notice shall be considered properly and adequately served if a copy thereof is posted on the outside of the building or structure in question at least 10 days prior to the hearing and a notice of the hearing is published in a newspaper having general circulation in the city at least once not later than one week prior to the hearing. (1969, c. 1065, s. 1; 1971, c. 698, s. 1; 2000-164, s. 2; 2009263, s. 4.)

160A-429. Order to take corrective action.

If, upon a hearing held pursuant to the notice prescribed in G.S. 160A-428, the inspector shall find that the building or structure is in a condition that constitutes a fire or safety hazard or renders it dangerous to life, health, or other property, he shall make an order in writing, directed to the owner of such building or structure, requiring the owner to remedy the defective conditions by repairing, closing, vacating, or demolishing the building or structure or taking other necessary steps, within such period, not less than 60 days, as the inspector may prescribe; provided, that where the inspector finds that there is imminent danger to life or other property, he may order that corrective action be taken in such lesser period as may be feasible. (1969, c. 1065, s. 1; 1971, c. 698, s. 1; 1973, c. 426, s. 68; 1977, c. 912, s. 13.)

160A-430. Appeal; finality of order if not appealed.

Any owner who has received an order under G.S. 160A-429 may appeal from the order to the city council by giving notice of appeal in writing to the inspector and to the city clerk within 10 days following issuance of the order. In the absence of an appeal, the order of the inspector shall be final. The city council shall hear and render a decision in an appeal within a reasonable time. The city council may affirm, modify and affirm, or revoke the order. (1969, c. 1065, s. 1; 1971, c. 698, s. 1; 1973, c. 426, s. 69; 2000-164, s. 4.)

160A-431. Failure to comply with order.

If the owner of a building or structure fails to comply with an order issued pursuant to G.S. 160A-429 from which no appeal has been taken, or fails to comply with an order of the city council following an appeal, he shall be guilty of a Class 1 misdemeanor. (1905, c. 506, s. 15; Rev., s. 3802; 1915, c. 192, s. 19; C.S., s. 2774; 1929, c. 199, s. 2; 1969, c. 1065, s. 1; 1971, c. 698, s. 1; 1993, c. 539, s. 1094; 1994, Ex. Sess., c. 24, s. 14(c).)

160A-432. Enforcement.

(a)   [Action Authorized.] – Whenever any violation is denominated a misdemeanor under the provisions of this Part, the city, either in addition to or in lieu of other remedies, may initiate any appropriate action or proceedings to prevent, restrain, correct, or abate the violation or to prevent the occupancy of the building or structure involved.

(a1)   Repealed by Session Laws 2009263, s. 1, effective October 1, 2009.

(b)   Removal of Building. – In the case of a building or structure declared unsafe under G.S. 160A426 or an ordinance adopted pursuant to G.S. 160A426, a city may, in lieu of taking action under subsection (a), cause the building or structure to be removed or demolished. The amounts incurred by the city in connection with the removal or demolition shall be a lien against the real property upon which the cost was incurred. The lien shall be filed, have the same priority, and be collected in the same manner as liens for special assessments provided in Article 10 of this Chapter. If the building or structure is removed or demolished by the city, the city shall sell the usable materials of the building and any personal property, fixtures, or appurtenances found in or attached to the building. The city shall credit the proceeds of the sale against the cost of the removal or demolition. Any balance remaining from the sale shall be deposited with the clerk of superior court of the county where the property is located and shall be disbursed by the court to the person found to be entitled thereto by final order or decree of the court.

(b1)   Additional Lien. – The amounts incurred by the city in connection with the removal or demolition shall also be a lien against any other real property owned by the owner of the building or structure and located within the city limits or within one mile of the city limits, except for the owner's primary residence. The provisions of subsection (b) of this section apply to this additional lien, except that this additional lien is inferior to all prior liens and shall be collected as a money judgment.

(c)   [Nonexclusive Remedy.] – Nothing in this section shall be construed to impair or limit the power of the city to define and declare nuisances and to cause their removal or abatement by summary proceedings, or otherwise. (1969, c. 1065, s. 1; 1971, c. 698, s. 1; 2000-164, s. 3; 2001-386, s.2; 2001-448,s.2; 2002-118,s.2; 2003-23,s.2; 2003-42,s.1; 2004-6,s.1; 2007216, s. 2; 200859, s. 2; 20099, s. 2; 2009263, ss. 1, 3.)

160A-433. Records and reports.

The inspection department shall keep complete and accurate records in convenient form of all applications received, permits issued, inspections and reinspections made, defects found, certificates of compliance granted, and all other work and activities of the department. These records shall be kept in the manner and for the periods prescribed by the North Carolina Department of Cultural Resources. Periodic reports shall be submitted to the city council and to the Commissioner of Insurance as they shall by ordinance, rule, or regulation require. (1905, c. 506, ss. 30, 31; Rev., ss. 3004, 3005; 1915, c. 192, s. 12; C.S., ss. 2766, 2767; 1969, c. 1065, s. 1; 1971, c. 698, s. 1; 1983, c. 377, s. 7.)

160A-434.Appeals in general.

Unless otherwise provided by law, appeals from any order, decision, or determination by a member of a local inspection department pertaining to the State Building Code or other State building laws shall be taken to the Commissioner of Insurance or his designee or other official specified in G.S. 143-139, by filing a written notice with him and with the inspection department within a period of 10 days after the order, decision, or determination. Further appeals may be taken to the State Building Code Council or to the courts as provided by law. (1969, c. 1065, s. 1; 1971, c. 698, s. 1; 1989, c. 681, s. 7A.)

160A-435. Establishment of fire limits.

The city council of every incorporated city shall pass one or more ordinances establishing and defining fire limits, which shall include the principal business portions of the city and which shall be known as primary fire limits. In addition, the council may, in its discretion, establish and define one or more separate areas within the city as secondary fire limits. (1905, c. 506, s. 7; Rev., s. 2985; 1917, c. 136, subch. 8, s. 2; C.S., ss. 2746, 2802; 1961, c. 240; 1969, c. 1065, s. 1; 1971, c. 698, s. 1.)

160A-436. Restrictions within primary fire limits.

Within the primary fire limits of any city, as established and defined by ordinance, no frame or wooden building or structure or addition thereto shall hereafter be erected, altered, repaired, or moved (either into the limits or from one place to another within the limits), except upon the permit of the local inspection department approved by the city council and by the Commissioner of Insurance or his designee. The city council may make additional regulations for the prevention, extinguishment, or mitigation of fires within the primary fire limits. (1905, c. 506, s. 8; Rev., s. 2988; 1915, c. 192, s. 5; C.S., s. 2750; 1969, c. 1065, s. 1; 1971, c. 698, s. 1; 1989, c. 681, s. 8.)

160A-437. Restriction within secondary fire limits.

Within any secondary fire limits of any city or town, as established and defined by ordinance, no frame or wooden building or structure or addition thereto shall be erected, altered, repaired, or moved except in accordance with any rules and regulations established by ordinance of the areas. (1905, c. 506, s. 8; Rev., s. 2988; 1915, c. 192, s. 5; C.S., s. 2750; 1969, c. 1065, s. 1; 1971, c. 698, s. 1.)

160A-438. Failure to establish primary fire limits.

If the council of any city shall fail or refuse to establish and define the primary fire limits of the city as required by law, after having such failure or refusal called to their attention in writing by the State Commissioner of Insurance, the Commissioner shall have the power to establish the limits upon making a determination that they are necessary and in the public interest. (1905, c. 506, s. 7; Rev., s. 3608; C.S., s. 2747; 1969, c. 1065, s. 1; 1971, c. 698, s. 1.)

§ 160A439. Ordinance authorized as to repair, closing, and demolition of nonresidential buildings or structures; order of public officer.

(a)   Authority. – The governing body of the city may adopt and enforce ordinances relating to nonresidential buildings or structures that fail to meet minimum standards of maintenance, sanitation, and safety established by the governing body. The minimum standards shall address only conditions that are dangerous and injurious to public health, safety, and welfare and identify circumstances under which a public necessity exists for the repair, closing, or demolition of such buildings or structures. The ordinance shall provide for designation or appointment of a public officer to exercise the powers prescribed by the ordinance, in accordance with the procedures specified in this section. Such ordinance shall only be applicable within the corporate limits of the city.

(b)   Investigation. – Whenever it appears to the public officer that any nonresidential building or structure has not been properly maintained so that the safety or health of its occupants or members of the general public are jeopardized for failure of the property to meet the minimum standards established by the governing body, the public officer shall undertake a preliminary investigation. If entry upon the premises for purposes of investigation is necessary, such entry shall be made pursuant to a duly issued administrative search warrant in accordance with G.S. 1527.2 or with permission of the owner, the owner's agent, a tenant, or other person legally in possession of the premises.

(c)   Complaint and Hearing. – If the preliminary investigation discloses evidence of a violation of the minimum standards, the public officer shall issue and cause to be served upon the owner of and parties in interest in the nonresidential building or structure a complaint. The complaint shall state the charges and contain a notice that a hearing will be held before the public officer (or his or her designated agent) at a place within the county scheduled not less than 10 days nor more than 30 days after the serving of the complaint; that the owner and parties in interest shall be given the right to answer the complaint and to appear in person, or otherwise, and give testimony at the place and time fixed in the complaint; and that the rules of evidence prevailing in courts of law or equity shall not be controlling in hearings before the public officer.

(d)   Order. – If, after notice and hearing, the public officer determines that the nonresidential building or structure has not been properly maintained so that the safety or health of its occupants or members of the general public is jeopardized for failure of the property to meet the minimum standards established by the governing body, the public officer shall state in writing findings of fact in support of that determination and shall issue and cause to be served upon the owner thereof an order. The order may require the owner to take remedial action, within a reasonable time specified, subject to the procedures and limitations herein.

(e)   Limitations on Orders. –

(1)   An order may require the owner to repair, alter, or improve the nonresidential building or structure in order to bring it into compliance with the minimum standards established by the governing body or to vacate and close the nonresidential building or structure for any use.

(2)   An order may require the owner to remove or demolish the nonresidential building or structure if the cost of repair, alteration, or improvement of the building or structure would exceed fifty percent (50%) of its then current value. Notwithstanding any other provision of law, if the nonresidential building or

structure is designated as a local historic landmark, listed in the National Register of Historic Places, or located in a locally designated historic district or in a historic district listed in the National Register of Historic Places and the governing body determines, after a public hearing as provided by ordinance, that the nonresidential building or structure is of individual significance or contributes to maintaining the character of the district, and the nonresidential building or structure has not been condemned as unsafe, the order may require that the nonresidential building or structure be vacated and closed until it is brought into compliance with the minimum standards established by the governing body.

(3)   An order may not require repairs, alterations, or improvements to be made to vacant manufacturing facilities or vacant industrial warehouse facilities to preserve the original use. The order may require such building or structure to be vacated and closed, but repairs may be required only when necessary to maintain structural integrity or to abate a health or safety hazard that cannot be remedied by ordering the building or structure closed for any use.

(f)   Action by Governing Body Upon Failure to Comply With Order. –

(1)   If the owner fails to comply with an order to repair, alter, or improve or to vacate and close the nonresidential building or structure, the governing body may adopt an ordinance ordering the public officer to proceed to effectuate the purpose of this section with respect to the particular property or properties that the public officer found to be jeopardizing the health or safety of its occupants or members of the general public. The property or properties shall be described in the ordinance. The ordinance shall be recorded in the office of the register of deeds and shall be indexed in the name of the property owner or owners in the grantor index. Following adoption of an ordinance, the public officer may cause the building or structure to be repaired, altered, or improved or to be vacated and closed. The public officer may cause to be posted on the main entrance of any nonresidential building or structure so closed a placard with the following words: "This building is unfit for any use; the use or occupation of this building for any purpose is prohibited and unlawful." Any person who occupies or knowingly allows the occupancy of a building or structure so posted shall be guilty of a Class 3 misdemeanor.

(2)   If the owner fails to comply with an order to remove or demolish the nonresidential building or structure, the governing body may adopt an ordinance ordering the public officer to proceed to effectuate the purpose of this section with respect to the particular property or properties that the public officer found to be jeopardizing the health or safety of its occupants or members of the general public. No ordinance shall be adopted to require demolition of a nonresidential building or structure until the owner has first been given a reasonable opportunity to bring it into conformity with the minimum standards established by the governing body. The property or properties shall be described in the ordinance. The ordinance shall be recorded in the office of the register of deeds and shall be indexed in the name of the property owner or owners in the grantor index. Following adoption of an ordinance, the public officer may cause the building or structure to be removed or demolished.

(g)   Action by Governing Body Upon Abandonment of Intent to Repair. – If the governing body has adopted an ordinance or the public officer has issued an order requiring the building or structure to be repaired or vacated and closed and the building or structure has been vacated and closed for a period of two years pursuant to the ordinance or order, the governing body may make findings that the owner has abandoned the intent and purpose to repair, alter, or improve the building or structure and that the continuation of the building or structure in its vacated and closed status would be inimical to the health, safety, and welfare of the municipality in that it would continue to deteriorate, would create a fire or safety hazard, would be a threat to children and vagrants, would attract persons intent on criminal activities, or would cause or contribute to blight and the deterioration of property values in the area. Upon such findings, the governing body may, after the expiration of the twoyear period, enact an ordinance and serve such ordinance on the owner, setting forth the following:

(1)   If the cost to repair the nonresidential building or structure to bring it into compliance with the minimum standards is less than or equal to fifty percent (50%) of its then current value, the ordinance shall require that the owner either repair or demolish and remove the building or structure within 90 days; or

(2)   If the cost to repair the nonresidential building or structure to bring it into compliance with the minimum standards exceeds fifty percent (50%) of its then current value, the ordinance shall require the owner to demolish and remove the building or structure within 90 days.

In the case of vacant manufacturing facilities or vacant industrial warehouse facilities, the building or structure must have been vacated and closed pursuant to an order or ordinance for a period of five years before the governing body may take action under this subsection. The ordinance shall be recorded in the office of the register of deeds in the county wherein the property or properties are located and shall be indexed in the name of the property owner in the grantor index. If the owner fails to comply with the ordinance, the public officer shall effectuate the purpose of the ordinance.

(h)   Service of Complaints and Orders. – Complaints or orders issued by a public officer pursuant to an ordinance adopted under this section shall be served upon persons either personally or by registered or certified mail so long as the means used are reasonably designed to achieve actual notice. When service is made by registered or certified mail, a copy of the complaint or order may also be sent by regular mail. Service shall be deemed sufficient if the registered or certified mail is refused, but the regular mail is not returned by the post office within 10 days after the mailing. If regular mail is used, a notice of the pending proceedings shall be posted in a conspicuous place on the premises affected. If the identities of any owners or the whereabouts of persons are unknown and cannot be ascertained by the public officer in the exercise of reasonable diligence, and the public officer makes an affidavit to that effect, the serving of the complaint or order upon the owners or other persons may be made by publication in a newspaper having general circulation in the city at least once no later than the time that personal service would be required under this section. When service is made by publication, a notice of the pending proceedings shall be posted in a conspicuous place on the premises affected.

(i)   Liens. –

(1)   The amount of the cost of repairs, alterations, or improvements, or vacating and closing, or removal or demolition by the public officer shall be a lien against the real property upon which the cost was incurred, which lien shall be filed, have the same priority, and be collected as the lien for special assessment provided in Article 10 of Chapter 160A of the General Statutes.

(2)   If the real property upon which the cost was incurred is located in an incorporated city, the amount of the costs is also a lien on any other real property of the owner located within the city limits except for the owner's primary residence. The additional lien provided in this subdivision is inferior to all prior liens and shall be collected as a money judgment.

(3)   If the nonresidential building or structure is removed or demolished by the public officer, he or she shall offer for sale the recoverable materials of the building or structure and any personal property, fixtures, or appurtenances found in or attached to the building or structure and shall credit the proceeds of the sale, if any, against the cost of the removal or demolition, and any balance remaining shall be deposited in the superior court by the public officer, shall be secured in a manner directed by the court, and shall be disbursed by the court to the persons found to be entitled thereto by final order or decree of the court. Nothing in this section shall be construed to impair or limit in any

way the power of the governing body to define and declare nuisances and to cause their removal or abatement by summary proceedings or otherwise.

(j)   Ejectment. – If any occupant fails to comply with an order to vacate a nonresidential building or structure, the public officer may file a civil action in the name of the city to remove the occupant. The action to vacate shall be in the nature of summary ejectment and shall be commenced by filing a complaint naming as partiesdefendant any person occupying the nonresidential building or structure. The clerk of superior court shall issue a summons requiring the defendant to appear before a magistrate at a certain time, date, and place not to exceed 10 days from the issuance of the summons to answer the complaint. The summons and complaint shall be served as provided in G.S. 4229. The summons shall be returned according to its tenor, and if on its return it appears to have been duly served and if at the hearing the public officer produces a certified copy of an ordinance adopted by the governing body pursuant to subsection (f) of this section to vacate the occupied nonresidential building or structure, the magistrate shall enter judgment ordering that the premises be vacated and all persons be removed. The judgment ordering that the nonresidential building or structure be vacated shall be enforced in the same manner as the judgment for summary ejectment entered under G.S. 4230. An appeal from any judgment entered under this subsection by the magistrate may be taken as provided in G.S. 7A228, and the execution of the judgment may be stayed as provided in G.S. 7A227. An action to remove an occupant of a nonresidential building or structure who is a tenant of the owner may not be in the nature of a summary ejectment proceeding pursuant to this subsection unless the occupant was served with notice, at least 30 days before the filing of the summary ejectment proceeding, that the governing body has ordered the public officer to proceed to exercise his duties under subsection (f) of this section to vacate and close or remove and demolish the nonresidential building or structure.

(k)   Civil Penalty. – The governing body may impose civil penalties against any person or entity that fails to comply with an order entered pursuant to this section. However, the imposition of civil penalties shall not limit the use of any other lawful remedies available to the governing body for the enforcement of any ordinances adopted pursuant to this section.

(l)   Powers Supplemental. – The powers conferred by this section are supplemental to the powers conferred by any other law. An ordinance adopted by the governing body may authorize the public officer to exercise any powers necessary or convenient to carry out and effectuate the purpose and provisions of this section, including the following powers in addition to others herein granted:

(1)   To investigate nonresidential buildings and structures in the city to determine whether they have been properly maintained in compliance with the minimum standards so that the safety or health of the occupants or members of the general public are not jeopardized.

(2)   To administer oaths, affirmations, examine witnesses, and receive evidence.

(3)   To enter upon premises pursuant to subsection (b) of this section for the purpose of making examinations in a manner that will do the least possible inconvenience to the persons in possession.

(4)   To appoint and fix the duties of officers, agents, and employees necessary to carry out the purposes of the ordinances adopted by the governing body.

(5)   To delegate any of his or her functions and powers under the ordinance to other officers and agents.

(m)   Appeals. – The governing body may provide that appeals may be taken from any decision or order of the public officer to the city's housing appeals board or zoning board of adjustment. Any person aggrieved by a decision or order of the public officer shall have the remedies provided in G.S. 160A446.

(n)   Funding. – The governing body is authorized to make appropriations from its revenues necessary to carry out the purposes of this section and may accept and apply grants or donations to assist in carrying out the provisions of the ordinances adopted by the governing body.

(o)   No Effect on Just Compensation for Taking by Eminent Domain. – Nothing in this section shall be construed as preventing the owner or owners of any property from receiving just compensation for the taking of property by the power of eminent domain under the laws of this State, nor as permitting any property to be condemned or destroyed except in accordance with the police power of the State.

(p)   Definitions. –

   (1)   "Parties in interest" means all individuals, associations, and corporations who have interests of record in a nonresidential building or structure and any who are in possession thereof.

   (2)   "Vacant industrial warehouse" means any building or structure designed for the storage of goods or equipment in connection with manufacturing processes, which has not been used for that purpose for at least one year and has not been converted to another use.

   (3)   "Vacant manufacturing facility" means any building or structure previously used for the lawful production or manufacturing of goods, which has not been used for that purpose for at least one year and has not been converted to another use. (2007414, s. 1.)

Appendix L: Payments to Subcontractors

CHAPTER 22C

§ 22C1. Definitions.

Unless the context otherwise requires in this Chapter:

(1) "Contractor" means a person who contracts with an owner to improve real property.

(2) "Improve" means to build, effect, alter, repair, or demolish any improvement upon, connected with, or on or beneath the surface of any real property, or to excavate, clear, grade, fill or landscape any real property, or to construct driveways and private roadways, or to furnish materials, including trees and shrubbery, for any of such purposes, or to perform any labor upon such improvements, and shall also mean and include any design or other professional or skilled services furnished by architects, engineers, land surveyors and landscape architects registered under Chapters 83A, 89C or 89A of the General Statutes.

(3) "Improvement" means all or any part of any building, structure, erection, alteration, demolition, excavation, clearing, grading, filling, or landscaping, including trees and shrubbery, driveways, and private roadways, on real property.

(4) An "owner" is a person who has an interest in the real property improved and for whom an improvement is made and who ordered the improvement to be made. "Owner" includes successors in interest of the owner and agents of the owner acting within their authority.

(5) "Real property" means the real estate that is improved, including lands, leaseholds, tenements and hereditaments, and improvements placed thereon.

(6) "Subcontractor" means any person who has contracted to furnish labor or materials to, or has performed labor for, a contractor or another subcontractor in connection with a contract to improve real property. (1987 (Reg. Sess., 1988), c. 946, s. 1.)

§ 22C2. Performance by subcontractor.

Performance by a subcontractor in accordance with the provisions of its contract shall entitle it to payment from the party with whom it contracts. Payment by the owner to a contractor is not a condition precedent for payment to a subcontractor and payment by a contractor to a subcontractor is not a condition precedent for payment to any other subcontractor, and an agreement to the contrary is unenforceable. (1987 (Reg. Sess., 1988), c. 946; 1991, c. 620.)

§ 22C3. Time of payment to subcontractors after contractor or other subcontractor has been paid.

When a subcontractor has performed in accordance with the provisions of his contract, the contractor shall pay to his subcontractor and each subcontractor shall pay to his subcontractor, within seven days of receipt by the contractor or subcontractor of each periodic or final payment, the full amount received for such subcontractor's work and materials based on work completed or service provided under the subcontract. (1987 (Reg. Sess., 1988), c. 946.)

§ 22C4. Conditions of payment.

Nothing in this Chapter shall prevent the contractor, at the time of application and certification to the owner, from withholding such application and certification to the owner for payment to the subcontractor for: unsatisfactory job progress; defective construction not remedied; disputed work; third party claims filed or reasonable evidence that claim will be filed; failure of subcontractor to make timely payments for labor, equipment, and materials; damage to contractor or another subcontractor; reasonable evidence that subcontract cannot be completed for the unpaid balance of the subcontract sum; or a reasonable amount for retainage not to exceed the initial percentage retained by the owner. (1987 (Reg. Sess., 1988), c. 946.)

§ 22C5. Late payments to bear interest.

Should any periodic or final payment to a subcontractor be delayed by more than seven days after receipt of periodic or final payment by the contractor or subcontractor, the contractor or subcontractor shall pay his subcontractor interest, beginning on the eighth day, at the rate of one percent (1%) per month or a fraction thereof on such unpaid balance as may be due. (1987 (Reg. Sess., 1988), c. 946.)

§ 22C6. Applicability of this Chapter.

The provisions of this Chapter shall not be applicable to residential contractors as defined in G.S. 87 10(1a), or to improvements to real property intended for residential purposes which are exempted from the application of Chapter 83A of the General Statutes pursuant to G.S. 83A13(c)(1), or to improvements to real property intended for residential purposes which consist of 12 or fewer residential units. (1987 (Reg. Sess., 1988), c. 946.)

Appendix M: Statutory Liens on Real Property

CHAPTER 44A, ARTICLE 2

Part 1. Liens of Mechanics, Laborers, and Materialmen Dealing with Owner.

§ 44A7. Definitions.

Unless the context otherwise requires in this Article:

(1) "Improve" means to build, effect, alter, repair, or demolish any improvement upon, connected with, or on or beneath the surface of any real property, or to excavate, clear, grade, fill or landscape any real property, or to construct driveways and private roadways, or to furnish materials, including trees and shrubbery, for any of such purposes, or to perform any labor upon such improvements, and shall also mean and include any design or other professional or skilled services furnished by architects, engineers, land surveyors and landscape architects registered under Chapter 83A, 89A or 89C of the General Statutes, and rental of equipment directly utilized on the real property in making the improvement.

(2) "Improvement" means all or any part of any building, structure, erection, alteration, demolition, excavation, clearing, grading, filling, or landscaping, including trees and shrubbery, driveways, and private roadways, on real property.

(3) An "owner" is a person who has an interest in the real property improved and for whom an improvement is made and who ordered the improvement to be made. "Owner" includes successors in interest of the owner and agents of the owner acting within their authority.

(4) "Real property" means the real estate that is improved, including lands, leaseholds, tenements and hereditaments, and improvements placed thereon. (1969, c. 1112, s. 1; 1975, c. 715, s. 1; 1985, c. 689, s. 13; 1995 (Reg. Sess., 1996), c. 607, s. 1.)

§ 44A8. Mechanics', laborers', and materialmen's lien; persons entitled to claim of lien on real property.

Any person who performs or furnishes labor or professional design or surveying services or furnishes materials or furnishes rental equipment pursuant to a contract, either express or implied, with the owner of real property for the making of an improvement thereon shall, upon complying with the provisions of this Article, have a right to file a claim of lien on real property on the real property to secure payment of all debts owing for labor done or professional design or surveying services or material furnished or equipment rented pursuant to the contract. (1969, c. 1112, s. 1; 1975, c. 715, s. 2; 1995 (Reg. Sess., 1996), c. 607, s. 2; 2005229, s. 1.)

§ 44A9. Extent of claim of lien on real property.

A claim of lien on real property authorized under this Article shall extend to the improvement and to the lot or tract on which the improvement is situated, to the extent of the interest of the owner. When the lot or tract on which a building is erected is not surrounded at the time of making the contract with the owner by an enclosure separating it from adjoining land of the same owner, the lot or tract to which any claim of lien on real property extends shall be the area that is reasonably necessary for the convenient use and occupation of the building, but in no case shall the area include a building, structure, or improvement not normally used or occupied or intended to be used or occupied with the building with respect to which the claim of lien on real property is claimed. (1969, c. 1112, s. 1; 2005229, s. 1.)

§ 44A10. Effective date of claim of lien on real property.

A claim of lien on real property granted by this Article shall relate to and take effect from the time of the first furnishing of labor or materials at the site of the improvement by the person claiming the claim of lien on real property. (1969, c. 1112, s. 1; 2005229, s. 1.)

§ 44A11. Perfecting claim of lien on real property.

A claim of lien on real property granted by this Article shall be perfected as of the time provided in G.S. 44A10 upon the filing of the claim of lien on real property under G.S. 44A12 and may be enforced pursuant to G.S. 44A13. (1969, c. 1112, s. 1; 2005229, s. 1.)

§ 44A12. Filing claim of lien on real property.

(a)   Place of Filing. – All claims of lien on real property must be filed in the office of the clerk of superior court in each county where the real property subject to the claim of lien on real property is located. The clerk of superior court shall note the claim of lien on real property on the judgment docket and index the same under the name of the record owner of the real property at the time the claim of lien on real property is filed. An additional copy of the claim of lien on real property may also be filed with any receiver, referee in bankruptcy or assignee for benefit of creditors who obtains legal authority over the real property.

(b)   Time of Filing. – Claims of lien on real property may be filed at any time after the maturity of the obligation secured thereby but not later than 120 days after the last furnishing of labor or materials at the site of the improvement by the person claiming the lien.

(c)   Contents of Claim of Lien on Real Property to Be Filed. – All claims of lien on real property must be filed using a form substantially as follows:

CLAIM OF LIEN ON REAL PROPERTY

(1)   Name and address of the person claiming the claim of lien on real property:

(2)   Name and address of the record owner of the real property claimed to be subject to the claim of lien on real property at the time the claim of lien on real property is filed:

(3)   Description of the real property upon which the claim of lien on real property is claimed: (Street address, tax lot and block number, reference to recorded instrument, or any other description of real property is sufficient, whether or not it is specific, if it reasonably identifies what is described.)

(4)   Name and address of the person with whom the claimant contracted for the furnishing of labor or materials:

(5)   Date upon which labor or materials were first furnished upon said property by the claimant:

(5a)   Date upon which labor or materials were last furnished upon said property by the claimant:

    (6)   General description of the labor performed or materials furnished and the amount claimed therefor:

_____

Lien Claimant

Filed this _____ day of _____, _____

_____

                 Clerk of Superior Court

      A general description of the labor performed or materials furnished is sufficient. It is not necessary for lien claimant to file an itemized list of materials or a detailed statement of labor performed.

    (d)   No Amendment of Claim of Lien on Real Property. – A claim of lien on real property may not be amended. A claim of lien on real property may be cancelled by a claimant or the claimant's authorized agent or attorney and a new claim of lien on real property substituted therefor within the time herein provided for original filing.

    (e)   Notice of Assignment of Claim of Lien on Real Property. – When a claim of lien on real property has been filed, it may be assigned of record by the lien claimant in a writing filed with the clerk of superior court who shall note the assignment in the margin of the judgment docket containing the claim of lien on real property. Thereafter the assignee becomes the lien claimant of record.

    (f)   Waiver of Right to File, Serve, or Claim Liens as Consideration for Contract Against Public Policy. – An agreement to waive the right to file a claim of lien on real property granted under this Part, or an agreement to waive the right to serve a notice of claim of lien upon funds granted under Part 2 of this Article, which agreement is in anticipation of and in consideration for the awarding of any contract, either expressed or implied, for the making of an improvement upon real property under this Article is against public policy and is unenforceable. This section does not prohibit subordination or release of a lien granted under this Part or Part 2 of this Article. (1969, c. 1112, s. 1; 1977, c. 369; 1983, c. 888; 1999456, s. 59; 2005229, s. 1.)

§ 44Λ12.1 No docketing of lien unless authorized by statute.

    (a)   The clerk of superior court shall not index, docket, or record a claim of lien on real property or other document purporting to claim or assert a lien on real property in such a way as to affect the title to any real property unless the document:

        (1)   Is offered for filing under this Article or another statute that provides for indexing and docketing of claims of lien on real property; and

        (2)   Appears on its face to contain all of the information required by the statute under which it is offered for filing.

    (b)   The clerk may accept, for filing only, any document that does not meet the criteria established for indexing, docketing, or recording under subsection (a) of this section. If the clerk does accept this document, the clerk shall inform the person offering the document that it will not be indexed, docketed, or recorded in any way as to affect the title to any real property.

    (c)   Any person who causes or attempts to cause a claim of lien on real property or other document to be filed, knowing that the filing is not authorized by statute, or with the intent that the filing is made for an improper purpose such as to hinder, harass, or otherwise wrongfully interfere with any person, shall be guilty of a Class 1 misdemeanor.

(d)   A claim of lien on real property, a claim of lien on real property with a notice of claim of lien upon funds attached thereto, or other document purporting to claim or assert a lien on real property that is filed by an attorney licensed in the State of North Carolina and that otherwise complies with subsection (a) of this section shall not be rejected by the clerk of superior court for indexing, docketing, recording, or filing. (2001495, s. 1; 2005229, s. 1.)

§ 44A13. Action to enforce claim of lien on real property.

(a)   Where and When Action Commenced. – An action to enforce a claim of lien on real property may be commenced in any county where venue is otherwise proper. No such action may be commenced later than 180 days after the last furnishing of labor or materials at the site of the improvement by the person claiming the claim of lien on real property. If the title to the real property against which the claim of lien on real property is asserted is by law vested in a receiver or is subject to the control of the bankruptcy court, the claim of lien on real property shall be enforced in accordance with the orders of the court having jurisdiction over said real property. The filing of a proof of claim with a receiver or in bankruptcy and the filing of a notice of lis pendens in each county where the real property subject to the claim of lien on real property is located within the time required by this section satisfies the requirement for the commencement of a civil action.

(b)   Judgment. – A judgment enforcing a lien under this Article may be entered for the principal amount shown to be due, not exceeding the principal amount stated in the claim of lien enforced thereby. The judgment shall direct a sale of the real property subject to the lien thereby enforced.

(c)   Notice of Action. – In order for the sale under G.S. 44A14(a) to pass all title and interest of the owner to the purchaser good against all claims or interests recorded, filed or arising after the first furnishing of labor or materials at the site of the improvement by the person claiming the claim of lien on real property, a notice of lis pendens shall be filed in each county in which the real property subject to the claim of lien on real property is located except the county in which the action is commenced. The notice of lis pendens shall be filed within the time provided in subsection (a) of this section for the commencement of the action by the lien claimant. If neither an action nor a notice of lis pendens is filed in accordance with this section, the judgment entered in the action enforcing the claim of lien on real property shall not direct a sale of the real property subject to the claim of lien on real property enforced thereby nor be entitled to any priority under the provisions of G.S. 44A14(a), but shall be entitled only to those priorities accorded by law to money judgments. (1969, c. 1112, s. 1; 1977, c. 883; 2005229, s. 1.)

§ 44A14. Sale of property in satisfaction of judgment enforcing claim of lien on real property or upon order prior to judgment; distribution of proceeds.

(a)   Execution Sale; Effect of Sale. – Except as provided in subsection (b) of this section, sales under this Article and distribution of proceeds thereof shall be made in accordance with the execution sale provisions set out in G.S. 1339.41 through 1339.76. The sale of real property to satisfy a claim of lien on real property granted by this Article shall pass all title and interest of the owner to the purchaser, good against all claims or interests recorded, filed or arising after the first furnishing of labor or materials at the site of the improvement by the person claiming a lien.

(b)   Sale of Property upon Order Prior to Judgment. – A resident judge of superior court in the district in which the action to enforce the claim of lien on real property is pending, a judge regularly holding the superior courts of the said district, any judge holding a session of superior court, either civil or criminal, in the said district, a special judge of superior court residing in the said district, or the chief judge of the district court in which the action to enforce the claim of lien on real property is pending, may, upon notice to all interested parties and after a hearing thereupon and upon a finding that a sale prior to judgment is necessary to prevent substantial waste, destruction, depreciation or other damage to said real property prior to the final determination of said action, order any real property against which a claim of lien on real property under this Article is asserted, sold in any manner determined by said judge to be commercially reasonable. The rights of all parties shall be transferred to the proceeds of the sale. Application for such order and further proceedings thereon may be heard in or out of session. (1969, c. 1112, s. 1; 2005229, s. 1.)

§ 44A15. Attachment available to lien claimant.

In addition to other grounds for attachment, in all cases where the owner removes or attempts or threatens to remove an improvement from real property subject to a claim of lien on real property under this Article, without the written permission of the lien claimant or with the intent to deprive the lien claimant of his or her claim of lien on real property, the remedy of attachment of the property subject to the claim of lien on real property shall be available to the lien claimant or any other person. (1969, c. 1112, s. 1; 2005229, s. 1.)

§ 44A16. Discharge of record claim of lien on real property.

(a)   Any claim of lien on real property filed under this Article may be discharged by any of the following methods:

    (1)   The lien claimant of record, the claimant's agent or attorney, in the presence of the clerk of superior court may acknowledge the satisfaction of the claim of lien on real property indebtedness, whereupon the clerk of superior court shall forthwith make upon the record of such claim of lien on real property an entry of such acknowledgment of satisfaction, which shall be signed by the lien claimant of record, the claimant's agent or attorney, and witnessed by the clerk of superior court.

    (2)   The owner may exhibit an instrument of satisfaction signed and acknowledged by the lien claimant of record which instrument states that the claim of lien on real property indebtedness has been paid or satisfied, whereupon the clerk of superior court shall cancel the claim of lien on real property by entry of satisfaction on the record of such claim of lien on real property.

    (3)   By failure to enforce the claim of lien on real property within the time prescribed in this Article.

    (4)   By filing in the office of the clerk of superior court the original or certified copy of a judgment or decree of a court of competent jurisdiction showing that the action by the claimant to enforce the claim of lien on real property has been dismissed or finally determined adversely to the claimant.

    (5)   Whenever a sum equal to the amount of the claim or claims of lien on real property claimed is deposited with the clerk of court, to be applied to the payment finally determined to be due, whereupon the clerk of superior court shall cancel the claim or claims of lien on real property or claims of lien on real property of record.

    (6)   Whenever a corporate surety bond, in a sum equal to one and onefourth times the amount of the claim or claims of lien on real property claimed and conditioned upon the payment of the amount finally determined to be due in satisfaction of said claim or claims of lien on real property, is deposited with the clerk of court, whereupon the clerk of superior court shall cancel the claim or claims of lien on real property of record.

(b)   The clerk may release funds held or a corporate surety bond upon receipt of one of the following:

    (1)   Written agreement of the parties.

    (2)   A final judgment of a court of competent jurisdiction.

(3)   A consent order. (1969, c. 1112, s. 1; 1971, c. 766; 2005229, s. 1; 2011411, s. 3.)

Part 2. Liens of Mechanics, Laborers, and Materialmen Dealing with One Other Than Owner.

§ 44A17. Definitions.

Unless the context otherwise requires in this Article:

(1)   "Contractor" means a person who contracts with an owner to improve real property.

(2)   "First tier subcontractor" means a person who contracts with a contractor to improve real property.

(3)   "Obligor" means an owner, contractor or subcontractor in any tier who owes money to another as a result of the other's partial or total performance of a contract to improve real property.

(4)   "Second tier subcontractor" means a person who contracts with a first tier subcontractor to improve real property.

(5)   "Third tier subcontractor" means a person who contracts with a second tier subcontractor to improve real property. (1971, c. 880, s. 1.)

§ 44A18. Grant of lien upon funds; subrogation; perfection.

Upon compliance with this Article:

(1)   A first tier subcontractor who furnished labor, materials, or rental equipment at the site of the improvement shall be entitled to a lien upon funds that are owed to the contractor with whom the first tier subcontractor dealt and that arise out of the improvement on which the first tier subcontractor worked or furnished materials.

(2)   A second tier subcontractor who furnished labor, materials, or rental equipment at the site of the improvement shall be entitled to a lien upon funds that are owed to the first tier subcontractor with whom the second tier subcontractor dealt and that arise out of the improvement on which the second tier subcontractor worked or furnished materials. A second tier subcontractor, to the extent of the second tier subcontractor's lien provided in this subdivision, shall also be entitled to be subrogated to the lien of the first tier subcontractor with whom the second tier contractor dealt provided for in subdivision (1) of this section and shall be entitled to perfect it by notice of claim of lien upon funds to the extent of the claim.

(3)   A third tier subcontractor who furnished labor, materials, or rental equipment at the site of the improvement shall be entitled to a lien upon funds that are owed to the second tier subcontractor with whom the third tier subcontractor dealt and that arise out of the improvement on which the third tier subcontractor worked or furnished materials. A third tier subcontractor, to the extent of the third tier subcontractor's lien upon funds provided in this subdivision, shall also be entitled to be subrogated to the lien upon funds of the second tier subcontractor with whom the third tier contractor dealt and to the lien upon funds of the first tier subcontractor with whom the second tier subcontractor dealt to the extent that the second tier subcontractor is entitled to be subrogated thereto, and in either case shall be entitled to perfect the same by notice of claim of lien upon funds to the extent of the claim.

(4)   Subcontractors more remote than the third tier who furnished labor, materials, or rental equipment at the site of the improvement shall be entitled to a lien upon funds that are owed to the person with

whom they dealt and that arise out of the improvement on which they furnished labor, materials, or rental equipment, but such remote tier subcontractor shall not be entitled to subrogation to the rights of other persons.

(5)   The liens upon funds granted under this section shall secure amounts earned by the lien claimant as a result of having furnished labor, materials, or rental equipment at the site of the improvement under the contract to improve real property, including interest at the legal rate provided in G.S. 245, whether or not such amounts are due and whether or not performance or delivery is complete. In the event insufficient funds are retained to satisfy all lien claimants, subcontractor lien claimants may recover the interest due under this subdivision on a pro rata basis, but in no event shall interest due under this subdivision increase the liability of the obligor under G.S. 44A20.

(6)   A lien upon funds granted under this section is perfected upon the giving of notice of claim of lien upon funds in writing to the obligor as provided in G.S. 44A19 and shall be effective upon the obligor's receipt of the notice. The subrogation rights of a first, second, or third tier subcontractor to the claim of lien on real property of the contractor created by Part 1 of Article 2 of this Chapter are perfected as provided in G.S. 44A23. (1971, c. 880, s. 1; 1985, c. 702, s. 3; 1995 (Reg. Sess., 1996), c. 607, s. 3; 2005229, s. 1.)

§ 44A19. Notice of claim of lien upon funds.

(a)   Notice of a claim of lien upon funds shall set forth all of the following information:

(1)   The name and address of the person claiming the lien upon funds.

(2)   A general description of the real property improved.

(3)   The name and address of the person with whom the lien claimant contracted to improve real property.

(4)   The name and address of each person against or through whom subrogation rights are claimed.

(5)   A general description of the contract and the person against whose interest the lien upon funds is claimed.

(6)   The amount of the lien upon funds claimed by the lien claimant under the contract.

(b)   All notices of claims of liens upon funds by first, second, or third tier subcontractors must be given using a form substantially as follows:

NOTICE OF CLAIM OF LIEN UPON FUNDS BY FIRST, SECOND, OR THIRD TIER SUBCONTRACTOR

To:

1. _____, owner of property involved.

(Name and address)

2. _____, general contractor.

(Name and address)

3. _____, first tier subcontractor against or through

(Name and address)   whom subrogation is claimed, if any.

4. _____, second tier subcontractor against or through

(Name and address)   whom subrogation is claimed, if any.

General description of real property where labor performed or material furnished:

_____

_____

General description of undersigned lien claimant's contract including the names of the parties thereto:

_____

_____

The amount of lien upon funds claimed pursuant to the above described contract:

$ _____

The undersigned lien claimant gives this notice of claim of lien upon funds pursuant to North Carolina law and claims all rights of subrogation to which he is entitled under Part 2 of Article 2 of Chapter 44A of the General Statutes of North Carolina.

Dated _____

_____, Lien Claimant

_____

(Address)

(c) All notices of claims of liens upon funds by subcontractors more remote than the third tier must be given using a form substantially as follows:

NOTICE OF CLAIM OF LIEN UPON FUNDS BY SUBCONTRACTOR MORE REMOTE THAN THE THIRD TIER

To:

_____, person holding funds against which lien upon funds is claimed.

(Name and Address)

General description of real property where labor performed or material furnished:

_____

_____

General description of undersigned lien claimant's contract including the names of the parties thereto:

_____

_____

The amount of lien upon funds claimed pursuant to the above described contract: $ _____

The undersigned lien claimant gives this notice of claim of lien upon funds pursuant to North Carolina law and claims all rights to which he or she is entitled under Part 2 of Article 2 of Chapter 44A of the General Statutes of North Carolina.

Dated: _____

_____, Lien Claimant

(Address)

(d) Notices of claims of lien upon funds under this section shall be served upon the obligor by personal delivery or in any manner authorized by Rule 4 of the North Carolina Rules of Civil Procedure. A copy of the notice of claim of lien upon funds shall be attached to any claim of lien on real property filed pursuant to G.S. 44A 20(d) or G.S. 44A 23.

(e) Notices of claims of lien upon funds shall not be filed with the clerk of superior court and shall not be indexed, docketed, or recorded in any way as to affect title to any real property, except a notice of a claim of lien upon funds may be filed with the clerk of superior court under either of the following circumstances:

   (1) When the notice of claim of lien upon funds is attached to a claim of lien on real property filed pursuant to G.S. 44A 20(d) or G.S. 44A 23.

   (2) When the notice of claim of lien upon funds is filed by the obligor for the purpose of discharging the claim of lien upon funds in accordance with G.S. 44A 20(e).

(f) Filing a notice of claim of lien upon funds pursuant to subsection (e) of this section is not a violation of G.S. 44A 12.1. (1971, c. 880, s. 1; 1985, c. 702, s. 1; 2005 229, s. 1.)

§ 44A 20. Duties and liability of obligor.

(a)   Upon receipt of the notice of claim of lien upon funds provided for in this Article, the obligor shall be under a duty to retain any funds subject to the lien or liens upon funds under this Article up to the total amount of such liens upon funds as to which notices of claims of lien upon funds have been received.

(b)   If, after the receipt of the notice of claim of lien upon funds to the obligor, the obligor makes further payments to a contractor or subcontractor against whose interest the lien or liens upon funds are claimed, the lien upon funds shall continue upon the funds in the hands of the contractor or subcontractor who received the payment, and in addition the obligor shall be personally liable to the person or persons entitled to liens upon funds up to the amount of such wrongful payments, not exceeding the total claims with respect to which the notice of claim of lien upon funds was received prior to payment.

(c)   If an obligor makes a payment after receipt of notice of claim of lien on funds and incurs personal liability under subsection (b) of this section, the obligor shall be entitled to reimbursement and indemnification from the party receiving such payment.

(d)   If the obligor is an owner of the property being improved, the lien claimant shall be entitled to a claim of lien upon real property upon the interest of the obligor in the real property to the extent of the owner's personal liability under subsection (b) of this section, which claim of lien on real property shall be enforced only in the manner set forth in G.S. 44A 7 through G.S. 44A 16 and which claim of lien on real property shall be entitled to the same priorities and subject to the same filing requirements and periods of limitation applicable to the contractor. The claim of lien on real property is perfected as of the time set forth in G.S. 44A 10 upon the filing of the claim of lien on real property pursuant to G.S. 44A 12. The claim of lien on real property shall be in the form set out in G.S. 44A 12(c) and shall contain, in addition, a copy of the notice of claim of lien upon funds given pursuant to G.S. 44A 19 as an exhibit together with proof of service thereof by affidavit, and shall state the grounds the lien claimant has to believe that the obligor is personally liable for the debt under subsection (b) of this section.

(e)   A notice of claim of lien upon funds under G.S. 44A 19 may be filed by the obligor with the clerk of superior court in each county where the real property upon which the filed notice of claim of lien upon funds is located for the purpose of discharging the notice of claim of lien upon funds by any of the methods described in G.S. 44A 16.

(f)   A bond deposited under this section to discharge a filed notice of claim of lien upon funds shall be effective to discharge any claim of lien on real property filed by the same lien claimant pursuant to subsection (d) of this section or G.S. 44A 23 and shall further be effective to discharge any notices of claims of lien upon funds served by lower tier subcontractors or any claims of lien on real property filed by lower tier subcontractors pursuant to subsection (d) of this section or G.S. 44A 23 claiming through or against the contractor or higher tier subcontractors up to the amount of the bond. (1971, c. 880, s. 1; 1985, c. 702, s. 2; 2005 229, s. 1.)

§ 44A 21. Pro rata payments.

(a)   Where the obligor is a contractor or subcontractor and the funds in the hands of the obligor and the obligor's personal liability, if any, under G.S. 44A 20 are less than the amount of valid liens upon funds that have been received by the obligor under this Article, the parties entitled to liens upon funds shall share the funds on a pro rata basis.

(b)   Where the obligor is an owner and the funds in the hands of the obligor and the obligor's personal liability, if any, under G.S. 44A 20 are less than the sum of the amount of valid claims of liens upon funds that have been received by the obligor under this Article and the amount of the valid claims of liens on real property upon the owner's property filed by the subcontractors with the clerk of superior court under G.S. 44A

23, the parties entitled to liens upon funds and the parties entitled to subrogation claims of liens on real property upon the owner's property shall share the funds on a pro rata basis. (1971, c. 880, s. 1; 1998 217, s. 4(d); 2005 229, s. 1.)

§ 44A 22. Priority of liens upon funds.

Liens upon funds perfected under this Article have priority over all other interests or claims theretofore or thereafter created or suffered in the funds by the person against whose interest the lien upon funds is asserted, including, but not limited to, liens arising from garnishment, attachment, levy, judgment, assignments, security interests, and any other type of transfer, whether voluntary or involuntary. Any person who receives payment from an obligor in bad faith with knowledge of a lien upon funds shall take such payment subject to the lien upon funds. (1971, c. 880, s. 1; 2005 229, s. 1.)

§ 44A 23. Contractor's claim of lien on real property; perfection of subrogation rights of subcontractor.

(a) First tier subcontractor. - A first tier subcontractor, who gives notice of claim of lien upon funds as provided in this Article, may, to the extent of this claim, enforce the claim of lien on real property of the contractor created by Part 1 of this Article. The manner of such enforcement shall be as provided by G.S. 44A 7 through 44A 16. The claim of lien on real property is perfected as of the time set forth in G.S. 44A 10 upon filing of the claim of lien on real property pursuant to G.S. 44A 12. Upon the filing of the claim of lien on real property, with the notice of claim of lien upon funds attached, and the commencement of the action, no action of the contractor shall be effective to prejudice the rights of the subcontractor without his written consent.

(b) Second or third subcontractor. -

(1) A second or third tier subcontractor, who gives notice of claim of lien upon funds as provided in this Article, may, to the extent of his claim, enforce the claim of lien on real property of the contractor created by Part 1 of Article 2 of the Chapter except when:

a. The contractor, within 30 days following the date the building permit is issued for the improvement of the real property involved, posts on the property in a visible location adjacent to the posted building permit and files in the office of the clerk of superior court in each county wherein the real property to be improved is located, a completed and signed notice of contract form and the second or third tier subcontractor fails to serve upon the contractor a completed and signed notice of subcontract form by the same means of service as described in G.S. 44A 19(d); or

b. After the posting and filing of a signed notice of contract and the service upon the contractor of a signed notice of subcontract, the contractor serves upon the second or third tier subcontractor, within five days following each subsequent payment, by the same means of service as described in G.S. 44A 19(d), the written notice of payment setting forth the date of payment and the period for which payment is made as requested in the notice of subcontract form set forth herein.

(2) The form of the notice of contract to be so utilized under this section shall be substantially as follows and the fee for filing the same with the clerk of superior court shall be the same as charged for filing a claim of lien on real property:

"NOTICE OF CONTRACT

"(1) Name and address of the Contractor:

"(2) Name and address of the owner of the real property at the time this Notice of Contract is recorded:

"(3) General description of the real property to be improved (street address, tax map lot and block number, reference to recorded instrument, or any other description that reasonably identifies the real property):

"(4) Name and address of the person, firm or corporation filing this Notice of Contract:

"Dated: _____

_____

"Contractor

"Filed this the ____ day of _____, ____.

_____

Clerk of Superior Court"

        (3)   The form of the notice of subcontract to be so utilized under this section shall be substantially as follows:

"NOTICE OF SUBCONTRACT

"(1) Name and address of the subcontractor:

"(2) General description of the real property where the labor was performed or the material was furnished (street address, tax map lot and block number, reference to recorded instrument, or any description that reasonably identifies the real property):

"(3)

        "(i)   General description of the subcontractor's contract, including the names of the parties thereto:

        "(ii)   General description of the labor and material performed and furnished thereunder:

"(4) Request is hereby made by the undersigned subcontractor that he be notified in writing by the contractor of, and within five days following, each subsequent payment by the contractor to the first tier subcontractor for labor performed or material furnished at the improved real property within the above descriptions of such in paragraph (2) and subparagraph (3)(ii), respectively, the date payment was made and the period for which payment is made.

"Dated: _____

_____

Subcontractor"

(4)   The manner of such enforcement shall be as provided by G.S. 44A 7 through G.S. 44A 16. The lien is perfected as of the time set forth in G.S. 44A 10 upon the filing of a claim of lien on real property pursuant to G.S. 44A 12. Upon the filing of the claim of lien on real property, with the notice of claim of lien upon funds attached, and the commencement of the action, no action of the contractor shall be effective to prejudice the rights of the second or third tier subcontractor without his written consent. (1971, c. 880, s. 1; 1985, c. 702, s. 4; 1991 (Reg. Sess., 1992), c. 1010, s. 1; 1993, c. 553, s. 13; 1997 456, s. 27; 1999 456, s. 59; 2005 229, s. 1.)

Part 3. Criminal Sanctions for Furnishing a False Statement in Connection with Improvement to Real Property.

§ 44A 24. False statement a misdemeanor.

If any contractor or other person receiving payment from an obligor for an improvement to real property or from a purchaser for a conveyance of real property with improvements shall knowingly furnish to such obligor, purchaser, or to a lender who obtains a security interest in said real property, or to a title insurance company insuring title to such real property, a false written statement of the sums due or claimed to be due for labor or material furnished at the site of improvements to such real property, then such contractor, subcontractor or other person shall be guilty of a Class 1 misdemeanor. Upon conviction and in the event the court shall grant any defendant a suspended sentence, the court may in its discretion include as a condition of such suspension a provision that the defendant shall reimburse the party who suffered loss on such conditions as the court shall determine are proper.

The elements of the offense herein stated are the furnishing of the false written statement with knowledge that it is false and the subsequent or simultaneous receipt of payment from an obligor or purchaser, and in any prosecution hereunder it shall not be necessary for the State to prove that the obligor, purchaser, lender or title insurance company relied upon the false statement or that any person was injured thereby. (1971, c. 880, s. 1.1; 1973, c. 991; 1993, c. 539, s. 406; 1994, Ex. Sess., c. 24, s. 14(c).)

National Association of State Contractors Licensing Agencies
NASCLA Membership Information

Membership Benefits

- Networking Opportunities with Industry Experts and Representatives

- Complimentary Copies of the Annual Membership Directory, Newsletter, Model Legislation, and *Contractor's State Licensing Information Directory (CSLID)*

- Reduced Registration Fees for NASCLA Annual Conferences & Training Seminars

- Access to the NASCLA Members Only Website *(*for State Members Only)*

    - *Member Reference Library* which includes consumer publications, NASCLA Model Legislation and other information

    - *Track Bills & State Legislation* NASCLA has partnered with a nationwide legislative tracking platform that tracks legislation across all 50 states and congress

    - *Top Regulatory Cases* affecting the construction industry and regulatory agencies

    - **Toolkit for Contractor Regulators* provides a variety of best practices from other states which state members can use to customize your very own programs without reinventing the wheel. Some of the highlighted programs include Elderly Abuse Prevention Program, Disaster Response Program and Understanding the Board's Role in a Legislative Environment to name a few!

    - *Community Forums* are available for *Executive Directors, Attorneys, *Public Information Officers, *Enforcement/Investigators, *IT Personnel, and Contractors. Communicate and engage with your counterparts nationally.

    - *Active Member Directory Search* allows you to search contact information for any NASCLA Member

To Apply for NASCLA Membership, please visit the following link: www.nascla.org

NASCLA's MISSION

"The National Association of State Contractors Licensing Agencies (NASCLA) promotes best practices and license uniformity for agencies that regulate the construction industry."

NASCLA®

NATIONAL ASSOCIATION OF STATE CONTRACTORS LICENSING AGENCIES

23309 N. 17th Drive
Building 1, Unit 110
Phoenix, Arizona 85027

Phone: (623) 587-9354

Fax: (623) 587-9625

www.nascla.org

APPLICANT INFORMATION

To become a member, please return this form with a check made payable to NASCLA at the address listed above or you may visit our website at www.nascla.org to register online for membership.

If you have any questions, please call NASCLA at (866) 948-3363.

MEMBERSHIP CLASSIFICATIONS

Please read the classifications below and check the box that best describes your membership classification.

❏ **Associate Member:** Limited to contractor trade associations, contractor firms, construction material suppliers, individual contractors, and regional (county, city or municipal) contractor licensing agencies.

$125.00 Annual Membership Fee.

❏ **State Member:** Limited to states that have enacted laws to regulate the business of contracting.

$475.00 Annual Membership Fee.

❏ **International Member:** Limited to regulatory agencies from other nations, countries or states other than the 50 United States of America and its territories.

$475.00 Annual Membership Fee.

❏ **Business Member:** Limited to firms whose business is related to the construction industry. These members shall not use the name of the association and its logo or in any manner refer to NASCLA in advertising, selling or soliciting.

$750.00 Annual Membership Fee.

❏ **Affiliate Member:** Limited to former employees and board members of state contractor licensing agencies who are not actively engaged in the contracting business.

$50.00 Annual Membership Fee.

Name: _____

Title: _____

Company: _____

City, State, Zip Code: _____

Phone: _____

Email: _____ Website: _____